THE

NEW
AMERICAN
NATION

1775–1820

A Twelve-Volume Collection of Articles on the Development of the Early American Republic

Edited by

PETER S. ONUF
UNIVERSITY OF VIRGINIA

A GARLAND SERIES

THE NEW AMERICAN NATION
1775–1820

Volume
10

★

STATE AND LOCAL POLITICS IN THE NEW NATION

Edited with an
Introduction by

PETER S. ONUF

GARLAND PUBLISHING, INC.
NEW YORK & LONDON
1991

Introduction © 1991 by Peter S. Onuf

Library of Congress Cataloging-in-Publication Data

State and local politics in the new nation / edited with an introduction by
Peter S. Onuf.
   p.   cm. — (New American nation, 1776–1815 ; v. 10)
   Includes bibliographic references.
   ISBN 0-8153-0445-5 (alk. paper) : $49.99
   1. United States—Politics and government—1783–1809. I. Onuf, Peter
S. II. Series.
   E164.N45   1991 vol. 10
   [E303]
   973 s—dc20
   [973]   91-15466
           CIP

Printed on acid-free, 250-year-life paper.
Manufactured in the United States of America

THE NEW AMERICAN NATION, 1775–1820

EDITOR'S INTRODUCTION

This series includes a representative selection of the most interesting and influential journal articles on revolutionary and early national America. My goal is to introduce readers to the wide range of topics that now engage scholarly attention. The essays in these volumes show that the revolutionary era was an extraordinarily complex "moment" when the broad outlines of national history first emerged. Yet if the "common cause" brought Americans together, it also drove them apart: the Revolution, historians agree, was as much a civil war as a war of national liberation. And, given the distinctive colonial histories of the original members of the American Union, it is not surprising that the war had profoundly different effects in different parts of the country. This series has been designed to reveal the multiplicity of these experiences in a period of radical political and social change.

Most of the essays collected here were first published within the last twenty years. This series therefore does *not* recapitulate the development of the historiography of the Revolution. Many of the questions asked by earlier generations of scholars now seem misconceived and simplistic. Constitutional historians wanted to know if the Patriots had legitimate grounds to revolt: was the Revolution "legal"? Economic historians sought to assess the costs of the navigation system for American farmers and merchants and to identify the interest groups that promoted resistance. Comparative historians wondered how "revolutionary" the Revolution really was. By and large, the best recent work has ignored these classic questions. Contemporary scholarship instead draws its inspiration from other sources, most notable of which is the far-ranging reconception and reconstruction of prerevolutionary America by a brilliant generation of colonial historians.

Bernard Bailyn's *Ideological Origins of the American Revolution* (1967) was a landmark in the new historical writing on colonial politics. As his title suggests, Bailyn was less interested in constitutional and legal arguments as such than in the "ideology" or political language that shaped colonists' perception of and responses to British imperial policy. Bailyn's great contribution was to focus attention on colonial political culture; disciples and critics alike followed his lead as they explored the impact—and limits—of "republicanism" in specific colonial settings. Meanwhile, the social historians who had played a leading role in the transformation of colonial historiography were extending their work into the late colonial period and were increasingly interested in the questions of value, meaning, and behavior that were raised by the new political history. The resulting convergence points to some of the unifying themes in recent work on the revolutionary period presented in this series.

A thorough grounding in the new scholarship on colonial British America is the best introduction to the history and historiography of the Revolution. These volumes therefore can be seen as a complement and extension of Peter Charles Hoffer's eighteen-volume set, *Early American History*, published by Garland in 1987. Hoffer's collection includes numerous important essays essential for understanding developments in independent America. Indeed, only a generation ago—when the Revolution generally was defined in terms of its colonial origins—it would have been hard to justify a separate series on the "new American nation." But exciting recent work—for instance, on wartime mobilization and social change, or on the Americanization of republican ideology during the great era of state making and constitution writing—has opened up new vistas. Historians now generally agree that the revolutionary period saw far-reaching and profound changes, that is, a "great transformation," toward a more recognizably modern America. If the connections between this transformation and the actual unfolding of events often remain elusive, the historiographical quest for the larger meaning of the war and its aftermath has yielded impressive results.

To an important extent, the revitalization of scholarship on revolutionary and early national America is a tribute to the efforts and expertise of scholars working in other professional disciplines. Students of early American literature have made key contributions to the history of rhetoric, ideology, and culture; political scientists and legal scholars have brought new clarity and sophistication to the study of political and constitutional thought and practice in the founding period. Kermit L. Hall's superb Garland series, *United States Constitutional and Legal History* (20 volumes, 1985), is another fine resource for students and scholars interested in the founding. The sampling of recent work in various disciplines offered in these volumes gives a sense of the interpretative possibilities of a crucial period in American history that is now getting the kind of attention it has long deserved.

Peter S. Onuf

INTRODUCTION

At the national level Federalists and Republicans offered alternative visions of American political economic development and foreign policy. The basis of party strength and the focus of electoral competition, however, were in the states. Before the advent of more modern forms of voter mobilization and party discipline in the 1820s, the national parties were little more than confederations of state organizations designed to gain control of the federal government. After Jefferson's election in 1800, the Republican succession was secured and national party competition diminished, notwithstanding a brief revival during the controversial War of 1812.

The study of state political history is essential to understanding national developments. Republican success was predicated on the erosion of Federalist support in key states. The Jeffersonians did not win power by popular appeals to an undifferentiated national electorate, but rather by building local support on the basis of local issues. Republican insurgents enjoyed marked success in Pennsylvania and New York, the most economically dynamic and socially diverse states in the union. Because Hamilton and the Federalists systematically fostered traditional patterns of Anglo-American trade, they alienated many manufacturers and mechanics who had expected the new government to protect and promote domestic manufactures. Anglophobic Irish immigrants gave a radical new dimension to Republican egalitarianism in urban precincts. The party of slaveholding southern planters thus mobilized the support of alienated and aspiring groups in the northern cities who sought to destroy privilege and equalize opportunity.

The social dimension of insurgent Republicanism was most apparent in New England where the Federalist ascendancy attempted to preserve church establishments. The Republicans' credibility as champions of popular rights was enhanced by Jefferson's and Madison's leadership in the campaign for disestablishment in Virginia, as well as by the party's advocacy of free speech and immigrants' rights in the late 1790s. In Massachusetts and Connecticut, local congregational control over the state churches and prudent concessions to Baptists and other "dissenters" enabled church establishments to survive the Revolution. But the steady growth of antiestablishment sects offered Republican managers the same kinds of opportunities provided by the influx of immigrants in the more heterogeneous Middle States.

State political developments reveal the extent—and limits—of "democratization" in post-Revolutionary America. If the bastions of privilege fell, or were at least shaken, by increasingly broad-based democratic electorates, then state legislatures and courts rigorously upheld property rights. In frontier regions from the Maine District of Massachusetts to the Northwest Territory (Ohio), Southwest Territory (Tennessee), Mississippi Territory, and Louisiana, Republicans campaigned for equal access to public property but never for redistributional policies that jeopardized vested interests. And everywhere in the new nation, from cities and long-settled rural areas to the rapidly extending frontiers, new concentrations of wealth and economic power quickly emerged.

Popular hostility to state-sanctioned monopolies and economic privilege did not stop the state governments from undertaking a vast array of initiatives that transformed the American economy. To the contrary, the democratization of politics legitimated public enterprise, especially in the development of transportation facilities, in order to promote market penetration and economic growth. Debunking the myth of laissez faire in early national history, Louis Hartz and Oscar and Mary Handlin showed in important studies of Pennsylvania and Massachusetts, respectively, that state governments did not hesitate to intervene where capital scarcity and an underdeveloped transportation network would have retarded development. Debates about internal improvements, as some of the essays in this volume show, did not center on the constitutionality of state action (as they did at the national level), but rather on the differential regional impact of specific proposals. The craze for state-sponsored improvements would not subside until the late 1830s and 1840s when depression, overbuilding, and massive indebtedness drove state governments to bankruptcy. L. Ray Gunn's *The Decline of Authority* (1988) provides the best overview and interpretation of the successive stages of state involvement in New York, where the Erie Canal, the greatest improvement of them all, was completed in 1824.

Legal historians have contributed some of the most interesting and controversial recent work on state politics. Richard E. Ellis analyzes Republican challenges to the Federalist-dominated judiciary in Massachusetts, Pennsylvania, and Kentucky in his *The Jeffersonian Crisis* (1971). The courts struggled to preserve their integrity while redefining their role under rapidly changing circumstances. Building on the seminal work of Willard Hurst, Morton Horwitz suggests that courts played an active role in facilitating capitalist development and imposing the resulting costs on the poor and marginal. Most critics reject Horwitz's "conspiracy" thesis and emphasize broad popular support for developmental policies, but it is clear that state governments played a crucial part in creating the conditions for rapid economic growth and all its unforseen consequences.

The essays in this volume, arranged on a state-by-state basis, provide only a sample of an enormously rich literature. The themes introduced here have by no means been exhausted. Good political histories for most states in this period remain to be written. Ongoing research should also clarify the connections between the democratization of politics, state activity in the economy, and the resulting redistribution and concentration of economic power.

Peter S. Onuf

ADDITIONAL READING

James M. Banner, Jr. *To the Hartford Convention: The Federalists and the Origins of Party Politics in Massachusetts, 1789–1815.* New York: Alfred A. Knopf, 1970.

Andrew R. L. Cayton. *The Frontier Republic: Ideology and Politics in the Ohio Country, 1780–1825.* Kent, OH: Kent State University Press, 1986.

Richard E. Ellis. *The Jeffersonian Crisis: Courts and Politics in the Young Republic.* New York: Oxford University Press, 1971.

Paul A. Gilje. T*he Road to Mobocracy: Popular Disorder in New York City, 1763–1834.* Chapel Hill: University of North Carolina Press, 1987.

L. Ray Gunn. *The Decline of Authority: Public Economic Policy and Political Development in New York, 1800–1860.* Ithaca, NY: Cornell University Press, 1988.

Oscar and Mary Flug Handlin. *Commonwealth: A Study of the Role of Government in the American Economy, 1774–1861.* Cambridge: Harvard University Press, 1947.

Louis Hartz. *Economic Policy and Democratic Thought: Pennsylvania, 1776–1860.* Cambridge: Harvard University Press, 1948.

Morton J. Horwitz. *The Transformation of American Law, 1780–1860.* Cambridge: Harvard University Press, 1977.

J. Willard Hurst. *Law and the Conditions of Freedom in the Nineteenth-Century United States.* Madison: University of Wisconsin Press, 1956.

Alan Taylor. *Liberty Men and Great Proprietors: The Revolutionary Settlement on the Maine Frontier, 1760–1820.* Chapel Hill: University of North Carolina Press, 1990.

Chilton Williamson. *American Suffrage: From Property to Democracy, 1760–1860.* Princeton, NJ: Princeton University Press, 1960.

Alfred F. Young. *The Democratic-Republicans of New York: The Origins, 1763–1797.* Chapel Hill: University of North Carolina Press, 1967.

CONTENTS

Volume 10—State and Local Politics in the New Nation

Douglas R. Littlefield, "Maryland Sectionalism and the Development of the Potomac Route to the West, 1768–1826," *Maryland Historian*, 1983, 14(2):31–52.

Douglas R. Littlefield, "The Potomac Company: A Misadventure in Financing an Early American Internal Improvement Project," *Business History Review*, 1984, 58(4):562–585.

Paul A. Gilje, "The Baltimore Riots of 1812 and the Breakdown of the Anglo-American Mob Tradition," *Journal of Social History*, 1980, 13(4):547–564.

John Lauritz Larson, "A Bridge, A Dam, A River: Liberty and Innovation in the Early Republic," *Journal of the Early Republic*, 1987, 7:351–375.

Harry Ammon, "The Formation of the Republican Party in Virginia, 1789–1796," *Journal of Southern History*, 1953, 19: 283–310.

Norman K. Risjord and Gordon DenBoer, "The Evolution of Political Parties in Virginia, 1782–1800," *Journal of American History*, 1974, 60(4):961–984.

Steven H. Hochman, "On the Liberty of the Press in Virginia: From Essay to Bludgeon, 1798–1803," *Virginia Magazine of History and Biography*, 1976, 84(4):431–445.

Michael E. Stevens, "Legislative Privilege in Post-Revolutionary South Carolina," *William and Mary Quarterly*, 1989, 46(1): 71–92.

Donald J. Ratcliffe, "The Experience of Revolution and the Beginnings of Party Politics in Ohio, 1776–1816," *Ohio History*, 1976, 85(3):186–230.

Andrew R. L. Cayton, "'A Quiet Independence': The Western Vision of the Ohio Company," *Ohio History*, 1981, 90(1):5–32.

ACKNOWLEDGMENTS

Volume 10—State and Local Politics in the New Nation

Alan Taylor, "The Disciples of Samuel Ely: Settler Resistance Against Henry Knox on the Waldo Patent, 1785–1801," *Maine Historical Society Quarterly*, 1986, 26:66–100. Reprinted with the permission of the Maine Historical Society. Courtesy of Yale University Sterling Memorial Library.

Gary J. Kornblith, "'Cementing the Mechanic Interest': Origins of the Providence Association of Mechanics and Manufacturers," *Journal of the Early Republic*, 1988, 8:355–387. Reprinted with the permission of Indiana University, Department of History. Courtesy of Yale University Sterling Memorial Library.

James R. Beasley, "Emerging Republicanism and the Standing Order: The Appropriation Act Controversy in Connecticut, 1793 to 1795," *William and Mary Quarterly, 1972,* 29:4 (Third Series): 587–610. Originally appeared in the *William and Mary Quarterly.* Courtesy of Yale University Sterling Memorial Library.

Barbara Graymont, "New York State Indian Policy after the Revolution," *New York History*, 1976, 57(4):438–474. Reprinted with the permission of the New York Historical Association. Courtesy of Yale University Sterling Memorial Library.

Alfred Young, "The Mechanics and the Jeffersonians: New York, 1789–1801," *Labor History*, 1964, 5(3):247–276. Reprinted with the permission of *Labor History.* Courtesy of Yale University Sterling Memorial Library.

Harvey Strum, "Property Qualifications and Voting Behavior in New York, 1807–1816," *Journal of the Early Republic*, 1981, 1(4):347–371. Reprinted with the permission of Indiana University, Department of History. Courtesy of Yale University Sterling Memorial Library.

Lee Soltow and Kenneth W. Keller, "New Jersey Wealth-holding and the Republican Congressional Victory of 1800," *New Jersey History*, 1982, 100(1–2):3–55. Reprinted with the permission of the New Jersey Historical Society. Courtesy of Yale University Sterling Memorial Library.

Martin S. Pernick, "Politics, Parties, and Pestilence: Epidemic Yellow Fever in Philadelphia and the Rise of the First Party System," *William and Mary Quarterly*, 1972, 29(4)(Third Series):559–586. Originally appeared in the *William and Mary Quarterly.* Courtesy of Yale University Sterling Memorial Library.

Roland M. Baumann, "Philadelphia's Manufacturers and the Excise Taxes of 1794: The Forging of the Jeffersonian Coalition," *Pennsylvania Magazine of History and Biography*, 1982, 106(1):3–39. Reprinted with the permission of the Historical Society of Pennsylvania. Courtesy of Yale University Sterling Memorial Library.

Kenneth W. Keller, "Cultural Conflict in Early Nineteenth-Century Pennsylvania Politics," *Pennsylvania Magazine of History and Biography*, 1986, 110(4):509–530. Reprinted with the permission of the Historical Society of Pennsylvania. Courtesy of Yale University Sterling Memorial Library.

Kim T. Phillips, "William Duane, Philadelphia's Democratic Republicans, and The Origins of Modern Politics," *Pennsylvania Magazine of History and Biography*, 1977, 101(3):365–387. Reprinted with the permission of the Historical Society of Pennsylvania. Courtesy of Yale University Sterling Memorial Library.

Douglas R. Littlefield, "Maryland Sectionalism and the Development of the Potomac Route to the West, 1768–1826," *Maryland Historian*, 1983, 14(2):31–52. Reprinted with the permission of the University of Maryland, Department of History. Courtesy of *Maryland Historian*.

Douglas R. Littlefield, "The Potomac Company: A Misadventure in Financing an Early American Internal Improvement Project," *Business History Review*, 1984, 58(4):562–585. Reprinted with the permission of Harvard Business School. Courtesy of Yale University Sterling Memorial Library.

Paul A. Gilje, "The Baltimore Riots of 1812 and the Breakdown of the Anglo-American Mob Tradition," *Journal of Social History*, 1980, 13(4):547–564. Reprinted with the permission of Carnegie Mellon University. Courtesy of Yale University Sterling Memorial Library.

John Lauritz Larson, "A Bridge, A Dam, A River: Liberty and Innovation in the Early Republic," *Journal of the Early Republic*, 1987, 7:351–375. Reprinted with the permission of Indiana University, Department of History. Courtesy of Yale University Sterling Memorial Library.

Harry Ammon, "The Formation of the Republican Party in Virginia, 1789–1796," *Journal of Southern History*, 1953, 19:283–310. Reprinted with the permission of the Southern Historical Association. Courtesy of Yale University Sterling Memorial Library.

Norman K. Risjord and Gordon DenBoer. "The Evolution of Political Parties in Virginia, 1782–1800," *Journal of American History*, 1974, 60(4):961–984. Reprinted with the permission of the *Journal of American History*. Courtesy of Yale University Sterling Memorial Library.

Steven H. Hochman, "ON THE LIBERTY OF THE PRESS IN VIRGINIA: *From Essay to Bludgeon, 1798–1803*," *Virginia Magazine of History and Biography*, 1976, 84(4):431–445. Reprinted with the permission of the Virginia Historical Society. Courtesy of Yale University Sterling Memorial Library.

Michael E. Stevens, "Legislative Privilege in Post-Revolutionary South Carolina," *William and Mary Quarterly*, 1989 46(1):71–92. Originally appeared in the *William and Mary Quarterly*. Courtesy of Yale University Sterling Memorial Library.

Donald J. Ratcliffe, "The Experience of Revolution and the Beginnings of Party Politics in Ohio, 1776–1816," *Ohio History*, 1976, 85(3):186–230. Reprinted with the permission of the Ohio Historical Society. Courtesy of *Ohio History*.

Andrew R. L. Cayton, "'A Quiet Independence': The Western Vision of the Ohio Company," *Ohio History*, 1981, 90(1);5–32. Reprinted with the permission of the Ohio Historical Society. Courtesy of *Ohio History*.

THE DISCIPLES OF SAMUEL ELY:
SETTLER RESISTANCE AGAINST HENRY KNOX
ON THE WALDO PATENT, 1785-1801

The Massachusetts General Court closed its 1785 session on the Fourth of July, the ninth anniversary of American independence. Just moments before the court adjourned, Major General Henry Knox's supporters pushed through a controversial bill confirming the Waldo Patent — a tract of thirty squares miles, or 576,000 acres of desirable land on the western shore of Penobscot Bay — to Knox and the other heirs of Brigadier General Samuel Waldo. In this manner, Knox exploited the absence of the bill's opponents, the legislators representing the more than six hundred families who had settled on the patent during the previous decade. During the Revolutionary War most of the Waldo heirs remained Loyalists, inspiring these settlers to move onto their patent in the expectation that the lands would be confiscated by the state and sold for token amounts to actual occupants. Knox's political maneuver launched the settlers prolonged, violent resistance to his land claims.[1]

The hastily drafted resolve included an ambiguous proviso: "that any person who may now be in possession of any lands within the limits of said patent, and who have been in possession of the same from any time before the 19th day of April, shall be quieted in such possession, upon such terms as shall hereafter be determined upon the General Court." Quieting referred to the General Court's policy of selling 100 acres for a token five dollars to those who had squatted on public lands during the Revolutionary War. Knox intended the year "1775" to follow "the 19th day of April," in order to exclude the overwhelming majority of the squatters who had settled after the war began. But in their haste his legislative servants left the year out, creating the impression that all pre-April 19, *1785*,

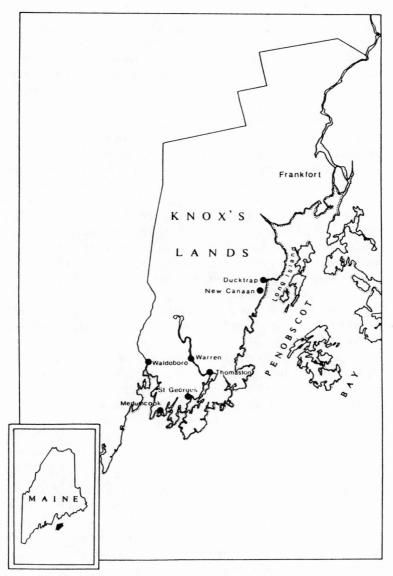

The Knox lands and Penobscot Bay's frontier towns, focus of settler resistance in post-Revolutionary War Maine.

settlers would be quieted. At the last moment Knox's servants noticed their mistake, but fearing that any attempt to correct it would exhaust the remaining members' dwindling patience and postpone consideration for another session, and perhaps sensing that the ambiguity would lull the doubts of some members, Knox's handlers pushed the misdrafted resolve through "in great haste."[2]

The resolve strengthened the heirs' legal right to demand payments from the settlers for their homesteads. If a settler refused, the heirs could institute an ejectment suit in the state courts to wrest away his lot of land, including any improvements — fences, clearings, and buildings. The heirs hoped that the threat of these suits would prove sufficient to bring the settlers to terms. In 1785 almost all of those settlers dwelled along the St. George's River or along the coast stretching from Broad Bay on the west to Penobscot River on the east. There were nine communities: Waldoborough, Meduncook (Friendship), Warren, Thomaston, St. George's (Cushing and St. George's), New Canaan, Ducktrap, Long Island (Islesboro), and Frankfort, the latter an extensive town that swept northward from Belfast along Penobscot Bay and up the Penobscot River. This string of new or greatly expanded communities attested that during the Revolution the Waldo heirs had lost complete control over the settlement process — over dispensation of access to land and over extraction of part of the enhanced value produced by settler labor applied to the forest, the fish, and the land. Henry Knox meant to regain that control.

By uniting against the proprietors, the settlers sought to frustrate legal actions by the heirs. After a fruitless visit to St. George's Valley in the fall of 1785, Samuel Winslow, one of the Waldo heirs, reported to Knox, "All the people that I spoke with behaved with great decency towards me but were evidently very circumspect & it is apparent they have agreed upon one mode of treating the proprietors." In some communities the settlers chose special town committees to represent their landed concerns; they pledged to follow the committees' lead, suffering none to seek a separate peace. By March 1786 Isaac Winslow Jr., Samuel Winslow's brother, was so "mortified at the present state of patent affairs" that he "heartily wished" that his family had never "had anything ever to do with them." Shortly thereafter the two brothers visited Long Island and were obliged to beat a hasty and ignominious retreat in "fear of rough usage." An August 1786 visit to the patent by Knox and the two Winslows did not improve relations. Knox offered to submit each settler's lot to three arbitrators — one chosen by the settler, one by the heirs, and the third by the first two — who would affix the price to be paid in three biennial payments without interest. The settlers rejected the compromise, insisting that the lands were their own and that they would pay nothing to men they perceived as wealthy parasites, most of whom had supported British efforts to "enslave" them. John Fitzgerald, an Irish-born Revolutionary War veteran who lived in Waldoborough, spoke for many when he insisted "that he had fought for the land and that he should think it a great hardship if he should be compelled to pay for it." The settlers hoped that the critical clause in the July 4 resolve would ultimately oblige the heirs to quiet every settler on the land before 1785 with 100 acres at five dollars.

Knox recognized the settlers' capacity for organized armed resistance and sensed their anxiety over the lack of warranty title to their lands. He knew that as long as the settlers stood together, the exercise of his legal power to attempt mass ejectments would spark bitter and sustained violence that would deter newcomers from the region and undermine local land values. Although hoping to obtain some land payments from these settlers, the General was willing to sell already occupied lands at a reduced rate in order to put his boundary lines around settler claims and preserve the unsettled lands in the backcountry for future sale at enhanced prices to their children and to newcomers.[4]

Returning to the patent with the Winslows in late August 1788, Knox offered to sell on terms amounting to four shillings

Portrait, after Gilbert Stuart, of Major-General Knox in Revolutionary War uniform. The cannon upon which Knox's left hand rests recalls his return from Fort Ticonderoga to Cambridge in January 1776, bringing the artillery which was used during the assault on British forces in Boston. Marriage to Lucy Flucker shortly before the war gave Knox access to the extensive Waldo Patent lands in Maine. Courtesy Maine State Museum.

($.67) per acre in three payments spread over five years, without interest. Moreover, instead of insisting upon scarce cash, he promised to accept payment in commodities such as lumber, cordwood, spars, staves, grain, or cattle, an important concession in the cash-short region. Knox promised to deliver a warranty deed once a settler met the first payment, taking a mortgage on the lot as security for the remaining two. The price — $67 per hundred acres — greatly exceeded the $5 that the "quieted" settlers on public lands paid, but the easy terms of credit, the ability to pay in commodities, the heirs' winking at parents signing for an additional lot or two for adolescent sons, the prospect of cherished warranty deeds, and the option of buying over one hundred acres were all tempting features. These terms particularly appealed to the most prosperous settlers who wanted to secure large tracts of especially valuable land. For instance, George and Philip Ulmer preserved their control over Ducktrap harbor and much of the Ducktrap watershed by buying 1,165 acres from Knox. The few with such

70

6

large claims had little to gain from the quieting alternative, which would limit them to 100 acres. The General shrewdly designed his proposal with the small settler elite in mind; he knew that when influential and economically pivotal men like the Ulmers embraced his terms many of their poorer neighbors would soon follow.[5]

Knox presented his proposed terms in a manner that pressured wavering settlers to accept quickly. He played on settler anxieties with hints that these were the best terms that would ever be extended. When the patent passed into the hands of the heirs' creditors or offspring, Knox intimated, the inhabitants would face harsher landlords. The General also exploited the poor communication between settlements by telling each in succession that the other communities had already embraced his terms, when frequently that was not true. Finally, Knox seems to have hinted that the terms would only stand if the General Court declined to mandate better quieting terms for the settlers. This led many to conclude that they had nothing to lose by signing on these terms; they still might avoid paying more than five dollars for a hundred acres.[6]

F earing isolation from their compatriots and worse terms in the future, 289, or about half of the 600 squatter families, embraced the heirs' offer. In all, Waldo Patent settlers signed for 32,784 acres, which at four shillings an acre promised the heirs a return of $21,856. Most of the holdouts dwelled in Islesborough and in predominately German Waldoborough. Apparently lacking a land committee and more vulnerable to misinformation because of their poverty and greater isolation, the settlers of Ducktrap and New Canaan proved particularly ripe for Knox's tactics. Although Knox initially found them the patent's "most hostile" settlers, in the end almost all grudgingly followed the Ulmers' lead in accepting the heirs' offer. When most of Ducktrap's settlers signed on September 24, their harder-line New Canaan neighbors anxiously asked for another meeting with the heirs. On September 30 they too embraced the proffered terms. Knox's special promise to allow

71

7

the local leading men to retain their mill seats seems to have loomed large in breaking down settler resistance. In Ducktrap and New Canaan a total of 81 residents with possession claims to New Canaan lots signed for a total of 13,837 acres, which, at four shillings an acre, promised the heirs $9,225 from those two communities alone. Since the 1790 census found only 87 families in the two communities, virtually all the residents in 1788 must have signed for their land.[7]

Knox left the patent satisfied with the terms secured and the division wrought in settler ranks. To encourage further doubts, the departing agents circulated a public "Notification" assuring the holdouts with calculated exaggeration that the heirs had "compromised with the great majority on terms highly advantageous to themselves & their families." The heirs enhanced the price for subsequent sales to between six and ten shillings ($1.00-1.67) per acre and promised another price increase in the near future. This placed psychological pressure on the holdouts and assured the signers that they had made a good bargain and that their interests lay with the proprietors in seeking a continued rise in local land values.[8]

But the ink on the agreements had scarcely dried when at least fifty residents of Ducktrap and New Canaan — over half the adult signers in those two settlements — took renewed stock of their poverty, their hopes of a General Court intervention, and their capacity for resistance. On October 18, 1788, they wrote to the heirs:

> We are each and every one of us very uneasy — that when we survey our naked families hear our creditors allso and [have] little or no provision to support us through the approaching winter and that we have to pay for the land that most of us payed largely for before [to original possessors] we find our difficulties to be such as is not equalled in any part of the Eastern Country (except in your Honrs. Patent) and we did not understand the true circumstances of the matter when we signed your Honr's obligation (for want of time to consider).

72

8

They asked "as children to a parent" either for a release from their agreement or for a much lower price. At the same time they protested to the court that the General's skill at stretching the truth had stampeded them into signing: "We think we are imposed upon by his representing things all in his own favour and taking advantage of the people's fears and ignorance by threatening to bring us to a federal court &c he knowing our circumstances to be very low indeed."[9]

Aware that such a release would encourage widespread remission from the heirs' terms, Knox flatly refused. The General dashed off a reply to the Ducktrap and New Canaan dissidents. He assured them it was utterly futile to expect any relief from the General Court, and for proof he enclosed a fresh copy of a new resolve "explaining" the 1785 document's vague but pivotal "quieting" clause. With half the settlers brought to terms, Knox concluded that the ambiguity in the clause had outlived its usefulness. In November 1788, exploiting the absence of the settlers' principal legislative spokesmen, Deacon Samuel Brown of Thomaston and Waterman Thomas of Waldoborough, the General obtained an explanatory resolve from the General Court that set 1775 as the year intended to follow "the 19th of April." This denied quieting to the great majority of Waldo Patent squatters: those who arrived either during or after the Revolutionary War. In this measure Knox's legislative servants violated the usual General Court practice of hearing both parties to a dispute, often through repeated extensions spanning several sessions, before holding a floor vote. By pushing through this "explanation," Knox meant to deprive holdouts of any hope that the General Court would intervene in their favor for a price lower than that offered by the heirs.[10]

Adding to settler apprehension, in the spring of 1789 several of the lesser Waldo heirs acting independently of Knox and the Winslows commenced trespass suits against all the settlers on Orphan Island (Verona) at the mouth of the Penobscot River. Many inhabitants regarded this as a precursor to massive ejectments brought by all the heirs against settler

73

9

holdouts throughout the patent. Consequently, the late 1788
and early 1789 petitions to the General Court protested that
Knox had practiced bad faith in securing an "explanation"
utterly contrary to their understanding of the original resolve
and to his repeated public assurances that he would seek no
alteration. Waldoborough's settlers insisted that unless the
General Court rescinded the explanation, they would "have
nothing to hope for but to be slaves to a set of men (The
Honorable H. Knox excepted) which have attempted to bring
us into bondage." The petitioners argued that the four shilling
price per acre would entail lifelong hardship:

> We have no lumber but cordwood which (to get one
> cord to market) will take one man and four oxen two
> days and then fetch but three shillings which ye
> petitioners want to purchase clothing for their
> children or pay their taxes which is more than they
> are able to pay, that with an addition of twenty
> pounds will involve many families in distress & mis-
> ery, as they have no other resource, many having but
> one cow, and some not as much as a cow and large
> families of small children.[11]

In the General Court, Deacon Brown and Waterman Thomas
conducted a passionate campaign for the explanatory resolve's
suspension. On the floor of the House, Deacon Brown furiously
insisted that the General had "cut the throats of the people by
obtaining that explanation." Brown and Thomas told Knox's
representative, General Henry Jackson, that "a *revolution*
would *certainly* take place on the patent unless they were
quieted in their possessions up to April 1785." Knox countered
that the settlers had simply misunderstood his words and
added, "The explanation can only affect the obstinately unjust.
Those who have compromised are not in the least affected by
it."[12]

Knox's legislative handlers rallied their supporters, particularly in the State Senate, a bastion of great property's interests, which to the General's delight not only rejected the
settlers' petitions, but ordered two of them burned as a demonstration of their disgust at the aspersions they cast on the

71

10

Land-poor settlers petitioned the General Court in Boston, arguing that if Knox's claims were upheld they would have "nothing to hope for but to be slaves." *Harpers Monthly,* 1872.

character of a fellow gentleman. In the House, Knox and his legislative allies practiced a strategy of delay, enlisting the support of House Speaker Dr. William Eustis of Boston to bottle up subsequent settler petitions in committees dominated by proprietary interests. When Waterman Thomas finally succeeded in June 1794 in securing House passage of a bill to send an investigative committee to the patent to hear settler complaints, Knox's servants used their greater strength in the State Senate to procure a continuation.[13]

Although triumphant in the legislature, the heirs' position among the settlers in the patent continued to erode. Land payments ground to a halt. In 1789 Knox's agents took in £262 in settler land payments; that plummeted to £35 in 1790; £33 in 1791; and £18 in 1792. From Ducktrap, George Ulmer wrote to the General in May 1790: "Your affairs here have not a verry pleasing prospect . . . Almost every one is flusht with the idea of getting their land for nothing. Circulating letters are sent from Penobscott to Waldoborough and St. Georges; and from them,

11

there are others sent to Penobscott and to this settlement." Community pressure restrained the few who remained willing to make payments to the heirs. In August 1791 Vose feared that "the unfriendly" settlers would cut away Ulmer's boom retaining the spars turned in on land account by some of his neighbors, "for there are many people in that quarter that are very angry that any person attempts to pay for their land."[14]

Few of the newcomers honored Knox's claim by applying for permits. On August 5, 1795, George Ulmer wrote to Knox: "The country settles much faster than it ever has done before; there are perhaps double the number on the land without permits to them that have them." In fact, Ulmer underestimated the number of new squatters without permits. During the decade 1790-1800, Ducktrap-New Canaan's combined population more than doubled from 87 to 206 families. During the same decade Ulmer issued only twenty-two permits. Knox faced not only the defection of most of the 1788 signers but a growing majority of new squatters in defiance of his claim. His prolonged absence, revived settler hopes of free land, and local population growth all combined to undermine Knox's fleeting control over the ongoing occupation of wild lands within the Waldo Patent.[15]

Resistance to Knox hinged upon three issues: the apparent injustice of a wealthy man demanding pay from the land's poor possessors; the suspect quality of Knox's title to the land; and the high price he charged for it. Nathan Knight of New Canaan insisted, "the state was rong in suffering any one man to possess so large a quantity of land." Knox recurrently promised, but just as recurrently failed, to deliver warranty deeds to those settlers who had made their first land payment. This aroused old suspicions of the Waldo Patent's legal bankruptcy, along with new fears that Knox's notorious financial difficulties would soon place his claim in the hands of creditors or heirs who would not honor his deeds. This was a frightening prospect to settlers intent upon safeguarding their children's status as land-holding free men. Finally, the poorer settlers particularly felt that they could not afford Knox's steadily

76

12

rising price without entailing prolonged sacrifices and suffering on their families. By 1796 Knox sought twelve to eighteen shillings ($2-3) per acre for his land, a rate at least three times that paid by the 1788 signers. Upon visiting the Waldo Patent, Alexander Baring, Knox's partner in another land speculation, the Bingham Purchase, concurred that the General was far "too enthusiastic" in his enhanced price; Baring considered it at least twice what the settlers could afford to pay.[16]

Knox's agents were especially concerned over the growing influence of the Reverend Samuel Ely of Ducktrap (in the portion that is now Northport). During a peripatetic career that mixed evangelical religion with an uncompromising populism, Ely acted throughout New England as the most consistent and forthright proponent of the Revolution as an opportunity for the common yeomanry to escape exploitation by their genteel rulers. He expressed a profound conviction that great men naturally sought to "enslave" the common folk. Timothy Dwight, the president of Yale College and voice of the Congregational and Federalist establishment in Connecticut, knew and detested Ely as a menace to genteel principles of good order: "He declared himself everywhere the friend of the suffering and oppressed and the champion of violated rights. Wherever he went he industriously awakened the jealousy of the humble and ignorant against all men of superior reputation as haughty, insolent and oppressive."[17]

Samuel Cullick Ely was born in the rural Connecticut town of North Lyme on November 6, 1740. He studied for the Congregational ministry at Yale, graduating in 1764. During the next year he began to preach in the northeastern Connecticut town of Somers. Dismissed on October 9, 1773, Ely patched together a modest living as an itinerant preacher in several of the new hill towns in Vermont and in western Massachusett's Hampshire County, returning periodically to his wife and young daughters in Somers. In January 1782 he emerged as the principal leader of "Ely's Rebellion" in western Massachusetts among hill farmers tired of heavy wartime taxation, expensive

77

13

government that seemed to benefit only the wealthy, and numerous debt suits brought by mercantile creditors. He insisted that these genteel rulers had perverted the Revolution for their own benefit and deprived the poor soldiery of their just pay by embezzling tax receipts. The county magistrates moved to behead the rebellion, arresting, trying, and convicting Ely of "treasonable practices." In March 1783 the General Court ordered Ely's release upon his posting a substantial bond, with his father and brother as sureties. The court stipulated that Ely would forfeit the sum if he did not keep quiet and stay out of the Commonwealth.[18]

Ely disappeared from sight until the 1790 Federal Census, which detected his presence with wife and daughter in Pownalborough's North Parish (Alna), a community long troubled with great proprietors. By June 1792, Ely had moved eastward, settling on the north side of "Ely's Brook" (now Shaw's Brook) at Ducktrap's (now Northport's) Saturday Point. Again he lived as an itinerant preacher among new and poor settlers, learning, in the process, of his new neighbors' hardships, hopes, and grievances — all so similar to what he had known among the hill folk of Vermont, northeastern Connecticut, and western Massachusetts. Conjoined with the settlers' frustrations, Ely's personal antipathy to great men proved explosive.[19]

Ely encouraged his neighbors to drive off Knox's surveyors and discipline those in their midst who spoke for the great proprietors. Ducktrap and New Canaan became the focal points of the conflict, as Ely's growing influence challenged the authority of George Ulmer, the area's wealthiest settler and preeminent proprietary supporter. In February 1793 Ulmer physically assaulted his new neighbor and then challenged him to a duel. In April Ely and his supporters exacted vengeance by tearing down the Ulmers' mill dam on the Ducktrap River, depriving the brothers of waterpower in the midst of the all-important sawing season. In June 1793 George Ulmer arrested Ely on charges of illegally performing two marriage ceremonies. A year later Ely escaped sentencing by presenting a letter of pardon from Governor Samuel Adams. In July 1793

78

14

one of Knox's land surveyors reported a threat from Micajah Drinkwater, "one of the GREAT SAMUEL ELY'S disciples who among others are going to prevent our surveying the seashore by Duck Trap &c, knock us on the head, break our instruments, moor us in Owl's Head Bay ... and ... say that even Genl. Knox himself will share the same fate if he attempts to take an active part in [the] enterprise." In September 1793 the Hancock court of General Sessions of the Peace convicted and fined Ely ten shillings for assaulting Job Pendleton, one of Knox's few supporters in Islesborough, "with a large stick."[20]

Ely also assumed the leading role in promoting the latest petitions from Ducktrap and New Canaan to the General Court. In October 1793 he drafted a forceful petition and secured 156 signatures from Ducktrap, New Canaan, and Islesborough. The petition informed the General Court that over two-thirds of the settlers were "so poor in purse and property that 'tis beyond their present ability & to human probability will remain so during their lives, to purchase or pay for their present premises." Ely carried the petition to Boston and lobbied the General Court on its behalf during the June 1794 term.[21]

Petitions from Ducktrap and New Canaan between 1788 and 1796 measure the local opposition to Knox's claim. The vast majority of the settlers in Ducktrap and New Canaan signed one or more of the following: the October 1788 letter to Knox for remission; Ely's October 1793 petition to the General Court and February 1796 letter to Ducktrap plantation's assessors; and Joseph Coombs's May 1796 petition to the General Court. Ely's petition alone claimed the allegiance of 103 settlers in the two communities, including nearly two-thirds of the 1788 signers (53 or 82) still there in 1790. A total of 112 adult males can be identified who persisted in the two communities during the years 1793-1797 when unrest peaked. Four out of every five (90 of 112) went on record against Knox's control.[22]

Two influences — prior frontier experience and relative poverty — played important roles in separating the ninety who chose Ely's path from the twenty-two who did not. The 1800

Federal Census for Northport and Ducktrap-New Canaan identify the place of origin for eighty-four of the former and twenty of the latter. Two-thirds (55 of 84) of the resisting settlers came either from elsewhere in mid-Maine, principally the Lincoln County coast, or from Nova Scotia, compared to but half (10 or 20) of those who stood by Knox. Prior frontier experience apparently taught men to distrust proprietors and encouraged settlers to trust in their ability to successfully resist proprietary power.

The resisting settlers were significantly poorer than those who declined to sign their petitions. The 1798 Federal Direct Tax returns provide property-holding evidence for seventy-seven resisting settlers and twenty collaborating settlers. Since all 112 lived in the two communities when the tax was taken, the fifteen who do not appear on the tax rolls apparently were considered without taxable dwellings and improved land. Thirteen of those fifteen were resisting settlers. Moreover, on average, those resisting settlers who possessed taxable property held less than half as much as the collaborators: $78 to $192 in average house value and $343 to $690 in real estate value. The two Ulmer brothers' combined $7,947 assessment represented 45 percent of the property value held by collaborators; but when they are excluded, the remaining eighteen were still 28 percent wealthier than the tax-paying resistors ($538 for the former and $421 for the latter). Those who could least afford to pay an outsider for title to their lands, and particularly those schooled by frontier experience to believe such payments were unnecessary and unjust, comprised those who defied Henry Knox.[23]

The settlers were further alarmed by the simultaneous efforts of the Kennebeck Proprietors, Twenty Associates, and Waldo heirs to extend their often overlapping survey lines deep into the backcountry. A series of proprietary surveys during the late fall of 1795 struck the inhabitants as a collusive effort to seal their fate. In Ely's words, "This chafed the minds of the people as a bear bereaved of her whelps." Armed settler bands, some reputedly involving up to three hundred men, intervened to order several survey parties to depart from the backcountry.

In late November a delegation of Balltown (Jefferson and Whitefield) settlers warned surveyor Benjamin Poor that "they were determin'd that no surveyor should run any line there at present" because the inhabitants were Revolutionary War veterans who had "fought" for the land once, "and were determined to fight for it again." In December, Clinton's leading settler, Simon Brown, demanded that Gershom Flagg cease his survey for the Plymouth Company, "as the land was the people's and not the company's," adding that "he had been in the service 6 years and fought for the land, and would have it."[24]

The most important incident concerned settler opposition to Ephraim Ballard's attempt to survey the Plymouth Patent's southeastern corner. This took Ballard's party into the heart of the new settlements founded by men and women who had moved up the Sheepscot and Damariscotta valleys in search of a refuge from the proprietary claims to Lincoln County's coastal lands. During early November in Newcastle and again in Nobleborough armed settlers turned Ballard's party away. A third attempt brought the persistent survey party to Balltown, the backcountry settlement where resistance was best organized. On November 12 they camped beside a brook north of Damariscotta Great Pond. In the middle of the night nine to ten armed men burst upon the campsite awakening the frightened survey party with shots into the air. Pressing a loaded musket to Ballard's chest the leader demanded, "deliver up, deliver up all, God damn you, deliver the compass, deliver up the papers, deliver up the cannister, God damn you, taking nothing out, if you do you are a dead man." Ballard delivered. To prevent resumption of the survey, the "Indians" smashed his compass and withdrew into the darkness, bearing away his map and survey notes.[25]

In the morning, six townsmen, all belonging to the household of Jonathan Jones, ventured out to guide Ballard's shaken men to safety. Jones was a local land speculator and the principal proprietary supporter in Balltown. Ballard described him as "a man of handsome property in that vicinity & who appears well attached to the government & laws." For this and other acts of assistance to Ballard's party, on the night of

81

17

Penobscot Bay scene, *Harpers Monthly*, 1877.

November 15 the insurgents burned Jones's two barns filled with grain and hay. Confident that no one would testify, the county magistrates decided not to risk arresting any suspects in the assault on Ballard's party or the burning of Jones's two barns.[26]

The absence of Knox and Ulmer in Boston for the winter inspired further militance throughout the region. Referring to the Balltown episodes, on February 10, 1796, an alarmed Thomas Vose wrote Knox, "The people's success in that undertaking seems to have given rise & encouragement to the inhabitants along thro' the back country to [New] Canaan & Ducktrap to plot & to covenant with each other, to pay you (as their expression is) a Jones' visit." He found that the settlers had collected "all the powder & lead in that country with a pretence of hunting." But, Vose noted, "Fire appears to be their favorite assistant." They reportedly hoped to drive Knox from the region by burning down his new Montpelier complex in Thomaston. Rumor held that several Balltowners involved in burning Jones's barns offered their expertise to the Ducktrap and Canaan people for driving out Knox and his agents. The new militance reached across the Penobscot River to the town of Penobscot (now Castine) where the lawyer Isaac Parker reported the settler resistance was "fast travelling east." A nocturnal fire badly damaged proprietor Leonard Jarvis's sawmill in Penobscot and an anonymous notice warned his agent-brother, Philip, to depart.[27]

In early February a mass meeting reportedly involving 200 men from New Canaan and nearby settlements subscribed to a written bond drafted by Ely. In a letter to Knox, Thomas Vose alleged that the settlers committed themselves, "under the most solemn obligations to extirpate you & and your agents from this country — [and] to abide by each other until the accomplishment of it, at the risk of their lives." Abner Milliken, captain of New Canaan's militia company, agreed to turn out his men to rescue any settler arrested for participating in the resistance. Referring to George Ulmer, Vose reported, "they pronounce him a traitor and propose to treat him accordingly when he returns." The settlers forwarded word to Ulmer that he must immediately remove himself and his effects from Ducktrap or suffer a "Jones visit."[28]

In the spring of 1796 the Ducktrap-New Canaan settler militance collapsed as suddenly as it had crested in the winter. On March 12 George Ulmer returned home armed with a new commission, secured with Knox's influence, as a justice of the peace; this invested Ulmer with enhanced prestige and power to arrest and imprison men suspected of riotous proceedings. He also bore a proclamation from Governor Samuel Adams denouncing the resistance and an order for Samuel Ely's arrest. Ulmer found that in New Canaan, Ducktrap, and Islesborough, "the combination was general with a few exceptions." But Ely's courage failed, and he took precipitous flight on the eve of Ulmer's return. This disheartened and confused the settlers, who consequently failed to carry out their threat to Ulmer.

Making the most of settler confusion, Ulmer immediately set about restoring his vigorous presence among the people. In a March 18 letter to Knox, he wrote, "I have endeavourd to mix in all the company I possibly could since my arrival, without the least fear and if they continue to shrink from their resolutions of opposition as they now appear to, by the time you arrive there will not be a man found that will own that he was in the least dissatisfied." As the new center of local attention,

83

19

Ulmer achieved a rapid reorientation of the oral exchanges upon which community consensus rested; settler conversation took on a new tone, stressing a love of order rather than a readiness to fight. Within a month Ulmer confidently informed Knox, "All is intirely tranquil ... amongue the people, there is not a person that appears to be the least opposed to your intrist, and but few that will own that they ever were." Knox's summertime return to Montpelier completed the transformation of public talk.[29]

George Ulmer took advantage of Ely's absence; when the parson failed to appear at the Hancock County Court on Common Pleas in April to answer the Ulmer brothers' suit against him for destroying their dam, the court automatically ruled for the brothers, awarding a ruinous sum of $349 in damages and legal costs, an amount twice what Ely possessed in real property. Ely briefly reappeared at his Northport home in September but again vanished before Knox's servants could arrest him.[30]

Why the dramatic shift in settler attitudes? The turning seasons contributed to the change from resistance to accommodation. Early winter was a season of relatively slack work and frequent visiting when settlers felt most closely knit to one another and could afford to attend meetings to exercise their anger. In early winter their larders were most full, nourishing a greater sense of independence from the credit nexus that tied them, through their leading men, to the external market. But late winter and spring were seasons of intense work and hunger that dispersed the settlers and discouraged attention to anything other than efforts to obtain food for their families. In addition, late winter's pinching circumstances restored the settlers' sense of vulnerability and dependence on provisions obtained on credit through leading men. George Ulmer noted the seasonal element in the ebbing resistance, labelling it "the reverse of the Philadelphia [yellow] fever: when the warm weather comes on wee shall hear no more of it."[31]

Joseph Thomas's new deed proved of equal importance with the onset of the heaviest work season and the renewed presence of social authority. On March 11, 1796, the day before Ulmer's return, Thomas Vose delivered to Thomas a warranty deed for 200 acres, Knox's first warranty deed to a lot of land in either New Canaan or Ducktrap. Vose exhorted Thomas to show it among his neighbors as evidence that the General did indeed dare to warranty his deeds. "Since Thomas has got his deed," George Ulmer reported, "they talk quite differently."[32]

Joseph Thomas was a very useful man to receive the first deed. First, unlike a George Ulmer, he was a rough-hewn man whose life was similar to that of his aggrieved neighbors. He began life in coastal Scituate, Massachusetts, and migrated to Jeremy Squam Island (a leading source of New Canaan's earliest settlers) at the mouth of the Sheepscot. Thomas married at Jeremy Squam in 1773 and during the Revolution moved eastward to become one of New Canaan's original settlers. Although he had been one of the October 1788 "revolters," unlike the great bulk of his neighbors he soon returned to Knox's fold and during what Ulmer called "the winter disorder of disaffection" continued to speak out in the General's favor. Consequently, Thomas's deed attested to the material benefit — warranty security — that accrued to those who stood by the General. Moreover, Thomas stood in the midst of an extensive kin network that promised to disseminate the deed's good effects to maximum advantage. Three other New Canaan settlers were his brothers and through their wives the Thomas clan was connected to the important Miller, Knight, and Higgins families. The Millers and the Knights ranked with the Thomases as the earliest and most influential families among the people and had been among Samuel Ely's most zealous disciples; their conversion promised to carry great weight among the rest of their neighbors.[33]

In sum, spring 1796 brought a sudden and dramatic reversal of the conditions that had promoted plans to drive Knox and his agents from the region. The effects of revived authority can be read in the reduced number and shifting distribution of signatures on Joseph Coombs's new petition to the General Court. Where 103 men signed Ely's October 1793 petition, only fifty-seven Ducktrap and New Canaan residents endorsed Coombs's. Thirty "holdovers" signed both; seventy-one "defectors" endorsed only the first, and twenty-seven "new signers" subscribed to only the second. Population turnover accounted for about a third (27 of 71) of the defectors, leaving forty-four 1793 signers who were still in the area in 1796 and so chose not to sign.[34]

It seems that most of the settlers who could afford to pay for their land — those for whom quality of title had been the chief reservation — were sufficiently impressed by Joseph Thomas's deed to withdraw from the resistance. Those least able to pay, and so more concerned with Knox's price, persisted in their opposition and were joined by other poor folk: their maturing sons and newcomers. More than ever, poor men of frontier origins predominated in the remaining opposition to Henry Knox. Where 68 percent of the 1793 signers (47 of the 69 whose place of origin is known) hailed from either mid-Maine or Nova Scotia, that proportion rose to 78 percent (21 of 27 holdovers and 18 of 23 new signers whose place of origin is known) of the 1796 signers. In short, a disproportionate number of defectors originally came from non-frontier areas with less of a tradition of resisting the authority of great men. The defectors also tended to be slightly more prosperous than holdovers; the thirty-nine defectors found on the 1798 Federal Direct Tax rolls owned an average of $426 in real estate compared to $377 for twenty-six holdovers. While the slightly more prosperous tended to drop out, still poorer men took their places: the twenty-two new signers on the 1798 tax list possessed an average of only $317. These men were poorer because, as a rule, they were either newcomers or young men just starting to develop their lots. On average, the 1796 signers were 16 percent poorer than the 1793 signers ($350 versus $407).[35]

That trend helps to account for the greater secrecy and desperation evident in settler behavior after Ulmer and Knox returned and Ely decamped. Although overt talk of "Jones' visits" lapsed, in late March George Ulmer noted, "Some still

Coastal farm clearing near Camden Hills, *Harpers Monthly*, 1877.

persist in heaving out threats, but in such a manner that it would be verry difficult to take hold of them." One day a group visited Ulmer's store and "after drinking freely" dropped hints that Knox "would sicken and die soon." Ulmer feared an attempt to poison the General, but it seems more likely that some frustrated and bitter settlers found recourse in a psychological war of suggestion. More tangibly, on the morning of July 15 George Ulmer awoke to look out toward Long Island and see "drifting about the bay" hundreds of spars that he had stored for Knox in two floating booms. In early September Ulmer and Knox again lost hundreds of spars through similar mischief.[36]

In March 1797 Knox's allies found still graver cause for concern. Evidence indicated that a few dissidents planned to take exemplary revenge on Knox and his leading supporters. Harris Ransom, a longtime boarder with Ely's family at Saturday Point, dropped alarming hints that led Ulmer to arrest and question him. Ransom testified that during Ely's last visit in September, eighty-two men joined with the parson in written bonds "to burn yours and many other people's houses, rob the stores, and burn the goods before the owners' faces, poison their cattle by mixing poison with salt, and putting in their fodder, and many other matters were to be done." Ely and his associates had planned to act in September, but held off until spring hoping that the General Court would pardon Ely and finally

87

respond to the settlers' repeated petitions. Ransom confessed and entered a guilty plea "in order to prove himselfe a good fellow as he term'd it" but refused to name any conspirators. Ulmer hustled Ransom across the bay to jail in Castine, Hancock County's shire town. Ulmer's fears of a rescue riot went unfulfilled, and Ransom was eventually released, apparently without trial.[37]

Ely's complete disappearance probably accounts for the failure of his latest scheme. During the winter, while Ransom and his associates held onto the written bond, Ely mounted an unsuccessful campaign to secure a pardon from the General Court. His last recorded words appeared later that year in a pamphlet entitled *The Deformity of a Hideous Monster Discovered in the Province of Maine by a Man of the Woods, Looking after Liberty*. The publication was devoted to assailing Knox, the Plymouth Company, the frontier's leading men, and Governor Samuel Adams. Ely expected martyrdom: "let me have a high scaffold that all may see a martyr die for the common cause of the people pleading for justice and true liberty." With that, Ely disappeared from sight. Two Ely family genealogies suggest that he died in Connecticut in 1795. Although the year is patently incorrect, it is possible that Ely did depart the Commonwealth to spend his remaining years in the state of his birth. In 1856 John L. Locke of Belfast recorded a tradition that Ely was drowned in Northport but gave no year. Destruction of Northport's vital records in the last century frustrates confirmation. Evidence from land deeds indicates that Ely's wife, Temperance, remarried in 1800 suggesting that the Parson died in 1799 or early 1800. For her second husband, Temperance took Islesborough's sixty-nine-year-old Shubael Williams, one of the island's earliest settlers and one of Samuel Ely's staunchest supporters. On July 16, 1803, Henry Knox conveyed title to Ely's eighteen-and-a-half acre lot on Saturday Point to Temperance for $87.50, punctuating the local demise of the resistance. No document survives to record what the General and his antagonist's widow thought or remembered on that occasion. Ironically, George Ulmer witnessed when Shubael Williams wrote his will on August 30, 1803.[38]

ADVERTISEMENT.

FOR THE BENEFIT OF THOSE,
WHOM IT MAY CONCERN.

T H E *Subscriber* has agreed, with all the *settlers*, seated on his back LANDS, and sold LANDS in the same quarter to numerous and respectable *Emigrants* from the *states Westward*, on principles promising them great prosperity and the establishment of harmony and *good order* throughout that fertile region. He conceives therefore, that this is the proper moment to announce in the most public and solemn manner that in future, *No usurpation of his lands will be tolerated.*

AS the LAND is, and will be surveyed into lots, no hope of impunity will arise from any supposed secrecy in the offence. Every regular *settler* has bound himself to discountenance and discover such lawless persons—It would be deemed madness among *Farmers* to suffer a WOLF to enter and remain among their sheep, much more so would it be for regular settlers after having *legally* engaged to pay a valuable confideration for their Lands to suffer an audacious usurper to enter and remain amongst them, SCATTERING THE SEEDS OF DISCORD, MISERY AND INSURRECTION WITH BOTH HANDS,

ANY Perfon therefore, who fhall in defiance of this notice, and in defiance of the laws, usurp lands of the Subscriber will be profecuted for the damages that may enfue ; fuffer the utter lofs of his labor and fixtures, and be refufed Land at any price whatever.

BUT the Young, Induftrious and orderly yeomanry and Artifts throughout New-England, are invited to view the Lands of the Subscriber, lying weft of PENOBSCOT-RIVER, and extending to within 15 miles of Kennebec-river, and contiguous to a line, on which it is in contemplation to open, and eftablifh a Turnpike-road from river to river.

THESE rich Lands are confidered by impartial Judges, foil fituation and climate combined, as affording as many at leaft, if not more advantageous, to young Agriculturifts, than any other within the United States.

THESE lands are to be fold for actual and immediate fettlement either for money or upon credit.

A perfect title and deeds of Warranty will be given on payment.

TIMBER and CORD-WOOD STEALERS throughout the PATENT, ftrip and wafte men who inftead of honeftly cultivating the foil, attempt meanly and infamously to gain property by this fpecies of theft, will incur, and receive all the punifhment, and pay all the damages, which the law fhall inflict ; and alfo all thofe, who fhall AID and ABET them in their unlawful conduct.

HENRY KNOX.

Montpelier, Thomaston,
St. George's River, Nov. 17, 1801

Nov. in Mass. Augusta, 1801

Knox's proclamation to the settlers. 1801. Courtesy Boston Athenaeum.

89

In 1797 a special commission proposed by Henry Knox and mandated by the General Court put an end to the speculation that the Commonwealth would eventually intervene to quiet the settlers. As Knox intended, the Waldo Patent Commission mollified enough settlers to bring the resistance to a halt. Henry Knox's lawyer, Nathan Dane, chaired the three-man "impartial" commission that set prices on a lot-by-lot basis. Each settler who had not already contracted with Knox to buy his lands could refer up to 100 acres of land already under his improvement; this intentionally excluded the 1788 signers.[39]

As a solution to the settlers' grievances, the Waldo Patent Commission fell far short of a blanket quieting act providing settlers with 100 acres for five dollars. Indeed, this measure was less favorable to the settlers than Knox's 1786 offer to have "mutually chosen" arbitrators set lot-by-lot prices. Prospect's land committee protested the commissioners prices: "It may be objected that the *rise* of land [values] has made these possessions worth more than in the period [1780s] before mentioned; but we beg leave to ask who was instrumental in the *rise* of these lands, or who made these lands more valuable than when in the state of nature? Was it not the settler?"[40]

As the October 1, 1797 deadline for submission drew nigh, many settlers concluded that the commission was their last best chance to obtain their lands at a relatively low price. In New Canaan, Ducktrap and Northport, forty-two settlers — roughly half the squatters who were newcomers since the 1788 signings — submitted, most during the final week of eligibility. The submissions were largely younger men or newcomers. As such, they tended to be poorer men who had previously opposed Henry Knox's claim. Twenty-seven appeared on the 1798 Direct Tax where, on average, they possessed a meager $299 in real property ($409 was the average in that poor area). Three in five had signed petitions against Knox and most (22 of 42) had signed the most recent petition in 1796.[41]

90

26

Once they had submitted, these settlers remained reluctant to hasten the day when the commissioners would assess payments. Knox's surveyors enjoyed little cooperation in completing the necessary survey plans of the submitted lots. By year's end, surveyor John Harkness had surveyed only half of the submitted lots in Northport-Ducktrap-New Canaan because so many settlers "war indefinite and delayed and said that they would have them surveyed another time." When early winter again removed Knox from the area and brought settlers into closer contact with one another, their talk again turned against the General and his agents. On February 4, 1798, George Ulmer informed Knox, "the winter disorder of disaffection so much prevails among our fickle inhabitants that I don't think I could collect two hundred dollars." But this residual disaffection was confined to delayed surveys and laggard payments from the 1788 signers; no one talked openly of "Jones' visits." [42]

With completion of the long-delayed surveys, the commissioners issued their awards on May 24, 1800. A total of 151 settlers throughout the patent received awards, 42 of them in Northport-Ducktrap-New Canaan. The settlers were to pay the amounts of their awards and interest (starting June 1, 1800) by October 1, 1801. Northport-Ducktrap-New Canaan submittees bought a total of 4,099 acres for $3,349, an average of $.82 per acre, a third to a fourth of the prevailing price Knox sought for his title in that area, but a bit more than what the 1788 signers had agreed to pay. In short, the commissioners acceded to Knox's wishes not to undercut the 1788 price and so increase discontent among the 1788 signers. The commission functioned as a face-saving measure that enabled Knox, on a one-time basis, to lower his official price sufficiently to further diminish the ranks of those opposed to his claim. [43]

Naturally, the settlers still did not much like the idea of paying a wealthy outsider for lands they considered their own, but the notion was more bearable amidst the new climate of confidence that every tomorrow would bring still higher land values for those with title. Even the poorest settlers, hardest

Situated on the St. George River, Montpelier was to be headquarters for Knox's many projects. Here, after years of acrimony, settlers converged to post notes and mortgages to receive warranty deeds to their lands. Maine Historical Society Collections.

pressed to scrape together the necessary payments, could sell their possessions and "right of signing" (the right to a Waldo Patent Commission award price) to more prosperous new-comers or local speculators eager to buy Knox's title at what were fast becoming bargain rates. Settler deeds in Northport-Ducktrap-New Canaan reveal that about half of the 1788 signers and Waldo Patent Commission submitees sold out their rights to others, who paid the General and received his title. This removed many poorer men, those who had comprised the body of the resistance from the area.[44]

In the fall of 1801 the last holdouts trooped to Montpelier to post notes and mortgages as double security for warranty deeds to their lots. Those squatters without signings, awards, or permits paid Knox $3.33 per acre. By 1804 Knox had disposed of title to most of the lands in the coastal towns. An investigation in that year found only 6,600 of Lincolnville's roughly 20,000 acres unsold. Some squatting persisted; 600 of

92

those acres were, in Knox's words, "recent usurpations, which are to be attended to." But such a small number of dispersed squatters posed no threat to Knox's control. Although their days of resistance were over, the inhabitants of Northport-Ducktrap-New Canaan continued to oppose Henry Knox vicariously by openly sympathizing with the backcountry folk who attacked Knox's survey parties in Lincoln Plantation (Thorndike) in 1800-1801. Writing from Ducktrap on July 9, 1801, George Ulmer informed Knox, "The people this way favour the insurgents very much and but few will take an active part against them."[45]

Knox's early supporters shared a portion of his spoils. They secured extensive tracts of valuable lands, including the most strategic combinations of timber, mill seats, and access to navigation, all for per-acre prices lower than those paid by their poorer neighbors for their less valuable lots. During the decade after 1794, when Knox issued deeds in Northport-Ducktrap-New Canaan, Philip and George Ulmer bought 3,668 acres for $5,230. Although the brothers obtained 18 percent of all the land Knox sold in those communities, they paid only 14 percent of the money Knox received for the land sales, amounting to just $1.42 per acre, compared to the average of $1.85 per acre paid by all others.[46]

With the cessation of hostilities against Henry Knox, the American Revolution came at last to an end for the inhabitants of the Waldo Patent. Contrary to their hopes, the Revolution had not wrought free wilderness lands for the poor man who got there first. Nonetheless, the terms obtained from Henry Knox did not represent a complete defeat. To break down resistance Knox had been obliged to offer terms that in price and warranty title compared favorably to those extended by Maine's other proprietors (although they were not nearly as good as those received by the squatters on state land). Once the Waldo Patent settlers acknowledged their dwindling options, they could conclude that they had protected their homesteads at a bargain rate. Knox, on the other hand, had established the limits of the coastal settlers' claims and had secured control

93

over the unsettled interior lands to the north and west — for which he planned to charge five to six dollars an acre. Consequently, the settlers' many children faced Knox's complete control over the wild lands that lay within a day's travel of their parents; if they wished to remain nearby, they stood to pay far more than their parents had to obtain smaller lots. Many would have to move beyond the Waldo Patent to find cheaper land.[47]

NOTES

[1] July 4, 1785, resolve in *General Court Resolves, 1785* (Boston, 1786, Evans no. 19090), p. 61; William Wetmore to Henry Knox, August 19, 1785, Henry Knox Papers (HKP hereafter) 51: 86, Massachusetts Historical Society (MHS hereafter).

[2] July 4, 1785, resolve in *General Court Resolves, 1785*, p. 61; William Wetmore to Henry Knox, August 19, 1785, HKP 51: 86, MHS.

[3] Samuel Winslow to Henry Knox, November 23, 1785, HKP 51: 97, MHS; Knox to Nathaniel Fales, March 1, 1785, HKP 51: 71, MHS; Knox to Warren's selectmen, August 26, 1786, HKP 51: 112, MHS; Knox to Thomaston's selectmen, August 26, 1786, HKP 51: 114, MHS; Knox to Philip and George Ulmer, August 29, 1786, HKP 51: 115, MHS; Knox to Mrs. Horwood January 13, 1789, HKP 52: 9, HKP 52: 9, MHS; James Hall to Knox, February 16, 1786, HKP, Box 1, Maine Historical Society (MeHS hereafter); October 4, 1788 entry in the second of Henry Knox's "Three Books on the Waldo Patent," MHS; Jasper Jacob Stahl, *History of Old Broad Bay and Waldoboro* (Portland, Maine, 1956), vol. 1: 533. For Fitzgerald's comment see September 18, 1788 entry in the first of Henry Knox's "Three Books on the Waldo Patent," MHS.

94

[4]Henry Knox to Mrs. S. L. Flucker, May 15, 1788, HKP 22: 41, MHS; Francois Alexandre Frederic, Duc de la Rochefoucauld-Liancourt, *Travels through the United States of North America* (London, 1799), vol. 1: 422.

[5]Henry Knox to Mrs. Horwood, January 13, 1789, HKP 52: 9, MHS; Lower Neck agreement, September 10, 1788, HKP 51: 144, MHS; Thomaston agreement, September 12, 1788, HKP 51: 148, 149, MHS; Ducktrap and New Canaan agreement, September 23, 1788, HKP 51: 154, MHS; Frankfort agreement, September 27, 1788, HKP 51: 161, MHS; Owl's Head agreement, October 2, 1788, HKP 51: 164, MHS; the second of Henry Knox's "Three Books on the Waldo Patent," MHS; for a somewhat distorted version see Alexander Baring to Hope and Company, December 3, 1796, in Frederick S. Allis, ed., *William Bingham's Maine Lands* (Boston: Colonial Society of Massachusetts, 1954), 37: 767.

[6]Henry Knox to Thomas Vose, January 10, June 21, 1789, HKP 23: 70, 24: 58, MHS; September 23, 24, 29, 30, 1788 entries in the second of Henry Knox's "Three Books on the Waldo Patent," MHS; copy of Ducktrap and New Canaan petition, n.d., c. January 1789, HKP 47: 42, MHS.

[7]For Ducktrap and New Canaan lists of signers see "Agreement at Ducktrap, 1788," HKP 52: 5, MHS; "Lists of Names who have signed General Knox's Proposals Since he left Ducktrap" in HKP Box 11, McHS; and "Subscribers in New Canaan, Northport & Ducktrap" in Henry Knox's Land Records Book, McHS.

[8]Henry Knox to Mrs. Horwood, January 13, 1789, HKP 52: 9, MHS; Waldo heirs to Captain George Ulmer, September 29, 1788, HKP 51: 162, MHS; Waldo heirs' "Notification," October 1, 1788, Eastern Lands Committee (ELC hereafter) Papers, Box 53, Massachusetts State Archives (MA hereafter); on Knox's shrewd psychology see Alexander Baring to Hope and Company, December 3, 1796, in Allis, ed., *Bingham's Maine Lands*, 37: 767; on Knox's plans for a further price rise see Knox to Isaac Winslow, Jr., June 28, 1789, HKP 24: 68, MHS.

[9]Ducktrap residents to Henry Knox, October 18, 1788, HKP 22: 164, MHS.

[10]Henry Knox to New Canaan's settlers, November 1788, HKP 51: 174, MHS; Henry Jackson to Knox, June 28, 1789, February 7, 1790, HKP 24: 66, 25: 127, MHS; Isaac Winslow, Jr., to Knox, June 21, 1789, HKP 52: 18, MHS; Resolve VIII, November 1, 1788, *General Court Resolves, 1788* (Boston, 1789, Evans no. 21248), p. 41.

[11]On the Orphan Island suits see 1791 Supreme Judicial Court (SJC hereafter) Record Book, July 1791, 194-195, 1794 Record Book, July 1794, 159, 167, Clerk's Office, Suffolk County Courthouse (SCCH hereafter), Boston, Massachusetts; on Knox's disassociation from those suits see Joseph Pierce to Knox, June 3, 1794, HKP 35: 130, MHS; Orphan Island petition to the General Court, June 18, 1789, *Maine Documentary History (MDH* hereafter), second series, vol. 22: 38-40; Nathaniel Palmer's petition to the General

Court, December 1788, *MDH*, 2d ser. vol. 22: 131; John Simonton et al. petition to the General Court, May 28, 1790, *MDH*, 2d ser. vol. 22: 362; the Waldoborough petition quoted is Waterman Thomas et al. to General Court, January 2, 1789, HKP 52: 7, MHS; David Fales to Henry Knox, April 3, 1789, HKP 23: 152, MHS; Isaac Winslow, Jr., to Knox, June 7, 1789, HKP 24: 42, MHS.

[12]Isaac Winslow, Jr., to Henry Knox, June 7, 1789, HKP 24: 42, MHS; Henry Jackson to Knox, June 28, 1789, HKP 24: 66, MHS; Knox to Thomas Vose, June 21, 1789, HKP 24: 58, MHS.

[13]Isaac Winslow, Jr., to Henry Knox, June 14, 21, 1789, HKP 24: 44, 52: 18, MHS; Henry Jackson to Knox, January 17, February 7, March 7, 1790, HKP 25: 100, 127, 162, MHS; Knox to Thomas Vose, April 18, 1790, HKP 27: 54, MHS; Dr. William Eustis to Henry Knox, March 6, 1790, HKP 25: 158, MHS. On the continued legislative stalemate see Henry Jackson to Henry Knox, February 13, 20, March 6, 1791, HKP 27: 140, 148, 156, MHS; Joseph Pierce to Knox, February 15, 1791, HKP 27: 142, MHS; Samuel Breck to Knox, February 20, 1791, HKP 27: 149, MHS; on Knox's strategy to bottle up settler petitions see Joseph Pierce to Knox, June 22, 29, 1794, HKP 35: 139, 145, MHS.

[14]For figures on the declining land payments see John Gleason Accounts, 1789-1794, HKP, MeHS; for the effect of petition continuations on payments see David Fales to Henry Knox, April 3, 1789, HKP 23: 152, MHS; Thomas Vose to Knox, September 9, December 14, 1789, HKP Box 1, MeHS and HKP 52: 28, MHS; Henry Jackson to Knox, November 15, 1789, HKP 25: 43, MHS; Isaac Winslow, Jr., to Knox, September 27, 1789, HKP 24: 175, MHS; Vose to Knox, March 30, 1790, HKP 26: 12, MHS; Jackson to Knox, July 4, 1790, HKP 26: 93, MHS; Isaac Winslow, Jr., to Knox, August 22, 1790, HKP 26: 153, MHS; George Ulmer to Knox, May 8, 1790, HKP 26: 45, MHS; on fears that Ducktrap's settlers would set Ulmer's spars adrift see Vose to Knox, August 22, 1791, HKP Box 2, MeHS.

[15]George Ulmer to Henry Knox, August 5, 1795, HKP 37: 159, MHS; the figures are a result of comparing names on the 1790 Federal Census returns with the names on the 1800 Federal Census returns for Northport and Ducktrap; on Knox's plans to prosecute see Knox to Isaac Winslow, Jr., June 28, 1789, HKP 24: 68, MHS; and Knox to Ulmer, October 1, 1795, HKP Box 3, MeHS.

[16]Nathaniel Knight's conversation is repeated in Thomas Vose to Henry Knox, March 6, 1796, HKP 38: 158, MHS; Moses Copeland to Henry Knox, April 2, 1789, HKP 23: 151, MHS; Knox to Thomas Vose, April 18, October 17, 1790, HKP 27: 31, 54, MHS; Vose to Knox, December 14, 1789, June 20, 1792, HKP 52: 28, 31: 150, MHS; Henry Jackson to Knox, May 1, 1791, HKP 29: 45, MHS; Vose to Jackson, May 14, 1794, HKP 35: 106, MHS; Samuel Ely, *The Unmasked Nabob of Hancock County or the Scales Dropt from the Eyes of the People* (Portsmouth, New Hampshire, 1796, Evans no. 31477), pp. 3-8;

96

The Appeal of the Two Counties of Lincoln and Hancock from the Forlorn Hope, or Mount of Distress; to the General Court, or to All the World (Portsmouth, New Hampshire, 1796, Evans no. 31477), pp. 20-21; Thomas Vose to Henry Knox, March 5, 6, 12, 1796, HKP 38: 155, 158, 37: 48, MHS; George Ulmer to Knox, April 7, 1796, HKP 39: 23, MHS. On price as an object see Thomas Vose to Knox, February 13, 27, 1796, HKP 38: 129, 144, MHS; John Rynier to Henry Knox, December 31, 1797, HKP Box 4, MeHS.

[17]Robert E. Moody, "Samuel Ely: Forerunner of Daniel Shays," *New England Quarterly* 5 (1932): 105-34; "Samuel Ely," in Franklin B. Dexter, *Yale Graduates*, vol. 3: 67-69. The Dwight quote appears in Timothy Dwight, *Travels in New England and New York* (New Haven, Connecticut, 1821), vol. 2: 189.

[18]Dexter, *Yale Graduates*, vol. 3: 67; Moody, "Samuel Ely," pp. 105-16; Dwight, *Travels*, vol. 2: 188-89.

[19]Pownalborough return for the 1790 Federal Census; on Ely preaching in Belfast for one summer see Joseph Williamson, *History of the City of Belfast in the State of Maine* (Portland, Maine, 1877), p. 229; and John L. Locke, "Sketches of the Early History of Belfast," *Republican Journal* (Belfast), May 29, 1856; on Ely's impact on his neighbors see James Nesmith to Isaac Parker, March 7, 1796, HKP 38: 160, MHS.

[20]On Ulmer assaulting Ely see Oliver Parker's Justice's Court record, April 13, 1793, in Hancock County Court of General Sessions of the Peace Files (CGSP hereafter), Box 77, Maine State Archives (MeSA hereafter); on the destruction of the Ulmers' dam see Philip and George Ulmer v. Samuel Ely, April 1796 in Hancock County Court of Common Pleas (CCP hereafter), Record Book, II: case no. 197; on Ely's pardon for performing irregular marriages see June 16, 1794 entry, Council Records, 32 (1793-1797): 184; see also Moody, "Samuel Ely," p. 123; and Commonwealth v. Samuel Ely, July 1794, in 1794 SJC Record Book, 176, SCCH; George Ulmer's account for June 1793 in Hancock County CGSP files Box 76, MeSA; Ebenezer Jennison's survey journal, July 2, 1793 entry, HKP 52: 53, MHS; on Ely's assault on Job Pendleton see Commonwealth v. Ely, September 1793 in Hancock County CGSP files Box 77, MeSA; see also Henry Knox to George Ulmer, September 5, 1793, HKP 34: 89, MHS.

[21]Waldo Patent petition, October 8, 1793, HKP 52: 50, MHS; Joseph Pierce to Henry Knox, June 3, 1794, HKP 35: 130, MHS.

[22]The names were collected from Ducktrap Plantation residents to Henry Knox, October 18, 1788, HKP 22: 164, MHS; Waldo Patent petition, October 8, 1793, HKP 52: 50, MHS; Samuel Ely et al. to Ducktrap Plantation assessors, January 27, 1796, HKP 38: 105, MHS; and Joseph Coombs et al. to the General Court, May 1796 in Related Papers filed with resolve of March 9, 1797, MA. The 112 men are those who appear on at least one of three listings for inhabitants of Ducktrap-New Canaan, 1788-1793 (the 1788 signers, the 1790 Federal Census, the November 10-12, 1793 list recorded in Hancock

County Deeds, October 4, 1794, III: 24) and on at least one of three listings for said inhabitants, 1797-1800 (1797 Waldo Patent Commission Submissions, vols. 1 and 2, MA; the 1798 Federal Direct Tax Returns; New England Historical and Genealogical Society (NEHGS hereafter); the 1800 Federal Census returns).

[23]The 1798 Federal Direct Tax returns for Northport and Ducktrap-New Canaan survive at NEHGS.

[24]Samuel Ely, *The Deformity of a Hideous Monster, Discovered in the Province of Maine, by a Man Looking after Liberty* ... MHS; Gershom Flagg to Joseph North, December 27, 1795, in Related Papers, February 27, 1796 resolve, MA; Benjamin Poor deposition, November 25, 1795 in related papers, January 29, 1799 resolve, MA.

[25]Ephraim Ballard to the Kennebeck Proprietors, January 1, 1796, Kennebeck Proprietors Papers (KPP hereafter), Box 4, MeHS; Philip Bullen deposition, January 1, 1796, in related papers, January 29, 1799 resolve, MA; Ephraim Ballard to the General Court, December 31, 1798 in related papers, February 1, 1799 resolve, MA; Ephraim Ballard deposition, November 20, 1795, Jonathan Jones, Jr., et al. deposition, January 5, 1796, both in related papers, January 29, 1799 resolve, MA.

[26]Jonathan Jones's petition to the General Court, n.d., c. January 1796; Jonathan Jones, Jr., et al. deposition, January 5, 1796, Thomas Trask, Jr., and Jonathan Trask depositions, June 9, 1797, all in related papers, January 29, 1799 resolve, MA; Ephraim Ballard to Jonathan Jones, November 18, 1795, KPP Box 4, MeHS; Jonathan Jones to the Kennebeck Proprietors, February 3, 1802, KPP Box 5, MeHS; on the decision not to seek arrests see Daniel Cony to James Sullivan, November 21, 1795, in related papers, February 27, 1796, resolve, HKP, MA.

[27]Samuel Waldo to Isaac Winslow, February 10, 1796, HKP 38: 123, MHS; Thomas Vose to Knox, February 10, 1796, Council Files Box 10 (March 1795-February 1797), MA; Isaac Parker to Henry Knox, March 1, 1796, HKP 38: 149, MHS.

[28]Thomas Vose to Henry Knox, February 10, 1796, in Council Files Box 10 (March 1795-February 1797), MA; Vose to Knox, February 13, March 5, 1796, HKP 38: 129, 155, MHS; Isaac Parker to Knox, March 1, 1796, HKP 38: 149, MHS; George Ulmer to Knox, March 18, 1796, HKP 38: 171, MHS.

[29]George Ulmer to Henry Knox, March 18, April 7, 1796, HKP 38: 171, 39:23, MHS; Ulmer to Thomas Vose, March 18, 19, 1796, HKP 38: 172, 173, MHS; see also Knox to Ulmer, July 6, 1796, HKP Box 4, MeHS.

[30]Thomas Knowlton and James Nesmith to Henry Knox, March 15, 1796, HKP 38: 169, MHS; George Ulmer to Knox, March 18, 1796, HKP 38: 171, MHS; Thomas Vose to Knox, March 19, 21, 1796, HKP 38: 173, 174; on Ulmer's suit see Philip and George Ulmer v. Ely, April 1796, Hancock County CCP Record Book, II: case no. 197; on Ely's return see Ulmer to Knox,

September 10, 1796, HKP 39: 142, MHS; Knox to Ulmer, September 27, 1796, HKP 39: 158, MHS; Knox to Richard Hunnewell, September 27, 1796, HKP Box 4, MeHS; Hunnewell to Knox, October 1, 1796, HKP 39: 162, MHS.

[31] On the absences of Knox and Ulmer see Thomas Vose to Knox, February 13, 1796, HKP, 38: 129, MHS; Henry Knox to Thomas Vose, February 28, 1796, HKP 38: 147, MHS; George Ulmer to Knox, March 18, April 7, 1796, HKP 38: 171, 39: 23, MHS.

[32] Thomas Vose to Henry Knox, March 12, 21, 1796, HKP 37: 48, 38: 174, MHS; George Ulmer to Knox, April 7, 1796, HKP 39: 23, MHS; Knox to Joseph Thomas, recorded July 25, 1797, Hancock County Deeds (HCD hereafter) 39: 173, Hancock County Courthouse (HCC hereafter).

[33] Joseph Miller, "Historical Sketch of the Town of Lincolnville," typescript, NEHGS; on Joseph Thomas's seeking a release from his signing see Ducktrap Plantation settlers to Knox, October 18, 1788, HKP 22: 164, MHS; on Joseph Thomas's vocal loyalty to Knox see George Ulmer to Knox, March 18, 1796, HKP 38: 171, MHS; for Thomas's genealogical connections I am indebted to Mrs. Priscilla Jones's Waldo County genealogical collection.

[34] Waldo Patent petition, October 8, 1793, HKP 52: 50, MHS; Joseph Coombs et al. to the General Court, May 1796, related papers, March 9, 1797 resolve, MA; 27 of the "defectors" cannot be found on either the 1797 list of submittees, the 1798 Federal Direct Tax returns, or the 1800 Federal Census; the 30 "holdovers" and 71 "defectors" add up to 101 rather than the 103 total signers to the 1793 petition because two of the names on the document are illegible.

[35] The 1798 Federal Direct Tax returns (NEHGS) or the 1800 Federal Census returns for Northport and Ducktrap-New Canaan provide the place of residence.

[36] George Ulmer to Henry Knox, March 18, July 15, September 10, 1796, HKP 38: 171, 39: 112, 39: 142, MHS; Knox to Ulmer, July 17, 1796, HKP Box 4, MeHS; Knox to Ulmer, September 14, October 12, 1796, HKP 39: 144, 167, MHS.

[37] George Ulmer to Henry Knox, March 3, 1797, HKP 40: 72, MHS; George Ulmer's J.P. Court, March 1, 1797, Hancock County CGSP files Box 77, MSA.

[38] Samuel Ely to the General Court, January 2, 1797, HKP 40: 42, MHS; Henry Knox to George Ulmer, March 12, 1797, HKP 40: 80, MHS; Ely, Deformity, p. 16; on the genealogies see Moody, "Samuel Ely," p. 134; Locke, "Sketches"; on Ely's Saturday Point property see George Ulmer to Henry Knox, July 15, 1803, HKP Box 7, MeHS; Ulmer to Knox, December 22, 1800, HKP Box 6, MeHS; on Williams's support of Ely see George Ulmer to Knox, March 18, 1796, HKP 38: 171, MHS; for Williams's August 30, 1805 will see Hancock County Probate, vol. 1: 415-16; John P. Farrow, History of Islesborough, Maine (Bangor, Maine, 1893), pp. 298-99. Farrow erroneously gives Shubael Williams's second wife's name as "Mrs. Temperance Easton."

99

[39]Resolve LX, March 9, 1797, *General Court Resolves, 1797* (Boston, 1797, Evans no. 32449), p. 72; Nathan Dane compiled a L21,13.5 account in legal work done for Knox April 1793-March 1796, HKP Box 4, McHS; John Sprague of Lancaster and Enoch Titcomb, Jr., of Newburyport were the other two commissioners.

[40]Prospect Land Committee to WPC, February 16, 1798, ELC Box 53, MA.

[41]Noah Miller to the WPC, August 14, 1797, ELC Box 53, MA; the list of settlers and their dates of submission can be found in Waldo Patent Commission Submissions, vols. 1, 2, MA.

[42]John Harkness to the WPC, January 1, 1798, ELC Box 53, MA; George Ulmer to Henry Knox, February 4, 1798, HKP Box 5, McHs.

[43]For a community-by-community breakdown of submissions see Waldo Patent Commissions Submissions, vols. 1: 1, 2: 1, MA.

[44]On rising prices see George Ulmer to Henry Knox, August 5, 1795, HKP 37: 159, MHS; Knox to George Washington, January 15, 1797, in Francis S. Drake, *Life and Correspondence of Henry Knox, Major General in the American Revolutionary Army* (Boston, Massachusetts, 1873), p. 114; Knox to Ulmer, November 13, 1801, HKP Box 6, McHS. On these transactions see La Rochefoucauld-Liancourt, *Travels*, vol. 1: 429-30.

[45]George Ulmer to Henry Knox, July 9, 1801, HKP 44: 22, MHS. The results of the Lincolnville investigation appear in the May 18, 1804, entry of Henry Knox's "Journal," Montpelier, Thomaston, Maine.

[46]The 137 deeds issued by Knox to Northport and Lincolnville lands, 1795-1804, sold a total of 20,475 acres for $36,335.

[47]For fuller discussion of these themes see Alan Taylor, "Liberty-Men and White Indians: Frontier Migration, Popular Protest, and the Pursuit of Property in the Wake of the American Revolution," Ph.d dissertation, Brandeis University, 1985.

A native of Maine, Alan Taylor graduated from Colby College in 1977. He received his Ph.D. in 1986 from Brandeis University for his dissertation, "Liberty-Men and White Indians," a study of the Maine frontier after the Revolution. He holds a postdoctoral fellowship at the Institute of Early American History and Culture. He is grateful to Robert A. Gross, Marvin Meyers, and Laurel Thatcher Ulrich for reading and criticizing this article, to Isabel Maresh, Betsy Moshier, the Honorable David Nichols, Danny D. Smith, and especially the late Priscilla Jones for genealogical assistance, and to Karen Bowden and Julia Walkling of the Maine Humanities Council for the council's generous support, moral and financial.

100

"CEMENTING THE MECHANIC INTEREST": ORIGINS OF THE PROVIDENCE ASSOCIATION OF MECHANICS AND MANUFACTURERS

Gary J. Kornblith

In September 1785, the artisans of Providence, Rhode Island, received a circular from members of the recently established Association of Tradesmen and Manufacturers of the Town of Boston. Warning that "the late system of commerce, pursued since the peace, of importing such articles as can be manufactured among ourselves . . . must eventually prove ruinous to every mechanical branch in America," the Bostonians urged craftsmen in other communities to form their own organizations and join in a nationwide effort to raise the "united voice of the tradesmen and manufacturers of America."[1]

Mr. Kornblith is a member of the Department of History, Oberlin College, in Oberlin, Ohio.
 The author gratefully acknowledges the assistance of Carol Lasser, James M. Banner, Jr., Charlotte Briggs, Michael Dieckmann, Heather Hogan, Karen Merrill, John M. Murrin, Eric Phillips, Steven J. Ross, Lynne Withey, Alfred F. Young, and the staffs of the American Antiquarian Society, Oberlin College Library, Rhode Island Historical Society Library, and Rhode Island State Archives. Funding for this study was provided by a Samuel Foster Haven Fellowship, American Antiquarian Society; a Shreve Postdoctoral Fellowship, Princeton University; an Albert J. Beveridge Grant for Research in the History of the Western Hemisphere, American Historical Association; Grants-in-Aid for Research and Development, Oberlin College; a Robert and Eleanor Biggs Fellowship in the Social Sciences, Oberlin College; and the Student Aid for Educational Quality Program, Dana Foundation.
  [1] *The United States Chronicle: Political, Commercial, and Historical* (Providence, R.I.), Sept. 22, 1785.

JOURNAL OF THE EARLY REPUBLIC, 8 (Winter 1988). © 1988 Society for Historians of the Early American Republic.

Providence artisans made no immediate reply, but three and a half years later they decided to act. On February 27, 1789, fourteen tradesmen gathered at the house of Elijah Bacon on the west side of town. With the Boston precedent in mind, they resolved unanimously to form "an Association, *for the Promotion of Home Manufactures, [for] cementing the Mechanic Interest,* and *for raising a Fund to support the Distressed.*"[2] The following week they met again, along with several other interested craftsmen, to adopt a constitution and to elect provisional officers. Styling themselves the Providence Association of Mechanics and Manufacturers, the group next petitioned the Rhode Island General Assembly for a charter of incorporation, which was duly granted on March 16. Before the month was out forty-six persons had paid the fee of 1 s., 6 d. required to join the Association.[3]

Compared to several other artisanal organizations founded in late eighteenth-century America, the Providence Association of Mechanics and Manufacturers proved to be highly inclusive and successful. A year after its inception it boasted "more than Two Hundred Members,—among which we reckon nearly all the Mechanics of Reputation in the Town."[4] Within five years, it commanded the respect of the local gentry and townspeople generally, and it continued to play a major role in Providence affairs until after the Civil War.[5] This article explores the founders' motivations and objectives, analyzes the composition of the Association's initial membership, and details the organization's fledgling efforts to fulfill its institutional goals. Particular attention is paid to the associates' strategies for shaping the political economy of the new nation.

---

    [2] Records of the Providence Association of Mechanics and Manufacturers (hereafter PAMM Records), Association Minute Books, I, Feb. 27, 1789; Letter to the Mechanics and Manufacturers of Boston, Apr. 30, 1789, *ibid.*, May 18, 1789; Minutes of Members Present at the First Meetings, PAMM Records, Papers, 1789. The PAMM Records are located at the Rhode Island Historical Society Library, Providence.
    [3] PAMM Records, Association Minute Books, I, Mar. 4, 7, 23, 30, 1789; Petitions to the Rhode Island General Assembly, XXIV, 141 (Rhode Island State Archives, Providence).
    [4] PAMM Records, Association Minute Books, I, May 10, 1790.
    [5] For scholarly accounts of the later history of the Association, see John S. Gilkeson, *Middle-Class Providence, 1820-1940* (Princeton, N.J. 1986), esp. ch. 2; Gary John Kornblith, "From Artisans to Businessmen: Master Mechanics in New England, 1789-1850" (2 vols., Ph.D. diss., Princeton University 1983), II, chs. 12-13, *passim*; and William Gerald Shade, "The Rise of the Providence Association of Mechanics and Manufacturers: A Workingman's Organization, 1789-1850" (M.A.T. thesis, Brown University 1962).

A number of historians have argued in recent years that American artisans developed their own brand of republicanism during and after the revolution, one that challenged elitist assumptions and promoted egalitarian values. In his important study of Baltimore mechanics, for example, Charles G. Steffen contrasts the mechanics' "radical" republicanism to the "conservative" republicanism of merchants and lawyers.[6] In a summary of his extensive research on Boston, New York, and other cities, Alfred F. Young characterizes artisan republicanism as "a conviction that mechanics were citizens entitled to equal rights and to an equal voice in their government, a pride of craft, and a pride in labor as the source of wealth."[7] By these accounts, what distinguished artisan republicanism from other variants was, above all else, its assertion of democratic principles within a cosmopolitan context.

Yet there is scholarly disagreement about the relationship between artisan republicanism and the development of liberal capitalism in America. On one side of this debate are historians who identify urban artisans as one of the first occupational groups to embrace openly the principles of self-interest, private gain, and an unfettered market economy. In his insightful analysis of Tom Paine's Philadelphia, Eric Foner finds that during the revolution master craftsmen forsook their commitment to the precepts of a traditional "moral economy" and "increasingly looked to the self-regulating market as the only legitimate arbiter of their economic activity."[8] More generally, Joyce Appleby contends that from the 1760s forward "the popular agitators in the urban politics in America elevated their goals to a universal law of self-interest." While Appleby does not question the artisanal commitment to democratic values, she argues forcefully that democracy and possessive individualism developed hand in hand. To the dismay of an American gentry still committed to "the austere truths of classical republicanism," she explains, ambitious tradesmen and other men-on-the-make "endorsed the liberal vision of a society of undifferentiated competitors."[9]

---

[6] Charles G. Steffen, *The Mechanics of Baltimore: Workers and Politics in the Age of Revolution, 1763-1812* (Urbana, Ill. 1984), 281.

[7] Alfred F. Young, "Revolutionary Mechanics," in *Working for Democracy: American Workers from the Revolution to the Present*, ed. Paul Buhle and Alan Dawley (Urbana, Ill. 1985), 8. Young explains his conception of artisan republicanism at greater length in "'By Hammer and Hand All Arts Do Stand': Mechanics and the Shaping of the American Nation, 1760-1820" (unpub. paper in author's possession).

[8] Eric Foner, *Tom Paine and Revolutionary America* (New York 1976), 173.

[9] Joyce Appleby, "The Social Origins of American Revolutionary Ideology," *Journal of American History*, 64 (Mar. 1978), 954, 949.

On the other side of this debate are historians who emphasize the communal dimension of artisan republicanism and highlight the persistence of cooperative values rooted in a handicraft mode of production. A leading exponent of this view is Sean Wilentz, whose brilliant study of New York City portrays the artisan ideal as the achievement of personal independence within a society of public-spirited citizens. In such a society, Wilentz explains, "Men's energies would be devoted, not to personal ambition or profit alone, but to the commonwealth." While he does not claim this ideal was ever fully realized, he does contend that it curbed tendencies toward possessive individualism. According to Wilentz, in short, "the rule of virtue" remained ascendant within New York trades until well into the nineteenth century.[10]

No single case study is likely to resolve this scholarly controversy. Yet a close examination of the early history of the Providence Association of Mechanics and Manufacturers allows further insight into the social ethos underlying artisanal behavior in the early republic and thus may serve to move the debate forward in a constructive fashion.

Boasting a population of approximately six thousand inhabitants in 1789, Providence over the previous half-century had evolved from a coastal village into a regional entrepôt and international seaport. In the years leading up to the revolution, a Providence town meeting later recalled, "extensive foreign trade . . . furnished business and support for all its numerous dependents and invigorated every class of people in town"—including "shipwrights, housewrights, masons and all sorts of mechanics and laboring men."[11] But the war brought disruption, inflation, and depression. While Providence escaped the ravages of British occupation, it endured a lengthy blockade of Narragansett Bay that forced local merchants to re-route their trade through other ports. When they attempted to revive old commercial patterns after the end of hostilities, they found the lucrative West Indies market closed to American vessels and English demand diminished by high duties on whale oil and other American products.

---

[10] Sean Wilentz, *Chants Democratic: New York City and the Rise of the American Working Class, 1788-1850* (New York 1984), 102. See also Steven J. Ross, *Workers on the Edge: Work, Leisure, and Politics in Industrializing Cincinnati, 1788-1890* (New York 1985), esp. ch. 1.

[11] Providence Town Meeting Records, VI, Jan. 29, 1778 (microfilm, Providence Public Library), quoted in Nancy Fisher Chudacoff, "The Revolution and the Town: Providence, 1775-1783," *Rhode Island History*, 35 (Aug. 1976), 72.

Unable to pay for the British goods they imported, they sank into debt to London creditors and curtailed their commercial activities. Local artisans, among others, suffered the consequences.[12] Although a state tariff passed in 1785 provided a measure of protection from foreign competition, the low level of consumer demand threatened many artisans with immediate impoverishment and posed for others the prospect of declining opportunities for years to come.[13]

Complicating this economic crisis was Rhode Island's peculiar political predicament. As in several other states, representatives of the commercial and agrarian interests battled in the legislature over questions of debt, taxation, and paper money. But, unlike elsewhere, in Rhode Island the agrarian interest gained a near total victory. In the spring of 1786, the self-styled Country party won control of the general assembly and promptly passed an act for the emission of paper currency as legal tender. Thereafter the so-called Mercantile party was kept on the defensive. When the summons went out for a convention in Philadelphia to revise the Articles of Confederation, Rhode Island declined to send a delegation. Once the proposed Constitution was conveyed to the states for their approval, the Country party, fearing the elimination of paper money and the loss of state autonomy, blocked repeated efforts by Federalists in the legislature to call a ratifying convention. Although the general assembly belatedly agreed to sponsor a public referendum on the Constitution in March 1788, it did so in full confidence that a majority of freemen, voting in their respective town meetings, would reject the document. Most Federalists chose to boycott the proceedings rather than accord them legiti-

---

[12] Chudacoff, "Revolution and Town," 71-89; Franklin Stuart Coyle, "The Survival of Providence Business Enterprise in the American Revolutionary Era (1770-1785)" (M.A. thesis, Brown University 1960); Franklin Stuart Coyle, "Welcome Arnold (1745-1798), Providence Merchant: The Founding of an Enterprise" (Ph.D. diss., Brown University 1972), chs. 3-6; James B. Hedges, *The Browns of Providence Plantations* (2 vols., Cambridge, Mass. 1952; Providence 1968), I, chs. 12-14; Lynne Withey, *Urban Growth in Colonial Rhode Island: Newport and Providence in the Eighteenth Century* (Albany, N.Y. 1984), chs. 5-6. For general histories of Providence, see Welcome Arnold Greene, *The Providence Plantations for Two Hundred and Fifty Years* (Providence 1886); John Hutchins Cady, *The Civic and Architectural Development of Providence, 1636-1950* (Providence 1957); and Patrick T. Conley and Paul R. Campbell, *Providence: A Pictorial History* (Norfolk, Va. 1982).

[13] On the passage of the state tariff, see John Russell Bartlett, ed., *Records of the Colony (State) of Rhode Island and Providence Plantations in New England* (10 vols., Providence 1856-1865), X, 115; and Merrill Jensen, *The New Nation: A History of the United States During the Confederation, 1781-1789* (New York 1950), 294.

macy, and the Constitution went down to defeat by a margin of over ten to one.[14]

Throughout these political controversies, Providence artisans consistently supported the town's commercial leaders. After the introduction of paper money and the passage of penal legislation to enforce its use in the summer of 1786, local mechanics joined merchants in closing their shops rather than accept paper bills on par with specie. (Not until a Providence judge signaled he would not impose the penalties prescribed by law did normal operations resume.)[15] When the Mercantile party nominated William Bradford to stand for election against incumbent governor John Collins in the spring of 1787, a sizable majority of Providence mechanics cast their ballots for Bradford, who easily carried the town but lost statewide by an overwhelming margin.[16] And when the Constitution was submitted to the freemen for consideration a year later, artisans followed the merchants' lead in shunning the referendum. Only one vote was recorded in Providence—implicit evidence of the town's strongly Federalist disposition.[17]

---

[14] Frank Greene Bates, "Rhode Island and the Formation of the Union," Columbia University *Studies in History, Economics and Public Law*, 10 (1898), 107-166; Hillman Metcalf Bishop, "Why Rhode Island Opposed the Federal Constitution," *Rhode Island History*, 8 (Jan., Apr., July, Oct. 1949), 1-10, 33-44, 85-95, 115-126; Patrick T. Conley, *Democracy in Decline: Rhode Island's Constitutional Development, 1776-1841* (Providence 1977), 74-130; John P. Kaminski, "Democracy Run Rampant: Rhode Island in the Confederation," in *The Human Dimensions of Nation Making: Essays on Colonial and Revolutionary America*, ed. James Kirby Martin (Madison, Wis. 1976), 243-269; Irwin H. Polishook, *Rhode Island and the Union, 1774-1795* (Evanston, Ill. 1969), 131-201.

[15] Edwin M. Stone, *The Life and Recollections of John Howland, Late President of the Rhode Island Historical Society* (Providence 1857), 101-105; *United States Chronicle*, July 27, 1786. Notwithstanding their refusal to accept paper money at par, both merchants and mechanics proved willing to borrow it from the state when it served their purposes. Forrest McDonald, *We the People: The Economic Origins of the Constitution* (Chicago 1958), 331-335; Grand Committee Office Account Books "A" & "B," 15-16 (Rhode Island State Archives).

[16] Providence Town Meeting Records, VII, Apr. 18, 1787 (microfilm, Providence Public Library). Of the 69 voters who later joined the Association, 48 supported Bradford, 16 supported Collins, and 5 cast unmarked ballots. Record linkage between *ibid.* and PAMM Membership File, 1789-1790, compiled from PAMM Records, Signature Book and Association Minute Books, I.

[17] William R. Staples, *Annals of the Town of Providence, from Its First Settlement, to the Organization of the City Government, in June, 1832* (Providence 1843), 321; Polishook, *Rhode Island and the Union*, 199.

Yet even as artisans cooperated politically with the commercial elite, they harbored deep resentment. Local merchants, after all, had contributed to the economic crisis by flooding the domestic market with foreign manufactures right after the war. And, following the introduction of paper money, merchants took advantage of state law to pay artisans in depreciated currency or truck. In a letter published in the local press on February 5, 1789, "An injured Mechanic" complained bitterly that there were *"few* who pay *Money* to their Workmen, *or even Articles at Money Price."* *"Remove the Beam from thine own Eye,"* he advised local merchants, *"then shalt thou see clearly to take the Mote from thy Brother's Eye."*[18]

Out of this tension within the local Federalist coalition emerged the decision to establish the Providence Association of Mechanics and Manufacturers. Among the organization's founders were several of the town's most prestigious tradesmen. William Barton, who chaired the meeting at Elijah Bacon's house on February 27, 1789, had risen from corporal to colonel during the War for Independence and had gained fame for his capture of General Richard Prescott; he currently served as one of Providence's delegates to the Rhode Island General Assembly.[19] Barzillai Richmond and Charles Keene, the Association's first president and vice-president, respectively, had each sat on the town council and in the general assembly before the revolution; Keene, who rose from captain to major in the militia during the war, also sat in the assembly during the 1780s.[20] Likewise Amos Atwell, the Association's first treasurer, had sat on the council and served as a justice of the peace before the revolution, sat in the general assembly in 1776, attained the rank of lieutenant-colonel commandant during the war, and served on the town council in the early 1780s.[21] As individuals, these men had already achieved social respectability and political influence. Now they hoped to mobilize Providence mechanics as a whole to achieve common goals through corporate means.

In their petition for a state charter, the Association's founders identified as their primary objective "encouraging and promoting

---

[18] *United States Chronicle*, Feb. 5, 1789.

[19] Edwin M. Stone, *Mechanics' Festival* (Providence 1860), 44; Staples, *Annals of Providence*, 652.

[20] Stone, *Mechanics' Festival*, 40; Staples, *Annals of Providence*, 651-652, 657; Providence Town Meeting Records, VII, *passim*; Joseph Jenckes Smith, comp., *Civil and Military List of Rhode Island* (2 vols., Providence, 1900-1901), I, *passim*.

[21] Staples, *Annals of Providence*, 651-652, 658; Smith, *Civil and Military List*, I, *passim*.

such Manufactures as will be advantageous to this State, and the United States,—and to extend the same as far as may be useful to the Community.''[22] To achieve this goal, they believed Rhode Island would have to join the Union and Congress would have to pass a protective tariff. Although the founders were careful not to raise the question of ratification with a hostile legislature, they made their position clear in a circular sent to artisans elsewhere in Rhode Island at the end of April 1789. ''We are ardently wishing for the Time when this State may be reunited with our Sister States, under one general Head,'' they declared. For then ''the united Voice of that Class of Citizens to which both you and we belong may be heard by that Body which we hope will be composed of true Patriots, who will not hesitate to despise the Gewgaws of Foreigners when set in Competition with the solid Advantage resulting from the Encouragement being given to our own Manufactures.''[23]

While the founders portrayed the encouragement of American manufactures as consonant with the general good, it would be naive to assume they were motivated purely by a sense of public virtue rather than by concern for private benefit.[24] Indeed, in retrospect, they resemble a modern interest group lobbying for government favors more than a group of classical republicans valiantly forgoing personal gain for the sake of the commonweal. Yet they were not liberal individualists. In establishing their institutional priorities, the founders drew on the rich tradition of European guilds and craft companies to emphasize the principles of cooperation and mutual assistance within the trades.[25] Without asserting an exclusive privilege to govern local crafts, the founders sought to strengthen internal craft discipline and collective self-regulation by mandating that members obey ''any Regulations'' henceforth adopted by the practitioners of their respec-

---

[22] Petitions to Rhode Island General Assembly, XXIV, 141.

[23] Circular Letter to the Mechanics and Manufacturers of Newport, East Greenwich, Etc. in this State, Apr. 29, 1789, PAMM Records, Association Minute Books, I, May 18, 1789.

[24] On the dangers of taking ''the rhetoric of virtue'' at face value, see John Patrick Diggins, *The Lost Soul of American Politics: Virtue, Self-Interest, and the Foundations of Liberalism* (New York 1984), esp. 23-24, 85-99, 347-365.

[25] The founders attributed ''the Degree of Eminency to which the Manufactures of Europe have arrived during the present Century . . . principally . . . to the Encouragement which the Artizans in the different Branches have received from Societies formed for that express Purpose, and to the Mechanics themselves being associated together under the Sanction of the Laws.'' *The Charter, Constitution and Bye-Laws of the Providence Association of Mechanics and Manufacturers* (Providence 1789), 13.

tive trades.[26] The founders had in mind price lists of the sort long maintained by Providence house carpenters, and they may also have anticipated rules setting standards for workmanship, limiting entry into a craft, or fixing wages for employees.[27] Through the support of such measures to curb the competitive pressures of the marketplace, the founders hoped to enhance both the social solidarity and economic security of the mechanic interest.

For similar reasons, the Association assumed guild-like authority for arbitrating disputes between members. Any member harboring a complaint against "a Brother Member" was required, on penalty of expulsion, "to lay the Case before the Association for their opinion," rather than to resort to the courts.[28] Nor did the Association's judicial responsibilities stop there. In cases where a complaint was lodged "by an Inhabitant of this Town, who may think himself defrauded by bad Manufactures being sold him by any Member . . . ; or by any Member not compleating his Contracts in a workmanlike Manner, or by extravagant Charges," the Association pledged it would investigate the matter promptly and "endeavour that Justice be done to the Parties."[29] In serving these disciplinary functions, the Association would not only enforce a code of honorable conduct among its members but also elevate their reputation within the general community.

Notwithstanding such efforts to inspire cooperation and maintain effective order within the trades, some mechanics were bound to suffer hardships in the pursuit of a decent livelihood. To the Association's founders, poverty seemed an ordinary fact of life, not a badge of bad character or personal sin. Even the most diligent and upright mechanic might succumb to the disability of disease, the uncertainty of market conditions, or other calamity beyond human control. To provide a degree of insurance against a devastating loss of income, the Association's officers were empowered to offer aid to "any Member . . . who may, through Sickness or Misfortune, fall into Want."[30]

Under the terms of the charter, funds could also be allocated "for the Purpose of promoting Industry, and giving a just Encouragement

---

[26] PAMM Records, Association Minute Books, I, Mar. 30, 1789; *Charter, Constitution and Bye-Laws*, 24.
[27] *Rules for House-Carpenters Work, in the Town of Providence* (Providence 1796), [2].
[28] *Charter, Constitution and Bye-Laws*, 24.
[29] *Ibid.*, 27.
[30] *Ibid.*, 24.

to Ingenuity.''[31] At a time when Providence lacked a bank or other institutional source of capital, such an investment might make the difference between the success and failure of a struggling enterprise. Whether helping the impoverished or the innovative, the strategy was to advance the welfare of artisans through mechanisms of mutual assistance, not by trusting wholly in the justice of the unregulated marketplace.

To carry out their corporate program, the founders designed a highly democratic organization headed by officers elected annually by the members at large. The officers included a president, vice-president, treasurer, secretary, and an eleven-person committee of correspondence that acted as an all-purpose executive body. While in practice older and wealthier individuals tended to be chosen, in principle any member of the organization was eligible to hold office. Equally important, major policy decisions remained in the hands of the general membership, which was required to meet at least four times per year and which at the outset assembled, on average, more than twice that often.[32]

Under the terms of the Association's constitution, "any Mechanic or Manufacturer" resident in Providence for at least three months was eligible to join the organization upon nomination by an officer and approval by the existing membership. Bylaws adopted in June 1789 added two restrictions. One effectively excluded merchants who engaged in manufacturing as a secondary pursuit—persons like local magnates Moses Brown and Welcome Arnold. The other bylaw limited the admission of journeymen to those who had served a regular apprenticeship in Providence or could by other means demonstrate their good character.[33]

In practice, the Providence Association attracted members from a wide array of trades. Occupational data have been developed for 130

---

[31] *Ibid.*, 11.

[32] *Ibid.*, 16-22; PAMM Records, Association Minute Books, I.

[33] PAMM Records, Association Minute Books, I, June 17, 1789; *Charter, Constitution and Bye-Laws*, 24-25. Unfortunately for the historian, neither the constitution nor the bylaws specified a definition of "mechanic" or "manufacturer." In contemporary usage, the former was the broader term, encompassing all who pursued a trade that demanded knowledge of a "mystery" and mastery of an art. "Manufacturer," by comparison, connoted a person who transformed raw materials into finished articles (manufactures) either by means of his own labor, by way of supervising other people's labor, or by utilizing machinery. Yet so long as large-scale industrial enterprises remained rare, the distinction between "mechanic" and "manufacturer" remained vague.

of the 218 individuals who joined the organization by the end of 1790. The members of this subset were distributed broadly among the clothing trades (16 percent), metal trades (15 percent), building trades (14 percent), leather trades (14 percent), maritime trades (12 percent), and furniture trades (12 percent); the remainder pursued such assorted occupations as baking, hairdressing, printing, and undertaking. (For a more complete breakdown, see Table 1.) How closely this occupational distribution matched the distribution of tradesmen within the town as a whole cannot be determined, but clearly the Association's appeal extended broadly across the spectrum of local craft specialties.[34]

It also extended broadly across the range of local property holdings. As Table 2 indicates, the distribution of property assessments among Association members nearly paralleled that among Providence taxpayers as a whole in 1790. Thus 25 percent of the 185 members located on the tax list were assessed for no property, as compared to 24 percent of all Providence taxpayers, and this pattern of similarity extended far up the assessment hierarchy. Only at the apex was there a noteworthy divergence. Of Association members, Amos Atwell alone ranked among the top 5 percent of Providence taxpayers—a select group that possessed nearly half the assessed property in the town. Moreover, even Atwell's holdings paled by comparison to those of the town's five wealthiest merchant princes—Joseph Nightingale, John Innes Clark, and the brothers Brown (Nicholas, John, and Moses)—who among them owned more property than all the Association members combined. Yet if none of the members was fabulously rich,

---

[34] Major sources of information on the members' occupations include PAMM Records, Signature Book; *ibid.*, Association Minute Books, I; List of Census Organizers, July 19, 1791, *ibid.*, Papers, 1791; Coyle, "Survival of Providence Business Enterprise," 41-60; Stone, *Mechanics' Festival*, 40-72; Wendell D. Garett, "Providence Cabinetmakers, Chairmakers, Upholsterers and Allied Craftsmen, 1756-1838: A Check List," *Antiques*, 90 (Oct. 1966), 514-518; Joseph K. Ott, "Recent Discoveries Among Rhode Island Cabinetmakers and Their Work," *Rhode Island History*, 28 (Winter 1969), 3-25; Joseph K. Ott, "More Notes on Rhode Island Cabinetmakers and Their Work," *Rhode Island History*, 28 (May 1969), 49-52; Joseph K. Ott, "Still More Notes on Rhode Island Cabinetmakers and Allied Craftsmen," *Rhode Island History*, 28 (Nov. 1969), 111-121; Joseph K. Ott, "Rhode Island Housewrights, Shipwrights, and Related Craftsmen," *Rhode Island History*, 31 (May-Aug. 1972), 65-79.

TABLE 1

Members' Occupations
Providence Association of Mechannics and Manufacturers, 1789-90

Occupational Category and Trade	Number of Members
Book and Printing Trades	3
Bookbinder	1
Papermaker	1
Printer	1
Building Trades	18
Bricklayer	3
Carpenter	3
House carpenter	2
Housewright	5
Mason	2
Painter	2
Stonecutter	1
Cloth and Clothing Trades	21
Cardmaker	1
Clothier	1
Cotton manufacturer	1
Cotton spinner	1
Cotton worker	1
Fringe, lace and web weaver	1
Hatter	5
Tailor	10
Clockmaking Trades	3
Clockmaker	1
Watchmaker	2
Food and Hospitality Trades	5
Baker	4
Innkeeper	1
Furniture Trades	15
Cabinetmaker	12
Chairmaker	3
Leather Trades	18
Cordwainer	3

Leather Trades (cont.)

Currier	2
Leather dresser	2
Saddler	5
Shoemaker	1
Tanner	5

Maritime Trades	16
Blockmaker	4
Boatbuilder	1
Sailmaker	3
Ship carpenter	1
Ship joiner	1
Shipwright	6

Metal Trades	20
Blacksmith	9
Brass founder and fire engine maker	1
Coppersmith	2
Goldsmith	2
Silversmith	1
Tinman	2
Tinplate worker	2
Toolmaker	1

Packaging and Transportation Trades	5
Box maker	1
Cooper	2
Chaisemaker	1
Wheelwright	1

Personal Service Trades	4
Barber	1
Dentist	1
Hairdresser	1
Undertaker	1

Soap and Candle Trades	2
Soap maker	1
Tallow chandler	1

Unknown	88

Total	218

Sources: See note 34.

JOURNAL OF THE EARLY REPUBLIC

TABLE 2

Distribution of Property Assessments, Providence Taxpayers and
Members of the Providence Association of Mechanics and
Manufacturers, 1790

N (Town) = 999; N (Assn.) = 186

Property Assessment (£)	Frequency		Cumulative Frequency	
	Town	Assn.	Town	Assn.
0	24%	25%	24%	25%
1-10	24	27	49	53
11-40	25	26	74	79
41 +	26	21	100	100

60-90	10	9	89	95
91-140	6	4	95	99
141 +	5	1	100	100

Sources: See note 35.

neither were they uniformly poor. Most associates possessed at least a modicum of taxable wealth.[35]

---

[35] PAMM Membership File, 1789-1790; Providence Town Tax Valuation List, Nov. 1790 (Rhode Island Historical Society Library); computerized version of Providence Town Tax Valuation List, Nov. 1790, produced by Lynne Withey. Occasionally persons and partnerships were enumerated more than once on the tax list. As a result, the 185 members located on the tax list accounted for 186 separate entries. Calculations of town and Association frequencies were based on the number of entries, not individuals, involved. A notice issued by the town assessors indicates that they based assessments on listings of real and personal property supplied by the inhabitants; assessments clearly did not measure full market value. Providence *Gazette*, Oct. 30, 1790.

Behind the diversity in members' property holdings lay differences in age, experience, and ambition. Among the members assessed for a poll but no property were journeymen and young masters like James Waterman, a tallow chandler who started his own business in late 1789. Upon taking over a shop on the west side of town, Waterman described his immediate circumstances and long-term aspirations in a newspaper advertisement. Acknowledging his youth and "the Want of that Experience which he purposes to make, by a strict Application of 20 or 30 years, should he live so long," he asserted "that, in the above-said Term, he will endeavour progressively, to make such Proficiency, as Art and Industry, added to his natural Capacity will enable him to." Although he might never produce "Tallow-Candles, equal in appearance, or Quality to Virgins-Wax, or Spermaceti, nor make Wicks of Cotton of a better Quality than such as is Imported," he hoped "to give such general Satisfaction, as to incite the repeated Favours of those, who have once commenced [as] his Customers."[36] His goal, in short, was not to acquire great wealth or fame but to attain what contemporaries termed a "competence"— a modest yet secure level of property that assured one's good standing in the community.

Associates who ranked in the middle of the tax hierarchy tended to be further along in their careers than Waterman, and many had already achieved the competence he aspired to. Printer Bennett Wheeler and cabinetmaker Job Danforth provide cases in point.

A native of Halifax, Nova Scotia, where he served an unpleasant apprenticeship to the king's printer, Wheeler made his way to Providence after gaining his freedom in 1776. Over the next two years, with time out for militia duty, he worked as a journeyman, first for job printer John McDougall and then for John Carter, publisher of the Providence *Gazette*. At the end of 1778, to Carter's everlasting resentment, Wheeler entered the employ of Solomon Southwick, in Attleborough, Massachusetts, and a few months later Southwick invited Wheeler to become his partner and run the business. They promptly moved their operations to Providence, where they launched the town's second newspaper, *The American Journal and General Advertiser*. Southwick soon withdrew from the partnership, but Wheeler continued publishing the paper until August 1781. During this time he attained the rank of captain in the state militia and married the daughter of a landed gentlemen. On January 1, 1784, after two years

---

[36] *United States Chronicle*, Dec. 24, 1789.

devoted to job printing, Wheeler started another paper, the *United States Chronicle: Political, Commercial, and Historical.* Despite his personal opposition to paper money, he opened the pages of the *Chronicle* to advocates of the Country party and gained a sizable readership. In 1787-1788 he served as collector of the excise for Providence County, and in 1789 he was elected the first secretary of the Association of Mechanics and Manufacturers. In 1790, with a wife and five children to support, he paid taxes on two separate estates, one assessed a £15 and the other—a "half house and field"—at £20.[37]

Born in 1745, Job Danforth had opened his cabinetmaking business in Providence before the revolution, and in 1790 was assessed for £40. His operations remained modest in scope, however. While at least one of his seven sons assisted him in the shop, he employed no journeymen and apparently did most of the work himself. He produced furniture on a custom basis—making chairs, desks, tables, and bedsteads to order—but the pace of work was irregular. Thus during the summer months Samuel Danforth—Job's oldest son—alternated between working in the shop and laboring in a neighbor's field or the family's garden. (Samuel also found time to read the classics, borrowing works by Homer, Plato, Thucydides, and other authors from a local library.) Job himself did some carpentry and farming on the side to supplement his income and also sometimes rented out space in his shop on a temporary basis. In all he earned approximately £88 per year in 1789-1790, of which he received little in cash. Given the shortage of specie and depreciation of paper currency, he often accepted payments in kind (*e.g.*, wood, cloth, or produce) and settled accounts on the basis of personal notes or orders drawn on third parties. By such means, he was able to protect his competence in hard times but not to accumulate capital on a sustained basis.[38]

As might be expected, members who ranked toward the top of the tax list operated larger and more diverse enterprises than their less propertied peers. Leather dresser Levi Hall advertised that he not

---

[37] Diary of Bennett H. Wheeler, 1-21 (Rhode Island Historical Society Library); Providence Typographical Union Number Thirty-Three, *Printers and Printing in Providence, 1762-1907* ([Providence] 1907), 14-16, xci; H. Glenn Brown and Maude 0. Brown, *A Directory of Printing, Publishing, Bookselling and Allied Trades in Rhode Island to 1865* (New York 1958), 179; Providence Town Tax, Nov. 1790.

[38] William M. Pillsbury, "Earning a Living, 1788-1818: Job Danforth, Cabinetmaker," *Rhode Island History*, 31 (May-Aug. 1972), 81-93; Samuel Danforth's Journal and typescript of same (American Antiquarian Society, Worcester, Mass.); Providence Town Tax, Nov. 1790; Ott, "Recent Discoveries," 19-20.

only dressed "in the neatest Manner, Buck, Doe, Moose, Carraboo, Cabareater, Goat and Lamb Skins," but also employed "Breeches and Glove-makers, who perform their Work equal to any in this Country, and for Strength and Neatness superior to any imported." Nor was Hall's business limited to retailing items on a custom basis. He regularly kept "Articles on Hand with which [to] furnish Shop-keepers, in Town and Country, on such terms as will afford them equal Profit with other Goods."[39] When he died in June 1789, at the age of 45, his wife Sarah took over the enterprise, and in 1790 his estate was assessed for the impressive sum of £140.[40]

Yet if they boasted relatively extensive operations, the Association's wealthier members usually remained practicing mechanics. Take, for example, the brothers Joel and Michael Metcalf. Tanners and curriers by trade, they sold, among other items, "good Hemlock and Oak tanned SOLE-LEATHER . . . ; good curried NEAT's LEATHER, and CALF-SKINS; BOOT-LEGS; Harness, Saddle and Chaise LEATHER."[41] In the year ending June 22, 1789, they purchased 1,372 calf skins and 367 sides of other animal hides as raw material, and in 1790 they were jointly assessed for £110 in taxable property plus another £10 for "the store they improve." But according to their surviving business papers, they paid wages to at most one journeyman and a woman (perhaps a housekeeper) on a regular basis.[42] Even assuming they had the unpaid help of one or more apprentices or family members, it appears they were directly engaged in the arduous (and odorous) process of scraping, washing, soaking, and pounding skins into leather.[43] Unlike modern capitalists, they operated as well as owned the means of production.

The account books of mason Zephaniah Andrews tell a similar story. Assessed for £120 in 1790, Andrews was among the richest mechanics in Providence. He owned a wharf and rented out stores and a house in addition to carrying on his trade. But carry on his trade he did. While he sometimes employed a journeyman to help him, he

---

[39] *United States Chronicle*, Feb. 5, 1788.

[40] Providence *Gazette*, July 4, 1789; Providence Town Tax, Nov. 1790.

[41] *United States Chronicle*, Apr. 9, 1789.

[42] Metcalf Papers, Accounts, bundle 1 (Rhode Island Historical Society Library); Providence Town Tax, Nov. 1790.

[43] On the technology of tanning and currying, see Edwin Tunis, *Colonial Craftsmen and the Beginnings of American Industry* (New York 1965), 32-34; and Peter C. Welsh, *Tanning in the United States to 1850: A Brief History* (Washington, D.C. 1964), chs. 1-2.

personally laid bricks as well as designed iron doors, whitewashed rooms, and bundled hay. Among his customers were the town's leading merchant princes, yet like Job Danforth he was commonly paid in truck rather than cash. Despite the speculative outlook suggested by his investments in real estate, Andrews at the age of 51 was still essentially a master artisan working with his own hands and trading his products directly for other goods as part of a local network of simple commodity exchange.[44]

For all their diversity, then, the early members of the Providence Association of Mechanics and Manufacturers shared a common identity as small-scale producers operating in a town dominated economically by a coterie of merchant princes and in a state dominated politically by a multitude of farmers. By banding together, the members hoped to affirm their social worth, provide mutual assistance in times of need, and gain leverage over public policy. As they sought to achieve cohesion among themselves, moreover, they reached out to make contact with artisans in other places and to develop a continental network of mechanic organizations devoted to like purposes.

On April 29 and 30, 1789, six weeks after the Association obtained its charter, the committee of correspondence dispatched letters to the mechanics and manufacturers of nearly two dozen communities throughout Rhode Island and the United States. To mechanics inside Rhode Island, it described local developments, urged speedy reunification with the other states, and expressed a desire for government encouragement of American manufactures. To mechanics outside Rhode Island, the committee recommended the creation of mechanic associations "in all the capital Towns in America." In addition to enhancing cooperation within the trades, such organizations could supply the new Congress with "the fullest Information" available on American manufacturing conditions. "We have to lament, it is true," the committee acknowledged, "that this state is not considered at present as one of the United States under the new Government." But it assured artisans elsewhere that Rhode Island would soon rejoin the Union and "that the Mechanics and Manufacturers of this Town are not in Principle separated from their Brethren in the other States."[45]

---

[44] John Andrews Papers, Series I—Zephaniah Andrews Papers, Accounts, 1790-1810 (Rhode Island Historical Society Library); Providence Town Tax, Nov. 1790; Stone, *Mechanics' Festival*, 114.

[45] Circular Letter to Mechanics in this State, Apr. 29, 1789, and Circular Letter

These communications drew an uneven response. Artisans in most places failed to reply, but those in a handful of communities sent letters of congratulations and moral support. Mechanics from East Greenwich, Rhode Island, a smaller town on Narragansett Bay, avowed their "unanimous agreement in sentiment" with the Providence membership, at least on the aim of encouraging domestic manufacture. (They omitted any reference to ratification of the federal Constitution.)[46] Artisans from Newburyport, Massachusetts, affirmed that "some general plan . . . is necessary in order to place our manufactures upon a more respectable footing," though they admitted that they themselves had not "gone into the Spirit of Associating." Correspondents from New York applauded the "zeal which appears in the Mechanical Association of your patriotic town" and celebrated the mounting determination across the continent "to promote our internal Wealth . . . and to rescue our Character from the Disgrace of a commercial Dependence." The Providence brethren could rest secure, the New Yorkers added, that notwithstanding Rhode Island's peculiar status, "our undiminished affections are still expanded to embrace you."[47]

As these replies trickled in during the late spring and early summer of 1789, Rhode Island's political crisis intensified. In June, over five hundred Providence townspeople signed a petition pleading with the general assembly to call a state ratifying convention as soon as possible. Under current circumstances, the petitioners explained, "many industrious tradesmen and mechanics, are compelled to emigrate for want of employment, and many more who once lived in a comfortable manner, are now distressed, and only waiting to dispose of their property, to remove also." According to the petitioners, ratification would solve the present crisis and prevent a worse disaster from developing.[48]

Notwithstanding this and other Federalist appeals, the general assembly continued to reject motions for a ratifying convention until January 1790. By then the state's public debt had been retired, the

---

to the Mechanics and Manufacturers at Philadelphia, New York, Etc. in the United States, Apr. 30, 1789, PAMM Records, Association Minute Books, I, May 18, 1789.

[46] Reply from East Greenwich, May 5, 1789, PAMM Records, Association Minute Books, I, May 18, 1789.

[47] Letter from Newburyport, May 27, 1789, and Letter from New York, May 29, 1789, PAMM Records, Association Minute Books, I, June 17, 1789.

[48] *United States Chronicle,* June 26, 1789.

legislation making paper money legal tender had been rescinded, and Federalists were threatening to summon their own convention if the legislature would not do its duty. With Governor John Collins breaking a tie vote in the upper house, the general assembly finally relented on January 16. A call went out for the election of convention delegates on February 9 and for the opening of the ratifying convention in South Kingston on March 1.[49]

These developments set the stage for Providence artisans to assert their political independence from the mercantile interest. Operating outside formal organizational channels but applying the cooperative principles fostered by the Association of Mechanics and Manufacturers, local tradesmen exercised their concerted power by electing one of their own to be a convention delegate.

On the evening of February 6, 1790, local mechanics gathered at General Thayer's tavern to decide on a nominee.[50] According to recollections recorded by John Howland a half century later, the idea for the meeting originated with William Barton, himself an aspiring candidate. "This was a new project," Howland explained, "as there had not usually been any distinction of class in choice."[51] In the past, artisans had periodically won election to important political offices in Providence, including the posts of town selectman and representative to the general assembly. But the men elected had been chosen on the basis of their personal reputations, not as representatives of the mechanic interest. Moreover, they had been nominated by a select group of wealthy gentlemen, not by a large gathering of common artisans. The conclave at Thayer's tavern applied the democratic edge of artisan republicanism to break this tradition. In the words of "Alpha," a contemporary observer who defended the mechanics' meeting in the press, "The Mechanics and other Freeman of this Town have been a long Time duped by a certain Class of Men—but, thank God, the Scales have fallen from their Eyes, and they have opened them to a Sense of their Liberties."[52]

---

[49] On the assembly's decision to call a ratifying convention, see William R. Staples, *Rhode Island in the Continental Congress, with the Journal of the Convention that Adopted the Constitution, 1765-1790* (Providence 1870), 627-631; Bates, "Rhode Island and the Formation of the Union," 175-179; Polishook, *Rhode Island and the Union*, 211-213; John P. Kaminski, "Political Sacrifice and Demise—John Collins and Jonathan J. Hazard, 1786-1790," *Rhode Island History*, 35 (Aug. 1976), 91-93.

[50] *United States Chronicle*, Feb. 11, 1790.

[51] John Howland Papers, Recollections (1840), 134-135 (Rhode Island Historical Society Library).

[52] *United States Chronicle*, Feb. 11, 1790.

By Howland's account, the assembled artisans first asked Amos Atwell and then Zephaniah Andrews to be their candidate, but each declined the nomination. The meeting then turned to Barton, who eagerly accepted. The question remained how to secure victory at the forthcoming town meeting, where each seat on the four-person Providence delegation would be filled by a separate election. To maximize their chances of success, the mechanics agreed to vote for Barton for the third spot and otherwise to support the regular nominees.[53]

Federalist leaders did not take this challenge to their hegemony lightly. Upon getting word of the mechanics' plans, they designated John Innes Clark, their most popular nominee, to stand for the third spot opposite Barton. "This was not expected or wished for by the mechanics," Howland remembered, "as Clark would have been their choice if he had not been brought down from the first to the third position." But the artisans stuck by their agreement and elected Barton over merchant opposition. Clark was so upset by his loss that he initially refused nomination to the fourth place on the delegation, relenting only after the town meeting unanimously insisted upon his selection.[54]

Over the next few weeks, local mechanics paid an economic price for their display of political independence. According to complaints brought before the Association of Mechanics and Manufacturers, "several worthy members [were] dismissed from their Employ, in consequence of voting their sentiments at the last town meeting—they being contrary to the sentiments of their employers."[55] Artisans had achieved collective strength in the polis, but they remained individually vulnerable in the marketplace.

When the ratifying convention met during the first week of March, William Barton took an active part in the proceedings. While he did not present himself as a spokesman for the mechanic interest per se, his evident distrust of merchants and avowed concern for the urban poor set him apart from other Federalists. He defended the provision in Article I, section 4, empowering Congress to regulate federal elections on the grounds that it might prevent electoral abuse by the "mercantile influence" at the local level.[56] Yet he attacked

---

[53] John Howland Papers, Recollections (1840), 134-135.
[54] *Ibid.*; Providence Town Meeting Records, VII, Feb. 8, 1790.
[55] PAMM Records, Association Minute Books, I, Apr. 5, 1790.
[56] *Theodore Foster's Minutes of the Convention Held at South Kingston, Rhode Island, in March, 1790, Which Failed to Adopt the Consitution of the United States,* ed. Robert C. Cotner (Providence 1929), 45.

the prospect of a federal capitation or poll tax as patently unfair. "The Congre[ss]men of Fortune do not feel for the Common People," he charged—an unusual objection for a Federalist to raise.[57] Barton also criticized the Constitution for barring congressional interference with the slave trade before 1808 and urged the trade's immediate elimination.[58] In the end, however, he strongly endorsed ratification. When Antifederalists moved to suspend the proceedings without holding a vote on the Constitution, he warned that further delay in rejoining the Union would hurt "the Poor and the Needy."[59] But he failed to persuade the opposition and on March 6 the convention voted to suspend its proceedings for two and a half months pending further consultation with the people at large.[60]

The convention's failure to ratify the Constitution left the tradesmen and other residents of Providence dismayed. Antifederalist sentiment continued strong in rural parts of the state, and the Country party retained control of the general assembly in the April elections.[61] In a letter to the artisans of Trenton, New Jersey, in early May, the Association of Mechanics and Manufacturers reiterated its concern about Rhode Island's isolation from the Union. "The Citizens of our State subsist in a great Measure by Trade," the Association explained, "and the Embarrassments we labour under at present are discouraging to the middling and poorer Classes of People."[62] After years of setbacks and growing frustration, the freemen of Providence prepared to take drastic measures. On May 24, the day the ratifying convention was due to resume deliberations in Newport, the Providence town meeting publicly threatened to secede from Rhode Island if approval of the Constitution were not forthcoming.[63]

The town meeting's resolve was never tested. On May 29, by a vote of 34 to 32, the convention formally ratified the Constitution, and after a long and bitter struggle Rhode Island belatedly yet peace-

---

[57] *Ibid.*, 54.

[58] *Ibid.*, 59, 53, 74.

[59] *Ibid.*, 88.

[60] For further analysis of these proceedings, see Polishook, *Rhode Island and the Union*, 215-223.

[61] *Ibid.*, 223-226.

[62] PAMM Records, Association Minute Books, I, May 10, 1790.

[63] Staples, *Annals of Providence*, 347-348. Among the committee that drafted the town meeting's resolution were two members of PAMM, Gershom Jones and Zephaniah Andrews.

fully rejoined the United States.[64] Providence artisans greeted the news with relief and joy. The Association of Mechanics and Manufacturers noted proudly that William Barton had been entrusted with reporting the convention's decision to President George Washington, and on June 4 the Association sent a message of its own to the nation's chief executive. "The Mechanics and Manufacturers of this town," the Association declared, "feel a Confidence in the Wisdom and Patriotism of the Legislature of the United States—that they will do all in their Power to promote the Manufactures, as well as the Agriculture of our Country." The Association added politely that "this Confidence is greatly strengthened by the consideration that you, Sir, are at the Head of it."[65]

In fact, however, members of the Association harbored doubts about the national government's commitment to American industry. While they praised federal "commercial Regulations" that stood to benefit domestic producers and pledged to uphold "said Laws . . . by discountenancing and discouraging Smuggling," they thought the impost on imported manufactures was too low.[66] On July 21, 1790, the committee of correspondence dispatched a letter to Boston asking mechanics there to lead a campaign for higher duties on articles that "are now, or might, with due encouragement be made among us, in considerable quantities." The existing tariff was unfair, the committee complained. Because of different patterns of consumption, "the poor Manufacturer, in many instances, must pay more than the rich Farmer, and in proportion to his Interest double what is paid by the opulent Merchant." Mechanics deserved better. "While we are by the Labour of our Hands, and draught on our purses, contributing largely to the Emolument of our Country," the committee argued,

---

[64] Records of the Newport proceedings are included in Staples, *Rhode Island in the Continental Congress*, 666-680. See also Bates, "Rhode Island and the Formation of the Union," 196-200; Polishook, *Rhode Island and the Union*, 228-230; and Conley, *Democracy in Decline*, 113-114.

[65] Letter of Introduction for Col. William Barton, June 1, 1790, and Address to the President of the United States, PAMM Records, Association Minute Books, I, June 4, 1790. Washington responded with a courteous note of thanks, and when he visited Providence in August, Association members joined in the procession honoring the president. Washington to the Association, *ibid.*, I, July 12, 1790; *United States Chronicle*, Aug. 19, 1790.

[66] PAMM Records, Association Minute Books, I, June 4, 1790. The Association sent a copy of its resolution regarding smuggling to Secretary of the Treasury Alexander Hamilton, who replied with applause for the effort. Hamilton to B. Wheeler, June 14, 1790, *ibid.*, Papers, 1790.

"it seems but reasonable that Government should, so far as is consistent with the Collection of a sufficient Revenue, encourage us, by laying such Duties on foreign Goods . . . as will enable the Manufacturers of America to sell their goods as low as Foreigners."[67] Artisan virtue, in short, merited its just reward: the protection and promotion of artisan self-interest.

To achieve this goal, the committee proposed the creation of a nationwide network of artisan conventions. Under this plan, artisans would gather in their separate communities to elect delegates to state conventions which would, in turn, send representatives to a single national convention. The national convention would have the authority to speak for the mechanic interest of the entire country. While the committee acknowledged that circulating petitions from town to town might also prove effective, it argued that the system of tiered conventions was likely to produce "a more unanimous and hearty agreement" among artisans throughout the United States.[68]

Although in several respects the proposal resembled earlier efforts to establish a string of mechanic associations in major towns, it possessed more radical implications. James Madison and other framers of the Constitution had hoped that by establishing a continental republic with a strong central government they would curb the influence of popular factions and place governmental power securely in the hands of an enlightened elite. Some Federalists went so far as to suggest that aside from electing duly qualified representatives, the people at large had little or no legitimate role to play in setting national policy.[69] The members of the Providence Association of Mechanics and Manufacturers clearly disagreed. While they would have denied that they comprised a "faction" in the contemporary sense of the word—to their own minds, their aims coincided with the public good—they openly insisted on the right of common citizens to organize in their own behalf and on the right of interested parties to influence the decision-making process at the highest levels of government. At the same time, by advocating a tiered system of mechanic conventions, the members sought to transcend the limits of localistic concerns and overcome the obstacles to popular mobilization posed by

---

[67] Providence Committee of Correspondence to Boston, July 21, 1790, *ibid.*, Association Minute Books, I, July 26, 1790.

[68] *Ibid.*

[69] Gordon S. Wood, *The Creation of the American Republic, 1776-1787* (Chapel Hill 1969), esp. ch. 12; Richard Buel, Jr., *Securing the Revolution: Ideology in American Politics, 1789-1815* (Ithaca, N.Y. 1972), ch. 5.

the extensive size of the republic. Had the Association's plan been implemented, it might have hastened the democratization of the American polity as well as the diversification of the American economy.

But the project proved too ambitious to undertake. Two weeks after making its proposal, the committee of correspondence received a reply from Benjamin Austin, Jr., and Sarson Belcher, erstwhile leaders of the Association of Tradesmen and Manufacturers of the Town of Boston. Although the Boston organization was now defunct, they had raised the convention idea with several former members. "Those gentlemen with whom we have conversed," Austin and Belcher reported, "are of the opinion that, at present, we had better decline taking up the business on so extensive a plan as is proposed by you." As a more modest alternative, the Bostonians proposed establishing a continental network of committees of correspondence that would draft and circulate a petition to Congress.[70]

Nothing more came of the convention proposal, but the Providence members continued to work for greater government assistance to American artisans. In the fall of 1790 the Association organized a local census of manufactures to collect information for a possible national appeal along the lines suggested by the Boston correspondents.[71] It also petitioned the state legislature for an expansion of Rhode Island's inspection system to include certain manufactures in addition to the agricultural exports already designated. Goods certified by the state, the members reasoned, would be easier to market in distant places—places beyond the reach of a local producer's reputation.[72]

While the petition for state inspection met with no success, the census of manufactures served its purpose.[73] In July 1791, six months after the Association completed its survey of local industry, Secretary of the Treasury Alexander Hamilton circulated a request for informa-

---

[70] Benjamin Austin, Jr., and Sarson Belcher to Providence, Aug. 1, 1790, PAMM Records, Association Minute Books, I, Aug. 16, 1790.

[71] PAMM Records, Association Minute Books, I, Aug. 30, Sept. 13, 1790.

[72] Ibid., Oct. 18, 22, Nov. 5, 1790; Petitions to the Rhode Island General Assembly, XXV, 56. The items specified in the petition included hats, chaises and other carriages, saddler's work, cotton and wool cards, scribbling cards, boots and shoes, tanned and curried leather, and edge-tools.

[73] Over the course of two years, the Association's petition for state inspection was referred to a committee, misplaced, reintroduced, sent to another committee, and eventually forgotten. Petitions to the Rhode Island General Assembly, XXV, 56, XXVI, part 2, item 11.

tion on the condition of American manufactures. Both John Dexter, the supervisor of revenue for Rhode Island, and Theodore Foster; one of the state's federal senators, relayed Hamilton's inquiry to the Association of Mechanics and Manufacturers.[74] Welcoming the opportunity to be heard in the nation's highest councils, the Association promptly dispatched a copy of its census to Dexter and also initiated another, expanded investigation of manufacturing in Providence and vicinity. The results of the latter survey were sent to Dexter in mid-October.[75] He duly forwarded them to Hamilton, who assimilated the relevant findings before transmitting his Report on Manufactures to Congress on December 5, 1791.[76]

In its second survey, the Association compiled information not only on the variety and volume of local manufactures but also on the aspirations and frustrations of the persons who produced them. Attitudes varied from trade to trade. Practitioners of a handful of crafts expressed satisfaction with current conditions and optimism about the future. Blockmakers, for example, celebrated their prosperity: "Workmen more than get Employ. Materials Plenty, and easily obtained." Similarly, the town's only fringe and web weaver declared confidently that his products were "equall to any, and at a lower Rate than can be imported, so that the Maker . . . wishes for nothing but to be known." And edge-tool manufacturers, brass founders, and cardmakers conveyed no sense of anxiety about present circumstances in their respective trades.[77]

The practitioners of several other trades, however, claimed they suffered major economic hardships as a result of destructive competition from abroad. Though hatmakers calculated that their production for 1791 would surpass that for 1790 by a third, they complained bitterly, "The Duty on imported Hats is so small that it does not operate as a Check on Importations, where long practised, especially where Trade is managed by the Agents of Foreigners, who . . . will do all in their Power to discourage the Manufactures of the Country

---

[74] John S. Dexter to Charles Keene, Theodore Foster to Charles Keene, PAMM Records, Association Minute Books, I, July 11, 1791.

[75] PAMM Records, Association Minute Books, I, July 11, 19, Oct. 10, 1791; draft of letter to Dexter, Oct. 12, 1791, PAMM Records, Papers, 1791.

[76] "Report of a Committee Appointed to Obtain Information on Manufacturing in Providence," enclosure from John Dexter to Alexander Hamilton, Oct. 1791, *The Papers of Alexander Hamilton*, ed. Harold C. Syrett *et al.* (27 vols., New York 1961-1981), IX, 441-449.

[77] *Ibid.*, quotations at IX, 443, 444.

where they acquire their Wealth.'' Tanners and curriers declared, ''The Embarassment on the Business of Tanning and Currying at present and for some Time past hath been very considerable, owing to the large Quantities of Leather imported from the West Indies, the Duty on which is small in Proportion to many other Articles.'' Likewise, boot and shoe makers bemoaned the heavy ''Importation from Europe, which tends to undervalue the Price of our Work,'' while clockmakers, silversmiths, chocolate manufacturers, soap and candle makers, and paper manufacturers also joined the chorus of concern about foreign imports.[78]

So sharp were a number of the complaints that the report's compilers worried lest it seem impertinent. But they assured themselves that ''instead of living under a Government which spurns at the Subject, for the Representation of any Thing that operates as a Grievance, those who fill the first Offices in Government are encouraging them to make such Representations, as may serve to give necessary Information.'' To underscore this point, they reaffirmed their faith in the rectitude and virtue of Congress. ''We doubt not,'' they concluded, ''that altho there are very few in Congress whose *immediate Interest* is concerned, yet a sincere Regard for the *general Interest* will animate that truly honorable Body to give all the Encouragement which they can (consistent with a proper Regard to the Revenue) to that Class of Citizens who in Proportion to their Property pay so large a Share of the public Expence.''[79]

Hamilton had already written a number of drafts of his report to Congress before the Providence findings reached his office. At most they influenced his recommendations for assistance to specific industries, not his central arguments.[80] In the final version of his report, he proposed higher duties on imported chocolate and coarse paper, two items of particular concern to Providence tradesmen. But he also concluded that hatmaking required no additional protection, and he wavered on the question of increasing the impost on foreign leather.[81] More generally, he showed greater interest in the promotion of large-

---

[78] *Ibid.*, quotations at IX, 443, 444.

[79] *Ibid.*, IX, 449.

[80] On the drafting of Hamilton's Report on Manufacturers, see *ibid.*, X, 1-340; Jacob E. Cooke, ''Tench Coxe, Alexander Hamilton, and the Encouragement of American Manufactures,'' *William and Mary Quarterly*, 32 (July 1975), 369-392; and John R. Nelson, Jr., ''Alexander Hamilton and American Manufacturing: A Reexamination,'' *Journal of American History*, 65 (Mar. 1979), 984-995.

[81] *Papers of Hamilton*, X, 336, 334, 331, 321-322.

scale industrial enterprise than in the encouragement of small-scale handicraft operations.[82] Congress, in turn, shied away from a comprehensive program to develop manufacturing, but in May 1792, it raised the tariff on most imports by a modest amount (commonly from 7.5 percent to 10 percent ad valorem). Nearly everything identified by Providence producers as deserving greater assistance was included.[83]

The Providence Association of Mechanics and Manufacturers took no public notice of this favorable outcome, however. By the time Congress acted, the clamor for protection had subsided. A revival of the coastal trade and overseas commerce spurred local economic growth, and craftsmen shared the benefits of renewed prosperity.[84] As a result, the Association of Mechanics and Manufacturers abandoned its campaign for government assistance and concentrated instead on local strategies of collective self-help.

From its inception, the Association had emphasized the importance of cooperation among local artisans, and in accordance with the bylaws it both adjudicated conflicts involving associates and supplied material aid to members in distress. Over the course of its first five years, the Association handled four disputes over matters such as the delay in payment of a bill. In each case, the Association achieved a settlement "without the Cost, Difficulty, Delay and Ill Blood, almost always attending Suits at common Law."[85] Not until 1798 did the Association encounter a case it could not resolve to the mutual satisfaction of the parties concerned.[86]

Providing assistance to needy members and their families proved a more challenging task. When Elijah Bacon's shop burned down in the fall of 1790, the Association organized a subscription to help cover

---

[82] Nelson, "Alexander Hamilton and American Manufacturing," 971-995; Drew R. McCoy, *The Elusive Republic: Political Economy in Jeffersonian America* (Chapel Hill 1980; New York 1982), 132-135, 152-161.

[83] *Annals of Congress*, 2d Cong., Appendix, 1363-1370.

[84] *United States Chronicle*, May 10, Nov. 1, 1792; Withey, *Urban Growth in Colonial Rhode Island*, Appendix B. See also Hedges, *The Browns of Providence Plantations*, II, chs. 1-3; and Peter J. Coleman, *The Transformation of Rhode Island, 1790-1860* (Providence 1963, 1969), ch. 2.

[85] PAMM Records, Association Minute Books, I, May 10, 28, 1790, Sept. 12, Oct. 10, 1791, Jan. 9, 1792; Providence Committee of Correspondence to Newport Association of Mechanics and Manufacturers, Mar. 5, 1792, *ibid.*, Association Minute Books, I, Apr. 2, 1792 (quotation); *ibid.*, Committee of Correspondence Minute Book, Mar. 25, May 20, June 17, 1793.

[86] *Ibid.*, Select Committee Minute Books, I, Sept. 24, 1798.

the loss.[87] When John Petty, Jr., took sick a year later, the Association gave him five dollars in financial aid—the equivalent of roughly one week's pay.[88] But when Lemuel Edmons fell ill in the fall of 1792 and his condition continued to deteriorate through the spring of 1793, the Association reached the limits of its generosity. Twice it granted Edmons five dollars, and it later agreed to donate the money collected in fines for nonattendance at meetings of the committee of correspondence. Upon his application for additional funds, however, the Association decided that in fairness to other members who might need assistance, it could not provide long-term financial support. Instead it recommended that he return to his place of legal settlement, where he was entitled to public relief, and offered to defray his moving expenses. Resigned to this fate, Edmons thanked his associates "for their Care and attention" and promptly died before he could leave town.[89]

Like European trade corporations, the Association of Mechanics and Manufacturers sought to assure a dignified funeral for deceased members and to supply aid to their surviving dependents.[90] Thus, upon Lemuel Edmons' death, the committee of correspondence arranged for his burial, and it later took charge of placing two of his sons in craft apprenticeships.[91] In 1795 the Association procured a hearse, palls, and bier to reduce the cost of funerals for members and their relatives.[92]

Aside from resolving disputes and helping the distressed, the Association served as a forum where members could share their views as

[87] Ibid., Association Minute Books, I, Oct. 22, 1790.

[88] Ibid., Committee of Correspondence Minute Book, Oct. 17, 1791. On wage rates during the early 1790s, see Carroll D. Wright, Historical Review of Wages and Prices: 1752-1860, Sixteenth Annual Report of the Massachusetts Bureau of Statistics of Labor (Boston 1885), 54-56.

[89] PAMM Records, Association Minute Books, I, Oct. 8, 1792, Aug. 26, 1793 (quotation); ibid., Committee of Correspondence Minute Book, Apr. 4, Aug. 28, 1793; copy of letter from Z. Andrews to L. Edmons, May 20, 1793, ibid., Papers, 1792-1793.

[90] In France under the Old Regime, "Nothing could state more eloquently either the corporation's concern for the whole person or the permanence of the members' commitment to the trade and to one another than the centrality of funerals in the corporation's ceremonial life." William H. Sewell, Jr., Work and Revolution in France: The Languaqe of Labor from the Old Regime to 1848 (Cambridge, Eng. 1980), 36.

[91] PAMM Records, Committee of Correspondence Minute Book, Aug. 28, 1793, Mar. 6, 12, 18, 30, 1795; ibid., Association Minute Books, II, Mar. 16, 1795, Mar. 14, 1796.

[92] Ibid., Association Minute Books, II, Oct. 12, Nov. 9, 1795.

equals and gain valuable experience in the art of public speaking. Although plans for a mechanics' hall came to naught, the Association brought artisans together on a regular basis to discuss matters of mutual interest and concern. "By the free and methodical discussion of all Questions, as well as the Decorum, and order observed in our Meetings," the committee of correspondence explained, "the Members obtain some Notion of public Proceedings, which in some Measure prepares any of them, who may be called to serve their Fellow-Citizens, in a more public capacity."[93] As an institution, the Association steered clear of electoral politics, and the scenario leading to William Barton's selection as a delegate to the ratifying convention was not repeated. But, as individuals, members put their political skills to good use. The number of associates elected to the town council rose from one in 1789 to two in 1790 through 1792, then to three in 1793 and 1794.[94]

More intangible yet perhaps most important, the Association promoted an esprit de corps among local artisans and enhanced both their self-respect and their social standing in the community at large. To quote the organization's own assessment, "As a class of Citizens, it serves to promote an honorable Idea of the several mechanical pursuits in which we are engaged—instead of repining that Providence has not destined us, to move in a higher Sphere."[95] Even amid growing prosperity, artisans remained sensitive to condescending treatment by the local gentry. By reinforcing their pride in themselves, upholding the principles of honesty and fair exchange within the trades, and publicizing their service to the community, the Association raised the mechanic interest to a social plane on par with its commercial and agricultural counterparts.

The public celebration of the Association's fifth anniversary signaled the mechanics' attainment of respectability. On April 14, 1794, the members, by prior design, interrupted their annual election meeting for a short procession through the streets of Providence and an oration at the Baptist Meeting House by the Reverend James Wilson,

---

[93] Letter to Newport Association of Mechanics and Manufacturers, Mar. 5, 1792, *ibid.*, Association Minute Books, I, Apr. 2, 1792.

[94] *United States Chronicle*, June 11, 1789, June 10, 1790, June 9, 1791, June 14, 1792, June 13, 1793, June 12, 1794.

[95] Letter to Newport Association of Mechanics and Manufacturers, Mar. 3, 1792, PAMM Records, Association Minute Books, I, Apr. 2, 1792.

pastor of the Beneficent Congregational Church.[96] Wilson in his remarks traced the history of the mechanic arts from biblical times to the present, hailed their positive influence on civilization, enumerated personal and social factors that promoted their development, and offered an optimistic assessment of their potential in the American republic. The United States might be "the Land of Husbandry," he reasoned, but for agriculture to flourish manufactures would have to grow and mature. Members of the Association were the pioneers of a balanced economy as well as the agents of benevolence. "Whilst with circumspection you pursue the great ends for which you are embodied," Wilson proclaimed, "you shall not only benefit yourselves, your country will rejoice; the husbandman seek your mart, and the merchant your commodities." Noting that "the Son of God was a Carpenter," he concluded with the assurance that "your avocations are honourable."[97]

A year later, upon the occasion of the Association's sixth anniversary, the Reverend Jonathan Maxcy, president of Rhode Island College, expanded on this theme. "You gentlemen," he told the assembled members, "have the satisfaction to reflect, that the employments you pursue, are the chief sources of convenience, opulence and power. Your exertions not only promote your own but the interests of society."[98] Thus did the town's leading religious and intellectual figure lend his authority to the mechanics' assertion of their social equality and productive contribution to the commonweal.

The willingness of the local gentry to accept the Association of Mechanics and Manufacturers as a beneficial institution helps to explain the persistence of the Federalist coalition in Providence long after it had splintered in other major cities. In New York prominent merchants for years opposed the incorporation of the General Society of Mechanics and Tradesmen, and several of the society's officers joined the Democratic-Republican opposition by the mid-1790s.[99] But

---

[96] *Ibid.*, Association Minute Books, II, Apr. 14, 1794; Providence *Gazette*, Apr. 19, 1794.

[97] James Wilson, *An Oration Delivered before the Providence Association of Mechanics and Manufacturers, at their Annual Election, April 14, 1794* (Providence 1794), quotations at 23, 26, 27.

[98] Jonathan Maxcy, *An Oration, Delivered Before the Providence Association of Mechanics and Manufacturers, at their Annual Election, April 13, 1795* (Providence 1795), 15.

[99] Alfred Young, "The Mechanics and the Jeffersonians: New York, 1789-1801," *Labor History*, 5 (Fall 1964), 252-258. Formed in 1785, the New York group finally received a state charter in 1792; the Providence Association marked the occasion by sending a letter of congratulations. Letter to New York, June 18, 1792, PAMM Records, Association Minute Books, I, July 9, 1792.

in Providence, the leadership of the Association of Mechanics and Manufacturers remained predominantly Federalist throughout the decade, and the members at large—like Providence freemen generally—voted overwhelmingly for John Adams over Thomas Jefferson in the critical election of 1800.[100] Not that local artisans slavishly followed the merchants' lead. In 1799, the Association took the initiative in petitioning the general assembly for free schools, and in 1800 it memorialized the Congress for a higher tariff.[101] At the turn of the nineteenth century, the members displayed a modicum of political independence.

Considered as a whole, the early history of the Providence Association of Mechanics and Manufacturers illuminates the dual character of artisan republicanism in the postrevolutionary era. On the one hand, the Providence associates consistently emphasized the importance of cooperation and solidarity among themselves, what they called "cementing the mechanic interest." On the other hand, as the term "mechanic interest" itself implied, the members recognized that society consisted of different groups competing aggressively for both private gain and public power. "It is true," the committee of correspondence stated explicitly on one occasion, "that Mankind never engage in any Pursuit to such Advantage as when it is evidently for their own Interests."[102] The members knowingly and skillfully joined in this contest for worldly aggrandizement. Consequently they tailored their institutional program to meet their shifting needs and aspirations, not to fulfill a transcendent vision of the public good. When economic conditions were bad, they called for government interven-

---

[100] Association members voted for Federalist electors by a ratio of 12 to 1; freemen as a whole voted for Federalist electors by a ratio of 9 to 1. The poll list for this election is located in the Providence Town Meeting Minutes, 1800-1808, Nov. 19, 1800 (Rhode Island Historical Society Library). The PAMM Membership File, 1800, was compiled from PAMM Records, PAMM Signature Book, *passim*; *ibid.*, Association Minute Books, I, II, *passim*; *The Charter, Article of Agreement, Bye-Laws, Rules and Regulations of the Providence Association of Mechanics and Manufacturers* (Providence 1798), 37-40.

[101] PAMM Records, Association Minute Books, II, Feb. 4, 1799, Oct. 17, 1800. On the campaign for free schools and its limited success, see William G. Shade, "The 'Working Class' and Educational Reform in Early America: The Case of Providence, Rhode Island," *The Historian*, 39 (Nov. 1976), 3-7; Francis X. Russo, "John Howland: Pioneer in the Free School Movement," *Rhode Island History*, 37 (Nov. 1978), 111-122.

[102] Letter to Newport Association of Mechanics and Manufacturers, July 6, 1792, PAMM Records, Association Minute Books, I, July 9, 1792.

tion; when economic conditions were good, they rested content with the status quo.

How, then, should one construe behavior that was neither highly individualistic nor truly communitarian? Modifying Tocqueville's dictum, it may be useful to characterize the social principle underlying artisan conduct as the doctrine of self-interest *collectively* understood.[103] More than either "a universal law of self-interest" narrowly interpreted or "the rule of virtue" as classically conceived, this principle proved suitable to the development of democratic capitalism in America.

---

[103] For Tocqueville's discussion of the doctrine of self-interest properly understood, see Alexis de Tocqueville, *Democracy in America*, ed. J.P. Mayer, trans. George Lawrence (Garden City, N.Y. 1969), esp. 525-528.

Emerging Republicanism and the Standing Order: The Appropriation Act Controversy in Connecticut, 1793 to 1795

James R. Beasley*

S CHOLARS examining the political development of Connecticut in the early national period have generally emphasized the immutability of Federalism and the late rise of Republicanism as compared to the early appearance of organized political opposition in other New England states, especially Massachusetts. In 1905 M. Louise Greene mistakenly identified the Democratic-Republican party as successor to the antifederalist faction of 1789 and thus distorted her entire discussion of the rise of an organized faction opposing the Connecticut Standing Order.[1] Greene's assertion was corrected by Richard J. Purcell in 1918 in what still remains the most comprehensive published study of Connecticut from 1775 to 1818. Purcell claimed that "Connecticut's opposition party was of late birth," and offered as support for this claim the argument that after the ratification of the Constitution "the factions [Federalists and antifederalists] were merged, for they were not at odds over questions of local import." Believing that "during the decade, 1790-1800, there was practically no political life in the modern sense," Purcell placed the formal beginnings of Republicanism in Connecticut in 1800.[2] Recent scholarship is in general accord with Purcell's contention that Republicanism arrived late in Connecticut. Noble E. Cunningham, Jr., says that although political parties in some states were fairly well defined by 1796, "outside of Boston, New England displayed few obvious signs of party organization." In discussing Connecticut Republicanism,

* Mr. Beasley is a graduate student at Tufts University. He wishes to thank Professors Robert J. Taylor of Tufts University and J. Earl Thompson, Jr., of Andover Newton Theological School for their suggestions.
[1] M. Louise Greene, *The Development of Religious Liberty in Connecticut* (Boston, 1905), 393-408.
[2] Richard J. Purcell, *Connecticut in Transition, 1775-1818* (Washington, D. C., 1918), 227, 229.

WILLIAM AND MARY QUARTERLY

Cunningham, like Purcell, begins with the organizational activities pre-
cipitated by the national election in 1800 and says that "there can be
little doubt that Republicans were more active in Connecticut in 1800
than they had been before and were for the first time threatening the
Federalist ascendancy."[3]

However, the establishment of 1800 as the formal organizational date
of Connecticut Republicanism does not preclude earlier expressions of Re-
publican-type sentiment or the prior occurrence of serious threats to
Connecticut's political and ecclesiastical establishment, which certainly
became identified with the Federalist ascendancy. Indeed, the opposition
faction emerging out of the controversy in the mid-1790s over what to
do with Connecticut's Western Reserve was marked by characteristics
which scholars identify with the state's Republican Party after 1800 and
which demonstrate the ideological affinity of the emerging group with
later Republicanism in other states and in the national government—
a vigorous anticlericalism, calls for "the purity and secrecy of elections"
and for the extension of the suffrage, and attacks upon a political
oligarchy.[4] Moreover, several of the leaders of this nascent opposition
took prominent roles in the Connecticut Republican Party after
its formal organization. For convenience, then, it may not be amiss
to label this emerging political faction "Republican" and its opponents
"Federalist," if it is understood that formal party organization and direct links with such groups in other states had to await the interjection
into state politics of domestic and foreign policy issues which were already influencing the development of parties "in Congress and in the affairs of the national government."[5]

From May 1793 until May 1795 the question of whether to sell Connecticut's Western Reserve—and what to do with any money actually
realized—occasioned debate in every session of the General Assembly,
elicited widespread popular comment including articles in every news-

[3] Noble E. Cunningham, Jr., *The Jeffersonian Republicans: The Formation of
Party Organization, 1789-1801* (Chapel Hill, 1957), 114, 208. See also William A.
Robinson, *Jeffersonian Democracy in New England* (New Haven, 1916), 38-41;
and Norman L. Stamps, "Political Parties in Connecticut" (Ph.D. diss., Yale University, 1950), 8-10.
[4] Cunningham, *The Jeffersonian Republicans*, 204-209; Purcell, *Connecticut in
Transition*, 129, 156, 209-210; Paul Goodman, *The Democratic-Republicans of
Massachusetts: Politics in a Young Republic* (Cambridge, Mass., 1964), 76-77.
[5] Cunningham, *The Jeffersonian Republicans*, 49.

72

paper published in the state, and led to heated discussions in town meetings and ecclesiastical societies.[6] The Appropriation Act controversy, as it came to be called because it centered on an act of 1793 providing for the expenditure of the proceeds from land sales in the Western Reserve, dramatically exhibited the extent of deep-seated resentment against Connecticut's political order and seriously weakened the stranglehold of the Congregationalist establishment on Connecticut politics.[7]

Connecticut's sea-to-sea charter had granted her an indefinite western boundary between the parallels forty-one degrees and forty-two degrees, two minutes, which constituted the state's southern and northern boundaries. The vagueness of the charter led Connecticut and her neighboring colonies into heated, occasionally bloody disputes over boundaries and territorial jurisdictions. There was a difference of opinion, too, among Connecticut residents as to whether the colony should assert her claim to western lands and, if the claim was made, how to use the land most profitably. As early as October 1772 an anonymous writer in the *Connecticut Courant* proclaimed Connecticut's right to the western lands and suggested that a part of the land might be sold "to defray all the public charges of the colony." The Reverend Benjamin Trumbull repeated this proposal in April 1774 and added that a public fund resulting from the land sale might also "enrich our college and support all the schools in the colony." The next month Ebenezer Hazard of New York, in a petition asking the Connecticut General Assembly to sell to him and his associates the land between Pennsylvania's western boundary and the

[6] There were 13 newspapers published in Connecticut during the period 1793-1795: *American Mercury* (Hartford), *American Telegraphe* (Newfield), *Connecticut Courant* (Hartford), *Farmers Chronicle* (Danbury), *Farmers Journal* (Danbury), *Hartford Gazette, Litchfield Monitor, Middlesex Gazette* (Middletown), *Connecticut Journal* (New Haven), *Connecticut Gazette* (New London), *Norwich Packet, Weekly Register* (Norwich), *Windham Herald.*
[7] Accounts of the Appropriation Act controversy have usually been cursory. The most comprehensive account of the issue is Charles J. Hoadly *et al.*, eds., *The Public Records of the State of Connecticut* (Hartford, 1894-), VIII, xiii-xvii, hereafter cited as *Conn. State Records.* The editors of Volume VIII, Leonard W. Labaree and Catherine Fennelly, have done an admirable job of chronicling the events relating to the controversy, but they do not attempt to provide much analysis of the significance of the politico-ecclesiastical skirmish. See also Charles Roy Keller, *The Second Great Awakening in Connecticut* (New Haven, 1942), 63; Purcell, *Connecticut in Transition,* 75-76; Greene, *Religious Liberty,* 380-392.

Mississippi River, suggested that the £10,000 income from the sale might be used "to give additional Support to the College at New Haven, or the inferior but important Seminaries throughout the Colony."[8]

Nothing came of these early proposals for utilizing the western lands, however, and in September 1786 Connecticut ceded all her western claims to Congress, "reserving" a strip of territory extending westward from the western boundary of Pennsylvania one hundred and twenty miles and bounded on the south and north by extensions of Connecticut's southern and northern boundaries.[9] This Western Reserve remained intact until May 1792 when the state granted five hundred thousand acres of "firelands" to the citizens of the Connecticut shore towns who had suffered property losses at the hands of British troops during the Revolutionary War.[10] The question of what to do with the remaining portion of the Reserve inaugurated the Appropriation Act controversy in 1793.

At the May 1793 session the General Assembly appointed a committee of eight to dispose of the remaining lands. Although the committee received authorization to sell, it could not make the sale final until six months after the adjournment of the session.[11] A pseudonymous writer, "Cato," reflecting almost two years later upon the events of May 1793, charged the Congregational clergy with initiating the move to sell the lands. "Cato" claimed that the preachers had pressured their supporters in the Assembly to proceed with the sale of the lands in hope that the proceeds might go toward the support of the clergy and thus strengthen their declining social standing. The clergy was, he charged, bent on "blowing up the sparks of faction and party spirit."[12]

Whatever the precise motivation for selling the lands, the action did create "sparks" in Connecticut politics. "Cato's" charge, coming so long after the event, also took account of what happened in the October 1793 session of the Assembly, when legislators passed an act assigning receipts from the sale of western lands to a perpetual fund, the income of which

---

[8] Julian P. Boyd and Robert J. Taylor, eds., *The Susquehannah Company Papers* (Ithaca, 1962-), V, xxxix-xlii, 48; VI, 109, 259.

[9] Harlan Hatcher, *The Western Reserve: The Study of New Connecticut in Ohio* (Indianapolis, 1949), 20-21.

[10] *Conn. State Records*, VII, 448-472.

[11] *Ibid.*, VIII, 16-17. No records of debates or votes on the resolution to appoint the committee can be found in newspapers, the *Conn. State Records*, or in the Journals of the House of Representatives, May 1791-May 1808, manuscripts in the Connecticut State Library, Hartford. The Connecticut Council kept no journal.

[12] *Am. Merc.*, Apr. 6, 1795.

was to be granted to "the several Eclesiastical Societies Churches or Congregations of all denominations" to be used for the support primarily of ministers and secondarily of "Schools of Education."[13] This Appropriation Act provoked widespread reaction. Numerous pseudonymous articles for and against the act filled Connecticut's newspapers from October 1793 to May 1794, and thirteen towns adopted denunciatory resolutions during the winter and spring of 1793-1794.[14]

When the Assembly met in May 1794, opponents introduced in the house a bill to repeal the Appropriation Act, thereby renewing the contest. Popular interest in the issue is evident from the publication of the entire house debate in the newspapers.[15] Finally, the lower house voted for repeal, only to have the Council of Assistants veto its action.[16] The General Assembly then assured the continuation of the controversy by directing the committee on the sale of the lands to receive no proposals for another six months.[17]

The newspaper and town meeting debates continued from May until October 1794, when the Assembly reconvened. The lower house promptly passed a second repeal bill.[18] This time, however, the Council realized the general unpopularity of the act and took steps to appease the opposition and yet salvage what it could. Rejecting the repeal bill for a second time, the Council presented for the representatives' approval a bill which would grant the income from the land sales to local school districts, to be used for the support of schools or the ministry as the district might decide by a majority vote.[19] The representatives, indicating

[13] *Conn. State Records,* VIII, 100-101.

[14] Typical articles are in *Conn. Cour.,* Oct. 23, 1793; *Conn. Jour.,* Nov. 6, 1793; *Am. Merc.,* Nov. 18, 1793, Feb. 10, Mar. 31, Apr. 14, 1794. Resolutions opposing the act were adopted by Stratford, Huntington, Derby, Norwalk, Cheshire, New London, Saybrook, Groton, Milford, Wallingford, Guilford, Redding, and Ashford. See *Conn. Jour.,* Dec. 19, 1793, Jan. 23, Feb. 13, 27, Mar. 13, 27, Apr. 17, 1794; *Conn. Gaz.,* Mar. 13, 27, 1794; *Farmers Chron.,* Jan. 6, 1794; *Wind. Her.,* May 3, 1794.

[15] *Conn. Gaz.,* May 19, 26, 1794. The debate is printed in *Report of the Superintendent of Common Schools, to the General Assembly, May Session, 1853* (Hartford, 1853), 73-95.

[16] *Am. Merc.,* May 19, 1794; House Journal, Mar. 24, 1794.

[17] *Conn. State Records,* VIII, 145.

[18] House Journal, Oct. 22, 1794; *Am. Merc.,* Nov. 3, 1794.

[19] The Council bill is in *Conn. Cour.,* Nov. 3, 1794. From 1717 to 1793 the towns, parishes, and ecclesiastical societies were responsible for supervising the financing and operation of schools. By an act of May 1794, the Assembly shifted the responsibility to newly authorized school districts. The school districts were

that they wanted to consult their constituents before passing on the proposal, ordered it carried over to the next session.[20]

The Council's proposal, published in the newspapers, provoked debate once more in the press, town meetings, and ecclesiastical societies. In the session of May 1795, the opposition faction secured key alterations in the Council's proposal of October 1794, and when the bill repealing the Appropriation Act of 1793 finally passed, it provided that the proceeds from the sale of western lands would be assigned to a perpetual fund, the income of which was to go to the school districts in the state for the support of schools. If any school districts should vote by a two-thirds majority to apply any part of its share to the support of the ministry, it might appeal to the legislature, and, upon receiving permission to do so, divide the money among the different churches in the district in proportion to their respective memberships.[21]

The day after the School Fund Act passed, a joint committee reported in favor of selling the Western Reserve as soon as the state received an offer of at least one million dollars.[22] During the next few months the committee appointed to sell the lands negotiated a sale for $1,200,000 to a syndicate consisting primarily of Connecticut residents that later organized as the Connecticut Land Company. At the October 1795 session, the General Assembly accepted and approved the committee's report on the sale.[23] Thus, after many years of worrisome disputes and two full years of acrimonious debate Connecticut succeeded in disposing of her Western Reserve and establishing a permanent school fund.

The very fact that the fund was for schools and not for the support of churches, as originally proposed, indicates the transformation that occurred in the Connecticut politico-ecclesiastical order between 1793 and 1795, a dramatic change brought about by the activities of an emerging opposition faction in Connecticut politics. Certainly there was opposition to the Connecticut political and ecclesiastical establishment before 1793, but the local contest over the disposition of the Western Reserve moved the opponents of the Standing Order to the unity of expression and elemental organization that is recognizable as incipient Republicanism.

---

allowed to tax themselves for the support of schools, to choose tax collectors, and to locate the schools. See *Conn. State Records*, VIII, 138.

[20] *Am. Merc.*, Nov. 3, 1794.
[21] *Conn. State Records*, VIII, 237-239.
[22] *Ibid.*, 249-250.
[23] House Journal, Oct. 15, 1795; *Conn. State Records*, VIII, 304; *School Supt. Report*, 103-107.

The debate set off by the passage of the Appropriation Act on October 27, 1793, gained momentum rapidly, and when the Assembly met in May 1794, Chauncey Goodrich of Hartford declared that the opposition to the act centered on two questions: "One, whether any appropriation be expedient, the other, whether the appropriation now made be the most beneficial"?[24] Actually, a third question was initially involved in the controversy—whether the lands ought to be sold at all—but this concern was short-lived. The consensus for selling the lands was so strong among both Federalists and Republicans that when Thaddeus Benedict of Redding resurrected the inquiry in the house debate of May 1794, the Speaker promptly declared him out of order on the ground that his observations were "not pertinent to the question before the House."[25]

Few had shown the reluctance of Benedict to selling the western lands, and those who did never made this point basic to their objections to the Appropriation Act. Many of the Republican leaders were land jobbers and speculators who thus had a personal financial interest in the sale, and they did not, of course, want it delayed because appreciation in the value of the lands would diminish their anticipated profits as potential agents of the sale and settlement of the Reserve. Several prominent Republicans—among them Gideon Granger, Jr., Daniel Holbrook, William Judd, Oliver Phelps, and Moses Cleveland, who was named general agent to survey the land—became members of the Connecticut Land Company, which purchased the Reserve in 1795.[26] The "no-sale" argument could have been used in the Republican fight against the Appropriation Act, especially since it emphasized a great financial benefit for the state. Personal financial interest, however, triumphed over concern for public good or even political expediency, and Chauncey Goodrich's observations on the central issues in the controversy proved accurate.[27]

On the question of the expediency of an immediate appropriation of the proceeds from the proposed land sale, those opposing the Appropriation Act argued that the income should be put in the state treasury and held for future public exigencies. Ephraim Kirby of Litchfield, who

[24] *School Supt. Report*, 82.
[25] *Ibid.*, 75.
[26] Hatcher, *Western Reserve*, Chaps. 2-3.
[27] The speeches in the house debate of May 1794 are the basic sources for the present delineation of the major issues in the controversy. There were numerous articles in the newspapers, but the arguments found there were effectively reiterated and enlarged by the representatives in debate.

became a leading Connecticut Republican, spoke of "innumerable sudden and unforeseen events" which might require the immediate application of large sums of money. "Moreover," Kirby asserted, "it has ever been found convenient in all well regulated governments to have some resources . . . as a security against accidents and provision for such exigencies as might suddenly demand their strength."[28]

In answer the Federalists pointed to two inherent dangers in delaying appropriation. In the first place, some felt that the Assembly would be shirking a moral and political duty if it failed to appropriate the funds. Hezekiah Bissell said of the Assembly's responsibility: "Here is a trust committed to the present generation, in the course of human events; and for which we are holden and bound to account—we are in duty bound so to manage with, and preserve it, as that it may not be wasted and lost."[29] The foremost danger, however, lay in the inevitable struggle among greedy interests which would follow the placing of so large a sum in the public treasury, where it might be appropriated by whoever gained the favor of the legislature. Numerous applications for grants of every description would flood the Assembly and particular interests would govern its disposition. William Moseley rhetorically described the way applications would be granted: "Each applicant states his case in language best adapted to engage the attention and excite the passions in his favor; little proof is produced and little required. Some member from the vicinity of the applicant states to the house, that he believes the facts stated in the petition are true, and the rest of the members from the best feelings that can influence the human heart, compassion for supposed distress, and a disposition to distribute ample justice, grant the prayer."[30] Such grants, however, "would afford no relief to the people at large."

The efforts of Republicans to block any appropriation of the Western Reserve proceeds appear, however, to have stemmed more from a fear of the bounty being usurped by the Federalist-minded Congregational clergy than from a genuine belief that the money should be held for future exigencies. The strategy of these Republicans was to effect a compromise: they doubted that the Federalists would for the present be coerced into any other use of the money, but to leave the proceeds in

[28] School Supt. Report, 76.
[29] Ibid., 79.
[30] Ibid., 87.

the state treasury might buy time for drumming up support and making some other appropriation of the funds.

The second major issue of the contest, as Goodrich rightly observed, was "whether the appropriation now made be the most beneficial." Most of the Federalist politicians who participated in the house debate of May 1794 or wrote articles for the newspapers adamantly supported the appropriation to ecclesiastical societies. Primarily they contended that the Appropriation Act would promote virtue, religion, and learning. A pseudonymous newspaper writer doubted that "a more pious act, one better founded on the principles of sound policy, of justice and of liberality of sentiment, ... [ever] passed the legislature of this or any other state." The act, "Philanthropos" felt, would cultivate and maintain "the virtues and freedom which render a commonwealth rich, formidable, peaceful, honorable, and happy."[31]

William Hart of Saybrook pointed to more specific reasons for granting the funds primarily to churches and secondarily to schools. He lamented the deplorable condition of churches and schools, hoping to overcome the opposition by arousing its sympathy. "It is a well known fact," he asserted, "that in many parts of this State we have small poor societies, which have for many years been laboring under intolerable burthens, and in many instances have not been able to support a preached gospel among them, nor to provide for the education of their children."[32] A writer in the *American Mercury* offered an even more precise case for the effects of financial debility on religious and educational institutions. "Cimon" began his article with the postulate that "no public office can be advantageously filled unless the pecuniary emolument resulting from it will enable the person employed in it, to support himself comfortably, without his being obliged to have recourse to some other business." From this maxim the writer moved to show that schoolmasters and clergymen in Connecticut did not receive such a salary. Connecticut's clergy, according to "Cimon," received an average of eighty to one hundred pounds a year, schoolmasters about forty shillings a month. "What man," asked "Cimon," "can support a family on that?" Moreover, such poor salaries meant that no well-qualified man would spend his life in teaching, and so public education suffered.[33]

[31] *Am. Merc.,* May 19, 1794.
[32] *School Supt. Report,* 92.
[33] *Am. Merc.,* Apr. 14, 1794.

All eight Federalists who participated in the house debate of May 1794 were convinced that the best use of the proposed state income was to support the churches, and they united most of their colleagues behind them.[34] Republicans, on the other hand, were anxious to leave the money from the land sale in the state treasury unappropriated, and this was the one positive goal they sought. Although there were isolated suggestions for other uses of the anticipated proceeds, it is difficult to identify these as either Republican or Federalist, since most were given anonymously and expressed sectional interests rather than factional divisions. Expressions of sectional bias were only a minor element in the Appropriation controversy; opposition to the act had arisen because of basic social, religious, and political concerns.

Believing that the successful passage of the Appropriation Act marked the culmination of the maladministration of the Standing Order, the Republican leaders now called for a complete review of the political process in Connecticut. More than any other individual, Ephraim Kirby, the lawyer from Litchfield, stood forth as the champion of governmental reform. When the Council vetoed the bill to repeal the Appropriation Act in May 1794, Kirby sensed that widespread disapprobation of the Council's action created the proper atmosphere in which to unleash his attack on the Assistants. His series of articles in the *American Mercury* in the fall and winter of 1794-1795 was the result. In the articles Kirby detailed the evils of Connecticut politics and suggested corrective measures. He began with the premise that "there are instances in society where is becomes the duty of the people to call government to account." The Appropriation Act of 1793 was such an instance. It was, however, only a result of cumulative evil, and Kirby wished to direct the attack not so much at repeal (although he felt that to be essential also) but toward the oppressions of a "gradually established aristocracy."[35]

The "aristocracy" that Kirby assaulted was the upper house of the Connecticut General Assembly, the Council of Assistants. Its members often elected year after year with little or no opposition as a result of

[34] The eight were Hezekiah Bissell, Jonathan Brace, Chauncey Goodrich, William Hart, Joseph Hopkins, Elijah Hubbard, William Moseley, and Abraham Pierson. See *School Supt. Report*, 73-95.
[35] *Am. Merc.*, Aug. 11, 1794. Kirby signed the letters "Cassius." See Elisha Hyde to Ephraim Kirby, Aug. 27, 1974, Ephraim Kirby Papers, Duke University, Durham, N. C.

a peculiar election system, the Council wielded a heavy veto power for which it could not easily be held accountable.[36] Kirby charged that the Council was under the control of the people "rather in name than in fact" and that elections to it were "a specious form, an artful show, an apt delusion, calculated to bewilder and mislead the people." "And no wonder, that in a legislative body organized like this," he continued, "there are interests different from those of the people." Such entrenchment of a select group in an important governmental body was contrary to the "principles of representative government." Public officials should be changed frequently, "lest they feel secure in office, expect their places as matter of course, and grow negligent about consulting the good of their constituents." The only way to change the "tyranny of aristocracy" in Connecticut was to remove the present Council and elect men who would represent the interests of the people.[37]

Realizing that the Federalist Council could not be overturned under the traditional election process, Kirby proposed basic changes. Under the existing system elections were held in town meetings each September to nominate twenty men for the twelve places on the Council. Among those twenty the freemen "as a matter of course" included the incumbent councillors. The nominations were, moreover, presented to the freemen in the April town meetings with the nominees listed according to seniority in office, regardless of the number of votes each had received in the fall nominations. "Hence upon this plan of arrangement," Kirby explained, "it always happens, that the existing members of the Upper House are placed the first upon the nomination: and . . . finding ourselves unacquainted with the comparative merits of the several candidates, we bestow our suffrages upon those who are placed the first upon the list."[88] Kirby recommended that in the future nominees appear on the list in the order of nominating votes received. He also advocated the use of the secret ballot, both in the nominations and in the April elections. Unless these reforms were introduced, it could be "clearly predicted, that without supernatural aid, fatal consequences will finally ensue."[39]

Besides writing the newspaper articles, Kirby also corresponded with key Republican colleagues such as William Judd and Elisha Hyde,

[36] Purcell, *Connecticut in Transition*, Chap. 5.
[37] *Am. Merc.*, Aug. 11, Sept. 1, 8, 1794.
[88] *Ibid.*, Aug. 11, 1794.
[39] *Ibid.*, Aug. 11, Sept. 1, 1794.

gaining their support along with that of other opponents of Federalism.[40] But Kirby and his colleagues realized that they could not rely solely on personal correspondence and "letters to the editor" to bring about reform. Concerted effort—effort that would provide at least the rudiments of political organization—was required. As early as the fall of 1793, shortly after the passage of the Appropriation Act, there had been signs of cooperative activity against the Standing Order. A number of town meetings had adopted resolutions that created committees "to confer with similar committees of other towns upon prudent measures for preventing the contemplated appropriation."[41] The Federalists did not overlook such activity, as William Moseley's comment in the house debate of May 1794 evidenced: "If then the public mind is inflamed on this subject, it is an unnatural inflammation, a *forced warmth* . . . [and] the probability that the uneasiness complained of originates from *undue exertions* to produce it is a strong objection . . . against the repeal."[42] These "undue exertions" marked the beginning of a campaign which grew in intensity until the Appropriation Act was repealed in May 1795.

One result of local political activity was a change in the composition of the lower house between October 1793 and May 1794. The Appropriation Act passed in the former month by a vote of 84 to 69, but the repeal bill passed in the latter by a count of 108 to 57. The tremendous gain for the opposition forces from October 1793 to May 1794 resulted not from a conversion of supporters of the act but from their replacement by representatives charged by their constituents to vote for repeal.[43] In the elections of May 1794, moreover, several of the men who replaced supporters of the act became key leaders in the opposition. Four of

[40] Hyde to Kirby, Aug. 27, 1794, William Judd to Kirby, Oct. 13, 1794, Kirby Papers.

[41] *Conn. Jour.*, Mar. 13, 1794; *Conn. Gaz.*, Mar. 27, 1794; *Farmers Chron.*, Jan. 6, 1794.

[42] *School Supt. Report*, 88, italics mine.

[43] In May 1794, 31 towns sent 39 new representatives to the Assembly who supported the repeal of the act and who voted opposite to their predecessors, while 5 towns sent 5 new representatives who opposed the repeal bill and who voted opposite to their predecessors. Thus, 39 Federalists were replaced by Republicans, while only 5 Republicans were replaced by Federalists. Moreover, no representative who voted on the Appropriation Act and the repeal bill changed his vote. This information results from my tabulation of individual votes on appropriation and repeal in the Assemblies of October 1793 and May 1794. The votes were published in the *Conn. Jour.*, Nov. 6, 1793, and the *Am. Merc.*, May 19, 1794. The representatives are listed by town in *Conn. State Records*, VIII, 84-86.

them—Elisha Hyde, Gideon Granger, Jr., Ephraim Kirby, and William Judd—appeared among the leaders of Republicanism after 1800.[44] Their position as stalwarts in this earlier battle against the Standing Order provided a further indication that incipient Republicanism was clearly emerging in Connecticut.

Kirby and his fellow Republicans were not only busy educating the public to the evils of the Appropriation Act and working for the election of Republicans to the lower house, but they were also conducting an active, though unsuccessful, campaign to oust the entrenched councillors. Kirby pleaded with the freemen to offer more than moral support to the campaign against the Assistants, telling the voters that "three-quarters of the Freemen in the state may earnestly wish for a change, and be completely defeated. If they [the freemen] are in quest of this object," he said, "they must omit to vote for the persons whom they do *not* like . . . and they must in some measure unite their votes upon persons whom they *do* like."[45]

To help the freemen unite their votes, the Republican leaders prepared lists of men for election to the Council as alternatives to the traditional "deacons' seat" nomination lists.[46] The Republicans distributed the lists throughout the state, posted them in taverns and inns, and talked to voters about them at every opportunity. It was no random distribution. The Republicans appear to have planned a canvass of every Connecticut county, enlisting colleagues to coordinate activities in their local areas. Elisha Hyde reported campaign progress to Kirby in a letter of August 27, 1794: "The nominations which you sent are gone out into Tolland County and Windham County, and Mr. Gilbert seems to be skilled in the business of soliciting support." Hyde also told of his own efforts to keep informed of party activities around the state: "I have had several interviews with Col. M and Brother P who stand firm and are very active in the cause of Republicanism in Windham County."[47] In enlisting support, Republican leaders were careful to offer encouragement to prominent men who were potential backers. William Judd wrote, for example, to Kirby on October 13, 1794, that the Republicans were

[44] Purcell, *Connecticut in Transition*, 217, 232, 255, 272.

[45] *Am. Merc.*, Sept. 1, 1794.

[46] On traditional methods of nomination see Purcell, *Connecticut in Transition*, 214-215.

[47] *Am. Merc.*, Sept. 1, 1794, Mar. 30, Apr. 6, 1795; *Nor. Packet*, Apr. 2 1795; Hyde to Kirby, Aug. 27, 1794, Kirby Papers.

"in danger of loosing Capt. Cowler from the interests of the faithful unless some attention is paid to him to set him in the right road." The captain felt "as tho the Federalist Ministerial party would more safely lead him to promotion of which he is very fervid," a possibility that frightened Judd, who felt the captain was "too valuable a character for us to loose."[48]

In the end, the Republicans were not successful in their move to dislodge the Council; indeed, they did not break the grip of the Federalist body until 1818. However, their campaign against the Council did add weight to their assault on the Appropriation Act and helped to bring the Standing Order to the rebuff of May 1795.

Opposition to the Appropriation Act was not based solely on the need for political reform: the Republicans' struggle against the establishment also illustrates the religious controversy that surrounded the disposition of the western lands. Part of the opposition to the Appropriation Act centered on a realization that most of the proceeds would fall into the hands of the largest religious body. One should not, however, view the religious issue primarily as a dissenter fight for a share of the funds from the proposed land sale, although historians have generally attributed the repeal of the Appropriation Act to the fervent opposition of dissenting sects. M. Louise Greene first advanced such an interpretation in her 1905 study of religious liberty in Connecticut, describing the "turning point" of the contest in the following terms: "At the May session of the Assembly, 1794, the Baptists from all over the state thronged the steps of the capitol at Hartford, angered almost to the point of precipitating civil war. There John Leland addressed them, . . . setting forth Connecticut's departure from the glorious freedom mapped out by her founders. . . . The result of the widespread hostility was the attempt at the May session of 1794 to repeal the offensive law."[49] The dissenters in Connecticut were, she concluded, beginning to realize that gaining voting power was the surest way to overthrow the "vexatious laws" which repressed them, and the "western land bills had demonstrated the intense opposition of the dissenting minority."[50]

Contrary to Greene's belief, Leland delivered the sermon from which

[48] Judd to Kirby, Oct. 13, 1794, Kirby Papers.
[49] Greene, *Religious Liberty*, 387-389.
[50] *Ibid.*, 392.

she quoted, *A Blow at the Root,* not at Hartford in 1794, but at Cheshire, Massachusetts, in 1801.[51] Leland spoke, in fact, of working in his parish in Cheshire in the spring of 1794 and did not mention being in Hartford for the May session of the Assembly, although if there had been a meeting as crucial as that which Greene describes, Leland would almost certainly have noted it.[52] Furthermore, there is no mention in standard Baptist histories of a mass meeting of Baptists in Hartford in May 1794,[53] and the comparatively small size of dissenting sects at this time makes it doubtful that dissenters could have displayed so much political power.[54] Indeed, as Purcell points out, the Anglicans, one of the largest dissenting groups, were often loyal to the Federalist position. Dissenters and radical Congregationalists, in fact, might have formed an effective Republican coalition, but the dissenters had few well known political leaders and the two groups did not unite successfully until 1816.[55] Dissenters, no doubt, opposed the appropriation to churches because they knew the established church would benefit most from it, but to say that they led the fight against the act is to distort the evidence.

Emphasis on the activities of dissenters in the repeal of the Appropriation Act obscures the existence of politico-religious discord within Connecticut Congregationalism and the important role which some Congregational laymen played in the early development of Republicanism in the state. The setback which the Standing Order suffered in the repeal of the Appropriation Act was primarily the work of members of the established church, suggesting that Congregationalism cannot be equated simply with Federalism and that nascent Republicanism was not exclusively a faction of dissenters.[56] The broad support, for example,

[51] Purcell, *Connecticut in Transition,* 432; John Leland, *A Blow at the Root* (New London, Conn., 1801).
[52] L. F. Greene, ed., *The Writings of the Elder John Leland, including some events in his life, written by himself with additional sketches, etc.* (New York, 1845), 178.
[53] Isaac Backus, *A Church History of New-England . . . ,* III (Boston, 1796); Jesse L. Boyd, *A History of Baptists in America Prior to 1845* (New York, 1957); Henry S. Burrage, *A History of the Baptists in New England* (Philadelphia, 1894).
[54] See Franklin Bowditch Dexter, ed., *The Literary Diary of Ezra Stiles,* III (New York, 1901), 464, for a view of the comparative strength of religious bodies at the time of the controversy.
[55] Purcell, *Connecticut in Transition,* 61, 332-336.
[56] At least 8 of the 10 Republicans participating in the house debate of May 1794 were Congregationalists. Ephraim Kirby of Litchfield was an Anglican and the religious affiliation of John Watson of Canaan is unknown. The 8 Congrega-

that the Republican leadership had in the town meetings which sent representatives to the Assembly to oppose the Appropriation Act came largely from Congregationalists.[57] In a state where the large majority of citizens were at least professing Congregationalists, the Republicans could hardly have won such a contest without having attracted many Congregationalists' votes.

Political discord appeared among both laity and clergy. Although most of the Congregational clergy united in support of the Federalist political establishment,[58] a few vocally supported the Republican faction "and did so in the conviction that Republicanism embodied the first principles of evangelical Christianity." One such was David Austin, who after 1795 broke "with his 'Federalist brethren'" and began a career of "itinerant Republican exhortation." Perhaps more important for the Appropriation Act controversy was the Republican pastor at New Milford, the Reverend Stanley Griswold. Griswold attacked both the rigidity of the new orthodoxy in Connecticut and the Federalist political position. Active in the Republican campaign for Jefferson in 1800, he was often the featured speaker at Republican meetings. During the Appropriation Act controversy the New Milford pastor occasionally told his people how the Federalists had violated the "true Republican

---

tionalists—Henry Allen (Windsor), Thaddeus Benedict (Redding), Moses Cleveland (Canterbury), Gideon Granger, Jr., (Suffield), Daniel Holbrook (Derby), William Judd (Farmington), Elisha Payne (Canterbury), and Charles Phelps (Stonington)—were, with Kirby, clearly the leaders against the Appropriation Act. See Mary B. Brewster, *St. Michael's Parish, Litchfield, Connecticut, 1745-1954* (Litchfield, Conn., 1954), 61; Henry R. Stiles, *The History and Ancient Genealogies of Ancient Windsor, Connecticut; including East Windsor, South Windsor, Bloomfield, Windsor Locks, and Ellington, 1635-1891*, II (Hartford, 1891), 383; Charles Burr Todd, *The History of Redding, Connecticut* (Newburgh, N. Y., 1906 [orig. publ. New York, 1880]), 198; *Records of the Congregational Church in Canterbury, Connecticut, 1711-1844* (Hartford, 1932), 63, 86; *Records of the Congregational Church in Suffield, Conn., 1710-1836* (Hartford, 1941), 141; Samuel Orcutt, *The History of the Old Town of Derby, Connecticut, 1642-1880, with Biographies and Genealogies* (Springfield, Mass., 1880), 283, 296-297; Sylvester Judd, *Thomas Judd and His Descendants* (Northampton, Mass., 1856), 19-20; *Confession of Faith and Covenant of the Congregational Church in Farmington, Conn.* (Hartford, 1900), 18-20; Richard Anson Wheeler, *History of the Town of Stonington* (Mystic, Conn., 1900), 319-320.

[57] Many of these towns are among those which Purcell points out as being strongly Congregationalist. See above, n. 42; Purcell, *Connecticut in Transition*, 44-45, 96-97.

[58] Keller, *Second Awakening*, 56.

principles" of liberty, equality, and benevolence.[59] It is difficult to say how much influence Griswold had in the Republican fight against the Appropriation Act, but in his own locality he was probably an important leader. Being able to express his Republican sentiments before the majority of churchgoers in New Milford, he probably influenced the choice of two new representatives in May 1794 to replace men who had voted for the Appropriation Act.[60] Moreover, Griswold's political sentiments were sufficiently familiar to his fellow clergymen in Litchfield County that they harassed him for his Republicanism.[61] Influential Republican clergymen, however, were rare among Congregationalists, and Solomon Blakslee, an avid Federalist himself, was probably accurate when he declared that "scarcely a minister can be found who favors the Republicans."[62]

More important for the political disunity within Congregationalism was the presence of an influential and vocal group of laymen who opposed their religious leaders. As Republicans they attacked the religious establishment on two specific points: the traditional conception of the ministry and the tight grip that the established church held on educational institutions. Concerned that clergymen would benefit from the appropriation, Republicans pointed out, however, that their apprehension about "clerical endowment" evidenced no distaste for virtue, morality, or religion, avowing that they were "sensible of the importance of religion in society" and always willing to contribute their "proportion toward giving religion an honorable support."[63] They were, therefore, not "infidels" as their opponents often branded them, yet in their opposition to the Appropriation Act, the Republicans did display a vigorous anticlericalism.[64] Charles Phelps, a Congregationalist layman from Stonington,

[59] Alan Heimert, *Religion and the American Mind: From the Great Awakening to the Revolution* (Cambridge, Mass., 1966), 535-537, 541-543.
[60] *Conn. State Records*, VIII, 129; *Am. Merc.*, Nov. 6, 1793, May 19, 1794.
[61] Heimert, *Religion and the American Mind*, 542.
[62] Solomon Blakslee, *A Sermon* (Norwich, Conn., 1795), 18.
[63] *School Supt. Report*, 75, 78.
[64] Edmund S. Morgan, *The Gentle Puritan: A Life of Ezra Stiles, 1727-1795* (New Haven, 1962), 410-412, writes of "an intensification of . . . anticlericalism" in the last two decades of the 18th century. "As the [Connecticut] ministers spun out the fine thread of metaphysics, their congregations grew cool and hostile, and complaints against the clergy became ever more common." In the 1790s Republicanism "lent new strength to the arguments." For example, Republicans, demanding that Yale teach more practical subjects, derisively charged that the school's curriculum was "well adapted to training clergymen: since clergymen

expressed the general attitude when he said, "We ought to be on our guard against putting power or wealth into the hands of the clergy." These anticlericalists feared making the ministers independent. Finding "themselves enriched by the funds which . . . [were] provided for their support," the preachers would become secure and would not "be faithful, diligent, and attentive to visiting their people; but they . . . [would] become negligent, and instead of minding the proper duties of their office, they . . . [would] be taken up with useless controversies and altercations."[65]

More frightening to the Republicans than clerical independence alone was the inevitable reinforcement of the socio-political influence which the clergy already wielded. The early Republicans recognized the clergy as the single most powerful group in Connecticut and were convinced that any success in effecting political or ecclesiastical reforms would largely depend upon how much power the Republicans could wrest from them. The Appropriation Act would certainly strengthen the clergy and broaden their influence. Moses Cleveland especially did not like the clergy "deviating from their proper line of duty, and assuming that which belongs to the province of others." Cleveland's cohorts similarly accused the clergy of being "political intriguers," and William Judd of Farmington's First Congregational Church stated frankly that the Appropriation Act might "establish a clerical hierarchy inconsistent with the spirit of toleration, or the principles of republicanism, (from which evil good Lord deliver us and our posterity)" and result in the state being "subjected to ecclesiastical tyranny."[66] Scholars have long recognized anticlericalism as "a chief plank" of the Republican party after 1800.[67] Republicans, however, made anticlericalism a political plank before 1800—its importance in the platform of those opposing the Appropriation Act illustrates the ideological affinity between the emerging faction of 1794 and the formally organized party of 1800. Obviously, because the Republicans were aware of the ironclad grip which the clergy held on Connecticut social and political life, they opposed them as obstacles to political and social reform.

Another point of contention between clerical Federalists and lay Republicans was the role of the church in Connecticut's educational

served no useful purpose anyhow, it was appropriate for them to acquire useless knowledge."

[65] *School Supt. Report,* 76.

[66] *Ibid,* 78, 79, 81, 84, 88, 91; *Am. Merc.,* Apr. 6, 1795.

[67] Purcell, *Connecticut in Transition,* 331; Robinson, *Jeffersonian Democracy,* 129-132.

system. The Republicans' alternative to the Appropriation Act was to use the western lands proceeds as a fund to benefit the state's schools.[68] Before such a school fund could be administered impartially, however, they believed the schools had to be removed from control by the "smothering establishment of religion."[69] For years the local schools had generally been under the watch and care if not the support of the churches[70] and, as the Republicans charged, were "subservient to the whims of clerical overseers." The clergymen chose the schoolmasters and "very frequently turned away respectable scholars because of their supposed unnatural sentiments." Moreover, the Republicans charged that Congregational ministers, through their intimate contact with the schools, were able to impress young minds with a sense of the "important public role of the clergy."[71]

To remove the schools from ecclesiastical control the Republicans fought for the establishment of school districts governed by a council of elected representatives. Gideon Granger, Jr., a prominent Republican leader and member of the First Congregational Parish in Suffield, drew up the school district program and was instrumental in the passage of an act establishing the new system in May 1794. [72] The Congregational clergy and their Federalist colleagues deplored the idea of changing Connecticut's traditional educational system. To remove the schools from the control of the ecclesiastical societies was, said Thomas Day, a pastor from Litchfield, "to deny our children an education under the guidance of morality."[73] The clergy denied any political conniving in their supervision of the schools. Herman Daggett of New London assured his hearers that all the clergy had ever dreamed of doing was impartially providing for the "literary education of all children." Furthermore, said Daggett of his fellow clergymen, "no class of men has contributed more to the worth of our schools of education."[74]

[68] Conn. State Records, VIII, 138-139.
[69] Wind. Her., Apr. 4, 1795.
[70] Robert Middlekauff, Ancients and Axioms: Secondary Education in Eighteenth-Century New England (New Haven, 1963), 63-67; Conn. State Records, VIII, 138.
[71] Am. Merc., Apr. 14, 1794, Apr. 6, 1795; Purcell, Connecticut in Transition, 63-64.
[72] Conn. State Records, VIII, 138; Dictionary of American Biography, s.v. "Granger, Gideon, Jr."; Franklin Bowditch Dexter, Biographical Sketches of the Graduates of Yale College with Annals of the College History, IV (New York, 1907), 546-547.
[73] Thomas Day, An Oration (Litchfield, Conn., 1796), 26.
[74] Herman Daggett, A Sermon (New London, Conn., 1794), 35-36.

The most elaborate defense of the Congregational clergy's close relationship to the public schools was that of Timothy Dwight in his
oration on the Appropriation Act. Dwight began by reminding his
audience that he had long been interested in the education of youth
and as a result had discovered "that all parents, even the most vicious,
wish their children to be virtuous." Thus, Dwight said, it may be assumed
that the entire community, with very few exceptions, "consider the
education of their children to virtuous conduct as a primary object."
Such an accomplishment, however, required more than "precept"; it
required "example." It was most important, then, "that there should always exist, in every part of our country, men obligated to an example of
the strict and blameless life." No men were so qualified to serve in this
capacity, he concluded, as the clergy.[75]

Dwight's oration, delivered two months before the passage of the
act reorganizing the schools, was an expression of fear that the Standing
Order would lose an important means of maintaining its control over
Connecticut society if the new school districts were instituted. Passage of
the educational reform bill made the Federalists work even harder to
retain the Appropriation Act, but the new legislation had provided
Republicans with an alternative use for the Western Reserve funds. The
result was the pitched battle of May 1795 in the Assembly in which
Republicans demonstrated the strength that they had mustered since
October 1793 by repealing the Appropriation Act and establishing the
school fund.

A final element of disunity within Connecticut's established church
stemmed from the Standing Order's theological inheritance. The Congregational clergy of the 1790s had translated New England theology
into a socially and politically conservative ideology which Alan Heimert
describes as "defensive ecclesiasticism."[76] The theological differences between Old and Consistent Calvinists were "largely overlooked" while
such men as Timothy Dwight and Lyman Beecher rallied "Con-

[75] *School Supt. Report*, 101.
[76] Heimert, *Religion and the American Mind*, 353-354, 377-378, 399, 535. On
the theological controversy, see Keller, *Second Awakening*, 31-35; Morgan, *The
Gentle Puritan*, 20-44; Charles E. Cunningham, *Timothy Dwight, 1752-1837: A
Biography* (New York, 1942), 107-109; Sydney E. Ahlstrom, ed., *Theology in
America: The Major Protestant Voices From Puritanism to Neo-Orthodoxy*
(Indianapolis, 1967), 41-43; Richard L. Bushman, *From Puritan to Yankee: Char-
acter and the Social Order in Connecticut, 1690-1765* (Cambridge, Mass., 1967),
196-220; Sidney Earl Mead, *Nathaniel William Taylor, 1786-1858: A Connecticut
Liberal* (Chicago, 1942), 12-23, 95-127.

gregational Calvinists of all shades to the defense of the Standing Order and religion against the inroads of infidelity and democracy."[77] Many laymen, however, did not welcome this new religious scheme, and even in the land of steady habits "there were Calvinists who resisted the conversion of their religion into an engine of Federalist partisanship."[78] Following the New Light emphases on religious toleration and the responsibility of the ruler, some Congregationalist laymen of the 1790s developed a general resentment against snobbish, politically powerful ecclesiastics. This dissatisfaction with the clergy found organized expression in early Republicanism.

The Appropriation Act controversy is a vivid illustration that the Congregational laity were dissatisfied with their preachers' violations of the "liberty" and "equality" demanded by moral law as set forth by Edwardsean Calvinism. When they attacked the program of appropriation that the clergy supported, the laymen could be confident that they were at once assaulting the materialistic selfishness and the political obtrusiveness of the clergy.[79]

In the course of the electioneering in the fall of 1794, Elisha Hyde wrote confidently to Ephraim Kirby: "I believe the foundation is now laid to overturn the old Gothic building which has been propped by Priestcraft encroachments on the Constitution."[80] Repeal of the Appropriation Act at least partly confirmed Hyde's optimistic projection. The new act of May 1795 was exactly opposite to what the Federalists had initially desired in appropriating the Western Reserve proceeds and represented a serious blow to their autocratic sway over Connecticut politics. Although the establishment of the school fund in 1795 does not mark the final defeat of Federalism or a decisive triumph of Republicanism in Connecticut, it does show that the battle between these two factions certainly had a spirited beginning in the mid-1790s.

Shortly after the repeal of the Appropriation Act, Timothy Stone informed his congregation that "a recent Act of the General Assembly has greatly injured the cause of civil order and virtue in this state." Most distressing for Stone was the knowledge that the legislative action was a "public victory for the anti-ministerial faction." Moreover, "Infidelity" was behind this upheaval in Connecticut society, and unless soon checked

[77] Mead, *Taylor*, 122.
[78] Heimert, *Religion and the American Mind*, 535-536.
[79] *School Supt. Report*, 78, 89.
[80] Hyde to Kirby, Aug. 27, 1794, Kirby Papers.

it would "bring to ruin all piety and morality in the state."[81] The Appropriation Act controversy did more than point to the existence of an attack on the Standing Order; it displayed "the source from whence cometh that evil attack."[82] Federalist ministers knew that the Republican faction was led by many of their own laymen and this fact contributed greatly to the preachers' fears and to their resulting defense of traditional socio-political relationships. The establishment had suffered internal injury in the fracas surrounding the Appropriation Act and even though it remained intact for another twenty years, there was substantial evidence of the rapid growth of a disgruntled laity.

The importance of these politico-ecclesiastical transformations in late eighteenth-century Connecticut goes beyond simply illustrating the genesis of political factionalism and the disunity within Congregationalism. They also illustrate attitudes toward methods for achieving general social reform. Conflicting ideologies and interests of Republicans and Federalists, clergy and laity, dissenters and members of established churches, led to attempts by each to gain or protect the kinds of institutions which they deemed essential to a successful experiment in republican government. Motivated by multiple interests and principles, some of which are no doubt indiscernible, Republicans and Federalists expressed in the Appropriation Act controversy the tension which arises between reformers and protectors of the status quo.

Although the conflict concerned the appropriation of a large sum of money, economic interest was not the key motivating force behind participants in the Appropriation controversy. Republicans tried, of course, to make political fuel out of the supposed material interest of the Congregational clergy, but these arguments were minor ones in the Republican barrage and were well refuted by the Federalists. Actually, the ministers could have received little personal financial benefit from the act, although the grant to the churches would have strengthened the overall financial position of Congregationalists. But the Congregational churches were facing no particular economic crisis and the ministers and their fellow Federalists were concerned about something beyond a cash grant. Nor were the Republicans' interests primarily financial. Many of the Republican leaders were loyal Congregationalists and yet they opposed an appropriation which would funnel the bulk of the western lands proceeds into their local churches.

[81] Timothy Stone, *A Sermon* (Hartford, 1795), 27, 29-30.
[82] *Ibid.*, 30.

Both factions, then, were more interested in the broad issue of social change than in economic benefit: Republicans viewed themselves as socio-political reformers while Federalists were intent on defending the existing order. The Republicans knew that the issue was "more than the mere disposal of a sum of money."[83] When Elisha Hyde spoke of tearing down the "old Gothic building," he knew he referred to an old and powerful institution in Connecticut society. Yet Hyde, as most other Republicans, would have agreed with Ephraim Kirby that such institutions, if left alone, "may encroach upon our liberties, and by little and little, aspire to arbitrary power."[84] The Federalist spokesmen were just as certain that there would be numerous attempts to damage the "civil, social, and religious institutions wisely formed by our ancestors." In the event of such attacks upon "steady habits" it was thought that "the security of . . . liberty, the principles of republicanism, and the continuance of . . . prosperity depend solely on a persevering attention and encouragement to . . . the wise institutions adopted by our ancestors."[85]

One means by which the Federalists could restrain the democratic impulses appearing in their midst was to convince the voters that the state had a responsibility to support true religion in the interest of society at large. Convinced that true religion was synonymous with Congregationalism, the Federalists saw the Appropriation Act as a step toward retaining the establishment of religion which they felt was essential to to a society honoring God and promoting harmony among the people. For Chauncey Goodrich the Appropriation Act assured the continuation of a relationship in which "the principles of order co-operate with those of liberty."[86] It is true that establishment meant only tax support for the Congregational Church and that laws restricting the freedom of dissenters had been considerably relaxed, but Federalists knew that the bond between civil and religious realms went beyond the tax dollar— it meant the control of such key institutions as education and civil government. In the face of post-Revolutionary intrusions of "infidelity," "immorality," and "democracy," Federalists seized the Appropriation issue as an opportunity for securing the shaky position of the Standing Order.

[83] *Am. Merc.*, Apr. 6, 1795.
[84] *Ibid.*, Mar. 30, 1795.
[85] *School Supt. Report*, 83, 87.
[86] *Ibid.*, 83.

Republicans were as anxious to broaden the political process as were the Federalists to keep it narrow. When the power of rulers invades the freedom of the people, proclaimed Ephraim Kirby, "then the people must dissolve the corrupted ties of degenerated society, and let loose the destroying Angel, till tyrants have been taught . . . what it is to feel the indignation of . . . a finally incensed people."[87] The Republicans were very aware that decisions affecting public policy were most often influenced by two groups in Connecticut society: the Council of Assistants and the Congregational clergy. It was at these two centers of power that the reformers directed their attack, and the Appropriation Act served as a perfect target for Republican animosity.

The reform impulse in late eighteenth-century Connecticut was generated not by a group of radicals from outside the Standing Order but rather by many who were part of the so-called Federalist-minded institution of Congregationalism. The established church had indeed long supported the status quo and most of its clergy still adhered to that position, but a progressive group of laymen were finally leading the way in tearing down the old alliance. It does not follow, however, that the methods employed by the reformers were traditional or generally acceptable to the establishment. Campaigning and electioneering seemed to many a disgraceful way of achieving one's political ends. The Federalists cried loud and long that if a man was worthy of public office his fellows would recognize his virtue and naturally choose him as their leader. Similarly, to withhold from a clergyman the respect due his political and moral advice was an affront to a man whom God had endowed with particular astuteness in these matters. Republicans were employing radical methods in pressing their reforms, but many coming out of the establishment church believed that the best way to accomplish their goals was to change the old system from within. Thus, they concentrated on getting men into the political system who would represent their interests. In this they were dramatically successful in the elections of May 1794. To suggest that successful social reform is not the monopoly of extra-establishment radicalism may seem contrary to current notions; however, events in Connecticut during the 1790s demonstrate that an internal reform impulse can, as it was in that historical setting, be effective.

[87] *Am. Merc.*, Aug. 11, 1794.

New York State Indian Policy
After the Revolution

By BARBARA GRAYMONT

An examination and analysis of the process by which the Iroquois gave up almost all of their lands in central and western New York. Dr. Graymont is in the Department of History and Economics at Nyack College, Nyack, N.Y.

A t the close of the Revolutionary War, the Six Nations Indians held the territory that today includes most of central New York, all of western New York with the exception of the military posts at Oswego and Niagara, much of northern and western Pennsylvania, and large areas in Ohio and southward. To the Six Nations, or Iroquois, this was their sovereign domain. They considered themselves to be members of a sovereign confederacy, on a diplomatic par with the European nations with whom they had conducted treaties in the past. Unfortunately for them, the unity of their confederacy had been shattered during the war as the constituent member nations drifted apart to support either Great Britain or the United States.

Not that the individual nations of the Six Nations Confederacy were at all times united. Most Senecas supported the British, but some Senecas remained neutral. Most Mohawks supported the British and even left their homes and fled to Canada or Niagara to join themselves to the King's cause, but a few Mohawks stayed behind at Fort Hunter in a friendly neutrality. Most Oneidas and Tuscaroras supported the United States and suffered greatly during the war because of this support, but a minority of these two nations attached themselves to the British. The Onondagas

An earlier version of this paper was presented at a conference on "New York in the New Nation" at State University College at Oneonta, April 26, 1974.

New York History OCTOBER 1976

Territory of the Six Nations. From Donaldson, The Six Nations of New York *(1892).*

were early split three ways—pro-British, pro-United States, and neutralist—until the Van Schaick expedition of April 1779 forced the Onondaga nation wholly into the British column.[1]

Now, after the war, only the Oneidas, Tuscaroras, and Senecas felt at all secure about their territory—the Oneidas and Tuscaroras because they were on the winning side, and the Senecas because they were the most numerous tribe and the most westerly, farthest removed from their American enemies.

The boundary between the white settlements and the Six Nations was known as the "Line of Property," or, "Old Treaty Line," negotiated by the Indians and Sir William Johnson at the Treaty of Fort Stanwix in 1768. In New York, the line ran southward from a point on Wood Creek, between Oneida Lake and Fort Stanwix, to the source of the

1. For a comprehensive discussion of the Six Nations' part in the war, see, Barbara Graymont, *The Iroquois in the American Revolution* (Syracuse: Syracuse University Press, 1972).

Unadilla River, down around the Great Bend in the Susquehanna River, then westerly to Tioga. It then ran southwesterly
through Pennsylvania and Virginia, and then south to the
Alabama region. This treaty was an attempt on Johnson's
part to set precisely a boundary that was but vaguely
described in the Proclamation of 1763, and, incidentally, also
to enrich himself and his fellow land speculators with the
additional Indian acreage in New York Province that would
now be on the white man's side of the line.[2]

Unfortunately for the Mohawks the treaty left their settlements entirely to the eastward of the line, on the white man's
side. This meant that after the Revolutionary War, there
would be little or no chance of these Mohawks returning
to settle in close proximity to the whites whose homes they
had ravaged and whose relatives they had slain during the
hostilities.

But it was this Old Treaty Line that the Six Nations
would insist upon as a boundary between them and the whites
during their subsequent negotiations with the Americans at
the end of the war. That they ultimately failed was a result
of their weak military position, their abandonment by
the British, their poverty, their disunity, the conflicting
sovereignties between Congress and New York State, the
weakness and indifference of the federal government,
and the insatiable land hunger of the New Yorkers. In
their disunity and in their destitute economic circumstances,
the Indians were no match for the hard bargaining of the New
York State Indian Commissioners.

New York State Indian policy after the Revolution can
be succinctly summarized under three headings:

1. Extinguish any claim of the United States Congress to
sovereignty over Indian affairs in the State of New York.
2. Extinguish the title of the Indians to the soil.
3. Extinguish the sovereignty of the Six Nations.

The Articles of Confederation, which had been adopted
in 1781, gave control of Indian affairs to Congress.

2. Francis S. Philbrick, *The Rise of the West 1754-1830* (New York: Harper
Torchbook, 1965), pp. 30-33.

Article IX, Section 4 stated: "The United States in Congress assembled shall also have the sole and exclusive right and power of . . . regulating the trade and managing all affairs with the Indians, not members of any of the states. . . ." Section 1 of the same article said: "The United States in Congress assembled, shall have the sole and exclusive right and power of determining on peace and war" and of "entering into treaties and alliances."

The specific wording of the Article left room for debate. Where was the boundary of New York State? Did it extend westward only to the Line of Property, described by the Treaty of Fort Stanwix in 1768, or did it extend westward to Niagara? Did the Six Nations, in the words of the 1832 Supreme Court decision in *Worcester v. Georgia*, form "a distinct community, occupying its own territory, with boundaries accurately described, in which the laws of Georgia [New York] can have no force, and which the citizens of Georgia [New York] have no right to enter but with the assent of the Cherokees [Six Nations] themselves or in conformity with treaties and with the acts of Congress"? Or were the Six Nations members of New York State? Like Governor Wilson Lumpkin of Georgia and President Andrew Jackson in 1832, Governor George Clinton and the New York State Indian Commissioners in 1784 had no question as to the status of *their* Indians. To the New York executive, and to the legislature, the Six Nations were members of New York State. Clinton said as much in his speeches to the Indians at the 1784 state treaty with them.

Brethren! The Right and Power of managing all Affairs with the Indians, not Members of any of the States, is vested in Congress, who have, as We are informed, appointed Commissioners for the Purpose. We [the New York State Indian commissioners] are appointed by a Law of the Legislature of this State, to superintend Indian Affairs within the same, by Virtue of which We are authorized and required to enter into Compacts and Agreements with any Indians residing within this State. It is in Consequence of this Law and these Powers that We appear now to treat with You our Brethren, with whom, when our present Differences are adjusted, We are inclined to live as heretofore, on Terms of the most sincere Friendship: in Testimony whereof we give You this [wampum] Belt.[3]

3. Franklin B. Hough, *Proceedings of the Commissioners of Indian Affairs Appointed by Law for the Extinguishment of Indian Titles in the State of New York* (Albany: Joel Munsell, 1861), p. 50.

Surprisingly, the Six Nations seem to have accepted this concept. Their spokesman, Joseph Brant, in his reply to Clinton's speech, stated, "We have considered the Confederation of the United States, the Constitution of this State and the Law under which You act and are fully sensible of your Right, as Commissioners of this State, in treating with Us the six Nations who live and reside within its Limits." Paradoxically, the Indians also considered themselves to be members of sovereign Indian Nations. They did not seem to grasp the significance of nationhood and territoriality in the white man's terms while later giving up their territory by treaty to a subsidiary state of the United States. But to talk of an independent nation within the state of New York was as inconceivable to Governor Clinton as an independent Cherokee nation within the state of Georgia was to Governor Lumpkin many years later. New York would not compromise its sovereignty by recognizing the independent sovereignty of any Indian nation within its borders.[4]

As far as the New Yorkers were concerned, their state boundaries were described by the colonial grant given by the King, Indian occupants notwithstanding. This meant that after 1780 when it gave up its claim to western lands, New York claimed Lake Erie and the Niagara River as its western border, and not the Old Treaty Line of 1768.

As a common decency, New York State recognized Indian title to the land still occupied by the original Indian inhabitants and would seek legally to buy that title, but it did not recognize Indian sovereignty over the soil. It was a fine distinction. Sovereignty had belonged not to the Indians, but to the European power that moved in upon the Indians, and, ultimately, to the state of New York, which was the successor to the British colony of New York. The old European imperial concept was that any area not claimed by a Christian prince belongs to any other Christian prince whose representatives could lay a claim to it for him. In discussing this problem, Vattel, the great eighteenth-century authority on international law, stated that "erratic nations"

4. Brant's speech is in *ibid.*, p. 60. See Governor Clinton's rejection of the Oneidas' offer at the 1785 treaty to lease some of their land to New York State. That, said Clinton, "would make the Government of the State tributary to You." *Ibid.*, p. 97.

in the New World occupied far more land than they had need of and, since their "unsettled habitation" gave them no "true and legal possession" of these vast regions, the overpopulated countries of Europe might lawfully take possession of whatever lands they needed.[5]

Clinton's view that the Indians were members of the State of New York led him and the State Indian Commissioners to feel that the commissioners of the Continental Congress had no business poking their long noses into New York State affairs. The Governor and his commissioners thus did everything in their power in terms of behind-the-scenes maneuvering to thwart the mission of the Continental commissioners who sought to conclude a peace with the Six Nations in 1784.

During the war years, New York State was much too occupied with the hostilities and the defense of its frontiers to take an active interest in land speculation in Indian country. Also, the state officials were content to have Indian affairs conducted by the Congressional Indian Commissioners for the Northern Department: Philip Schuyler, Oliver Wolcott, Joseph Hawley, and Turbot Francis. Of these men, the New Yorker, Philip Schuyler was by far the most active and most prominent of the Indian commissioners. But while the war was in progress, New York did take steps to guard its own interests in regard to Indian affairs. On October 23, 1779, the New York Legislature designated the governor and four Indian commissioners to look out for New York's interests at any peace negotiations with the Indians.[6]

With the end of hostilities, Congress adopted a report on Indian peace on October 15, 1783. This report demonstrated

5. Emmerich de Vattel, *The Law of Nations*, edited by Joseph Chitty (Philadelphia: T. & J. W. Johnson & Co., 1872), Book I, Chap. XVIII, Sect. 209, pp. 99-100. Also see the opinion of John Tabor Kempe, Attorney General of the Province of New York, in William Johnson, *The Papers of Sir William Johnson*, edited by James Sullivan and others (Albany: State University of New York, 1921-1965), XI, 817-819; A. Pearce Higgins, "International Law and the Outer World, 1450-1648," in *Cambridge History of the British Empire*, edited by J. Holland Rose and others (Cambridge: Cambridge University Press, 1929), I, 193. In British practice, "it was the characteristic of our own feudal tenures, which held that the ultimate ownership of the soil was the property of the crown." James E. Thorold Rogers, *A Manual of Political Economy* (Oxford: The Clarendon Press, 1876), p. 169.

6. Thomas C. Cochran, *New York in the Confederation* (Philadelphia: University of Pennsylvania Press, 1932), p. 99.

the esteem the Congress held for the friendly Oneidas and Tuscaroras by assuring them of their inviolate right to their country, until such time as they should voluntarily desire to dispose of any of their lands.[7] Finally, on March 19, 1784 Congress appropriated $15,000 for use of the commissioners who would negotiate a treaty of peace with the Six Nations.[8]

Even before this time, and five months before the preliminary articles of peace were signed, the New York Legislature on July 25, 1782 moved to expropriate the Six Nations country for military bounty lands, the country of the Oneidas and Tuscaroras excepted.[9]

Early the following year, New York took steps to exert control over Indian affairs within its borders. A statute of March 25, 1783 empowered the Council of Appointment to appoint three Indian commissioners, who, acting with the governor, would have control over Indian affairs.[10] The Legislature was to validate the acts of the commissioners before they could take effect. Specifically, however, the Indian commissioners were to secure to the Oneidas and Tuscaroras their rights in appreciation for their loyal service during the war.

On July 27, 1783, the Council made the following appointments as Indian Commissioners: Abraham Cuyler, Peter Schuyler, and Henry Glen. Major Peter Schuyler was a relative of General Philip Schuyler, a resident of Albany, and a member of the Assembly. He later became a member of a notorious land company that sought to evade New York's constitutional provision against private individuals conducting land negotiations with the Indians without a license from the state. Schuyler and his cronies

7. United States Continental Congress, *Journals of the Continental Congress 1774–1789* (Washington, D.C.: United States Government Printing Office, 1904–1937), XXV, 687 (hereafter, *JCC*).

8. *Ibid.*, 747; Papers of the Continental Congress, Item 30, II, f. 213 (hereafter, PCC).

9. *Laws of the State of New-York, Commencing with the first Session of the Assembly after the Declaration of Independency, and the Organization of the New Government of the State, Anno 1777* (Poughkeepsie, N.Y.: John Holt, 1782 [sic]), Sixth Session, Chapter XI, 267–268.

10. *Laws of the State of New York passed at the Session of the Legislature held in the years 1777, 1778, 1779, 1780, 1781, 1783 and 1784, inclusive, Being the First Seven Sessions* (Albany: Weed, Parsons and Company, 1886), Chapter XLVIII, pp. 290, 595.

in the New York Genesee Company of Adventurers, as it was called, secured fraudulent 999 year leases from the Six Nations and also separately from the Oneidas. These leases were promptly voided by the legislature.

The Continental Congress was well aware of New York's activities in Indian affairs, and its members duly alarmed. Of particular concern was New York's determination to use the Indian country for military bounty lands. New York's laws in this regard were quoted in a report to Congress on October 3, 1783, with a recommendation that "if it shall appear that the persisting in such grants and appropriations may so far irritate the Indians, as to expose the United States to the dangers and calamities of Indian war; that then it will be proper for the Commissioners to report the difficulties which shall so occur . . . to the legislature of the State of New York; and in such case, it is earnestly recommended to the Legislature of New York, to revise the laws . . . so as to prevent the calamities of a new rupture with the Indians."[11] But in response to the strenuous objections of James Duane, prominent New York member of Congress, this passage was deleted from the report.[12]

The New York Legislature met in January of 1784 and proceeded to assert New York's sovereignty in Indian affairs within its own borders. Philip Schuyler, a member of the New York Senate, and the most prominent of the Congressional Indian Commissioners in the Northern Department, took the leadership in drafting measures to strengthen New York's control in Indian matters. He was named to a special Indian Committee to seek measures "to extend the Powers of the Commissioners of Indian Affairs." This committee reported on March 12, 1784. With some changes, the bill was approved by the Senate on March 22, 1784.[13] The bill, called "An Act to Appoint His Excellency the Governor of this State, or Person administering the Government thereof for the Time being, and the Commissioners therein designated to Superintend Indian Affairs," was sent to the Assembly, where it was

11. *JCC* XXV, pp. 602, 642–43, 680–95.

12. *Ibid.,* 642–43.

13. *Journal of the Senate of the State of New York, Seventh Session* (New York: E. Holt, 1784), pp. 41, 56, 57, 65–66.

passed without change on April 6, 1784. One of its
provisions was to permit the Governor and Commissioners
to associate with them such other persons as they would
deem helpful to the work of the commissions.[14]

It is of interest to note that Schuyler, while serving
in the New York Senate drafting a law to strengthen
New York's control of Indian affairs, still considered
himself a Congressional Indian Commissioner. New federal
Indian commissioners had been appointed by Congress on
March 4, 1784, and Schuyler's name was not among them.
But he did not know of this arrangement at the time,
until notice was sent later in March to Governor Clinton.
As far as Schuyler was concerned, until that notice came,
he was still serving as a Congressional Indian Commissioner;
yet, he felt no conflict of interest.[15]

When Clinton received official notice from Congress
informing him of the new federal Indian commissioners
just appointed, Schuyler drafted a strong resolution which
set forth New York's sovereignty over Indians considered
members of their state and directed the Governor not to
permit the commissioners "of the United States or of any
state or power whatsoever, to hold any conference or
negotiate any session of country from the said Indians
without the express permission of the Legislature," and
to warn the Congressional commissioners that any treaty they
had in mind would be contrary to the Articles of Confederation. This resolution was not passed, but its terms were
enforced by Clinton, insofar as lay in his power, when

14. *Journal of the Assembly of the State of New York, Seventh Session* (New York:
E. Holt, 1784), pp. 32, 63, 92, 93, 110–11.
15. In requesting compensation from Congress in 1786 for his work as Indian
Commissioner, Schuyler figured the term of his service from July 13, 1775 - March 1,
1784, at which latter date "a New Arrangement took place." But Schuyler did not
know of this new arrangement at the time he was framing New York's Indian
policy. Philip Schuyler's Memorial to Congress, April 14, 1786, PCC, Item 41, XI,
383–84; Mary-Jo Kline, "The Continental Congress and New York - Oneida
Relations 1782–1788," unpublished paper, pp. 6–7. On March 4, 1784, George Rogers
Clark, Nathanael Greene, Stephen Higginson, Oliver Wolcott, and Richard
Butler were appointed Indian commissioners by Congress and on March 12
they received their commissions. Only Butler and Wolcott later served. On April 8,
1784, Congress also appointed Philip Schuyler, who declined being accepted as an
afterthought. Arthur Lee was then appointed, *JCC*, XXV, 680–95; *ibid.*, XXVI,
134, 152–55; Mifflin to Commissioners, March 22, 1784, PCC, Item 16, pp. 295–96;
Mifflin to Schuyler, April 8, 1784, *ibid.*, pp. 299–300. The original commission to
Schuyler, dated April 8, 1784, is in the Schuyler Papers, Indian Papers, Box 14, New
York Public Library.

the Congressional representatives attempted to negotiate a treaty with the Six Nations later that year at Fort Stanwix.[16]

Governor Clinton's attitude was one of complete non-cooperation with Congress on Indian matters, even though during the war he had been glad for the assistance of Congress in this field. In fact, the State planned to hold a treaty with the Six Nations just as quickly as possible, before the Congressional commissioners arrived, to make peace and to secure a land cession.

New York issued a call to the hostile Six Nations to assemble at Fort Herkimer to conduct a treaty with the state and reestablish the former peaceful relations. The Indians replied favorably, but considered Fort Herkimer and German Flats too far, and instead designated Fort Stanwix. Clinton and his commissioners thereupon made arrangements to undertake the treaty negotiations, securing the services of Peter Ryckman, a long-time Indian trader, as messenger and interpreter.

When Arthur Lee, one of the Congressional commissioners, arrived in New York, he found Clinton uncooperative and reluctant to provide a guard of troops for the Congressional treaty.[17] Lee therefore wrote to Congress from New York on August 4, 1784:

16. Edmund C. Burnett, ed., *Letters of Members of the Continental Congress* (Washington, D.C.: Carnegie Institution of Washington, 1923-1933), VII, p. 477 and note 2; Resolution, n.d., Schuyler Papers, Indian Papers, Box 14, NYPL; Kline, "New York-Oneida Relations," p. 7.

17. Hough, pp. 18, 20-21. In a later communication to the Congressional commissioners dated August 13, 1784, however, Clinton went to great lengths to explain that he could not supply troops to garrison the frontier posts since the "Legislature of the State who alone were competent to this business" had already adjourned and it would "be impracticable to convene them together again"; and furthermore it would not be urgent for them to convene since it was too late in the season to garrison the posts and no order had arrived in Canada ordering evacuation of the posts anyway. He promised that he was "authorized to draw from the Militia a force sufficient if any should be necessary, to protect the Commissioners of Congress in negociation with the Indians and this will in great measure save the unnecessary expence attending a present permanent force." As for the upcoming federal treaty with the Six Nations, he warned: "I shall have no objection to your improving this incident to the advantage of the United States, expecting however and positively stipulating that no agreement be entered into with the Indians residing within the jurisdiction of this State, with whom only I mean to treat, prejudicial to its rights." George Clinton, *Public Papers of George Clinton*, edited by Hugh Hastings and others (Albany: State of New York, 1900-1914), VIII, pp. 332-33.

On my arrival here I found the Governor was at Albany, where he proposes soon to hold a treaty with the Six Nations, & I am informed that the Chiefs of the more western tribes are expected to attend. How far this state has a right to hold such treaties the Committee must judge. But while the Indians are induced to believe by such proceedings that there are distinct, independent & perhaps jealous Powers to treat with them they will certainly avail themselves of it much to the disadvantage of the general Confederation. The treaty is held under an Express Act of the Legislature.[18]

On August 19, 1784, Arthur Lee and Richard Butler, Congressional commissioners, wrote to Clinton from New York City suggesting whether the business he had to conduct with the Indians might "not be more properly transacted at the same time with and in Subordination to the General Treaty," that is, the treaty the representatives of Congress intended to hold. "Such Conduct on the Part of the State of Pennsylvania," Lee and Butler continued, "has been generally approved for its Wisdom and Confederal Policy. It is with a View that this State may have an Opportunity of shewing the same Respect for the Confederation and may avail itself of the same Advantages that We have the honor of communicating to your Excellency our Determination to meet the Indians of the six Nations at Fort Stanwix on the 20th of September next."[19] Butler and Lee might as well have been talking to the wind.

The New York State treaty, or conference, with the Six Nations was held at Fort Stanwix August 31–September 10, 1784.[20] The opening speech by the Governor was devoted to calming the well-founded fears of the Oneidas and Tuscaroras that the state meant to take their lands. Clinton assured these nations that the state had no such intention, but rather, in accordance with the state constitution of 1777, was determined to protect Indian lands from unscrupulous individuals who would attempt to negotiate private purchases. Having thus put the minds of the friendly nations at rest, he turned to the former four hostile nations and offered them peace. In the picturesque speech of forest diplomacy, Clinton announced that he thereupon rekindled the ancient

18. PCC, Item 56, pp. 129-30.
19. Hough, pp. 29-30.
20. The negotiations are in *ibid.*, pp. 11-66.

council fire of friendship that had united their ancestors "in hopes that no future Events may ever arise to extinguish it; but that You and We and the offspring of us both may enjoy its benign Influence, as long as the Sun shall shine or the Waters flow."[21] But, he added, in exchange for the sufferings they had caused New York during the war, they ought to provide compensation by a land grant, and that grant should include Niagara and Oswego.

Joseph Brant, chief spokesman for the hostile nations, replied that they were glad to accept peace but were not empowered to give a land grant. They considered New York's request just, however, and would recommend such a grant to their confederacy. As for Oswego and Niagara, these had been granted long ago by the Six Nations to the British and now passed to the Americans by the treaty of peace with Great Britain, Brant reminded Clinton.

The treaty, if it may be so called, thus ended inconclusively. Pacific intentions were exchanged, but no land had passed out of the possession of the Indians, as Clinton had hoped.

Before the Governor and the Board of Commissioners finally quitted Fort Stanwix for Albany, they met on September 14, 1784 and decided it would be for the best interests of the State to leave two representatives behind to watch the every move of the United States Commissioners at their upcoming treaty, to be held in a few weeks with the Six Nations at Fort Stanwix. The two men left behind were Major Peter Schuyler, one of the commissioners for the State, and Peter Ryckman, the interpreter. The instructions given Peter Schuyler are revealing. They read as follows:

> You are to remain at this Place with Mr. Peter Ryckman, who is to attend You, to observe the Conduct of the Commissioners of Congress in their proposed Treaty, and take Notes of their daily Proceedings. You will attend their public Speeches & Answers and find out the Objectives they have in View; and where You find they have in View anything that may eventually prove detrimental to the State, You are to use your best Endeavours to counteract and frustrate it.[22]

21. *Ibid.*, p. 49.
22. *Ibid.*, p. 63.

George Clinton, by Ezra Ames, about 1812. New York State Historical Association.

The United States treaty with the Six Nations was held at Fort Stanwix during the month of October 1784. Early in the proceedings, the commissioners warned the Indians "that a treaty with an individual State without the sanction of Congress would be of no validity."[23] In the light of the multitudinous treaties conducted in later years between New York and the Indians, it was a warning that would fall on deaf ears, especially when the New York commissioners and Governor Clinton would continually assure the Indians that they were carrying on in the ancient tradition "in which Treaties have been conducted between You and Us and our Ancestors."[24] Confused over conflicting sovereignties, the Indians gave in to the pressure exerted on them by New York State during the 1780s and 1790s and continued to conduct treaties with the state.

Although the Congressional commissioners had publicly advertised even before leaving Albany for the treaty grounds that no liquor would be permitted at the negotiations, three New York suttlers arrived with a supply of liquor for

23. Commissioners to Congress, October 5, 1784, PCC, Item 247, p. 133; *ibid.*, Item 56, pp. 137–40.
24. Hough, p. 50.

sale to the Indians. Before the treaty formally opened, therefore, the commissioners ordered Lieutenant John Mercer to confiscate all the liquor until the end of the treaty, when it would be returned to the owners. The three suttlers went before the sheriff of Montgomery County and swore out a writ against Mercer, which the commissioners refused to honor, and ordered the sheriff to leave. The dignity of the United States could not be compromised by submission to an inferior power. Also, the commissioners ordered confiscation of the liquor belonging to Peter Schuyler and Peter Ryckman. Furthermore, they ordered sentries stationed around the treaty grounds to keep the New York commissioners away. The final report of the commissioners to Congress regarding the treaty detailed the "great inconveniences from the conduct of the Governor of this state, in attempting to frustrate the treaty; and the consequent licentiousness of some of its citizens. . . ."[25]

So irate were the suttlers and their friends, that the commissioners had to take Lieutenant Mercer with them when they left for Pennsylvania, en route to subsequent Indian negotiations. Writing to the President of Congress from Carlisle on November 20, 1784, and introducing Lieutenant Mercer as the bearer of the message, they informed the President that "we had no other way of rescuing him in the State of New York but by bringing him with us." They further explained, "nothing but the indispensable necessity of abandoning the treaty, or suppressing the sale of spirituous liquors, would have engaged us in a measure so disagreeable and hazardous, as that of opposing Civil process. . . ."[26]

The Treaty of Fort Stanwix of 1784 between the Congress and the Six Nations promised, "The Oneida and Tuscarora nations shall be secured in the possession of the lands on which they are settled." Once the treaty had been signed by the delegates and ratified by Congress, however, the federal government abandoned the Oneidas and Tuscaroras,

---

25. Commissioners to Congress, October 1784, PCC, Item 56, pp. 137–40. For a more comprehensive description of the negotiations and the Indian reaction to the treaty, see Graymont, *Iroquois in the American Revolution,* pp. 259-84.

26. Richard Butler and Arthur Lee to President of Congress, November 20, 1784, PCC, Item 56, pp. 313-15.

and their dependents, the Stockbridges and Brothertons, to the mercy of New York State, which would in only four years deprive these friendly nations and tribes of their entire land holdings, with the exception of the small acreages surrounding their respective villages.

In December of 1784 the Continental Congress and the capital of the United States moved to New York City. The members of Congress would now be fully apprized through the New York newspapers of New York State's activities in the realm of Indian affairs. The fact is, however, that once Congress had concluded peace with the Iroqouis at Fort Stanwix, its members showed no concern that New York continued to negotiate Indian treaties throughout the 1780s and 1790s and thus infringed on Congress's treaty-making powers. Only the Massachusetts delegates in Congress were disturbed over New York's efforts to relieve the Indians of their land, but not because such efforts compromised the sovereignty of Congress or exploited the Indians. Rather, Rufus King and Elbridge Gerry, Massachusetts delegates in Congress, were distressed because the New Yorkers were ignoring the Massachusetts claims to western New York lands.[27]

In early 1784, Massachusetts had revived its claims to a broad strip of land running from its present western border through New York State. The 1629 grant to Massachusetts by the King was a sea-to-sea charter. Now in 1784, Massachusetts again claimed all the land westward between 42°.02′ and 44°.15′ north latitude and asked Congress to settle the boundary dispute. Congress on June 3, 1784 requested the two states to bring the matter to a federal court.[28] After much delay and quibbling over

27. Rufus King to Elbridge Gerry, April 18, 1785, Rufus King Papers, New-York Historical Society. In her unpublished paper, "The Continental Congress and New York - Oneida Relations 1782-1788," Mary-Jo Kline has demonstrated conclusively that each member of Congress was officially supplied with copies of the New York newspapers on each day of publication and that these newspapers carried full accounts of New York State Indian negotiations and land acquisitions. On March 3, 1785, Charles Thomson, Secretary of Congress, placed subscriptions for forty copies of each of the following papers to be delivered to Congress: Shepard Kollock's *Gazette, Loudon's New-York Packet,* and J. McLean's *Independent Journal.* On August 26, 1785, Thomson added the *New-York Journal and Daily Patriotic Register* to the subscription list. Charles Thomson to Sundry Printers, March 1, 1785, and March 3, 1785, Burnett, *Letters of Members of the Continental Congress,* VIII, pp. 49, 52-54; Resolution of August 26, 1785, *JCC,* XXIX, p. 663.

satisfactory judges, the two state legislatures in 1786 decided on direct negotiation rather than court action. The issue was finally settled at a meeting of the two sides in Hartford, Connecticut in December of 1786. New York granted to Massachusetts the right to preempt from the Indians 230,400 acres of land between the Owego and Chenango Rivers, and almost all of the present state of New York west of a line extending from the Pennsylvania border north along Seneca Lake to Lake Ontario. In return, New York retained governmental control of this territory.[29]

Massachusetts was further granted the right to "hold treaties and conferences with the native Indians relative to the property or right of soil of the said lands and territories hereby ceded" or, to grant the same preemptive rights to individuals to purchase from the Indians.[30]

While the two states were still in the early stages of the controversy, however, the New York legislature in March and April of 1785 began discussion of a new bill to appropriate Indian lands. The bill was finally passed on April 11, 1785 and was called, "An Act to facilitate the Settlement of the Waste and unappropriated Lands within the State and for repealing the Act therein mentioned." The Act "therein mentioned" was that passed on May 10, 1784, also for encouraging "the Settlement of the waste and unappropriated Lands within this State." As the 1785 act explained, the previous year's act "would be attended with great Delays in the Execution thereof." The new act therefore proposed to speed up settlement by causing "Advertisements to be published in the several News-papers printed within this State, giving Notice that upon and after a certain Day therein to be specified, not less than two, nor more than three Months from the Time of publishing the said Advertisements, that Locations upon the Lands so described in the said Advertisements will be received in the Office of the Surveyor-General of this State." Also, as soon as any future cession of land was obtained from the Indians, it was to be the duty of the Indian commissioners to advertise these lands for sale.[31] As a result,

---

28. *JCC*, IV, p. 444.

29. Cochran, *New York in the Confederation*, pp. 95–96.

30. *JCC*, XXXIII, pp. 626–27.

the state's treasury would be promptly reimbursed for the expenses connected with conducting the Indian treaties, the state would soon be fully settled by tax-paying land holders, and the privileged land speculators would have reaped a handsome profit.

Under the provisions of this act, Governor Clinton and the State Indian commissioners met with the Oneidas and Tuscaroras at Fort Herkimer beginning on June 23, 1785

31. *Laws of the State of New-York, Passed by the Legislature of said State, at their Last Meeting of the Eighth Session* (New York: Samuel Loudon, 1785), Chapter LXVI, pp. 57–60. (This section is bound in one book with *Laws of the State of New-York, Passed at the first Meeting of the Eighth Session, 1784.*)

Good Peter. Courtesy of Yale University Art Gallery.

and requested a huge land cession between the Chenango and Unadilla rivers, as far south as the Great Bend in the Susquehanna River and the Pennsylvania border. Good Peter, the Oneida spokesman, protested vigorously. This, he said, was their beaver and deer hunting territory—the place where they obtained their meat to eat and skins for clothing.

After much wrangling back and forth between the two sides, and a factional dispute among the Indians, Good Peter retired and Peter the Quartermaster, also known as the Beech Tree, stepped forward as chief Indian spokesman. The Oneidas and Tuscaroras, he said, agreed to a cession almost as big as originally requested in exchange for the money and goods they saw displayed before them. The treaty was thereupon concluded, with a grant of $11,500 in goods and money to the Indians.[32]

The Oneidas and Tuscaroras had taken their first step toward their extinction as a nation. Ironically, these two peoples who had suffered most severely for their steadfast loyalty to the Americans during the war in their protection of the New York frontier, would be the first to fall before the land greed of their former allies.

Though the Continental Congress did not protest this treaty, there was a sharp retort from Massachusetts. Alerted by a letter from Rufus King, their delegate in Congress, the Massachusetts legislature directed the governor to write to Clinton reminding him of the "impropriety" of New York's opening a land office to deal in lands in the disputed area.[33]

Governor James Bowdoin of Massachusetts wrote a strong protest to Clinton on July 18, 1785. "An attempt by either State," he said, "to purchase of the Natives their right in that territory, and to dispose of, grant, or settle any part of it, while their respective claims, (submitted to the decision of Commissioners mutually chosen, under the authority of Congress) remain undecided, would, as

32. Hough, pp. 66–116.

33. The letter from King was dated May 27, 1785 and was read in the Senate June 6, 1785. The joint resolution of the Massachusetts Senate and House was dated June 22, 1785. Massachusetts State Archives, "Journal of the Massachusetts Senate," pp. 50–51, 111; "Journal of the House of Representatives," pp. 81, 143. (Both journals in manuscript.)

we conceive, be judged by the states disinterested, as altogether improper." Referring to the recent Treaty at Fort Herkimer, he reminded Clinton, "we cannot entertain a thought that either your Excellency or your Legislature can intend, or will suffer, the cession or grant of lands made to your State by those Indians, to operate, in any respect whatever, to the disadvantage of this Commonwealth."[34]

New York State was still determined to pressure the Indians into further land sales. Accordingly, on March 1, 1788 the legislature passed "An Act appointing Commissioners to hold Treaties with the Indians within this state. . . ." This act appointed the Governor and the following commissioners: William Floyd, Ezra L'Hommedieu, John Lawrence, Richard Varick, Samuel Jones, Egbert Benson, and Peter Gansevoort.[35] Gansevoort's place on the commission was the result of expert lobbying on the part of his younger brother, Leonard Gansevoort, who was a member of the Continental Congress. As Leonard explained in a letter to Peter:

> On my arrival at Poughkeepsie I was informed that the Legislature had under consideration a Law for the appointment of Commissioners of Indian affairs that it had already passed the Assembly who had appointed six Gentlemen, it occurred to me instantly that if I could procure your name to be added to the Number, it would serve as a Basis to my future operations & designs, upon which I waited on Genl Schuyler expressed to him my wishes, he complied without hesitation and promised he would not fail to nominate you on the succeeding Day in Senate where the Bill then Lay and assured me that he was happy I had mentioned you for he had conceived it a reflection · upon the Northern part of the State that the Commissioners was all taken from the Southern & Middle part of the State and he knew no Person more Proper than yourself from our Quarter and added that he would exert his Influence to get you appointed. I then spoke to General of my Friends in the Assembly who in like Manner promised that if the Bill should be amended in Senate they would cheerfully give it their concurrence, hence, I am persuaded that the Legislature will insert your Name in the Bill if it is not already done—you will easily perceive the good Use that can be made of it.[36]

34. James Bowdoin to George Clinton, July 18, 1785, *Public Papers of George Clinton,* VIII, pp. 393–94.

35. Hough, p. 117.

36. Leonard Gansevoort to Peter Gansevoort, March 5, 1788, Gansevoort Military Papers, VII, NYPL. The history of this important Dutch family has been written

The Gansevoorts were clearly looking out for their own interests in getting a seat on the Indian Commission.

The commissioners met on March 3 and voted to hold a treaty with the Indians at Fort Schuyler (Stanwix) on the 10th of July, 1788.[37]

Before the treaty was held, the governor and the legislature were occupied with voiding the fraudulent 999 year leases obtained from the Indians by the New York Genesee Company of Adventurers—a group of eighty land speculators including John Livingston, Peter Schuyler, Abraham Cuyler, James Dean, Peter Ryckman, Abraham Schuyler, Robert Troup, Matthew Visscher, and other prominent individuals. This abbreviated list includes the names of several former Indian commissioners and associates along with the two interpreters, Dean and Ryckman. James Dean, a confidant of the Oneidas, had once served in religious work among these people. The purpose of the 999 year leases of the Genesee Company was to circumvent the provision of the state constitution which forbade private purchase of Indian lands without express license from the Legislature.[38]

The lease with the Six Nations, concluded November 13, 1787, turned over to the lessees a huge tract of land beginning at Canada Creek, seven miles west of Fort Stanwix, extending "thence Northeasterly to the Province of Quebec; thence along said Line to the Pennsylvania Line; thence East on the said Line or Pennsylvania Line to the Line of Property so called by the State of New York; thence along the said Line of Property to Canada Creek aforesaid," including all improvements, rights of way, "Waters, Water Courses, Mines, Minerals, Easements and Appurtenances whatsoever," except those tracts that the chiefs and sachems might reserve for themselves and their heirs. For this enormous grant of land the chiefs and sachems of the Six Nations or their heirs were to receive "the yearly Rent or Sum of Two Thousand Spanish Milled Dollars." A second lease with the Oneidas, concluded January 8, 1788, gave over to the enterprising land speculators another enormous tract consisting of most of that portion of Oneida

by Alice P. Kenney, *The Gansevoorts of Albany* (Syracuse: Syracuse University Press, 1969).

37. Hough, p. 117.

38. A complete list of the shareholders and copies of the two leases, with commentary, are in Hough, pp. 119n–128n.

territory that had not already been granted to New York State
by the Treaty of Fort Hunter in 1785. For this lease, the
Oneidas were to receive $1,000 annual rent "for the first ten
Years, and increasing after that Time at the Rate of $100
annually until the sum amounted to $1,500, which was to re-
main the annual Rent afterwards." The lessees agreed to
share the profits of any mines with the Oneidas.[39]

Massachusetts agents were also active among the Indians in
1788. In April of that year the Massachusetts General Court
sold the preemptive rights to the New York tract to Oliver
Phelps and Nathaniel Gorham. Phelps and Gorham lost no
time in conducting a purchase agreement with the Indians.
They held a treaty at Buffalo Creek, in Seneca country, in
July of 1788 and bought from the Indians 2,600,000 acres of
land.[40]

New York State ratified the Constitution of the United
States on July 26, 1788. Article I, Section 10, Paragraph 1 of
the Constitution says in no uncertain terms that "No State
shall enter into any Treaty, Alliance, or Confederation. . . ."
And Article II, Section 2, Paragraph 2 specifically grants the
treaty making power to the President of the United States, "by
and with the Advice and Consent of the Senate." These
Constitutional provisions the State of New York blithely ignored throughout much of the remainder of the eighteenth
century and the early years of the nineteenth century as
it proceeded to make a multitude of treaties with the Six
Nations or separately with their constituent nations.

At the Treaty of Fort Schuyler held with the Indians in
September of 1788, Clinton and the commissioners secured
the complete cession to the state of the Onondaga and Oneida
lands, small reservations set aside for their personal use
excepted. Since the Indians had already been softened up for
a land sale by the Genesee Company with their perpetual
leases, Clinton and the commissioners had a rather easy time

39. *Ibid.*

40. Joseph Brant to George Clinton, July 9, 1788, Hough, pp. 160–67. For an excellent
account of the land companies operating in western New York at this period, see
Barbara Ann Chernow, "Robert Morris: Land Speculator, 1790–1801," Chapter II,
unpublished Ph.D. dissertation, Columbia University, 1974. For older accounts,
see Orsamus Turner, *Pioneer History of the Holland Purchase of Western New
York* (Buffalo: Jewett, Thomas & Co., 1849); and Orsamus Turner, *History of the
Pioneer Settlement of Phelps & Gorham's Purchase, and Morris' Reserve* (Rochester:
W. Alling, 1852).

of it. The Indians' lack of sophistication in real estate matters was nothing short of amazing.

On September 12, 1788, the commissioners concluded a treaty with the Onondagas which stated: "First, the Onondagoes do cede and grant all their Lands to the People of the State of New York forever." In this ceded tract, the Onondagas were to "hold to themselves and their Posterity forever" a certain area around their village for their reservation. The ceded tract was a huge area running from Lake Ontario southward to the Pennsylvania line. For this enormous cession, the State paid "one thousand French Crowns in Money and two hundred Pounds in Cloathing" and an annuity of "five hundred Dollars in Silver" forever, but the Onondagas might at any time elect to have this money annuity paid in clothing if they so wished. [41]

On September 22, 1788, a similar treaty was concluded with the Oneidas. The first article stated, "The Oneidas do cede and grant all their Lands to the People of the State of New York forever." Secondly, out of these ceded lands, a tract was designated as an Oneida reservation which the Oneidas would hold forever—never to be leased or sold. But a residue tract was stipulated where the Oneidas might make leases of no longer than twenty-one years. For the loss of their country, the Oneidas received "one thousand Dollars in Money, two thousand Dollars in Clothing and other Goods, and one thousand Dollars in Provisions; and also five hundred Dollars in Money to be applied towards building a Grist Mill and Saw Mill at their Village," plus an annuity of "six hundred Dollars in Silver," which latter might be paid in whole or in part in clothing or provisions if the Oneidas gave proper notice to the Governor. Finally, the Stockbridge and Brotherton Indians, dependents of the Oneidas, were guaranteed their reservations. [42]

Assuming the rather unlikely possibility that the New York Genesee Company of Adventurers would have been in existence 999 years from the date of the leases, the Indians would have eventually secured a somewhat more favorable financial return from the company than from the State of New York.

41. Hough, pp. 197–203.
42. *Ibid.,* pp. 241–47.

The next year, a treaty was held between the New York State Indian Commissioners and the Cayuga Indians at Denniston's Tavern in Albany, February 12-25, 1789. At that time, the Cayugas also ceded their whole country to "the People of the State of New York forever," a small tract of land for a reservation excepted. The payment for this huge cession, which extended from Lake Ontario to the Pennsylvania border, was "five hundred Dollars in Silver" down, and "one thousand six hundred and twenty-five Dollars" on the first of June. An annuity of "five hundred dollars in Silver" was granted on the same terms as to the Oneidas and Onondagas.[43]

On July 22, 1790, Congress adopted "An Act to Regulate Trade and Intercourse with the Indian Tribes." This Trade and Intercourse Act spelled out and enforced the Constitutional provisions of federal control in Indian matters. The Act stated that no person might carry on trade or intercourse with the Indians without special federal government license. Also, and most important:

> That no sale of lands made by any Indians, or any nation or tribe of Indians within the United States, shall be valid to any person or persons or to any state, whether having the right of pre-emption to such lands or not, unless the same shall be made and duly executed at some public treaty held under the authority of the United States.[44]

This provision New York would ignore continually well on into the nineteenth century as it conducted Indian treaties, save for a brief period during John Jay's governorship (1795-1801) and in 1802 when federal commissioners were present at four treaties. Certain prominent elements in New York State leadership were determined to win the struggle with the federal government for sovereignty in Indian affairs.

On March 11, 1793, the New York State Legislature passed "An Act relative to the Lands appropriated by this State, to the use of the Oneida, Onondaga and Cayuga Indians." By the terms of this act, Israel Chapin, John Cantine, and Simeon De Witt were appointed New York State agents

43. *Ibid.*, pp. 307-308. The entire negotiation is covered on pp. 266-313.

44. U.S. Stat., I, 137-38. See also the discussion in Francis Paul Prucha, *American Indian Policy in the Formative Years* (Lincoln: University of Nebraska Press, 1970 [first published by Harvard University Press, 1962]), pp. 2-3, 45-46.

to convene the Indians of the Oneida, Onondaga and Cayuga nations severally, and at their usual place of residence, and being so convened, to propose to the said nations severally, that they should quit claim to the people of the state, so much of the rights reserved to them, in the lands appropriated to their use by this state, as they may think proper to dispose of, and that for every square mile of the lands to which the rights so by them to be quit-claimed, the people of the state shall pay the Indians an annuity not exceeding the sum of five dollars in perpetuity, the first payment whereof shall be made on the execution of such quit-claim by said Indians. . . ."[45]

This act further provided that the attorney general of the state and the clerk and treasurer of the local counties in which the Indian lands were situated, "and the successors in office of said officers," were to be "vested with the property, the rights whereof the said Indians shall chuse to retain, as trustees for the said Indians, to prevent any encroachments on the said rights and property, and to bring suits for trespass thereon, and to prosecute the same to effect for the benefit of said Indians." In addition, provision was made for transfer of these rights to "the said officers and their successors" whenever the Indians should choose to convey those rights.[46]

It is clear from the terms of this act that New York State intended to maintain complete control over Indian affairs and transfers of Indian real property within its borders, without recourse to the federal government.

Acting under the authority granted by this piece of legislation, John Cantine and Simeon De Witt, agents for the State of New York, held a treaty with the Onondagas, at the Onondaga village, on November 18, 1793. The state agents were not licensed by the federal government, and no federal agent was present as required by the Trade and Intercourse Act of 1790. In direct defiance of federal law, then, the agents proceeded to secure for the state two large tracts of land from the Onondagas. In the words of the treaty, the Onondagas "do release and quit claim to the People of the State of New York forever all rights reserved to the said Onondagoes in and to so much

---

45. *Laws of the State of New-York, Comprising the Constitution, and the Acts of the Legislature, since the Revolution, from the First to the Twentieth Session, Inclusive* (New York: Thomas Greenleaf, 1797), III, 73.

46. *Ibid.*

of the lands appropriated to their use by the said State commonly called the Onondaga Reservation as it is comprehended within the two tracts of land (To wit) . . . . '[47]

In late 1794, the federal government asserted its prerogative in Indian affairs by conducting two treaties with the Iroquois. The first, concluded on November 11, was held at Canandaigua, New York, with Secretary of War Timothy Pickering as the negotiator for the United States, and reaffirmed a perpetual peace and friendship between the Six Nations and the United States. By the second article of the treaty, the United States government acknowledged "the lands reserved to the Oneida, Onondaga, and Cayuga nations, in their respective treaties with the State of New York, and called their reservations to be their property," and promised that the United States would never claim those lands or disturb the Indians in their use; "but the said reservations shall remain theirs, until they choose to sell the same to the people of the United States, who have the right to purchase." Article 3 delineated the boundaries of the Senecas and gave them the same assurances of peaceful occupation and ownership. The intent of the government was to secure the Indians in the lands which they claimed as theirs and to recognize the engagements made by the Indians with the state prior to the adoption of the Constitution, not to give blanket endorsement to continuing state Indian treaties.[48]

The second treaty conducted by Pickering was concluded on December 2 and was with the Oneida, Tuscarora, and Stockbridge Indians. The treaty compensated these nations for their losses in the late war.[49]

Not to be outdone by the United States government's intrusion into what it considered its domain, the New York legislature on April 9, 1795 passed a very lengthy and

47. The treaty is in *Report of Special Committee to Investigate the Indian Problem of the State of New York, Appointed by the Assembly of 1888. Assembly Document 51* (Albany: The Troy Press Company, 1889), pp. 195-97. Quotations from pp. 195 and 196.

48. *American State Papers. Indian Affairs* (Washington, D.C.: Gales and Seaton, 1832), I, 545. For a careful evaluation of Timothy Pickering's role in Indian affairs, see Edward Hoke Phillips, "Timothy Pickering at His Best—Indian Commissioner, 1790-1794," *Essex Institute Historical Collections*, Vol. CII, No. 3 (July, 1966), pp. 163-202.

49. *American State Papers. Indian Affairs*, I, 546.

involved act entitled: "An Act for the better Support of the
Oneida, Onondaga, and Cayuga Indians, and for other
Purposes therein mentioned."[50] The ostensible purpose of
this act, as stated in its preamble, was to settle
the differences and difficulties that had arisen between the
Indians and their white neighbors to whom they had leased
large portions of their land, and to make the property
more productive to the Indians. To carry out this end,
the governor, Philip Schuyler, John Cantine, John
Richardson, and David Brooks, "or any three of them,"
were appointed state agents "to make such arrangements with
the Oneida, Onondaga, and Cayuga tribes of Indians
respectively, relative to the lands appropriated to their use,
as may tend to promote the interest of the said Indians,
and to preserve in them that confidence in the justice of
this state, which they have so repeatedly evinced to
entertain."[51]

Far from being an act to prosper the three Indian groups
mentioned, however, it was a law designed to secure more
land sales from them for the benefit of the state and its white
inhabitants. The State's tactic in making Indian land more
productive for Indians was to buy it from them. The small sum
paid and the annuity together would amount to far less than
the sum for which the acreage would be sold, the taxes the
land would yield in the future, and the profit that could be
made from these purchases and sales by white speculators.
The Indians were rapidly being drawn into the white man's
money economy because their smaller and smaller land
holdings could no longer satisfy their economic needs. This
law even provided for allotting Indian lands in severalty,
with the lots so designated officially surveyed for each Indian
family, provided the Indians agreed. Such an arrangement
would have eventually weakened tribal control over Indian
lands.

By this act, the state also agreed to pacify the disgruntled
Onondagas, who felt they had been imposed upon in a

50. *Laws of the State of New-York, Comprising the Constitution and the Acts of the
Legislature, since the Revolution, from the First to the Twentieth Session, Inclusive*
(New York: Thomas Greenleaf, 1797), III, 236–42. This act was passed during the
Eighteenth Session of the legislature. A seventeen-page handwritten copy of the
act is also in the Schuyler Papers, Box 15, New York Public Library.

51. *Laws of the State of New-York* . . . (New York: Thomas Greenleaf, 1797), 236.

previous land sale to the state, by increasing their annuity from $410 to an escalating annuity of no more than $800. And a previous tract of land that had been "appropriated to the common use of the Onondaga Indians" and the people of New York State and which presently was "unproductive of any income to the said Indians," was to be purchased either in whole or in part from the Onondagas in exchange for a perpetual annuity not to exceed $500.[52]

As for the Oneidas and Cayugas, "the residue of any of the lands beyond what may be appropriated in the manner aforesaid, the said agents shall in their discretion stipulate perpetual annuities ... after having appropriated a part thereof to the maintenance of the public school in each tribe, in which Indian children shall be taught. *Provided,* That such annuities severally, shall not exceed an annual interest of six per cent. on the principal sum which would arise from the sale of such residue, if the same was sold at four shillings per acre."[53]

The act then explained in elaborate detail how this land which was to be obtained from the Indians at four shillings per acre should be surveyed and laid into lots and the lots sold at public auction to the highest bidder, *"Provided,* That none of the said lots shall be sold for less than sixteen shillings an acre."[54]

The Council of Revision, consisting of Governor George Clinton, Chief Justice Robert Yates, and Justice Egbert Benson, vetoed this bill, believing that it was "improper to become a law" since it was not in the best interest of the Indians and did not live up to the promises made by both houses of the legislature in concurrent resolution on February 13, 1794. This resolution had stated: "His Excellency the Governor, was requested to confer with the Indians then in the city of Albany, and to give them the fullest assurances of the continued friendship of the State towards their brethren the Six-Nations, and that the legislature would protect and secure them in the possession and enjoyment of their reservation, according to the agreements made with their several nations, and were ready to make any further disposition

52. *Ibid.,* pp. 237, 238.
53. *Ibid.,* p. 237.
54. *Ibid.,* p. 238.

thereof for their *sole* benefit, whenever the wishes of their respective nations shall be made thereon for that purpose."[55]

Since the Indian land was to be bought for four shillings an acre and to be sold for no less than sixteen shillings an acre, which latter the Council deemed the true value, the act was "not a *disposition* for the sole benefit of the Indians," but rather "a *disposition* three fourths of which at least will be for the benefit of the *State*." The Council concluded, "The restrictions therefore on the agents in respect to the *amount* of the annuities to be stipulated by them, is inconsistent with the *assurances* contained in the above recited resolutions, and which, agreeably to the request of both houses were made to the Indians by his Excellency the Governor."[56]

The veto of the Council of Revision went first to the Senate, where it was overruled. Then the Assembly also voted down the Council's objection by a two-thirds majority on a roll call vote, the division being 29–13. The members of the legislature thus proved themselves to be even more covetous of securing Indian lands at bargain rates than was Governor Clinton.[57]

With the authority given them by this act of April 9, 1795, four of the New York Commissioners, John Richardson, Philip Schuyler, John Cantine, and David Brooks, began preparations for holding several Indian treaties that summer. Richardson made these intentions known to Israel Chapin, Jr., who, in April had been appointed to succeed his father as the federal government's Superintendent of the Six Nations, and requested him to have the interpreter Jasper Parrish assemble the Cayuga and Onondaga nations at Scipio for the treaties. Richardson further noted that he could not supply Chapin with the law authorizing the treaty as it was "very lengthy to coppy."[58]

Much alarmed by this news which had been relayed to him by Israel Chapin, Jr., and by New York State's open defiance of Congress and the Constitution, Pickering submitted the

55. *Journal of the Senate of the State of New-York. At Their Eighteenth Session . . .* (New York: Francis Childs, 1795), p. 89.

56. *Ibid.*

57. *Ibid.*; *Journal of the Assembly of the State of New-York, At Their Eighteenth Session . . .* (New York: Francis Childs, 1795), pp. 180–81.

58. Israel Chapin, Jr. to Timothy Pickering, May 6, June 13, July 31, 1795; Pickering to Chapin, June 29, July 3, 1795, O'Rielly Papers, XI, 17, 26, 29, 30, 33, New-York Historical Society.

matter to the Attorney General of the United States, inquiring "Whether the State of New York has a right to purchase from the Six Nations or any of them the lands claimed by those nations and situate within the acknowledged boundaries of that State without the intervention of the general government." [59]

The Attorney General submitted his opinion emphatically in the negative:

By the Constitution of the United States, Congress has power to regulate commerce with the Indian Tribes, and by the act of 1 March 1793, it is expressly enacted, That no purchase or grant of lands, or of any title or claim thereto, from any Indians or nation or tribe of Indians, within the bounds of the United States, shall be of any validity in Law or equity, unless the Same be made by a treaty or convention entered into pursuant to the Constitution, that it shall be a misdemeanor in any person not employed under the authority of the United States in negotiating such Treaty or convention directly or indirectly to treat with any such Indians, nation or tribe of Indians for the title or purchase of any lands by them held or claimed &c.

The language of this act is too express to admit of any doubt upon the question unless there be something in the circumstances of the case under consideration to take it out of the general prohibition of the law.

Nothing of this kind appears on the documents submitted to the attorney General. It is true, that by treaties made by the State of New York with the Oneidas, Onondagas and Cayugas, previous to the present Constitution of the United States, those nations ceded all their lands to the people of New York, but reserved to themselves and their posterity forever (for their own use & cultivation, but not to be sold, leased or in any other manner disposed of to others,) certain tracts of their said lands, with the free right of hunting & fishing &c. So far therefore as respects the lands thus reserved the treaties do not operate further than to secure to the state of New York the right of preemption: but subject to this right they are still the lands of those nations, and their claims to them, it is conceived cannot be extinguished but by a treaty holden under the authority of the United States, and in the manner prescribed by the laws of Congress. [60]

Pickering thereupon sent a copy of the opinion to Israel Chapin, Jr. on June 29, 1795, along with a strong covering letter of his own, warning the superintendent "that you are to give no aid or countenance to the measure [the treaty]; as it is repugnant to the law of the United States made to regulate trade and intercourse with the Indian tribes," and to warn

59. "Opinion of the Atty General to Secty of War re State Indian Treaties, June 16, 1795," O'Rielly Papers, XI, 27.
60. Ibid.

the Indians "that any bargains they make at such a treaty will be void." In addition, he sent a copy of the Attorney General's opinion to Governor George Clinton.[61]

Feeling that Governor Clinton was the major problem in the New York defiance of the federal government, Pickering appended the following P. S. to Chapin's letter: "All difficulties on this subject I expect will cease as soon as Mr. Jay's administration commences. I shall advise him of all that has passed."[62]

John Jay, who had been negotiating with Great Britain the treaty that bears his name, arrived back in New York on May 28, 1795 during the counting of the votes in the New York gubernatorial election. On June 5, Jay's election as governor was announced. He resigned as Chief Justice of the United States on June 29 and became governor of New York on July 1, 1795.[63]

But preparations for the Indian treaties had evidently progressed too far to be stopped. Owing to the slowness of the eighteenth-century mail service, the negotiation of the first two treaties in July was perhaps not known by Jay in time for his intervention. Less understandable, considering Jay's more conciliatory attitude toward the federal government, was the fact that a treaty was held in Albany with the Oneidas in September of that year, when Jay's administration was already more than two months underway. Here again, the determination of the state Indian commissioners and the slowness of communication may have been the deciding factor.[64]

Israel Chapin, Jr. did not receive Pickering's letters of June 29 and July 3 warning him to have nothing to do with the treaty until July 31, after two treaties had already been concluded. On July 27, 1795, the state commissioners secured a land grant from the Cayugas at the Treaty of Cayuga Ferry. All the Cayugas had left to give was their reservation. This

61. Pickering to Chapin, Jr., June 29, 1795, O'Rielly Papers, XI, 29.

62. Ibid.

63. Frank Monaghan, John Jay, (New York and Indianapolis: The Bobbs-Merrill Company, 1935), pp. 405-406.

64. Instructions from Governor John Jay to Israel Chapin, Jr. respecting the annuities to be paid the Cayugas and Onondagas under the 1795 treaties are in O'Rielly Papers, Vol. XI, p. 50, NYHS. Jay clearly accepted the legality of these treaties, or, at least, accepted them as a fait accompli.

was further whittled away, leaving them with about six square miles for themselves and their posterity forever. In exchange, the state promised to pay the Cayugas $1,800 immediately and $1,800 on the following June first, and $1,800 "annually forever thereafter." This sum was paid until the war of 1812, at which time the State ceased to pay, arguing that the support of the Canadian Cayugas for Britain in the war abbrogated the treaty. The case was in dispute for years and finally in the 1920s was submitted to international arbitration. The judgment was awarded to Great Britain and the Cayugas.[65] Long before that time, however, the Cayugas in New York State were left without an acre to call their own since the state had long since persuaded them to sell the last of the lands that had been promised to them and their posterity forever.[66]

On July 28, 1795, the Onondagas and the commissioners concluded a treaty. This agreement raised the Onondaga annuity from a previous treaty from $410 to $800. In regard to the lands previously held in common by them and New York State, the Onondagas sold their Salt Lake, the lands surrounding it, and the right of way, to the State of New York for $700 at once and an annuity of $700 and one hundred bushels of salt "forever thereafter." These payments were in addition to the annuities already received under the terms of the Treaty of Fort Schuyler of 1788.[67]

65. Chapin, Jr. to Pickering, July 31, 1795, O'Rielly Papers, Vol. XI, p. 33. A parchment original of this treaty, with endorsements for annuities, is in the Cayuga Museum of History and Art, Auburn, New York. Another parchment original, with endorsements to 1809, is in the Public Archives of Canada. The writing on this latter copy had faded to the point where it was necessary to make a transcript copy on November 19, 1951. MS Group 19, F - Indians, No. 9 Cayuga Indians, Public Archives of Canada. The treaty is printed in *Report of Special Committee to Investigate the Indian Problem of the State of New York, Appointed by the Assembly of 1888. Assembly Document 51* (Albany: The Troy Press Company, 1889), pp. 224–28. Interpreters listed for the treaty were Israel Chapin, James Dean, and Jasper Parrish. A manuscript copy of the treaty is in the Schuyler Papers, Box 15, New York Public Library.
The members of the international arbitration commission who settled the Cayuga claim were Dean Roscoe Pound of Harvard Law School, Sir Charles Fitzgerald representing Great Britain, and Alfred Nerinez of Belgium as president of the tribunal. For the American argument before this tribunal, see *American and British Claims Arbitration, Cayuga Indians. Oral Argument by Fred K. Nielsen, Agent and Counsel for the United States* (Washington, D.C.: Government Printing Office, 1926).

66. Most of the Cayugas in New York today, being entirely without a reservation of their own, live among the Senecas on the Cattaraugus Reservation. There are a few Cayugas intermarried with Indians from other reservations and living in these communities.

Philip Schuyler. Tibbets Collection, New York State Library, Albany.

During the progress of these treaties, Chapin was still ignorant of the true nature of affairs since he would not receive Pickering's instructions until after the treaties were concluded. He had requested the commissioners to provide him with the state law which authorized them to hold the treaty, "or even to shew it to me when at the treaty," but received no satisfaction. He then "enquired of Genl Schuyler how he construed the law of Congress in regard to holding treaties with the Indians tribes? He made very little reply by saying it was well where it would correspond with that of an Individual state."[68] Schuyler's reply, and the general attitude of the legislature and the governor, were clear examples of the philosophy of interposition.

Once Chapin was apprized of the law, he hurried forward to the Oneida village to block the proposed treaty. He care-

67. *Report of Special Committee to Investigate the Indian Problem of the State of New York, Appointed by the Assembly of 1888. Assembly Document 51*, pp. 199-203. The agents for New York State at both treaties were Philip Schuyler, John Cantine, David Brooks, and John Richardson. Interpreters were Israel Chapin, James Dean, and Jasper Parrish. A manuscript copy of this July 28 treaty, and Schuyler's speeches to the Onondagas, are in the Schuyler Papers, Box, 15, NYPL.

68. Chapin, Jr. to Pickering, July 31, 1795. O'Rielly Papers, Vol. XI, p. 33, NYHS.

fully explained to the Indians the contents of Pickering's letter, to which they listened intentively. After his address, the New York State agents put strong pressure upon the Oneidas to part with yet another portion of their land, for which they offered the Oneida Nation $4000 annually.

In a letter to Pickering, Chapin described the debate that ensued among the Oneidas, and the growing resentment that the Indians felt over the treatment they had received from the State:

> The Indians considered on the offer day after day without returning any answer, some were for selling as they wished to injoy the money they should receive annually for in a short time they would be of[f] the stage and it would be left for their posterity to injoy; others for reasons I had impressed upon them did not incline to sell and on the nineth days consideration made their reply to the Commissioners in telling Genl Schuyler what fine things he had promised them the beginning of the War, that if they would remain peaceable they should never want for nothing, and as they had formerly got their lands for a trifle and as they come out to do them good they wished they would pay them the just value, and the sum they had offered them was not equal to the value of the land. [69]

Though the commissioners failed on this occasion, they had better success in September of the same year, when they held a treaty with the Oneida representatives at Albany and purchased 100,000 acres from them. [70]

During the years 1796, 1797, and 1798, there were three Indian treaties held by New York State, all of which had a federal representative present at the request of Governor John Jay. The first of these was concluded on May 31, 1796 in New York City with the Seven Nations of Canada, represented by delegates from the Caughnawaga and St. Regis reservations. These Indians, though speaking the Mohawk language, were not a part of the Six Nations Confederacy. Their reservations had been formed as a result of Roman Catholic missionary enterprise. Good Stream and Thomas Williams from Caughnawaga and Colonel Louis Cook and William Gray from St. Regis were delegates for the Indians. Abraham Ogden was the United States commissioner and

69. Chapin, Jr. to Pickering, August 19; 1795, O'Rielly Papers, Vol. XI, p. 34.

70. Chapin, Jr. to Pickering, October 9, 1795, *ibid.*, p. 42. The treaty, concluded on September 15, 1795, is in *Report of Special Committee to Investigate the Indian Problem of the State of New York, Appointed by the Assembly of 1888. Assembly Document 51*, pp. 244–48.

Egbert Benson, Richard Varick, and James Watson were the agents for New York State. The "sole object" of this negotiation "was to enable the State of New York to extinguish, by purchase, the claim or right of these nations or tribes of Indians to lands within the limits of the state."[71] By the terms of this treaty, the Seven Nations of Canada gave up all land previously claimed by them in the State of New York save for a tract six miles square for the St. Regis reservation, in exchange for an initial payment and a perpetual annuity.[72]

The second treaty was held in Albany on March 29, 1797 with the Mohawks who had formerly lived at Fort Hunter and Canajoharie, but who were now situated on the Bay of Quinté and the Grand River in Canada. These Canadian land grants had been given to these Loyalist Indians by the British government at the urging of General Frederick Haldimand in appreciation for their services to the Crown during the Revolutionary War and in compensation for their loss of land on the American side of the border. But the Mohawks continued to press for settlement of their claim for their abandoned lands in New York State. New York therefore held a treaty with these Mohawks before United States Commissioner Isaac Smith. Present for the claimants were Joseph Brant and John Deserontyon. Chief Cornplanter of the Senecas was also present as a witness. The New York Commissioners were Abraham ten Broeck, Egbert Benson, and Ezra L'Hommedieu. As a final settlement for their lands, the State paid the Mohawks $1,000 plus $600 expenses.[73]

The third treaty was concluded on June 1, 1798 with the Oneidas at their central village of Kanowalohale and was

71. *American State Papers. Indian Affairs*, I, 617. The Seven Nations of Canada had been a confederacy of Algonkian and Iroquoian nations formed by the French during the French and Indian War. The membership consisted of: Caughnawaga (a mixed Iroquoian settlement dating from the seventeenth century, which later adopted the Mohawk language), Lake of Two Mountains Oka (Mohawk), Lake of Two Mountains Oka (Algonquin), Lake of Two Mountains (Nipissing), St. Francis (Abnaki), Lorette (Huron), Oswegatchie (Cayuga and Onondaga). When the Oswegatchie mission was closed, these Indians went to live among the Akwesasne Indians at St. Regis, and the latter then became a part of the Seven Nations. The capital was Caughnawaga, which had been the parent of the St. Regis settlement.

72. A sum of £1233/6/8 and an additional sum of £213/6/8, New York currency, were to be paid on August first. The annuity, to be paid "on the third Monday in August, yearly forever," was £213/6/8. The treaty and negotiations are in *American State Papers. Indians Affairs*, I, 616–620.

73. Hough, 329n.; *American State Papers. Indian Affairs*, I, 636.

initiated at the request of the Indians. Joseph Hopkinson of Pennsylvania was the 'United States Commissioner and Egbert Benson, Ezra L'Hommedieu, and John Taylor were the New York agents. The state secured another significant land grant for the sum of $500, of which $300 had already been advanced prior to the treaty at the request of the needy Oneidas. In addition, the treaty provided for an annuity of $700 as further compensation.

Here, then, we have the story of the precipitate decline of the Six Nations. In less than fifteen years, New York State had reduced this mightiest of all Indian confederacies to a nullity. The white man had taught the Indian to regard land as a commodity—something that could be bought and sold. This had been a concept totally alien to Indian tradition. But in making this partial transition to a money economy, the Indians in general seemed incapable at that period of making a full transition to the white man's ideology in regard to land and its ultimate value, both in their terms and in white man's terms. They were, in fact, suspended between two ideologies in their concept of both the land and their own economy. As a result, their economy and their society would soon be in a shambles. At this point, the Six Nations entered upon the reservation period, with its resultant demoralization and social disruption, so capably described by Anthony F. C. Wallace in his *Death and Rebirth of the Seneca*.[74] From having once been a mighty confederacy composed of six sovereign nations, feared by whites and Indian neighbors alike, whose alliance was eagerly sought by the Europeans, they now descended to the status of mere tribal villages.

Vattel defines nationhood as follows: "Nations or states are bodies politic, societies of men united together for the purpose of promoting their mutual safety and advantage by the joint efforts of their combined strength." Further, Vattel continues, "a weak state, which, in order to provide for its safety, places itself under the protection of a more powerful one, and engages, in return, to perform several offices equivalent to that protection, without however divesting itself of the right of government and sovereignty,—that state, I say, does not, on this account, cease to rank among the sovereigns

74. Anthony F. C. Wallace, *Death and Rebirth of the Seneca* (New York: Alfred A. Knopf, 1970).

who acknowledge no other law than that of nations."[75]

As required in international law for recognition as a nation or state, the six groups maintained their political structure, and even the structure of their confederacy. But where was the Six Nations Confederacy? And where, indeed, were the constituent nations of that Confederacy? The Eastern Door of the Confederacy, the Mohawks, had moved to Canada. The Akwesasne Indians at St. Regis, far to the north, mostly Mohawks, and the Caughnawagas in Quebec, had never been a part of the Six Nations Confederacy but had been members of the alliance known as the Seven Nations of Canada. Thus the Eastern Door of the old Confederacy, its eastern defense, was now removed and the breach would not be repaired until 1888 with the admission of the St. Regis Indians to the Confederacy to replace the absent Mohawks.

A large portion of those Iroquois who had supported the British in the Revolutionary War were now living along the Grand River in Canada. This great population shift to Canada thus weakened the real power of the Iroquois remaining in their old territory, now comprised by New York State. As pressure for real estate sales intensified, the Cayugas finally sold out their entire reservation and either removed to Canada or went to live with the Senecas in western New York. In the early nineteenth century, the largest portion of the Oneida Nation moved to Wisconsin, leaving only a few kinsmen behind in New York State—most of them living on the Onondaga Reservation, and a few owning a very small tract of land in central New York. In 1849 a band of Oneidas moved over into Canada and settled along the Thames River in Upper Canada.

The Confederacy also very soon became divided, with a separate confederacy being set up on each side of the border. This divided territorial status, divided political structure, and small remaining acreages would make it difficult if not impossible to maintain their status as "nations or states" in terms of international law. Nor were they any longer free to make treaties with any European power they chose, as in the past, for the European states had ceased to recognize the Iroquois nations as sovereign, independent entities.

What the Indians did not seem to comprehend at the time

75. Vattel, *Law of Nations*, "Preliminaries," p. liv; Chap. I, pp. 1, 2.

was that nationhood, in all practicality, was not merely a matter of ethnic identity and ongoing village government, but was a state of being that required a land base, and a fairly extensive one at that. The Indian economy, the Indian religious ritual cycle—which was largely agricultural in its concepts—the Indian world view, and the Indian culture in general, as well as Indian political and diplomatic power, required a large land base. Without the land, their society degenerated and their power was no more.

The Indian nations could not exist as independent entities when their constituent members were pensioners of the white man. In buying these vast amounts of land from the Six Nations New York State destroyed Indian independence and sovereignty.

The ancient Covenant Chain of friendship between the Six Nations and the whites had become a fetter to bind the Indian, to reduce him to poverty that the white man might prosper. And the Indian might sometimes wonder, in his humiliation, what had become of that old friendship—a friendship that the white man had assured him would last "as long as the sun shall shine or the waters flow."

THE MECHANICS AND THE JEFFERSONIANS:
NEW YORK, 1789-1801

by ALFRED YOUNG

In 1789, on the eve of George Washington's inaugural, New York was a solidly Federalist town. In the Congressional election of 1789, the city chose a Federalist by a vote of 2,342 to 373; in the gubernatorial poll it voted against George Clinton, anti-Federalist Governor, 833 to 385.[1] And the mechanics of all ranks were overwhelmingly Federalist. They poured forth to celebrate Washington's inauguration just as they had marched in 1788 to celebrate ratification of the Constitution. They were active in nominating Federalists and they voted Federalist.[2] "Almost all the gentlemen as well as all the merchants and mechanics," Virginia's Senator Grayson observed in 1789 "combined together to turn [George Clinton] out" while the "honest yeomanry" alone supported him.[3] In 1790 anti-Federalists did not even go through the motions of nominating Assembly or Congressional candidates.

From 1789 to 1801 the major thrust of New York City politics was the effort of the anti-Federalists, then the Republicans, to win back the following they enjoyed in the immediate post-war years and establish a new one among the rapidly expanding electorate.[4] Of necessity this was an effort to win support among the mechanics.

For the old anti-Federalist leaders this was a formidable task. George Clinton, the party chieftain and governor since 1777, was an Ulster county lawyer and landholder whose reputation was built on his services in the Revolution as a staunch Whig, wartime governor

---

[1] *Greenleaf's New York Journal and Patriotic Register*, Apr. 9, 1789 (hereafter cited as *New York Journal*); [New York] *Daily Advertiser*, Apr. 27, 1789.

[2] In 1788 Federalist legislative and convention candidates were endorsed at meetings of master carpenters, and at a meeting of "the respectable mechanics and tradesmen," *Daily Advertiser*, Apr. 24, 28, 29, 1788.

[3] William Grayson to Patrick Henry, June 12, 1789, W. W. Henry, ed., *Life, Correspondence and Speeches of Patrick Henry* (3 vols., New York, 1891), III, pp. 389-95.

[4] For a brief survey, Sidney Pomerantz, *New York, an American City, 1783-1803* (Columbia University Studies in History, Economics and Public Law, No. 442, New York, 1938), chs. 2, 3.

ALFRED YOUNG *is Associate Professor of History at Northern Illinois University*

and foe of Tories.[5] Anti-Federalist political support came primarily
from the independent small farmers of Long Island, the west bank of
the Hudson and the upper Hudson valley.[6] In New York City the
small circle of Clintonian leaders, while men of lowly origins, were all
successful merchants, as their homes in the fashionable part of lower
Manhattan attested.[7] John Lamb, for example, was Collector of the
Port, a lucrative position;[8] Marinus Willett was the county sheriff;[9]
Melancton Smith was busy with various speculations, some of them
in William Duer's group.[10] Henry Rutgers was born to wealth which
made him one of the city's largest landlords.[11] Only one officer of the
General Society of Mechanics and Tradesmen, John Stagg, their old
radical Whig compatriot, acted with the Clintonians; while the only
artisan in their circle,[12] Ezekial Robbins, a wealthy hatter, was not
even a member of the Mechanics Society.[13] They had, in fact, better
connections among merchants than mechanics.

In 1791-92 when the Livingston family defected from the Federalists to form a coalition with the old anti-Federalists, they brought with
them no special strength among the mechanics. They were city merchants and lawyers, and owners of tenanted estates in the upper Hudson valley. Indeed before the Revolution, in 1768-69, the Delancey
faction had been able to win over mechanics against William Livingston of the famed "whig triumvirate,"[14] and in 1774-76 the radical

[5] E. Wilder Spaulding, *His Excellency George Clinton, Critic of the Constitution* (New York, 1938), chs. 7-12.
[6] E. Wilder Spaulding, *New York in the Critical Period, 1783-1789* (New York, 1932), chs. 5, 12. Forrest McDonald, *We The People. The Economic Origins of the Constitution* (Chicago, 1958), pp. 283-300.
[7] For the leaders see "Minutes of the Republican Society" (1788), John Lamb Papers, N.Y. Hist. Soc. and Box 5 of Lamb Papers, *passim*.
[8] Isaac Q. Leake. *Memoirs of the Life and Times of General John Lamb* (Albany, 1850), pp. 296-98, 351-55; *American State Papers, Miscellany*, I, pp. 57-58, 60-62, for Lamb's income as collector.
[9] Daniel E. Wager. *Col. Marinus Willet: The Hero of the Mohawk Valley* (Utica, 1891), pp. 45-47.
[10] Robin Brooks, "Melancton Smith, New York Anti-Federalist, 1744-1798" (unpub. doctoral diss., University of Rochester, 1964), ch. 2.
[11] L. Ethan Ellis, "Henry Rutgers," *Dictionary of American Biography* VIII, pp. 255-56; "Tax Lists or Assessments on the Real and Personal Property" (New York City, June, 1796), Ms. N.Y. Hist. Soc., in particular for the seventh ward.
[12] See Roger Champagne, "The Sons of Liberty and the Aristocracy in New York Politics, 1765-1790" (unpub. doctoral diss., University of Wisconsin, 1960), p. 481. For Stagg on Clinton's election committee, *New York Journal*, Apr. 2, 1789.
[13] "Minutes of the General Society of Mechanics and Tradesmen," Dec. 1, 1794, Dec. 23, 1795 (typescript at the office of the Society, New York City); for his house see James Wilson, *Memorial History of the City of New York* (4 vols. New York, 1891-93), III, pp. 150-52.
[14] Roger Champagne, "Family Politics versus Constitutional Principles: The New York Assembly Elections of 1768 and 1769," *William and Mary Quart.*, 3rd ser., XX

mechanic factions usually were at loggerheads with conservatives led by Robert R. Livingston (senior and then junior), Philip Livingston and John Jay and William Duane, related to the Livingstons by marriage.[15] The memory of Chancellor Robert R. Livingston's veto of the charter for the General Society of Mechanics in 1785 was even fresher.[16] Moreover Aaron Burr, the young lawyer sent to the United States Senate in 1791 by the Livingstons and Clinton, in 1785 was the only city Assemblyman who had voted against the charter.[17] Thus the loose coalition that became the "republican interest" as far as New York City politics went—the Clintons, the Livingstons and Burr—were in reality three factions in search of a following.

They found this following in stages in a long uphill battle. Their first victory did not come until the end of 1794 when they won the Congressional seat by a vote of about 1,850 to 1,650.[18] They did not win an Assembly election until 1797, and in the closing years of the decade all the elections were nip and tuck. In the famous "battle of 1800"—the election that determined that the state's electoral votes would be cast for the Jefferson-Burr ticket—the Republicans took the assembly by 3,050 to 2,600 and squeaked through the congressional race 2,180 to 2,090 votes. Not until 1801 did they win a majority of the £100 freeholder electorate privileged to vote for Governor. Thus even at the end of the Federalist era, New York was not quite a safe Republican town; Federalists in defeat retained a sizable following. Analysis of the election returns leads to the conclusion that the mechanics who in 1789 were overwhelmingly Federalist, by 1800-01 were divided: most were Republican; a good number stayed Federalist. The task, then, that confronts the historian is to explain how various segments of the mechanic population left the house of Federalism in response to the successive issues of the 1790s.

I

Through most of Washington's first administration, from 1789 through 1792, the honeymoon of mechanic Federalist and merchant

(1963), 57-79; Milton Klein, "William Livingston: American Whig" (unpub. doctoral diss., Columbia University, 1954), chs. 13, 15.
[15] Becker, *New York, 1763-1776, passim.*; Champagne, "Sons of Liberty," ch. 7 and pp. 439-40.
[16] George Dangerfield, *Robert R. Livingston of New York, 1746-1813* (New York, 1960), p. 197; for the veto, Charles Z. Lincoln, ed., *Messages From The Governors* (Albany, 1909), II, (1777-1822), pp. 228-233.
[17] Nathan Schachner, *Aaron Burr: A Biography* (New York, 1937), pp. 84-85.
[18] The returns for this and subsequent elections are given below.

Federalist continued. The sources of Federalist popularity among mechanics were several. Federalists were the party of the Constitution; they also appeared as the party of the Revolution. The Tories in their camp took a back seat; Colonel Alexander Hamilton ran the party and it was not missed that John Laurence, their first Congressman, had married the daughter of the famed "Liberty Boy," Alexander McDougall.[19] Federalists were also the party of George Washington, an object of universal veneration while the city was the nation's capital in 1789-90. "Poor men love him as their own," said a character in a play by the New York dramatist, William Dunlap.[20] The fact that the city was the capital also helped; anti-Federalists complained that the Federalist "electioneering corps" included "the masons, stone cutters, the carpenters and the mortar carriers" employed in refurbishing city hall as Federal Hall.[21]

In drawing up slates at election time Federalists accommodated mechanics. In the 1789 election when mechanics and merchants each nominated an assembly ticket, Hamilton presided over a meeting of delegates from both groups which drew up a satisfactory coalition ticket.[22] Hamilton claimed, with apparent impunity, in *Federalist* Essay Number 35 that "Mechanics and manufacturers will always be inclined with few exceptions, to give their votes to merchants, in preference to persons of their own professions and trades. Those discerning citizens are well aware that the mechanic and manufacturing arts furnish the materials of mercantile enterprise and industry."[23] But just to make sure, for years Federalists ran one or more leading mechanics, including leaders of the General Society, on their annual assembly ticket.[24]

[19] Charles W. Spencer, "John Laurence," *Dictionary of American Biography*, VI, pp. 31-32.
[20] Cited in Martha Lamb, *History of the City of New York* (2 vols., New York, 1880), II, p. 352.
[21] "Civis," *New York Journal*, Apr. 9, 1789.
[22] Miscellaneous Notes and Memoranda for April, 1789, Alexander Hamilton Papers, N.Y. Hist. Soc.; for the nominations, *Daily Advertiser*, Apr. 8, ff, 1789.
[23] Jacob Cooke, ed., *The Federalist*, Essay 35, (Middletown, Conn., 1961), p. 219.
[24] The mechanics elected as Federalist Assemblymen and the year of their election were: 1789: Anthony Post, carpenter and President of the General Society; Francis Childs, printer of the Federalist *Daily Advertiser* and Vice President of the Society, and Henry Will, pewterer, an incorporator of the Society; 1790: William W. Gilbert, silversmith, and Will; 1791: John Wylley, tailor, and Will; 1792: Gilbert and Wylley; 1793: Robert Boyd, blacksmith, Richard Furman, painter and glazier and Jotham Post, either a druggist or carpenter; 1794: Furman and Post; 1795: Furman, Post and Alexander Lamb, a cartman; 1797: (ticket defeated); 1798: Furman; 1799: John Bogert, iron monger, Jacob Sherred, painter, Anthony Steenback, mason and

In their policies in the first Congress, Federalists made good on some of their promises during the ratification controversy. The city's mechanics petitioned for tariff protection at once, pointing out to their brethren that "foreign importations were highly unfavorable to mechanic improvement, nourishing a spirit of dependence, defeating in a degree the purpose of our revolution and tarnishing the luster of our character."[25] Congressman Laurence neatly balanced the interests of his constituency, pleading for higher duties on beer, candles, hemp, and cordage, (manufactured by the city's artisans), for lower duties on rum, madeira, and molasses, (imported by the West Indies merchants), couching the latter plea on behalf of the poor—"that part of the community who are least able to bear it."[26] Early in 1792 Congress passed another mildly protective tariff bill while the anti-Federalist position was sufficiently blurred for Hamilton to be able to claim that "this faction has never ceased to resist every protection or encouragement to arts and manufactures."[27]

Hamiltonian finance was generally supported in the city as in the state as a whole. Funding drew only a few whimpers of protest in the city; in fact it was John Stagg, the Clintonian mechanic, who helped squelch a petition that appeared among veterans on behalf of Madison's proposals for discrimination.[28] Assumption struck sparks only among the old anti-Federalist foes of "consolidation." While Hamilton's "Report on Manufactures" does not seem to have drawn any special accolades from mechanics, his overall performance as Secretary of the Treasury gave him a prestige that outlasted his party's. On his retirement in 1795 a group of building craftsmen offered to build him

---

Anthony Post, carpenter; 1800 and 1801, defeated; see *New York Civil List* (Albany, 1869 edn.), 130-148 for assemblymen; for identifications, see *New York Directory* (New York, annually) and "Minutes of the General Society of Mechanics and Tradesmen, 1785-1832," *passim*. For a published list of the members of the Society, Thomas Earle and Charles C. Congden, eds., *Annals of the General Society of Mechanics and Tradesmen of the City of New York, 1785-1889* (New York, 1882), appendix.

25 A letter to the Mechanics Society of Boston in "General Society of Mechanics Minutes," at November 18, 1788; the petition is in *American State Papers: Finance* (Washington, 1832), I, pp. 8-9.

26 Joseph Gales and W. C. Seaton, eds, *The Debates and Proceedings in the Congress of the United States, 1789-1824* (42 vols., Washington, 1834-56), 1st Cong., 1st sess., Apr. 14, 1789, 131, 133-34, 150, 153; Apr. 24, pp. 205-06. Hereafter cited as *Annals of Congress*.

27 An unpublished ms. fragment (1794) in Hamilton Papers, Lib. of Congress, Microfilm, also reprinted in Beard, *Economic Origins*, pp. 246-47.

28 *Daily Advertiser*, Feb. 3, 22, 1790. Stagg was active in putting down the movement in the Society of Cincinnati.

a house at their own expense,[29] and after his death in 1804 the General Society went into mourning for six weeks.[30]

The first sign of a serious mechanic alienation from the merchants came in 1791, when the General Society's new petition for incorporation was "treated with contemptuous neglect" by the state assembly which in the same session granted a charter to the Bank of New York, the merchants' favorite. Some of the old mechanic consciousness, last apparent in 1785-86 when the charter was first rejected, now revived. "Mechanics," said a writer in Greenleaf's anti-Federalist organ, "those who assume the airs of 'the well born' should be made to know that the mechanics of this city have equal rights with the merchants, and that they are as important a set of men as any in the community."[31] Another man pushed the issue further:

> Who will deny that a republican government is founded on democratic principles? . . . That the manufacturing interest, from its nature is, and ever will remain of the democratic denomination, none can deny. Why then incorporate large monied interests, and no democratic ones? Should we not have a wholesome check to the baneful growth of aristocratic weeds among us?[32]

In the Spring elections of 1791 the mechanics refused to go along with the merchants ticket, nominating instead a slate that included one of their officers and two leaders of the burgeoning Tammany Society. Four of their candidates won—"our motley city representatives," Robert Troup called them in his alarmed report to Hamilton.[33] And the following year the mechanics charter sailed through the legislature.

Once chartered, the Society grew from about 200 members in 1792 to about 600 in 1798, most of them master craftsmen. Chartered "only for charitable purposes" as the society regretfully explained, it occasionally made small loans to its members besides acting as a benefit

---

29 Griffith J. McRee, *Life and Correspondence of James Iredell* (2 vols. New York, 1857), II, p. 442.
30 Martha Lamb, "The Career of a Beneficient Enterprise," *Magazine of American History*, XX: 2 (Aug., 1889), 94. I have found no evidence of mechanic testimonials in a search through the Hamilton Transcripts, Col. Univ. Lib. I am indebted to Harold Syrett, Editor of The Hamilton Papers, for the opportunity to make use of the transcripts. Nor is there any such evidence in Broadus Mitchell, *Alexander Hamilton, The National Adventure, 1788-1804* (New York, 1962) or in John C. Miller, *Alexander Hamilton, Portrait in Paradox* (New York, 1949).
31 A Friend to Equal Rights, *New York Journal*, Mar. 30, 1791.
32 "Leonidas," *ibid.*, Feb. 22, 1792.
33 For nominations, *New York Journal*, Apr. 13, 16, 1791; *Daily Advertiser*, June 2, 1791; Robert Troup to Alexander Hamilton, June 15, 1791, Hamilton Transcripts, Col. Univ. Lib.

society.[34] And while it eschewed partisan politics, it nonetheless had the effect it anticipated of "uniting us as brethren in common interests."[35]

Mechanics expressed some of this same spirit by flocking into the Tammany Society, described confidentially by its organizer as "a political institution founded on a strong republican basis whose democratic principles will serve in some measure to correct the aristocracy of the city."[36] Founded in 1789, it had 300 members by the Fall of '91; and perhaps 200 more by 1795, among whom mechanics were the most numerous. Its first chief Sachem was William Mooney, an upholsterer and paper hanger.[37] Its leaders stressed its democratic rather than its class character. Tammany "united in one patriotic band," William Pitt Smith of the Columbia faculty exclaimed, "the opulent and the industrious—the learned and the unlearned, the dignified servant of the people and the respectable plebeian, however distinguished by sentiment or by occupation."[38] The organization was not political, and its leadership at first was predominantly Federalist. But the fact that anti-Federalists were active in Tammany and the Assemblymen elected in 1791 were Tammany figures were both omens of its political potential.[39]

The little appreciated "bank war" and "panic" of 1792 brought to a boil such disillusionment with the Federalist honeymoon as then existed.[40] After the Bank of the United States was chartered and a threat of a coalition of its New York branch with the Bank of New York loomed in 1791, there was a movement to charter a third bank led by "the disappointed in the direction of the existing banks," foremost among whom were the Livingstons.[41] While the origins of the

[34] "Minutes of the General Society," passim. The usual loan was £100 or £150; on Mar. 2, 1796, the society had £500 on loan, on Mar. 7, 1798, £1250.
[35] A letter to the Mechanics Society of Providence, ibid., at Nov. 7, 1792. For the charter see Laws of the State of New York, 13th sess.,ch. 26.
[36] John Pintard to Jeremy Belknap, Oct. 11, 1790 cited in Edwin P. Kilroe. Saint Tammany and the Origins of the Society of Tammany . . . (New York, 1913), pp. 136-37.
[37] Peter Paulson, "The Tammany Society and the Jeffersonian Movement in New York City, 1795-1800," New York History, XXXIV (1953), p. 50.
[38] William Pitt Smith, "An Oration Before the Tammany Society, May 12, 1790," New York Magazine or Literary Repository, I (1790), pp. 290-95, at 294.
[39] For the officers see New York Directory (1789-1792). Pintard was elected to the Assembly in 1790 and failed in 1791 when William Pitt Smith and Melancton Smith were elected. See New York Journal, Apr. 22, 1790, Daily Advertiser, June 2, 1791.
[40] Alfred Young, "The Democratic Republican Movement in New York State, 1788-1797" (unpub. doctoral diss., Northwestern University, 1958), ch. vii and Joseph S. Davis, Essays in the Earlier History of American Corporations (2 vols., Harvard Economic Studies, XVI, Cambridge, Massachusette, 1917), II, ch. 2.
[41] Alexander Macomb to William Constable, Feb. 21, 1792, Constable Papers, N.Y. Pub.

venture were speculative, "men of all classes flocked" to subscribe to its stock, as Edward Livingston claimed in extolling its advantages to "persons of small capital" and victims of the lending "favoritism" of the Bank of New York.[42] Hamilton fought the new venture desperately; by March he knew that the "bank mania" was "made an engine to help the governor's [Clinton's] re-election."[43] In April the "prince of speculators," William Duer, Hamilton's recently resigned Assistant Secretary, collapsed, and the bubble inflated by speculation in bank stock, securities, and land burst. Duer brought down with him not only leading merchants like the Livingstons but a host of common folk from whom he had borrowed to the hilt: "shopkeepers, widows, orphans, butchers, carmen, gardeners, market women," a businessman recorded, "ever the noted bawd Mrs. McCarty." All business, including that of construction, halted; and "the mechanics began to feel the effect of the failures."[44] Small wonder, then, that a mob of about 400-500 threatened Duer's life at the debtor's jail,[45] or that Republicans "made bitter use" of Hamilton's "attachment to Colonel Duer" in the elections.[46] In the gubernatorial poll of 1792 Clinton ran better than he ever had in the city, receiving 603 votes, to 729 for John Jay, or 44 per cent of the total.[47]

In the Congressional election late in 1792 William Livingston—elected previously as a Federalist Assemblyman—offered the Federalists their first national challenge. "That whore in politics," as a Hamilton's informant called him,[48] Livingston made a special appeal to the Mechanics Society for support, claiming to be responsible for their charter. He was also identified with an unsuccessful appeal to

---

Lib.; see also Seth Johnson to Andrew Craigie, Jan. 21, 1792, Craigie Papers, III, No. 70, Amer. Antiq. Soc.

42 Reported in Johnson to Craigie, Jan. 22, 1792, *ibid.*, No. 71; see also "Decius," *New York Journal*, Feb. 15, 1792 and a spate of articles, *Daily Advertiser*, Feb. 7-29, 1792, *passim*.

43 See Alexander Hamilton to William Seton, cashier of the Bank of New York, Jan. 18, 24, Feb. 10, Mar. 19, 21, 1791; the quotation is from James Tillary to Hamilton, Mar. 1, 1792, all in Hamilton Transcripts, Col. Univ. Lib.

44 Johnson to Craigie, Mar. 25, Apr. 18, 1792, Craigie Papers, III, Nos. 73, 76. Amer. Antiq. Soc.; *New York Journal*, Mar. 28, 1792.

45 Benjamin Tallmadge to James Wadsworth, Apr. 19, 1792, Wadsworth Papers, Conn. Hist. Soc. and ms. fragment [Apr. 1792], N.Y.C. Misc. ms., Box 14, N.Y. Hist. Soc.

46 James Watson to James Wadsworth, Apr. 3, 1792, Wadsworth Papers, Conn. Hist. Soc. and Johnson to Craigie, Apr. 15, 1792, Craigie Papers, III, No. 75 Amer. Antiq. Soc.

47 *Daily Advertiser*, June 2, 1792.

48 James Tillary to Hamilton, Jan. 14, 1793, Hamilton Transcripts, Col. Univ. Lib.; for Livingston, Wilson, *Memorial History of the City of New York*, III, pp. 79-80.

make New York City's appointive mayor elective.[49] In a cloudy campaign in which party lines were not clearly drawn, Livingston received 700 votes to 1,900 for the successful Federalist, John Watts.[50]

Through these minor political crises, the leaders of the Mechanics Society did not break with the Federalists. They turned down Livingston's plea for support; it was not only "repugnant to their objects to participate in elections," but he was "an improper person."[51] Similarly they refused to endorse Governor Clinton in 1792[52] or Melancton Smith when he successfully sneaked into the Assembly in 1791. In the Spring of 1793 several officers of the Mechanics Society, including Robert Boyd, the radical Whig blacksmith, were still on the Federalist assembly ticket giving the party an easy victory.[53] In short, at the end of the first Washington administration, despite a smouldering discontent with Federalism in the city, mechanics of the substantial sort and mechanics as a whole had not left the house of Federalism.

II

The parting of the ways came in Washington's second term, and the precipitant was Federalist foreign policy. The French Revolution was an initial stimulus in 1793. When the French frigate *L'Embuscade*, did battle with the English man of war *Boston* off Sandy Hook some nine boatloads of New Yorkers went out to cheer the French victory while on the shore fistfights broke out between "Whig" and "Tory" cartmen.[54] The arrival of Citizen Edmund Genêt prompted the first open mass meeting of the decade and a welcoming committee was formed whose secretary was White Matlack, a well-to-do brewer and iron manufacturer.[55] As a young doctor walked through the poor east side section, he heard "a dram shop full of Frenchmen singing 'Carmagnole.' The next shop I came upon some person was singing 'God

---

[49] *Journal of the Assembly of the State of New York*, 15th sess., 151; "Atticus," *New York Journal*, June 17, 1792.

[50] *New York Journal*, Feb. 20, 1793. Livingston was not endorsed by anti-Federalist or Republican leaders either for Congress or for the Assembly the following spring; see Philip Ten Eyck to John B. Schuyler, Apr. 3, 1793, Schuyler Papers, Misc., N.Y. Pub. Lib.

[51] "General Society Minutes," Jan. 9, 1793; *New York Journal*, Jan. 12, 1793.

[52] See the election committees in *New York Journal*, Feb. 25, Mar. 21, 1792.

[53] *Ibid.*, May 29, June 1, 1793.

[54] Alexander DeConde. *Entangling Alliance: Politics and Diplomacy Under George Washington* (Durham, N.C., 1958), pp. 269-70.

[55] *New York Journal*, Aug. 7, 10, 1793; Rufus King to Alexander Hamilton, Aug. 3, 1793, Charles King, ed., *The Life and Correspondence of Rufus King* (6 vols., New York, 1894-1900), I, p. 493.

Bless Great George' and which immediately procured a parcel of
hearty curses upon his majesty from the rest of the company."[56]

Actually it was Britain and not France that proved the real catalyst.
By early 1794, because the thin wall of Federalist tariff protection was
not holding the line against the competition of British manufactures,
craft groups once again dispatched petitions to Congress.[57] Then news
of massive British depredations against American ships and of a British threat to renew Indian war electrified all classes; it brought the
possibility of war to the state's unprotected frontier and the city's unprotected harbor. Thus Republican proposals—in Congress, Madison's
old bill for discrimination against British shipping; in New York,
Governor Clinton's demand to fortify the harbor and the Livingstons'
strident cry for war—caught full sail the most violent wave of Anglophobia since the Revolution.[58] At a meeting sponsored by Republicans,
White Matlack was the principal speaker and mechanics were so
prominent that a Federalist satirist derided the "greasy caps" in a
mock epic poem. At each good point made by a speaker, he jibed:[59]

> Hats, caps and leathern aprons flew
> And puffs of wondrous size and jerkins blue

In the same flurry of patriotism the city's Democratic Society came
into being: its leaders were merchants and lawyers; its members, according to one of them, "are composed of and mingle with every class
of citizens"; its meetings, according to a Federalist critic, were attended by "the lowest order of mechanics, laborers, and draymen."[60]

---

[56] Alexander Anderson, "Diary," Jan. 9, 1794, Ms., Columbiana Col., Col. Univ. Lib.; see
also entries for July 31, Aug. 8, 1793.
[57] *Annals of Congress*, 3rd Congress 1st sess. Petitions were received from the following
New York City artisans: manufacturers of hand bellows (Feb. 3, 417), nail manufacturers (Feb. 21, 458), hatters (Mar. 5, 478). From other cities petitions
came from manufacturers of metal buttons, tobacco, hemp, nails, paint, bar iron,
glass, hats, and hosiery, 482, 1023, 1131, 432, 256, 475, 452, 453, 456, 523, 522.
For support for protection from Tammany, see *New York Journal*, Nov. 27, 1795.
[58] DeConde, *op. cit.*, ch. 3. John C. Miller, *The Federalist Era, 1789-1801* (New York,
1960), ch. 9.
[59] *New York Daily Gazette*, Mar. 4, 1794; "Acquiline Nimblechops," [psued.] *Democracy,
An Epic Poem* . . . (New York, 1794), attributed, falsely, I believe, to Brockholst
Livingston.
[60] William Woolsey to Oliver Wolcott, Jr., Mar. 6, 1794 cited in Eugene P. Link.
Democratic Republican Societies, 1790-1800 (Columbia Studies in American Culture
No. 9, New York 1942), 94; "Address . . . by the Democratic Society of New York,"
May 28, 1794, Broadside, N.Y. Pub. Lib. Of 43 men known to be members of the
Society, a very incomplete number, it has been possible to identify them as follows:
merchants, 14; craftsmen, 12; public officials, 2; lawyers, 4; teachers, 2; unidentified,
13. For analysis of the comparable Philadelphia society in which 32.8% were
craftsmen, see *ibid.*, pp. 71-73.

A dramatic change in city opinion was apparent in the Spring of 1794 when the Commissioners of Fortifications, headed by Governor Clinton, called for volunteer labor to erect a fort on Governor's Island.[61] For weeks, the Republican paper reported, "hardly a day has passed . . . without a volunteer party of fifty to one hundred" putting in a day's labor.[62] A British visitor described it vividly:

> Marching two and two towards the water side . . . a procession of young tradesmen going in boats to Governor's Island to give the state a day's work . . . drums beating and fifes playing . . . with flags flying. Today the whole trade of carpenters and joiners, yesterday the body of masons; before this the grocers, school masters, coopers and barbers; next Monday all the attorneys and men concerned in the law, handle the mattock and shovel the whole day, and carry their provisions with them.[63]

And of course he could have added more: The Democratic Society, Tammany, the General Society of Mechanics, "all the true Republican carpenters," "the patriotic Republican sawyers," "the patriotic sailmakers"—so they called themselves in the papers—the journeymen hatters, cordwainers, peruke makers, hairdressers, tallow chandlers, tanners and curriers; in short, it was the Constitutional parade of 1788 all over again but under different leadership. And there was also something new: the most recent immigrants to the city styling themselves "Irish laborers," "English Republicans," and the "patriotic natives of Great Britain and Ireland."[64]

The Republicans reaped a political harvest quickly. Early in April 1794, Chancellor Robert R. Livingston advised his younger brother, Edward, not to run again for the Assembly. "The mechanics and cartmen" were Federalist; "I find no class of people on which you can depend."[65] A few weeks later in elections held after the work on the fort had just begun, Federalists won but the Republican vote unexpectedly zoomed from a high of 500 in 1793 to a range of 1,200 to

[61] "Proceedings of the Commissioners of Fortifications for the City of New York and its Vicinity," (1794-1795), Ms., N.Y. Hist. Soc.
[62] *New York Journal*, May 10, 1794.
[63] Henry Wansey, *The Journal of an Excursion to the United States of North America in the Summer of 1794* . . . (Salisbury, Eng., 1796), reprinted in Bayrd Still ed. *Mirror for Gotham* (New York, 1956), pp. 65-66. I have changed the order of several sentences.
[64] See *New York Journal*, Apr. 26, 30, May 3, 7, 10, 24, 28, June 18, 21, 1794. See also I. N. P. Stokes, comp. *Iconography of Manhattan Isle* (6 vols., New York, 1915-1928), V, 1307.
[65] Robert R. to Edward Livingston, Apr. 10, 1794, R. R. Livingston Papers, N.Y. Hist. Soc.

1,400.[66] Then in the Congressional poll of December 1794-January 1795 Edward Livingston risked a race against John Watts, the Federalist incumbent. A lawyer and city resident, a member of the aristocratic Hudson Valley family known as "Beau Ned" (the young dandy),[67] he was presented to the voters as "the poor man's friend," a "good Whig," and "a good Republican and true friend of the French." Watts was described as a "Tory," "a paper man," "an opulent merchant" and "a friend to British measures."[68] The year before, when Livingston ran for the Assembly, he received 214 votes; he now won 1,843 to 1,638.[69]

In this changing climate the General Society of Mechanics and Tradesmen shifted perceptibly. John Stagg, the Clintonian and radical Whig, was returned as President; later he presided at the public meeting at which Livingston was nominated.[70] At its Fourth of July dinner in 1794, the Society toasted "the republican societies of the City of New York"; the following year it accepted an invitation from the Democratic Society for a joint celebration of Independence Day with them, Tammany and the Coopers Society. A committee worked out the details of an observance that was repeated every year thereafter: a parade to a church (militia officers seated in front of the pulpit, the mechanics to the right of the center aisle, the Democrats to the left, Tammany and the Coopers off to either side aisle), a ceremony consisting of the reading of the Declaration of Independence followed by a patriotic oration by a Republican leader.[71] The typical mechanic could now be portrayed in Republican hues: he was, according to a writer in the Republican paper, a hard working man who eschewed high living, opposed the "haughty well born," saved to buy a lot in the suburbs for his old age, and enjoyed a family gathering at home where his children beat time to "Yankee Doodle" and "Carmagnole."[72]

---

66 New York Journal, June 7, 1794.
67 William Hatcher, Edward Livingston: Jeffersonian Republican and Jacksonian Democrat (Baton Rouge, 1940), ch. 1; Charles H. Hunt, Life of Edward Livingston (New York, 1964), chs. 1-3.
68 William Miller, "First Fruits of Republican Organization: Political Aspects of the Congressional Elections of 1794," Penn. Mag. Hist. and Biog. LXIII (1939), 118-43; Young, op. cit., pp. 616-20.
69 New York Journal, Feb. 7, 1795 cf. to returns, ibid., May 29, June 1, 1793.
70 New York Journal, Nov. 26, 29, Dec. 3, 1794.
71 New York Journal, July 5, 1794; "General Society of Mechanics Minutes," June 3, 24, July 1, 1795 and for the seating arrangements, June 7, 1798.
72 "See to That," New York Journal, Dec. 27, 1794.

Thus, the first Republican breakthrough came in a revival of "The Spirit of 76." Over the next few years Republicans had great difficulty transferring this new strength, which came on a national issue, to state elections.[73] They were also unable to sustain mechanic Republicanism on national questions, as the vicissitudes of the Jay Treaty fight of 1795-96 illustrated. A "town meeting" protesting the treaty was attended by from 5,000 to 7,000 people. It was held at the noon lunch hour when, according to an irate Federalist, "our demogogues always fix their meetings in order to take in all mechanics and laborers—over whom they alone have influence."[74] The poorer workers were especially noticeable: cartmen with their horses, "the hodmen, and the ash men and the clam men," as were recent immigrants—Scotsmen, Irish, English and French.[75] When the vote was taken to damn the Treaty, according to one contemporary, "there was not a whole coat" among them. The Livingstons were "supported by a few of the principal citizens, the rest being made up of men of the lower class." Others claimed, however, that the leaders did not have "a majority of the lower class," or that several hundred sided with Hamilton.[76] By the Spring of 1796, after Washington signed the treaty and Republicans in the House threatened to hold up its enforcement, anti-treaty sentiment faded. Playing on the fear of war and threatening economic coercion, Federalists were able to collect some 3,200 signatures on a pro-Treaty petition.[77] Republicans by contrast turned out less than half of the previous year's opponents at a public rally, one-third of whom, a Federalist charged, "as is usually the case were negroes, sweeps, boys, Frenchmen, and curious people." The "merchants and traders," he insisted, and "the substantial mechanics" backed the Treaty.[78]

The claim was probably justified. In the Congressional election at the end of 1796 James Watson, a wealthy merchant, received the Fed-

---

[73] For returns in the 1795 gubernatorial elections, *New York Journal,* June 3, 1795.
[74] Benjamin Walker to Joseph Webb, July 24, 1795 in W. C. Ford, ed. *Correspondence and Journals of Samuel Bacheley Webb* (3 vols., New York, 1894), III.
[75] Grant Thorburn, *Forty Years Residence in America* . . . (Boston, 1834), 37-40.
[76] Seth Johnson to Andrew Craigie, July 23, 1795. Craigie Papers, III, No. 97, Amer. Antiq. Soc.; "Slash," *New York Journal,* July 25, 1795 for the remark about "not a wholecoat;" Benjamin Walker cited in footnote 74.
[77] Alexander Hamilton to Rufus King, Apr. 24, 1796, Hamilton Transcripts, Col. Univ. Lib. For pressure by insurance underwriters, "Circular letter by Nicholas Low, Archibald Gracie and Gulian Verplanck, New York, May 3, 1796," Broadside, N.Y. Pub. Lib.
[78] William Willcocks, a New York City Federalist Assemblyman, in *Albany Gazette,* May 2, 1796.

eralist nomination after four others had turned it down because, in
Hamilton's words, "he had gotten a strong hold of most of the leading
mechanics who act with us."[79] Edward Livingston recovered his lost
ground to win a second term by a safe margin of 2,362 to 1,812 votes.
But his vote, a contemporary accurately put it, came from wards
"chiefly inhabited by the middling and poorer classes of the people."[80]
Thus at the end of the second Washington administration the city's
working population was split: the Federalists retained a good section
of the "substantial mechanics" while the Republicans had the "middling and poorer classes" in an unstable constituency.

III

Republicans did not consolidate this foothold until they mastered
the art of exploiting the class antagonisms of the poor, threats to the
economic interests of particular crafts, and the aspirations of new
immigrants.

Poverty in New York went hand in hand with population growth
and economic progress.[81] The city, the worldy-wise LaRochefoucauld
observed in 1796, "like all great towns contains at once more riches
and more wretchedness than towns less populous and commercial."[82]
A petition from one group of workers pointed out that "house rent,
fuel, provisions and prices of everything necessary for the support of
a family have been rising." In the winter of 1796-97 some 600 unem-
ployed journeymen petitioned for public assistance because many "by
reasons of large families" were "in want of sufficient fire and wood."[83]
For newcomers housing was the worst problem. The upper-east side
near the shore—the seventh ward—was the city's worst slum. As a
doctor described it, it had "narrow, crooked, flat, unpaved, muddy
alleys" filled with swamps, stagnant water, "little decayed wooden
huts," some inhabited by several families; all was wafted by an intoler-

[79] Hamilton to Rufus King, Dec. 16, 1796, Hamilton Transcripts, Col. Univ. Lib.
[80] "Impartial History of the Late Election," *New York Journal*, Dec. 27, 1796; Argus,
Jan. 20, 1797.
[81] Pomerantz, *op. cit.*, 199-225; Morris, *Government and Labor in Early America*, 200 ff.
[82] F. A. F. de La Rochefoucauld-Liancourt, *Travels Through the United States of America,
in the Years 1795, 1796, 1797* (2 vols., London, 1799), II, p. 205.
[83] "Petition of the Repackers of Beef and Pork to the State Legislature, Jan. 24, 1795,"
Misc., Ms., N.Y.C. No. 86, N.Y. Hist. Soc.; "Jehosphapet," [New York] *Evening
Post*, Jan. 14, 1795; "To the Inhabitants of the City of New York," *Argus*, Jan. 14,
1797.

able stench from garbage piled in the streets, putrefying excrement at the docks and a tan yard in their midst.[84] Understandably, when a yellow-fever epidemic claimed 700 lives in the summer of 1795, it was here that the toll was heaviest.[85]

Discontent bred of such conditions was ready for political exploitation. By 1795 there were 900 more voters in the £100 electorate for a total of 2,100 but there were 2,300 more 40 shilling renters, or a total of 5,000. Moreover, the poorer voters were concentrated in the newly-built parts of town, the fifth and especially the seventh wards along the East River, and the fourth and especially the sixth to the west along the North (or Hudson) River. In the seventh, known as the "cartman's ward," there were 870 40-shilling voters to 311 £100 voters; in the sixth the proportion was 1,298 to 223. Here was the Republican potential.[86]

The pent-up class feeling erupted in the election of the Spring of '96 which, as Hamilton put it, "in view of the common people . . . was a question between the rich and the poor because of the 'vile affair of whipping Burke and McCredy'."[87] Thomas Burk and Timothy Crady—Federalists could not get their names straight—were ferrymen, recent Irish immigrants who got into an altercation with Gabriel Furman, an arrogant Federalist alderman of the wealthy first ward. Accused of the crime of "insulting an alderman" they were tried without due process before a court of three aldermen and a Federalist Mayor intent upon making an example of the "impudent rascals," and were sentenced to two months in jail (Burk got twenty lashes as well).

William Keteltas, a young Republican lawyer, took this case of the "oppression of the innocent poor" to the State Assembly, demanding impeachment of the city official.[88] After a Federalist committee exonerated them and Keteltas turned his guns on the Assembly, he was called before the Bar of the House and asked to apologize. He refused

---

[84] Dr. Elihu Hubbard Smith, "Letters to William Bull . . . on the Fever" in Noah Webster, Jr., comp., *A Collection of Papers on the Subject of Billious Fevers* (New York, 1796), pp. 66-74.

[85] Matthew Davis, *A Brief Account of the Epidemical Fevers* (New York, 1796), pp. 58-67 for a list of the dead, 6, 16-17 for housing. For verification, Dr. Richard Bayley, *An Account of the Epidemic Fever* (New York, 1796), 59-66, 122 and *Argus*, Oct. 17, 1795.

[86] See Table 1, in introduction above; for the electoral census of 1795 by wards, see Supplement to the *Daily Advertiser*, Jan. 27, 1796.

[87] Hamilton to Rufus King, May 4, 1796, Hamilton Transcripts, Col. Univ. Lib.

[88] For a full account, Young, *op. cit.*, ch. 20; for a brief account, Pomerantz, *op. cit.*, pp. 263-68.

and was found guilty of contempt, whereupon the tumultuous crowd that had jammed the Assembly carried him off to jail in a handsome arm chair midst cries of "The Spirit of '76." An issue of class justice had been transformed into one of free speech. After a month of agitation from "the iron gate," Keteltas was released and escorted home by a cheering crowd. That was a Tuesday; on Friday Republicans nominated him as one of their twelve Assembly candidates. When Federalists mocked the "ragamuffins" who paraded for Keteltas, Republicans claimed them as "the men by whose mechanical labours the necessaries and conveniences of life are prdouced in abundance"; it was "such men as these [who] were the triumphant victors at Breed's Hill, at Saratoga, at Yorktown." The Federalists won, but the Republican slate hit its highest peak thus far.[89]

In the September 1796 municipal elections Republicans for the first time capitalized on local issues. The Common Council was in the hands of conservative Federalist merchants elected by a tiny handful of voters.[90] Republicans railed at the Mayor and Council for dispensing arbitrary justice, failing to curb forestalling in the markets, neglecting to keep the streets clean, and increasing expenditures and taxes. They elected two men, both of whom were disqualified on technicalities, then re-elected one of them, Jacob Delamontagnie, a secretary of the Democratic Society, by an even wider margin.[91]

Early in 1797 Republicans took up the cause of a single craft, the seventy-five members of the Association of Tallow Chandlers and Soap Makers, whose factories the state legislature ordered removed from the city proper to the outskirts of towns—on the grounds that their fumes were a cause of epidemic. The chandlers petitioned the Assembly. The Republican Brockholst Livingston became their counsel, and at their request Dr. Samuel Latham Mitchill, the Columbia scientist and Tammany orator, prepared a pamphlet-length treatise exonerating the chandlers' "pestilential vapors," blaming the fever on "septic acid vapors," his favorite theory.[92] The chandler issue boiled

---

[89] *New York Journal*, Apr. 15, 19, 22, especially "A Dialogue Between an Old Tory and a Young Republican," *ibid.*, Apr. 22.
[90] Pomerantz, *op. cit.*, pp. 64-76.
[91] In the *New York Journal*, "An Elector," Sept. 20; "A Citizen," Sept. 22; "A Freeholder," Sept. 22; and an editorial paragraph, Sept. 29, 1796; for the contested election, Arthur Peterson, *Minutes of the Common Council of the City of New York* (19 vols., New York, 1917), II, pp. 284-86; Pomerantz, *New York*, pp. 120-22.
[92] For the petition, Assembly Papers, Box 5, No. 113, New York State Lib.; for news-

through March; in April the Republicans nominated Mitchill for the Assembly on a slate that included a tanner, a hatter, a sailmaker, and the two aldermen elected in the wake of the Keteltas affair. Federalists capitulated, endorsing half the Republican ticket, an unheard of event, and Republicans won their first Assembly election of the decade, their vote ranging between 1,600 and 2,100 to a scant 600 to 700 for the Federalists.[93] In 1800 Dr. Mitchill, the tallow chandlers' hero, was the successful Republican candidate to replace Edward Livingston in Congress.

Republicans also won over another group, the cartmen. Numbering more than 1,000 by 1800, they were known for their "quick tempers" and "mistreating their horses." Normally they chafed under the regulations of the city fathers.[94] In the ferryman affair a doggerel verse on broadside reminded the cartmen of their own trouble with Major Richard Varick:[95]

He often sits upon a bench
Much like unto a judge, sir.
And makes the wretches bosom wrench
To whom he owes a grudge sir.

But now he does a great offense
It is no thing to mock at
He takes away the cartmen's pence
And puts them in his pocket.

By 1798 the cartmen were Republican enough for the Federalists to gerrymander the outlying seventh ward ("the cartmen's ward") out of the city into the Westchester congressional district. In the 1799 Assembly elections Federalist merchants stood at the polls and "used all their influence with the cartmen" with some success.[96] The next year "Independent Cartman" appealed to his brethren not to submit again to such merchant pressure: who will do the work if not us?

---

paper accounts, *New York Journal*, Feb. 18, 23, Mar. 8, 11, 1797; Samuel L. Mitchill, *The Case of the Manufacturers of Soap and Candles in the City of New State Stated and Examined* (New York, 1797); Mitchill to Robert R. Livingston, June 9, 1797, Misc., ms., N.Y. Hist. Soc.; Livingston to Mitchill, July 18, 1797, R. R. Livingston ms., N.Y. State Lib.

[93] *New York Journal*, June 4, 1797.

[94] Kenneth and Anna M. Roberts, trans. and ed., *Moreau de St. Mary's American Journey (1793-1798)* (New York, 1947), pp. 124-25, and 127, 158-59, 162 for other observations on labor in the city; "Regulations of the Cartmen . . . 1795," Broadside, Lib. of Congress.

[95] "The Strange and Wonderful Account of a Dutch Hog," (New York, 1796), Broadside No. 7765, N.Y. State Lib.; Varick was Dutch for hog.

[96] Peter Jay to John Jay, May 3, 1799, John Jay Papers, Col. Univ. Lib.

"Will their puny clerks carry the burdens which we do?"[97] The cartmen resisted and as a result there were only eighteen cartmen in the
crowd when Hamilton, in 1801, appeared at a meeting of cartmen
and appealed to "my dear fellow citizens."[98]

From the mid-'90s on, Republicans also spoke in clear tones to the
city's new immigrants. Federalists were not without experience in
dealing with nationality groups politically.[99] But to the French, Scots,
English, and especially the Irish recent arrivals who ran up the cost
of charity at the alms house, hated England and allegedly brought in
yellow fever, Federalists were cool or hostile.[100] Republicans, by contrast, formed the "Society for the Assistance of Persons Emigrating
from Foreign Countries." They turned out en masse to welcome
Joseph Priestly and in their press, Irish and Scots could read reports
of struggles for liberty in their native lands.[101] Congressman Livingston, during the xenophobia of 1798 to 1800, eloquently opposed the
Alien Law, even introducing a petition from Irish aliens of New York,
and in the Assembly Aaron Burr fought the proposed constitutional
amendment to bar Federal office to naturalized citizens.[102] The political
fruits fell accordingly. "The poor Irish and French," one Federalist
was convinced, were enough to carry the sixth and seventh wards for
Jefferson in 1800.[103]

IV

In the closing years of the decade Republicans also picked up some
of the issues that from the 1780s on had been of concern to master me-

---

[97] "An Independent Cartman," *Republican Watch-Tower*, Apr. 30, 1800 and in the same
issue "To the Cartmen of New York," "To the Cartmen," by "Eighteen Hundred,"
and report of a meeting; "Leonidas" *ibid.*, Mar. 14, 1801 claimed that only 1,150 of
1,500 votes were cast in the 1800 election as a result of threats.
[98] "A Cartman," *Republican Watch Tower*, Apr. 25, 1801.
[99] To take the Germans as an example: In 1788 Federalists candidates were endorsed "at
a very numerous meeting of Germans," (*Daily Advertiser*, Apr. 28, 1788); in 1790
the German Society, claiming to be rebuffed by the merchants, offered support to the
mechanics' ticket if they nominated a German (*New York Gazette*, Apr. 20, 1790).
[100] See Alfred Young, "New York City in the Hysteria of 1798 to 1800" (unpub. Master's
thesis, Col. Univ., 1947), pp. 92-101.
[101] "Society for the Assistance of Persons Emigrating From Foreign Countries . . . June
30, 1794," Broadside, N.Y. Hist. Soc.; for their constitution, *New York Journal*,
June 25, 1794 and philosophy, Thomas Dunn, A.M. *A Discourse . . . October 21,
1794 Before the New York Society . . .* (New York, 1794); for Priestley's Welcome,
Edgar Smith, *Priestley in America, 1794-1804* (Philadephia, 1920), pp. 21-40.
[102] *The Speech of Edward Livingston on the Third Reading of the Alien Bill* (Philadelphia, 1798) also in *New York Journal*, July 14, 1798; *Annals of Congress*, 5th Congress, 1st Sess., Feb. 12, 1799, p. 2884; Schachner, *Aaron Burr*, 152.
[103] Phillip Livingston to Jacob Read, Feb. 23, 1801, reprinted in *Col. Univ. Quart.*
XXIII (June, 1931), p. 200.

chanics. For one, they committed themselves to tariff protection. In the General Society a committee headed by the Republican sailmaker, George Warner, drafted a letter lamenting the growth of foreign importations; they were "an influence highly unfavorable to mechanical improvement, nourishing a spirit of dependence, defeating in a degree the purpose of our Revolution, and tarnishing the luster of our national character"—the very language was that used by Federalist mechanics in 1789.[104] In 1801 a mass meeting of "the mechanics and manufacturers of New York City" sent a memorial to Congress beseeching the "protecting hand of government."[105] As the reign of Jefferson approached, "A Song for Hatters" expressed the expectations of other artisans:[106]

Before the bad English Treaty,
Which Jay with that nation has made
For work we need make no entreaty
All Jours were employed at their trade.

Philadelphia she then had a hundred
New York she had fifty and more
In the first scarce the half can be numbered
In the last there is hardly a score. . . .

And what has occasion'd this failing,
And caus'd us to fall at this rate
'Tis the English, whose arts are prevailing
With our Great rulers of state. . . .

When shortly in our constitution
A Republican party will sway
Let us all then throw in a petition
Our grievance to do away . . . .

---

[104] "General Society of Mechanics Minutes," Jan. 16, Feb. 6, Feb. 20, Mar. 6, Apr. 3, 1799 reprinted in Earle and Congdon. eds., *Annals,* pp. 241-42. The letter was drafted, agreed to, and reconsidered at a special meeting, then rejected. Thus there was a division in the society on the question which may also account for the first recorded contest for officers, Jan. 4, 1800. The fact that George Warner, an active Republican, was chairman of the drafting committee leaves no doubt as to the Republican position.

[105] *American Citizen,* Mar. 19, Mar. 21, Apr. 10, 1801. George Warner was secretary to this committee; another petition was sent to the state legislature requesting bounties for the production of sheep to encourage the wool industries, signed by a number of Republicans, *American Citizen,* Feb. 14, 1801.

[106] "A New Song," by J. C. [James Cheetham, hatter and co-editor of the paper], *Republican Watch-Tower,* Feb. 21, 1801; for other evidence of Republican support for manufactures, Minutes of the Tammany Society, Dec. 1, 1800, ms., N.Y. Pub. Lib., for a debate; *Argus,* Nov. 27, 1795 for a Tammany toast; *New York Journal,* Apr. 15, 1797, June 8, 1799.

> That our party in Congress may now rule
> Let each voter for liberty stir
> And not be to England a base tool
> When Jefferson aids us and Burr.

Republicans again took up the cause of freer banking facilities. But where the Livingstons' frontal assault of 1792 failed, Aaron Burr in 1799 managed the camouflaged Bank of Manhattan through the legislature with finesse.[107] While the new bank was primarily of concern to aspiring merchants, it is symptomatic of the mechanic interest in credit that some two dozen members of the Mechanics Society were among the charter stock subscribers.[108] The new bank, Republicans boasted, broke the "banking monopoly" and struck a blow at usury, an object of special contempt to many working class patrons of the city's money lenders.[109]

From 1797 on, Republicans also committed themselves clearly to direct representation of master mechanics on their assembly tickets. In 1798 they repeated their success of the previous year by running four artisans on their ticket; in 1799 they ran six new ones. Even the famous all-star slate Aaron Burr assembled for the battle of 1800 had a place on it for George Warner, sailmaker, Ezekial Robbins, hatter, and Phillip Arcularius, tanner.[110]

The inroads Republicans made among mechanics of all types was confirmed by Federalist tactics from 1798-1801. For a while during the "half war" with France and the "reign of terror," Federalists basked in a glow of X.Y.Z. patriotism as some mechanics turned against the Republicans—now the so-called "French party"—just as they had deserted

---

107 Beatrice Rubens, "Burr, Hamilton and the Manhattan Company," *Polit. Sci. Quart.*, LXXII (1957), 578-607 and LXIII (1958), pp. 100-125.

108 Bank of Manhattan, *A Collection of 400 Autographs Reproduced in Facsimilie from the Signatures of the Original Subscription Book of the Bank of Manhattan* (New York, 1919).

109 *New York Journal*, Jan. 8, Feb. 12, 15, 1800; "Philander, *American Citizen*, Apr. 28, 29, 1800; for a debate, "Minutes of the Tammany Society," Mar. 31, 1800, Ms., N.Y. Pub. Lib.

110 The mechanic candidates on the Republican ticket were: for 1797: Phillip Arcularius, tanner, Ezekial Robbins, hatter, and George Warner, sailmaker; for 1798: Arcularius, Robbins, Arthur Smith, mason and John Wolfe, boot and shoemaker; for 1799: Joshua Barker, manager of an air furnace, Ephriam Brasher, goldsmith, John Brower, upholsterer, Matthew Davis, printer, Benjamin North, carpenter and William Vredenbergh, grocer. For excellent details: Anne B. Seeley, "A Comparative Study of Federalist and Republican Candidates in New York City" (Unpublished master's thesis, Col. Univ., 1959). Of 16 Republican candidates of mechanic background nominated over the entire decade Mrs. Seeley found the tax evaluations of about half of them to be high, e.g., £1200 to 5850 and about half to be low, £100 to 400

the Federalists in 1794-95 as the British party. It was almost a second honeymoon of mechanic and merchant as the Mechanics Society toasted "Millions for defense, not one cent for tribute," Tammany substituted "Yankee Doodle" for "The Marseillaise," and mechanics paraded en masse in Washington's funeral cortege. But the Federalist attitude to Republican mechanics was by this time fatally ambivalent. Besides threatening mechanics with the loss of their jobs, they beat the nativist drums, challenging naturalized aliens at the polls and attempted to suppress the city's two Republican papers. At election time when they sought to woo mechanics, Republicans warned about "the avowed despisers of mechanics who may for a few days intermingle with honest men in order to deceive them."[111] Federalists also voted the poor from the alms house and courted free Negroes with promises of office holding and "enormous supplies of home crackers and cheese."[112] And in the election of 1800 when Hamilton was unable to induce men of "weight and influence" to run, he arranged an Assembly slate filled with unknown artisans: a ship chandler, a baker, a bookseller, a potter, a shoemaker, a leather inspector, and spoiled the image only by including Gabriel Furman "the man who whipped the ferrymen."[113] Federalist tactics thus can only be described as desperate and to no avail. Mechanic interest was unsurpassed in the voting in the Spring of 1800: "all business was suspended, even the workmen deserted the houses they were building";[114] yet Federalists lost the city.

The election returns for 1800 and 1801 indicate that the mechanics were preponderantly Republican yet were divided in their allegiances. The fact that there were two categories of voters—the £100 freeholders alone qualified to vote for Senators and Governor, and the 40 shilling renters allowed to vote only for Assemblymen—enables us to differentiate roughly the voting patterns of the various strata of mechanics. (see Table 3) First, about two thirds of the Republican vote—in 1800, about 2,200 of 3,100 votes; in 1801, 2,400 of 3,600 votes—came from the Assembly voters, the 40 shillings renters who in effect were the poorer mechanics, the cartmen, petty tradesmen and journeymen. Sec-

---

[111] *Argus,* Apr. 20, 1799; see James Smith, *Freedom's Fetters. The Alien and Sedition Acts* (Ithaca, N.Y., 1956), pp. 204-220, 385-417; Young, "New York City in the Hysteria of 1798-1800," *passim.*

[112] "To a Certain Man," *American Citizen,* Apr. 24, 1801.

[113] Matthew L. Davis to Albert Gallatin, Apr. 15, 1800, Gallatin Papers, N.Y. Hist. Soc.; see also Robert Troup to Rufus King, Mar. 9, 1800, in C. King, ed., *Correspondence of Rufus King,* III, pp. 207-08.

[114] Peter Jay to John Jay, May 3, 1800, Jay Papers, Col. Univ. Lib.

ondly, about one half of the total Federalist vote came from this same group—in 1800, 1,300 of their 2,600 votes; in 1801, 1,100 of 2,150 votes. Thirdly, Republicans also had significant support among the £100 freeholders who included the master craftsmen—43 per cent or 876 voters in 1800, 54 per cent or 1,266 voters in 1801. As a Republican editor proudly pointed out, this refuted the Federalist contention that Jefferson and Burr were supported only by "persons of no property."[115]

TABLE NO. 3

THE NEW YORK CITY ELECTIONS OF 1800 and 1801

| | 1800 | | | | 1801 | | | |
| | Asssembly | | Senate | | Assembly | | Governor | |
Ward	Rep.	Fed.	Rep.	Fed.	Rep.	Fed.	Rep.	Fed.
1	172	245	47	130	208	222	82	145
2	200	434	74	213	217	375	112	209
3	250	438	75	185	284	365	104	194
4	412	330	124	179	426	274	145	162
5	458	370	139	147	545	313	170	148
6	814	363	187	108	919	267	289	89
7	786	485	231	164	1052	353	364	145
Total vote	3092	2665	877	1126	3651	2169	1266	1090

Sources: for 1800, *American Citizen*, May 5, 1800; for 1801, *Republican Watch-Tower*, May 6, 1801.

Analysis of the returns by wards confirms this political division among both prosperous and poorer mechanics. In the sixth and seventh wards with the greatest proportion of poor voters and recent immigrants, where Republicans made their greatest effort to get out the vote,[116] they received more than half of their total city vote in 1800 and 1801. Yet Federalists also had a following here, 800 voters in 1800, reduced to 600 the following year. By contrast, the second and third wards at the bottom of Manhattan, the centers of the fashionable wealthy merchant residences,[117] through the entire decade gave the

---

[115] *American Citizen*, May 4, 1801; see also Aaron Burr to William Eustis, Apr. 28, 1801, Eustis Ms., Mass. Hist. Soc.

[116] For 1800 Matthew L. Davis to Albert Gallatin, May 1, 1800, Gallatin Papers, N.Y. Hist. Soc. Notices of meetings: *American Citizen*, Apr. 22, 25, 1800; Peter Jay to John Jay, May 3, 1800. Jay Papers, Col. Univ. Lib., John C. Miller, *Alexander Hamilton*, p. 512.

[117] Wilson, *Memorial History of New York*, III, 150-52, for a list of 250 homes assessed at over £2000 in 1798; Stokes, *Iconography of Manhattan Island*, V, p. 1374; Beard, *Economic Origins*, pp. 382-87, erred in lumping the first with the second and third; it was more mixed; see "Impartial History of the Late Election," *New York Journal*, Dec. 27, 1796, for comment that remains valid for 1800.

154

Federalists almost a two to one margin. The fourth and fifth wards, the midtown on both the west and east side, which were probably the most "middling" in the city, divided about evenly between the two parties. In 1802 Republicans confirmed the class basis of their support in the poorer wards when they divided the city into two congressional districts. They created their own safe district by placing the sixth and seventh wards in together with the fourth, giving the first, second, third and fifth wards to the Federalists in a district which also included Brooklyn and Richmond. Federalists did not even run a candidate in the Republican district, while Republicans ran one in the Federalist area with "no hopes of success."[118]

By 1800-01 Republican support among mechanics, it is reasonable to hypothesize, came from: 1.) master craftsmen and journeymen in many trades, especially the less prosperous ones; 2.) craftsmen as a whole in trades whose interests Republicans espoused, such as tallow chandlers and shoemakers; 3.) craftsmen in those trades most in need of protection from British manufacturers such as hatters and tanners; 4.) cartmen as a whole; 5.) newer immigrants, especially the Irish,[119] French[120] and to a lesser extent the Scots,[121] and English, 6.) mechanics who had been patriots in the Revolution and responded to the revival of the "Spirit of '76."

The numerically smaller following of the Federalists may well have come from 1.) the more "substantial mechanics" in many trades to whom Hamilton's appeal for the Federalists—as the party that brought "unexampled prosperity"—was meaningful;[122] 2.) craftsmen least in need of protection, such as the building trades; 3.) poorer tradesmen

---

118 Editorial, *American Citizen,* Apr. 30, 1802.
119 For Republican organizations among the Irish: for the United Irishmen of New York, *Time Piece,* July 6, Aug. 30, 1798 and *Argus,* Mar. 18, 1799; for "Republican Irishmen," *American Citizen,* July, 1800 and July 9, 1801; for Hibernian Provident Society, *Republican Watch Tower,* Mar. 18, 28, 1801; for Hibernian Militia Volunteers, Link, *op. cit.,* p. 184.
120 For the variety of political opinions among the French see F. S. Childs, *French Refugee Life in the United States: An American Chapter of the French Revolution* (Baltimore, 1946), pp. 70-75; *Moreau de St. Mary's American Journey, passim;* for a French newspaper of a Republican cast see George P. Winship, "French Newspapers in the United States from 1790 to 1800," *Bibliographic Society of America Papers,* XIV (1920), pp. 134-47.
121 For the Calendonian Society, decidedly Republican, see [New York] *Evening Post,* Dec. 22, 1794; *Argus,* Dec. 3, 1795; *New York Directory for 1796,* unpaged; for a conservative Scot's observations on the "hot characters" among his fellow migrants, Grant Thorburn, *Forty Years Residence,* pp. 23, 37-40, 92.
122 New York *Commercial Advertiser,* Apr. 11, 1801 and *An Address to the Electors of the State of New York* (Albany, 1801).

most closely dependent on and most easily influenced by merchants, such as the service trades; 4.) American-born mechanics and New England migrants who felt their status threatened by the influx of "foreigners";[123] 5.) new immigrants, anxious to differentiate themselves from their radical countrymen, especially the English;[124] and 6.) mechanics of a loyalist or neutralist background who were made uneasy by the revival of anti-Toryism.

V

The New York Republicans, it should be clear, did not become a labor party. The Clintons, Livingstons and Burrites, and other merchants, landholders, lawyers and office holders ruled the party. Moreover, they had the support of a substantial segment of the merchant community, although not the men at the apex of economic power in the city.[125] Nor did the mechanics become even an organized wing of the party, bargaining for nominations as they had with the Federalists early in the decade. Republicans always found a place for a few mechanics on their twelve-man Assembly slate and for many others on their electioneering committees. Mechanics were members, though not leaders, of the Democratic Society and leaders as well as members of the Tammany Society. George Warner, sailmaker, or Matthew Davis, printer,[126] were speakers at the annual Republican celebration of Independence Day; James Cheetham, a former hatter,[127] was influential as an editor and pamphleteer; and early in the 1800s a number of tanners were active enough to win a reputation as the "tannery yard clique" and "the swamp clique." But there was no assertive workingmen's faction among the Republicans as there would be in the Jacksonian era.[128] And me-

---

[123] See the toasts of a "Yankee Fraternity," *Daily Advertiser*, July 10, 1798.

[124] For a short-lived Federalist paper founded by a recent English migrant, John Mason Williams, see [New York] *Columbian Gazette* (April 4-June 22, 1799), especially the prospectus April 6 and valedictory, June 22.

[125] Alfred Young, "The Merchant Jeffersonians: New York as A Case Study," (unpub. paper delivered before the Miss. Valley Hist. Ass'n., Apr., 1954).

[126] Matthew Davis, while best known as Burr's amanuensis for *Memoirs and Correspondence of Aaron Burr*, was a printer, publisher of the short-lived [New York] *Evening Post* (1795), then co-publisher of [New York] *Time Piece* (1797). He was active in Tammany and the Mechanics Society, was the Independence Day orator in 1800, and the organizer of the Society for Free Debate (1798).

[127] James Cheetham, a recent English immigrant and a hatter by trade, became co-editor of *American Citizen* and *Republican Watch-Tower* (1801-ff), a leading pamphleteer and the first biographer of Thomas Paine (1809).

[128] Frank Norcross, *History of the New York Swamp* (New York, 1901), 8-11; Lee Benson, *The Concept of Jacksonian Democracy: New York as a Test Case* (Princeton, 1961); Walter Hugins, *Jacksonian Democracy and the Working Class: A Study of the New York Workingman's Movement, 1829-1837* (Stanford, 1960).

chanic support was as much the product of the courting by Republican politicians as it was of the demands of the labor movement.

Nor were Republicans put to the severe test of choosing between wage workers and master craftsmen in labor disputes. Republicans, it is apparent, were sympathetic to the craft organizations. They celebrated the Fourth with the Mechanics and Coopers Societies, pleaded the cause of the Association of Tallow Chandlers, and opposed the use of prison labor to manufacture shoes, an issue close to the hearts of cordwainers.[129] While there were a few strikes late in the decade, there was no trial of "a combination of labor" as "a criminal conspiracy" until 1809-10.[130]

Nonetheless Republican thought was unmistakably shaped by the party's mechanic constituency. There was, to be sure, a tinge of agrarianism to some Republicans: a glorification of the yeomanry among the upstate anti-Federalist leaders; an idealization of the rural virtues in the aristrocratic landholder Robert R. Livingston[131] (who signed his newspaper articles "Cato"); a contempt for the hateful city in the poet-editor, Philip Freneau.[132] But, understandably, Chancellor Livingston, who fearfully vetoed the Mechanics Society charter in 1785, praised the aggressive tallow chandlers in 1797 as "those respectable and useful citizens."[133] By the late 1790s, when Republican writers analyzed the political alignment of social classes, they found a place for mechanics in the Republican coalition. The concept might be that "farmers and mechanics & co" were the "laborers, men who produce by their industry something to the common stock of commodity" opposed by the unproductive classes,[134] or it might be that "farmers, merchants, mechanics and common laboring men" have a "common interest" against "the great landholders and monied men."[135] The General Society of Mechanics and Tradesmen, for its part, found a place for a picture of a plowman on its membership certificate side by side with a house

129 "A Shoemaker," *American Citizen*, Apr. 23, 1801; "To the Shoemakers," *Republican Watch-Tower*, Apr. 22, 1801; "A Shoemaker to the Journeymen Shoemakers," *ibid.* Apr. 25; Report of the Commissioners of the Prison, *Albany Register*, Mar. 3, 1801.
130 Richard Morris, "Criminal Conspiracy and Early Labor Combinations in New York," *Polit. Sci. Quart.*, LVII (1937), pp. 51-85.
131 Robert R. Livingston, "Address to the Agricultural Society of the State of New York," *New York Magazine*, VI (Feb., 1795), pp. 95-102.
132 Lewis Leary, *That Rascal Freneau. A Study in Literary Failure* (New Brunswick, N.J., 1941), pp. 260-65, 275.
133 Robert R. Livingston to Samuel L. Mitchill, July 18, 1797, Livingston Ms., N.Y. State Lib.; for the veto see note 16 above.
134 "To Farmers, Mechanics and other Industrious Citizens," *Time Piece*, May 14, 1798.
135 "Scrutator," *New York Journal*, Apr. 19, 1797.

carpenter and a shipwright, all beneath a slogan "By Hammer and Hand All Arts Do Stand."[136]

Perhaps the New York Republican leaders, who were neither agrarian-minded nor commercial-minded in the strict sense, will be best understood as spokesmen for productive capital. Three of the four merchant presidents of the Democratic Society, for example, invested in such productive ventures as a linen factory, a thread factory, a mine and spermaceti candle works.[137] Chancellor Livingston, who is well known for promoting the steamboat, also experimented with manufacturing paper and reducing friction in millstones. "Mechanicks is my hobby horse," he told Joseph Priestley.[138] He was the President and Samuel L. Mitchill the Secretary of the Society for the Promotion of Agriculture Arts and Manufactures. Mitchill was also a pioneer in industrial chemistry, and sympathized with the goal of protection for American manufactures. He congratulated Hamilton on his "Report on Manufactures" in 1792; as Republican chairman of the House Committee on Commerce and Manufactures, in 1804 he sponsored a tariff program.[139]

New York Republicans also took up the social reforms favored by their mechanic constituents. Tammany, for example, at one dinner toasted in succession "the speedy abolition" of slavery, "a happy melioration of our penal laws" and "the establishment of public schools."[140] William Keteltas, the hero of the ferrymen's *cause célèbre*—when incarcerated in the debtor's prison—edited a paper, *Prisoner of Hope*, which pleaded the debtor's plight.[141] Edward Livingston, in his first

---

136 Lamb, "The Career of a Beneficent Enterprise," *op. cit.;* a membership certificate is on exhibit at the General Society, New York City.
137 Henry Rutgers established a "bleach-field and thread manufactory" (*Daily Advertiser,* May 12, 1791); James Nicholson was chairman of the New York Manufacturing Society (*New York Directory for 1790*, p. 135) and was interested in a textile venture (Joseph Garlick to Nicholson, Mar. 15, 1798, Misc. Ms., Nicholson, N.Y. Hist. Soc.); Solomon Simpson had an interest in the New York Iron Manufacturing Company, was part owner of a lead mine and a founder of the American Minerological Society and co-owner of a spermaceti candle factory (Morris Schappes, "Anti-Semitism and Reaction, 1795-1800" *Pubs. of the American Jewish Hist. Soc.* XXVIII, Part 2 [Dec., 1948], 115-16).
138 Dangerfield, *op. cit.*, pp. 284-289.
139 Lyman C. Newall, "Samuel Latham Mitchill," *Dictionary of American Biography,* VII, pp. 69-70; Mitchill to Hamilton, Dec. 3, 1792, Hamilton Transcripts, Col. Univ. Lib.; Joseph Dorfman, *The Economic Mind in American Civilization, 1606-1865* (New York, 1946), I, pp. 324-25.
140 *New York Journal*, "Extraordinary" page, Dec. 6, 1794; for the Mechanics Society reform sentiment see "Minutes of the General Society" July 1, 1795.
141 *Forlorn Hope*, Mar. 24-Sept. 13, 1800; for a rival debtor's paper also edited by a Republican, see *Prisoner of Hope*, May 3-Aug. 23, 1800.

term in Congress, began the reform of the criminal code, a subject that would become a life-long concern.[142] Contrary to the contention of some historians, Republicans also lent active support to abolition.[143] Reform was bi-partisan and several measures came to fruition when John Hay was governor, but the urban Republicans imparted a warm humanitarianism to a frosty anti-Federalism and a crusading egalitarian flavor to the genteel philanthropic humanitarianism of the city's merchants and ministers. Equally important Republican orators instilled the environmentalist concepts of the enlightenment that justified a permanent program of reform.[144]

Neither mechanics nor Republicans made much of an issue of political reform, especially during George Clinton's long tenure as governor from 1777-95. The restrictive suffrage provisions in the state constitution and its unique Council of Appointment and Council of Revision were occasionally discussed but not widely protested.[145] Typically, when Tunis Wortman examined the question of abolishing the property qualification to vote, in his political treatise of 1800, the city's leading democratic theorist contented himself with summarizing the pros and cons and ended by saying the question was "not decided."[146] In 1801, when Republicans sponsored the first constitutional revision convention, they permitted universal male suffrage in the election of delegates, but restricted the convention itself to reforming the Council of Appointment.[147]

After 1801, their mechanic constituency cautiously beckoned the Republicans towards reform on the municipal level where only freeholders of £20 or more were permitted to vote for Aldermen and the Mayor was appointed. For a while Republicans were content to broaden suffrage in their own way. Wortman as county clerk was

---

[142] *Annals of Congress*, 4th Cong., 1st Sess., pp. 254-55, 257, 304-07, 1394.
[143] See Young, "Democratic Republican Movement," pp. 768-69.
[144] Tunis Wortman, *An Oration on the Influence of Social Institutions Upon Morals and Human Happiness . . . before the Tammany Society May 12, 1795* (New York, 1796); and DeWitt Clinton, *An Oration on Benevolence Delivered before the Society of Black Friars . . . November 10, 1794* (New York, 1795).
[145] I saw no signs of interest in suffrage reform in the Minutes of the Mechanics or Tammany, the toasts offered at their celebrations or in the expressions of the Democratic Society; for pro universal suffrage articles in *Time Piece:* "On Some of the Principles of American Republicanism," May 5, 1797; "Political Creed," Aug. 21, 1797; "Communication," Oct. 6, 1797; and "Universal Justice," Nov. 10, 1797.
[146] Tunis Wortman. *Treatise Concerning Political Enquiry and the Liberty of the Press* (New York, 1800), pp. 195-97.
[147] Jabez Hammond. *History of Political Parties in the State of New York* (2 vols., Cooperstown, 1846), I, ch. 6.

observed "running to the poll with the books of the Mayor's court under his arm, and with a troop of ragged aliens at his tail." He was also one of the organizers of "faggot voting," a process by which a group of propertyless Republicans were qualified to vote by the joint temporary purchase of a piece of real estate.[148] When the courts ruled out faggot voting, Republicans demanded that the voting qualifications be lowered at least to the 40 shilling leasehold requirement in Assembly elections; they also asked for the elimination of plural voting and voice voting and for the popular election of the Mayor.[149] By 1804 they won all but the last of these demands.[150]

It might be argued that Republicans did more within the framework of the existing political institutions to provide a greater place for mechanics. Like the old anti-Federalists, Republicans were generally distrustful of the wealthy. Unlike the anti-Federalists, who had confidence only in the yeomanry, Republicans included a role for mechanics among the *Means for the Preservation of Political Liberty*, as George Warner entitled his oration. The trouble, as this sailmaker put it, was that "tradesmen, mechanics, and the industrious classes of society consider themselves of too little consequence to the body politic."[151] Republicans defended the right of mechanics to scrutinize political affairs in "self-created" societies and to instruct their representatives at "town meetings." When Federalists mocked such pretensions, Republicans delighted in taunting them with their own epithets, signing their newspaper articles "one of the swinish multitude" or "only a mechanic and one of the rabble." Republicans also upheld the election of mechanics to public office against Federalist scoffers who "despise mechanics because they have not snored through four years at Princeton."[152]

The mechanic vote and viewpoint guaranteed that Republicans, in their political philosophy, would abandon the old anti-Federalist suspicion of the Constitution. For converts from Federalism like the Livingstons there was never any problem. Other Republicans straddled the constitutional question: Keteltas said he was "neither a Federal

---

[148] John Wood, *A Full Exposition of the Clintonian Faction* (Newark, 1802), 20-21; Pomerantz, *op. cit.*, pp. 208, 134.
[149] James Cheetham, *Dissertation Concerning Political Equality and the Corporation of New York* (New York, 1800).
[150] Pomerantz, *op. cit.*, 133-145; Chilton Williamson, *American Suffrage From Property to Democracy 1760-1860* (Princeton, 1960), pp. 161-64.
[151] George Warner. *Means for the Preservation of Public Liberty . . . delivered before the Mechanics, Tammany, Democratic and Coopers Societies, July 4, 1797* (New York, 1797), pp. 12-13.
[152] *Argus*, Apr. 8, 1799.

nor anti-Federal."[153] Wortman, however, was tempted to revert to the old anti-Federalist view, and to indict the Federalists of '98. He began to collect materials for a book that would expose "the secret convention of 1787 and its members . . . , [and the] intrigues and artifices made use of, for the purpose of compelling the adoption of the constitution." But the book that appeared in 1800—Wortman's *Treatise Concerning Political Inquiry and the Liberty of the Press*—was a libertarian disquisition devoted to the Constitution and Bill of Rights.[154] Republicans could hardly have done otherwise, for their mechanic supporters were men who had paraded for the Constitution in 1788 or had since migrated to the new democracy in order to seek its blessings. To George Warner, the sailmaker and soldier, "the same American spirit which animated to the contest the heroes of the Revolution" prevailed in directing the national convention of '87 to the constitutional establishment of the liberty we at this day enjoy."[155] Thus the city's Republicans, like the mechanics, were both nationalistic and democratic in their outlook.

And now to return to the question posed in the introduction as to the character and continuity of the political conflict between the years 1774 and 1801. Beyond any question, in the 1790s the mechanics were important in New York City politics. Charles Beard's observation that "neither the Republicans nor the Federalists seem to have paid much attention to capturing the vote of the mechanics" was based on inadequate evidence. In the effort to construct the party conflict as one of "agrarianism" vs "capitalism," Beard did not allow a sufficient place for the mechanics to whom even Jefferson referred sympathetically as "the yeomanry of the city."[156] Carl Becker's projection of the conflict of the 1760s into the 1790s was misleading in another way.

---

[153] "A Dialogue Between 1776 and 1796," *New York Journal*, Jan. 29, 1796.
[154] Tunis Wortman to Albert Gallatin, Feb. 12, 1798, Gallatin Papers, N.Y. Hist Soc. For the book see Leonard Levy, *Legacy of Suppression, Freedom of Speech and Press in Early American History.* (Cambridge, Mass., 1960), pp. 283-89.
[155] Warner, *Means for the Preservation*, pp. 9, 19; in the same pro-constitution vein see Samuel L. Mitchill, *An Address . . . July 4, 1799* (New York, 1800), pp. 7, 20; Matthew L. Davis, *An Oration . . . July 4, 1800* (New York, 1800), 15; for a hint of the old anti-Federalist attitude, George Eacker, *An Oration . . . July 4, 1801* (New York, 1801), pp. 10-11, all delivered before the several societies.
[156] Beard, *op. cit.*, p. 466; Jefferson to Thomas Mann Randolph, May 6, 1793, Paul L. Ford, ed., *The Writings of Thomas Jefferson* (10 vols., New York, 1892-1899), VI, p. 241.

The implication of the continuity of mechanic allegiances—radical Whig to anti-Federalist to Jeffersonian—is insupportable. Mechanics who clearly were Federalist in 1788 remained safely Federalist until 1794 and the substantial mechanics a good deal longer, many of them through 1801 and beyond. Mechanics did not always behave as one unified class in politics. Nor can the Republicans be understood as a mechanic party if that was Becker's implication.

And yet Becker's thesis remains attractive. There was an intense struggle in New York City in the 1790s for "who shall rule at home," and if not strictly a class conflict, within it were the elements of a clash between "the privileged and the unprivileged" involving the mechanics as Becker suggested. The plot, dialogue and even character types of the 1790s bear a striking resemblance to the drama of the pre-Revolutionary era. Once again the battle cry that stirred the mechanics was British policy, the cause was American Independence, and the ideology was patriotism or "the spirit of '76." Other insistent mechanic demands thread through the last three decades of the century: for democratic participation, for social recognition, for protection for American manufactures. The new leaders of the 1790s, the Livingtsons, resumed something of their pre-war position as aristocratic republicans at the head of the "popular party." The new mechanics' hero of the late 1790s, William Keteltas, was Alexander McDougall of 1769 all over again, a second "John Wilkes of America." The methods, too, were similar: the town meetings, the popular political societies, the churning printing presses. The symbolism of the July Fourth celebration perhaps completes the picture. Thus Jeffersonian Republicans of New York City, with due allowance for the rhetoric of politics, could claim that they were heirs to the "spirit of '76" and that the "revolution of 1800" was indeed the consummation of the Revolution of 1776.

162

PROPERTY QUALIFICATIONS AND VOTING BEHAVIOR IN NEW YORK, 1807-1816

Harvey Strum

Historians David H. Fischer, J. R. Pole, and Richard P. McCormick have argued that the growth of democracy in the United States began before the Jacksonian period. Studies by McCormick and Pole revealed a sudden expansion of voter participation between 1800 and 1816, and Fischer has labeled the period "America's age of Democratic revolution." This brief analysis, concentrating on New York during the latter half of the period designated, reinforces the view that there was a growing democratization of politics at this time. Changes in political structure, both formal and informal, also contributed to a decline in deferential politics.[1]

Studying the period of 1807-1816 provides an opportunity to compare the New York gubernatorial election of 1807, when two

---

Mr. Strum is a member of the Department of History at Syracuse University.

[1] David H. Fischer, *The Revolution of American Conservatism: The Federalist Party in the Era of Jeffersonian Democracy* (New York 1965), 187-192 (the quotation is at 191); J. R. Pole, "Suffrage and Representation in Massachusetts: A Statistical Note," *William and Mary Quarterly*, 3d Series, 14 (Oct. 1957), 560-592, and 15 (July 1958), 412-416; J. R. Pole, "Suffrage and Representation In Maryland from 1776 to 1810: A Statistical Note and Some Reflections," *Journal of Southern History*, 24 (May 1958), 218-225; J. R. Pole, "The Suffrage in New Jersey, 1770-1807," *Proceedings of the New Jersey Historical Society*, 71 (Jan. 1953), 39-61; Richard P. McCormick, "Suffrage Classes and Party Alignments: A Study in Voter Behavior," *Mississippi Valley Historical Review*, 46 (Dec. 1959), 397-410; Richard P. McCormick, *The History of Voting in New Jersey* (New Brunswick 1953). For the growth of democracy in New York see Dixon Ryan Fox, *The Decline of Aristocracy in the Politics of New York* (New York 1919); Jabez D. Hammond, *The History of Political Parties in the State of New York* . . . (2 vols., Albany 1842); Alvin Kass, *Politics in New York State, 1800-1830* (Syracuse 1965); Alfred Young, *The Democractic Republicans of New York: The Origins, 1763-1797* (Chapel Hill, N.C. 1967).

JOURNAL OF THE EARLY REPUBLIC, 1 (Winter 1981). ©1981 Society for Historians of the Early American Republic.

factions of the Republican party fought for dominance, with events between 1808 and 1816 when the Federalists reemerged as a major threat to continued Republican control of New York. Possibly the resurgence of Federalism and renewed Republican-Federalist conflict, Fischer has hypothesized, "served to stimulate an expansion of popular participation." When applied to New York, however, Fischer's thesis needs a major qualification — well organized factions of the Republican party, as was demonstrated in the 1807 election, could generate as much political participation as Federalist-Republican rivalry. New York's warring Republican factions proved quite adept in mobilizing voters.[2]

During 1807 Daniel Tompkins emerged as a major figure in New York politics. Elected governor in 1807 and reelected three times (1810, 1813, and 1816), Tompkins demonstrated the importance of appearing as one of the people before the Age of Jackson and the Log Cabin and Hard Cider campaign of 1840. Campaigning as the "Farmer's Boy," Tompkins symbolized the growing democratization of New York political life because he was a candidate "without personal wealth or important family connections."[3]

The competition by Federalists and Republican factions encouraged the democratization of New York politics by mobilizing voters and by producing a de facto liberalization of New York's restrictive electoral laws. Under the 1777 constitution of New York and the 1801 Act for Regulating Elections, only men possessed of freeholds worth at least $250 could vote for governor, lieutenant governor, and state senator. Men owning a freehold worth $50 but less than $250 or renting tenements for $5 per year could vote for assemblymen and congressmen.

Both Federalists and Republicans proved willing to ignore the state's laws and allow voters eligible to vote only for the assembly and Congress to vote for governor. In their competition for votes, Federalists and Republicans made voting fraud an integral part of New York politics and illegally expanded the electorate. Any lingering commitment to a deferential society disappeared as both

---

[2] Fischer, *American Conservatism*, xv. For another modification of Fischer's thesis see James H. Robbins, "Voting Behavior in Massachusetts, 1800-1820: A Case Study" (Ph.D. diss., Northwestern University 1970), 129.

[3] Ray W. Irwin, *Daniel D. Tompkins* (Kingsport, Tenn. 1968), 56; Alexander C. Flick, ed., *History of the State of New York* (10 vols., New York 1933-1937), VI, 47.

parties mobilized and competed for popular support. Republican and Federalist campaign appeals and the widespread evasion of the electoral laws weakened the deferential society from above, while anti-landlord agitation and petitions by the disenfranchised to legally broaden the franchise undermined from below.[4]

In 1801 the Federalists lost control of both houses of the state legislature and the gubernatorial office. The party went into a rapid political decline, and by 1806 it held no seats in the state senate, only two of seventeen congressional seats, just nineteen of one hundred and twelve assembly seats, and it did not bother to offer a candidate in the 1804 gubernatorial contest. With the Federalists defeated and no longer a threat, the Republicans split into warring factions. George Clinton, his nephew De Witt Clinton, and the younger Clinton's brother-in-law, Ambrose Spencer, led one faction while Robert R. Livingston, his brother-in-law Morgan Lewis, and Brockholst Livingston led the Livingstonians. Aaron Burr emerged as chief of a third faction, the Burrites.

The Clintonians joined with the Livingstonians to isolate Burr and deny his followers any share of the political offices controlled by the Republicans. When George Clinton retired from the governorship in 1804 to become vice president, the Clintonian-Livingstonian coalition chose Morgan Lewis as their gubernatorial candidate. Trying to break out of his political isolation, Burr challenged Lewis. The remnant of the Federalists split. While the majority backed Burr, a minority of Federalists led by Alexander Hamilton refused to support Burr.[5]

By accepting Federalist support, Burr alienated most rank and file Republicans, and the vast majority of Republicans voted for

---

[4] For studies of voting behavior and property qualifications besides those listed above see Robert E. Brown, *Middle-Class Democracy and the Revolution in Massachusetts, 1691-1780* (Ithaca 1955); Jackson Turner Main, *The Social Structure of Revolutionary America* (Princeton 1965); Chilton Williamson, *American Suffrage: From Property to Democracy, 1760-1860* (Princeton 1960); Kirk H. Porter, *A History of Suffrage in the United States* (Chicago 1918); Marchette Chute, *The First Liberty: History of the Right to Vote in America, 1619-1850* (New York 1969). For a different analysis of deference see Ronald P. Formisano, "Deferential-Participant Politics: The Early Republic's Political Culture, 1789-1840," *American Political Science Review*, 68 (June 1974), 473-487.

[5] For a detailed analysis of the internecine Republican warfare between 1801-1816, see Hammond, *Political Parties*, I, 164-402.

Lewis. Burr's defeat and his subsequent slaying of Hamilton re-moved Burr as a force in New York politics. With Burr gone, the Clintonians and Livingstonians began to fight for control of the Republican party and the state's patronage. By forming a coalition with the Federalists, the Livingstonians obtained a majority in the assembly.

Controlling a majority in the assembly was crucial to obtain-ing control of the state's patronage. From 1777 to 1821, the as-sembly annually elected one senator from each of the state's four senatorial districts to the Council of Appointment. The four senators and the governor formed the council and it had the power to appoint sherriffs, mayors of cities, and almost all other state and county officers — the major source of patronage and political power.

Once the Livingstonians controlled the Council of Appoint-ment they immediately ousted the Clintonians from state, county, and municipal offices. Angered at his removal as mayor of New York City, De Witt Clinton and his backers challenged Lewis for reelection by nominating Daniel Tompkins. In an effort to counter the Livingstonian-Federalist alliance, the Clintonians formed a coalition with some of the former Burrites in 1806. Other Burrite leaders, however, refused to join with Clintonians. At a meeting at Abraham Martling's tavern in New York City, the dissident Burrites joined with the Livingstonians and other anti-Clinton Republicans to form the Martling Men. Since many of them be-longed to the Tammany Society the two groups soon became syn-onymous. Determined to destroy the Clintonians and especially De Witt Clinton, the Martling Men repeatedly challenged the Clintonians for control of the New York City Republican party.

Against this backdrop of intense Republican party fac-tionalism the 1807 gubernatorial campaign took place. During the campaign the Clintonians portrayed Tompkins as a simple "Farmer's Boy" running against Morgan Lewis, an in-law of the aristocratic Livingstons. Tompkins garnered 53 percent of the vote and defeated Lewis. About 93 percent of the voters went to the polls compared to 88 percent in 1801 when the Federalists fielded a gubernatorial candidate. Surviving records indicate high voter turnout in the legislative races with New York City reporting 75 percent, Kings County 80 percent, Oneida County 78 percent,

Ulster County 82 percent, and Columbia County 90 percent.[6]

The defeat of Lewis, combined with the victory of Clintonians in most of the assembly races, left the Clintonians in total control of the Republican party and the state. Almost immediately, the Clintonians removed all of the Livingstonians from public office. Clintonian control, however, proved short-lived. Anger at the imposition of the embargo led many New York farmers to vote Federalist. In 1808, 80 percent participated in the state senate election and 67 percent in the congressional contests. While the Clintonians retained control the Federalists doubled the number of assembly seats they held from twenty-four to forty-seven. With the Embargo Act still an issue, voter turnout rose by 28 percent in 1809 as the assembly went Federalist for the first time since 1799. Key counties that switched from Republican to Federalist reported significant increases in voter participation. Otsego's rate jumped 44 percent and Ontario's 20 percent. Even counties that remained Republican reported sharp voting increases as the Republicans mobilized the party faithful in an unsuccessful effort to prevent a Federalist victory.[7]

The Federalists removed virtually every Republican from appointed state office, and this loss of patronage provided the catalyst for a temporary unification of the warring Republicans. During the campaign Republicans portrayed the Federalist gubernatorial candidate, Jonas Platt, as antidemocratic and an advocate of views suited to courtiers abroad but not to Americans. Tompkins defeated Platt and the Republicans won about two thirds of the assembly seats and twelve of the seventeen congressional seats. Approximately 90 percent of the gubernatorial voters went to the polls and 70 percent of the electorate voted in the congressional contests. Voter turnout in the gubernatorial race increased 9 percent over the 1809 state senate races and 20 percent

---

[6] The election returns information is from New York Gubernatorial Returns, 1807, Consortium for Political Research (University of Michigan, Ann Arbor), hereafter cited as CPR; Hudson *Balance*, May-June 1807; New York *American Citizen*, May 1807; and New York *Evening Post*, May 1807.

[7] *Ibid.*, May 1808; New York Congressional Returns, 1808, CPR. The CPR returns contained results for counties; town tallies were taken from the press: Albany *Balance*, May 12, 1809, and Hudson *Bee*, May 2, 1809.

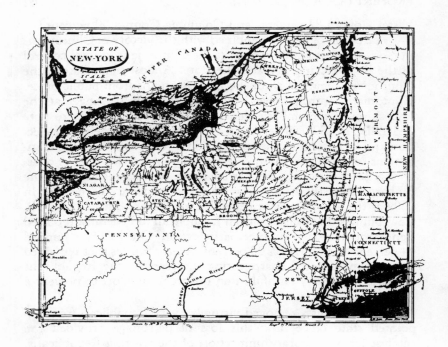

New York Counties, 1813

From Horatio Gates Spafford, *A Gazetteer of the State of New York* (Albany 1813).
Courtesy of the author.

over the 1807 gubernatorial race. During the 1810 election the
Republicans benefited from higher voter participation.[8]

With the Federalists defeated, the Republicans again split over
control of the party and the state's patronage. In 1811 a three way
race developed for lieutenant governor between Federalist
Nicholas Fish, Republican De Witt Clinton, and Marinus Willett,
the candidate of the Tammany-Livingstonian coalition. In an
effort to obtain the support of President James Madison, the Tammany-Livingstonian coalition described itself as Madisonian.
Morgan Lewis tried to persuade the president to back the anti-

---

[8] Hudson *Bee*, January-May 1810; New York *Columbian*, January-May 1810;
New York *Public Advertiser*, January-May 1810; Cooperstown *Otsego-Herald*, January-May 1810.

Clinton forces and remove all Clintonians from federal patronage positions. The Tammany-Livingstonian plan to obtain presidential support and discredit Clinton with Republican voters failed. Clinton won and Willett received only 5 percent of the vote. About 65,000 voters cast ballots for lieutenant governor, a drop of 14,500 votes from 1810. Divisions in party ranks did not threaten Republican control of the assembly, and they retained two thirds of the seats.[9]

With the threat of war and a new embargo, foreign policy dominated the 1812 assembly elections, and the Federalists won control of the legislature. Voter turnout among gubernatorial-senatorial voters remained about the same as in 1811, but voter participation increased by 13 percent in the counties of northern and western New York as citizens came out to protest against the new embargo. During special congressional elections in December 1812 the war was the major issue. Federalists won nineteen of twenty-seven seats in spite of Republican gerrymandering, and for the first time since the 1792 elections the Federalists won a majority of the state's congressional seats. Prior to the election Clinton had tried to form an alliance with the Federalists, but it fell apart outside of New York City. Between 63 and 65 percent of the voters cast ballots, a drop of 15,000 from 1810.[10]

In the spring of 1813 Governor Tompkins ran for a third term against Federalist Stephen Van Rensselaer. Tompkins and Ambrose Spencer joined with other anti-Clintonians to drop Clinton from the ticket. A year before, Tompkins and Spencer had broken with Clinton because of his ambiguous position on the state charter of the Bank of America. Clinton had refused to join Spencer and Tompkins in condemning the state charter because some of the men who backed Clinton for president favored the charter. Therefore, while a majority of the state's Republican legislators endorsed Clinton's presidential bid, Tompkins and Spencer supported Madison. In addition, Clinton's flirtation with the Federalists and his ambiguous position on the war angered Tompkins and Spencer, who engineered his removal from the

---

[9] Morgan Lewis to James Madison, May 12, 1811, Reel 13, James Madison Papers (Library of Congress); Albany *Balance*, June 18, 1811; Hudson *Bee*, May 10, 1811; New York *Spectator*, May-June 1811.

[10] New York Congressional Returns, 1812, CPR; New York *Evening Post*, December 1812; New York *Columbian*, December 1812.

ticket. In retaliation, Clinton tried to sabotage Tompkins' reelection, but his plan backfired and most of his followers deserted him. As in 1807 with Lewis and 1804 with Burr, whenever a Republican leader appeared to be openly flirting with the Federalists, the majority of Republicans abandoned that leader.[11]

During the campaign Republicans reminded voters that Tompkins was a man of modest means and a friend of the poor while Van Rensselaer was a landowner with seven thousand tenants. A Republican editor described Van Rensselaer's tenants as "subject to . . . more than Egyptian bondage," and Republican campaigners warned that the election of Van Rensselaer was "a direct and sure means of creating a dangerous aristocracy." The May 1813 voter turnout jumped from 67,500 to 83,000 (23%) over that of May 1812, as about 95 percent of the electorate went to the polls to give Tompkins a third term. Returns available for the assembly races indicate that there too voters flocked to the polls. Most counties reported returns in the 72-80 percentile, a significant rise over 1812. In the assembly races, however, the Federalists managed to retain their majority in spite of Tompkins' victory.[12]

In late December 1813, the British burned Buffalo and neighboring settlements, and the following spring the embargo on trade was removed. These two events enabled the Republicans to win two thirds of the assembly seats and twenty-one of twenty-seven congressional seats in the 1814 spring election. Two Clintonian Republican leaders, Solomon Southwick and Philip Van Cortlandt, ran for the state senate and Congress, respectively. Both lost, once again demonstrating that rank and file Republicans would not vote for Republicans tainted with Federalism. A small group of pro-war Federalists, known as the Coodies, split off in 1814 and ran a separate assembly slate in New York City, but it won only 0.8 percent of the vote. About 85 percent of the senatorial-gubernatorial voters cast ballots and about 73 percent of the electorate voted for congressional and state assembly candidates.[13]

---

[11] Buffalo *Gazette*, April 27, 1813.

[12] Albany *Argus*, April 16, 1813. See also New York *Columbian*, March-May 1813; Cherry Valley *Otsego Republican Press*, March 26, 1813; Hudson *Bee*, March-May 1813; Gubernatorial Returns, 1813, CPR.

[13] New York *Evening Post*, May 1814; New York Congressional Returns, 1814, CPR; New York *Columbian*, May 1814.

Even though the war ended before the 1815 spring election, it emerged as the major issue. Federalists picked up twenty-two assembly seats to equal the Republican total of sixty-three. The Republicans, however, under rather dubious circumstances, disqualified one of the Federalists to obtain a 64-62 majority. About 85 percent of the senatorial voters participated in the election and 73 percent of the total electorate voted for assemblymen. In 1816 Tompkins defeated Federalist Rufus King for governor, as approximately 95 percent of the gubernatorial voters went to the polls. About 82 percent of New York voters took part in the legislative races with the Republicans winning two thirds of the seats.[14]

Gubernatorial contests brought out the most voters as suggested by the voter peaks in 1807, 1810, 1813, and 1816. High voter participation in New York gubernatorial races fits in with the pattern evident throughout the nation during the first two decades of the nineteenth century. New York also had relatively high voting percentages in the legislative races. This evidence confirms work done by Pole and McCormick for other states, but suggests a modification of Fischer's emphasis on Federalist-Republican rivalry. A spirited contest between two well organized Republican factions in 1807 proved as effective in drawing voters as the direct Federalist-Republican rivalry.[15]

Issues, party organization, and factional and interparty rivalry all contributed to voter participation. Of the foreign policy issues arising out of the Anglo-American confrontation the embargo had the most impact on bringing out voters. Occasionally, local issues also mobilized the electorate. In 1808, for example, when residents of Bethel, in Sullivan County, met to decide upon separation from Lumberland, "not a stone was left unturned. Every one voted who had the legal right to do so, and some who had no right." Moreover, an analysis of the voting behavior of lower income New Yorkers eligible to participate only in legislative elections suggests that they had a lower rate of turnout than the higher income gubernatorial voters. With the exception of New York City, where

---

[14] New York Congressional Returns, 1816, Gubernatorial Returns, 1816, CPR; New York *Evening Post*, May 1815, 1816; New York *Commercial Advertiser*, May 1815, 1816.

[15] For a detailed analysis of New York voting patterns and election tables between 1807-1815, see Harvey Strum, "New York and the War of 1812" (Ph.D. diss., Syracuse University 1978).

TABLE I
Electoral Censuses of 1807 and 1814[1]

County	1807 Gubernatorial[2] Voters	1807 Assem.-Congress. Voters $50 Freeholders	1807 Tenants	1814 Gubernatorial Freeholders $250 or more	1814 Freeholders' Less than $250 but over $50	1814 Tenants over $5/year
Albany	3,745(62%)	178(3%)	2,156(35%)	3,069(56%)	106(2%)	2,301(42%)
Allegany	66(19%)	—	278(81%)	135(22%)	11(2%)	473(76%)
Broome	583(54%)	78(9%)	487(37%)	917(60%)	34(5%)	528(35%)
Cayuga	2,236(61%)	338(9%)	1,123(30%)	3,180(58%)	286(5%)	2,060(37%)
Chautauqua	—	—	—	430(67%)	115(18%)	95(15%)
Chenango	1,570(57%)	333(12%)	841(31%)	1,961(52%)	140(4%)	1,651(44%)
Clinton	688(51%)	87(6%)	583(43%)	635(50%)	28(2%)	620(48%)
Columbia	2,968(66%)	91(2%)	1,466(32%)	3,232(61%)	119(2%)	1,966(37%)
Cortland	—	—	—	1,042(68%)	122(8%)	376(24%)
Delaware	1,498(61%)	160(6%)	806(33%)	1,928(62%)	181(6%)	1,018(33%)
Dutchess	4,191(62%)	179(3%)	2,382(35%)	3,783(57%)	151(2%)	2,751(41%)
Essex	517(42%)	214(17%)	510(41%)	621(40%)	71(4%)	874(56%)
Franklin	—	—	—	183(40%)	17(4%)	252(56%)
Genesee	477(24%)	128(6%)	1,318(70%)	745(19%)	43(1%)	3,197(80%)
Greene	1,643(67%)	101(4%)	711(29%)	1,867(65%)	69(3%)	925(32%)
Herkimer	1,722(58%)	55(2%)	1,197(40%)	2,020(59%)	71(2%)	1,347(39%)
Jefferson	835(42%)	219(12%)	914(46%)	1,039(37%)	107(4%)	1,641(59%)
Kings	584(58%)	5(1%)	408(41%)	695(57%)	23(2%)	507(41%)
Lewis	574(52%)	72(7%)	450(41%)	614(52%)	71(4%)	499(42%)
Madison	2,220(74%)	246(8%)	521(18%)	2,508(63%)	126(3%)	1,378(34%)
Montgomery	3,512(67%)	220(4%)	1,484(29%)	4,166(64%)	163(3%)	2,108(33%)
New York	3,000(24%)	20(1%)	9,334(75%)	3,141(22.5%)	17(0.5%)	10,763(77%)
Niagara	—	—	—	418(29%)	78(5%)	955(5%)
Oneida	3,501(64%)	357(7%)	1,550(29%)	4,088(60%)	304(4%)	2,524(36%)
Onondaga	2,331(65%)	227(4%)	1,134(31%)	2,748(59%)	201(4%)	1,729(37%)
Ontario	2,806(57%)	297(6%)	1,786(37%)	4,499(50%)	312(3%)	4,285(47%)
Orange	2,583(68%)	123(3%)	1,109(29%)	3,081(61%)	1,521(3%)	1,787(36%)
Otsego	3,254(67%)	378(8%)	1,228(25%)	3,746(59%)	151(2%)	2,505(39%)
Putnam	—	—	—	857(57%)	43(3%)	599(40%)
Queens	1,891(69%)	178(7%)	638(24%)	2,065(64%)	153(5%)	922(31%)
Rensselaer	3,103(66%)	123(3%)	1,502(33%)	3,426(58%)	136(2%)	2,362(40%)
Richmond	513(72%)	45(6%)	153(22%)	584(71%)	41(5%)	199(24%)
Rockland	766(78%)	65(7%)	153(15%)	838(73%)	63(6%)	245(21%)
St. Lawrence	616(72%)	151(17%)	93(11%)	880(60%)	175(12%)	401(28%)
Saratoga	2,997(68%)	139(3%)	1,290(29%)	3,275(64%)	87(2%)	1,758(34%)
Schenectady	—	—	—	1,043(57%)	51(2%)	751(41%)
Schoharie	1,468(64%)	146(6%)	783(33%)	1,850(57%)	185(6%)	1,209(37%)
Seneca	912(57%)	110(7%)	582(36%)	1,768(54%)	151(5%)	1,351(41%)
Steuben	250(27%)	23(3%)	647(70%)	588(32%)	46(2%)	1,247(66%)
Suffolk	2,610(80%)	142(4%)	507(16%)	2,898(78%)	168(5%)	643(17%)
Sullivan	—	—	—	643(62%)	23(2%)	381(36%)
Tioga	485(44%)	39(4%)	565(52%)	702(44%)	45(3%)	842(53%)
Ulster	2,498(65%)	253(7%)	1,100(28%)	2,727(65%)	239(6%)	1,223(29%)
Warren	—	—	—	699(53%)	58(4%)	564(43%)
Washington	3,289(65%)	164(3%)	1,585(32%)	3,434(63%)	111(2%)	1,942(35%)
Westchester	2,657(72%)	96(3%)	906(25%)	2,773(65%)	137(3%)	1,380(32%)
Total	71,159(58.7%)	5,800(4.8%)	44,330(36.5%)	87,541(58%)	5,231(3%)	59,104(39%)[4]

[1] Source: *Journal of the Assembly of the State of New York, 1808* (Albany 1808), unpaginated lists of returns between 181 and 182; *ibid., 1814* (Albany 1815), 233-273, 503.
[2] Men possessing freeholds worth $250 or more.
[3] Men possessing freeholds worth between $50-249 or voters renting tenements for at least $5 a year.
[4] Total includes 26 electors in Albany and 62 in New York entitled to vote for the assembly because they were freemen in 1777.

the Republicans usually ran better among the citizens eligible to vote only for assemblymen and congressmen, there was on the whole little difference in the voting behavior between gubernatorial and legislative voters.[16]

Surprisingly, New York's property qualifications for voting based upon freeholds under the 1777 constitution and an 1801 act of the legislature proved most restrictive on the western frontier, in parts of northern New York between Lake Champlain and Lake Ontario, and in New York City — not in the landlord dominated counties of the upper Hudson Valley. Most frontier settlers in western New York rented their land, which disqualified them from legally voting for governor. In 1795, when Ontario County included all of New York west of Seneca Lake, 83 percent of the county's voters qualified to vote for governor. By 1814, this had dropped to 50 percent in Ontario, 29 percent in Niagara, 22 percent in Allegany, 19 percent in Genesee, 44 percent in Tioga, and 32 percent in Steuben County. In the north country, the property qualifications had their most restrictive impact in Jefferson, Essex, and Franklin counties (37, 40, and 40 percent, respectively). Thirty-two percent of New York City voters could legally cast ballots in the 1795 gubernatorial election. By 1814, only 22.5 percent qualified. At the termination of the War of 1812, 16, 9, 7, and 13 percent, respectively, of the voters in the fifth, sixth, seventh, and tenth wards could participate in gubernatorial elections. These wards had the highest concentrations of urban poor and, consequently, the lowest percentage of gubernatorial voters. By comparison, 61 to 66 percent of the electorate qualified to vote for governor in the landlord dominated counties of the upper Hudson Valley.[17]

Property qualifications disenfranchised young men, mechanics, and laborers without families. In 1811, Rensselaer

---

[16] James Eldridge Quinlan, *History of Sullivan County* [New York] ... (Liberty, N.Y. 1873), 232-237; McCormick, "Suffrage Classes," 408, also concluded that there was little difference in voting behavior between the two groups of electors.

[17] These data were derived from the 1807 and 1814 New York electoral censuses. *Journal of the Assembly of the State of New York, 1808* (Albany 1808), 181-182; *Journal of the Assembly of the State of New York, 1815* (Albany 1815), 233-273, 503; Franklin B. Hough, ed., *Census of the State of New York, for 1855* ... (Albany 1857), ix-x, xli-xliii, plate III.

County Republicans denounced the restrictive impact of property qualifications because it prevented from one fifth to one fourth of the free citizens over twenty-one from voting. Historian Chilton Williamson has estimated that 78 percent of the adult white males could vote in 1821, but Richard P. McCormick has suggested, in the figures presented below, that between 1801 and 1821 property qualifications excluded about one third of the adult white males over twenty-one from voting:

Year	Adult White Males (AWM)	Total Electors	Percent of AWM	$250 Electors	Percent of AWM	Other Electors	Percent of AWM
1801	125,000	85,907	68.7	52,058	41.6	33,849	27.1
1807	170,000	121,289	71.3	71,159	41.8	50,130	29.5
1814	239,000	151,846	63.5	87,491	36.6	64,355	26.9
1821	299,500	202,510	67.6	100,490	33.5	102,020	34.1

Additional data compiled by this author from the 1814 electoral census and presented in Table I compare the gubernatorial voters and the total electorate with the white male population over eighteen. Statewide, 39 percent of the males over eighteen could vote for governor and 67 percent could vote for the assembly and Congress.[18]

Efforts at franchise reform began in the 1790s when several Republican legislators recommended extension of the franchise, but the legislature refused to change the electoral laws. Hoping to end Federalist control of the New York City Common Council, Republicans urged the state legislature to lower the property qualification for voting in New York municipal elections. Over objections raised by the Council of Revision, the assembly did so. Republicans in the senate, however, refused to agree with their colleagues and lower the property qualification from $50 to $5; instead they compromised by lowering it to $25 in 1804.[19]

---

[18] Williamson, *American Suffrage*, 197; McCormick, "Suffrage Classes," table IV, 405. The 1814 electoral census included data on the number of males over 18, but did not provide data for those over 21. Contemporary accounts of the extent of disenfranchisement may be found in the files of Ontario County Republicans, February 6, 1812, Assembly Papers (New York State Library, Albany), and Hoosick Republicans, February 12, 1811, Hoosick MSS (New-York Historical Society, New York, N.Y.).

[19] The Council of Revision, consisting of the state's supreme court judges, the chancellor, and the governor, ruled on the constitutionality of the state laws.

The reluctance of many Republicans to alter existing property qualifications continued to prevent additional franchise reform. In 1811, Rensselaer County Republicans called for the elimination of all property qualifications. Raising the Revolutionary War argument of no taxation without representation, Rensselaer Republicans asked if all free citizens shall have the right to vote "or be circumscribed by the qualifications of property."[20] The following year a convention of Republican delegates from the towns of Ontario County petitioned the legislature to enlarge the franchise. The delegates complained that men "who pay taxes and who are compelled to serve in the militia" could not vote. Ontario Republicans desired an extension of the franchise to include all males over twenty-one and elimination of the distinction between gubernatorial and assembly-congressional voters. "Your petitioners cannot believe," they argued, "that property is . . . any proof of superior virtue, discernment or patriotism."[21]

A dozen Republicans, nevertheless, joined with the minority Federalists in 1811 to table the call for a constitutional convention to amend the state's electoral laws. While the Republican party controlled the assembly with a two to one majority, it refused to endorse and support an extension of the franchise. During the first party system, therefore, neither Federalists nor Republicans favored franchise extension. Their positions on enlarging the franchise or restricting it depended on which party or Republican faction would gain or lose politically by the particular law.[22]

It could disallow any bill, but had to act within ten days of receiving it. The legislature could override with a two thirds vote. For information on efforts to reform the franchise see Williamson, *American Suffrage*, 121, 124, 162-163. For details on the 1804 extension of the New York City franchise see Minutes of the Council of Revision, April 4, 1804, 308-309, Reel 9, Executive Records, Early State Records (New York State Archives, Albany); New York *Morning Chronicle*, December 27-28, 1802; New York *American Citizen*, December 27, 1802-January 4, 1803; January-February, November 1804; New York *Commercial Advertiser*, February 1, 1804; New York *Evening Post*, April 10, 1804; and "Burghers and Freemen of New York," *Collections of the New-York Historical Society* (New York 1885), XVIII, 297-365.

[20] Hoosick Republicans, February 12, 1811, Hoosick MSS. See also Canandaigua *Ontario Messenger*, March 5, 1811; Salem *Washington Register*, April 11, 1811.

[21] Ontario County Republicans, February 6, 1812, Assembly Papers.

[22] Norwich *Chenango Weekly Advertiser*, March 1811.

Instead of enlarging the franchise, the Republicans tried to restrict it by attempting to neutralize the pro-Federalist free black vote. Over the objections of Federalists in the Council of Revision the legislature in 1811 passed a law requiring all free blacks to carry certificates proving their freedom in order to vote. Four years later, again over objections from Federalists on the Council of Revision, the Republican majority upheld a new law requiring registration of free blacks and requiring free blacks to produce the registration to vote. The cost involved amounted to an indirect poll tax. To no avail free blacks staged public protests against the curtailment of their voting rights. The hostility within the Republican party to free blacks emerged during the 1821 convention to revise the state constitution. While the property requirement for whites was reduced to a taxpaying requirement the Republicans ignored Federalist protests and required blacks to have a $250 freehold to vote.[23]

During the first party system a form of franchise extension did exist — voting fraud. Enlarging the franchise by fraud permitted political leaders to retain a greater degree of control over the voters than merely extending the franchise would allow. Political leaders enlarged the franchise by illegally speeding the naturalization process of immigrants, permitting aliens with borrowed naturalization certificates to vote, and allowing voters legally eligible to participate only in assembly and congressional elections to vote for governor and state senator. Another method involved fagot holdings. A wealthy landowner or politician temporarily assigned deeds to enough land to tenants or poorer partisans to permit them to vote. In 1800, Daniel Tompkins joined with thirty other Republicans to purchase a house on the tontine plan so that all could vote.[24]

The Federalists were especially upset at the Republicans for al-

---

[23] Albany *Balance*, April 9, 1811; Salem *Washington Register*, April 18, 1811; Hudson *Bee*, April 26, 1811; New York *Evening Post*, April 15, 1811; New York *Examiner*, April 26, 1815; New York *Gazette*, April 15, 20, 1815; Minutes of the Council of Revision, April 5, 1811, 206-208, March 29, 1813, 20-22; Dixon Ryan Fox, "The Negro Vote in Old New York," *Political Science Quarterly*, 32 (June 1917), 252-275; Williamson, *American Suffrage*, 278; Hammond *Political Parties*, II, 18, 21.

[24] Dixon Ryan Fox, *Aristocracy*, 144; [Joseph A. Scoville], *The Old Merchants of New York* (6 vols., New York 1863), I, 281; Gustavus Myers, *The History of Tammany Hall* (New York 1901), 17-18; Williamson, *American Suffrage*, 159-161; Irwin, *Tompkins*, 44.

lowing the immigrant Irish to vote illegally. During the debate on lowering the property qualifications for municipal elections Federalists expressed the fear that Common Council members would henceforth be "chosen by all such 'unhappy fugitives from distress arriving in this land' " who could rent a tenement for $25 a year. When the Federalists lost the 1807 assembly election they blamed their defeat upon *"the votes of foreigners."* New York *Evening Post* editor William Coleman believed the Irish produced 60 percent of the Republican vote in the city. Lax enforcement of the naturalization laws by Republican election inspectors and judges allowed Irish immigrants to qualify for citizenship in "half the time" the law required. Both Republicans and Federalists agreed that New York City courts naturalized approximately two thousand Irish immigrants between January and May 1807.[25]

Questioning the integrity of these new citizens, Coleman claimed the Irish "did not know a ballot box from a bank bill." Federalists charged that the Republicans permitted the illegal voting of aliens, speeded the naturalization process, bought votes, and created phony freeholds in upstate New York. After the 1810 election Federalists claimed that the Republicans created voters from "the dregs of the people, by Quit Claim deeds." A newly made voter would cast his ballot and then "assign his deed to another." Republicans accused the Federalists of purchasing votes, allowing slaves to vote as free blacks, and creating fagot voters. "Many Federalists who were not worth one cent" perjured themselves to vote. In reality, both Republicans and Federalists competed in illegally enfranchising people. Alden Spooner, a Brooklyn Republican editor, printed in 1812 a satirical poem, "The Qualified Voter":

By the big book of rules which our lawyers wrote,
No man unassess'd, is permitted to vote;
Yet, said one to his neighbor, in these party days,
They will vote, tho unable one shilling to raise,
You mistake, said the other, in grog shops and stores
And Brooklyn Hotels, they have rais'd *many scores!*[26]

[25] New York *Commercial Advertiser*, February 1, 1804; New York *Evening Post*, May 4, 12, 1807; David B. Ogden to William Meredith, May 6, 1807, William Meredith Papers (Historical Society of Pennsylvania).

[26] New York *Evening Post*, May 12, 1807; Goshen *Orange County Patriot*, May 8, 1810; New York *Commercial Advertiser*, May 7, 1810; New York *Public Advertiser*, May 8, 1810; Brooklyn *Long Island Star*, April 29, 1812. See also Robert Troup to Rufus King, April 24, 1807, Rufus King Papers (New-York Historical Society).

TABLE II
Gubernatorial Elections, 1807 and 1814[1]

County	1807			1814		
	Eligible Voters	Votes	Turnout	Eligible Voters	Votes	Turnout
Albany	3,745	3,079	82%	3,072	2,888	94%
Allegany	66	65	98%	135	252	197%
Broome	583	396	68%	848	789	93%
Cayuga	2,236	2,112	94%	3,182	2,991	94%
Chautauqua	—	—	—	430	555	129%
Chenango	1,570	1,967	125%	1,960	2,058	105%
Clinton	688	612	89%	634	590	93%
Columbia	2,968	2,819	95%	3,237	3,043	94%
Cortland	—	—	—	1,047	1,026	98%
Delaware	1,498	1,293	86%	1,746	1,659	95%
Dutchess	4,191	3,186	76%	3,779	3,250	86%
Essex	517	706	137%	621	758	122%
Franklin	—	—	—	183	216	118%
Genesee	477	812	170%	746	1,961	263%
Greene	1,643	1,393	85%	1,869	1,663	89%
Herkimer	1,722	1,745	101%	2,025	1,883	93%
Jefferson	835	1,380	165%	1,039	1,528	147%
Kings	584	534	91%	694	673	97%
Lewis	574	830	145%	616	542	88%
Madison	2,220	2,170	98%	2,518	2,266	90%
Montgomery	3,512	3,095	88%	4,165	3,707	89%
New York	3,000	3,479	116%	3,152	3,625	115%
Niagara[3]	—	—	—	419	775	185%
Oneida	3,501	3,609	103%	4,033	4,557	113%
Onondaga	2,331	2,424	104%	2,762	2,431	88%
Ontario	4,515	4,425	98%	2,806	2,702	96%
Orange	2,583	2,243	87%	2,747	1,868	68%
Otsego	3,254	2,991	92%	3,745	3,408	91%
Putnam	—	—	—	857	737	86%
Queens	1,891	1,295	72%	2,054	1,664	81%
Rensselaer	3,103	3,047	98%	3,425	3,288	96%
Richmond	513	486	95%	586	510	87%
Rockland	766	628	82%	838	545	65%
St. Lawrence	616	455	74%	789	868	110%
Saratoga	2,997	2,721	91%	3,172	3,013	92%
Schenectady	—	—	—	1,047	995	95%
Schoharie	1,468	1,195	81%	3,263	1,697	52%
Seneca	912	750	82%	1,776	1,527	86%
Steuben	250	300	120%	537	526	98%
Suffolk	2,610	1,949	75%	2,911	2,445	84%
Sullivan	—	—	—	639	358	56%
Tioga	485	324	67%	700	602	86%
Ulster	2,498	2,108	84%	2,737	2,162	79%
Warren	—	—	—	699	650	93%
Washington	3,289	3,227	98%	3,445	3,204	93%
Westchester	2,657	1,915	72%	2,785	2,228	80%
Total	71,159	66,042	93%[2]	87,413	83,042	95%

[1] Source: *Journal of the Assembly of the State of New York, 1808* (Albany 1808), unpaginated lists of returns between 181 and 182; *ibid.*, 1814 (Albany 1815), 233-273, 503.

[2] In 1801, 88 percent of the eligible voters turned out.

[3] Includes Cattaraugus.

According to Martin Van Buren, during the 1810 election the Federalists and Republicans competed in making voters in Columbia County. The Republicans contributed one third and the Federalists two thirds of the six hundred illegal voters in the county. Columbia County had about 3,000 eligible gubernatorial voters but 3,742 cast ballots, confirming Van Buren's statement. Similarly, New York City had only 3,000 eligible gubernatorial voters, but over 3,700 voted. Jefferson County, which had only 1,000 eligible voters in 1814, managed to cast 2,100 votes.[27]

Evidence of widespread electoral fraud was not confined to the 1810 election. During the 1807 election Genesee County, with only 477 gubernatorial voters, produced 812 votes (170%). Steuben County's tally equaled 132 percent of the eligible electorate. Additional evidence of voting irregularities surfaced in thirty towns in six other central and western New York counties, in twenty-five towns in five northern counties, and in a scattering of towns in five counties in the Hudson Valley.[28]

During the 1813 gubernatorial election, Federalist Congressman Thomas R. Gold charged that the Republican towns of Western and Floyd in Oneida County gave "double the votes they have freeholders." Available vote tallies confirm Gold's charge:

	Repub. Votes	Fed. Votes	Total	Eligible Voters	Turnout
Floyd	151 (73%)	55 (27%)	206	115	179%
Western	210 (94%)	15 (6%)	235	129	182%

In Cayuga County, a Federalist editor reported, "young men and even boys were permitted to vote for Tompkins." Returns from Dryden and Locke, which had vote totals of 134 percent and 169 percent respectively and which went for Tompkins (95% and 74%), substantiate the Federalist complaint. According to another

[27] Martin Van Buren to De Witt Clinton, April 28, 1810, De Witt Clinton Papers (Special Collections, Columbia University, New York, N.Y.). See also Goshen *Orange County Patriot*, May 8, 1810; New York *Commercial Advertiser*, May 7, 1810; Albany *Balance*, May 2-20, 1810; New York *Public Advertiser*, May 8, 1810; Cooperstown *Otsego Herald*, May 19, 1810.

[28] This statement is based on a town by town analysis of voter participation during the 1807 election. Most of the towns with over 100 percent tallies went to Tompkins.

Federalist, Genesee County reported almost "twice as many more votes" for Daniel Tompkins than there were voters. Genesee's record turnout of 263 percent confirms the charge. Vote totals exceeded 100 percent in eight other counties and numerous towns throughout the state with Tompkins emerging as the primary beneficiary. During the 1814 state senate election flagrant violations of the electoral laws appeared in eight counties in western and northern New York. In fact, throughout the first party system voting fraud in New York was an integral part of the political process.[29]

Widespread evasion of the electoral laws took place in the gubernatorial and state senate races, especially in New York City and in the counties in western and northern New York. While Van Buren's admission suggests that the Federalists were more adept at creating voters in the upper Hudson Valley, the Republicans more successfully made voters in western New York. There, New England immigrants in collusion with Republican politicians and election inspectors circumvented the election laws. On the Holland Land Purchase, for example, the majority of settlers had emigrated from Vermont where they had the right to vote. Holland Land Company policy of not granting deeds to settlers until they paid in full for the land, however, disenfranchised most of the settlers. In 1807, only one fifth of the potential voters owned sufficient property to vote. Disregarding the property qualifications, the Vermonters went to the polls in 1807, but Federalists challenged their right to vote. When the Federalists tried to stop them from voting illegally, the settlers used their fists to enforce their right to vote. "The Consequences," observed Joseph Ellicott, resident agent for the company and Republican party leader, "was that more quarreling and Blows passed which occasioned bloody

---

[29] Thomas R. Gold to Charles Webster, May 2, 1813, Simon Gratz Papers (Historical Society of Pennsylvania); Binghamton *Political Olio*, May 25, 1813; New York *Spectator*, June 9, 1813. See also Albany *Register*, May 28, 1813; New York *Evening Post*, May 1-June 1, 1813; New York *Courier*, May 31, 1815; Lansingburgh *Gazette*, June 8, 1813; "Report of Illegal Voting," 1812-1815, Box 42, Tibbits Family Papers (New York State Library). The table was compiled from an 1813 broadside, "Towns, Counties and Districts of New York" (New York State Library), and data from the electoral census of 1814 in the *Journal of the Assembly of the State of New York, 1815* (Albany 1815), 233-271.

Noses and black Eyes than has been done . . . ever since the Commencement of the Sales on the Company's Lands."[30]

Even before the confrontation, Ellicott had persuaded the company to lower its cash requirement from full purchase price to 25 percent. This was still too much for most settlers and Ellicott subsequently induced the company to reduce the cash requirement to 10 percent. Ellicott, in order to placate the settlers, gave out deeds on easy terms "without giving too much attention to the accuracy of the number of acres of cleared land involved." This policy of creating voters enabled Ellicott to enlarge the Republican party base in western New York, strengthen his position as a Republican party leader, and divert the anger of the settlers toward the Federalists for trying to prevent them voting.[31]

Republican party dominance in parts of western New York meant "in some towns in the western district it is absolutely unsafe for a federalist to appear at the polls unless he disguises his principles and conceals his vote." This dominance enabled the Republicans to ignore electoral restrictions when it suited their political purposes. After the 1813 gubernatorial election, Federalist editor Reuben Close complained that Genesee County, "where most people hold their land on contracts, and therefore have no right to vote for governor," gave Tompkins a nine hundred vote majority. After 1800, with the increasing flow of New England immigrants into western New York, it was the Republican party which benefited most from electoral fraud.[32]

Electoral fraud created a de facto lowering of the property qualifications for voting in gubernatorial and senatorial races, mitigated the impact of restrictive electoral laws, and significantly enlarged the potential electorate. It did not, however, create universal male suffrage. The petitions by Republicans in Ontario and Rensselaer counties and the resistance of legislators to enlarging the electorate legally suggest that universal male suffrage did not exist. Rather, electoral fraud permitted large numbers of assembly-congressional voters to cast ballots illegally for gubernatorial and

[30] William Chazanof, *Joseph Ellicott and the Holland Land Company: The Opening of Western New York* (Syracuse 1970), 104; Williamson, *American Suffrage*, 196, 199-200.
[31] Chazanof, *Ellicott*, 105.
[32] Binghamton *Political Olio*, May 25, 1813.

senatorial candidates in New York City and in western and northern New York. Electoral fraud enabled Republican and Federalist politicians to control who voted and when they voted; this gave the politicians control over a part of the electorate which would be lost if universal suffrage existed either legally or de facto.

A de facto enlargement of the electorate coincided with the decline of deference in New York. The dominance of the Republican party and the subsequent proscription of Federalists marked the decline of deference. Even those Federalists who "were most eminent in council or in the field" during the Revolution, such as the Jays, Morrises, and Van Rensselaers, could not obtain appointment to "the humblest office." Instead, observed Gouverneur Morris, "let a wretch, whose crimes have driven him from his native land, come forward, his head close cropt, the countenance of a savage, with the manners of a blackguard, and the doors of office fly open." Republicans appointed men not only loyal to the Republican party but men loyal to the particular Republican faction in power. The repeated purges during the factional Republican wars enshrined the spoils system as an integral part of the New York political process. The spoils system, "a new and peculiarly democratic system of political corruption," contributed to the decline of deference.[33]

Voting behavior and election rhetoric reflected the change in attitude. The inability of William North, Judge William Cooper, and Jacob Morris to control the voters in Schenectady and Otsego counties after 1800 demonstrated a declining respect for deference. In 1812, when Pierre Van Cortlandt, Jr. and Valentine Morris ran for Congress in the Westchester-Rockland district, voters rejected both of these members of prominent Westchester families and elected Peter De Noyelles. In 1814 voters rejected Phillip Van Cortlandt and Morris again to elect an obscure politician, Jonathan Ward. An issue, support for the war and President

---

[33] New York *Examiner*, June 26, 1814 (a manuscript copy of this article is in the Gouverneur Morris Papers, Columbia University); Fischer, *American Conservatism*, 195. Perhaps the first assault on a deferential style of politics took place in 1777 when George Clinton defeated Philip Schuyler in the gubernatorial race, and the raucous style of New York politics in the 1790s contributed to its decline, but the first two decades of the nineteenth century saw a far more rapid decline of deferential politics. See Alfred F. Young, *The Democractic Republicans of New York: The Origins, 1763-1797* (Chapel Hill 1967), and Hammond, *Political Parties*, I, 5.

Madison, meant more to the voters than a candidate's social background. The repeated reelection of Daniel Tompkins, "The Farmer's Boy," especially his defeat of the patroon of Rensselaer Manor, Stephen Van Rensselaer, further demonstrated the declining respect for a candidate's social standing.

At a campaign rally in Duanesburgh, Schenectady County, in 1810, Republicans advised the assembled mechanics, laborers, and farmers to elect men of their own kind. A spokesman asked, "does a nobleman . . . know the wants of the farmer and the mechanic? If we give such men the management of our concerns, where is our INDEPENDENCE and FREEDOM?" and he cautioned the voters not to elect "men whose aristocratic doctrine teaches that the rights and representative authority of the people are vested in a few proud nobles." During the 1810 campaign the Republicans attacked Jonas Platt, the Federalist candidate, for favoring elected representatives voting their conscience rather than merely reflecting the will of their constituents.[34]

During the Fourth of July celebrations of 1809 John Irving reminded the braves of St. Tammany that the United States did not have the burden of a titled nobility demanding deference based on "birth and not . . . merit." While Americans honored men of superior merit or virtue they were "still only considered as equals." Irving portrayed the United States as a society based on the equality of man. Deferential politics had no place in a nation of free men. Republican rhetoric undermined any lingering commitment New Yorkers might have had to a deferential society.[35]

Growing discontent with landlord domination in the Hudson Valley further demonstrated the declining commitment to a deferential society. Tenants on Livingston Manor appealed to Governor Tompkins against the "detestable, wicked practices" of the Livingston family. When the Livingstons ejected squatters in the summer of 1812 it led to the shooting of one man and to a con-

---

[34] "Duanesburgh Republican Nomination, March 17, 1810," Broadside (Schenectady County Historical Society, Schenectady, New York). See also *Public Advertiser*, January-April 1810; New York *Columbian*, February-April 1810; Troy *Farmer's Register*, February-April 1810; and Poughkeepsie *Political Barometer*, February-April 1810.

[35] John T. Irving, *Oration Delivered on the 4th of July, 1809, Before the Tammany Society* . . . (New York 1809). See also Seth Parsons, "Oration, July 4, 1809," Hoosick MSS.

frontation between a posse and supporters of the displaced squatters. The squatters evaded the posse, sent Livingston's tenant packing, and placed the ejected squatters back on their farms. Other tenants on the manors of the Livingstons in Columbia County and the Van Rensselaers in Rensselaer County brought lawsuits against their landlords. When Gerardus Hardenbergh tried to evict squatters from the Neversink Valley on the Harden-bergh Patent in Ulster and Sullivan counties, the squatters killed him. At the news of Hardenbergh's death the local populace ex-pressed great joy and toasted his killers. Public opinion so strongly favored the killers that local authorities dared not prosecute his murderers.[36]

Republicans capitalized upon the anti-landlord sentiments. Hillsdale, the center of anti-landlord agitation in Columbia County, voted the most solidly Republican of any town in the county. Martin Van Buren represented tenants in Columbia and Rensselaer counties against their Federalist landlords. During the 1813 gubernatorial campaign, Republicans sought to discredit Stephen Van Rensselaer by describing his tenants as little more than slaves. Republicans warned voters that Van Rensselaer's elec-tion was "a direct and sure means of creating a dangerous aristocracy."[37]

Federalists indirectly encouraged the decline of deferential politics by encouraging voter participation, mobilizing the electorate, and by trying to demonstrate that their republican cre-dentials were better than those of their opponents. In an effort to mobilize voters, Federalists established town, district, and ward committees. According to Elisha Williams, the Federalists ad-monished the faithful to vote, and "the doubtful are plied by every honest means that they may be saved." To counteract Tammany and other Republican party organizations, the Federalists created

---

[36] Committee of the People of the Manor of Livingston to Governor Daniel Tompkins, June 15, 1812, Box 5, Daniel Tompkins Papers (New York State Library); Hudson *Northern Whig*, August 24, 1812; Buffalo *Gazette*, September 8, 1812; Quinlan, *Sullivan County*, 232-237; Cooperstown *Otsego Herald*, May 1808.

[37] Albany *Argus*, April 16, 1813. See also the correspondence, legal papers, and autobiography of Martin Van Buren for 1808-1812, Van Buren Papers (Library of Congress); New York *Columbian*, March-April 1813; Cherry Valley *Otsego Republican Press*, March 26, 1813; Albany *Argus*, March-April 1813; and Hudson *Bee*, March-April 1813.

the Washington Benevolent Society and the Whig Society and
established chapters throughout the state.[38]

To save the state from continued Republican rule, Federalists
adopted Republican campaign techniques. During the 1807 election campaign, for example, Washington Irving "talked handbill
fashion with the demagogues and shook hands with the mob . . . ."
As David H. Fischer noted, "Federal appeals to the people, like
those of the Whigs in 1840, bordered upon pure demagoguery." In
1807, Federalists appealed to anti-Irish nativism and rechristened
their party the American party in an effort to win votes. When
this failed they tried in 1810 to obtain the votes of all ethnic
minorities. Federalists organized black and German-American
campaign committees and sang:

Come Dutch and Yankee, Irish, Scot
    With intermixed relations;
From whence we came, it matters not;
    We all make, now, one nation.[39]

In an effort to counteract the Republican portrayal of Daniel
Tompkins as "The Farmer's Boy," Federalists described their
gubernatorial candidate, Jonas Platt, as a man of the people
"whose habits and manners are as plain and republican as those of
his country neighbors." Platt was not "a city lawyer who rolls in
splendor and wallows in luxury." During the 1807 campaign,
when the Republicans charged that the Federalists believed that
only the wealthy should govern, Federalists counterattacked.
Henry Rutgers, the leader of the Republican assembly slate in New
York, was described by the Federalists as an "over grown
landlord" and as a man "of immense wealth."[40]

Hoping to demonstrate their superior republican credentials,
Federalists in 1809 assailed the legislative caucus as a subversion of
republican principles and an "assumption of power highly

---

[38] Elisha Williams to Ebenezer Foote, March 24, 1809, Albany Federal Committee to Ebenezer Foote, January 17, 1809, Ebenezer Foote Papers (New York
State Library); New York General Committee to William Price, February 15,
1809, Kernan Family Papers (Cornell University, Ithaca, New York).

[39] George S. Hellman, *Washington Irving, Esquire: Ambassador at Large from
the New World to the Old* (New York 1925), 70; Fischer, *American Conservatism*,
163-179; "Platt and Liberty," Broadside (New York Public Library).

[40] Utica *Patriot*, January 16, 1810; Goshen *Orange County Patriot*, April 10,
1810; New York *Evening Post*, April 27, 29, 1807. See also Canandaigua *Ontario
Repository*, March 6, 1810; New York *Commercial Advertiser*, April 1807.

derogatory to freemen."[41] They pointed to their use of district conventions to nominate candidates as proof of their commitment to
popular nomination of candidates. While the Republicans debated
adopting a state convention instead of the legislative caucus, the
Federalists pioneered its use in 1812.

In their appeals for votes, Federalists proved as willing as Republicans to praise the people and portray themselves as the
champions of the common man. When a Republican congressman
condemned opposition to the embargo as rebellion, Barent
Gardenier, Federalist congressman representing Ulster and
Greene counties, replied, "I cannot find a word to express my ideas
at having the majesty of the people assailed in this way; and, as a
Representative of the people, I will not endure it; it is
abominable."[42]

During the 1808 campaign, Schenectady Federalists articulated a vision of the people's role in government remarkably
similar to the Republicans. To these Federalists, the American
government "was formed for the people, not the people for the
government." Citizens had the right to dissent from government
policy and to throw out of office men who violated the public
trust. When a government ceases to maintain the "safety, honor
and welfare of the people," it loses its mandate to rule, and the
people have a right to elect men who will fulfill these obligations.
In the United States, "all power emanates from the people."[43]

While New England immigrants settling in western New York
joined the Republican party and liberalized New York's electoral
laws, New Englanders who settled in Albany County helped
democratize the Federalist party. "Some few aristocratic Dutchmen, who have established . . . *wealth* as the criteria of merit, and
Dutch descent as their indispensible requisite of a public office,"
wrote Yankee immigrant Ebenezer Baldwin, objected to the
nomination of Connecticut born John Lovett as the Federalist
candidate for Congress. The strength of the Yankees in Albany
County, however, overwhelmed them. Another Federalist, writing
to Congressman Harmanus Bleecker, believed it "desirable, both
to the candidates . . . and to the citizens generally, that the people

[41] New York *Evening Post*, February 23, 1809.
[42] *Annals of Congress*, 10th Cong., 2d sess., 1260.
[43] *A Report on the Present Alarming State of National Affairs* (Schenectady 1808), 3-7, 10-11, 14.

should have an opportunity of expressing their opinion generally and fairly" on the nomination of candidates.[44]

Many Federalists did not like the changes they saw. "It is indeed lamentable that we have no hope of relief from *the principle of democracy*," wrote Bleecker. For men of virtue, Federalists, "national councils in which wheelwrights, innkeepers and butchers make a figure cannot be respectable." The growing feeling of equality affected even the servants. "Uncle Peter has a great deal of trouble with his Servants," Peter Jay informed his father, and "they become more and more ungovernable."[45] Even though the Federalists waged a rear guard fight against the increasing democratization of society, their efforts to mobilize voters and their campaign rhetoric helped promote the democratization of New York politics.

The mass involvement of the voters, the de facto liberalization of the election laws, and the growing discontent of the disenfranchised paved the way for the adoption of universal male suffrage in the 1820s. Any lingering commitment to a government based on deference disappeared as both Republicans and Federalists mobilized, praised, and competed for popular support. Tompkins' "Farmer's Boy" campaigns demonstrated the importance of appearing as one of the people. New Yorkers refused to show deference to their elected officials and they refused to elect men who expected deference. Republican appeals to equalitarianism directly and indirectly encouraged anti-landlord agitation. Confrontation and lawsuits by squatters and tenants against the remnants of the manor system and the murder of Gerardus Hardenbergh demonstrated the declining respect for a deferential society. Republican and Federalist campaign appeals, combined with their encouragement of evasions of the electoral laws, assaulted the deferential society from above; anti-landlord agitation, petitions to broaden the franchise, high voter participation, ungovernable servants, and the fists of Vermonters undermined it from below.

---

[44] Ebenezer Baldwin to Roger Baldwin, April 6, 1812, Ebenezer Baldwin to Rebecca Baldwin, April 24, 1812, Box 15, Simeon Baldwin Papers (Yale University Library, New Haven, Conn.); R. Bennett to Harmanus Bleecker, March 18, 1813, Reel 4, Lloyd Smith Collection (Morristown National Historic Park, New Jersey).

[45] Harmanus Bleecker to H. Sedgwick, June 12, 1812, Sedgwick Papers (Massachusetts Historical Society, Boston); Peter A. Jay to John Jay, April 5, 1811, Jay Papers (Columbia University).

New Jersey Wealth-holding and the Republican Congressional Victory of 1800

LEE SOLTOW AND KENNETH W. KELLER

STUDENTS of the history of New Jersey politics in the early national period have often attempted to explain how party antagonisms stemmed from economic, social, cultural, and regional divisions in the state. Several excellent monographs and articles have appeared describing these party conflicts, but among the authors of these works there is substantial disagreement about the relative importance of wealth as a source of political conflict. Early local historians like Alfred Heston saw the rise of Jeffersonian Republicanism as a product of a Methodist and Presbyterian rebellion against Quakers, "who were Federalists almost to a man."[1] Walter Fee, who wrote the first important monograph on the party history of early national New Jersey, concluded that the Republicans represented the economic and political interests of common men. To Fee, Jefferson's party fought against Federalist "aristocracy" to defend the "average citizen" and the principles of 1776 from domestic elites and foreign domination.[2] J. R. Pole saw the New Jersey Republicans as representing a constituency of small farmers, some artisans, and poorer classes, but the Republicans' advocacy of these groups' interests took place in a relatively equalitarian society with a "substantial degree of equality among the dominant farming population."[3] Jackson Turner Main's analysis of the Confederation period viewed sectional rivalry between the old provinces of East and West Jersey as the chief theme in postrevolutionary history. This sectionalism, Main argued, "revived after Independence" because of old economic and cultural differences between the two regions.[4] Richard P. McCormick saw the sectional split as continuing into the 1790s for the same "historical, geographical, social, cultural, and economic differences," but McCormick nevertheless perceived New Jersey as essentially homogeneous with "no jarring antagonisms between classes or sections, or between metropolis or hinterland; no established aristocratic elite capable of monopolizing power and no self-conscious minority groups chafing under a sense of oppression." In McCormick's view, tensions between rich and poor were of minor importance. Republicans succeeded because of superior organization and leadership, not because they were genuinely champions of popular interests.[5] Carl E. Prince was even less convinced that Republicans truly represented the economic interests of the common man. Republicans exploited issues, but were not true democrats. Their appeal was based on the attractive personalities of Republican leaders.[6] These pronouncements on the role of economic and other factors in the development of parties are all the more surprising and confusing since none of the authors has attempted to measure economic differences between Federalist and Republican constituencies in the era of party formation in any systematic way. This paper attempts to fill that void by examining wealth-holding in New Jersey as parties began to organize themselves. If party differences represented actual differences in wealth-holding among the parties' constituencies, then perhaps these revisionists, like others, are in need of revising.

Political parties, or organized networks of committees established to nominate persons for office and elect them, began to appear in New Jersey about 1798. The Republicans, followers of Thomas Jefferson, were the first to organize intercounty networks of party committees in New Jersey, for the Federalists, who dominated the state's politics in the 1790s, were suspicious of extragovernmental systems with the purpose of organizing the state's electorate. Federalists preferred to create party committees by using Federalist legislative caucuses or general countywide meetings to nominate and to campaign. Republicans promoted their establishment by instituting a system of delegates chosen in each township for the purpose of representing local followers in the organization and decision-making of other party committees at higher county and state levels. Not until the congressional election of 1800 did these early party organizations spread sufficiently throughout the state to qualify New Jersey as a practitioner of organized party politics. New Jerseyans recognized the labels "Federalist" and "Republican" by 1800 as representing not only sets of principles, but also organizations. Both of these parties, however primitive and incomplete their organizations may have been, had developed intercounty structures and were appealing to voters with distinctive rhetoric and programs. The congressional election of 1800 was the first real test of how the parties' rhetoric and programs attracted groups whose votes the parties hoped to win.[7]

New Jersey Republican rhetoric and programs in 1800 showed again and again that the party of Jefferson aspired to win the votes of small farmers, mechanics, tradesmen, and what eighteenth century people called "the middling sort." The Republicans commonly denounced "aristocracy," merchants, lawyers, judges, bankers, speculators, landjobbers, stockjobbers, and swindlers.[8] If we can accept their rhetoric at face value, they believed that power (which the Federalists possessed) and wealth were synonymous, as a Republican "Lay Preacher" said.[9] Republicans saw their party as the defender of the "honest labourer," "industrious mechanic," and "respectable farmer."[10] Republicans did not profess to lead a social revolution that would put the poor in the seats of power, but they did promise to stop the oppression of the poor. Republican writers counseled voters to elect "those who are neither rich nor poor: for the first is an aristocrat, and the latter is a slave—generally speaking; and are unfit for government."[11] The thrust of Republican rhetoric in New Jersey was unmistakable— Jefferson's followers saw themselves as rivals of the rich and powerful.

Of course not all Republican rhetoric in New Jersey used arguments so clearly connected with antagonisms between the rich and the not-so-rich. To cast a wider net, the Republicans portrayed themselves as defenders of personal liberty, which the Federalists' Alien and Sedition Acts had threatened. Jeffersonians inveighed against these laws as outrageous, unconstitutional assualts upon the press and immigrants.[12] They represented themselves as friends of conscience and devotees of true religion, and not priestcraft, special privileges for a state church, or the mixing of politics and preaching.[13] They exploited popular Anglophobia by assailing British impressment practices, while they exalted the virtues of popular democratic militia (rather than a Federalist-inspired volunteer standing army or navy).[14] They championed few taxes and economy in government.[15] In a rare Dutch-language appeal entitled "Een Aanspraake aan de Duytsche Burgersvan den Staat van Niew Jersey," Republicans emphasized that they were the party of frugality and the opponents of New England (Federalist) efforts to create a national church.[16] But though the Republicans frequently appealed to voters by discussing issues that were not directly linked to differences between the well-to-do and those less well off, in New Jersey appeals rooted in economic differences issued from the presses of Republican printers more frequently than appeals of any other form.[17]

Federalist rhetoric and programs attempted to reply by representing their mission as the defense of prosperity and order from the onslaughts of the French Revolution, foreigners, and avaricious, Republican-controlled neighboring states. In their public statements, Federalists seldom emphasized any sense of being an elite, although on occasion their pamphleteers would stigmatize their enemies as being refugees from penury.[18] When Federalist pamphleteers resorted to economic arguments to win votes, they stressed the efforts of John Adams's administration to promote American commerce, which brought riches to all. Federalists wanted vigorously to compete with Britain for markets; they were not the King's toadies.[19] Frenchmen, whom Federalists uniformly identified as the Republicans' allies, imperiled the commerce of the seas by impressing American tars. Federalist financial reforms, like the funding system of Alexander Hamilton, were designed to restore prosperity for everyone by liquidating the war debt from the American Revolution.[20] They claimed to be defenders of economic liberty and "the freedom of the private contract." These wise policies, they asserted, assured America of prosperity, restored confidence in the public credit, promoted town growth and economic development, and created higher wages for labor[21] According to Morris County Federalists in 1800, the principal critics of the Federalists' programs were the large states that tried to saddle small New Jersey with burdens. Republican-controlled Virginia, New York, and Pennsylvania wanted to destroy the federal constitution so they could place tariff duties on goods New Jersey needed.[22] The Federalists of New Jersey tried to persuade voters that they spoke for the well-being of "the merchant; the husbandman; the artizan; the laborer: every class of the community," the whole social organism, and not one single economic interest.[23] Republican assertions that their party was the farmers' party were nonsense. Federalists gleefully pointed out that the Republicans' congressional ticket of 1800, which was supposed to consist of farmers, really represented the professional classes of physicians and generals more than common cultivators.[24]

While they maintained that they took the economic interests of all to heart, New Jersey's Federalists also placed great emphasis on their party's defense of inherited cultural values of the community. They ceaselessly accused Jefferson of being an infidel; his followers were deists and "prophaners of the Sabbath."[25] New Jersey Federalist addresses made specific appeals to Quakers, who respected "unviolated conscience," shunned conscripted service in a popular militia, and cherished peace and neutrality, the watchwords of the diplomacy of John Adams. Burlington County Federalists addressed their constituents in the center of New Jersey Quakerdom by extolling the Federalists' role in suppressing the slave trade.[26] Federalists called attention to the danger from foreigners in general and from France in particular.

Some polemicists identified the Republicans as an amalgam of the "French faction" united with aliens.[27] Federalist rhetoric in the campaign of 1800 betrays a tendency to avoid confrontation between economic groups, to champion the common interests of all members of the social organism, and to divert voters' attention from differences between the wealthy and the middling to issues involving threats to established values and the "rock of ORDER."[28]

Election of 1800

Using arguments like these, both parties went into combat to elect a slate of five congressmen at the election to be held December 23 and 24, 1800.[29] To the Republicans' chagrin, New Jersey's Federalist-dominated legislature had enacted a law stipulating that congressmen would be chosen that year at large, rather than in congressional districts. Federalists hoped that a general election would allow them to sweep the state with a victory, since Republican organizational efforts before 1800 had been concentrated in the counties stretching west from Newark—Essex, Morris, and Sussex. The Federalist plans encouraged Republicans to intensify efforts to organize a party committee network in the campaign of 1800, the first in which any Republican party ticket would be set before the voters on a statewide basis. Both parties organized state committees and nominated slates for Congress. The Federalists' state nominating meeting picked Aaron Ogden, Colonel Peter D. Vroom, Assembly Speaker William Coxe, Jr., the attorney James M. Imlay, and General Franklin Davenport. A short time later, Republicans chose as their slate former state treasurer James Mott, Dr. John Condit, Dr. Ebenezer Elmer, General William Helms, and the laborer Henry Southard.[30]

When the results of the congressional election were counted after Christmas, Republicans discovered that they had won their first statewide victory by a slim margin of about 700 votes. Statewide, the Republicans had won about 51 percent of the vote. Table I indicates the majorities by which Federalists and Republicans carried each county.[31] The centers of the Republicans' support were in the counties that Republicans dominated in earlier elections: Essex (containing Newark and Elizabeth) was 78 percent Republican, whereas about 91 percent of Morris County went for the Jeffersonians.[32] Sussex County also went Republican, but the precise percentage by which it voted so is unclear, because newspapers did not list the exact number of votes each slate received in Sussex and other counties. The Republicans had also attracted voters deep inside old West Jersey, formerly regarded as safe for Federalism. In southern New Jersey, the counties of Salem, Cumberland, and Cape May went to the Republicans by slim margins. They seem to have done best here in Cumberland County, the home of congressional candidate Dr. Ebenezer Elmer. The level of participation at the election ground was quite high: about 70 percent of New Jersey's eligible voters cast ballots.[33] The voters' response to the new party networks demonstrated the effectiveness of party organization in turning out the electorate.

Table I

MARGINS OF VICTORIES (MAJORITIES) BY FEDERALISTS AND REPUBLICANS IN 1800, NUMBER OF WHITE MEN AGED 26 AND OVER, AND POLITICAL SCORES.[a]

	Majority	White Men Aged 26+	Political Score
Federalist			
Burlington	1,945	3,518	+55
Somerset	756	1,849	+41
Hunterdon	963	3,238	+30
Middlesex	645	2,652	+24
Gloucester	450	2,514	+18
Bergen	307	2,485	+12
Monmouth	255	3,054	+ 8
Republican			
Cape May	25	461	− 5
Salem	152	1,829	− 8
Cumberland	178	1,414	−13
Essex	2,430	3,369	−72
Sussex	2,500	3,442	−73
Morris	2,418	2,760	−88

Source: U.S Census Office, *Second Census,* 1800; [Philadelphia] *American Daily Advertiser,* January 4, 1801.
[a]Percents of majorities who were white men aged 26 and over are expressed as a positive score for Federalist majorities and a negative score for Republican majorities.

By examining the election results in 1800 it may be possible to identify characteristics of the constituencies from which Republicans and Federalists drew their support. Unfortunately, for most counties, New Jersey's newspapers reported only the majorities both tickets obtained. The absolute totals county by county would help identify the voters' preferences more clearly than majorities, but reported majorities may be used to group the counties of New Jersey in relationship to one another as Republican or Federalist.

These rankings are not identical to the proportions of Republican and Federalist voters in each county in 1800. But if they are linked to a rough estimate of the number of eligible voters in each county, they will serve the purpose of providing a picture of the intensity of party dominance in one county or another. The federal census of 1800 gives figures that may be used for expressing the relationship between a party majority and the number of eligible voters in each county.[34] The 1800 census shows the numbers of men between the ages of sixteen and twenty-six as well as between the ages of twenty-six and forty-five and over, but it does not establish a category using age twenty-one, the age at which eligible New Jerseyans could vote. By using federal counts of men aged twenty-six and over for each New Jersey county, we can approximate the size of each county's voting population. The federal census counts of men aged twenty-six and over are not identical to New Jersey's voting population, for a few of these men could not meet New Jersey's liberal suffrage requirements. This method also overlooks men aged twenty-one to twenty-six, and ignores adult free blacks and women. Free blacks and women were technically eligible to vote in New Jersey, but when they did cast ballots newspapers reported their appearance at the polling ground with amazement.[35] In 1800 voting by women and free blacks must have been highly unusual. Expressing the 1800 majorities as a proportion of the white men aged twenty-six and older in each county yields a close approximation of party support across the state. If we arbitrarily count all Republican proportions as mathematically negative and all Federalist proportions as mathematically positive, we shall have established a political scale for measuring party dominance in each county. If every adult white man aged twenty-six and over in a county had voted Republican, that county's political score would have been -1.0. If every adult white man aged twenty-six and over had voted Federalist, that county's score would have been $+1.0$. If a county's adult white men aged twenty-six and over had been equally divided between Republicans and Federalists, the political score would have been

0. By comparing these scores, shown in table I, with records of wealth-holding in New Jersey's counties, it will be possible to see whether appreciable economic differences existed between Federalist and Republican constituencies.

Land and Housing Values

Fortunately, comprehensive records of wealth-holding in New Jersey do exist for the year 1798. These records provide a convenient tool for estimating New Jersey wealth-holding at the time of the 1800 congressional balloting. These data yield the best, most uniformly measured, and most comprehensive estimate of New Jersey's wealth that we have for the era in which political parties arose. They appear in the records of the U.S. Direct Tax of 1798. On July 9, 1798, Congress passed an act ordering that all dwelling houses and lands in the United States be valued and that all slaves be enumerated. On July 14, 1798, Congress enacted the first federal direct tax in American history. This direct tax of 1798 was designed to provide the government with revenue to prepare for a possible war with France, which many Americans expected as Franco-American diplomatic relations worsened during the administration of the Federalist President John Adams. These revenue measures established a carefully defined, uniform measurement of the value of all dwelling houses, outbuildings, and lands. Slaves of all ages and both sexes were to be counted so taxes could be levied upon their masters. Since the abstracts assessors returned cover all New Jersey counties, these records provide a source for measuring wealth-holding available nowhere else.[36]

The measurement of land and housing values to reflect overall wealth of a society may not provide a complete picture of a community's wealth-holding patterns, since personal property (except for slaves in these records) is not included in the estimates of wealth. There were those in the eighteenth century who did believe that the best indication of any society's wealth was its investment in land and housing, which were the basis of the direct tax estimates of national wealth-holding along with investment in slaves. The Reverend Dr. John Witherspoon, president of the College of New Jersey (now Princeton University), had been an advocate of exactly such a measurement of wealth-holding as early as the Second Continental Congress in 1776. Witherspoon, who with fellow New Jersey delegates to the Congress had opposed using population as a measurement of wealth, argued that "the value of lands and houses was the best estimate of the wealth of a nation. This is the true barometer of wealth."[37]

The direct tax of 1798 valued about 2.8 million acres of privately held New Jersey land and 38,580 dwellings and outbuildings. It was only improved farmland and other property under title that the tax of 1798 assessed. The tax commissioners of 1798 distinguished between land on which dwellings and outbuildings sat and all other land. The value of the land upon which dwellings and outbuildings were located was included in the assessment value of the dwelling houses in the abstracts of their values. It is not possible, then, to say what the value of town lots occupied with dwelling houses may have been. All other land occupied was valued. The valuations the assessors made are accurate reflections of land values within each county. With one exception, all the acreage assessed in the state in 1798 was valued in assessors' districts that lay exactly within the boundaries of the New Jersey counties. The one exception to the rule was the sparsely populated township of Little Egg Harbor in easternmost Burlington County in the region between the pine barrens and the coastal marshes on the Atlantic. This region, which may have contained an iron furnace and little else, was valued with the property values of Monmouth County, which lay to its immediate north. All estimates made in this paper include this small and barely populated township of Burlington County in the estimates of Monmouth County's wealth. Accordingly, the values examined here for these two counties will be slightly altered from what they truly were. With these caveats in mind, it is now possible to survey New Jersey's wealth-holding in 1798 and link it with party preferences in 1800.

Table II displays the total value of houses and lands in New Jersey's counties grouped according to Federalist or Republican voting in 1800, and per white men aged twenty-six and over. The table clearly shows that there were differences in wealth in both land and housing in Federalist and Republican counties of 1800. The Federalist counties had an average land value per white man aged twenty-six and over of $975.67; for the Republican counties, a substantially lower figure of $642.33 appears. By using correlation techniques, it is possible to express the relationship between Federalist dominance and landed wealth per white man aged twenty-six and over. The squared correlation coefficient of landed wealth-holding and the political scores computed from voting majorities is .63, a figure about as high as one can reasonably expect to find between such variables.[38] A line of regression plotted between the political scores computed from voting majorities in

1800 (Y) and the value of land of 1798 per white male inhabitant age twenty-six and over in 1800 (X) can be described by the regression equation $Y = -1.47 + .0016X$.

The regression line that this equation describes reveals that economic condition, especially landed wealth-holding, was closely connected with Federalist dominance in New Jersey in 1800.[39] The higher the average value of land in a county, the more likely it was to be Federalist.

Table II

AVERAGE VALUES OF DWELLING HOUSES AND LANDS IN NEW JERSEY IN 1798 PER WHITE MALE INHABITANT AGED 26 AND OVER.[a]

	Dwelling Houses ($)	Land ($)	Value of Dwellings per WM 26+ ($)	Value of Land per WM 26+ ($)
Federalist				
Burlington	1,525,440	3,215,901	433.61	914.13
Somerset	697,997	2,087,552	377.50	1,129.02
Hunterdon	1,044,944	3,466,179	322.71	1,070.47
Middlesex	997,562	2,500,190	376.16	942.76
Gloucester	664,717	2,635,872	264.41	1,048.48
Bergen	681,508	2,448,562	274.25	985.34
Monmouth	865,759	2,485,921	283.48	813.99
Total	6,477,927	18,840,177	335.47	975.67
Republican				
Cape May	73,755	240,438	159.99	521.56
Salem	428,415	1,653,115	234.24	903.84
Cumberland	336,955	1,117,554	238.30	790.35
Essex	1,566,665	2,087,968	465.02	619.76
Sussex	357,451	1,675,207	103.85	486.70
Morris	501,293	1,752,624	181.63	635.01
Total	3,264,534	8,526,906	245.92	642.33
Total New Jersey	9,742,461	21,367,083	298.99	839.87

Source: See footnote 36 and the federal census of 1800.
[a]Land means privately held, improved land under title. Land on which houses and outbuildings sat was valued with the value of dwelling houses.

Table III shows estimates of the population density of Federalist and Republican counties. By calculating the number of acres per white man aged twenty-six and over in each county, it becomes clear that Republicans came from slightly more densely populated areas than Federalists did. This conclusion should be no surprise, since the centers of New Jersey's Republican organization were the counties of Essex (site of Newark and Elizabeth) and Morris (site of Morristown). There were about 88.42 acres of land per white man aged twenty-six and over in the Federalist counties; in the Republican counties there were about 81.42 acres

Table III

ACRES OF LAND IN 1798 IN FEDERALIST AND REPUBLICAN COUNTIES AND ACRES PER WHITE MEN AGED 26 AND OVER.[a]

	Acres of Land	Acres per WM 26+
Federalist		
Burlington	267,583	76.06
Somerset	176,232	95.31
Hunterdon	292,859	90.44
Middlesex	194,955	73.51
Gloucester	325,300	129.40
Bergen	171,380	68.97
Monmouth	279,113	91.39
Total	1,707,422	88.42
Republican		
Cape May	72,284	156.80
Salem	160,439	87.72
Cumberland	207,974	147.08
Essex	112,722	33.46
Sussex	317,933	92.37
Morris	209,495	75.90
Total	1,080,847	81.42
Total New Jersey	2,788,269	85.57

Source: See footnote 36 and the federal census of 1800.

[a]Land means privately held, improved land under title. Land on which houses and outbuildings sat was valued with the value of dwelling houses.

per white man aged twenty-six and over. Some counties of both persuasions had relatively sparse populations: Cape May, Cumberland, and Gloucester counties had relatively large acreages per white man aged twenty-six and older. Federalist Bergen County, across the Hudson from New York City, was also more densely settled, as were the central counties of Somerset and Middlesex, which included Princeton, Perth Amboy, New Brunswick, and the town of Somerset.

Table IV summarizes the average value of an acre and a dwelling house assessed in each county. In all cases but one, the

Table IV

AVERAGE VALUES OF AN ACRE AND A DWELLING HOUSE IN 1798 IN NEW JERSEY FEDERALIST AND REPUBLICAN COUNTIES.

	Value of an Acre of Land[a] ($)	Number of Dwelling Houses	Value of a Dwelling House ($)
Federalist			
Burlington	12.02	4,055	376.19
Somerset	11.85	1,663	419.72
Hunterdon	11.84	2,914	358.59
Middlesex	12.83	2,894	344.70
Gloucester	8.10	2,304	288.51
Bergen	14.29	3,004	226.87
Monmouth	8.91	3,108	278.56
Total	11.03	19,942	324.84
Republican			
Cape May	3.33	630	117.07
Salem	10.30	1,752	244.53
Cumberland	5.37	1,590	211.92
Essex	18.52	2,812	557.14
Sussex	5.27	2,549	140.23
Morris	8.37	2,182	229.74
Total	7.89	11,515	283.50
Total New Jersey	9.82	31,457	309.71

Source: See footnote 36.
[a]Land means privately held, improved land under title. Land on which houses and outbuildings sat was valued with the value of dwelling houses.

higher the land values were, the higher the values of housing would be in the same county. The exception to this rule was Bergen County, which had highly valued lands but less highly valued housing. It may have been that Bergen county houses differed from houses elsewhere in New Jersey because of their distinctive architectural characteristics and modest appearance. Thomas Jefferson Wertenbaker's study *The Middle Colonies* pointed out that Bergen County had a housing design unique to New Jersey and southern New York: the Flemish cottage. Housing built according to this design was long, low, usually made of stone, with few dormers (hence few windows), one room in width, and of modest appearance.[40] The New Jersey Dutch, who formed about 40 percent of Bergen's population, were especially fond of this frugal building style.[41] Since the assessed value of every house was based on the number of rooms, stories, and windows and building materials a house possessed, it is likely that Bergen County houses received values somewhat lower than those of other New Jersey dwellings, in which there were more rooms, more than one story, and dormers with windows. With the exception of Bergen and Monmouth counties, all the Federalist counties in 1800 had housing values higher than the average total value of a house in the Republican counties. The only Republican county with a higher average value of a dwelling than the Federalist average total was Essex County, where town sites drove up housing values. Also, the only Republican county with a higher average total value of an acre than the Federalist counties was Essex. No Federalist county had a lower average total value of an acre than the average total value of an acre in the Republican counties.

An examination of housing values shows that dwellings in Federalist counties were more highly valued than those in Republican counties, although the gap between Federalist and Republican counties' housing values was not as wide as it was for land values. Table IV shows that the average value of a dwelling house in Federalist areas was $324.84, whereas in Republican counties it was $283.50. Table V indicates the percentage of dwelling houses in each range of value the direct tax assessors recorded when they assessed houses and table VI cumulates those values for dwellings valued at $100 or more and at $1,000 or more. Table VI expresses the number of houses at these ranges of value as a percentage of the total number of dwelling houses in the county and then adjusts each result to the total number of white men aged twenty-six and over in 1800. As table VI shows, in Federalist counties 64.1 percent of the dwelling houses had values over $100, while in the Republican counties 60.3 percent of the dwell-

Table V

PERCENT OF DWELLING HOUSES IN 1798 BY VALUATION IN NEW JERSEY FEDERALIST AND
REPUBLICAN COUNTIES.

	Number of Dwellings	$100 or less	$101–$500	$501–$1,000	$1,001–$3,000	$3,001–$6,000
Federalist						
Burlington	4,055	39.6	35.1	17.4	7.7	0.3
Somerset	1,663	19.2	51.7	24.7	4.0	0.5
Hunterdon	2,914	26.6	56.7	14.9	5.0	0.5
Middlesex	2,894	33.9	45.2	15.3	5.1	0.5
Gloucester	2,304	27.1	57.8	10.8	4.1	0.2
Bergen	3,004	55.7	33.9	9.1	1.3	0.2
Monmouth	3,108	41.4	41.7	13.4	3.4	0.1
Total	19,942	36.4	44.6	14.7	4.6	0.3
Republican						
Cape May	630	65.9	31.9	2.2	0	0
Salem	1,752	42.0	45.0	10.1	2.9	0
Cumberland	1,590	39.3	52.4	5.9	2.5	0
Essex	2,812	11.9	51.1	24.7	11.2	1.1
Sussex	2,549	63.4	31.6	4.4	0.6	0.04
Morris	2,182	38.6	52.6	7.3	1.3	0
Total	11,515	39.7	45.3	10.8	3.9	0.3
Total New Jersey	31,457	37.6	44.8	13.3	4.3	0.3

Source: See footnote 36.

202

ings were so valued. The Federalist counties with smaller proportions of dwelling houses valued over $100 than the Republican counties were Monmouth and Bergen. The only Republican county with a higher proportion of dwellings valued over $100 than the Federalist counties was Essex. The Flemish cottages of Bergen County and the towns of Essex County produced these divergences from the general trend. Bergen was not the most strongly Federalist county in 1800: its political score was a low + 12 and 43 percent of its voters cast ballots for Republicans in 1800. Monmouth may have been even less enthusiastically Federalist in 1800, for its political score was +8. Housing values adjusted to

Table VI

DWELLINGS BY VALUATION AND NUMBER OF DWELLINGS PER WHITE MALE INHABITANT AGED 26 AND OVER IN 1798 IN NEW JERSEY FEDERALIST AND REPUBLICAN COUNTIES

	Dwellings at $100+ N	%	Dwellings at $100+ per WM 26+	Dwellings at $1,000+	Dwellings at $1,000+ per WM 26+
Federalist					
Burlington	2,449	60.4	0.696	321	0.091
Somerset	1,343	80.8	0.726	74	0.040
Hunterdon	2,244	77.0	0.693	161	0.050
Middlesex	1,911	66.0	0.721	161	0.061
Gloucester	1,680	72.9	0.668	99	0.039
Bergen	1,332	44.3	0.536	43	0.017
Monmouth	1,822	58.6	0.597	110	0.036
Total	12,781	64.1	0.662	969	0.050
Republican					
Cape May	215	34.1	0.466	0	0
Salem	1,016	58.0	0.556	51	0.028
Cumberland	965	60.7	0.683	39	0.028
Essex	2,477	88.1	0.735	347	0.103
Sussex	934	36.6	0.271	17	0.005
Morris	1,334	61.1	0.483	28	0.010
Total	6,941	60.3	0.523	482	0.036
Total New Jersey	19,722	62.7	0.605	1,451	0.045

Source: See footnote 36.

reflect each county's white male population aged twenty-six and over also show Federalist counties as being more well-to-do. As table VI shows, the number of dwellings valued over $100 per white man aged twenty-six and older is 0.662 in Federalist counties and 0.523 in Republican counties. A comparison of the figures for the houses evaluated at $1,000 or more per each white man aged twenty-six or over also shows Federalist counties as being wealthier: in the Federalist counties there were 0.050 houses valued at $1,000 or more, and in the Republican counties 0.036. The squared correlation coefficient between housing values and Federalist voting is .51. The strength of Republicanism in the towns of Essex County, where houses had high values, makes this result less dramatic than the coefficient for landed wealth.

Table V, which displays the number of houses within various ranges of value, suggests that there may have been greater inequality of housing values in the Federalist counties. Some Federalist counties had a rather high proportion of low-valued houses: about 55.7 percent of Bergen's houses, 41.4 pecent of Monmouth's, and 39.6 percent of Burlington's were valued at less than $100. In each of these counties, however, there were houses valued at the higher levels of housing values recorded in the tax abstracts: about 0.2 percent of Bergen's, 0.1 percent of Monmouth's, and 0.3 percent of Burlington's houses were valued within the $3,001–$6,000 range. Among the Republican counties only Essex County approached these in the number of highly valued houses: 1.1 percent of Essex's dwellings were valued at $3,001–$6,000.

Slaves

At the end of the eighteenth century New York and New Jersey were the northern states with the largest slave populations. The distribution of New Jersey's 10,128 chattel slaves in 1798 was another sign of wealth-holding, although not as reliable a one as the measurements of land and houses.[42] Table VII shows that the average number of chattel slaves per white male inhabitant aged twenty-six and older was 0.16 in Republican counties and 0.40 in the Federalist counties. Quakers did not keep slaves, so their presence in Burlington, Gloucester, Cape May, Salem, and Cumberland counties, all of which had Quaker meetings in the eighteenth century, lowered the number of slaves that might have otherwise appeared.[43] The largest concentration of slaves in New Jersey occurred in Bergen County, which had a high proportion of Dutch inhabitants. There were more slaves in Bergen County in 1798 than there were white male inhabitants over age twenty-six in 1800. Perhaps the high concentration of slaves in Bergen County can be explained by the tendency of the Dutch not to emancipate their slaves. Historians of Bucks County, Pennsylvania, have found high concentrations of slaves in Dutch settlements there.[44] The French traveler Brissot de Warville found that the New York Dutch kept their slaves in bondage even when emancipation began to spread in the north. The Dutch, he said were "a people less willing than others to part with property."[45] The largest concentration of slaves in the Republican counties appears in Essex County. Slave population concentrated in northern towns in the early republic. In spite of the Quaker opposition to slavehold-

Table VII

NUMBER OF SLAVES IN 1798 IN NEW JERSEY FEDERALIST AND REPUBLICAN COUNTIES AND SLAVES PER WHITE MALE INHABITANT AGED 26 AND OVER.

	Slaves	*Slaves per WM 26+*
Federalist		
Burlington	120	0.034
Somerset	1,701	0.912
Hunterdon	1,133	0.350
Middlesex	1,140	0.430
Gloucester	54	0.022
Bergen	2,583	1.039
Monmouth	1,317	0.431
Total	8,048	0.417
Republican		
Cape May	73	0.158
Salem	34	0.019
Cumberland	56	0.040
Essex	906	0.269
Sussex	338	0.098
Morris	673	0.244
Total	2,080	0.157
Total New Jersey	10,128	0.311

Source: See footnote 36.

ing and the accumulation of slaves in towns where Republicans were strong, once again a measure of wealth-holding puts the Federalist counties ahead of the Republican ones.

Age and Birthrate

It could be possible that these differences in wealth-holding existed because the population in Federalist areas was older than in Republican ones. Older people tend to own more property than younger people. But the wealth differences uncovered here cannot be explained on the basis of age differences in these two groups of counties. Federalist areas did not have older populations more likely to accumulate wealth, nor were birth rates in Federalist areas much greater than in Republican ones. The average age of men twenty-six and older, estimated from the federal census, was 41.7 years in Federalist counties and 41.2 in Republican ones. The birth rates in these groups of counties can be estimated by determining the proportion of children (aged fifteen and under) to women (aged sixteen to forty-four). In the six Republican counties the rate of births was 2.64, and in the Federalist counties it was 2.67.[46] These wealth differences, then, were not dependent on age stratification in the two groups of counties.

Economic Differences in Voting

These results suggest that the Republican appeal to farmers, mechanics, and the middling sort succeeded remarkably in attracting people of less prosperity than those who voted Federalist. In every county wealthier constituencies in 1798 voted Federalist in 1800, and less wealthy ones voted Republican. Certainly in New Jersey economic differences, however closely they were linked to sectionalism between East and West Jersey, were the major influence on how constituencies voted. Cultural and religious characteristics of groups may have modified the overall tendency for constituencies to consider property first in making political choices, but in the cases of the state's two most distinctive cultural groups, the Quakers and the Dutch, cultural traits reinforced tendencies to vote according to economic interests.

Quakers opposed Republican support of a conscripted militia; frugal Dutchmen on highly valued land supported conservative economic policies that would protect what they had accumulated. In no New Jersey county was there a non-English ethnic group large enough to dominate the county's politics. Moreover, the constituencies' allegiances displayed in the congressional election of 1800 lasted throughout the age of Jefferson, at least as long as the Federalists were able to survive as a party. Wealthy Somerset, Middlesex, and Burlington counties, along with Bergen County, remained Federalist for another decade. Poorer Sussex, Morris, Salem, Cumberland, and Essex counties remained loyal to Republicanism. Cape May County, with its Quaker population, flirted with Federalism, while Hunterdon County, site of the state capital of Trenton, edged toward Republicanism after the Jeffersonians began to take over New Jersey's state government. Gloucester and Monmouth counties shifted back and forth between the two parties over the next decade.[47] The economic rhetoric of the Republicans, in general, worked well among most New Jersey voters. It transformed the state's politics so that Federalists were not to control the state again except for brief periods.

These indications that wealth-holding played an important role in New Jersey politics should not necessarily be seen as typical of all states in the early national years. A recent study of "Chesapeake politics" in Maryland, Virginia, and North Carolina emphasizes that wealth differences and struggles between creditors and debtors were of prime importance there.[48] The best study we have of New York politics in the years up to 1797 portrays the Republicans as a party of farmers and mechanics, but one that was flexible enough to open its doors to wealthy men who were suspicious of the mixing of riches and political power.[49] A recent study of the nation's most culturally complex state, Pennsylvania, sees some connection between landed wealth and Federalism, while an older study of Federalist Delaware suggests that culture, religion, ideology, and party leadership qualities were of greater importance than riches in keeping Federalism ascendant.[50] New Jersey's class antagonisms may not have been "jarring," but enough conflict existed between the richer inhabitants and middling farmers and artisans to make the political difference in 1800.

Notes

[1] Alfred M. Heston, ed., *South Jersey: A History, 1664–1924*, vol. 1 (New York, 1924), 154.
[2] Walter R. Fee, *The Transition from Aristocracy to Democracy in New Jersey, 1789–1829* (Somerville, N.J., 1933), 100–102.
[3] J. R. Pole, "Jeffersonian Democracy and the Federalist Dilemma in New

Jersey, 1798–1812," in *Proceedings of the New Jersey Historical Society*, 74 (October 1956): 270, 286.

⁴ Jackson Turner Main, *Political Parties before the Constitution* (Chapel Hill, N.C., 1973), 7, 157, 164.

⁵ Richard P. McCormick, *Experiment in Independence: New Jersey in the Critical Period, 1781–1789* (New Brunswick, N.J., 1950), 305:6; Richard P. McCormick, *The Second American Party System: Party Formation in the Jacksonian Era* (Chapel Hill, N.C., 1966), 124, 126–27.

⁶ Carl E. Prince, *New Jersey's Jeffersonian Republicans: The Genesis of an Early Party Machine, 1789–1817* (Chapel Hill, N.C., 1967), 247–51. Prince found that regional differences between old West and East Jersey were "never far from the surface of New Jersey politics . . . [and] may be found at the root of several of the most prominent post-1800 intra-party struggles." He also found that the Republican party "like the society of which it was a part, was essentially classless in an economic sense after 1800." Prince, 98–99, 147.

⁷ Pole, "Jeffersonian Democracy," 263–69; Prince, *N.J.'s Jeffersonian Republicans*, 61–65.

⁸ [Newark] *Centinel of Freedom*, August 5, 26, November 25, 1800; *Address of the Republican Committee of the County of Gloucester, N.J.* [broadside], December 15, 1800.

⁹ *Centinel of Freedom*, September 9, 1800.

¹⁰ Ibid., April 1, 1800.

¹¹ Ibid., September 23, 1800.

¹² Ibid., January 7, 21, April 29, September 2, October 7, December 2, 1800; [Elizabeth] *New Jersey Journal*, October 7, 14, 1800.

¹³ *New Jersey Journal*, October 7, 14, 1800; *Centinel of Freedom*, February 25, July 8, July 29, August 5, 12, 26, September 2, 23, 30, October 7, 22, 1800; from Bergen County, see [Carlisle, Pa.] *Carlisle Gazette*, October 22, 1800. Republicans tried to appeal to Quakers and Presbyterians in their partisan manifestos. Federalists were just as skilled in using religious arguments for their candidates. Presbyterians may have formed the core of the Republican party in New Jersey. Prince found that among the county leadership of the Republican party, thirteen of twenty-three leaders whose religious affiliations could be identified, were Presbyterian (Prince, *N.J.'s Jeffersonian Republicans*, 147). Occasionally announcements of Republican meetings in newspapers indicate that the presiding officer of a party meeting was called a "moderator." Among Presbyterians, the word "moderator" is used to designate the presiding officer in a church court, congregational meeting, session, presbytery, or general assembly. See Vergilius Ferm, ed., *An Encyclopedia of Religion* (New York, 1945), 497–98. The term "moderator" was never used to designate the chairman of party meetings in neighboring Pennsylvania. Presbyterians also used the term "clerk" or "stated clerk" to identify the secretary of church meetings. This term "clerk" also appears in New Jersey to designate the secretary of political meetings. It is never used among Pennsylvania Republicans.

¹⁴ *New Jersey Journal*, October 14, 1800; *Centinel of Freedom*, February 1, March 11, 25, April 1, 22, 29, May 27, July 1, September 2, October 7, December 2, 1800.

¹⁵ *Centinel of Freedom*, July 22, 1800; *New Jersey Journal*, October 7, 1800.

¹⁶ *Centinel of Freedom*, October 7, 1800.

¹⁷ Fee, *Aristocracy to Democracy*, 100–118.

¹⁸ Pole, "Jeffersonian Democracy," 286; *Address to the Federal-Republicans of the State of New Jersey . . . .*, November 13, 1800, *New Jersey Journal*, November 25, 1800.

19 *An Address to the Citizens of the County of Morris* [broadside] (Morristown, N.J., 1800).

20 *An Address to the Federal Republicans of Burlington County* [broadside], September 24, 1800 (Trenton, N.J., 1800).

21 *An Address to the Citizens of the County of Morris.*

22 Ibid.

23 *Address to the Federal Republicans of the State of New Jersey. . . .*, November 13, 1800.

24 Prince, *N.J.'s Jeffersonian Republicans*, 65.

25 *Centinel of Freedom*, July 29, August 26, September 2, 1800.

26 *An Address to the Federal Republicans of Burlington County.*

27 *Address to the Federal Republicans of the State of New Jersey.*

28 *Address to the Federal Republicans of Burlington County.*

29 New Jersey held its election for members of the General Assembly on a different day from the congressional election. Voters chose assemblymen on October 14, when every county except Essex, Morris, and Sussex elected legislators who voted with Federalists.

As late as 1799, some announcements of tickets in New Jersey contained no indication of the party preferences of assembly nominees. (*Centinel of Freedom*, September 10, 1799.) Party identifications were common in 1800. The party attachments of the two 1800 congressional tickets were clearly made known throughout the state.

30 Prince, *N.J.'s Jeffersonian Republicans*, 61-74; *Centinel of Freedom*, November 18, 1800.

31 [Philadelphia] *American Daily Advertiser*, January 4, 1801; *Centinel of Freedom*, January 6, 1801.

32 Every township in Essex County went Republican except Elizabeth, which cast 59 percent of its 947 total votes for Federalists. Newark cast 83 percent of its 1,655 votes for Republicans. Morris County cast 91 percent of its 2,962 votes for Republicans. Of Bergen County's 1,600 votes cast, 57 percent were for Federalists. (*Centinel of Freedom*, December 30, 1800.)

33 The 70 percent turnout estimate is Richard P. McCormick's. See Prince, *N.J.'s Jeffersonian Republicans*, 65. Liberal suffrage regulations allowed most adult males to vote. Free blacks and women could also vote, but they rarely did so. Free black and female suffrage was abolished in 1807. See Chilton Williamson, *American Suffrage from Property to Democracy, 1760-1860* (Princeton, N.J., 1960), 85, 104, 212, 280.

34 U.S. Census Office, Second Census, 1800. *Return of the Whole Number of Persons within the Several Districts of the United States. . . .* (Washington, D.C., 1801).

35 Williamson, *American Suffrage*, 180; *Centinel of Freedom*, December 2, 1800; Richard P. McCormick, *The History of Voting in New Jersey* (New Brunswick, N.J., 1953), 98-99. According to McCormick, women were occasionally "herded to the polls" by partisans. Female voting promoted "outrageous frauds" (McCormick, *Voting*, 98-99).

36 A general discussion of the law and statistics is given in Lee Soltow, "America's First Progressive Tax," *National Tax Journal* 30 (March 1977): 53-58. Descriptions of data appear in National Archives and Records Service, *United States Direct Tax of 1798: Tax Lists for the State of Pennsylvania* [pamphlet accompanying microcopy no. 372] (Washington D.C., 1963); *Annals of Congress*, vol. 9, 5th Cong., 3d Sess., Acts of July 4 and 14, Appendix 3757-3786. See also Timothy Pitkin, *A Statistical View of the Commerce of the United States* [reprint of 1816 edition] (New York, 1967), 377-78.

NEW JERSEY WEALTH-HOLDING / 53

[37] John Witherspoon quoted in Thomas Jefferson's *Autobiography* in Adrienne Koch and William Peden, eds., *The Life and Selected Writings of Thomas Jefferson* (New York, 1944), 32.

[38] The squared correlation coefficient of .63 indicates that about 63 percent of the statistical variance in the voting margin can be accounted for by the value of landed wealth.

[39] For an explanation of regression methods, see Charles M. Dollar and Richard J. Jensen, *Historian's Guide to Statistics: Quantitative Analysis and Historical Research* (Huntington, N.Y., 1971), 56–87.

[40] Thomas Jefferson Wertenbaker, *The Founding of American Civilization: The Middle Colonies* (New York, 1938), 66–76, 153.

[41] William Nelson, Austin Scott, and E. S. Sharpe made an estimate of the ethnic composition of New Jersey's counties for the U.S. Census Bureau in 1909. According to these local historians, in 1790 Bergen County was 40 percent Dutch. It was the most ethnically heterogeneous county in the state. Persons of English descent comprised more than 50 percent of the population of every New Jersey county, except for Hunterdon, where the English amounted to 30 percent, Middlesex, where there were 48 percent, Cape May, where there were 50 percent, and Bergen, where Nelson et al. estimated they amounted to 15 percent. The next largest ethnic groups in these counties were the Germans (25 percent) and Dutch (25 percent) in Hunterdon, the Germans (20 percent) and Scots (20 percent) in Middlesex, the Swedes (40 percent) in Cape May, and the English (15 percent) in Bergen. The English population of Cape May had come from New England settlements and Yankee outposts on Long Island. The Nelson et al. estimates appear in the U.S. Department of Commerce and Labor, *A Century of Population Growth* (Washington, D.C., 1909), 119–20. Historians who have criticized *A Century of Population Growth* for overestimating the proportion of persons of English descent in America regard the Nelson estimates as "excellent." See American Historical Association, *Annual Report for the Year 1931, Proceedings,* 1:129. Thomas Purvis's revised estimates of the ethnic composition of New Jersey are found in his article in this issue of *New Jersey History;* his figures were compiled too late to be used in this article.

[42] There were 12,422 slaves in New Jersey in 1800. See Edgar J. McManus, *Black Bondage in the North* (Syracuse, N.Y., 1973), 175–79.

[43] Lester J. Cappon, ed., *Atlas of Early American History: The Revolutionary Era, 1760–1790* (Princeton, N.J., 1976), 38.

[44] W.W.H. Davis, *The History of Bucks County, Pennsylvania* (Doylestown, Pa., 1876), 793–98.

[45] Durand Echeverria, ed., *New Travels in the United States of America 1788 by J. P. Brissot de Warville* (Cambridge, Mass., 1964), 227.

[46] U.S. Census Office, Second Census, 1800. Those twenty-six to forty-four and forty-five and older are given an age of 33 and 55, respectively, as suggested by data for 1850 appearing in Lee Soltow, *Men and Wealth in the United States, 1850–1870* (New Haven, Conn., 1975).

[47] The voters of Monmouth and Cape May counties were closely divided in 1800. If numerous voters in Cape May County were of New England extraction, they may have preferred the Federalist party, for New Englanders tended to vote Federalist when they emigrated to places outside New England like Pennsylvania's Luzerne and Erie counties or Ohio's Western Reserve or the Ohio Company Purchase of southeastern Ohio. The presence of these New Englanders and Cape May County's Quakers may have strengthened the Federalist interest in Cape May in spite of the fact that the county was a poor one. In this case cultural ties may have overcome the force of economic interest.

Monmouth County was one of the poorer Federalist counties, so economic circumstances may have weakened its allegiance to Federalism. See Prince, *N.J.'s Jeffersonian Republicans*, 70–130; Fee, *Aristocracy to Democracy*, 124, 128–38, 159; McCormick, *Voting*, 88. Possibly, differences in wealth were sharpening by the end of the eighteenth century. The New Jersey General Assembly was becoming increasingly conscious of the social problems associated with poverty in 1799–1800, for legislators passed several acts to assist the poor, relieve insolvent debtors, and establish workhouses in New Jersey's counties. See *Centinel of Freedom* March 19, June 25, November 26, 1799.

[48] Norman K. Risjord, *Chesapeake Politics: 1781–1800* (New York, 1978).

[49] Alfred F. Young, *The Democratic-Republicans of New York: The Origins: 1763–1797* (Chapel Hill, N.C., 1967).

[50] Kenneth W. Keller, *Rural Politics and the Collapse of Pennsylvania Federalism*, (*Transactions of the American Philosophical Society*, vol. 72, part 6, 1982); John A. Munroe, *Federalist Delaware: 1775–1815* (New Brunswick, N.J., 1954).

Politics, Parties, and Pestilence: Epidemic Yellow Fever in Philadelphia and the Rise of the First Party System

Martin S. Pernick*

THE omens were not auspicious for Philadelphia in the summer of 1793. Unusually large flocks of migrating pigeons filled the day-time sky. By night a comet streaked the heavens. Increased numbers of cats were dying, their bodies putrefying in the streets and sinkholes, as the rains that usually washed them away were replaced by prolonged drought. Most ominously, the swarms of flies seemingly indigenous to the city had been driven off by a dense mass of "moschetoes" that hung over the city like a cloud.[1] Warned by these signs and portents, the learned Philadelphia medical community had prepared itself for the appearance of a somewhat more virulent strain of "autumnal fever" than was usual. By early August, though, the doctors were puzzling over isolated cases of a new disease involving yellowing of the skin and vomiting of an unknown black substance. On August 19, Dr. Benjamin Rush, signer of the Declaration of Independence and dean of Philadelphia medicine, proclaimed that yellow fever had returned to the city for the first time since 1762.

Initial disbelief turned rapidly to panic as the death toll mounted. By the end of the month between 140 and 325 Philadelphians had died of the fever. On one October day, 119 dead were buried. Between August 19 and November 15, 10 to 15 percent of the estimated 45,000 Philadelphians perished, while another 20,000, including most government officials, simply fled.[2] An extralegal committee of citizen volunteers, called upon

---

* Mr. Pernick is an instructor in the Pennsylvania State University College of Medicine, Milton S. Hershey Medical Center, Hershey.

[1] J. H. Powell, *Bring Out Your Dead: The Great Plague of Yellow Fever in Philadelphia in 1793* (Philadelphia, 1949), 1-64; Charles E. A. Winslow, *The Conquest of Epidemic Disease: A Chapter in the History of Ideas* (Princeton, 1943), 198.

[2] Powell, *Bring Out Your Dead*, 8-12, 219, 232. The exact number of deaths is

213

by the mayor following the hasty departure of the regular municipal officers, gradually brought the panic under control. Growing slowly from a nucleus of ten men who answered Mayor Matthew Clarkson's September 10 call, the committee commandeered the vacant Bush Hill estate for use as a hospital, set up an orphanage, distributed food, firewood, clothes, and medicine to the poor, buried the abandoned corpses, and undertook a complete cleanup of the city.[3]

Good intentions and hard work were not enough; the hospital could do little when no cure was known. Sanitary efforts were random at best when no one understood the cause of the sickness. The city of Philadelphia needed immediate resolution of three crucial medical questions: what caused the fever and how might its spread and recurrence be averted? how should the sick be treated? and should the people evacuate or stay?

Philadelphia was the medical capital of the United States. Franklin's Pennsylvania Hospital, the prestigious College of Physicians, and the American Philosophical Society combined to attract to the city the best of the new nation's scientific and medical talent. But the medical problems posed by yellow fever were simply not soluble by even the best eighteenth-century physicians—or, more accurately, medical science alone provided no definitive way of choosing from among the scores of conflicting causes, preventives, and cures, each presented as gospel by its learned advocates. This uncertainty provided the opening by which influences quite removed from medical science entered the medical debate.[4]

Philadelphia in 1793 was not only the medical center of America but the political capital of a new republic as well. And in politics as in medicine, the presence of a large body of experts did little to expedite agreement. In fact, 1793 found the political leadership of the nation more

unknown. The figure 4,040, derived from burial lists, includes deaths from all causes in the city but does not include the many fever victims buried elsewhere. The burial lists are appended to Mathew Carey, *A Short Account of the Malignant Fever,* . . . 4th ed. (Philadelphia, 1794). See also Richard H. Shryock, *Medicine and Society in America, 1660-1860* (New York, 1960), 82, 108.

[3] Powell, *Bring Out Your Dead*, 143, 242-243.

[4] Erwin H. Ackerknecht, "Anticontagionism Between 1821 and 1867," *Bulletin of the History of Medicine*, XVI (1948), 562-593. An opposing view is J. B. Blake, "Yellow Fever in Eighteenth Century America," *Bulletin of the New York Academy of Medicine*, XLIV (1968), 681.

divided than at any time in its short past. The year began amid an increasingly bitter verbal duel between Treasury Secretary Alexander Hamilton, writing in John Fenno's *Gazette of the United States,* and Secretary
of State Thomas Jefferson, whose views appeared in Philip Freneau's
National Gazette. The battle, begun over fiscal policy, took on added
significance with the news at midspring that Revolutionary France had
executed America's benefactor, Louis XVI, and had declared war on
England. Jefferson and his followers feared English "monarchism" as
much as Hamilton and his supporters detested French "anarchy." The
arrival of Citizen Genêt, the new French Republican Minister to the
United States, inspired sympathetic popular demonstrations in Philadelphia and elsewhere, events organized in part by the newly formed
Pennsylvania Democratic Society. The exact purposes of this organization may well have been as unclear to the founders as they are to modern
historians, but everyone agreed that it was pro-French and pro-
Republican.[5]

In spite of such signs of pro-French sympathy, Jefferson's political
standing underwent a marked decline in the summer of 1793. Hamilton
gained increased influence over foreign policy within the administration
following the April Neutrality Proclamation, while Genêt's rapid success in alienating almost everyone in America further discouraged Jefferson. On July 31, Jefferson notified Washington of his intention to resign
by year's end.

Local Philadelphia politics grew more involved following the arrival
in early August of over two thousand French refugees from the black
revolution in Haiti. Unlike the earlier royalist refugees, the new arrivals
included many white radicals and moderates, ousted when the slaves
seized control of the revolutionary movement.[6]

Both Hamilton and Jefferson feared dividing the young Republic,
but their debate provided the core around which local and congressional
factions crystalized to form the first institutional American party system.
As Jeffersonians became Democratic-Republicans and Hamiltonians became Federalists, both sought to arouse public interest by taking sides

[5] Eugene P. Link, *Democratic-Republican Societies, 1790-1800* (New York,
1942); Harry M. Tinkcom, *The Republicans and Federalists in Pennsylvania, 1790-
1801: A Study in National Stimulus and Local Response* (Harrisburg, 1950).
[6] Frances S. Childs, *French Refugee Life in the United States, 1790-1800: An
American Chapter of the French Revolution* (Baltimore, 1940), 22, 103, 142-143,
159.

in a variety of local or nonpolitical disputes. Local factions likewise often tried to identify their cause with a national party for ideological, rhetorical, political, or moral support against their local rivals. In either case local antagonisms were deepened and prolonged while the national party gained new grass roots significance.[7] Not surprisingly, the national parties first found themselves embroiled in local issues in the capital city of Philadelphia. The medical controversies generated by the 1793 epidemic over the cause of the disease, its proper treatment, and the conduct of those caught in the crisis, thereby became an integral chapter in the history of the first party system.

Since it was not until 1901 that Walter Reed demonstrated the process by which the *Aëdes aegypti* mosquito transmits yellow fever from an infected person to a healthy one, Philadelphia physicians of 1793 divided bitterly over the cause of the epidemic. Doctors who saw the roots of the disease in domestic causes—the poor sanitation, unhealthy location, or climatic conditions of Philadelphia itself—disputed those who placed the blame on the unhealthy state of the still disembarking refugees and their ships. In fact, both sides were right, since a yellow fever epidemic requires both locally bred mosquitoes and an initial pool of infected persons, such as the exiled Haitians. In 1793, however, there was simply no known medical theory to resolve the dispute.[8] The etiological debate revealed, moreover, a medical community split along partisan political lines. In general, Republican physicians, including the refugee doctors, believed the

[7] A general picture of the events and mechanisms of party development may be found in Joseph Charles, *The Origins of the American Party System* (New York, 1956); Noble E. Cunningham, Jr., *The Jeffersonian Republicans: The Formation of Party Organization, 1789-1801* (Chapel Hill, 1957); Richard Hofstadter, *The Idea of a Party System: The Rise of Legitimate Opposition in the United States, 1780-1840* (Berkeley and Los Angeles, 1969); and Richard P. McCormick, *The Second American Party System: Party Formation in the Jacksonian Era* (Chapel Hill, 1966).

[8] Winslow, *Epidemic Disease*, 195, 200, 231. Related to, but distinct from, the etiology question was the problem of contagion. Almost all importationists believed the fever contagious, but advocates of a local origin differed over whether it could become contagious after appearing. For examples, see David Nassy, *Observations on the Cause, Nature, and Treatment of the Epidemic Disorder Prevalent in Philadelphia* (Philadelphia, 1793), 13; Benjamin Rush, *An Enquiry Into the Origin of the Late Epidemic Fever in Philadelphia* (Philadelphia, 1793), 14; Benjamin S. Barton, "On Yellow Fever," n.d. [1806?], Benjamin Smith Barton Papers, Delafield Collection, American Philosophical Society, Philadelphia.

fever to be local. The "importationists" were almost all nonpartisans or Federalists.

Dr. Michael Leib, a founder of all three branches of the Philadelphia Democratic Society and a member of the key correspondence committee of the "mother society," argued the domestic origin case before the College of Physicians. Joining him was his old professor, Dr. Rush, an outspoken opponent of Hamilton. Rush, a founding fellow of the College, leader of the medical school faculty, and probably the best known physician in Philadelphia, insisted that "miasmata" from local swamps and "effluvia" from unsanitary docks bred the fever. A second member of the Democrats' correspondence committee, Dr. James Hutchinson, who as Secretary of the College and Physician of the Port was responsible for deciding to admit or bar the refugee ships, reported to Pennsylvania Governor Thomas Mifflin on August 26, "It does not seem to be an imported disease; for I have learned of no foreigners or sailors that have hitherto been infected." Dr. Jean Devèze, himself a refugee, attributed importationism to ignorance and party influence.[9]

The advocates of importation included Philadelphia's lone confessed Federalist physician, Dr. Edward Stevens, a future diplomat and close boyhood friend of Hamilton. The other leading importationists were Drs. Adam Kuhn, Isaac Cathrall, and William Currie. Although prominent in the profession, they took no part in party politics in 1793. On November 26, after Hutchinson's death in the epidemic enabled Kuhn and his supporters to gain a majority, the College of Physicians passed a resolution firmly asserting, "No instance has ever occurred of the disease called the *yellow fever*, having been generated in this city, or in any other parts of the United States . . . but there have been frequent instances of its having been imported." The resolution was the work of Drs. Thomas Parke, John Carson, and Samuel P. Griffitts, none of whom was politically active in 1793.[10] Benjamin Rush had resigned from

[9] Powell, *Bring Out Your Dead*, 43-44; Carey, *Short Account*, 12; Benjamin Rush, *An Account of the Bilious Remitting Yellow Fever* . . . (Philadelphia, 1794); *Dictionary of American Biography*, s.v. "Hutchinson, James"; Jean Devèze, *An Enquiry into, and Observations upon; the Causes and Effects of the Epidemic Disease* (Philadelphia, 1794), 16; Powell, *Bring Out Your Dead*, 36-44. On the importance of the correspondence committee, see Edward Ford, *David Rittenhouse: Astronomer-Patriot, 1732-1796* (Philadelphia, 1946), 190.

[10] Records of the College of Physicians, I (1787-1812), 175, Nov. 19, 1793, College of Physicians of Philadelphia; Rush, *Account*, 146; Adam Kuhn, Yellow Fever Manuscripts (1794), 6, College of Physicians of Philadelphia, Philadelphia;

the College a few days earlier. Benjamin Smith Barton was the only Republican physician in Philadelphia to support importationism in this
epidemic.[11] (See Table I)

TABLE I

1793 PARTY AFFILIATIONS OF PHYSICIANS WHO EXPRESSED
AN OPINION ON THE CAUSE OF YELLOW FEVER

	Republicans	Federalists	Uncommitted
Importationists - 10	1	1	8
Domestic Origin - 14	6	0	8

Note: Twenty-four Philadelphia physicians, the most prominent third of the practicing
healers in town, left evidence of their opinions on the cause of the fever. One-third
of this medical elite was actively involved in the earliest stages of party building.
While this degree of participation led to a qualitatively significant interrelationship
between politics and medicine, the number of individuals involved was too small
to judge their statistical significance.

Politics entered the issue by different doors with different doctors. As
a topic for medical debate "The Origin of Pestilential Fevers" was an
old favorite, and several physicians were committed to one side or the

Stacey B. Day, ed., *Edward Stevens: Gastric Physiologist, Physician and American
Statesman* (Montreal, 1969); William Currie, *A Treatise on the Synochus Icteroides,
Or Yellow Fever* . . . (Philadelphia, 1794), 1, 67, 84; Currie, *An Impartial Review
of that Part of Dr. Rush's Late Publication* . . . *In Which His Opinion is Shewn
to be Erroneous; the Importation of the Disease Established; and the Wholesome-
ness of the City Vindicated* (Philadelphia, 1794), 6-14.

[11] Rush, *Account,* 146; *Independent Gazetteer* (Philadelphia), Jan. 22, 1794;
Benjamin S. Barton to Thomas Pennant, Apr. 11, 1794, Barton Papers. Later epidemics in 1797 and 1798 introduced some blurring of party lines. By 1797, Republican Dr. Caspar Wistar had definitely joined the importationists. See College of
Physicians of Philadelphia, *Facts and Observations Relative to the Nature and
Origin of the Pestilential Fever* . . . (Philadelphia, 1798), 43, 52; Samuel D. Gross,
ed., *Lives of Eminent American Physicians and Surgeons of the Nineteenth Century*
(Philadelphia, 1861), 134-135; College of Physicians Records, I, 216, 225, 250. The
political allegiance of Dr. William Shippen, Jr., is uncertain. An importationist, he
chaired a largely Republican town meeting in 1795 but also appeared in the rolls
of the Federalist marching society. See *Ind. Gaz.,* Nov. 30, 1793, July 25, 1795; and
General Roll of McPherson's Blues, Hollingsworth Manuscripts, Business Papers
Miscellaneous, undated, Historical Society of Pennsylvania, Philadelphia. An unlikely suggestion was made that Shippen did not know who was behind the 1795
meeting, "thus committing himself as a puppet to be moved at the pleasure of
very bungling artists." *Gazette of the United States* (Philadelphia), July 25, 1795.
Dr. Charles Caldwell continued to champion localism even after his 1796 conversion to Federalism, but in 1793 he was loyal to both the politics and the medicine
of Benjamin Rush. See Charles Caldwell, *Autobiography* (Philadelphia, 1855),
174, 182, 254, 267, 278; Caldwell to James Hutchinson, Aug. 1, 1793, Hutchinson
Papers, Am. Phil. Soc.

other before 1793. One such was Benjamin Rush. His 1789 comments belittling both importationism and its advocates created hostilities which may help explain why few importationists would join Rush in the Jeffersonian councils.[12]

For most physicians, though, the whole issue remained a somewhat remote subject for scholarly speculation until the crisis of 1793 suddenly forced each practitioner to choose a course of immediate action. Many turned for guidance to trusted colleagues—teachers and friends whose opinions on medical, political, and other matters they had shared in the past.[13] In addition, Republican doctors were the most likely to have come in contact with the localist doctrines which dominated French medicine. In the case of Dr. Hutchinson, politics may have influenced medical decisions more directly. An importationist prior to the epidemic, the Republican port physician apparently switched to localism to avoid closing the city to the French refugees.[14]

Like the physicians, the political leaders of Philadelphia split by party over the cause of the fever. Although Republican editor Freneau vehemently condemned the disputes of the medical men, declaring that "no circumstance has added more to the present calamity," he actually strongly supported a local origin. He made his viewpoint clear in the following poem:

> Doctors raving and disputing,
> Death's pale army still recruiting—
>   What a pother
>   One with t'other!
> Some a-writing, some a-shooting.
>
> Nature's poisons here collected,
> Water, earth, and air infected—
>   O, what pity.
>   Such a City,
> Was in such a place erected![15]

[12] Benjamin Rush, *Medical Inquiries and Observations* (Philadelphia, 1789); Carl Binger, *Revolutionary Doctor: Benjamin Rush, 1746-1813* (New York, 1966), 228.

[13] Rush, for one, expected just such deference from former students. See L. H. Butterfield, ed., *Letters of Benjamin Rush*, II (Princeton, 1951), 681.

[14] Powell feels Hutchinson was "obviously confused." *Bring Out Your Dead*, 43. See also n. 23 below.

[15] "Pestilence," quoted *ibid*.

On September 23, the *National Gazette* published a discussion of more than a dozen theories of the origin of the disease without once mentioning the possibility of its being imported.[16] In medicine as in politics only one's opposition was seen as the "divisive faction." Local Republican civic leaders like editor Andrew Brown and merchants John Swanwick and Stephen Girard supported Dr. Devèze's explanation that burying the dead inside the city had produced the disease. Jefferson explained to Madison that the fever was "generated in the filth of Water street."[17]

On the other hand, Philadelphia Federalists John Fenno, Oliver Wolcott, Thomas Willing, Benjamin Chew, Levi Hollingsworth, J. B. Bordley, Ebenezer Hazard, Bishop William White, and printer Benjamin Johnson led their party in publicly proclaiming yellow fever a foreign disease.[18] In his days as a Federalist after 1794, William "Peter Porcupine" Cobbett, the Anglo-American pamphleteer, penned a series of libelous attacks on Rush's theories. But in 1793, as a supplicant of the patronage of Secretary Jefferson and a tutor to the refugees, Cobbett spoke of the yellow fever as a typical product of the unhealthy American climate.[19]

More than one-third of the most prominent national and local political leaders in Philadelphia took a public position on the cause of the epi-

[16] *National Gazette* (Philadelphia), Sept. 23, 1793.

[17] Thomas Jefferson to James Madison, Sept. 1, 1793, in Andrew A. Lipscomb and Albert E. Bergh, eds., *The Writings of Thomas Jefferson* (Washington, D. C., 1903), IX, 214-215; *Federal Gazette* (Philadelphia), Dec. 17, 21, 28, 1793; *Gaz. of U. S.*, Dec. 18, 1793. Democratic Society leader Israel Israel requested the city to dig sewers following the epidemic. Israel to Clarkson, Jan. 29, 1794, Philadelphia Streets and Alleys Manuscripts, Hist. Soc. of Pa.

[18] For Fenno, see Nathan Goodman, *Benjamin Rush: Physician and Citizen, 1746-1813* (Philadelphia, 1934), 198; for Wolcott, see Charles Francis Jenkins, *Washington in Germantown* . . . (Philadelphia, 1905), 76; for Willing and Chew, see College of Physicians of Philadelphia, *Additional Facts and Observations Relative to the Nature and Origin of the Pestilential Fever* (Philadelphia, 1806), 10, 11; for Hollingsworth, see "An Old Resident" [Hollingsworth] to David Claypoole, Hollingsworth MSS; for Bordley, see J. B. Bordley, *Yellow Fever* (Philadelphia, 1794); for Hazard, see "Hazard Letters," Massachusetts Historical Society, *Collections*, 5th Ser., III (1877), 338, and Powell, *Bring Out Your Dead*, 86; for White, see Bird Wilson, *Memoir of the Life of the Right Reverend William White, D.D.*, . . . (Philadelphia, 1839), 158, 288; for Johnson, see Benjamin Johnson, *Account of the Rise, Progress, and Termination of the Malignant Fever* (Philadelphia, 1793), 5.

[19] Lewis Saul Benjamin [Lewis Melville], *The Life and Letters of William Cobbett in England & America, Based upon Hitherto Unpublished Family Papers* (New York, 1913), 85-87.

demic. (See Table II) With few exceptions the Republicans backed a domestic source of the fever, while Federalists largely blamed importation. Governor Mifflin, who endorsed importation theories, has been called a Republican although he usually appeared as the nonpartisan "Father of his State." Benjamin Franklin Bache, editor of the Republican *General Advertiser,* believed the disease imported but blamed the *British* West Indies, later calling the fever "a present from the English." The least typical was Republican printer Mathew Carey, who included his native Ireland as well as the French islands among the possible sources of the fever.[20] Timothy Pickering, an intimate friend of Dr. Rush, was probably the only Federalist leader in Philadelphia to claim the yellow fever as a domestic disease.[21]

TABLE II

OPINIONS ABOUT THE CAUSE OF YELLOW FEVER HELD BY THE
POLITICAL LEADERSHIP OF PHILADELPHIA

	Importationist	Domestic Origin	Unknown
Republicans - 9	1	4	4
Uncommitted - 6	1	1	4
Federalists - 16	3	1	12

Note: Tables II, III, and IV examine the views of Philadelphia's major officeholders and editors: the federal executive officers, Pennsylvania's U. S. Senators, the Philadelphia delegations to the Third Congress and to the state legislature, the governor and the secretary of state of Pennsylvania, the mayor of Philadelphia, and the editors or publishers of Philadelphia's English language newspapers. All party affiliations are as of 1793.

[20] For Mifflin, see Powell, *Bring Out Your Dead,* 52-53, Samuel Hazard *et al.,* eds., *Pennsylvania Archives,* 4th Ser., IV (Harrisburg, 1900), 264-269, and Tinkcom, *Republicans and Federalists,* 72, 112, 219-220; for Bache, see Donald H. Stewart, *The Opposition Press of the Federalist Period* (Albany, 1969), 137; for Carey, see Mathew Carey, *Observations on Dr. Rush's Enquiry into the Origin of the Late Epidemic Fever in Philadelphia* (Philadelphia, 1793), and Carey, *Short Account,* 67.
[21] Charles W. Upham, *The Life of Timothy Pickering,* III (Boston, 1873), 56, 62. Some Federalists from rival cities, such as Harrisburg's Alexander Graydon, encouraged the idea that Philadelphia was an unhealthy place. Alexander Graydon, *Memoirs of a Life* (Harrisburg, 1811), 336-338. However, most Federalist merchants in New York, Baltimore, and Trenton remained importationists, leading the local efforts to cut off the trade of their stricken rival. See *General Advertiser* (Philadelphia), Sept. 18, 20, 23, 1793; and James Weston Livingood, *The Philadelphia-Baltimore Trade Rivalry 1780-1860* (Harrisburg, 1947). Even anticontagionist New York Federalist Noah Webster believed this Philadelphia epidemic contagious. Noah Webster, *A Collection of Papers on the Subject of Bilious Fevers* (New York, 1796), 233.

The party leaders, moreover, moved rapidly to exploit the many political implications they discovered in the medical controversy. Federalists used the importation doctrine to back demands for the quarantine or exclusion of the radical French, and for limitations on trade with the French islands, while Republican merchants saw importationism as a cover for plans to wreck their lucrative trade with the West Indies. Girard and Dr. Devèze denounced the proposed quarantine as "disastrous to commerce," but in June 1798, during the "Quasi-War" with France, the newly drafted quarantine laws were in fact successfully invoked to block the immigration of suspected Haitian subversives.[22]

A novel twist was provided by Dr. Currie's theory that the disease originated on board the French privateer Sans Culotte, which brought a prize to Philadelphia in July. Accusing both the French and Port Physician Hutchinson, the Federalists charged that sickness on the ship had been covered up to protect the Republican political and financial stake in her activities. Benjamin Johnson blamed the epidemic on the French "licensed plunderers of the Ocean," adding that "if particular men had done their duty; and had not betrayed more indulgence to French cruizers, than genuine friendship for this city," the disease would have been averted.[23] Federalist charges fed a growing Francophobia. "AMOR PATRIAE" warned Philadelphians not to trust the city's benevolent French physicians. Persistent rumors that the wells had been contaminated preparatory to a French invasion led to threats of mob violence against the hapless refugees.[24]

Although the Federalists talked of closing all trade with the French islands, they seemed far more anxious to arouse public suspicion of the French and the Republicans than to create any precedent for a government embargo on commerce. Indeed, the Federalist merchants feared that localism was part of a Republican conspiracy to discredit Philadelphia and all large commercial centers and to force relocation of the

[22] Harry Emerson Wildes, *Lonely Midas: The Story of Stephen Girard* (New York, 1943), 121, 126; Albert J. Gares, "Stephen Girard's West Indian Trade, 1789-1812," *Pennsylvania Magazine of History and Biography*, LXXII (1948), 316; J. Thomas Scharf and Thompson Westcott, *History of Philadelphia, 1609-1884* (Philadelphia, 1884), I, 493.
[23] Johnson, *Account*, 5, 9; *Dunlap's American Daily Advertiser* (Philadelphia), Dec. 20, 1793; Rush, *Account*, 147. Leib and others defended Hutchinson against the charges raised by the College. *Gen. Adv.*, Nov. 30, Dec. 10, 1793.
[24] *Ind. Gaz.*, Dec. 14, 1793; Henry D. Biddle, ed., *Extracts from the Journal of Elizabeth Drinker* (Philadelphia, 1889), 193.

capital in a rural setting. Richard Peters warned Timothy Pickering against Rush's doctrine on October 22: "His Assertion that the Philadelphia Hot beds produced this deadly Plant is . . . a mischievous Opinion . . . and will be eagerly caught at by the Anti Philadelphians. Stifle this Brat if you can."[25] Rush noted the result by October 28: "A new clamor has been excited against me in which many citizens take a part. I have asserted that the yellow fever was generated in our city. This assertion they say will destroy the character of Philadelphia for healthiness, and drive Congress from it."[26] John Beale Bordley wrote an importationist pamphlet for the admitted purpose of convincing Congress to remain in Philadelphia. Federalist editor John Fenno worried that the domestic origin theory would "not only render multitudes uneasy and interrupt the usual course of business, but injure the interest and reputation of the city in several respects."[27]

Such political fears could easily distort medical objectivity. "Is there a city in the world," asked Levi Hollingsworth, "kept cleaner than Philadelphia?" The College of Physicians answered flatly, "No possible improvement with respect to water or ventilation can make our situation more eligible"—this at a time when Philadelphia had no sewage system, no fresh water supply, and no provision for regular garbage disposal![28]

Republicans did attack large cities as unhealthy, and Jefferson later expressed confidence that the "yellow fever will discourage the growth of great cities in our nation."[29] Yet most Republicans protested that they wanted not to destroy commercial cities but to preserve them through sanitary reform.[30] Federalist fears of a plot to move the capital also

[25] Richard Peters to Timothy Pickering, Oct. 22, 1793, Timothy Pickering Papers, Massachusetts Historical Society, Boston, quoted in Butterfield, ed., *Rush Letters*, II, 729-730. Pickering may have shown the letter to Rush. Fearing government restrictions on trade, one Federalist importationist appealed to the benevolence of the merchants and ship captains to impose a voluntary quarantine. "A Philadelphian," in *Occasional Essays on the Yellow Fever* . . . (Philadelphia, 1800), 8-11, 13.

[26] Benjamin Rush to Julia Rush, Oct. 28, 1793, in Butterfield, ed., *Rush Letters*, II, 729.

[27] Goodman, *Benjamin Rush*, 198; Bordley, *Yellow Fever*, 1; Blake, "Yellow Fever," *Bull. N. Y. Academy of Medicine*, XLIV (1968), 682.

[28] "An Old Resident" to Claypoole, Hollingsworth MSS; College of Physicians, *Facts and Observations*, 24.

[29] Jefferson to Rush, Sept. 23, 1800, in Lipscomb and Bergh, eds., *Writings of Jefferson*, X, quoted in Charles N. Glaab, *The American City: A Documentary History* (Homewood, Ill., 1963), 52.

[30] For example, *Fed. Gaz.*, Dec. 6, 21, 1793; John Redman Coxe Letters on the

proved groundless. In the debates over whether or not Congress could legally meet elsewhere to avoid the fever, the Republicans, for strict constructionist reasons, favored convening in Philadelphia.[81]

The Federalist endorsement of importation proved to be a very effective and popular position as the idea of a native American plague irritated a highly sensitive patriotic nerve. Rush noted that "Loathsome and dangerous diseases have been considered by all nations as of foreign extraction."[82] Importationists made much of the widely held feeling that independent America was the New Eden. Reaching the farthest extreme of this argument, one importationist asserted in 1799 that the doctrine of domestic fevers was "treason," perhaps hoping that the Alien and Sedition Acts gave the Federalists the power to deport foreign diseases along with foreign agitators.[83]

The people of Philadelphia urged their officials to agree on specific actions to prevent the return of yellow fever, but the political implications of the issue made adoption of any single course of action unacceptable. Thus, immediately following the 1793 epidemic, Pennsylvania and other threatened states undertook *both* quarantine and sanitary reform projects. Simple political compromise provided a way around the bitter medical deadlock.[84] Considering the state of medical knowledge in 1793, the imposition of a political settlement may well have been the best result that could have been expected.

In 1793, the division between medicine and theology was still young. Not everyone in Philadelphia believed the cause of the plague was strictly medical; rather, the wrath of the Deity appeared to many as manifest in the fever, and before the debate over the epidemic had ended, theology, like medicine, had become enmeshed in political developments. The devout saw most early American diseases, such as cholera

Yellow Fever [1794], 139, College of Physicians of Philadelphia; Joseph McFarland, "The Epidemic of Yellow Fever in 1793 and Its Influence Upon Dr. Benjamin Rush," *Medical Life*, XXXVI (1929), 468. Both sides in the medical split claimed to be the true friends of commerce. Blake, "Yellow Fever," *Bull. N. Y. Academy of Medicine*, XLIV (1968), 681.

[81] Powell, *Bring Out Your Dead*, 260-263. Constitutional principles did not limit the state's power to move its own capital out of Philadelphia in 1799 as a result of the yellow fever. Scharf and Westcott, *Philadelphia*, I, 501.

[82] Rush, *Account*, 147.

[83] College of Physicians, *Facts and Observations*, 15-16; Butterfield, ed., *Rush Letters*, II, 798; Hazard et al., eds., *Pa. Arch.*, 4th Ser., IV, 269.

[84] Blake, "Yellow Fever," *Bull. N. Y. Academy of Medicine*, XLIV (1968), 681.

and typhoid, as punishment for the individual sins of vicious immigrants and slothful poor. Unlike these diseases, though, yellow fever was spread not by poor individual hygiene but by infected mosquitoes which could and did bite high and low with complete republican egalitarianism. Some physicians even declared that blacks and the West Indian immigrants were more immune than respectable white Philadelphians, a costly error. At any rate, the pious saw the yellow fever as a communal punishment rather than as retribution against individual sinners.[35]

The issue that remained, of course, was to identify and root out those communal transgressions which had provoked the pestilence. With no shortage of suggestions as to where the country was going astray, the Republicans first gave political content to the religious debate. At the very height of the plague, Freneau devoted front page coverage to a series of articles and letters which pointed to the pride and vanity of the communal leaders as the major transgression. Mathew Carey joined in the attack. And Benjamin Rush, the Enlightenment man of science, commented in retrospect, "I agree with you in deriving our physical calamities from moral causes. . . . We ascribe all the attributes of the Diety to the name of General Washington. It is considered by our citizens as the bulwark of our nation. God would cease to be what He is, if he did not visit us for these things."[36]

Federalists too put the religious issue in political harness. An official thanksgiving-fast sermon by the Reverend William Smith linked the pestilence with French immorality and with the "wild principles and restless conduct of their partisans here, impatient of all rule and authority."[37] Connecticut Senator Chauncey Goodrich saw the divine anger resulting from Republican adoration of Genêt, while Alexander Graydon recalled the "state of parties in the summer of 1793, when the metropolis of Pennsylvania, then resounding with unhallowed orgies at the dismal butcheries in France, was visited with a calamity which had much the appearance which heaven sometimes sends to purify the heart."[38]

[35] For a discussion of the theological perception of cholera, 1832-1866, see Charles E. Rosenberg, *The Cholera Years: The United States in 1832, 1849, and 1866* (Chicago, 1962). See also Shryock, *Medicine and Society*, 94; Butterfield, ed., *Rush Letters*, II, 659; Horace W. Smith, *Life and Correspondence of the Rev. William Smith, D.D.,* . . . I (Philadelphia, 1880), 395; *Gen. Adv..* Jan. 8, 1794.

[36] Rush to William Marshall, Sept. 15, 1798, in Butterfield, ed., *Rush Letters*, II, 807. Rush also blamed party spirit in general. See also *Natl. Gaz.*, Oct. 9, 12, 16, 1793; Carey, *Short Account*, 10.

[37] Smith, *Life of William Smith*, I, 392.

[38] Graydon, *Memoirs*, 335; Stephen G. Kurtz, *The Presidency of John Adams:*

A peculiar coincidence gave added depth to these speculations, for the fever had miraculously appeared just as Philadelphia completed construction of what one Republican termed its "Synagogue for Satan"—the city's new Chestnut Street Theater. Many in Revolutionary America saw the theater as an extremely complex negative symbol, part bordello and part palace. The new theater, with fluted marble columns and pure golden ornaments, was indeed palatial.[39] While a few Republicans like Swanwick owned stock in the theater company, the major backers were prominent Federalists.[40] They in turn tried to portray opposition to the theater as a Republican scheme to subvert private property. One Francophobe detected the same "rigourous enthusiasm" which spawned the French Revolution motivating the foes of the drama. Opponents of the stage did appeal to Anglophobic, antimonarchical, and Republican imagery to justify their cause, although not all Republicans were antitheater.[41]

Philadelphia's embattled defenders of public virtue had all but given up when the epidemic provided the ammunition for yet another crusade. Sixteen of the city's leading clergymen joined with the Quakers in petitioning the state to shut the new theater. "We conceive that the solemn intimations of Divine Providence in the late distressing calamity which has been experienced in this city, urge upon us in the most forcible manner the duty of reforming every thing which may be offensive to the Supreme Governor of the Universe." Devout Republicans found it significant that "the actors and retainers of the stage, who actually arrived here at the time when the fever raged with the utmost violence," were Englishmen.[42] The opponents of stage plays eventually lost their struggle, even with the arguments gained from the epidemic.

The Collapse of Federalism, 1795-1800 (Philadelphia, 1957), 190; Charles D. Hazen, Contemporary American Opinion of the French Revolution, Johns Hopkins University Studies in Historical and Political Science, XVI (Baltimore, 1897), 185-186.
[39] Natl. Gaz., Oct. 16, 1793; Scharf and Westcott, Philadelphia, II, 966-967.
[40] Scharf and Westcott, Philadelphia, II, 966-967.
[41] Gaz. of U. S., Dec. 19, 28, 1793; Gen. Adv., Jan. 6, 1794; Arthur Hornblow, History of the Theatre in America, I (Philadelphia, 1919), 174-175; Natl. Gaz., Oct. 16, 1793.
[42] Gaz. of U. S., Dec. 14, 26, 1793, Feb. 8, 1794; René La Roche, Yellow Fever . . . (Philadelphia, 1855), 73; William Priest, Travels in the United States of America . . . (London, 1802), 13; [John Purdon], A Leisure Hour; or a Series of Poetical Letters, Mostly Written During the Prevalence of the Yellow Fever (Philadelphia, 1804), 27.

The issue, however, helped strengthen the growing bond between Quakers and Republicans in Philadelphia.[43]

Medical science today can do little more to cure a case of yellow fever than it could in 1793, a sobering fact that helps explain the continued controversy over the treatment of the disease long after the question of etiology had been shelved. The number of treatments attempted in the sheer desperation of the Philadelphia epidemic was astounding, yet the medical community rapidly split into two main schools. One favored the use of "stimulants"—quinine bark, wine, and cold baths—a method long used in both British and French West Indies. Opposing these "bark and wine murderers," a second group advocated the "new treatment" concocted by Dr. Rush, who believed it advisable to draw an amount of blood which we know today to be in excess of the quantity possessed by most people, and whose doses of mercury caused severe disfiguration of the teeth and skin. But by eighteenth-century standards his "experimental" approach appeared more advanced than the "traditional" bark cure.[44]

Many factors helped determine which doctors adopted what cure, not the least of which was chance. Rush himself tried the bark and wine method before his "discovery" but lost three of four patients. Another variable was the infamous, tangled infighting among Philadelphia physicians. Almost any medical opinion rendered by Benjamin Rush eventually drew the ridicule of Dr. William Shippen, the man Rush had hauled before a court-martial over their disagreements in the Revolution.[45] Partisan differences were at first unimportant in a doctor's choice

[43] Several leading Republican literary figures remained aloof from this alliance. Bache, whose son-in-law was an actor, was accused of misrepresenting rank and file Republican sentiment on the theater for family reasons. Roger Griswold, *The Republican Court; or, American Society in the Days of Washington* (Philadelphia, 1854), 316; *Gen. Adv.*, Jan. 10, 1794. On Jan. 8, though, Bache attributed his stand to anticlericalism. See also Mathew Carey, *Autobiography* (New York, 1942 [reprint of 1837 ed.]), 29.

[44] W. H. Hargreaves and R. J. G. Morrison, *The Practice of Tropical Medicine* (London, 1965), 183-185; Powell, *Bring Out Your Dead*, 64, 125, 292. Wine is generally not a stimulant although it was believed to be one. Chris Holmes, "Benjamin Rush and the Yellow Fever," *Bull. Hist. Med.*, XL (1966), 246-262, believes Rush's cures were not lethal, but does not fully distinguish patients like Hazard, who left Rush after one or two treatments, from those who stayed for the full course of bloodletting.

[45] David Freeman Hawke, *Benjamin Rush, Revolutionary Gadfly* (Indianapolis,

of a cure. True, Rush counted among his followers many ardent Republicans such as Dr. Leib, Dr. George Logan, the Quaker pacifist, Dr. Benjamin Say, and most of his former students. However, a large body of Republican "bark and wine doctors" included Hutchinson, Dr. Benjamin Smith Barton, and the French-trained Bush Hill staff under Devèze and Girard. Republican bark doctors did learn the cure from the French refugees, while the Federalist Dr. Stevens and other non-Republican physicians adopted the procedure from the British or Dutch islands, but their actual methods of treating patients were almost identical. Although it was inaccurate, many Philadelphians persisted in the conviction that there was a "Republican cure" and a "Federalist cure."[46]

The man initially responsible for politically polarizing this nonpartisan jumble was Alexander Hamilton. Seeing an opportunity to do a favor for an old friend, Hamilton published a glowing personal tribute to Dr. Stevens, attributing his own recovery to the bark and wine cure. In so doing, Hamilton could not resist a sneer at his old critic, Dr. Rush. Hamilton's tool, Secretary of War Henry Knox, followed, airing his thoughts on Rush a few days later. The local and national Federalist press took the cue and began a barrage of political-sounding attacks on Rush's cure, terminated only by the 1799 libel judgment against Cobbett. Fenno's unkind attempt to derive Rush's bloodletting from that of the French terror resulted in a libel action against him as well, but the case was never tried.[47]

By simply declaring long enough and loud enough that bark and wine was the Federalist cure, these editors were able to make a considerable political issue out of a basically nonpartisan dispute. Their appeal was meant to gain political support among the many users of the mild wine and quinine therapy while personally discrediting Rush. The political element in the attack on bleeding seemed obvious to Rush. "I think it probable that if the new remedies had been introduced by any other per-

1971), 208-223, 236-240; Powell, *Bring Out Your Dead*, 78; Goodman, *Benjamin Rush*, 90-116.

[46] Powell, *Bring Out Your Dead*, 82, 153, 203; George Logan to "Citizen Bache," in *Gen. Adv.*, Sept. 18, 1793; Harold Syrett and Jacob E. Cooke, eds., *The Papers of Alexander Hamilton*, XV (New York, 1969), 325, n. 1. Say's party affiliation is derived from Tinkcom, *Republicans and Federalists*, 240.

[47] *Dunlap's Adv.*, Sept. 13, 1793; Syrett and Cooke, eds., *Hamilton Papers*, XV, 331-332; Powell, *Bring Out Your Dead*, 135; Goodman, *Benjamin Rush*, 215; Jenkins, *Washington in Germantown*, 25.

son than a decided Democrat and a friend of Madison and Jefferson, they would have met with less opposition from Colonel Hamilton," Rush complained. "Many of us," he later told Gen. Horatio Gates, "have been forced to expiate our sacrifices in the cause of liberty by suffering every species of slander and persecution. I ascribe the opposition to my remedies in the epidemic which desolated our city in 1793 chiefly to an unkind and resentful association of my political principles with my medical character."[48] Rush did not deny the Federalist charge that his cures were associated with his politics. Attacked as a democrat, he replied as a democrat, hoping to rally Republican political support for his medical views. Rush declared his cure the only truly egalitarian form of medicine in that it was easy to master and could be practiced by anyone with little formal training. Putting his beliefs into practice, he trained a group of free blacks as itinerant bleeders during the epidemic and published "do-it-yourself" directions in the newspapers, actions which did not endear him to the guardians of the professional mysteries any more than to the Federalists. Rush declared it unnecessary "to send men educated in colleges . . . to cure . . . pestilential disease," assuring his followers that "men and even women may be employed for that purpose, who have not perverted their reason by a servile attachment to any system of medicine." "All that is necessary," he added, "might be taught to a boy or girl twelve years old in a few hours."[49]

Rush also adopted the Federalists' derogatory identification of his cures with the French Revolution, affirming "I am in the situation of The French Republic surrounded and invaded by new as well as old enemies, without any other allies." He went so far as to imply that the true treatment, no less than the true politics, could be derived in good democratic fashion: "The people rule here in medicine as well as government." The best cure could be decided by the will of the majority. On

[48] B. Rush to J. Rush, Oct. 3, 1793, to Horatio Gates, Dec. 26, 1795, to John Dickinson, Oct. 11, 1797, in Butterfield, ed., *Rush Letters*, II, 701, 767, 793; Goodman, *Benjamin Rush*, 203, 209.

[49] McFarland, "Yellow Fever and Dr. Rush," *Med. Life*, XXXVI (1929), 486-487; John E. Lane, "Jean Devèze," *Annals of Medical History*, N.S., VIII (1936), 220; Margaret Woodbury, *Public Opinion in Philadelphia, 1789-1801*, Smith College Studies in History, V (Northampton, Mass., 1920), 16; Goodman, *Benjamin Rush*, 208. Some Republican bark physicians agreed that Rush's cures were egalitarian but denied that political Republicanism required opposition to medical elitism. See letter of "Citizen Robert, M.D.," *Gen. Adv.*, Dec. 6, 1793, whose combination of titles reflects his attempt to combine egalitarianism and professional distinctions.

October 2, Rush wrote to Elias Boudinot that "Colonel Hamilton's remedies are now as unpopular in our city as his funding system is in Virginia or North Carolina."[50]

Public support of bark and wine by several prominent Federalists gave credence to its reputation as the "Federalist cure." Rush, however, failed in his attempt to rally the Republican leadership behind his "egalitarian" medicine. Prominent Republican leaders largely ignored the issue on which Republican physicians were themselves divided. (See Table III)

TABLE III

OPINIONS ABOUT THE CURE OF YELLOW FEVER HELD BY
THE POLITICAL LEADERSHIP OF PHILADELPHIA

	Bark and wine	Mercury and bleeding	Unknown
Federalists - 16	4	1	11
Uncommitted - 6	0	0	6
Republicans - 9	1	0	8

Republican "bark and wine" physicians denied that bleeding was the Republican cure, but they could not compete for public attention with the colorful and prolific Dr. Benjamin Rush. Many Republican "bark doctors" were refugees, barred from political office and lacking public influence, and Hutchinson's death deprived them of their most prominent and articulate spokesman. The failure of "bark and wine" Republicans to counter the publicity attracted by Hamilton and Rush made the cure of yellow fever seem a clear-cut party issue.[51] Moreover, the injection of politics into this medical debate probably had some adverse side effects. The partisan taint of arguments against mercury and bleeding delayed rejection of the Rush cure long after the medical evidence pointed to its inefficacy and danger.

The first days of the epidemic produced a mad scramble to escape town. Benjamin Rush warned all who could to leave the city; even his bitter rivals Drs. Shippen and Kuhn took his advice this time and quickly departed. The panic was so great that "many people

[50] Powell, *Bring Out Your Dead*, 201; Butterfield, ed., *Rush Letters*, II, 692.
[51] McFarland, "Yellow Fever and Dr. Rush," *Med. Life*, XXXVI (1929), 462.

thrust their parents into the streets, as soon as they complained of a headache."[52] Exceptions to the general exodus soon appeared, however. Most of the physicians stuck to their posts. Rush, following his discovery of a "cure," publicly advised everyone to remain in town. The French, familiar with the disease and trained to believe it noncontagious, did not flee. Many shopkeepers and middle-class merchants with no one to look after their affairs, and the poor with no place else to go, stayed as well. A handful of true philanthropists remained. As the epidemic wore on, observers noted that the leaders of each of these groups were often Republicans.[53]

Several Federalists did play major roles in the heroic relief work. Mayor Clarkson organized the citizens' committee while Samuel Coates and John Oldden headed a merchants' distribution organization which handled supplies for the mayor. Coates, an intimate of Rush and Girard, was nonetheless a Federalist and was often criticized by Girard for his Francophobia.[54] Levi Hollingsworth and Caspar W. Morris joined the merchants' group. Clement Humphreys, son of the shipbuilder, remained at his post as a guardian of the poor. Three Federalist clergymen, William Smith, William White, and Robert Blackwell, also remained to comfort the ill. Although these nine men were the only identifiable Federalists at all involved in the organized relief work, an additional five, Jacob Hiltzheimer, Postmaster Timothy Pickering, ex-Postmaster Ebenezer Hazard, Congressman Thomas FitzSimmons, and John Stillé, chose not to join the organized effort but rendered important aid to their families and neighbors individually.[55]

[52] Goodman, *Benjamin Rush*, 183.
[53] Stephen Girard to Pierre Changeur & Co., Sept. 11, 1793, Girard Papers, Am. Phil. Soc.; Powell, *Bring Out Your Dead*, 175, 179-180.
[54] Powell, *Bring Out Your Dead*, 179, 242. Samuel Coates is not to be confused with William Coates, a founder of the Democratic Society. Henry Simpson, *The Lives of Eminent Philadelphians, Now Deceased* (Philadelphia, 1859), 218; *Gaz. of U. S.*, Dec. 14, 1793.
[55] Carey, *Short Account*, 27, 28. Carey seems to slight Federalists in his stories of heroism. For their side, see also Jacob Cox Parsons, ed., *Extracts from the Diary of Jacob Hiltzheimer, of Philadelphia* (Philadelphia, 1893), 195-197; Smith, *Life of William Smith*, I, 379; Upham, *Life of Pickering*, III, 62; "Hazard Letters," Mass. Hist. Soc., *Colls.*, 5th Ser., III (1877), 334; Powell, *Bring Out Your Dead*, 138; and Simpson, *Eminent Philadelphians*, 908-922. For party affiliations of Morris (as of 1798), see letter of Nov. 19, 1798, Hollingsworth MSS; of Humphreys, see Scharf and Westcott, *Philadelphia*, I, 490; of Hollingsworth, see David Hackett Fischer, *The Revolution of American Conservatism: The Federalist Party in the*

Active Republicans, however, performed the greatest share of the work. Of the eighteen men cited in the minutes as the leaders of the citizens' committee, nine were definitely Republicans, one was the brother of an ardent Republican, and seven could not be identified with either party. The mayor was the only Federalist. The Republican leaders of the committee were Vice-chairman Samuel Wetherill, Secretary Caleb Lownes, Stephen Girard of Bush Hill, Israel Israel (orphans), Mathew Carey (printing), Jonathan Dickinson Sergeant (counsel), James Sharswood (accounts), James Kerr (orphans), and John Connelly (accounts). Treasurer Thomas Wistar was the brother of Republican Dr. Caspar Wistar.[56] The other committeemen were Andrew Adgate (at large), Peter Helm of Bush Hill, Daniel Offley (at large), Joseph Inskeep (at large), John Letchworth (orphans), Samuel Benge (burials), and Henry Deforest (supplies).

Three of the four members of the key correspondence committee which ran the Democratic Society were leaders in fighting the fever. Two, Hutchinson and Jonathan Dickinson Sergeant, lost their lives while caring for the sick. The third was Dr. Leib, who had charge of Bush Hill in the first chaotic days of its existence. Alexander B. Dallas, the fourth member, claimed with some justification that his state office required him to follow the state government to its exile in Germantown.[57] At least seventeen men listed as active in the Democratic Society played major roles in aiding the sick. Israel Israel directed the relief and orphanage work of the committee. Well-known in Philadelphia for

Era of Jeffersonian Democracy (New York, 1965), 339; of Hiltzheimer and Fitz-Simmons, see Tinkcom, Republicans and Federalists, 138, 152. In addition, Samuel Pancoast of the merchants' committee was listed as a Federalist by 1817. Scharf and Westcott, Philadelphia, I, 588.

[56] For Wetherill, see Simpson, Eminent Philadelphians, 940, and Tinkcom, Republicans and Federalists, 252; for Lownes, see Scharf and Westcott, Philadelphia, I, 477; for Girard, see Link, Democratic Societies, 75-76; for Israel, see Powell, Bring Out Your Dead, 178; for Carey, see Carey, Autobiography; for Sergeant, see Dictionary of American Biography, s.v. "Sergeant, Jonathan Dickinson"; for Sharswood, see Simpson, Eminent Philadelphians, 885; for Kerr and Connelly, see Minute Book of the Democratic Society, 29, 47, Hist. Soc. of Pa., and Scharf and Westcott, Philadelphia, I, 507, 588; for Wistar, see Powell, Bring Out Your Dead, 179. The list of leaders of the committee was compiled from names most frequently cited in Minutes of the Proceedings of the Committee Appointed on the 14th September, 1793 (Philadelphia, 1848); and Carey, Short Account, 95.

[57] Powell, Bring Out Your Dead, 72, 87, 179; Ford, David Rittenhouse, 190; Kenneth R. Rossman, Thomas Mifflin and the Politics of the American Revolution (Chapel Hill, 1952), 225.

his Revolutionary War exploits and for his antifederalism, Israel was treasurer of the Democratic Society. The president of the Society, David Rittenhouse, went on call with his nephew Dr. Barton, arranging for free treatment of the poor. After the death of his son-in-law Sergeant, Rittenhouse left town briefly, but returned before the end of the epidemic to resume his work.[58]

The Quaker Dr. George Logan was an ardent Democrat who had left both medicine and Philadelphia in 1781. Returning now from his retirement at Stenton near Germantown, he served as the committee's inspector at Bush Hill, from where he reported to the world the incredible efforts of the managers, "Citizens Girard and Helm." The one-eyed merchant Girard, who almost alone turned Bush Hill from a pest-house to a hospital, was also active in the Democratic organization.[59] The labors of Dr. Rush, who formally joined the Society in early 1794, were comparable to those of Girard. Visiting hundreds of patients while ill himself, Rush stuck to his post even after the death of his sister. Also members of the Democratic group were John Connelly and James Kerr of the citizens' committee; George Forepaugh, Jeremiah Paul, William Robinson, Sr., James Swaine, and William Watkins of the merchants' committee; volunteer John Barker; and John Swanwick, owner of the committee's orphanage. Others of Republican persuasion cited for their roles were aldermen Hilary Baker and John Barclay, and merchants' committeeman Caspar Snyder.[60]

[58] Powell, *Bring Out Your Dead*, 177; Ford, *David Rittenhouse*, 190-192.

[59] Helm was Girard's assistant in charge of "external affairs." He was a second generation German-American but little else is known of him. The chronology of Bush Hill is as follows: Aug. 31—Mayor authorizes seizure of estate, hospital set up under Leib and others; Sept. 16—Girard and Helm volunteer to manage and administer the hospital for the committee; Sept. 18—Girard appoints Devèze to assist Leib and the medical staff; Sept. 21—Leib resigns in dispute over the proper cure. Powell, *Bring Out Your Dead*, 140-172.

[60] Democratic Society Minute Book, 29, 39, 42, 47, 48, 52, 95; Link, *Democratic Societies*, 77, 90; Carey, *Short Account*, 20, 27, 30, 37; Tinkcom, *Republicans and Federalists*, 57, 84, 283. Snyder is identified as of 1799 in Scharf and Westcott, *Philadelphia*, I, 507, 588. There were two John Barclays; this one was president of the Republican Bank of Pennsylvania. Duplication of names makes it impossible to say whether merchants' committeeman William Clifton was the Federalist poet or one of two shopkeepers of that name. Likewise, William Sansom, Guardian of the Poor, may have been either the Federalist or the Republican of that name. Simpson, *Eminent Philadelphians*, 210; General Roll of McPherson's Blues, Hollingsworth MSS; J. Hardie, *The Philadelphia Directory and Register . . .* (Philadelphia, 1793), 182 and *passim*.

Among Philadelphia newspapers, only Republican Andrew Brown's *Federal Gazette* appeared throughout the epidemic, keeping the remaining citizens in touch with the relief workers.[61] Freneau, who vowed to publish for as long as possible, held on longer than any editor except Brown. The *National Gazette* last appeared on October 16, a victim of financial losses rather than of editorial dereliction. His work ended, Freneau did not flee the city but remained until mid-December.[62]

The list of Republican heroes also included Frenchmen. In addition to Devèze, all four physicians' aides and most of the staff at Bush Hill were French. The French specialist in tropical medicine, Citizen Robert, hearing of the epidemic while en route to France, rushed to Philadelphia from Boston in what one writer termed a "confirmation of the sincere attachment of the French patriots, to the truly republican Americans!" The largest individual contribution to the relief fund came from Citizen Genêt. Even "THE REPUBLICAN SEAMEN OF FRANCE" got involved, forming Philadelphia's only intact fire company during the epidemic. Freneau credited them with saving the city from the fate of London.[63]

While Republicans dominated the relief work, Federalists often joined the ranks of the refugees, not necessarily from cowardice, as Republicans charged, but rather because of their belief in importation and contagion. No prominent importationist leaders of either party stayed in Philadelphia. The one anticontagionist Federalist official remained; the one importationist Republican fled. (See Tables IV, A and B) Illustrative of the disappearance of Federalists was the case of the Dutch Minister, Francis Van Berkle, who believed himself ill. Since Dr. Stevens had left for New York, Hamilton (from his refuge in Albany) suggested that the minister consult Oliver Wolcott on the use of bark and wine. The minister soon discovered that Wolcott too was gone. Tired of looking for someone to instruct him in the "Federalist cure," Van Berkle was treated by Rush and recovered.[64]

[61] Powell, *Bring Out Your Dead*, 85-86. To avoid confusion over the new implications of its old name, the *Federal Gazette* became the *Philadelphia Gazette* on Jan. 1, 1794. Clarence S. Brigham, *History and Bibliography of American Newspapers, 1690-1820*, II (Worcester, Mass., 1947), 91.
[62] Lewis Leary, *That Rascal Freneau: A Study in Literary Failure* (New Brunswick, N. J., 1941), 240-246; Dumas Malone, *Jefferson and the Ordeal of Liberty*, Vol. III of *Jefferson and His Time* (Boston, 1962), 142.
[63] *Natl. Gaz.*, Sept. 11, Oct. 9, 1793; Scharf and Westcott, *Philadelphia*, II, 1606; *Minutes of the Committee*, 232.
[64] Powell's account, *Bring Out Your Dead*, 135, differs from Rush's version

TABLE IV

A. PERSONAL REACTIONS OF PHILADELPHIA'S POLITICAL LEADERSHIP

	Stay	Flee	Unknown
Federalists - 16	5	8	3
Uncommitted - 6	1	4	1
Republicans - 9	4	4	1

B. FURTHER ANALYSIS OF PERSONAL REACTIONS
OF THOSE POLITICAL LEADERS WHOSE RESPONSE IS KNOWN

	Importationists		Domestic Origin		Unknown	
	stay	flee	stay	flee	stay	flee
Federalists - 13	0	3	1	0	4	5
Uncommitted - 5	0	1	0	1	1	2
Republicans - 8	0	1	3	1	1	2

It appeared that the Republicans would receive high praise for their efforts. Benjamin Rush "is become the darling of the common people and his humane fortitude and exertions will render him deservedly dear," noted one observer.[65] Bravery and leadership make popular American campaign fare, and the Republicans were not slow to present their political bill for services rendered. Among the first to make an issue of bravery was Jefferson, whose Revolutionary War record had recently come under unkind Federalist scrutiny. His scornful cut at Hamilton as the Treasury Secretary prepared to flee is considered by Dumas Malone to have been Jefferson's most vicious political remark. "His family think him in danger," wrote Jefferson, "and he puts himself so by his excessive alarm. He has been miserable several days before from a firm persuasion he should catch it. A man as timid as he is on the water, as timid on horseback, as timid in sickness, would be a phenomenon if his courage of which he has the reputation in military occasions were genuine. His friends, who have not seen him, suspect it is only an autumnal fever he has." Jefferson also attacked Henry Knox, who had already fled, but after waiting to make sure Hamilton had

of the Van Berkle business, B. Rush to J. Rush, Oct. 3, 1793, in Butterfield, ed., *Rush Letters*, II, 701. Wolcott fled with Knox in early September. Jenkins, *Washington in Germantown*, 22.

[65] Powell, *Bring Out Your Dead*, 123.

really gone first, Jefferson himself left town over a week ahead of his planned departure.[66]

Freneau took over the task of castigating the "deserters." His poem, "Orlando's Flight," ridiculed the fugitives:

> On prancing steed, with spunge at nose,
> From town behold Orlando fly;
> Camphor and Tar where'er he goes
> Th' infected shafts of death defy—
> Safe in an atmosphere of stink,
> No doctor gets Orlando's chink.

Freneau also implied it was greed that made the fugitives so anxious to preserve themselves. Speaking of the afterworld, he concluded:

> Monarchs are there of little note,
> And Caesar wears a ragged coat.
>
> .   .   .   .
>
> Blame not Orlando if he fled,—
> *So little's got by being dead.*[67]

The last evacuees had not yet returned when a special election brought the heroism issue to the fore. State Senator Samuel Powel, Philadelphia's beloved Revolutionary War mayor, had died of the fever. On December 12, a Republican meeting put forth the name of Israel Israel for Powel's seat. Israel's platform was simple and direct. He was "a gentleman whose philanthropy on a late melancholy occasion is well known, and whose firm and steady attachment to the people will, it is hoped, bring forth the united suffrages of the citizens in his favour."[68] The Federalist response came swiftly. The day after the Israel nomination, Fenno revealed a move to draft Mayor Clarkson as the Federalist choice. In an

[66] Jefferson to Madison, Sept. 8, 1793, in Paul Leicester Ford, ed., *The Writings of Thomas Jefferson*, VI (New York, 1895), 419; Malone, *Jefferson and the Ordeal of Liberty*, 140-142.

[67] *Natl. Gaz.*, Sept. 4, 1793. The version in Powell, *Bring Out Your Dead*, 240, is not the original 1793 poem but a printed edition of 1795. The original attacks all deserters; the later one absolves all but the fleeing physicians. Condemnation of the fugitives often stressed their wealth. *Gaz. of U. S.*, letter of Feb. 20, 1794.

[68] *Dunlap's Adv.*, Dec. 14, 1793; Nathaniel Burt, *The Perennial Philadelphians: The Anatomy of an American Aristocracy* (Boston, 1963), 156-157. "Nomination," "platform," etc. are all useful metaphors in spite of the anachronism.

attempt to outdo the Republicans, Clarkson's backers asserted that "gratitude demands a particular tribute of acknowledgement to him for his assiduity, and perseverance in relieving the distresses of our fellow citizens during the calamity from which we have just emerged."[69] Clarkson, however, was content to be mayor, and the nomination went instead to William Bingham, the extremely wealthy associate of the powerful Willing-Morris partnership. Bingham had followed the progress of the fever from his New Jersey shore retreat. The actual management of his campaign, however, was placed in the hands of relief workers John Oldden and John Stillé. Their efforts apparently countered the appeal of Israel's candidacy, and Bingham won the December 19 contest by a three to two margin.[70]

The return of the "deserters" further complicated Republican use of the heroism issue. While many of the Federalists had fled the fever, most of the evacuees were not Federalists. One-third of all Philadelphians had left, and the majority of the rest remained hidden behind locked doors, venturing out only for necessities. Their initial gratitude toward the members of the committee was mingled with a good deal of shame, guilt, and envy. As one perceptive reviewer noted in commenting on Mathew Carey's account of the epidemic, "To panegyrize our contemporaries, without attracting censure on ourselves, requires a very delicate hand."[71] The Republicans realized that a campaign based solely on praising their own heroics while damning the opposition's defections was politically unwise. They usually attempted to temper their attacks by expressing sympathy with the difficulties encountered by the fugitives, many of whom had been brutally repulsed by the panicked citizens of neighboring cities.[72]

The returnees meanwhile countered criticism with charges of their own, terming the epidemic a "doctors' harvest." The citizens' committee was attacked as too expensive and as growing insolent with power. "Unless the Committee feel *tickled* with their employment," wrote one critic, "they ought to surrender it to the Guardians of the

---

[69] *Gaz. of U. S.,* Dec. 13, 1793.

[70] *Ibid.,* Dec. 14, 20, 1793; Robert C. Alberts, *The Golden Voyage: The Life and Times of William Bingham, 1752-1804* (Boston, 1969), 246. Out of 14,000 eligible, only 1,282 Philadelphians came out to vote. *Ind. Gaz.,* Dec. 21, 1793.

[71] *Dunlap's Adv.,* Dec. 14, 1793.

[72] Syrett and Cooke, eds., *Hamilton Papers,* XV, 332n; Carey, *Short Account,* 93; Powell, *Bring Out Your Dead,* 216-232.

poor, who are competent to the service, and who will perform it at a *much less expence* and *with far less state*." Rush's black bleeders were easy targets for Federalist charges of profiteering. Actually, the committee and most physicians offered free medical service to the poor, while Rush even distributed free mercury. Yet the boast of Rush's student, Dr. Mease, that the fever had made his fortune for life, and the activities of Samuel Wetherill, whose drug business took precedence over his committee duties, gave the charges just enough credibility to undermine the Republican appeal to public gratitude.[73] A common complaint charged the committeemen with usurping powers reserved for the traditional political elite. "The bulk of them," wrote one resentful critic, "are scarcely known beyond the smoke of their own chimnies."[74] Further, many Philadelphians simply wished to forget the entire painful scene as quickly as possible. The heroes of the epidemic were living reminders of the horror and the suffering. "If the disease has disappeared as it no doubt has, every momento of its existence should disappear with it, that the citizens may once more enjoy repose."[75]

Despite the strenuous efforts of the party organization, Republican heroism was a complete flop as a political issue. A 1797 election in which Israel Israel had defeated Federalist Benjamin Morgan was invalidated when Morgan claimed his backers had been disenfranchised by holding the election while the Federalists were "driven from their homes" by the epidemic of that year. With the fleeing Federalists safely home again, the hapless Israel lost the second election despite heavy contributions from Girard and Sharswood.[76]

The yellow fever struck a Federalist Philadelphia in 1793 and left both local and national Federalist rule considerably strengthened. For one thing, the epidemic seriously weakened the national

[73] *Gen. Adv.*, Dec. 2, 1793; Butterfield, ed., *Rush Letters*, II, 736; Johnson, *Account*, 28; Powell, *Bring Out Your Dead*, 87, 178. Carey printed rumors of black profiteering similar to Johnson's but he hastily withdrew them. Richard Allen, *Life Experiences and Gospel Labors* . . . (Philadelphia, 1933), 34-35.

[74] *Gen. Adv.*, Dec. 2, 3, 1793; *Fed. Gaz.*, Dec. 9, 14, 1793.

[75] "HOWARD," in *Gen. Adv.*, Jan. 8, 1794; see also Nov. 27, 1793.

[76] Tinkcom, *Republicans and Federalists*, 176-179; John Bach McMaster, *The Life and Times of Stephen Girard, Mariner and Merchant*, I (Philadelphia, 1918), 352. The career of Israel Israel and his role in Philadelphia class politics is traced in John K. Alexander, "The City of Brotherly Fear: The Poor in Late Eighteenth Century Philadelphia," in Kenneth T. Jackson and Stanley K. Schultz, comps., *Cities in American History* (New York, 1972), 86-90.

Republican organization. The deaths of Hutchinson and Sergeant eliminated two of the four men responsible for creating and directing new Democratic Society branches. Years later, John Adams declared that these two deaths alone saved the nation from an imminent revolution.[77] The collapse of the *National Gazette* under the financial strain of the epidemic created another void which Bache's *Aurora* could not immediately fill. Even the little-noted death of Citizen Dupont, the French Consul, had its political effect, leaving France's critical relations with the United States in the hands of a vice-consul for months until the arrival of a replacement for Genêt.

In issues as well as institutions the Federalists gained, at least in the short run. The Republicans were unable to convert their heavy organizational losses into an effective sympathy vote. By denying any local source of the pestilence, the Federalists won much national chauvinist and local booster support, while their espousal of importationism heightened American Francophobia. In addition, the Federalists managed to identify their opponents with Benjamin Rush's advocacy of a dangerous and controversial remedy. Although Philadelphia Republicans found some additional Quaker support in the theater issue, the national party gained at best a minor new point against large cities.[78]

More important, the epidemic served to introduce new issues and attract new supporters to the two developing parties, thereby extending and broadening the base of the new party system. This development was sometimes local in its origins, as in the debate over the cause of the fever, where the already politically polarized local controversy introduced issues that the national politicians adopted and used. In other issues, such as the bleeding v. bark debate, a nonpolarized initial conflict had political meaning imposed from the outside by the intervention of national leaders. Furthermore, the process of giving political significance to social issues was highly selective. The issue which seemed logically closest to politics was that of courage and leadership, but despite the efforts of the local antagonists and the party organization, human feelings of gratitude proved too flimsy a foundation on which to build a political platform.

[77] Charles Francis Adams, ed., *The Works of John Adams,* . . . X (Boston, 1856), 47. Jefferson declared the death of Hutchinson to be as great a setback as the Genêt fiasco. Merrill D. Peterson, *Thomas Jefferson and the New Nation: A Biography* (New York, 1970), 508.
[78] Tinkcom, *Republicans and Federalists,* 173.

Political influence in late eighteenth-century medicine did not always signify irresponsible meddling. Political compromise permitted concerted public action to fight future epidemics at a time when medical opinion seemed hopelessly deadlocked, although the political significance of the potentially lethal Rush "cure" helped assure its continued use, needlessly endangering the lives of patients.

Finally, not everyone was willing to be drawn into partisan debate over a medical question. Expressing the hope that the next epidemic might be met by the united efforts of "all parties" in the City of Brotherly Love, an anonymous satirist poked fun at both the Federalist and Republican views of the fever:

Be patient ye vivid sons of mercury with the medical baptisms of your *cold bath brethren*. For had that therapentic process been tried under the cataract of Niagara, no body can tell the wonders which might have been produced by it . . .

Cease ye yellow fever heroes to censure, those of your brethren whose delicacy of nerves and previous engagements called them suddenly chrochet and forceps a la main to Nootka Sound, to catch Others and Beavers. Be assured, important discoveries have been made by the Jaunt.

Lend a kind ear to the graduates of Montpelier, who inform you that the late disease arose from the burying grounds in the heart of your city, since in France they never bury the dead under Churches, but in balloons high up in the air.[79]

Ye learned and long robed sons of Esculapius, pity and pardon poor Absolam Jones and Richard Allen,[80] two sable Ethiopians, who being ignorant of the Greek and Latin languages, were under the necessity of curing their patients *in English*.[81]

But neither the political nor the medical debates would be silenced so simply.

[79] Jean Pierre Blanchard had recently introduced the city to the French hot air balloon.

[80] Two of Rush's black apprentices.

[81] *Gaz. of U. S.*, Dec. 23, 1793.

THE
Pennsylvania
Magazine
OF HISTORY AND BIOGRAPHY

Philadelphia's Manufacturers and the Excise Taxes of 1794: The Forging of the Jeffersonian Coalition

THE WHISKEY INSURRECTION in Pennsylvania is a familiar event. Supposedly, the insurrection, arising from opposition to the federal excise tax, was centered in the four western counties. Individualism, frontier spirit and economic deprivation were the underlying causes for the uprising. The tax revolt is further regarded as an important chapter in the constitutional and economic history of the early republic. Other opponents of the excise in the other sections of the United States—Kentucky, western Virginia, Carolina back country and Georgia—are depicted in the same agrarian mold.[1] Historians

*This article was presented in a somewhat abbreviated form at the forty-ninth meeting of the Pennsylvania Historical Association held at Wilkes-Barre on October 17-18, 1980. The author wishes to thank Steven R. Boyd and Alfred F. Young for their helpful suggestions.

[1] For a comprehensive study of the rebellion in Pennsylvania see Leland D. Baldwin, *Whiskey Rebels, The Story of a Frontier Uprising* (Pittsburgh, 1939). Jacob E. Cooke, "The Whiskey Insurrection: A Re-Evaluation," *Pennsylvania History*, XXX (July, 1963), 316-346, is still the best summary of what has been written on the subject. Forrest McDonald, *Alexander Hamilton, A Biography* (New York, 1979), 255-256, 297-303, restates the traditional view of the event.

have left the impression that the farmers of rural America were the only interest group to face economic hardship when the national government sought to develop revenues by the imposition of excise taxes in 1791 and 1794. Such an interpretation has prevailed because historians of the Federal Era have not considered all of the provisions of the Revenue Acts of 1794. Most important, they have overlooked the existence of significant agitation in the seaboard towns over the extension of the excise.[2]

This article explores the contours of urban opposition to the introduction of indirect taxes in Philadelphia during the years 1794-1797. Because that protest differed in form and content from the excise rebellion in rural America, the administration of George Washington did not use military force in the spring and summer of 1794 to put down an urban insurrection. But the city's protests, including petition campaigns, meetings, and electioneering, generated consequences for the Federalist party that probably exceeded the political significance of the rural rebellion. Indeed, the agitation over the excise taxes in urban America helped to forge the Democratic-Republican movement in Philadelphia by allowing Republicans to draw on the support of self-conscious occupational groups who felt economically threatened by the excise tax placed on manufacturers.[3]

In 1789, Philadelphia was an important manufacturing center and promoter of mechanical arts, the hub of a regional economy and the principle commercial entrepot of the country.[4] The city contained

[2] This subject was not developed either in Harry M. Tinkcom, *The Republicans and Federalists in Pennsylvania 1790-1801: A Study in National Stimulus and Local Response* (Harrisburg, 1950), chap. 6, or in Richard G. Miller, *Philadelphia—The Federalist City: A Study of Urban Politics, 1789-1801* (Port Washington, N.Y., 1976). Passing references to an urban response to the excise tax exist, however, in the earlier studies of William Miller, "The Democratic Societies and the Whiskey Insurrection," *The Pennsylvania Magazine of History and Biography (PMHB)*, LXII (July, 1938), 324-349; Eugene P. Link, *Democratic-Republican Societies, 1790-1800* (New York, 1942), 76-78.

[3] These views were originally presented in the author's, "The Democratic-Republicans of Philadelphia: The Origins, 1776-1797" (unpublished Ph.D. diss., Pennsylvania State Univ., 1970), chap. 10.

[4] According to one English traveller Philadelphia was "the London of America." Henry Wansey, *An Excursion to the United States of North America in the summer of 1794*, 2nd ed. (Salisbury, 1798), 57. For an excellent secondary description of Philadelphia, see Ethel M. Rasmusson "Capital on the Delaware: the Philadelphia Upper Class in Transition, 1789-1801," (unpublished Ph.D. diss., Brown Univ., 1962), chap. 3.

large-scale manufacturers, small-scale manufacturers and rank-and-file artisans. Exclusive of carpenters, masons, and other skilled workers, the city and suburbs of Northern Liberties and Southwark, with a total population in 1790 of 43,000, had some 2200 persons (or one-quarter of the adult males) who might properly be identified as manufacturers—that is, individuals who were engaged in the production of such articles as beer, distilled spirits, carriages, flour products, hats, leather, pearl, ash, rope, shoes, sugar, textiles, timber, tobacco products, etc. At least one-half of these articles were produced locally and sold in both an internal and external market.[5]

The manufacturers' prominence came as the result of continuous growth and development since the 1760s. The non-importation movements of the 1760s and 1770s stressed the development of household and other predominantly small scale manufacturers. Before the American Revolution Philadelphians depended upon England for the bulk of their manufactured goods, but during the immediate post-war years the "industrial sector" challenged the "commercial-maritime" sector for attention and sought the support and patronage of the Pennsylvania General Assembly for loans, subsidies and other preferential treatments.[6] Many large-scale manufacturers also formed partnerships in order better to serve the needs of a growing urban center. This non-British capitalization—along with the state's aid of protective duties, use of water power, and the adoption of modern techniques of production and marketing—was most conspicuous in the brewing, carriage-making, distilling, snuff-making, sugar refining and tanning industries.[7] The long struggle for economic independence

---

[5] Thomas J. Scharf and Thompson Westcott, *History of Philadelphia, 1609-1884* 3 vols. (Philadelphia, 1884), III, 2230, 2251, 2285. To understand the occupational structure of Philadelphia, by wards, I have depended upon the little used November 1793 Septennial Census Returns, Record Group (RG) 7, Records of the General Assembly, Div. of Archives and Manuscripts (State Archives), Pennsylvania Historical and Museum Commission.

[6] For this story see Charles S. Olten, *Artisans for Independence, Philadelphia Mechanics and the American Revolution* (Syracuse, N.Y., 1975). Robert L. Brunhouse, *The Counter-Revolution in Pennsylvania, 1776-1790* (Harrisburg, Pa, 1942), 115-116, 134-135, 142, 151-152, 172-173, 181-182, 195.

[7] On the formation of business partnerships to raise capital, see John R. Commons et al., *History of Labour in the United States* 4 vols. (New York, 1918-1935), I, chap. 3; Curtis P. Nettles, *The Emergence of a National Economy, 1775-1815* (New York, 1962, 1969), 69-75. The manufacturers used mercantile models. Harry D. Berg, "The Organization of Business in Colonial Philadelphia," *Pennsylvania History*, X (1943), 155-177.

coincided with the struggle for political independence.[8]

Before analyzing how this economic group was tested in the 1790s, it is helpful to understand what is meant by the term "large-scale manufacturer." Laboring in the aforementioned industries and running a manufactory, the manufacturer either worked for himself or with a partner. He thus manufactured outside the small shop and garrett, usually employed journeymen and workers for a wage, and where possible used newer methods and tools. The large-scale manufacturer who combined the functions of merchant and artisan was often required to make a considerable investment in plant and equipment. In the industries of snuff-making and sugar refining, for example, the leading manufacturers were retailers as well as wholesalers; filled orders at pre-arranged prices; and exposed themselves to foreign competition and to the risks of owning raw materials, stocking goods, extending credit and operating in a modern marketplace subject to price and market fluctuations. In short, these were independent businessmen who needed capital to operate and who sought to improve their station by taking advantage of the buoyant economy of the leading seaport. By 1800 many of the large-scale manufacturers had become members of the economic elite of Philadelphia.[9]

These manufacturers increased their political participation when economic interests took sides on issues involving the nature and functions of the national government. For instance, on the eve of George Washington's inauguration as president of the United States in April 1789, Philadelphia's manufacturers stood solidly behind the Federalist party. They were not only an important voting bloc in favor of the Federal Constitution, but had also provided support for Federalist candidates in the first Congressional and Presidential elections. In joining the party of Federalism, the manufacturers demonstrated their belief that the new national government would advance the interests of

[8] Olten, *Artisans for Independence*, 117-119. See also the insightful analysis of this struggle in Eric Foner's, *Tom Paine and Revolutionary America* (New York, 1976), chap. 2.

[9] Philadelphia's economic elite lacked cohesion and distinctiveness, often engaged in economic conflict, and its members came from all social groups. Robert Gough, "Towards a Theory of Class and Social Conflict: A Social History of Wealthy Philadelphians, 1775 and 1800" (unpublished Ph.D. diss., Univ. of Pennsylvania, 1977), 285-287, 564-567, 621-642. Gough also rejects the author's view that a struggle existed between competing economic elites. This writer contends that Gough's study supports, on an individual basis, the significance of the large-scale manufactures as wealthy and prominent members of Philadelphia society.

home manufacturers and foster a self-sufficient American economy. Indeed, a strong national government would put an end to the conflicting legislation of separate states and offer manufacturers better protection against imports. There also was some anticipation of discriminatory duties on British tonnage and goods imported on foreign vessels.[10]

The buoyant enthusiasm of the manufacturers and their sense of a dawning of a "new era" under the banner of protection was evident on July 4, 1788, when Philadelphians commemorated the ratification of the Federal Constitution.[11] Figuring prominently in the "Federal Procession" of leading citizens and occupational groups were members of eighty-eight trades who organized and marched in separate groups, carrying "flags, devices and machines." One such machine was a large stage sponsored by the Manufacturing Society on which carding and spinning machines displayed the manufactory of cotton. Among the other groups present were ten brewers, one hundred and fifty coachmakers and their allied branches, twelve distillers, seventy tobacconists, and thirty-six sugar refiners. Outfitted in the dress of their vocations the manufacturers carried slogans or mottos on banners that read: "home-brewed is best"; "no tax on American carriages"; and "may government protect us." One of the ten toasts offered honored "the agriculture, manufactures, and commerce of the United States."[12]

The parade, considered by some observers the greatest spectacle in eighteenth-century Philadelphia, testified to the importance of manufacturing in Philadelphia's multi-faceted economy. This grand celebration indicated how far the respective trades had come in both economic and political esteem and showed the ambitions and expectations of the various groups. Indeed, the parade could be viewed as part of the lobbying effort of Philadelphia's manufacturers who wanted a federal tariff shield to protect them from the British goods flooding the Phil-

[10] The 1789 debate in the House of Representatives is reported in *The Debate and Proceedings in the Congress of the United States, 1789-1824*, compiled by Joseph Gales (Washington, D.C., 1834-56), I, 183-199, 294-302, et passim [*Annals of Congress*]. The best study of the nation's attempt at commercial independence and regulation, is Vernon G. Setser, *The Commercial Reciprocity Policy of the United States, 1774-1829* (Philadelphia, 1937), especially chap. 4.

[11] Francis Hopkinson, "Account of the Grand Federal Procession in Philadelphia, July 4, 1788," *American Museum*, IV (July, 1788), 55-78.

[12] *Ibid.*, especially pages 60-61, 65, 68-69; L.H. Butterfield, ed., *Letters of Benjamin Rush* 2 vols. (Princeton, N.J., 1951), I, 470-477.

adelphia market. Aided by the well-organized Pennsylvania Society for the Encouragement of Manufacturers and the Useful Arts, an advocate since 1785 of duties on competitive imports and the admittance of scarce raw materials duty free, the manufacturing community during the First Congress also lobbied for protection directly with the "federal" representatives Thomas Fitzsimmons and George Clymer.[13]

Obviously, the expectations of the manufacturers had to be weighed against the complicated demands of other interest groups. Some sectors of the urban economy had long standing ties to Britain and others had developed newer markets to the Orient, France, and, by means of navigation of the Mississippi River, the West. Capitalization of economic activity and access to credit also varied among groups. Some individuals (the house carpenter, butcher, and the baker) sold goods in the naturally protected local consumer's market and others (hatters, ironmongers, shoemakers, sugar refiners and tobacconists) competed with British imports. And, as Jacob Price has argued, certain occupations fell in both the industrial and service sectors and worked for the local and external markets.[14] Placed against such a background of economic diversity one might well understand why the manufacturers experienced only modest success in protecting their interests.

The nation's first tariff act of 1789 epitomized the manufacturers' ambiguous position in the government's hierarchy of interests. The act enumerated a long list of specific duties, and five classes of goods carrying *ad valorum* rates. Among those articles listed for protection were

[13] Thomas Fitzsimmons to Benj. Rush, April 20, 1789, Gratz, Historical Society of Pennsylvania (HSP). *Annals of Congress*, (1st Cong., 1st & 2nd Sess.), passim; Linda Grant DePauw et al., editors, *Documentary History of the First Federal Congress, 1789-1791* 3 vols. (Baltimore, Md., 1977), III, 60, 72, 350, 370, 388, 395, 451, 458.

[14] Jacob Price, "Economic Function and the Growth of American Port Towns in the Eighteenth Century," *Perspectives in American History*, edited by Donald Fleming and Bernard Bailyn (Cambridge, Mass., 1974), VII, 132-133. Large-scale manufacturers were proto-merchants. A sugar house, for instance, required some $16,000 worth of sugar-baking apparatus, plus capital of at least $50,000 and a good measure of credit. To engage in the manufacture of snuff for a profit required £5,000 to purchase and stock the materials, plus monies for house rent, machinery, wages for journeymen, and the frequent repair of mill dams damaged by flood waters. James T. Callender, *A Short History of the Nature and Consequences of Excise Laws* (Philadelphia, 1795), 107, 112 (hereafter cited as Callender, *History of the Excise Laws*).

beer, carriages, cordage, shoes, sugars, snuff and tobacco products.[15] Manufacturers in the industrial sector immediately criticized the act's encouragement and protection clause as providing either the wrong type or not enough protection. For instance, early in the second session of the First Congress, Philadelphia distillers complained that a "greater difference" of duties should be placed on imports of rum and molasses, and the manufacturers of tobacco products from Philadelphia and New York City petitioned about possible duties being placed on the articles they exported in order to produce revenue to pay for the assumption of state debts.[16] From Philadelphia alone members of at least five other native industries—coachmakers, cordage, mustard-makers, shipwrights and tanners—voiced their differences over the original legislation and the attempt to provide further increases in revenue by means of excises.[17] When the tariff law was later amended in the same session to provide for the effectual collection of duties and to increase them by only about two and one-half percent, revenue considerations took precedence over the encouragement and protection to manufacturers.[18]

During the third session of the First Congress an excise tax, discussed even before the enactment of the tariff of 1789, followed as the "next logical step for the Federalists beyond the existing customs arrangements."[19] Still, during its first years, the Washington administration seemed prepared to favor manufacturers more than merchants and shopkeepers by relying more heavily on customs or tonnage duties than on excise taxes. Secretary of the Treasury Alexander Hamilton, in his 1791 "Report on Manufacturers," proposed to create a city of manufactories in New Jersey.[20] Help was received from Assistant Secretary

[15] "An Act for laying a Duty on Goods, Wares, and Merchandises imported into the United States," in Richard Peters, ed., *The Public Statutes at Large of the United States from. . .1789 to March 3, 1845* 8 vols. (Boston, 1848-1850), I, 24-27. Hereafter cited as Peters, ed. *U.S. Statutes.*

[16] The memorial is cited in DePauw, ed., *Doc. Hist. of 1st. Federal Congress,* III, 60 and n.

[17] *Ibid.,* III, 72, 370, 388, 395, 451, 458.

[18] "An Act to provide more effectually for the collection of the duties. . .," Peters, ed., *U.S. Statutes,* I, 145-178. *Annals of Congress* (1st Cong., 2nd Sess.), I, 1721-1722, 1724.

[19] *Ibid.* (1st Cong., 3rd Sess.), II, 2321-2322, 2339-2340. Quote in William D. Barber, "Among the Most Techy Articles of Civil Police: Federal Taxation and the Adoption of the Whiskey Excise," *William and Mary Quarterly (WMQ),* 3rd Series, XXV (Jan., 1968), 70.

[20] Prospectus of the Society for Establishing Useful Manufactures, August 1791, Report on Manufacturers, and Hamilton's Final Version (Dec. 5, 1791), in Harold C. Syrett and others, eds., *The Papers of Alexander Hamilton* (New York, 1961-1977), IX, 145-147, X, 266, 295-296 (hereafter cited as Syrett, ed., *Papers of Hamilton*).

Tench Coxe of Philadelphia, a merchant and a member of the local Society of Manufacturers.[21] In Philadelphia, however, the industrial experiment, commonly called the S.U.M., did not attract wide support.[22]

Although Hamilton's public image has been that of an advocate of American manufacturing,[23] Philadelphia's manufacturing community early questioned his economic stabilization program because it appeared to forsake a highly developed division of labor as the essence of social progress and economic independence. According to Professor Drew McCoy, "the Report on Manufacturers seems to describe a society ominously reminiscent of the English system that Franklin and the Revolutionaries had rejected."[24] Gradually the worst fears of manufacturers were confirmed: protection against British competition proved inadequate, and reliance upon domestic taxation to produce income increased sharply.[25] At a time when American agriculture and commerce were very prosperous, Hamilton's economic stabilization program, which depended upon ties to British manufacturing power, left little room for support to America's manufacturers.[26] Seeking either more protection or the retention of existing schedules, certain classes of manufactures in 1794 faced instead the prospect of being burdened with excise taxes and of having protection subordinated to other national goals.

[21] Jacob E. Cooke, *Tench Coxe and the Early Republic* (Chapel Hill, N.C., 1978), 182-189, and "Tench Coxe, Alexander Hamilton and the Encouragement of American Manufacturers," *WMQ*, 3rd Ser., XXXII (July, 1975), 369-392.

[22] "A Mechanic," *Independent Gazetteer* (Philadelphia), Aug. 18, 1792. For the reply and rebuttal, see also "Detector" and "A Manufacturer," *ibid.*, Sept. 1 1792; Frederick B. Tolles, *George Logan of Philadelphia* (New York, 1953), 116-122; Baumann, "Democratic Republicans of Philadelphia," 344-345, 370-372.

[23] This view is well established in the literature of the period. Less well known is the fear held by citizens of economic decline and ruin, and of the need to expand employment opportunities and the urban economy; see John K. Alexander, *Render Them Submissive: Responses to Poverty in Philadelphia, 1760-1800* (Amherst, Mass., 1980), 6, 13-15, 33, 77-78. Billy G. Smith, "The Material Lives of Laboring Philadelphians, 1750 to 1800," *WMQ*, 3rd Ser., XXXVIII (April, 1981), 163-202.

[24] Drew R. McCoy, *The Elusive Republic: Political Economy in Jeffersonian America* (Chapel Hill, N.C., 1980), 153.

[25] Rudolph M. Bell, *Party and Faction in American Politics, The House of Representatives, 1789-1801* (Westport, Conn., 1973), chap. 5, especially pages 96-100, 104.

[26] John R. Nelson, Jr., "Alexander Hamilton and American Manufacturing: A Reexamination," *Journal of American History*, LXIV (March, 1979), 971-995, offers a corrective to the idea that Hamilton was a strong advocate of American manufacturing.

The first real test of the 1789 Federalist commitment to protect manufacturers, a test also of the political coalition molded during the ratification contest, came during the spring of 1794 when the Washington administration also faced an unexpected crisis in foreign affairs. News of the massive British depredations against American ships and of a British threat to renew Indian war on the western frontier angered many Philadelphians.[27] James Madison revived his proposals for discriminatory tonnage duties and restrictions on British trade policies that Federalists had side-tracked in 1789 and again in 1791.[28] Madison's 1794 "commercial resolutions" constituted Congress's response to Britain's failure to enter into a trade agreement with the United States. Thus, the resolves were aimed at forcing Britain to improve her ways, breaking the British monopoly of the import trade; and encouraging American manufacturing and ship building.[29]

Anti-British views were warmly received in Philadelphia, and were echoed by import-export merchant John Swanwick at a series of well attended mercantile meetings held in Philadelphia on March 8, 15 and 16, 1794.[30] The wealthy Swanwick, a business partner in the firm of Willing, Morris and Swanwick and a member of the Pennsylvania General Assembly, did not act strictly out of political gain or economic interest. In mid-1790, while still a Federalist, Swanwick authored an article entitled, "Thoughts on the Commerce of the United States," in which he insisted that commerce, navigation, agriculture and manufacturing were mutually dependent.[31] Swanwick called for higher tariff barriers as a way to develop commercial reciprocity and for discrimi-

---

[27] Baumann, "Democratic Republicans of Philadelphia," chap. 9, especially pp. 452-469.

[28] See James Madison's speech in the first session, Third Congress, *Annals of Congress*, IV, 155-156, and Appendix, 1417. The resolves were actually based on a report, dated Dec. 16, 1793, prepared by Thomas Jefferson and Tench Coxe; it will be found in Paul L. Ford, ed., *The Writings of Thomas Jefferson* 10 vols. (New York, 1892-99), VI, 470-484.

[29] See the discussions in Irving Brant, *James Madison: Father of the Constitution, 1787-1800* (Indianapolis, 1950), 389-393; Dumas Malone, *Jefferson and the Ordeal of Liberty* (Boston, 1962), 154-160.

[30] The meetings were reported in the Philadelphia newspapers. *Gazette of the United States*, Mar. 24, 25, 31, April 10; *General Advertiser*, Mar. 10, 11, 13, 18, 21, 1794. For an analysis, see the author's "John Swanwick: Spokesman for 'Merchant-Republicanism' in Philadelphia, 1790-1798," *PMHB*, XCVII (April, 1973), 159-161.

[31] The pamphlet appeared in the *Universal Asylum and Columbian Magazine* (Philadelphia), V (July 1, 1790), 24-26. When reprinted in Mathew Carey's *American Museum*, XII (August, 1792), 89-97, it included a reply by Dr. Thomas Ruston and a defense by Swanwick. Swanwick to Carey, [undated], Lea & Febiger Collection, 1785-1796, HSP.

nation against foreign vessels. In 1794 the "merchant-Republicans" and the "manufacturer-Republicans" warmly supported Madison's resolves and they offered numerous alternatives to the policies pursued by the Federalists to American commerce and manufactures.[32]

In addition to the call for commercial retaliation, both state and federal governments responded to the Anglo-American crisis. In Pennsylvania Governor Thomas Mifflin demanded that the harbor along the Delaware River be fortified, stationed an artillery company at Mud-Island, and readied the state militia.[33] The Washington administration sent John Jay as a special envoy to Great Britain to seek ways to improve relations, and, with the approval of Congress, authorized an expensive national defense program, including the construction of six frigates, the raising of an army of fifteen thousand, and the placing of eighty thousand militia in a state of readiness.[34] These expenditures, along with the possible drying up of import duties owing to dislocations in trade, raised the prospect of a federal deficit unless new taxes were levied.

If the Washington administration asked Congress to raise revenues to pay for the new defense programs and the interest on the public debt, it faced major difficulties. Five years of experience had shown that tax measures were neither easily written into law nor administered since the choices were limited to direct taxes (those on real estate, general assessments on property of all kinds and on polls) and indirect taxes (excises and custom duties). Taxes were also still a battleground between federal and state governments.[35] The issue was drawn, however, when Secretary Hamilton, siding with those who believed existing revenues

[32] These alternatives are summarized in the author's, "Swanwick," 160-161.

[33] The *Pennsylvania Archives* (Series I-IX) edited by Samuel Hazard et al., 138 vols. (Harrisburg, Pa., 1838-1935), Series 9, vol. I, 767-768, 772-777; Scharf and Westcott, *Philadelphia*, I, 476-477.

[34] *Annals of Congress* (3rd Cong., 1st Sess.), III, 485-504; *Gazette of the United States* (Philadelphia), Apr. 26, 1794.

[35] The controversy was best captured in the Philadelphia newspapers. See in particular the exchange between "Warren" (pro-excise tax) and "Pluma" (anti-excise tax) appearing in the *General Advertiser*, May 17, 24, 26, June 3, 9, 1794 and elsewhere. Also see "From a Correspondent," May 7, 9, 16; *ibid*, and "Hancock," June 6; "Pluto," June 12, 1794 in *ibid*. Unsigned article, April 26, and "A Plain Spoken Man," *American Daily Advertiser*, May 10, 1794.

would be inadequate by at least $621,000, recommended the enlargement of excise taxes.[36]

The Revenue Act of 1794, which passed in the House of Representatives as a series of separate tax bills during the first nine days of June, is an overlooked piece of tax legislation.[37] Specifically, a duty of eight cents per pound upon all snuff manufactured for sale and a duty of two cents per pound was placed upon all snuff manufactured for sale and a duty of two cents per pound on all refined sugar. Drawbacks equal to the duty paid were allowed on all snuff and refined sugar exported, provided the quantity exported was not less than twelve dollars in value. On account of the duties paid on raw sugar imports, three cents per pound was added to the drawback allowed on refined sugar.[38] There also was a carriage duty or rate that ranged from two to ten dollars depending upon the type of vehicle.[39] Other legislation in 1794 reduced import duties on carriages and parts of carriages by nearly seventy percent from 15 to 4½ percent *ad valorem*.[40] Duties were placed on wines and foreign distilled spirituous liquors sold by retailers, who also had to obtain a five dollar license.[41] Likewise, property sold at auction received a levy based on a schedule of rates for all auction sales, and the auctioneers had to obtain a license.[42] Warmly debated but not favorably acted upon were proposals to tax stock transfers, to adopt a stamp tax, and to increase tonnage duties.[43]

The manner in which the duties were to be levied and collected by federal revenue officials, a continuation of procedures begun in 1791, troubled the manufacturers. In most cases manufacturers had to give a $5,000 bond as a way to ensure accurate reporting of the daily quantity

[36] Syrett, ed., *Papers of Hamilton, XVI, 4. Annals of Congress* (3rd Cong., 1st Sess.), 597, Appendix, 1307-1311. The debate was started on May 1, 1794 and it lasted for five weeks.

[37] The best summary of the passage of these bills is to be found in Bell, *Party Faction*, chap. 5.

[38] "An Act laying certin duties upon Snuff and Refined Sugar" (June 5, 1794), Peters, ed., *U.S. Statutes*, I, 384-390.

[39] "An Act laying duties upon Carriages for the conveyance of Persons," (June 5, 1794), *ibid.*, I, 373-376.

[40] "An Act laying Duties of Goods, Wares and Merchandise imported into the United States" (June 4, 1794), *ibid.*, I, 391-392.

[41] "An Act laying duties on licenses for selling Wines and foreign distilled spirituous liquors by retail," (June 5, 1794), *ibid.*, I, 376-378.

[42] "An Act laying duties on property sold at Auction," (June 9, 1794), *ibid.*, I, 397-400.

[43] *Annals of Congress* (3rd Cong., 1st Sess.), IV, 666, 670, 699, 726, 740-741; Bell, *Party and Faction*, 104-107.

of production of the article. Forfeiture of a bond would result if the manufacturer omitted an entry or neglected to pay the required duties. Inspectors also were to be given six hours notice when the article was to be exported. The large-scale manufacturers characterized as excessive and expensive regulation, the inspection of exports, along with the oaths, fines, court costs and so forth.[44] Finally, while the revenue bill of 1794 did not cover all of the goods or articles manufactured in Philadelphia, there existed a possibility that in the future other articles could be taxed under this system.[45] Remembering the Boston port bill of 1774, the opponents to the excise legislation argued that "if the system of excise is not early checked, it will hamstring, in turn, every manufacture in America."[46]

Philadelphia's manufacturers considered the excise system a "real grievance" because it represented a revised policy. Manufacturers believed that they should receive special encouragement (protection) from state and national government in order to insure the nation's economic independence from England. They were also not convinced of their ability to pass on the extra cost to the consumer. Certainly they were not about to remain in a political alliance that provided direct benefits to merchants and not to manufacturers. Thus, because the excise threatened, either directly or potentially, the interests of virtually every manufacturer in Philadelphia, the subject of the enlargement of the excise law proved controversial. In responding to the apparent economic threat and the lack of commitment to develop manufactures, the large-scale manufacturers advanced the same arguments as the opponents of the excise tax placed on distilled spirits in 1791 (viz., that they were being made victims of unconstitutional, discriminatory and confiscatory taxes).[47] They argued that the state should levy indirect taxes and that the federal exise was more than revenue producing. Drawing upon the 1791 debates of Pennsylvania's General Assembly,[48] the

[44] These views are best summarized in Callender, *History of the Excise Laws*, Section II, 56-116.
[45] *American Daily Advertiser* (Philadelphia), Apr. 26, 1794.
[46] James Thompson Callender, *History of the United States for 1796* (Philadelphia, 1797), 8. See also the remarks by Samuel Smith, *Annals*, IV, 1115-1117.
[47] These arguments are ably summarized in Barber, "Most Techy Articles of Civil Police," 58-84. Callender, *History of 1796*, 202.
[48] The 1791 resolves denouncing the excise tax, although primarily written by Albert Gallatin, were actually introduced in the General Assembly by Francis Gurney, a Philadelphia merchant. *Journal of the First Session of the House of Representatives*. . .(Philadelphia, 1791), 94-95, 98, 101, 104, 107-109, 112-113, 138, 142-149.

urban critics also concluded that they would never have ratified such a provision in the Federal Constitution if they had realized that excise taxes were to "become one of the first, and favourite resources of government."[49] The protest of 1794 took on additional significance because its organizers tied it with other anti-administration protests through the Democratic Republican clubs, and they abandoned traditional restraints on electioneering by openly campaigning for candidates opposed to the excise. In doing so, they left behind the deferential politics of an earlier age as the manufacturers of Philadelphia sought to participate in society and government as equals of the gentry.[50]

The principal leaders of the excise protest in Philadelphia consisted of a handful of large scale tobacconists (Gavin Hamilton, Thomas Leiper and John Hankart) and sugar refiners (Jacob Morgan, J. Dorsey, Frederick A. Muhlenberg, and Isaac and Edward Pennington). Serving together on the local committee that organized the several public meetings held in Philadelphia during May 1794, they also prepared the series of memorials directed to the House, Senate and President Washington in which Philadelphia's manufacturers of tobacco products and sugar asserted that the excise tax would prove economically destructive to the reasonable profits of their industries and a detriment to the growth of manufacturing throughout the country. A select committee formed to meet with a committee from the Senate to explore tax alternatives. Finally, the city's manufacturers of tobacco and sugar tried to organize a national petition campaign against the excise tax.[51] They attempted to communicate with the manufacturers in New

[49] Gavin Hamilton and Thomas Leiper were embittered by the course of events during the framing of the excise bill. Apparently Alexander Hamilton had invited the tobacconists to his office to discuss the subject of the manufacture of tobacco so as not to injure the industry. But the original draft, which contained an excise of four cents per pound on tobacco, was expunged by the House Ways and Means Committee and increased to eight cents before the bill was reported to the whole House. Callender, *History of Excise Laws*, 48.

[50] The breakdown of deference in politics was speeded up by the American Revolution. Richard A. Ryerson, *The Revolution Is Now Begun: The Radical Committees of Philadelphia, 1765-1776* (Philadelphia, 1978), 3-4, 77-88, and chap. 8. See also Ronald P. Formisano, "Deferential-Participant Politics: The Early Republic's Political Culture, 1789-1840," *American Political Science Review*, LXVIII (1974), 473-487.

[51] Callender, *History of the Excise Laws*, 70-75, 86-88. On the national campaign, see the exchange of letters, dated April 24 and 29, 1794, cited as "A.Z., " in the *American Daily Advertiser* (Philadelphia), May 2, 1794. A reading of the *Annals of Congress* in 1794 also suggests that cooperation existed among the manufacturers in the seaboard towns. Reference is also made to communications in the Minutes of the Democratic Society of Pennsylvania, 60-63, typescript, HSP.

York City, but for unknown reasons a concerted national effort never materialized.

In entering the political arena, these manufacturers demonstrated close and intelligent attention to detail. For instance, the meetings of May 2, 7 and 8 were held at 5 P.M., a time calculated to be most convenient to the journeyman manufacturers or tradesman who labored for about eight to ten dollars per week in these industries. Believing that the only way to defeat the administration's revenue plans was to organize all the manufacturers in and around the city and county of Philadelphia, the organizers drew up an address entitled "EXCISE—Citizens Attend!" which requested the city's large and small scale manufacturers to attend a general meeting to be held in the State House yard on 8 May 1794. A special invitation was extended to the manufacturers of malt, hops, beer, ale, cider, starch and hair powder, chocolate, cocoa paste, vinegar, glass, candles, soap, paper and paste board, leather and skins, iron, and all who opposed the excise. Those who gathered at Independence Square unanimously adopted a set of resolves, which condemned the excise and proclaimed "republicanism."[52]

We are fortunate to have a contemporary account of this Philadelphia protest meeting written by Samuel Hodgdon, an Army storekeeper for the War Department.

> By six o'Clock about three hundred of the lower class of people were assembled, when for want of more respectable characters Colonel Morgan, Mr. Leiper, Neddy Pole and Mr. Pennington wer[e] called on to preside. The meeting being thus organized, without further ceremony the Moderator, Morgan, handed to the Secretary Pennington, a number of resolutions cut and dried—and asked the Mob whether they should be read, all vociferated yes. The Secretary after making apologies for want of better lungs, read the resolutions (which were lengthy) through. Leiper then came forward to address the rable, his speech was worthy of such an orator—he attempted to explain, and then bitterly complained of the meditated tobacco and snuff excise as he was taught by the resolution-writer to call the duty. He said the whole fraternity were not able to raise the money, or give the requested security. Pole next came forward to complain of the injuries intended on the Auctioneers, having finished his

[52] My recounting of this event is based on Callender, *History of the Excise Laws*, 66-75, and a reading of the Philadelphia newspapers cited below.

reading and speech, without one word of debate the question on the resolutions were called for. The Moderator desired to be informed whether they would take them up separately or together, all being satisfied with the debates and fully understanding the merits of the resolutions they agreed to pass them in gross; which was instantly done—and three cheers ended the meeting. The spectators of the farce whom I took to be more than two thirds of the persons present, were distress'd to see with what facility a few demagogues could mislead and abuse an ignorant but harmless people. I shall say nothing of the resolutions more than that they were well wrote, impertinent and insidious;[53]

The eyewitness account offers some clues as to the class of citizens who attended the meeting as well as who led the proceedings. Hodgdon described the crowd as "lower class" and "ignorant but harmless people." The leaders were characterized as misguided demagogues only a bit more respectable than their audience.

Hodgdon's characterization of the event reflects his inherited Federalist outlook of deferential expectations. He minimized the status of the leaders involved in the protest and the substance of the interests they represented. The manufacturers of tobacco products and sugar were clearly of a higher socio-economic group than Hodgdon assumed, largely because occupational classifications in Philadelphia were changing in this "age of Merchant-Capitalism" (Table I). In fact, the manufacturers who led the excise protest compare favorably to many of the persons who led and dominated the Federalist Party.[54] Compared to Federalist leaders, fewer manufacturers owned a chair or sulky and held

[53] Hodgdon to Hamilton, May 9, 1794, Syrett, ed., *Papers of Hamilton, XVI*, 397. The resolutions appear in the *Gazette of the United States* (Philadelphia), May 10, 1794. See also *General Advertiser* (Philadelphia), 3 June 1794; there is a response by "Pluma," in *ibid.*, June 9, 1794. "Anti-Protextus" also poked fun of these well-to-do manufacturers for not being willing to pay their fair share of the taxes. *Ibid.*, May 26, 1794.

[54] This view is based on my reading and study of the Philadelphia County Tax Assessment Ledgers, 1770-1854 (Record Group 1), Archives of the City and County of Philadelphia, Philadelphia, Pa. By 1820, for example, the tobacconist ranked third behind the merchant and physician on an occupational rank order based on mean wealth. Stuart M. Blumin, "Mobility in a nineteenth-century American City: Philadelphia, 1820-1860" (Ph.D. dissertation, Univ. of Pennsylvania, 1968), 66. My own survey of the tax assessment books leads me to conclude that by 1794 the tobacconists, sugar refiners and distillers or brewers had already moved up the occupational rank order behind the "Gentlemen," merchant, doctor and/or lawyer. Other occupations in the manufacturing community, such as watchmakers, tinsmiths, tanners, iron mongers and shipwrights, also ranked high.

fewer servants, livestock and ounces of plate. Still, such protest leaders
as Gavin Hamilton, Sr. (Chestnut Ward and Blockley), John Hankart
(North Mulberry Ward and Bristol), Thomas Leiper (Middle Ward
and North Market Ward), Jacob Lawerswyler (South Mulberry
Ward), Jacob Morgan (South Mulberry Ward), and F.A. Muhlenberg (South Mulberry Ward) were on an average but one or two steps
below the import or export merchant on the economic ladder. The
medium assessed personal tax of these six manufacturers was £150. The
1794 personal tax of Philadelphia's three Federalist members to Congress was £166.[55] Far from being among the ignorant propertyless,
these manufacturers would soon come to dominate the economy of the
City of Philadelphia and they were far more successful than their
numbers might suggest.

The life of Thomas Leiper, a manufacturer who achieved prominent
economic and political fame, is representative of the ambitious, aspiring manufacturers. After emigrating from Scotland to the United
States in 1763, Leiper soon came to Philadelphia to work for his cousin
Gavin Hamilton, a pioneer in the snuff business in the country. This
relationship turned into a business partnership, which was dissolved by
mutual consent sometime during or after the American Revolution in
order to bring their sons into the business. Leiper, who married
well—Elizabeth Gray, daughter of William Gray of Gray's Ferry—
became a prominent member of the 1st Troop, Philadelphia City
Cavalry, St. Andrews Society, and the Democratic Society of Pennsylvania.[56] By 1794 the Leipers and Hamiltons were among the principal wholesale and retail merchants in the city. Leiper, although he
started later, actually prospered more than his kinsman. He accumulated a considerable fortune based on snuff mills, stone quarries, public
securities and numerous pieces of urban real estate. In 1794 he had an
assessed evaluation of nearly £20,000 for his properties in Philadelphia

[55] Tax Assessment Ledgers, 1770-1854, RG 1, Archives of the City and County of Philadelphia, passim. The 1794 personal taxes for the Federalists were as follows: Robert Morris
(£100); George Clymer (£100); and Thomas Fitzsimmons (£200). Social status, though closely
related to wealth or occupation, was a very important independent variable. See also Gough,
"Towards a Theory of Class and Social Conflict," chaps. 6, 13.

[56] John H. Frederick, "Thomas Leiper," *DAB*, XI, 154. This theme is presented in Carl
Bridenbaugh, *The Colonial Craftsman* (New York, 1950), 165; and in Sam Bass Warner Jr.'s,
The Private City: Philadelphia in Three Periods of its Growth (Philadelphia, 1968), chap. 1.

City and Delaware County.[57] His finest urban dwellings were rented to distinguished persons, such as French merchant Theophiles Cazenove, Secretary of the Commonwealth Alexander James Dallas, Supreme Court Justice James Wilson and Secretary of State Thomas Jefferson.[58] Leiper, who supported the American Revolution by contributing large sums of money and participating in the First City Troop's active field service, had become by 1789 one of the leading advocates of government support to promote, defend and protect, individually and collectively, manufacturing enterprises and to sustain a self-sufficient American economy.[59] He was a firm believer in what historian Louis Hartz describes as mixed enterprises.[60] Tobacconists Jacob Benninghove, John Hankart, Isaac Jones, and Philip Stimmel also were parvenues who took advantage of free and mixed enterprise and experienced occupational mobility.[61] In battling with state and national governments over taxation and tariff protection they acted to insure that they would not long remain second-class citizens in the new republic.

The leading sugar refiners also possessed wealth. Jacob Morgan, F.A. Muhlenberg and Jacob Lawerswyler, Isaac and Edward Pennington, Charles Schaffer, John Corman and Matthew Lawler, John Bartholomew and J. Dorsey and Peter and Henry Miercken were well-to-do and they were among the economic leaders of Philadelphia's manufacturing community. Most of them owned their own homes and possessed personal belongings that included horses, cows, plate and riding chairs. Like the tobacconists they had benefited from the city's increased wealth and enjoyed many of the new luxuries in life.

Two conclusions can be drawn about the size and wealth of this group. If the manufacturers of sugar and tobacco appear to have been

[57] Tax Assessment Ledgers, 1794, Philadelphia City, Archives of the City and County of Philadelphia, Philadelphia, Pa. Searches were also made in Philadelphia City and Delaware county in the National Archives and Records Service, United States Direct Tax of 1798; Tax Lists for the State of Pennsylvania, Microcopy No. 372 (Washington, 1963).

[58] *Ibid.*, Reel 1, frames 109, 262, 418, 420, 423, 426, 477-478. Tax Assessment Book, Middle Ward, 1794, 44, 46-47, Archives of the City and County of Philadelphia.

[59] *DAB*, XI, 154, Henry Graham Ashmead, *History of Delaware County, Pennsylvania* (Philadelphia, 1884), 661-663, 742, 751-753; Henry Simpson, *The Lives of Eminent Philadelphians, Now Deceased* (Philadelphia, 1859), 648-650.

[60] Louis Hartz, *Economic Policy and Democratic Thought: Pennsylvania, 1776-1860* (Cambridge, Mass., 1948), 3, 7, 82ff.

[61] An assessment of their tax records suggests that these persons were successful entrepreneurial minded manufacturers who hoped to achieve upper class standing in Philadelphia.

small in number, totaling under 100, they were vocal and certainly possessed the potential to rouse the entire manufacturing community and the laborers dependent upon those industries. Of the approximately 2,200 manufacturers in Philadelphia, the new excise taxes, directly affected at least fifteen percent including the producers of ale, beer, cider, hops, malt, chocolate, cocoa, paste, vinegar, candles, glass, soap, paper and paste board, starch and hair powder, leather and skins, and iron.[62] Perhaps the indirect or potential effect mobilized other manufacturers, as well as auctioneers, brokers, cardmakers, coachmakers, innkeepers and stationeers. The ability of this core group, highly concentrated in a few wards, to merge the interests of the manufacturers with the city's Democratic Republican societies, heightened the political impact.

Although the city's two Democratic societies—the German Republican Society and the Democratic Society of Pennsylvania—formed before the spring of 1794, the protest of the manufacturers provided the clubs with an issue and a source for new support. The societies apparently enjoyed greater unity and momentum as a result of the enthusiastic support they received from the manufacturers.[63] Little is known about the activities of the German Republican Society during the year 1794. The Society's April 1793 constitution reveals that its members planned to concern themselves with maintaining a Republican government and searching for ways to improve themselves.[64] Only persons of German "blood" could join; officers were elected the first Wednesday in January.[65]

The constitution and circulars of the Democratic Society of Pennsylvania, suffused with international republicanism and an emphasis on the cultivation of "rational liberty," explicitly endorsed the promotion of the country's infant industries and the exclusion of British goods.[66]

---

[62] The figure used here for the number of manufacturers in Philadelphia is the one cited in Tench Coxe's *A View of the United States of America* (Philadelphia, 1794), and subsequently reported in Davies, *Some Account of the City of Philadelphia*, 82; and later in Scharf and Westcott, III, *Philadelphia*, 2230.

[63] Baumann, "Democratic Republicans of Philadelphia," 448-449.

[64] Link, *Democratic Republican Societies*, 6-8.

[65] *Neue Philadelphische Correspondenz* (Philadelphia), April 9, 16, 1793. I am indebted to Kenneth Keller for this information.

[66] Link, *Democratic Republican Societies*, 11-12.

The Philadelphia Society, on April 10, 1794 before the excise was debated in Congress, had resolved:

> That this society considering and believing that the general welfare of our country is involved in promoting necessary manufacturers as far as is consistent with our situation in giving full employment and comfortable support to our fellow citizens; it is expected that the members of the Democratic Society will have sufficient patriotism to prefer and make use of the manufacturers of their own country, confident that by creating a demand for them we shall afford them that substantial encouragement and support particularly necessary at this time.[67]

In appealing to the nation's general welfare, full employment and patriotism, the Democratic Society attracted manufacturers, especially the producers of snuff, tobacco and sugar. Of the 315 members of the society, more than a quarter can be identified as craftsmen. Signers of the memorials and resolutions protesting the excise on tobacco and sugar are listed on the membership rolls of the two societies. Among the tobacconists and snuffmakers in the Philadelphia society were George Brown, Michael Lawler, Thomas Leiper, Christian Schaffer, and William Watkins; while the sugar refiners were Matthew Lawler, Jacob Morgan, Isaac Pennington and Conrad and Peter Sybert.[68] Although the occupations of the general membership in the German Republican Society remains a great mystery, Eugene P. Link argues that urban support for the club came from manufacturers, and we do know that manufacturers dominated its leadership. Henry Kammerer (papermaker) was president; Jacob Lawerswyler (sugar refiner) was vice-president and Christopher Kucher (sugar refiner) was treasurer. The meetings of the Democratic Society of Pennsylvania," usually held at 8 P.M. at the German Lutheran schoolhouse, often followed the scheduled 5 P.M. excise protest gatherings. "Doubtless these men [protestors]," writes Link, "were responsible for introducing resolutions passed by the two Philadelphia organizations condemning excise

[67] Minutes, Dem. Society of Pennsylvania, p. 74, HSP.

[68] Baumann, "Democratic-Republicans of Philadelphia," Appendix I, Table 3, "Democratic Society Membership By Occupation," 598-601. My analysis of the membership, based on a reading of the manuscript minutes of the society, has recently been confirmed by Philip S. Foner, *The Democratic-Republican Societies, 1790-1800 A Documentary Sourcebook of Constitutions, Declarations, Addresses, Resolutions, and Toasts* (Westport, Conn., 1976), 7, 42.

taxes and pledging devotion to the American manufacturing interests."[69]

Because the formation of the Democratic Society of Pennsylvania occurred two years after the passage of the 1791 excise on distilled liquors, one should not draw any firm conclusions about any position that the society might or might not have taken before 1794. The excise tax was a small issue in the local elections of 1792.[70] Once the report to enlarge the number of products to be covered under law came before the House of Representatives in the spring of 1794, the Society wasted no time in identifying with the manufacturers' grumblings over the proposed excise taxes. On May 8, for instance, the organization issued resolves declaring that its membership opposed excises "on salt and coal, on sugar and snuff, on boots and shoes, on spirits, coffee, carriages and cheese."[71] Declaring that these infant industries required the "fostering care of government" and would be ruined by the burdens of taxation, the Society argued that an excise system would lead to fraud, great expense for collection and the unnecessary appointment of placemen whose salaries and other requisites would be greater than the tax itself. The manufacturers faced reluctantly the prospect of having to pass on this tax to the consumer, but, more important, they preferred "republican taxes" which were direct in their object, equal in assessment, and economical in collection.[72]

The aforementioned declarations were, of course, drawn up to win the support of the manufacturing community. New members were attracted to the Society with some success. After the club issued the so-called "infant industries" resolution, at least forty new persons joined between May and July 1794, including manufacturers James Burges McCoy, Conrad Seyfert, Robert Cochran, Henry Bellegeau, Samuel

[69] Link, *Democratic Republican Societies*, 90. The quote is on page 78.

[70] Baumann, "Democratic-Republicans of Philadelphia," 344-347, 370-374.

[71] The original minutes of the May 8, 1794 meeting of the Dem. Society of Pennsylvania are incomplete. Quoted words in John Bach McMaster, *A History of the People of the United States*...8 vols. (New York, 1883-1913), II, 188. The full minutes are printed in the *American Daily Advertiser* (Philadelphia) May 12 and 13, 1974.

[72] *Ibid.*, Unsigned article, April 26; "A Plain Spoken Man," May 10, 1794, in *ibid*.

Johnson, Michael Lawler, Robert McGee, David Ogden, Jacob Morgan and George Rehn (Rein).[73]

Contemporaries, though, such as James Madison, Oliver Wolcott, Jeremiah Smith and Fisher Ames, attributed the societies' opposition to the excise to base political motives and an attempt to embarrass the Washington administration. "The discontent as to the excise law has probably been stirred up for some electioneering purpose, and will subside, of course," wrote James Madison on May 19, "unless fostered by other excises now in agitation here, to wit, on manufactured tobacco and refined sugar. . . ."[74] The political unrest was widely reported in the Philadelphia press.[75] The Democratic-Republicans in and out of Congress, however, failed in their effort to organize a successful campaign, although they succeeded in having the stamp tax bill rejected. "All opposition to the new excises, though enforced by memorials from manufacturers," wrote Madison, "was [in] vain."[76]

Although the manufacturers, the societies, and Republican party could not defeat the excise tax, they did not give up the battle. Republicans, in particular, knowing that the manufacturers of tobacco products, sugar, distilled spirits and carriages resented the excise tax and that other manufacturers in the city feared coverage extended on other articles or products, moved to draw this important following solidly into their ranks. Alexander Graydon observed that "a handle was made of the excise law."[77] In order to rekindle the body politic the Democratic Republican clubs made the inflexible Thomas Fitzsimmons, who had voted in favor of the Administration's six indirect tax

[73] The number was probably greater than forty. Unfortunately, the manuscript minutes of the two key meetings held by the society on April 17 and May 1, 1794, pages 77-84 and 89-94, are missing. The society, which admitted new members only when they were sponsored by another member, had averaged about nine new members per meeting. On May 1, 1794, when the Society celebrated St. Tammany's Day at the house of Israel Israel, Treasurer of the Democratic Society, some 800 persons attended. *General Advertiser* (Philadelphia) Apr. 24, May 3, 16; *Gazette of the United States* (Philadelphia) May 9, 1794. References to the celebration can also be found in the minutes, Dem. Society of Pennsylvania, 85-86, HSP.

[74] James Madison to James Madison, Esq., May 19, 1794, United States Congress, *Letters and Other Writings of James Madison* 4 vols. (Philadelphia, 1865), II, 16 (hereafter cited as *Madison* (Cong. ed.).

[75] The accounts of the excise can be found in all of the major party newspapers. See Donald H. Stewart, *The Opposition Press of the Federalist Era* (Albany, N.Y., 1969), 83-86, 89-90, 523.

[76] Madison to Jefferson, May 11, June 1, 1794, *Madison* (Cong. ed.), II, 14, 18. Quoted material on page 14; Baumann, "Democratic-Republicans of Philadelphia," 480-481.

[77] Alexander Graydon, *Memoirs of His Own Time* (Philadelphia, 1846), 390.

measures and who stood during his two terms in Congress as the champion of Secretary Hamilton's stabilization program, their bete noire.[78]

The strategy to unseat Fitzsimmons developed in early June. At meetings held on June 5 and 12, 1794, the Democratic Society defended the right of an individual to criticize government actions which tampered with constitutional liberty, and reminded the people that in times of peace interest in public concerns often lagged. Joining hands with the German Republican Society in the cause of liberty and in the anti-Fitzsimmons movement, the Democratic Society of Pennsylvania formed a task force on the excise and taxation. It also resolved to organize an election committee for the purpose of deciding "how far their Representatives are entitled to public confidence, by approving the good and dismissing the bad."[79] The tone of the fall political campaign was symbolically set forth during the Independence Day Dinner of 4 July 1794 when party revellers offered the toast: "EXCISE, may this baneful exotic wither in the soil of freedom."[80] In honor of Bastille Day, July 14, 1794, shipwrights and mariners, some of whom were members of the clubs, drank toasts to celebrate French independence.[81] These events reinforced the view that on matters of taxation and foreign policy Fitzsimmons no longer represented many interests in Philadelphia.

During the summer and fall months of 1794 the manufacturers in need of protective duties and opposed to excise taxes played a substantial role in the city's politics. No longer prepared to recognize the mercantile community as the city's natural leaders, they moved to ameliorate the provisions of the act of 1794 and to defeat one of its principal spokesmen. There was new involvement in ticket making to support their economic aspirations.[82] This process was complicated by the un-

[78] Bell, *Party and Faction*, 107; Baumann, "Swanwick," 163. With the exception of the sketch in the *DAB*, VI, 444-445, the only biography of Fitzsimmons is James A. Farrell, "Thomas Fitzsimmons, Catholic Signer of the American Constitution," *American Catholic Historical Society Record*, XXXIX (Sept. 1928), 175-224.

[79] Minutes, Dem. Society of Pennsylvania, p. 106-115, 117. HSP.

[80] *General Advertiser* (Philadelphia), July 8, 9, 10, 1794.

[81] *American Daily Advertiser* (Philadelphia), July 16, 1794.

[82] Minutes, Dem. Society of Pennsylvania, p. 117, HSP. See also Baumann, "Democratic-Republicans of Philadelphia," 483-484, 488ff. A battle was being waged over whether the election would be by districts. Tinkcom, *Republicans and Federalists*, 138-139.

anticipated acts of the insurgents at Braddock's field in western Pennsylvania in late July, which divided political ranks between moderates and radicals in Philadelphia and disrupted the activities of the city's two democratic societies.[83] The majority of the manufacturers and the members of the society held an ambivalent position. They could not condone the intemperate actions of the western insurgents because they believed that change had to be carried out through legal, constitutional channels. At the same time they also disapproved of the federal government's taxation program because they believed "Excise systems to be oppressive, hostile, to the liberties of the Country."[84]

While events were in progress to quell the rebellion in the four western counties of Pennsylvania, the manufacturers of tobacco products and sugar took their case to the Pennsylvania General Assembly which Governor Thomas Mifflin convened to deal with the crisis.[85] The manufacturers' memorial of 5 September 1794 carried the signatures of twenty-three snuff makers and thirteen sugar refiners.[86] The thirty-six memorialists sought the "interposition" and "influence" of the State legislature on the excise question as "the more immediate guardian of the rights and liberties of the citizens of Pennsylvania."[87] As precedent they cited the action taken by the Pennsylvania General Assembly on the original excise law on January 22, 1791, and they requested that body to exercise again its right to review the proceedings and acts of the United States Congress.[88] Because the excise law was never popular in

[83] For a discussion see Miller, "The Democratic Societies and the Whiskey Insurrection," 324-349; Link, *Democratic Republican Societies*, 45-49.

[84] Resolve of July 31, 1794, in Minutes, Dem. Society of Pennsylvania, 131, HSP.

[85] *Pennsylvania Archives* (Second Series), IV, 122-123; *ibid.* (Fourth Series), IV, 288-310.

[86] A copy of the memorial, with accompanying signatures, can be found in the *Gazette of the United States* (Philadelphia), Sept. 8, 1794. Subsequently, Henry and Peter Miercken asked that their names be removed from the memorial. *Gazette of the United States* (Philadelphia), Sept. 12, 1794. *Annals of Congress*, (3rd Cong., 2nd Sess.), V, 1191-1192.

[87] *Gazette of the United States* (Philadelphia), Sept. 8, 1794. For a general discussion of deliberations during the special session, see Baumann, "Democratic-Republicans of Philadelphia," 492-493.

[88] The Pennsylvania House of Representatives passed a resolution denouncing the first federal excise tax in February 1791 and the doctrine of instruction had been advanced during the debate over funding in 1790. William Maclay, *The Journal of William Maclay, United States Senator From Pennsylvania, 1789-1791*, (New York, 1890), 193, 199, 212, 220. See also above, note 48.

TABLE I

INDEX OF ASSESSED TAXES PAID

Value in Pounds	Tobacconists & Snuffmakers		Sugar Refiners		Brewers & Distillers		Coachmakers	
	Property	Personal	Property	Personal	Property	Personal	Property	Personal
0-25	12	12	4	3	3	7	6	14
26-50	0	15	1	5	1	3	1	4
51-100	2	5	0	7	1	7	2	2
101-250	4	3	2	1	2	3	6	0
251-500	9	0	1	0	2	0	2	0
501-1000	5	0	2	0	3	0	2	0
1001-2000	1	0	3	0	7	0	1	0
2001-2500	0	0	1	0	0	0	0	0
Over 2501	2	0	2	0	0	0	0	0
Unidentified	33	33	4	4	2	1	33	33

Source: Tax Assessment Ledgers, 1794, Philadelphia City, Archives of the City and County of Philadelphia. National Archives and Records Service, U.S. Direct Tax of 1798: Tax Lists on Microfilm for Pennsylvania (Washington, 1963).

TABLE II
INDEX OF RESIDENCY FOR
MANUFACTURERS OF TOBACCO PRODUCTS AND SUGAR

Ward and/or Suburb	Number w/Occupation	Number of Taxables (1793)
Bristol	10	175
Germantown	1	652
Northern Liberties (East & West)	8	2,651
N. Mulberry	13	971
S. Mulberry	10	1,295
North	9	950
Middle	4	702
South	0	354
Upper Delaware	7	323
Lower Delaware	3	196
High	2	266
Chestnut	2	154
Walnut	3	174
Dock	4	681
New Market	4	1,022
Southwark	7	1,800
Other Townships (County)	2	1,507
TOTAL	89	13,873

Source: Septennial Census Returns (November 1793), Record Group 7, Records of the General Assembly, Div. of Archives and Manuscripts, PHMC.

TABLE III
CONGRESSIONAL DISTRICT ELECTION, 1794
BY WARD AND PARTY

Ward	Republican Swanwick	Federalist Fitzsimons	Majority for Swanwick	Majority for Fitzsimons
New Market	166	165	1	
Dock	76	125		49
South	43	49		6
Walnut	17	34		17
Middle	120	114	6	
Chestnut	22	37		15
Lower Delaware	43	32	11	
Upper Delaware	46	35	11	
North	160	128	32	
High Street	35	36		1
South Mulberry	217	80	137	
North Mulberry	177	59	118	
TOTAL	1,222	874	316	88

Source: Philadelphia Gazette, Nov. 7, 1794.

TABLE IV
PHILADELPHIA CONGRESSIONAL ELECTION OF 1794
BY WARD AND PARTY

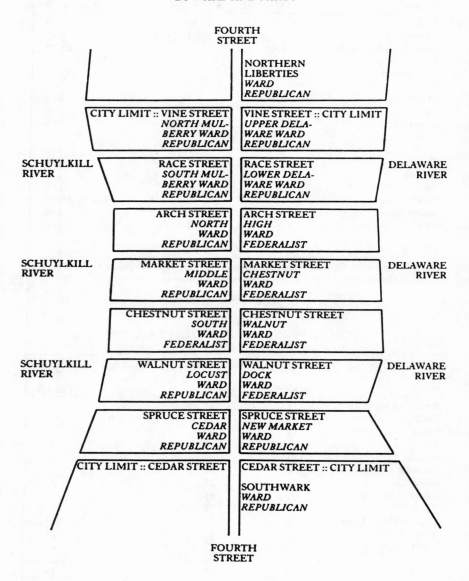

FOURTH
STREET

NORTHERN
LIBERTIES
WARD
REPUBLICAN

CITY LIMIT :: VINE STREET | VINE STREET :: CITY LIMIT
NORTH MUL- | *UPPER DELA-*
BERRY WARD | *WARE WARD*
REPUBLICAN | *REPUBLICAN*

SCHUYLKILL
RIVER

RACE STREET | RACE STREET
SOUTH MUL- | *LOWER DELA-*
BERRY WARD | *WARE WARD*
REPUBLICAN | *REPUBLICAN*

DELAWARE
RIVER

ARCH STREET | ARCH STREET
NORTH | *HIGH*
WARD | *WARD*
REPUBLICAN | *FEDERALIST*

SCHUYLKILL
RIVER

MARKET STREET | MARKET STREET
MIDDLE | *CHESTNUT*
WARD | *WARD*
REPUBLICAN | *FEDERALIST*

DELAWARE
RIVER

CHESTNUT STREET | CHESTNUT STREET
SOUTH | *WALNUT*
WARD | *WARD*
FEDERALIST | *FEDERALIST*

SCHUYLKILL
RIVER

WALNUT STREET | WALNUT STREET
LOCUST | *DOCK*
WARD | *WARD*
REPUBLICAN | *FEDERALIST*

DELAWARE
RIVER

SPRUCE STREET | SPRUCE STREET
CEDAR | *NEW MARKET*
WARD | *WARD*
REPUBLICAN | *REPUBLICAN*

CITY LIMIT :: CEDAR STREET | CEDAR STREET :: CITY LIMIT

SOUTHWARK
WARD
REPUBLICAN

FOURTH
STREET

266

Pennsylvania, either among Federalists or anti-federalists, there was reason to expect a favorable legislative response.[89] Yet for some unexplained reason, the memorial was never seriously taken up a second time by the General Assembly.

Unable to get the desired support in the legislature to review the law, the manufacturers and local political leaders now sought national as well as state and local ties. The Democratic-Republicans benefited from the failure of the Federalists to be responsive to manufacturers' needs and sentiments. The manufacturers did not select one of their own to challenge Fitzsimmons, but they found an anti-excise spokesman in John Swanwick, who had joined the Democratic Society on May 15.[90] To become the candidate of the Democratic-Republican party, of the societies, of "moderate" Federalists, of disgruntled merchants, of manufacturers and tradesmen and, in general, of the city's immigrants, Swanwick broke with existing political practice and openly sought the seat in Congress. His early federalism, wealth, status, and espousal of the interests of banking, insurance, and freer enterprises for the "arriviste," made Swanwick an ideal opponent to Fitzsimmons.[91]

Swanwick defeated Fitzsimmons by 248 votes (See Tables III-IV). His triumph met with a mixed response. According to James Madison, Swanwick's election represented "a standing change for the aristocracy." Subsequently, he wrote James Monroe that the election of a Republican at the commercial and political metropolis of the United States was "of itself, of material consequence," and it was so considered by the Federalists.[92] Federalist William Bradford thought the "contemtible" [sic] Swanwick owed his success "more to resentment against Fitzsimmons than to his own merits." "Many refused," he revealed,

---

[89] On the general opposition to the excise, see William Findley to Thomas Mifflin, Nov. 21, 1792, *Pennsylvania Archives* (Series 2), IV, 50; Charles Biddle, *Autogiography of Charles Biddle. . ., 1745-1821*, edited by James S. Biddle (Philadelphia, 1883), 262. Tinkcom, *Republicans and Federalists*, 91-94.

[90] Minutes, *Dem. Society of Pennsylvania*, 97, HSP. Baumann, "Swanwick," 161-163. Harry M. Tinkcom claims that Swanwick joined the society for business reasons in order to protest British interference with American commerce. Tinkcom, *Republicans and Federalists*, 85.

[91] Baumann, "Swanwick," 148ff, 156-163.

[92] Madison to Jefferson, Nov. 16, and Madison to Monroe, Dec. 4, 1794, *Madison* (Cong. ed.), II, 19, 25-26.

"to vote for either candidate and many voted for S[wanwick] in order to vote against F[itzsimmons]."[93] Perhaps Vice-President John Adams best summed up the results of the election when he wrote, "Swanwick may be for anything that I know as federal as his Rival."[94]

More specifically, Swanwick owed his election to Congress from the country's largest city to the events of 1794. Certainly, the two issues that hurt arch-Federalist Fitzsimmons were his conduct during the spring embargo and his vote for excise taxes. Especially damaging was the Republicans' cry, "Swanwick and no Excise."[95] Edmund Randolph reported that Fitzsimmons' conduct cost him support in the mercantile community and that the tax slogan gained support for Swanwick among the "less informed classes of men." In addition, Randolph noted that Chief Justice Thomas McKean, who had openly campaigned for Swanwick, remarked that at the last moment "the gentlemen" decided to vote for the "merchant-Republican."[96]

Swanwick won in Philadelphia City not because of any great upsurge of voters of little or no property, but because Fitzsimmons was unable to hold onto the traditional votes of merchants and large-scale manufacturers.[97] In particular, Swanwick found support among manufacturers hurt by the enlargement of the excise law and those in support of protective duties. The Democratic-Republicans clearly did not win over the votes of all manufacturers or artisans. An analysis of the returns by ward reveals that Swanwick carried seven of the twelve wards and that his greatest support came from the newer and middling-class wards of the City of Philadelphia (See Table 3). One recent authority has concluded that, while Philadelphia had a striking inequality of wealth distribution, the wards were marked by considerable occupational

[93] Bradford to Elias Boudinot, Oct. 17, 1794, Wallace Collection, II, 101, HSP. Fisher Ames wrote that "Here the supine good men let Swanwick get a nominal majority." Ames to Christopher Gore, Nov. 18, 1794, Seth Ames, ed., *The Works of Fisher Ames* 2 vols. (Boston, 1854), I, 152.

[94] Adams to Abigail Adams, Nov. 11, 1794, Adams Microfilm, Reel 377, Massachusetts Historical Society.

[95] Edmund Randolph to George Washington, Oct. 15, 1794, Washington Papers, Library of Congress (DLC).

[96] *Ibid.* Randolph to George Washington, Oct. 16. See also William Bradford to Washington, Oct. 17, 1794, Washington Papers, DLC.

[97] "A Mechanic," *Gazette of the United States* (Philadelphia), Sept. 27, 1794. The Democratic Republicans had nearly overturned the candidacy of Fitzsimmons during the ticket making. *General Advertiser*, (Philadelphia), Oct. 14, 1794.

diversity.[98] The 255 vote majority piled up by Swanwick in the peripheral wards of North and South Mulberry, the home of the German manufacturers hurt by the excise and threatened by foreign competition, proved decisive in overcoming Fitzsimmons' support in the core wards of Walnut and Chestnut and among the militia forces. (The late returns of the militia reduced Swanwick's winning margin to 58). Similarly, Swanwick proved he could hold his own against the incumbent in New Market, North and Dock wards, which contained the highest concentration of Irish.[99] Basic to the Federalists' defeat was their inability to recognize the self-esteem of merchant-manufacturers gained by their role in the Revolution and their support of the Federal Constitution in 1787.

The political results were similar in the second congressional district, composed of Philadelphia and Delaware Counties, where F.A. Muhlenberg defeated Samuel Miles by 146 votes.[100] Since the two candidates were sugar refiners by trade and had contacts in both political parties, the contest pitted an anti-excise candidate against a pro-excise candidate. Not only had Muhlenberg opposed the extension of the system as the Speaker of the House, but he also had signed a number of memorials of remonstrance, circulated in the city's counting houses and taverns, which were eventually forwarded to Congress. His business partner, Jacob Lawerswyler, was a consistent opponent to the excise tax. Samuel Miles' signature, on the other hand, was not found on any of the memorials. Benjamin Franklin Bache, editor of the *General Advertiser*, called for Muhlenberg's re-election because he had voted against the extension of the excise tax system. The Republican party editor remarked that this vote "will procure him the warm support of his former friends [Federalists] and indeed of every Republican."[101]

The election for seats in the General Assembly in Philadelphia and Delaware counties also showed Republican gains and support from the manufacturers. In Philadelphia County the entire Republican slate of

[98] Miller, *The Federalist City*, 8-13.

[99] Baumann, "Swanwick," 162, 165-166; for the late militia returns from western Pennsylvania, see the *General Advertiser* (Philadelphia), Oct. 21, 31, Nov. 5, 6, 8, 10, 1794.

[100] *Gazette of the United States* (Philadelphia), Oct. 8, 14; *General Advertiser* (Philadelphia), Oct. 13, 16, 1794. Samuel, Miles and Col. Jacob Morgan operated a sugar refinery together at 77 Vine Street. C.A. Browne, "Early Philadelphia Sugar Refiners and Technologists," *Journal of Chemical Education*, XX (1943), 522.

[101] *General Advertiser* (Philadelphia), Oct. 13, 1794.

candidates, sponsored at a meeting chaired by George Egert on October 8, was elected. Jacob Morgan, one of the principal protest leaders among the sugar-refiners and a member of the Democratic-Republican Society, received the highest number of votes.[102] In Delaware County John J. Preston and William West, alleged Republicans, won.[103] It is noteworthy that tobacco was raised and manufactured extensively in both counties. Bristol contained ten tobacconists or snuffmakers and there were ten more in the twin suburbs of Northern Liberties and Southwark. Leiper, certainly one of the principal spokesmen for support of manufacturers, lived in Delaware County as well as Philadelphia.[104]

The elections of 1794 in Philadelphia City and Philadelphia and Delaware counties were significant. With the exception of the races for the State Senate, which remained solidly Federalist,[105] the vote revealed that the newer mercantile and manufacturing interests, demanding expansion and diversification of the economy, were a growing political and economic force in an area becoming more urban and industrialized. Although their years of political and economic dominance were still in the future, the manufacturers had nevertheless used the issue of the excise taxes to rally the "interest." A "Correspondent" summed up the 1794 election as follows:

> From the state of the poll at our late election for a city member of Congress, the opinion of the people with regard to excise laws is clearly manifested. They have given a decided proof of their abhorrence of those revenue systems by excluding one of its most strenuous advocates. . .in the Federal legislature, and supplying his place with an acknowledged enemy to excises. The same reasons actuated the electors of the county in their choice of a Federal representative, and we have no doubt the same spirit prevailed in the Delaware State. . . .[106]

[102] *Gazette of the United States* (Philadelphia), Oct. 8, 13, 1794.

[103] *General Advertiser* (Philadelphia), Oct. 16, 1794.

[104] The count of tobacconists is based on a reading of the Philadelphia County Septennial Census, RG7, Records of the General Assembly, PHMC. On Thomas Leiper, see Ashmead, *Delaware County*, 661-662.

[105] *General Advertiser* (Philadelphia), Oct. 16; and *Gazette of the United States* (Philadelphia), Oct. 30, 1794; Tinkcom, *Republicans and Federalists*, 141-142.

[106] *General Advertiser* (Philadelphia), Oct. 17, 1794.

When the second session of the Third Congress convened on November 3, 1794, the issues of the first session were still very much on the minds of the representatives. Although House members were preoccupied with a resolution denouncing the "self-created" societies designed to place the "Republican interest" on the defensive, the most significant domestic issue was the raising of revenues to reduce the public debt. The call by some representatives that the excises be continued through 1801 sent shock waves through the manufacturing community. It was further stunned by Congressman William L. Smith, who, scoffing at the excise protestors, stated on December 23, 1794, that "there had been no petition or complaint against the snuff or sugar excises. They appeared as popular as any taxes could be expected to be."[107]

The tobacconists (snuffmakers) and sugar bakers answered Congressman Smith's assertion almost immediately by a petition.[108] They called for either the repeal or revision of the excise tax on refined sugar and tobacco products because excises placed on a domestically produced luxury brought foreign competition, oppressed the poor, and caused an increase in wages; the petitioners further explained that the public had resorted to white sugars of an inferior quality and that the manufacturer and not the consumer paid the excise. Taxing industry rather than wealth or property, they concluded, was contrary to the social compact of 1789. The manufacturers reasoned that extinguishing the public debt would be more cheerfully and effectively brought about through a general system of taxation on property of all descriptions. They regarded raising a tax on landed or personal property as neither "unjust" nor "impossible," but as the safest way to pay off the interest on the debt to 1801.[109]

The manufacturers added weight to their argument by demonstrating that the excise system had proven troublesome and costly. Not only

[107] Callender, *History of Excise Laws*, 91. See also *Annals of Congress* (3rd Cong., 2nd Sess.), IV, 1016. Congressman Smith's role in these proceedings is overlooked by George C. Rogers, Jr., *Evolution of a Federalist: William Loughton Smith of Charleston (1758-1812)* (Columbia, S.C., 1962), chap. 12.

[108] *Annals of Congress*, (3rd Cong., 2nd Sess.), IV, 1023. A copy was received by Tench Coxe, which he forwarded to Secretary Hamilton in a letter dated December 26, 1794, in Syrett, ed. *Papers of Hamilton*, XVII, 483-486.

[109] Callender, *History of the Excise Laws*, 92, 95-98.

had it failed to generate the expected new revenues, but there was every reason to conclude that the revenues had not equalled the expenses of a system that required a large force of revenue officers to maintain adequate surveillance over the country's manufacturers.[110] Congress was informed that six of the seven snuff mills in Pennsylvania closed at one time or another because of the 1794 excise taxes, while the seventh mill was open but remained on a precarious footing. Evasion of the taxes was easy, the petitioners added, if one either worked in his cellar and bolted his door or smuggled snuff by using a hand mill. Both methods were used in Philadelphia. Testimony before the 1795 select committee also indicated that the "excise had 'shut up the workhouses'" and that a number of sugar bakeries had been taxed out of business. In summary, the manufacturers contended that the excise law was "oppressive, unequal and consequently unjust."[111]

Congress debated the subject of extending revenues to reduce the public debt during the early months of 1795. The manufacturers of tobacco products and sugar in New York City, Baltimore and Philadelphia were regarded as the principal complainers but none were more vociferous than the Philadelphians.[112] Congressman Fitzsimmons, serving out his term, not only remained adamantly opposed to any changes in the present system, but also led the supporters of the present system.[113] Still, a House bill calling for changes in the taxing procedures was approved by the United States Senate on March 2, and the House concurred in the amended Senate version on March 3, 1795.[114] The fourteen-part act, which altered the provision of "An Act Laying Certain Duties Upon Snuff and Refined Sugar," essentially repealed the previous pound weight duties (eight cents duty on snuff) and laid them instead upon all mills employed in the manufacture of snuff at annual rates that varied according to the mode of production. The law required entries of the mills and a license before commencing business. If a person exported in quantities of not less than 300 pounds at one time, the duties on refined sugar were not altered.[115] He continued to

[110] *Annals of Congress* (3rd Cong., 2nd Sess.), IV, 1184.
[111] Callender, *History of the Excise Laws*, 101, 103.
[112] *Annals of Congress* (3rd Cong., 2nd Sess.), IV, 1191.
[113] *Ibid.*, IV, 1104. Baumann, "Swanwick," 166.
[114] *Annals of Congress* (3rd Cong., 2nd Sess.), IV, 843-844, 847, 849, 1281.
[115] "An Act to alter and amend the act entitled "An Act laying certain duties upon Snuff and refined Sugar," in Peters, *U.S. Statutes*, I, 426-430. J. Leander Bishop, *A History of American Manufacturers from 1608 to 1860. . .*2 vols. (Philadelphia, 1864), 61-62.

receive the drawbacks of six cents per pound. The new law had min-imized the so-called "evils" of the excise system by eliminating the visits of excisemen and removing the dangers of false and erroneous swearing as to the weight of the product, which varied in the snuff industry according to the day's temperature.

Even though the tobacconists and snuff-makers were instrumental in modifying the revenue law of 1794, they were still not fully satisfied, probably because the principle of excise taxation remained intact. "This law is a lesser evil than its predecessor, from which it differs as one broken leg differs from two; and this is," summed up an apologist for the anti-excise interest, "the utmost which can be said in defence of it."[116] And while Philadelphians debated the merits of John Jay's mission to England and the subsequent treaty, the city's manufacturers of tobacco products continued to work feverishly to regain their pre-1794 status. Because the issue had to compete for public attention with the controversy over Jay's Treaty, the manufacturers paid James Thompson Callender to write a pamphlet entitled *A Short History of the Nature and Consequences of Excise Laws; including Some Account of the Recent Interruption to the Manufactories of Snuff and Refined Sugar* (Philadelphia, December 7, 1795). The one-hundred-sixteen page pamphlet, released to all members of the two houses of Congress and to the principal officers of the federal government, coincided with the opening of the Fourth Congress.[117] The tract spelled out the so-called ruinous effects of the previous revenue measures, incorporating all of the memorials prepared on the subject, and contained as preface a short history of the nature and consequences of excise laws in England and Ireland.

In seeking alternatives to the excise, the snuff and sugar manufac-turers found an able and articulate spokesman in John Swanwick, who was re-elected to the Fifth Congress over Edward Tilghman. Phila-delphia and Delaware Counties, a key region in the country for tobacco and sugar manufactories, had as representatives Swanwick and F.A. Muhlenberg (Fourth Congress) and Swanwick and Blair McClen-achan, former President of the Democratic Society of Pennsylvania

[116] Callender, *History of the Excise Laws*, 104.

[117] Callender, *History of 1796*, 198; *Annals of Congress* (3rd Cong., 2nd Sess.), IV, 1410. James Thompson Callender's 1795 pamphlet on the *History of the Excise Laws* has generally been overlooked by scholars.

(Fifth Congress).[118] Between December 1795 and May 1797 the urban representatives busied themselves with presenting the memorials of snuffmakers and sugar refiners, calling for the repeal of the original legislation.[119] As a member of the Committee of Commerce and Manufacturers, Swanwick worked particularly hard for the repeal of the revenue law on tobacco products, including the eventual elimination of drawbacks (bounties), and voiced the general concerns of protectionist-minded manufacturers and direct tax advocates. Bounties, described as favored by Hamilton, were considered unrepublican. The actions of the memorialists, referred to as the "rebellious men," and the Philadelphia area representatives troubled other members of the House of Representatives. One of them sarcastically asked would the public be satisfied after learning that the important object of reducing the public debt "had been defeated by the means of half a dozen manufacturers of snuff and loaf sugar?"[120]

The chief argument for repeal was that the law seemed to defeat its own purposes—drawbacks being greater than the revenues. For instance, it was reported that large commercial mills that exported snuff, such as the Richard Gernon & Company, received drawbacks ten times as great as the taxes paid. In any event, after three years of detailed examination, countless memorials and local pressure, a majority in Congress finally yielded to the demands of the Philadelphians and decided that it was too difficult to make the excise tax equal and just and to prevent fraud. The Act had never produced, according to John Swanwick, "anything but uneasiness and dissatisfaction in whatever way the tax might be collected."[121] For Congress, repeal of the law eventually brought a negligible loss of funds to the Union, and the vexatious tax experiment that had produced a sinking fund rather than revenue was terminated.[122] Swanwick and others argued that additional stop-gap revenues might be more easily acquired through a national lottery system.[123]

---

[118] *Aurora* (Philadelphia), Oct. 13; *Philadelphia Gazette* (Philadelphia), Oct. 12, 1796; Baumann, "Swanwick," 166-167, 173-178.
[119] *Annals of Congress* (3rd Cong., 2nd Sess.), IV, 171; (4th Cong., 1st Sess.), V, 381, 636, 1406-1418; (4th Cong., 2nd Sess.), VI, 2074.
[120] Quoted words by Congressman Uriah Tracey, in *ibid.*, IV, 1186.
[121] *Ibid.*, (4th Cong., 1st Sess.), V, 1406, 1409. See references to the Richard Gernon & Co. and the method of drawbacks in Callender, *History of 1796*, 199-202.
[122] *Annals of Congress* (4th Cong., 1st Sess.), V, 1409.
[123] *Ibid.*, V, 1412.

The excise repealers in Congress, who were led by the Pennsylvania and Virginia delegations, were not yet able to overcome the strong objections of Congressman William L. Smith and other members of the House Ways and Means Committee.[124] Being forced to compromise, the Committee of Commerce and Manufacturers resolved to suspend rather than repeal the 1795 Act. On May 21, 1796, a suspension bill passed which terminated provisions of the act of March 3, 1795 until the end of the second session of the Fourth Congress (March 4, 1797).[125]

In 1796 and 1797 Philadelphia Manufacturers of tobacco products and sugar again fell short of their objective, repeal of the Revenue Act of 1794. Instead, their petitions for repeal were met with suspension of the act. As the members of the House developed new tax schemes and perfected the collection of old ones, the battle in Congress between the direct and indirect tax forces became more intense.[126] Pennsylvania's Congressional delegation and her manufacturers were especially involved in this process. Writing from Philadelphia, Fisher Ames complained that "the silly reliance of our coffee house and Congress pratlers on the responsibility of members of the people etc., is disgraced by every page of the history of popular bodies."[127]

The repeal forces, led by Albert Gallatin and John Swanwick, demanded that the federal government shift its revenue base from import duties and stopgap indirect taxes to a domestic land tax. A land tax would break the national government's dependence upon the commercial interests and allow for a foreign policy devoted to national needs rather than the payment of public creditors. The snuffmakers' petition of February 9, 1796, calling for the repeal of the law was once again answered by suspending the Act. The suspension was to run through the end of the first session of the Sixth Congress (May 14, 1800).[128] By the

[124] *Ibid.*, V, 1415, 1417-1418.
[125] *Ibid.*, V, 1417.
[126] This story has never been adequately told. See Henry C. Adams, "Taxation in the United States, 1789-1816," *John Hopkins University Studies in Political Science*, II, Nos. 5-6 (Baltimore, 1884), 5-79. Rudolph M. Bell's, *Party and Faction in American Politics* is limited to analysis of what happened in the House of Representatives.
[127] Ames to Alexander Hamilton, Jan. 26, 1797, Syrett, ed., *Papers of Hamilton*, XX, 487.
[128] *Annals of Congress* (4th Cong., 2nd Sess.), VI, 1562, 1565, 1569 [Feb. 27, 1797]. The petition of the manufacturers of snuff is in Callender, *History of 1796*, 197-203. This meant that the suspension ran through the second and third sessions of the Fifth Congress as well as the first session of the Sixth.

subsequent Act of April 24, 1800, the tax on tobacco products was finally repealed.[129] A similar measure, dated April 6, 1802, repealed the legislation of 1795 relating to sugar.[130] With the passage of these two Acts the eight-year controversy over the excise taxes ended.

*   *   *   *

The enlargement of the excise tax in 1794 had a substantial impact on the politics of Philadelphia. The manufacturers and tradesmen, who made up a majority of the city's population, ranged from journeymen to master artisans to affluent manufacturers. Solidly behind the Federalists in supporting the Constitution in 1789, many although not all of the manufacturers of products affected by the excise tax gradually shifted to the Republicans during the middle years of the 1790s. Led by the more wealthy sugar and tobacco manufacturers, and working initially through the Democratic Societies, the shift into the Republican camp between 1794 and 1800 in part can be attributed to dissatisfaction with Federalist tariff and excise policies. The Democratic-Republicans of Philadelphia became the spokesman for the self-conscious occupational groups or the anti-excise interest; the Republicans presented the manufacturers with an ideology that placed them on an equal footing with their counterparts in commerce and supported their claim to a share in political power. The Federalists, on the other hand, refused to adopt a political response that supported all of the demands of the manufacturers and that accepted the older justification for formed opposition to the policies of the Washington administration.[131]

If Philadelphia is to be considered a test case, this article confirms the recent revision by Alfred F. Young and others of the traditional view of Jeffersonian Republicans as either exclusively agrarian or as the poorer

[129] *Annals of Congress* (6th Cong., 1st Sess.), Appendix, 1495; "An Act to repeal the act laying Duties on mills and implements employed in the manufacture of Snuff," Peters, ed., *U.S. Statutes*, II, 54.
[130] "An Act to repeal the Internal Taxes," *ibid.*, II, 148-150. For John Swanwick's role in the tax repeal struggle on sugar, see *Annals of Congress* (4th Cong., 2nd Sess.), VI, 1885-1890, 2260-2262.
[131] This theme can be found in Richard Buel Jr.'s *Securing the Revolution: Ideology in American Politics, 1789-1815* (Ithaca, N.Y., 1972). According to Lance Banning, Hamilton's economic program and President Washington's courtly formality offered the Republicans a foil for "country" symbolism. *The Jeffersonian Persuasion: Evolution of a Party Ideology* (Ithaca, N.Y., 1978).

elements in the urban manufacturing interest.[132] To be sure, opposition to the Federalist system, consisting of funding, assumption, banks, and indirect taxes, was never limited to agrarian-minded ideologues. While in theory there was an abiding faith in the superiority of agriculture, in practice the Jeffersonians early abandoned free trade and often adopted full fledge mercantilist ideas before 1800. Federalist foreign policy and restrictions upon non-British commerce alienated Federalist merchants such as John Swanwick, Blair McClenachan, Stephen Girard and Charles Pettit in a way that led to "merchant-Republicanism."[133] Similarly, the larger, entrepreneurial-minded manufacturers such as Gavin Hamilton, Thomas Leiper, and Jacob Morgan opposed Hamilton's political economy that favored import merchants of British industrial goods at the expense of export merchants and domestic manufacturers. Contrary to Drew McCoy, the Jeffersonians did not support only small scale manufacturers because they were appropriate to a predominantly agrarian stage of society.[134] Instead, the evidence presented here documents the response of the large-scale manufacturers to Hamilton's taxation policies. Their opposition was not only limited to excise taxes placed on domestic manufactures but also involved protection to compete favorably in the international market and economic independence from Great Britain. Thomas Jefferson, taking his cues from early promoters like Tench Coxe, Albert Gallatin and James Madison, wrote in 1816 to Benjamin Austin that "experience has taught me that manufacturers are now as necessary to our independence as to our comfort."[135] There were, in short, entrepreneurial sources of Jeffersonianism. The urban variant of republicanism did not represent the main thrust of party strength, but it was a significant component.

Pennsylvania Historical and
Museum Commission   ROLAND M. BAUMANN

[132] Alfred Young, "The Mechanics and the Jeffersonians: New York, 1789-1801," *Labor History*, V (Fall, 1964), 247-276; Staughton Lynd, *Class Conflict, Slavery, and the United States Constitution* (Indianapolis, 1967), 267; Foner, *Paine and Revolutionary America*, 98-103; Baumann, "John Swanwick," 131-182; Howard B. Rock, *Artisans of the New Republic: Tradesmen of New York City in the Age of Jefferson* (New York, 1979). Nelson, "Alexander Hamilton and American Manufacturing," 971-995. Aleine Austin, *Matthew Lyon: 'New Man' of the Democratic Revolution, 1749-1822* (University Park and London, 1980).

[133] This point is developed in the author's "John Swanwick," 131-182.

[134] McCoy, *The Elusive Republic*, 107ff.

[135] Jefferson to Austin, Jan. 9, 1816, in Albert E. Bergh, ed., *The Writings of Thomas Jefferson* 20 vols. (Washington, D.C., 1903-04), XIV, 392.

Cultural Conflict
in Early Nineteenth-Century
Pennsylvania Politics

INTERPRETATIONS OF PENNSYLVANIA POLITICS have frequently stressed the cultural, ethnic, and religious sources of a series of eighteenth-century political controversies. Historians have seen the struggles of the 1750s as a conflict between Quakers and newly assertive Presbyterians, a conflict played out in the Revolution with a Presbyterian victory. In the Pennsylvania debates over a new national government in the 1780s, some historians have found a division between Calvinist and anti-Calvinist religious and ethnocultural groups. Other scholars interpret the rise of political parties in the 1790s, the development of the Democratic party, and the collapse of the Federalists within the context of a conflict among the Germans, new British immigrants, Presbyterians, and pacifist sectarians.[1] But after the rise to power of the Jeffersonian Democrats in 1799, accounts of Pennsylvania politics turn starkly away from ethnocultural explanations. Pennsylvania politics are said to have become a great struggle for office, or a battle of personalities, or a competition for transportation and communication improvements, or a "game without rules."[2] The most respected history of Jeffersonian Pennsylvania concludes that, "geographic, racial, and religious factors appear to have had little influence on party allegiances." The same author notes that

---

[1] For example see the writings of Frederick Tolles, *Meetinghouse and Countinghouse* (Chapel Hill, 1948); Charles H. Lincoln, *The Revolutionary Movement in Pennsylvania* (Philadelphia, 1901); Owen Ireland, "The Ratification of the Constitution in Pennsylvania," Ph.D. dissertation, University of Pittsburgh, 1966; Owen Ireland, "The Crux of Politics: Religion and Party in Pennsylvania, 1778-1789," *William and Mary Quarterly*, Third Series, 42 (1985): 453-475; Ethel Elise Rasmussen, "Capital on the Delaware: The Philadelphia Upper Class in Transition, 1789-1801," Ph.D. dissertation, Brown University, 1962; Kenneth W. Keller, *Rural Politics and the Collapse of Pennsylvania Federalism* (*Transactions of the American Philosophical Society*, 72, Part 6; Philadelphia, 1982).

[2] See Harry Tinkcom, *Republicans and Federalists in Pennsylvania* (Harrisburg, 1950); Sanford Higginbotham, *The Keystone of the Democratic Arch* (Harrisburg, 1952); Philip Shriver Klein, *Pennsylvania Politics, 1817-1832—A Game Without Rules* (Philadelphia, 1940).

279

among Germans, for example, "there is no indication that cultural factors had any effect on their political leanings." He stresses that personal leadership influenced their political choices far more than cultural factors.[3] The major study of the War of 1812 in Pennsylvania avoids any discussion of the Commonwealth's pacifist sectarians.[4] Yet it seems unlikely that the cultural and religious bases of late eighteenth-century political rivalries could disappear so dramatically when Pennsylvania became a Jeffersonian commonwealth after 1799. Indeed, ethnocultural antagonisms continued and had much to do with the course of Pennsylvania politics after the Jeffersonians came to power.

The consensus about Pennsylvania politics in the Jeffersonian era emphasizes growing factionalism and competition for patronage among Pennsylvania Democrats.[5] In the most commonly accepted narrative, Thomas McKean, who served for three terms as governor of the Commonwealth from 1799 to 1808, offended various factions within the Pennsylvania Democratic movement in administering the extensive appointments power of his office. This initial criticism of McKean's use of patronage was limited to Democrats of Philadelphia City and County, led by Michael Leib and the editor William Duane. Eventually this criticism spread to other sections of Pennsylvania. Although the Democrats who entered office pledged to make Pennsylvania's government more republican, McKean's conservatism soon had him at odds with the more radical members of the Democratic coalition. McKean himself had advocated revising the judicial system to make it more efficient and less expensive, but by 1803 it became clear that his antagonists had more far-reaching changes in mind. While McKean wished to preserve the authority of the courts and the dignity of the legal profession, his more radical Democratic adversaries attacked the bench and bar by demanding that justices of the peace—generally laymen—be given greater jurisdiction. They also advocated a system of arbitration to make Pennsylvania's citizens

---

[3] Higginbotham, *Keystone of the Democratic Arch*, 327-28.
[4] Victor Sapio, *Pennsylvania and the War of 1812* (Lexington, Kentucky, 1970).
[5] Pennsylvanians used a variety of names to designate political parties and factions in the early nineteenth century. I have chosen to use the word "Democrat" to designate the party also known as the "Republican," "Democratic-Republican," or "Jeffersonian Republican" party. Party names varied from county to county and election to election.

less dependent on lawyers. Pennsylvania Democrats soon plunged into a bitter and divisive controversy about judicial reform.

The quarrel forced McKean into an alliance with Pennsylvania's battered Federalists, who formed with him the nucleus of the "Quid" party. The Quids resisted radicalism and the demagogic appeals of McKean's critics. McKean had been easily re-elected governor in 1802, but during McKean's second administration tensions between the governor and his critics worsened. By 1805 McKean's foes tried to replace the Constitution of 1790 with a new document intended to give the Commonwealth's government a more popular tone.[6] When the movement for a new constitution failed by the spring of 1805, McKean's Democratic party enemies decided to replace him by nominating Simon Snyder for governor in 1805. McKean survived both a close election and a subsequent impeachment effort. Throughout these political quarrels, McKean vetoed one proposal after another to reform the operations of state government. Legislative efforts to override McKean's vetoes usually failed, and the last years of his administration were filled with animosity, disappointing Thomas Jefferson and the national Democratic administration.[7] The infighting ended in 1808, when the Democrats nominated and elected Snyder governor. The new administration seems not to have followed through on the political agenda of the reformers; instead, it devoted its attention to developing corporations to improve the transportation and communication systems of the Commonwealth and to the growing threat of war with Britain. The movement to democratize Pennsylvania government faded.

Why then had so little issued from the hopeful campaign to implement true Jeffersonian democracy in the Commonwealth? Why had the struggles to reform the constitution and to oust McKean led

---

[6] Champions of constitutional reform wanted to trim the power of the governor and Pennsylvania Senate, institute popular election of justices of the peace, limit the terms of militia officers, county officers and judges, strip the governor of his power to choose sheriffs, impose restrictions on changing state officials' salaries, and provide for a regular decennial convention to revise the state constitution. See William Duane, *Experience, the First Test of Government* (Philadelphia, 1806).

[7] Thomas Jefferson to George Logan, May 11, 1805, Logan Papers, Historical Society of Pennsylvania [hereafter, HSP]; Thomas Jefferson to Caesar Rodney, October 23, 1805, Gratz Collection, Old Congress, HSP.

nowhere? Why were the opponents of reform able to resist plans to transform Pennsylvania into a more republican society? Certainly, the popularity and political influence of persons who came to McKean's aid cannot be discounted. And the bitter personal rivalries between Philadelphia's Democratic leaders and other politicians were clearly destructive of a populist challenge to McKean and the alliance of moderate Democrats and Quids. But more fundamental causes brought the failure of reform. Voters feared the radicalism of McKean's opponents. The radical Jeffersonians were perceived as threatening cultural values dear to some of the Commonwealth's more important ethnic and religious subcultures. McKean's success in keeping hold of his office and resisting radical judicial innovation owed much to his sensitivity to the felt needs of diverse Pennsylvanians to preserve and enhance their ways of life. McKean was able to reassure members of these ethnic and religious communities that he would protect their distinctive practices from the assaults of radical ideologues whose programs threatened to homogenize the Commonwealth.

The oldest of these communities were pacifists: Quakers, Mennonites, Amish, Moravians, German Baptists, and Schwenkfelders. In the aftermath of the American Revolution in which many of them refused to bear arms or cooperate with the Commonwealth's militia system, these "defenseless Christians" had been harassed and ridiculed for their non-cooperation. Although some of them did not vote, by 1800 enough members of these pacifist sects did vote, and the group gained a significant influence, especially in southeastern Pennsylvania. The second subculture, sometimes overlapping the first, was the German-speaking community. Substantial numbers of Pennsylvanians continued to speak and understand only the German language. They hoped to continue using their mother tongue; they also wanted to be represented in local government by persons who could give them access to the public business in their native language. German speakers were suspicious of those who might try to coerce them into abandoning their language. A third and much smaller subculture were the "new Irish" who had come to America since independence. Many were filled with hatred of England for its suppression of the Irish Revolution of 1798. These new Irishmen were often poor; many worked as day laborers on canal and road construction projects. Unlike the large numbers of descendants of Ulster Protestants in Pennsylvania, the new Irish were often Roman Catholic. Various of the political issues of the McKean administration touched each of these subcultures and built support for it.

The best known debate of the McKean administration concerned judicial reform. Thomas McKean, who had served as the Chief Justice of the Commonwealth from 1777 to 1799, was well aware of the delays and inefficiencies in the administration of Pennsylvania justice. When he assumed the governorship in 1799, McKean recommended simplifying the system by abolishing the High Court of Errors and Appeals, expanding the county courts of common pleas, and redrawing the lines of judicial circuits so that judges could more easily ride to court sessions. Beyond making these proposals to the legislature, McKean removed from office Federalist judges and court clerks who—he claimed—were using the courts to punish enemies of the Federalist party. McKean appointed Democrats and some moderate Federalists in their places, naming—in addition—hundreds of local justices of the peace in places where such officers had not theretofore existed.[8]

McKean sought to address judicial inefficiency by removing incompetent officials. He also swept out at the same time those Federalists who had been hostile to him, renewing the appointments of Federalists who had shown him no personal animosity. In addition, he wanted to make the legal system itself more accessible. More zealous Democrats objected to his retention of moderate Federalists and they argued that the system was in need of fundamental reform. They wanted elected rather than appointed juries, and a system of lay arbitration for civil disputes. The reformers wanted to expand the authority of justices of the peace, so that disputes that could not be arbitrated could still be settled without lawyers and courts. McKean resisted these sweeping reforms. When legislators voted to expand the jurisdiction of justices in 1802 and 1803, McKean vetoed the bills on the grounds that they would increase litigation and weaken the system of trial by jury. The Democratic party split over the issue.[9]

[8] The Philadelphia *Democratic Press* of December 19, 1807, estimated that McKean had appointed one thousand justices of the peace during his administration. An extensive list of appointments of justices of the peace currently sitting in the Commonwealth appears in the *Journal* of the Pennsylvania House of Representatives for 1808-1809, 3-47.
[9] On the debate over judicial reform in Pennsylvania see Richard Ellis, *The Jeffersonian*

On the surface, the dispute over judicial reform had little to do with the interests and needs of subcultures within Pennsylvania's pluralistic society. The newspapers, especially in Philadelphia and in the state capital of Lancaster, reported extensively on the court reform debate. And political leaders like Leib and Duane were intensely involved in the controversy. But to many Pennsylvanians other issues were far more compelling. In the midst of the controversy the Democratic *Harrisburger Morgenröthe Zeitung* reported that the chief topics of conversation in rural Pennsylvania's interior towns of Harrisburg, Reading, and Sunbury were a church lottery, the route of a turnpike, the building of a bridge across the Schuylkill, and the imprisonment of a local woman for fraud.[10] Observers noted that rural farmers were too preoccupied with their crops to take much notice of the judicial debate. The German-speaking inhabitants of Pennsylvania, many of whom did not understand much English, ordinarily did not mix in court business. Indeed, rural German-language papers reported that people who spoke German exclusively were customarily excluded from jury service because they did not understand court proceedings.[11] Among the pacifist religious groups in the Commonwealth, nonlitigation was an established religious principle. Disputes within the Quaker and German-speaking sectarian groups were often settled without resort to courts.[12]

Nonetheless, the courts were important to the state's religious and ethnic communities. In the late eighteenth century, it had been common for Germans in rural Pennsylvania to receive some recognition when court appointments were made. McKean's predecessor,

---

Crisis (New York, 1971), 157-83; Elizabeth K. Henderson, "The Attack on the Judiciary in Pennsylvania, 1800-1810," *Pennsylvania Magazine of History and Biography* 61 (1937): 113-36; and G.S. Rowe, *Thomas McKean: The Shaping of an American Republicanism* (Boulder, Colorado, 1978), 333-59.

[10] *Harrisburger Morgenröthe Zeitung*, July 2, 1803.

[11] See the *Readinger Adler*, June 16, 1807; the *Harrisburger Morgenröthe Zeitung*, May 16, 1807. The Federalist *Lancaster Amerikanische Staatsbothe*, January 26, 1803, asserted that the Germans did not use the court system much because they did not understand English. English had been the official language since the days of Penn.

[12] The Mennonite writer Francis Herr asserted in 1790 that Quakers were more likely to use the courts than other pacifist sectarian groups. See Peter Brock, *Pacifism in the United States* (Princeton, 1968), 393. Of the pacifist groups considered here, the Quakers were the only native English-speakers, and so would have understood court business more readily.

Governor Thomas Mifflin, had responded positively to German communities that had petitioned for German-speaking justices of the peace.[13] When McKean took office, German leaders, confident that their votes had elected the governor, visited McKean and demanded a thorough purge of old officials in their communities. William Findley explained to Thomas Jefferson that he knew how McKean had made his judicial selections. Findley noted that "The leading Germans in many instances insisted on and procured the removal of all in their respective counties." McKean removed officials German political leaders deemed undesirable.[14] By 1800 the Germans had developed their own leaders who were politically powerful enough to demand that the governor appoint their supporters. McKean complied, placing German leaders and their supporters in his political debt.

German-speaking communities in rural Pennsylvania also wanted justices of the peace and associate judges on the county bench who could speak their language. McKean complied,[15] appointing so many Germans, according to the Democratic *Gettysburg Gazette*, that the greatest number of justices of the peace in the Commonwealth were German.[16] It was at the level of justice of peace that most German farmers were likely to have contact with the courts, for these officials dealt mostly with the collection of debts, a problem common in agricultural parts of the Commonwealth. Germans petitioned for the appointment of German-speakers and criticized the German language skills of candidates for appointment as justice.[17] Local meetings or-

[13] Keller, *Rural Politics*, 38-39.

[14] William Findley to Thomas Jefferson, March 14, 1804, Thomas Jefferson Papers, Library of Congress.

[15] The list of justices appointed by McKean in 1808-1809 indicates he appointed persons with German surnames as justices of the peace in the counties of Adams, Beaver, Bedford, Berks, Bucks, Centre, Cumberland, Dauphin, Erie, Fayette, Franklin, Huntingdon, Lancaster, Luzerne, Lycoming, Mifflin, Montgomery, Northampton, Northumberland, the City of Philadelphia, Philadelphia County, Somerset, Washington, Wayne, Westmoreland, and York. See *House Journal*, 3-47.

[16] *Gettysburg Gazette*, July 29, 1803. The *Gazette* noted that three-fourths of Pennsylvania's Germans were Democratic, and that the judges of York, Lancaster, Berks, Bucks, Dauphin, Northampton, and Mifflin Counties "are not of Irish and Scotch extraction, but many of them are German. . . . In almost every county, the Germans have their full share of the county offices, viz., commissioners, sheriffs, &c. &c."

[17] For example, see the petition to Thomas McKean of October 1-7, 1803, in which John

ganized political pressure to secure the appointment of German-speakers. On the Saturday before the gubernatorial election of 1805, Germans called a public meeting in Westmoreland County, where the population was at least one-third German, to press for the appointment of a German associate judge. About two hundred persons attended the meeting, which endorsed McKean for governor in the hotly fought 1805 election. A McKean supporter reported the events to Secretary of the Commonwealth Thomas McKean Thompson, McKean's nephew, forwarding as well a list of five local Germans loyal to the administration. McKean appointed one of them to the county bench.[18] These rural Germans did not share the radical hostility to the courts; they merely wanted their share of judicial appointments so that court business could be explained to them in their own language if necessary. McKean's careful attention to German-speakers' demands for representation and his cultivation of German leaders may have defused the issue of judicial reform among rural Germans. By the time of the judicial reform debates of the McKean administration, many Germans felt a proprietary interest in the system the urban radicals attacked. McKean's sensitivity to the needs of German leaders won him the endorsement of the powerful Muhlenberg and Hiester families in the election of 1805.

McKean's enemies argued that he showed contempt for rural Germans in his choice of justices. Possibly the best-known incident of the 1805 campaign involved anti-McKean politicians who solicited

---

Capp was recommended as justice of the peace in Harrisburg because he could read both English and German. Capp was appointed on January 2, 1804. (The petition is found in the Jacob Bucher Collection of the Dauphin County Historical Society, Harrisburg.) A petition from Mahonoy Township in Northumberland County, described in the petition as "a large German settlement," objected to the appointment of Samuel Rhoadermal because of his "having no learning, neither duch [sic] or english." Rhoadermal was not appointed. See undated petition of the inhabitants of Mahonoy Township, Northumberland Appointments File, McKean Administration, Bureau of Elections, Papers of the Secretary of the Commonwealth (RG 26), Division of Archives and Manuscripts, Pennsylvania Historical and Museum Commission, Harrisburg, [hereafter, PHMC].

[18] James Brady to Thomas McKean Thompson, October 15, 1805, Westmoreland County Appointments File, McKean Administration, Bureau of Commissions and Elections, Records of the Secretary of the Commonwealth (RG 26), PHMC. Governor McKean appointed Jacob Painter to be associate justice of the Westmoreland County Court of Common Pleas. Westmoreland County's German inhabitants had been demanding more German appointees since the 1790s. See Keller, *Rural Politics*, 18.

an appointment for justice in Northumberland County's Mahonoy Township, a settlement with a large German population. (Among the group was Simon Snyder, who was soon to challenge McKean for leadership of the Democratic party.) McKean had appointed a German named Adam Linkhart as justice in the township in January and was considering the appointment of Hugh Brunson, who could not speak German, to a second position. The politicians requested the appointment of Henry Latscha, presumably a German-speaker, but McKean refused. In one version of the story, McKean asserted that Latscha lacked popular support and other qualifications for the job and then lamented aloud that the movement to reform the constitution was the project of "geese and clodhoppers."[19] Leaving the governor, the disgruntled politicians spread the story of the confrontation to editors hostile to McKean. According to reports these editors circulated, McKean had called the inhabitants of Mahonoy "geese and clodhoppers," although he really had intended that phrase for constitutional reformers. The "clodhopper incident" spread across over the Commonwealth, usually in more garbled forms, so that by the summer some versions had McKean calling the Germans "clodhoppers," while others had him referring to Pennsylvania farmers as "clodpoles." Whatever the truth, the incident shows how important these local appointments had become and how easily political antagonists might seize upon supposed slights to ethnic groups. McKean's critics could not claim that he had failed to appoint a German-speaker, because he had made an appointment of a German-speaker a few months earlier. But they were quick to use McKean's outburst to anger Germans whose votes would be critical in the gubernatorial election of 1805.

---

[19] See *The Address of the Members of the General Assembly Agreed upon at a Numerous Meeting Held after a General Notice at Lancaster, April 3, 1805* [broadside]; "Facts in Plain Language," [Philadelphia] *General Advertiser*, May 20, 1805; *The Address of the Society of Constitutional Republicans Established in the City and County of Philadelphia*, 1805 [broadside]; Emerson Lee Derr, "Simon Snyder, Governor of Pennsylvania, 1808-1817," Ph.D. dissertation, Pennsylvania State University, 1960, 68. The politicians who came to visit McKean objected to the appointment of Brunson because he was not a Democrat. McKean responded that Brunson was well recommended. McKean thought that too many appointments had been proposed for people qualified only by their political affiliations. McKean may have been told that Brunson could speak German. [Philadelphia] *General Advertiser*, May 23, June 3, 1805.

A second set of political issues centering on reform of Pennsylvania's militia legislation involved pacifist sectarian religious groups. The militia—with 88,707 men between the ages of 18 and 45 enrolled in 1802—touched the lives of many inhabitants.[20] The largest foot militia in the nation, it was organized under the Fourth Militia Act, passed in April, 1799.[21] Both Thomas McKean and his critics agreed that the militia act needed revision, but they disagreed on how it should be changed. The sectarians thought the existing legislation too punitive to those who refused, out of conscience, to participate in the militia. Opposing them were radical Democrats who wanted to bolster provisions of the law that punished pacifist sectarians who refused to comply with the act. McKean and his advisors sided substantially with the sectarians, preferring a less punitive law that allowed latitude for conscientious objections. The Fourth Militia Act provided that white males of age were to enroll before the commanding officer in charge of their militia district. Those refusing to enroll—and this included pacifist sectarians—were automatically classified as "exempts," and their names were turned over to the county commissioners, who were to fine them six dollars.[22] Pacifists objected to the fine, regarding it as a form of cooperation prohibited by their scruples. Radical reformers wanted harsher penalties for noncompliance, advocating the disenfranchisement of persons who refused to enroll.[23] A legislative proposal to do that, introduced in February, 1800, intitated a newspaper debate that continued for two years.[24] As the debate began, McKean's political ally Tench Coxe advised him not to be swayed by extremists out to persecute the sectarians.

[20] This figure is reported in Commonwealth of Pennsylvania, *General Return of the Militia* (1802). See also the *Oracle of Dauphin*, April 12, 1802. The *Carlisle Gazette*, May 9, 1806, reported another count of 86,105. On August 7, 1807, the same newspaper reported 94,221 persons were enrolled.

[21] "An Act for the Regulation of the Militia of the Commonwealth of Pennsylvania," in James T. Mitchell and Henry Flanders, eds., *The Statutes at Large of Pennsylvania from 1682 to 1807*, 16:276-308.

[22] Mitchell and Flanders, 16:276-77.

[23] [Lancaster] *Amerikanische Staatsbothe*, February 26, 1800.

[24] See issues of the *Lancaster Amerikanische Staatsbothe* as noted above, and the *Harrisburger Morgenröthe Zeitung*, April 27, 1801; the *Philadelphische Correspondenz*, January 28, 1800; the *Lancaster Correspondent*, March 8, 1800, April 18, 1801; and the *Lancaster Intelligencer*, December 28, 1802.

It would have a good effect, and would I conceive be wise and humane, if some improvements could be made in the laws and executive proceedings by which militia fines are collected from the members of the societies of Menonists, Moravians, people called Quakers, and other churches professing *peace*. They have been sadly harassed, and injured by some inconsiderate men. That circumstance has occasioned many of them, who have been called to the legislature during the last 12 or 15 years [to] be unfriendly to the militia, and to favor regular troops. When our opponents [the Federalists] are continuing their abuse, their intrigues, their associations, their seductions and all their devices [,] it behooves the friends of republican government to render it as great and manifest an instrument of public justice and benefit as possible.[25]

Coxe advised the governor to be lenient with the pacifists for both humanitarian and political reasons. The legislature debated militia reform in its session late that year, but it did not produce any legislation on the militia until its 1801-1802 session. Meanwhile, petitions to McKean and the legislature urged that the statute be made less onerous to pacifists.[26] A Quaker address to McKean commended his administration; in March, 1802, the Quakers appealed to the legislature, noting that paying militia fines was contrary to their conscience and to the Charter of Pennsylvania. They reminded the legislature that some persons who had refused to cooperate had been imprisoned and their property distrained for non-payment of fines.[27] After much debate, the legislature passed and sent the Fifth Militia Act to McKean, who signed the bill on April 6, 1802.[28] The new measure

[25] Tench Coxe to Thomas McKean, July 17, 1800, Tench Coxe Papers, Box 82, HSP. Coxe's comments reveal that Democratic leaders were concerned about increasing political activity among pacifist sectarians in the early nineteenth century. In the years after the American Revolution, many pacifist sectarians refrained from voting. As the party battles of the 1790s intensified, more began to vote and some were even sent to the legislature. Undoubtedly, some pacifists refrained from voting in the early nineteenth century, but Coxe saw them as an important, politically active force. Voting patterns from regions with large sectarian populations indicate that they were participating more in politics. For the 1790s, see Kenneth W. Keller, "Diversity and Democracy: Ethnic Politics in Pennsylvania, 1788-1799," Ph.D. dissertation, Yale University, 1971, 185-200; 222-34; 247-52.
[26] Pennsylvania Senate *Journal*, 1800-1801, 108, 118, 124, 192, 197-203, 230, 249, 258, 266, 304. Pennsylvania House *Journal*, 1801-1802, 38.
[27] *Norristown Herald*, March 26, 1802; *Lancaster Journal*, March 27, 1802; [Philadelphia] *General Advertiser*, December 13, 1802.
[28] House *Journal*, 1801-1802, 214, 240, 308, 457, 495; Mitchell and Flanders, 17:174-218. No useful roll calls were recorded in the House *Journal* on this issue.

eased the provisions of its predecessor respecting exempts; it also guaranteed those who refused to comply the right to appeal to a militia board for exoneration from exempt status even if they neglected to choose exemption. In addition, the exempt fine was lowered from six to five dollars.[29] While the new measure was hardly the total triumph the sectarians wanted, it was certainly not the defeat that disenfranchisement would have represented.[30] The role of the McKean administration in the legislative debate over the militia law is not fully clear, but the governor's signature on the act and his commendations from pacifists indicate that he favored less rather than more punitive militia legislation.

Clear signs of some Democrats' hostility to the pacifists came as the widening war in Europe forced Pennsylvanians to re-examine their militia. Pacifists continued to appeal for modification of the militia laws in the legislature of 1802-1803.[31] In the next two leg-islatures, radical Democrats battling Thomas McKean gave further thought to tightening provisions about exempts. In the 1803-1804 session, a committee chaired by Cumberland County radical David Mitchell proposed that appeals for exempts be abolished.[32] Nathaniel Boileau (another McKean foe) of Montgomery County and Robert Giffen of Northumberland County also supported this proposal.[33] Although the House *Journal* recorded no votes on the issue, demands for stricter militia laws continued. Some of the radicals advocated a twenty dollar fine for anyone disavowing the militia law, and others closely associated with Snyder's candidacy (like Thomas Leiper and

[29] Mitchell and Flanders, 17:175-76.

[30] The debate over the treatment of the pacifists continued. On June 17, 1802, a public debate was held at Ker's Long Room in Philadelphia on the topic "Ought a man, whose principle is against fighting in defense of his country, be allowed to have a vote in the administration thereof." See [Philadelphia] *General Advertiser*, June 16, 1802.

[31] Pennsylvania House *Journal*, 1802-1803, 218, 310, 360, 557, 661; Pennsylvania Senate *Journal*, 1802-1803, 171, 229. No significant changes were made in the militia laws in 1803 on the grounds that the old act had not been in force long enough. For reports of the pacifists' petitions, see the *Carlisle Gazette*, February 23, 1803, March 16, 1803; the *Lancaster Intelligencer*, February 15, 22, 1803; and the [Lancaster] *Amerikanische Staatsbothe*, March 2, 1803.

[32] [Northumberland] *Republican Argus*, March 30, 1804.

[33] House *Journal*, 515.

John Steele) urged steeper fines.[34] But the radicals were unsuccessful. A meeting of delegates from fourteen Lancaster County townships warned the county's substantial pacifist population that the "revolutionists" wanted to "persecute men of all denominations"; the delegates reminded conscientious objectors that there would be "destruction to their earnings and possessions; [and to] those who have scruples of conscience against bearing arms, immediate disenfranchisement." The address was published in the pro-McKean *Lancaster Constitutional Democrat*.[35] A supplementary statute modifying the Fifth Militia Act passed the House of Representatives in April, 1805, and was signed by McKean. The measure did not abolish appeals; nor did it change the fines. McKean had taken the path of moderation.

The next major struggle over militia legislation occurred in the legislature of 1806-1807, after McKean's 1805 re-election to a third term in a close victory over Simon Snyder. With James Monroe and William Pinkney unable to secure an acceptable agreement with the British, Thomas Jefferson's diplomacy lay in shambles and war seemed likely. As arguments between the sectarians and the radicals intensified, William Duane's *Aurora* and the *Lancaster Intelligencer*, a paper that opposed McKean, endorsed the demands of Philadelphia militia units for double fines. At the same time, pacifists in Chester and Delaware Counties petitioned the legislature for mitigation.[36] The legislature passed the Sixth Militia Act in April, 1807, retaining the appeals process and lowering the fine from five dollars to four dollars.[37] Thirty-four of McKean's forty-three legislative supporters voted

[34] *Lancaster Wahre Amerikaner*, January 4, 1806, *Lancaster Constitutional Democrat*, September 17, 1805. Leiper signed a call to Philadelphia Democrats to form the Society of Friends of the People, an organization for Snyder and in favor of a convention to revise the constitution. Leiper was Vice-President of the Society of the Friends of the People. Steele had presided over a meeting of legislators that nominated Snyder for governor. [Philadelphia] *General Advertiser*, March 27, April 3, 1805.

[35] *Lancaster Constitutional Democrat*, August 27, 1805. See also the *Lancaster Wahre Amerikaner*, September 7, 21, 1805, the *Lancaster Journal*, September 6, 1805, and the *Dauphin Guardian*, October 5, 1805. Such charges multiplied as the gubernatorial election of October 1805 approached.

[36] [Philadelphia] *General Advertiser*, December 16, 1806, and *Lancaster Intelligencer*, March 24, 1806. For the petitions, see House *Journal*, 1805-1806, 356, 457.

[37] Mitchell and Flanders, 18:572-620. See page 575 for the lowered fine.

in favor of lowering the fine, while twenty-eight of Simon Snyder's thirty-five supporters voted against lowering the fine.[38]

Still dissatisfied with the legislation, McKean declared the Commonwealth's militia laws totally defective in his annual message to the legislature of 1807-1808. Legislators debated a supplement to the militia act in that session, and in March, 1808, voted whether to increase militia fines. Twenty-eight of thirty-nine Snyder supporters agreed, while thirty-four of thirty-eight pro-McKean legislators did not. The bill that passed and received McKean's signature included none of the radicals' demands about abolishing appeals, increasing militia fines and the fine for disavowal, or disenfranchising conscientious objectors.[39]

Throughout the struggle over militia reform, McKean and his supporters stood consistently on the side of moderation; they even succeeded in reducing militia fines in the face of radical sentiment for harsher penalties. McKean carried the heavily pacifist counties of Lancaster, Chester, Delaware, Bucks, and Montgomery in 1805; those counties gave him most of the edge he needed to defeat Simon Snyder and the radicals. In the election of 1808, which pitted Snyder against the resurrected Federalist James Ross, the sectarians again remembered the position of the pro-Snyder forces on militia reform.[40] While Ross and the Federalists carried only six counties in their unsuccessful

[38] House *Journal*, 1806-1807, vote of March 10, 1807.
[39] House *Journal*, 1807-1808, 319; Mitchell and Flanders, 18:829-34. My identification of the factional affiliations of legislators in the 1806-1807 and 1807-1808 sessions is derived from local newspapers and legislative journals for the period.
[40] One observer of sectarian participation in the campaign against Snyder in 1808 noted that the Quakers had shown "unexampled activity" in the election. See the [Philadelphia] *General Advertiser*, October 13, 1808. Rural Pennsylvania newspapers spread the word that if Snyder were elected, militia fines would increase and military tribunals would be given the power to assess the value of estates to be seized from those who disavowed the militia law. See the [Lancaster] *Volksfreund*, August 9, September 20, 1808; the *Cumberland Register*, July 26, August 31, 1808; the *Norristown Herald*, September 16, 23, 30, 1808; the *Lancaster Journal*, July 1, August 5, 12, September 2, 9, 1808; the *Lancaster Amerikanische Staatsbothe*, July 6, 13, 1808; the *Lancaster Weekly Advertiser*, July 9, 23, August 20, 27, September 24, 30, 1808; the *Lancaster Intelligencer*, July 26, August 30, 1808; the *Harrisburger Morgenröthe Zeitung*, July 16, 23, August 20, September 17, 1808; the *Pittsburgh Gazette*, July 27, September 7, 1808; the *Reading Weekly Advertiser*, September 10, 24, 1808; the *Readinger Adler*, August 2, 1808; the *Northumberland Gazette*, August 16, 1808; the *Oracle of Dauphin*, October 1, 1808; and the [Philadelphia] *Democratic Press*, August 23, 1808. See also the broadside *Bauern, Sehe hierher*. . . . (Lancaster, 1808).

gubernatorial campaign, Ross did win majorities in Lancaster, Chester, Delaware, and Bucks.[41]

The last major cultural conflict of importance to early nineteenth-century Pennsylvania politics was the growing hostility toward recent immigrants, especially those from Ireland. In the 1790s, the Federalist party had exploited anti-Irish sentiment. At that time, Democrats welcomed the Irish into their party and denounced England for its domination of Ireland. But after the Pennsylvania Democrats came to power, moderates like McKean began to express second thoughts about liberal immigration laws and especially about Irish radicalism. McKean and his allies came to identify recent Irish immigrants with anarchy, with hostility to the law and to the constitution, and with the movement to elect Simon Snyder.[42]

Irish immigration to the United States increased dramatically in the early years of the nineteenth century.[43] Most of these immigrants

---

[41] For the returns of 1805, see the [Philadelphia] *American Daily Advertiser*, October 26, 1805, and the House *Journal*, 1805-1806, 69. For the returns of 1808, see Senate *Journal*, 1808-1809, 80-81. The Snyderites, once in office, passed another supplement to the militia laws, an act of April 4, 1809. This measure contained no provisions to institute the demands of the extremists. See Mitchell and Flanders, 18:1172-73. The next significant alteration in the basic militia law of the Commonwealth did not occur until the passage of the Seventh Militia Act of March 28, 1814.

[42] Thomas McKean's suspicions of recent immigrants are surprising in the light of his having been president of the Hibernian Society of Philadelphia between 1790 and 1800. The Hibernian Society was a philanthropic organization of merchants, professional men, and skilled craftsmen of Irish descent that aided recent Irish immigrants. See John H. Campbell, *History of the Friendly Sons of St. Patrick and of the Hibernian Society* (Philadelphia, 1892), 315. By 1805, such philanthropic organizations were becoming politicized. A St. Patrick's Benevolent Society was organized in Philadelphia by Irishmen opposed to "the apostate" McKean. William Duane alleged that McKean no longer attended celebrations of St. Patrick's Day in Philadelphia, but did attend a meeting of the English St. George's Society at which Phineas Bond, the British consul, was present. The St. George society toasted the health of the royal family on the King's birthday. Duane quoted McKean that only a "few vagabond Irish" will vote for Snyder in 1805. See the [Philadelphia] *General Advertiser*, March 21, October 5, 1805.

[43] For some examples of reports on Irish immigration in rural Pennsylvania newspapers, see the *Harrisburger Morgenröthe Zeitung*, August 8, 1801; the *Readinger Adler*, July 21, 1801; the *Lancaster Journal*, August 1, 1801; the *Carlisle Gazette*, August 4, 19, 1801; the *Oracle of Dauphin*, July 26, 1802; May 21, 1808; the *Easton American Eagle*, October 11, 1802; the *Country Gazette of the United States*, October 26, 1804. See also Edward C. Carter, II, "A Wild Irishman under Every Federalist's Bed: Naturalization in Philadelphia, 1789-1806," *Pennsylvania Magazine of History and Biography* 94 (1970): 331-46.

were fleeing Britain's harsh suppression of the unsuccessful Irish risings of 1798 and 1803. These abortive revolutions were widely reported in the American press which told of the heroic deeds of Irish revolutionaries and published sympathetic histories of Ireland.[44] At the same time, another less favorable image also gained currency as stereotypes about comic, ignorant, whiskey-sodden Irishmen grew ever more common.[45] Hugh Henry Brackenridge, a political ally of Thomas McKean, published parts of his novel *Modern Chivalry* in Carlisle in 1804-1805. In episodes Brackenridge wrote during these years, Teague O'Regan, an Irish bogtrotter, becomes imbued with revolutionary notions he does not understand and launches a crusade (comically rendered) against learning, the law, and the constitution.[46] Even as these ethnic stereotypes gained in popularity, impoverished Irish immigrants moved into the Pennsylvania countryside as canal and road laborers or hardscrabble farmers. Soon xenophobic newspaper editors began reporting murders, duels, thefts, illegal voting, and other crimes allegedly perpetrated by Irishmen.[47] By the election of

[44] See the [Philadelphia] *General Advertiser*, September 14 to 28, 1803; the *Oracle of Dauphin*, September 25, 1803; June 23, 1804; the *Carlisle Gazette*, September 21, October 5, 1803; August 3, 1804; the *Northumberland Argus*, November 4, December 9, 1803. Archibald Loudon of Carlisle published collections of songs, poetry, and stories from Scotland and Ireland in 1804-1806. He also published a history of the rising of 1798, *The History of the Late Grand Insurrection*, in Carlisle in 1805. In 1802, William Duane published a compilation of pieces from the Irish press called *Extracts from The Press: A Newspaper Published in the Capital of Ireland*. Philadelphia printers published Francis Plowden's *An Historical Review of the State of Ireland* in five volumes in 1805-1806.

[45] For stereotypes about comic Irishmen, see the [Pittsburgh] *Tree of Liberty*, May 19, 1804; the [Lancaster] *Constitutional Democrat*, March 18, 1806; the [Carlisle] *Cumberland Register*, April 19, 1808; the *Adams Centinel*, December 3, 1800, January 21, 1801; the *Lancaster Journal*, April 18, 1801; the *Harrisburg Times*, February 15, 1808; the *Lancaster Intelligencer*, June 30, 1807. Newspapers like the *Tree of Liberty*, the *Cumberland Register*, and the *Constitutional Democrat* supported McKean.

[46] See Hugh Henry Brackenridge, *Modern Chivalry* (New York, 1962), 327-631.

[47] On the poor Irish in western Pennsylvania, see Gouverneur Ogden to William Meredith, July 18, 1803, in the Meredith Papers, HSP. See also the *Lancaster Amerikanische Staatsbothe*, May 20, October 21, 1801; July 6, 1808; the *Pittsburgh Commonwealth*, February 5, 1806; the *Adams Centinel*, July 6, 1808; the *Cumberland Register*, June 28, 1808; the *Pittsburgh Gazette*, October 23, 1801; the [Philadelphia] *General Advertiser*, October 24, 1801; the *Carlisle Gazette*, September 2, 1808. After a series of reports about alleged illegal Irish voting, one correspondent to the *Lancaster Intelligencer* of October 14, 1806, noted that "There is a great noise made about Irishmen!"

1805, Pennsylvanians were developing a new sense of urgency about Irish immigration.

Not surprisingly, politicians sought to capitalize on anti-Irish sentiment. Thomas McKean and his friends were soon opposing laws intended to widen political participation by new immigrants, especially those from Ireland. When the Jeffersonians took office in 1801, Thomas Jefferson had urged repeal of the Federalist-inspired Naturalization Act of 1798. This measure required a fourteen-year residency before an immigrant could become a citizen. Pennsylvania Democrats petitioned for its repeal. In April, 1802, Congress made naturalization less difficult by lowering the residency requirement to five years.[48] Some Democrats—notably editor William Duane—advocated even simpler naturalizations, asking the state to permit the procedure in the Commonwealth's courts of common pleas. Governor McKean demurred, noting that the legislature would have to grant this specific power to the courts.[49] When the legislature produced a bill in March, 1802, authorizing naturalization in state courts, the bill included a provision requiring only two-years' residence. The bill passed the Pennsylvania House, but it failed in the Senate.[50]

The effort to amend Pennsylvania's electoral law continued in the session of 1802-1803. Legislators swept aside opponents' objections that a two-year residency requirement was inconsistent with the federal Naturalization Act. Supporters argued that naturalization was a concurrent power shared with the federal government. Legislator John Ross of Easton (a McKean supporter) argued that the two-year requirement would bring in enough "new Irishmen" to overthrow the government.[51] The bill passed but was vetoed by McKean, who argued

---

[48] For reports of and solicitations for repeal, see the [Philadelphia] *General Advertiser*, December 24, 1801; the *Readinger Adler*, November 24, 1801; the *Lancaster Intelligencer*, December 23, 1801; February 3, 10, 1802. The five-year residency requirement re-established the period stipulated in the old naturalization act of 1795.

[49] *Oracle of Dauphin*, December 8, 1800; [Philadelphia] *General Advertiser*, February 2, 1802.

[50] See the *Lancaster Journal*, March 27, 1802; the *Readinger Adler*, March 30, 1802; the *Easton American Eagle*, March 27, 1802; the [Philadelphia] *General Advertiser*, April 5, 1802; the *Lancaster Amerikanische Staatsbothe*, April 7, 1802; the [Pittsburgh] *Tree of Liberty*, April 17, 1802.

[51] *Lancaster Journal*, February 19, 1803; *Carlisle Gazette*, March 9, 1803; *Norristown Herald*, March 4, 11, 1803; *Lancaster Intelligencer*, March 8, 1803. The *Carlisle Gazette*

that a longer residency was necessary "to wean immigrants from their prejudices, habits, and natural regard for their native land and to attach them to our own."[52] An attempt to override the veto failed.

The veto had important political repercussions. It drove another wedge between McKean and William Duane. According to one sympathizer in Philadelphia, it triggered rumors that a radical Democratic faction opposed to McKean was forming in the city.[53] But the veto seems to have been well received in rural Pennsylvania, where new Irishmen were not popular. The German editor Salomon Myer of York wrote McKean that "The rejection of the alien bill is universal with us."[54] At least as Myer saw it, Pennsylvanians endorsed McKean's caution about the new Irish.

The political consensus assumed that most recent immigrants and especially the "new Irish" tended toward political radicalism. McKean's third inaugural message denounced "political incendiaries, just landed on our shores, [who] attempt to acquire for sinister purposes the mastery of the passions and prejudices of the people."[55] William Findley, a man of Ulster descent, blamed opposition to McKean on "unprincipled emigrants." In a series of letters written under the pseudonym "Sidney," Findley complained that too many Irish and English radicals were emigrating to the United States.[56]

---

report quoted Ross saying that "foreigners had come among us with high wrought notions of liberty and equality such as could not be adopted here, with manners not in unison with the cool and mild temper of Americans, hostile to our general government, turbulent and presumptuous . . . [The law would] open all the jails of Europe to stock our country with their inhabitants." John Ross, a Democrat, had been nominated for the legislature by a Democratic meeting on July 29, 1799. See the [Philadelphia] *General Advertiser*, August 7, 1799. McKean had appointed him clerk of the orphan's court, recorder of deeds, and register of wills for Northampton County in 1800. McKean appointed John Ross of Easton commonwealth attorney to prosecute cases in Luzerne County about 1805. See Samuel Bryan to Joseph B. McKean, February 25, 1805, Society Collection, HSP.

[52] *Carlisle Gazette*, March 23, 1805.

[53] George Worrall to Tench Coxe, April 11, 1803, Coxe Papers, Box 72, HSP.

[54] Salomon Myer to Thomas McKean, March 19, 1803, Lamberton Manuscripts, Vol. 2, HSP. Another version of the electoral law passed the House without the two-year residency requirement. It received McKean's signature on April 4, 1803.

[55] See his message of December 17, 1805, in the House *Journal*, 1805-1806, 15.

[56] *Lancaster Constitutional Democrat*, October 29, 1805. Findley is identified as "Sidney" in the July 30, 1805, issue of the *Lancaster Constitutional Democrat*. His essays against the project to revise the constitution ran from July 2 to November 5, 1805. Findley wrote to

According to Andrew Gregg, another of McKean's supporters, recent emigrant editors were responsible for Pennsylvania's political confusion. Hugh Henry Brackenridge blamed the Commonwealth's political quarrels on "emigrant Hybernians." Tench Coxe informed Joseph Gales in a letter condemning McKean's radical opponents in Philadelphia that "*anticonstitutional* and *foreign* considerations govern them."[57] George Logue, whom McKean had appointed brigade inspector of the militia of Cumberland and Franklin Counties, reported that "All the disapointed [*sic*] office hunters of our county together with the new Irish has [*sic*] enrolled themselves against the re-election of our present Governor." And a political supporter from Butler County informed Thomas McKean Thompson in 1805 that "The Irish as far as came within my view were opposed to his [McKean's] re-election."[58] The Lancaster Democrat William Barton, another McKean appointee, blamed the attack on both constitution and courts on "ALIENS and NEWLY ADOPTED CITIZENS who are *overrunning the land*." To give such persons citizenship was "a national evil of vast magnitude."[59] McKean's supporters in the 1805 election openly attacked the Irish as the instigators of Snyder's candidacy.[60]

McKean on December 24, 1805, "When we made the Constitution [of 1790], I thought we made citizenship too cheap and endeavoured in vain to have it somewhat restrained. No other state is cursed with such a number of unprincipled emigrants who are prepared to be both the dupes and tools of any faction as Pennsylvania." William Findley to Thomas McKean, December 24, 1805, McKean Papers, Vol. 3, HSP.

[57] Andrew Gregg to Joseph Hiester, August 9, 1805, Society Collection; Hugh Henry Brackenridge to [A.J.Dallas], May 25, 1805, Alexander J. Dallas Papers, Correspondence; Tench Coxe to Joseph Gales, January 9, 1805, Coxe Papers; all at HSP.

[58] Letter of George Logue to Thomas McKean Thompson, July 31, 1805, Executive Correspondence; letter of John Gilmore to Thomas McKean Thompson, October 20, 1805, Washington County Appointments File, Bureau of Commissions and Elections; both in the Records of the Secretary of the Commonwealth (RG 26), McKean Administration, PHMC.

[59] William Barton, *The Constitutionalist* (Philadelphia, 1804), 5-13, 46-48.

[60] The Montgomery County address of McKean's supporters maintained that among the radicals "it was thought sufficient to delude the Germans of Pennsylvania, by nominating Mr. Snyder, who is a German, and as to the Irish, they were to be satisfied with an assurance that the Irish influence in Philadelphia would govern Snyder whenever he was chosen to govern the state." See the *Easton American Eagle*, September 14, 1805. Articles in the *Readinger Adler* played upon German rivalry with the Irish in Berks County by associating Snyderites with "newly arrived Irishmen." See the *Readinger Adler*, September 10, 1805. An address to the Constitutional Republicans in the *Cumberland Register*, October 1, 1805, asserted that in Chester, Montgomery, and Berks Counties, a party calling itself the "Sons of Ireland" was organizing to overturn the constitution and defeat McKean.

By the election of 1805, there had been a complete turnabout on the immigration issue. In 1799 the Federalists had attacked McKean as the candidate who would bring thousands of Irish rebels to American shores. Now McKean and his allies had adopted the nativist position, exploiting popular fear of the new Irish.

Other cultural and ethnic conflicts in early nineteenth-century Pennsylvania did not relate as directly to the divisions among factions in the Democratic party. Nearly all white Pennsylvanians, for example, condoned restrictions on the civil and political liberties of blacks. Blacks could not serve on juries or in the militia. In 1807 the legislature debated requiring blacks and mulattos to register with county prothonotaries and pay fees if they wished to seek employment.[61] These restrictive, racist measures were never a matter of political disagreement between McKean and his foes.

Another cultural issue not significant to Democratic party factionalism involved the creation of public schools. Germans and Quakers maintained large church-related school establishments. The Germans feared that public schools would destroy the German language and would hinder religious instruction in that language; the Quakers preferred not to endorse a public school system that might promote ideas contrary to the teaching of the Friends. But the debate over school legislation did not divide Democrats against each other.[62] McKean endorsed public schools, but he settled for an act providing free education for the poor, which Simon Snyder's administration altered only in minor details in 1809.[63]

Geographic and historic considerations sometimes took center stage in otherwise culturally nuanced political disputes. Proposals to support the construction of churches or academies through lotteries or to incorporate colleges and religious institutions were often fought out on the basis of local rivalries, usually between eastern and western Pennsylvania. Legislation to suppress vice and immorality, to regulate dueling, or to abolish slavery did not produce clear divisions among Democratic factions. In the conflict between Pennsylvanians and Yankee claimants to Luzerne County lands, neither wing of the

[61] *Lancaster Intelligencer*, February 11, 1806; *Lancaster Journal*, January 24, 1806.
[62] House *Journal*, 1804-1805, 345-46; House *Journal*, 1805-1806, 393.
[63] Mitchell and Flanders, 18:1171-72.

Democrats opposed strong support for the rights of the Pennsylvania claimants, though some Federalists supported the transplanted Yankees trying to win legal recognition of their titles.[64] Not every issue involving conflict among ethnic, cultural, or religious groups led to ongoing political alliances or political divisions.

The politics of cultural conflict might at times be overshadowed by other disagreements. The War of 1812 temporarily brought positions on international politics to the fore. Economic issues—monopolies and internal improvements—were always important, as were rivalries over patronage between competing politicians and their supporters. Only a false precision can conclusively determine which of these sources of political infighting dominated Pennsylvania politics. But it is incorrect to conclude from the evidence that cultural factors did not influence early nineteenth-century Pennsylvania politics because Pennsylvania Germans did not unite behind Simon Snyder in an ethnic bloc in the election of 1805.

By the first decade of the nineteenth century, Pennsylvania subcultures were no longer satisfied with simple ethnic or linguistic recognition accomplished through ticket-balancing.[65] Religious, linguistic, or cultural groups had special public policy agendas. These groups wanted access to the public business in their native language, protection from excessively punitive militia requirements, and the preservation of the ballot from supposedly corrupt alien influences. The politicians who stood with McKean against the radicals did not merely recognize the subcultures; rather, they shared power with emerging leaders, pursued public policies important to these groups, and responded to their fears. A new kind of ethnocultural politics emerged. The politics of ethnic recognition continued at the local

[64] George Worrall to Tench Coxe, February 5, 1802, Tench Coxe Papers; letter of Lord Butler, October 7, 1803, Northampton County Manuscripts, Box 1; both in HSP. Tench Coxe to Thomas McKean Thompson, February 21, 1803, Executive Correspondence, McKean Administration, Records of the Secretary of the Commonwealth (RG 26), PHMC. See also the *Luzerne Federalist*, October 22, 1803. Luzerne was one of three counties that voted for Federalist James Ross for governor in 1802 (the other two were Delaware and York). It went by a slim margin for McKean in 1805. In 1808 it was one of the six counties that voted for Federalist James Ross against Simon Snyder.

[65] I have described changing styles of ethnic politics in Keller, "Diversity and Democracy," 61-201.

level, but now Pennsylvania's subcultures were associated with one another in a political system in which they were represented by powerful leaders. Thomas McKean and his advisors understood this transformation of the political system. They kept their offices and held back radical reform because they accommodated themselves to political change.

Historians should be careful in making claims about the impact of cultural differences on politics. The divisions in Pennsylvania's Democratic party were not the culturally determined product of bloc voting by ethnic or religious subcultures. Nor were they merely the result of competition among factions organized around personalities. By the time Jeffersonians came to power in Pennsylvania, the sectarians, the German-speakers, and those who feared the new Irish were trying to achieve specific political objectives at odds with the radical Democratic agenda. The alliances they formed with Thomas McKean held the line against radical reform and kept the Commonwealth on a conservative path until Simon Snyder's election. Once Snyder became governor, economic development and patriotic indignation against the British assumed higher priorities and diverted him from pursuing the radical Democratic program. Pennyslvania was the largest laboratory for democracy in the early American republic. It had the largest electorate and nearly the most liberal suffrage requirements in the nation. The Commonwealth developed a growing political party system; a largely free labor economy with agricultural, commercial, and manufacturing sectors; an ethnically and culturally diverse population; a government not beholden to a religious establishment; and— for a time—the largest city of the republic. More than any other state, Pennsylvania was a pluralistic democracy that foreshadowed communities that did not appear until much later in the nation's history. It was there more than any place that one could see what democracy meant to early Americans. And to Pennsylvanians of the early nineteenth century, *democracy* meant a system by which local ethnic and religious subcultures claimed power and defended themselves against real or imagined threats that in the name of a majority sometimes attempted to homogenize the pluralistic commonwealth.

Mary Baldwin College   KENNETH W. KELLER

William Duane, Philadelphia's Democratic Republicans, and The Origins of Modern Politics

T
HE Jeffersonian era, once synonymous with the rise of democracy, now is viewed by historians as at most a transitional period in political culture, as yet more traditional than modern.* There is a growing scholarly consensus that politics in the early republic, both in ideas and practices, was closer to eighteenth-century patterns than to the voter-oriented, mass party politics of the 1840s and after. Richard Hofstadter, Michael Wallace, and others have taught us that party itself was still viewed as inherently pernicious. According to this thesis, it was another political generation before men recognized the potential benefits of democratic conflict; leaders of the early republic held to the Whiggish ideal of consensual harmony.[1] Similarly, recent studies of political practices in this era tend to the common conclusion that post-Revolutionary politics was still a gentleman's avocation. Partisan disputes, once viewed as fundamental, are now seen as mere

* The author wishes to thank R. Kent Newmyer of the University of Connecticut (Storrs) for judicious criticism of the manuscript.

[1] Hofstadter, *The Idea of a Party System: The Rise of Legitimate Opposition in the United States, 1780–1840* (Berkeley and Los Angeles, 1969); Wallace, "Changing Concepts of Party in the United States: New York, 1815–1828," *American Historical Review*, LXXIV (1968), 453–491. Lynn L. Marshall, "The Strange Stillbirth of the Whig Party," *ibid.*, LXXII (1967), 445–468, was the first major study to contrast the ideologies of the first and second party systems. On changing concepts of leadership and public service see Perry M. Goldman, "Political Virtue in the Age of Jackson," *Political Science Quarterly*, LXXXVII (1972), 46–62. Recent studies of the first party system which stress the links to traditional political thought are: Lance Banning, "Republican Ideology and the Triumph of the Constitution, 1789 to 1793," *William and Mary Quarterly*, 3d. ser., XXXI (1974), 167–188, and Daniel Sisson, *The American Revolution of 1800* (New York, 1974). For an excellent review of the literature on the ideology and political culture of the early republic, see Robert E. Shallhope, "Toward a Republican Synthesis: The Emergence of an Understanding of Republicanism in American Historiography," *William and Mary Quarterly*, 3d. ser., XXIX (1972), 49–80.

365

quarrels among contending elites.[2] Nor, it is argued, was the party organization into Federalists and Republicans so clearcut or advanced as formerly believed. Indeed, some have questioned the existence of a "first American party system."[3] Taken together these studies suggest, in effect, that for this period political history is elitist history, willy-nilly, with little to tell us about citizens below the leadership class.

Before the consensus hardens further, let us look at the problem with a new focus. A commendable trend toward state and local studies has substantially modified interpretations drawn from politics at the national level. But, as historians, we have not sufficiently analyzed the internal mechanisms of party, either local or national. Much of the significant political conflict of these years occurred, this essay contends, not so much between as *within* parties. We have tended too easily to dismiss intraparty strife as mere factionalism, ipso facto evidence of an old-fashioned politics still organized around personal and regional loyalties. Such an assumption assures that we will continue to have a history as written by the winners. Those who spoke for a party were not invariably its most representative members. Looking behind the public face of party, we may perhaps glimpse more clearly the concerns of activists and voters. To do so is to question the prevailing interpretations of the nature of politics in the early republic.

Politics in Philadelphia in the years just after 1800 may serve to illustrate the need for alternative interpretations. At first glance, the Philadelphia experience appears to verify the Hofstadter thesis about party instability. Pennsylvania's Republican Party, so crucial in the election of Thomas Jefferson, was considered a bulwark of Republican strength nationally. Yet by 1805 the party in Pennsylvania was broken, and two Republican candidates opposed each

[2] See, for example, the following state studies: Richard R. Beeman, *The Old Dominion and the New Nation, 1788–1801* (Lexington, Ky., 1972); Paul Goodman, *The Democratic-Republicans of Massachusetts: Politics in a Young Republic* (Cambridge, 1964); Carl E. Prince, *New Jersey's Republicans: The Genesis of an Early Party Machine, 1789–1817* (Chapel Hill, 1967).

[3] See Ronald P. Formisano's provocative critique and interpretation of "Deferential-Participant Politics: The Early Republic's Political Culture, 1789–1840," *American Political Science Review*, LXVIII (1974), 473–487.

other for governor. The schism began in Philadelphia as early as 1802, and quickly spread to statewide politics. It would be a mistake to regard this early breakdown into factionalism as proof of the weakness of party or of partisan thinking. The schism did, however, reveal tensions that were inherent within the Republican alliance. Once in power, the Republicans were forced to recognize that they held fundamentally differing notions about the meaning of party and about what kind of party they wanted. The conflict they experienced over these essential questions transformed the political character of Philadelphia.[4]

When the Republicans took office in 1801, five men could be said to hold the effective leadership of the party in Philadelphia: Alexander James Dallas, William Duane, Tench Coxe, George Logan and Michael Leib. Two others, not direct participants in city affairs, who influenced party developments there were Governor Thomas McKean and Secretary of the Treasury Albert Gallatin, Pennsylvania's representative in Jefferson's cabinet. Among the Philadelphians, Dallas and Duane were pre-eminent in influence.

Dallas was perhaps the most universally respected man within the party leadership, considered in some quarters "the life and soul of the Republican cause" in Pennsylvania. He was a Jamaican of Scottish background who emigrated to the United States at the end of the Revolution, entered law practice in Philadelphia, and rose in politics as a protégé and adviser of Governor Thomas Mifflin. From his position as Mifflin's Secretary of the Commonwealth, Dallas became the outstanding organizer of the Republican interest from the early 1790s onward. More skillful behind the scenes than as a public figure, Dallas eschewed elective office but continued in the powerful post of Secretary of the Commonwealth when his hand-picked candidate, Thomas McKean, was elected Governor in 1799. In 1801 he resigned his state office to accept President Jefferson's

[4] The interpretation offered here sharply differs from that implicit within the standard work on Pennsylvania politics in this era: Sanford W. Higginbotham, *The Keystone in the Democratic Arch: Pennsylvania Politics, 1800–1816* (Harrisburg, 1952). That book remains a highly useful factual account and an indispensable starting point for further study. See also Noble E. Cunningham, Jr., *The Jeffersonian Republicans in Power: Party Operations, 1801–1809* (Chapel Hill, 1963), 213–220, for a good, brief description of the Pennsylvania schism.

appointment as federal District Attorney. Dallas' position as the city's highest ranking Republican officeholder, his close friendship with Secretary Gallatin, and his influence over Governor McKean all ensured him of top political standing in Philadelphia.

William Duane, a newcomer and relative outsider, who was never part of Dallas' inner circle, was nonetheless the second most powerful Republican in the city as a consequence of his role as party editor. Duane had taken over the *Aurora* in 1798 following the death of Benjamin Franklin Bache and had built it into perhaps the most outstanding political newspaper in the country, an indispensable source of Republican strength in the election of 1800. Jefferson called it "the rallying point for the Orthodox of the whole union," "our comfort in the gloomiest days," and John Adams named Duane as one of the three or four men most responsible for his defeat.[5] Duane was an Irishman and former newspaper editor in Calcutta who had come to the United States in 1796 as a political refugee from the British Empire. A year earlier, the British government had expelled him from India as a "dangerous incendiary." Forcibly deported to London, he briefly became a speaker and writer for the radical London Corresponding Society, then opted to leave for America in search of a more congenial political atmosphere. Duane's rough political apprenticeship prepared him well to stand up to the so-called Federalist "reign of terror" of 1798 to 1800. As *Aurora* editor, he was continually harassed—indicted three times for seditious libel, threatened with deportation, dragged through the streets by rioters, beaten and whipped by a mob of officers for refusing to reveal a source. The courage that Duane showed in resisting intimidation established him as almost a folk hero in the minds of ordinary Republicans and that power over public opinion made him a force to be reckoned with in politics.[6]

In 1801 Dallas and Duane were cordial if hardly intimate political allies. Four years later they stood at the heads of opposing wings

[5] Jefferson to William Wirt, Mar. 30, 1811, William Wirt Papers, Maryland Historical Society; Adams to Benjamin Stoddert, Mar. 31, 1801, Charles Francis Adams, ed., *The Works of John Adams, Second President of the United States* . . . (Boston, 1850–1856), IX, 582; Adams to Christopher Gadsden, Apr. 16, 1801, *ibid.*, 584.

[6] See Kim Tousley Phillips, "William Duane, Revolutionary Editor" (doctoral dissertation, University of California, Berkeley, 1968).

of a party hopelessly divided over issues concerning the essential nature of party itself. The Dallas wing, formally named the Constitutional Republicans, was commonly known as the Quids. Duane's section called themselves the Democratic Republicans or, more frequently, simply the Democrats. For simplicity, the name Quids and Democrats will be used from the outset to distinguish the factions in the making.[7]

Philadelphia's Federalists, meanwhile, virtually disappeared as an organized party. "Truly humbled" by the Republican victories of 1799 and 1800, the Federalists temporarily secluded themselves in a self-imposed political exile. Their "utmost ambition" was keeping "Duane & his Gang from the supreme Power." To this end, when they voted, they voted Quid.[8]

The Federalists could bring themselves to cooperate with the Quids because they found them less socially offensive than the Democrats. In defeat, the Federalists were ready to concede that not all Republicans were Jacobins. Rather, as one of them put it, they "very obviously consisted of two classes of men." On one side were "all the well informed, well disposed citizens" and on the other was "crowded the *rubbish* of our community."[9] This suggestive social commentary, while overly simplistic, was nonetheless essentially accurate in pointing out the presence of class differences among Republicans that tended to separate them into Quids or Democrats.

The conflicting social elements that went into the party in formation made Republican unity in Philadelphia inherently precarious. During the 1790s, the Republicans had aimed to incorporate nearly everyone below the highest stratum of society. They had succeeded in steadily expanding their constituency, in part because the Federalist leaders were so patently exclusive. With them, in the

---

[7] President Jefferson dubbed the two groups the "moderates" and the "high-fliers." Jefferson to Gallatin, Mar. 28, 1803, Henry Adams, ed., *The Writings of Albert Gallatin* (Philadelphia, 1879), I, 119–120. His terms appropriately suggest the differing qualities of partisanship that were instrumental in the schism. The term "radicals," frequently used for the Democrats, is better avoided because of its anachronistic connotations.

[8] John Rutledge to Robert Goodloe Harper, Aug. 3, 1805, Robert Goodloe Harper Papers, Library of Congress.

[9] *Gazette of the United States*, "Ephraim," Mar. 11, 1801.

absence of the right credentials of family and social position, mere wealth and achievement were not sufficient claims to acceptability. Foreign birth, for example, was likely to disqualify a person for Federalist Party service.[10] As a result, ambitious men who lacked the social cachet to rise politically as Federalists tended to take their "talents to the best market."[11] The Republican Party leadership in 1800 was top heavy with such men. Merchants, lawyers, men of wealth and business prominence enjoyed an influence in the party that was wholly disproportionate to their numbers. The Republican voting strength came from the mechanic classes, the Germans and the Irish who lived in the working-class wards at the edges of the city and in the crowded, lower-class suburbs of the Northern Liberties and Southwark.

The social disparities within the party were bound to produce stress. As compared with the most prominent Federalists, all Republicans were social outcasts, but that basis for mutuality became rather strained once the common enemy was gone. Republican leaders from the commercial-professional wing of Quids, once in office, tended to display their own social pretensions. Ambitious for respectability for both themselves and their party, they were ready to slough off an identity with the party's less respectable elements by discouraging their participation in party affairs. Duane and those who became Democratic activists had a different conception. Their goal was to strengthen the partisan identity of mechanics and the ethnic minorities by drawing them into an active, ongoing involvement in the party apparatus.

The Democrats' efforts at party building were partially frustrated, for a time, by the Quids' reluctance to appear partisan. The trouble between them began over the question of patronage. Duane and the Democrats urged a "clean sweep" of the Federalists from office, while the Quids, led by Gallatin and Dallas, counselled

---

[10] This was evidently the case with A. J. Dallas. The burden of Federalist argument, against "counsellor Creole," as William Cobbett called him, was that he was an "arrogant assuming foreigner." *Porcupine's Gazette*, Aug. 5, 1798; *Gazette of the United States*, Sept. 11, 1799. See also *ibid.*, Apr. 17, Sept. 4, Dec. 18, 1799. The Federalists' nativism probably helps to account for the Republicanism of other rich, distinguished immigrants, such as Albert Gallatin, Stephen Girard, and Congressman John Swanwick.

[11] "A Westerner," commenting on Dallas, in *ibid.*, Aug. 6, 1799.

restraint and conciliation. Behind the opposing views on removals and patronage were conflicting attitudes toward the idea of party itself. The Quids were hesitant to do anything that might perpetuate the two-party system. If parties persisted, in Dallas' view, "each general election will involve the hazard of civil war." Therefore it was crucial to open the "door to reconciliation."[12] The Democrats, for their part, had no aspirations to consensual harmony. They wanted to defeat the Federalists, not absorb them, for they neither expected nor wished to see partisan conflict wither away.[13]

Philadelphia's Democrats of 1801 were as candid as the Jacksonians of the next generation in their appraisal of the political value of patronage. Seeing the advantage it had been to the Federalists, they concluded that it would be "political suicide" not to follow their example. A spoils system made better sense to them than dividing the "honours & profits" of government with political enemies.[14] Governor McKean had disappointed them with his patronage policy by ignoring party considerations in favor of his own relatives and personal associates.[15] New appointments, in their estimate, should be calculated to reward party loyalists and help consolidate "the republican interest."[16]

The leading Quids, with their eighteenth-century standards of political propriety, were disgusted by the "clamor" from the "office-hunting caitiffs." Appointments should be based on "integrity and capacity" alone, regardless of party affiliation, in Secretary Gallatin's opinion. If the Democrats' view were to prevail, it would reduce government to a business. To Gallatin, the demand for removals suggested that the "hard struggle" by Republicans was not fought on principle but for "the sake of a few paltry offices . . . mere ad-

12 Dallas to Gallatin, June 14, 1801, Gallatin Papers, New-York Historical Society. See Wilson Cary Nicholas to James Madison, May 1, 1801, Rives Collection, Madison Papers, Library of Congress, for a quintessential expression of the antiparty philosophy of Republican moderates.

13 See, for example, the unabashed partisanship in the survey of government clerks which "Citizen W. Duane" furnished to Gallatin in 1801, Gallatin Papers.

14 *Gazette of the United States*, quoting *Aurora*, Mar. 4, 1801; Thomas Leiper to Jefferson, Sept. 22, 1802, Jefferson Papers, Library of Congress.

15 McKean practiced what Ronald Formisano has characterized as "a *patron-client* type of patronage." "Deferential-Participant Politics," 479.

16 Duane to Jefferson, June 10, 1801, Jefferson Papers; Michael Leib to Gallatin, May 14, 1801, Gallatin Papers.

ministrative offices of profit."[17] The Quids themselves tended to see politics as a civic duty, if sometimes an unpleasant one.[18] To them, the Democrats appeared to be turning it into a profession.

The dispute over patronage crested in the spring of 1803 when the Democrats decided to take their case directly to the President. His caution in removals, as they saw it, was not a policy of his own choosing but the work of conservative advisers, especially Gallatin.[19] To give him the "pretext" he needed to justify a change in policy, the Democrats set out to rally public sentiment on the question through a series of local ward meetings. The Quids were enraged by the meddling, the efforts to stir public opinion on a subject they believed was better left to the discretion of government. In the end, the Democrats' petition campaign came to nothing. Jefferson drafted a friendly reply to be sent through William Duane, but Gallatin disliked its "appearance of apology" and on his advice the President withdrew it. But the dispute exposed an intensity of feeling that made it evident to most observers that schism in Philadelphia was inevitable.[20]

The schism broke wide open the following year when the Quids tried to stop Michael Leib's re-election to Congress. A similar attempt had been made two years earlier, but had been suppressed by party leaders bent on unity, including at that time both Dallas and Duane. In 1804 Leib's enemies would not be stopped. When they failed to defeat his nomination, the Quids bolted the Republican

---

17 Dallas to Gallatin, June 14, 1801, *ibid.*; William Jones to John Randolph, Mar. 19, 1803, Uselma Clarke Smith Collection, Historical Society of Pennsylvania (HSP); Leonard D. White, *The Jeffersonians: A Study in Administrative History, 1801–1829* (New York, 1951), 152; Gallatin to Jefferson, Aug. 11, 1803, *Writings of Albert Gallatin*, I, 135.

18 Dallas to Gallatin, Sept. 30, 1801, *ibid.*; William Jones to Jefferson, May 20, 1801, Jefferson Papers.

19 There was probably some truth to the Democrats' contention. Certainly Gallatin was more conservative than Jefferson at his most cautious. During his second administration, Jefferson made his own decisions on Pennsylvania appointments, independent of Gallatin, and the results favored the Democratic partisans. Thomas Leiper to Jefferson, Mar. 23, 1806, Jefferson Papers; Gallatin to Jefferson, Aug. 6, 1808, *Writings of Albert Gallatin*, I, 402.

20 Michael Leib to Mathew Carey, Dec. 12, 1802, Lea and Febiger Papers, HSP; Gallatin to Jefferson, Aug. 11, 1803, *Writings of Albert Gallatin*, I, 134–135; Jefferson to Duane, unsigned draft, July 24, 1803, Jefferson Papers; William Jones and others to Jefferson, draft, Feb. 12, 1803, Uselma Clarke Smith Collection; William Jones to John Randolph, Mar. 19, 1803, *ibid.*

ticket and, with the aid of Federalists, ran their own independent candidate against him. Leib survived the election, barely, but the Republican Party in Philadelphia was doomed. From that point on, Quids and Democrats openly competed for Republican votes as rival parties.[21]

On one level, Leib's troubles were the result of a personal rivalry with George Logan. The two, who had disliked each other since their days in the Democratic Republican Society, contested for exclusive leadership of Philadelphia County, those districts adjacent to Philadelphia but outside the city limits.[22] Logan, the Quaker pacifist and gentleman farmer, was popular in the rural areas of the county. But Leib, a German physician who had abandoned medicine for politics, had the clear advantage. He controlled the densely-settled Northern Liberties, which held more than 40 percent of the county's population and a majority of its Republican voters.[23] Moreover, Leib was the more astute—some said, unscrupulous—politician. Logan had the help, however, of his close friend Tench Coxe, a man almost without peer in political infighting. It was Coxe who directed the fight against Leib in 1804, and Leib launched a vendetta in retaliation which ultimately cost Coxe his federal appointment.[24]

But personal rivalries were not the whole story. The most damaging case against Leib was the charge that he was morally unfit for office. He was tarnished by a personal scandal, going back many years, that he may have defrauded the Penrose family of several thousand dollars in government securities. Although the charge was never proved conclusively, and the case was settled out of court,

[21] For fuller, somewhat differing accounts of the bolt from Leib in 1802 and 1804, see Higginbotham, *Keystone*, 43–45, 68–73, and Phillips, "William Duane," 148–153, 158–160, 164–170.

[22] *Ibid.*, 104–107; Minutes of the Democratic Society of Pennsylvania, 141–146, HSP; Eugene P. Link, *Democratic-Republican Societies, 1790–1800* (New York, 1942), 147–148; Frederick B. Tolles, *George Logan of Philadelphia* (New York, 1953), 141, 145, 233–234, 245–246.

[23] Higginbotham, *Keystone*, 62.

[24] Jacob E. Cooke, "Tench Coxe, Alexander Hamilton, and the Encouragement of American Manufactures," *William and Mary Quarterly*, 3d series, XXXII (1975), 369–392. Leib, in the United States Senate, succeeded in 1812 in abolishing the position of Purveyor of Public Supplies, held by Coxe since 1803. See Michael Leib from [John Steele or William Linnard?], Jan. 11, 1811, Society Collection, HSP; *Annals of Congress*, 12th Cong., 1st Sess. (Washington, 1853), 106, 1212–1213, 2257–2261.

Leib had failed to clear his name of suspicion.[25] In these circumstances, he could never have survived politically, despite his strength in his home district, except for the support of William Duane. The *Aurora* editor put his own reputation on the line in Leib's defense, and that decision opened a new chapter in Philadelphia politics.

Duane believed that Leib's only real crime, in the eyes of the Quids, was his Democracy. Other politicians, including Tench Coxe, had survived equal or worse scandals. Leib was to be ostracized, Duane was convinced, because he played a different style of politics from the gentlemen seeking to run the Republican Party as their own private club. Leib was not a club member by anybody's reckoning. He played street politics as Philadelphia had rarely seen it. His style was as distasteful to the Quids as to the Federalists before them. All this Duane charged and the Democrats agreed with him. In retrospect, the Quids may well have been right to dismiss Leib as an opportunistic demagogue. But the Democrats could not have conceded that, given the context of the quarrel. To them, the issue was greater than the personality of a single man. Therefore Leib was toasted around town as the pillar of democracy and his cause was made the symbol of a wider struggle.[26]

The Quids were dumbfounded by Duane's moral obtuseness, as they saw it. During the campaign of 1804, they reported, Duane remarked that morality was not a necessary quality in a legislator.[27]

25 Leib to Albert Gallatin, May 8, 1801, Gallatin Papers; *The Following Testimonials of the Conduct and Characters of Dr. Michael Leib and Colonel William Duane are Taken from the Records of the Supreme Court of Pennsylvania* ([Philadelphia], 1816), pamphlet, HSP; *Gazette of the United States*, Sept. 4, 1799, Apr. 17, 23, 25, 1801; *Freeman's Journal*, June 13, 14, Aug. 20, 1804.

26 See Phillips, "William Duane," 191–193. In "The Transformation of Urban Politics, 1700–1765," *Journal of American History*, LX (1973), 605–632, Gary B. Nash has argued that, as early as the mid-eighteenth century, Philadelphia and other cities experienced a democratization of political style and tactics which served to undermine the traditional political ethos. While it is significant that political elites learned to broaden their appeal and solicit the votes of the lower classes, Nash perhaps exaggerates the "tendency to shift power downward." As he notes, leaders retained their conservative social outlook. And lower-class voters were, at best, passive participants in the electoral process. Michael Leib, on the other hand, did not merely dabble in mass politics; he made it a fulltime occupation. He was consistent not sporadic in grounding his political fortunes squarely upon support from the masses and disdain for elites. And he envisioned working-class voters as active, indispensable partners in a political machine directed by himself.

27 *Freeman's Journal*, "Clonensis," July 20, 1804.

Perhaps he said it, perhaps not. But the sentiment perfectly summed up what Duane and the Democrats believed was at issue. In their opinion, *public* character not private reputation was the test of an officeholder. Personal morality, however genuine, was no guarantee of sound government. The job of an officeholder was to faithfully represent the will of his constituents—nothing more, nothing less.[28] With these views, Philadelphia's Democrats had come a long way from the political heritage of the eighteenth century, expressing a philosophy of politics customarily associated with the Jacksonian era.

It was precisely on this question—who is fit to govern in a representative democracy?—that Quids and Democrats contended throughout Pennsylvania in the gubernatorial election of 1805. The Quids claimed a superior weight of character that entitled them to recognition. The Democrats refused to defer to their self-estimation. More importantly, they challenged the very concept of a class of "natural leaders," more fit than ordinary men to represent the people wisely. In their opinion, the Quids' attitude was not only condescending but dangerous, a perversion of the meaning of popular sovereignty as they understood it. The Quids, indeed, saw themselves as "stewards" of society, offering their talents, their education, their wealth, the benefits of all their attainments in the public service. In this election, they were to be baffled and angered by the public's ingratitude.

In 1805 Governor Thomas McKean was forced to seek re-election to a third term without the endorsement of the Republican caucus, for the Country Democrats in the legislature at Lancaster had lost all patience with him. McKean was a thorough-going Quid. His aristocratic lifestyle and opinions were made doubly offensive by his personality—vain, arrogant, and notoriously ill-tempered.[29] In truth, Governor McKean had never been popular with the Democrats within the party. Since 1799 they had been obliged to tolerate him because of the influence of A. J. Dallas over party decisions. In

---

28 An especially clear statement of these views is in William Duane, *Experience the Test of Government: In Eighteen Essays. Written During the Years 1805 and 1806.* . . . (Philadelphia, 1807), pamphlet, HSP.

29 *Gazette of the United States,* Aug. 6, 12, 14, 16, 28, Sept. 9, 1799; Gail Stuart Rowe, "Power, Politics, and Public Service: The Life of Thomas McKean," 256–259, 270, 279, 323–324, and *passim* (doctoral dissertation, Stanford University, 1969).

1805 the Democrats rebelled and nominated one of their own number, Speaker of the House Simon Snyder, as the caucus choice for Governor. McKean's friends, led by Dallas, were now forced to organize the Quids officially into a third party to support the incumbent.

McKean and the Country Democrats had come to loggerheads on the issue of judicial reform. The legislature sought to simplify court procedures and create a new system of speedy, local justice, but the Governor thwarted their efforts with repeated vetoes.[30] During this phase of the developing quarrel, Duane and the Philadelphia Democrats remained essentially neutral. The city Democrats, while broadly sympathetic to the intentions of their rural colleagues, did not share their confidence in the democratic or reform potential of localism.[31]

The judicial reform issue, however, fully engaged the Philadelphians when it turned to the question of judicial life tenure. Here was an issue with the force to crystallize the ideological differences separating Democrats from Quids. To the Quids, with their paternalistic notions of government, any violation of judicial independence was unthinkable. As the Democrats saw it, judges were no more intended to be above the will of the people than any other officer of government.

The subject of judicial tenure came into sharp focus in January 1805 with the acquittal of three state Supreme Court Justices impeached for misconduct in the case of Thomas Passmore. Every Democrat agreed that the judges had been grossly arbitrary, but Dallas, speaking for the defense, had successfully argued that the judges had acted within their powers under the common law.[32] To Duane, the outcome of the trial illustrated two things: it demonstrated the latitude and discretion that the common law gave to 'udges to create law and thus to impose their personal vision on

30 On judicial reform in Pennsylvania, see *ibid.*, 51–58, 65–67, 77–81, 86–87, and Richard E. Ellis, *The Jeffersonian Crisis: Courts and Politics in the Young Republic* (New York, 1971), chaps. XI and XII.

31 For a sample of the *Aurora*'s progression on the issue, compare the editorials of Jan. 4, 1803, Mar. 22, 1804, and Feb. 1, 1805. On the geographic split, see *ibid.*, Jan. 4, 1803; Elizabeth K. Henderson, "The Attack on the Judiciary in Pennsylvania, 1800–1810," *Pennsylvania Magazine of History and Biography*, LXI (1937), 132.

32 Higginbotham, *Keystone*, 55–58, 66–67, 77–80; Ellis, *The Jeffersonian Crisis*, 165–170.

society; and it showed the failure of impeachment as a protective mechanism, proving the need to limit judicial tenure as a means to make judges responsible.[33]

City and Country Democrats allied, at this point, and campaigned together for judicial reform through amendment to the state Constitution. Their call for a constitutional convention became the focus of the gubernatorial contest between McKean and Snyder. The Democrats proposed a series of revisions which together would have shifted the balance of power in government, created by the Constitution of 1790, by weakening the judicial and executive branches and strengthening the lower house of the legislature.[34] Indeed, their stated intention was to restore the democratic structure and spirit of the state Constitution of 1776.[35] Evidently they miscalculated, however, in seeking to revive old constitutionalist sentiments among Republicans. By 1805 the constitutional issue, as such, was an abstraction without force to engage the close attention of voters. Even before this gubernatorial campaign was over, the Democrats began to retreat from their commitment and, ultimately, the idea of a constitutional convention was allowed to die quietly.[36]

While the Democrats were flexible on the constitutional issue, the Quids were not. Organized as the Society of Constitutional Republicans, they defended the Constitution of 1790 as if the safety of the republic hung in the balance. Their fears cannot be dismissed as exaggerated campaign rhetoric, for they were more alarmed in private than they were willing to admit publicly. To avoid alienating voters, they concealed their true feeling that tampering with the Constitution was an invitation to anarchy, and argued only that a convention would be inexpedient.[37]

---

33 These points are repeated in numerous editorials and guest articles in the *Aurora* during 1805. See, for example, *ibid.*, Jan. 28, 30, 1805.

34 Higginbotham, *Keystone*, 80–84, and chap. IV, *passim.*

35 For an especially clear statement, see Thomas Paine's letters "To the Citizens of Pennsylvania on the Proposal for Calling a Convention," *Aurora*, Aug. 31, Sept. 4, 7, 1805, reprinted in Philip S. Foner, ed., *The Complete Writings of Thomas Paine* (New York, 1945), II, 992–1007.

36 Higginbotham, *Keystone*, 94.

37 Dallas to Robert Smith, Apr. 11, 1805, in George Mifflin Dallas, *Life and Writings of Alexander James Dallas* (Philadelphia, 1871), 117; Dallas to Albert Gallatin, Jan. 26, 1805, Gallatin Papers; Gallatin to Dallas, Mar. 30, 1805, Simon Gratz Collection, HSP.

It is significant that Quids and Democrats differed in intensity
on this issue, for it suggests a crucial divergence in their political
thought. Behind their differing conceptions of the structure of
government was a deeper disagreement about the relevance of
structure itself. The best studies of the Revolutionary ideology have
taught us that constitutionalism was the genius of the age. All of
that generation, Federalists and Anti-Federalists alike, shared a
common faith that the success of the republican experiment depended upon the creation of balanced institutions of government
that would serve as a perpetual check against the abuse of power.
Recently, Lance Banning has argued that "Most of the inherited
structure of eighteenth-century political thought persisted in
America for years after 1789," and that the "intellectual universe"
of "constitutionalism" informed the origins and character of Republican Party thought.[38] These interpretations brilliantly illuminate the political philosophy of the Quids, and allow us to understand their passionate concern for the safety of the carefully balanced
Constitution of their state.

They cannot, however, serve to explain Democratic thought, for
the Democrats no longer entirely shared that common vocabulary
of political ideas. Subtly but surely, they were moving away from
the constitutionalist mode of thought toward the modern ideas of
partisans. They questioned whether governmental institutions, however designed, could be relied on to protect liberty. No system could
provide an automatic check on tyranny, William Duane argued.
"There is no *check*—and can be none—but the *people.*" The Democrats' goal, therefore, was not so much to alter the structure of
government as to go beyond it. Their trust was in direct action by
the people, through the mechanism of political party.[39]

The Democrats' partisan thinking is especially revealed in their
positive attitude toward conflict. Here they diverged sharply from
the classical eighteenth-century canon with its consensual ideal. The
fear of perpetual agitation had occupied the Framers of the Consti-

[38] Bernard Bailyn, *Ideological Origins of the American Revolution* (Cambridge, Mass.,
1967); Gordon S. Wood, *The Creation of the American Republic, 1776–1787* (Chapel Hill,
1969); Banning, "Republican Ideology and the Triumph of the Constitution," 173, 187–188.
[39] Duane, *Experience the Test of Government*, 7, and *passim*. This pamphlet is perhaps the
fullest, clearest expression of these views.

tution more than any single issue and they had structured the government, deliberately, as a buffering device to screen out conflict. The notion that conflict and agitation were inherently dangerous made parties abhorrent to this generation.[40] These ideas persisted among Philadelphia's Quids. That the Democrats were "noisy" was one of their most typical complaints. A. J. Dallas lamented that so long as William Duane had influence "the state, the United States will never enjoy quiet."[41] In truth, tranquillity was not their aim. On the contrary, the Democrats believed that continual agitation was essential to political health. In Duane's metaphor, "Like the continual motion of the sea, which preserves its sweet and its saline particles from evaporating, so does a continued rulling of the democratic waters prevent their stinking, stagnating, or being converted into a pestilential pool of monarchy, aristocracy or priestcraft."[42]

The traditional fear of conflict, Duane and others pointed out, was grounded in distrust of the people's capacity for self-government. It was the attitude of those who believed that "the sovereignty of the people is ideal and not real."[43] The Quids, indeed, understood popular sovereignty as the Founders had conceived it; through the principle of representation, they had found the means to ground government squarely on the consent of the people, yet, simultaneously, to eliminate the need for their immediate or direct involvement. The people ruled everywhere, yet nowhere.[44] Only through representation, the Quids agreed, could freedom and order be held in balance. The alternative was to permit individual "passions" and "interests" to overwhelm the "standard of reason, order and law." To them, this was the "crisis" now posed by the Democrats. They aimed to shatter the invisible barrier between the

---

[40] Hofstadter, *Idea of a Party System*, chap. II, provides an excellent summation of the ideas behind the creation of "A Constitution Against Parties."

[41] Dallas to Gallatin, Apr. 4, 1805, Gallatin Papers.

[42] *Aurora*, Apr. 1, 1805. Duane, using the pseudonym of Jasper Dwight, had brilliantly argued for the value of political conflict in his first political pamphlet in America, written in reply to George Washington's warning, in the Farewell Address, against the "baneful effects of the Spirit of Party." *A Letter to George Washington . . . Containing Strictures on His Address of the Seventeenth of September, 1796 . . .* (Philadelphia, 1796).

[43] Duane, *Experience the Test of Government*, 7–9.

[44] See Wood, *Creation of the American Republic*, 596–600, and Part Six, *passim*.

public and the government. "The object is to reduce government to its elements," according to Dallas, "rendering the immediate agency of the people perpetually necessary to every executive, legislative, elective, and judicial purpose."[45]

From their point of view, the Quids were right to see this moment as a crisis. Dallas correctly perceived the threat to traditional constitutionalism behind the Democratic program. The Democrats sought to revise the meaning of popular sovereignty, to transform theoretical principle into working reality. Their various constitutional proposals added up to a single demand for responsibility by every officer of government to his constituents. By this they meant not an abstract responsibility arising from a sense of obligation, but a constant, concrete dependence upon public opinion. Perpetual scrutiny was the only guarantee of faithfulness in office, in their opinion. To argue, as the Democrats did, for government "founded on public opinion" was to fly in the face of traditional political thought with its fear of "factious majorities." In their view, "a majority of the people," quite simply, "can not be a mob." On the contrary, "the *opinion of the majority*, in representative democracies, is the *only criterion*" of wise policy.[46] Consensus was the grand illusion of the past, majoritarianism the received faith of the future. Deliberately, self-consciously, Philadelphia's Democrats were pushing their countrymen toward that future.

The Democrats' expressed faith in the innate wisdom of majorities struck at the roots of the philosophy of stewardship. In this gubernatorial election, they set out to challenge society's so-called "natural leaders" and to disabuse them of their pretensions. No man better personified the claims of the "natural aristocracy" than Thomas McKean. As Governor, he was neither bashful nor discreet in demanding deference to his superior knowledge and experience.[47] On one notorious occasion he told a visiting delegation that he was

---

[45] Dallas to Gallatin, Jan. 26, 1805, Gallatin Papers; Dallas to Robert Smith, Apr. 11, 1805, in G. M. Dallas, *Life and Writings of Alexander James Dallas*, 117.

[46] *Aurora*, "Lucius," Mar. 17, 19, 24, 1808. See *ibid.*, "Regulus," Mar. 21, 23, 1805; Duane, *Experience the Test of Government*, 7–9, 14–16, 42–45, 51.

[47] See Rowe, "Power, Politics, and Public Service," 270, 323–324, and *passim*. See also, for example, McKean to George Logan, Feb. 19, 1803, Logan Papers, HSP; McKean to Joseph Hiester, July 31, 1807, Gregg Collection, Library of Congress.

plagued by "ignoramuses" and "clodpoles (or, if they please, clod-hoppers)" within his own party. His outburst set the theme for the 1805 campaign. The Democrats announced as criteria for their candidate that he "should not be a lawyer, and that a clod hopper should be preferred."[48] This was the Quiddish world turned upside down. "It is avowed here," reported Dallas, "and it will be in practice by the reformers everywhere, that lawyers, men of talents and education, men of fortune and manners, ought not to participate in the formation, or in the administration of a democratic govern-ment."[49] The malice toward lawyers was especially pronounced in this campaign. Lawyers as a group were uniformly opposed to radical judicial reform, convincing Democrats of a conspiracy by bench and bar. But beyond this timely reason for hostility, lawyers were a natural target. To the Democrats, lawyers as a class repre-sented an especially flagrant example of the arrogance of those who claimed a special competence for public leadership.[50] Personally, they preferred a clodhopper.

The Clodhopper candidate, Simon Snyder, was not elected in 1805. He became Governor three years later and served for three terms, the most popular Governor in Pennsylvania's history during this era. Thomas McKean, the incumbent, was returned by a narrow margin and served a harrowing three more years, threatened with impeachment and virtually devoid of party support. The official returns belied the real results of this election. In all its implications, it was a victory for the Democrats.

Privately, the Quids conceded defeat to William Duane. They had hoped to "rally the genuine Republicans," but had failed, and it was no secret that McKean "owes his re-election to the federal-ists." The *Aurora* had overwhelmed them, as they feared. In Albert Gallatin's postmortem judgment, Duane had "easily gained the victory for his friends. I call it victory," Gallatin admitted, "for the number of republicans who have opposed him . . . do not exceed one fourth or at most one third of the whole."[51]

---

48 Higginbotham, *Keystone*, 85–87.

49 Dallas to Robert Smith, Apr. 11, 1805, in G. M. Dallas, *Life and Writings of Alexander James Dallas*, 117.

50 See *Aurora*, Feb. 6, 12, 1802, for a strong, early expression of this view.

51 Dallas to Gallatin, Jan. 26, 1805, Gallatin Papers; Gallatin to Jean Badollet, Oct. 25, 1805, *ibid.*

To the Quids, Duane had become the monstrous symbol of every hated political tendency. That he perhaps spoke the true sentiments of Republicans was unthinkable to them. Most intolerable was the suggestion that he had "the confidence" of Thomas Jefferson. When a Federalist taunted a Quid that Duane was a friend of the President, the Quid beat him in a fistfight then wounded him in a duel.[52] The Quid, no doubt, felt consoled that he had vindicated Republican honor. But while the Federalist lost the fight, he won the argument.

Jefferson maintained a careful neutrality in this election which, in its effects, encouraged the Democrats and hurt the Quids. His failure to endorse the incumbent could easily be interpreted as a rebuff, especially after Duane's associate, Michael Leib, coaxed a letter from the President denying that he supported McKean. Leib campaigned from tavern to tavern flaunting the secret letter and "perhaps a thousand persons of the lowest class of society have already seen it," a Quid complained.[53] Jefferson's neutrality in the party schism was typical, reflecting his personal wish to avoid alienating anyone. But, at a number of points, he betrayed an affection for his "high-fliers," as he called them, that gives reason to question his reputation as a moderate partisan.[54]

What the Quids most wanted from the President, but failed to get, was an explicit renunciation of William Duane.[55] When he ignored their tacit demands, some Quids secretly turned bitter against Jefferson himself. A disenchanted A. J. Dallas, for example, dropped out of state politics and put the ultimate blame on Jefferson for the uncongenial atmosphere of Pennsylvania Republicanism. His "countenance, to the presumptions of the Aurora" was the

---

[52] Dallas to Gallatin, Apr. 4, 1805, *ibid.*; Duane to Joseph Clay, Dec. 12, 1805, Clay Papers, New York Public Library; William J. Duane to Clay, Dec. 16, 1805, *ibid.*

[53] Unsigned letter to Jefferson, Aug. 24, 1805, quoted in Cunningham, *Jeffersonian Republicans in Power*, 219; Leib to Jefferson, July 22, 1805, Jefferson Papers; Jefferson to Leib, Aug. 12, 1805, *ibid.*

[54] See note 19. Whether from friendship or shrewd political sense, Jefferson consistently supported Duane over the years. He believed, in sharp contrast to the opinion of moderates, that the "over zealous" Democrat reflected the attitudes of "a great portion of the republican body." Jefferson to James Madison, Aug. 16, 1803, Jefferson Papers.

[55] See Dallas to Gallatin, Apr. 4, 1805, Gallatin Papers; McKean to Jefferson, draft Feb. 18, 1805, Thomas McKean Papers, HSP; Jefferson to McKean, Mar. 3, 1805, *ibid.*

"true cause," in Dallas' opinion, "why no man of real character and capacity . . . has the power to render any political service."[56]

It is not surprising that the Quids had fallen for, compared with the Democrats, they were political amateurs. Elections are not won on debate alone, no matter how attractive the ideas. The Democrats' ideology clearly implied new forms of political action, and this the Democrats understood. They initiated political practices as advanced as their political thought. Their politics resembled the politics of the 1840s in sophisticated understanding of the role of party organization. Here, too, the example of Philadelphia offers reason to question the Hofstadter-Wallace timetable for the emergence of modern conceptions of party.

For a decade after 1800, Duane and Leib presided over a party organization of impressive depth and complexity.[57] The Democrats were the first politicians in the city's history to recognize that effective politics was a year-round occupation, not a seasonal distraction. The informal apparatus of the party operated constantly through a number of overlapping groups—political clubs, social clubs, ethnic fraternal associations and, largest of all, the militia. The uniformed volunteers of the Philadelphia Militia Legion were, in essence, a Democratic political army some 800 strong.[58] If he wanted to, a Democrat could go to some sort of party gathering most any night of a week, if only to the local tavern that served as the clubhouse in his neighborhood. There were picnics, parades, militia drills, Tammany meetings, fraternal dinners—a steady round of occasions all serving to keep the party's members socially involved and emotionally committed.[59] As a result when election season came around each fall, the party cadre could call upon the

---

56 Dallas to Gallatin, Apr. 21, 1811, Gallatin Papers. See Cunningham, *Jeffersonian Republicans in Power*, 220.

57 See Phillips, "William Duane," chap. IV, for a fuller discussion of the organization and social-cultural composition of the party.

58 A comparison of the roster of militia officers (*Pennsylvania Archives*, 6th Series, IV) with the names of Democratic party activists, compiled from newspaper sources, makes clear the connection between political ambition and militia service. Abundant, widely scattered evidence testifies to the party affiliation of the rank and file.

59 One important criterion of modern politics is the presence of "party as a reference group in the electorate." Formisano, "Deferential-Participant Politics," 481. By this criterion, Philadelphia's Democrats qualify as a modern party.

services of hundreds as campaign workers in their wards and districts.

Philadelphia's elections were won or lost on the neighborhood level.[60] The Democrats were the first to see this, and they left little to chance in their techniques for turning out the vote in the Democratic strongholds. By rolling up immense majorities in the four poorest wards, on the northern and southern fringes of the city, and in the slum-ridden Northern Liberties, they repeatedly managed to offset the large voting margins that the Federalist-Quid coalition enjoyed in the fashionable center of the city.[61]

The Democrats' core constituencies were Philadelphia's two largest ethnic minorities, the Irish and the Germans. As social outgroups, both had excellent class and cultural reasons to identify with the Democrats in their war on elitism. The majority of Germans were probably middling mechanics, but their economic status as skilled craftsmen was not matched by an equivalent social standing. While they were not ordinarily the victims of open bigotry, as were their immigrant parents and grandparents, they were still treated as a group apart and slightly suspect. No doubt they were sensitive to remembered cultural slights and to the covert prejudice that persisted.[62]

[60] This was particularly true in Philadelphia because of peculiarities in the election procedures which exaggerated the importance of ward-level elections. Phillips, "William Duane," 212–216.

[61] The characteristic geographic split in Philadelphia's voting pattern may be seen, for example, in the returns for Michael Leib's congressional race in 1804 and William Duane's defeat for the state senate in 1807. *Aurora*, Oct. 11, 1804; *Democratic Press*, Oct. 14, 1807. Using tax assessments, Stuart Blumin has estimated the wealth of each Philadelphia ward and district in 1820. "Mobility and Change in Ante-Bellum Philadelphia," in Stephen Thernstrom and Richard Sennett, eds., *Nineteenth Century Cities: Essays in the New Urban History* (New Haven, 1969), 187. Blumin's figures for 1820 may be used as a reliable general indicator of the city's economic profile in 1800–1810. A similar pattern of residential segregation by wealth existed as early as 1780. See John K. Alexander, "The City of Brotherly Fear: The Poor in Late-Eighteenth-Century Philadelphia," in Kenneth T. Jackson and Stanley K. Schultz, eds., *Cities in American History* (New York, 1972), 82–83, 93 n. 27. See also Anthony N. B. Garven, "Proprietary Philadelphia as Artifact," in Oscar Handlin and John Burchard, eds., *The Historian and the City* (Cambridge, Mass., 1963), 177–201, and Norman Johnston, "The Caste and Class of the Urban Form of Historic Philadelphia," *Journal of the American Institute of Planners*, XXXIII (1966), 344–349.

[62] On persistent prejudice toward Germans see, for example, Robert Liston to Lord Grenville, Nov. 5, 1799, British State Papers, Robert Liston Correspondence, Library of Congress; *Gazette of the United States*, Nov. 22, 1799; *Spirit of the Press*, Oct. 5, 1805, "A Lutheran," Jan. 1807, Oct. 1808, Aug. 1809; *The Tickler*, Sept. 28, 1808, Aug. 2, 1809. On the tendency to bloc voting by Germans, see Thomas Leiper to Jefferson, Sept. 19, 1802, Jefferson Papers.

The city's Irish were economically and socially just one step above the bottom, defined by the black population. As early as 1800, the immigrant Irish in Philadelphia competed with blacks for the same jobs and the same houses, the worst the city had to offer.[63] There was nothing covert about the prejudice they encountered. Irish-baiting became popular in America long before the potato famine. It can be dated, more or less exactly, to the mid-1790s with the rise and fall of the United Irish. Britain's suppression of the abortive rebellion drove thousands to America as refugees from political reprisals as well as from economic dislocation. A substantial minority of the newcomers were Catholic, but it was not the religion of the Irish that alarmed native-born citizens of this generation. Rather, the alleged radicalism of their politics was the prime source of suspicion and hostility.[64] They were shunned, too, for their poverty and for cultural habits that offended proper Philadelphians.

A political coalition of the Irish and the Germans became the backbone of the Democratic Party created by Duane and Leib. The Irish editor and the German physician each had solid foundations for popularity with his own ethnic constituency. When these two merged their political interests, it laid the groundwork for a formidable alliance. The various subgroups of the party tended to be organized along ethnic lines. Particular Tammany tribes and Legion companies, for example, were dominantly Irish or German in their membership. This innovation, more than any other, set Philadelphia's Democrats apart from the typical Republican organization. Party moderates everywhere resented the appeal to ethnic identities and would have agreed with Thomas Ritchie when he blamed Philadelphia's troubles upon the presence of Irish and Germans who could be organized into "clans and tribes for political purposes."[65]

63 Cedar ward, the poorest neighborhood in the city, was the center of South Philadelphia's "Irishtown" and also the center of black population. See the city census of 1808 in John Thomas Scharf and Thompson Westcott, *History of Philadelphia, 1609–1884* (Philadelphia, 1884), I, 537. W. E. B. DuBois noted that by 1800 immigrant Irish were displacing free blacks in jobs. *The Philadelphia Negro; a Social Study* (New York, 1967).

64 On the political motivation for emigration, see the hints in Maldwyn A. Jones, "Ulster Emigration, 1783–1815," E. R. R. Green, ed., *Essays in Scotch-Irish History* (New York, 1969), 55–56.

65 Quoted in Charles H. Ambler, *Thomas Ritchie: A Study in Virginia Politics* (Richmond, 1913), 31–32. See John Randolph to James M. Garnett, July 29, 1811, Randolph-Garnett Letter Book, Library of Congress.

321

The Democratic leaders were equally deliberate in their efforts to nurture a sense of fraternity between the party's two major ethnic components. They saw to it, for example, that Germans and Irish mingled at militia turnouts and similar social opportunities.

To expand on the ethnic advantage, the Democrats recruited new immigrants as partisans well before they became voters. The party set up appropriate machinery, of course, to encourage prompt naturalization. Moreover, Congressman Leib had helped to open up a loophole in the naturalization law that temporarily expanded the numbers eligible to become citizens.[66] Charges of fraudulent naturalizations and fraudulent voting by aliens were reiterated throughout the decade. Such charges, whatever their accuracy, testified to the Democrats' success in effectively organizing Philadelphia's ethnic minorities.

Two hazards threatened the stability of the Irish-German coalition: it could become the victim of a nativist backlash, or it might succumb to distrust aroused between its member groups. By 1810 these hazards had combined to destroy the ethnic alliance, but only after a decade.[67] Obviously, Philadelphia's Democrats had not mastered the art of stable mass politics. Still, their innovations as party-builders entitle them to identification as essentially modern partisans.

How should Philadelphia's political experience be understood? Were the city's Democrats wholly anomalous to their generation when they challenged the antiparty axioms of consensus and deference? Or did they represent a more widespread drive toward party and all that it stood for—the recognition of heterogeneity, the acceptance of conflict, the rejection of deference? The legitimization of party marked a profound transformation in American political culture, not complete until the 1840s. The Philadelphia example

---

[66] The naturalization act of 1804, introduced by Leib a year earlier, exempted aliens who had immigrated before 1802 from the requirement of filing first papers, or a declaration of intent, and permitted their naturalization upon the sworn testimony of a witness that they had resided in the United States for five years. The Democrats set up a committee on naturalization to encourage use of the special law, which continued as a regular feature of the party organization.

[67] Phillips, "William Duane," 279–287.

indicates that the process of transformation was underway well before the Jacksonian era.

Philadelphia's Democrats were "precocious partisans," to be sure.[68] Their complex urban environment gave them reason, earlier than most, to question the antiparty tradition. But if they were not typical, one suspects, neither were they unique. No doubt the impetus toward party was experienced at different rates in different places, and with varying degrees of success or frustration. Judging from Philadelphia, it seems likely that it appeared on a community level before it surfaced nationally. A look within Republican Party groups in other localities would probably reveal a similar struggle between traditionalists and modern partisans. While traditionalists tended to dominate for a while longer, the advocates of modern party were nonetheless working, if frequently unnoticed, to change the nature of political thought and practice in America.

In brief, the case of Philadelphia suggests the need to modify our understanding of the timing and the process for the emergence of modern politics. The first party system was a transitional period in politics, certainly. But it was a politics in transition, not so firmly rooted in eighteenth-century precedents as historians currently would have us believe. At present, we have distinguished too sharply between the supposed "traditionalism" of the first party system and the "modern" politics of the second. Such a demarcation, while it has been useful as a concept, tends ultimately to distort the complex reality of political change. To acknowledge this is simply to acknowledge what we know to be the complexity of the historical process.

The University of Connecticut, Groton   KIM T. PHILLIPS

[68] The phrase is Ronald P. Formisano's, "Deferential-Participant Politics," 473.

Douglas R. Littlefield

Maryland Sectionalism and the Development of the Potomac Route to the West, 1768–1826

Sectionalism is a fundamental characteristic of American frontier history. As Frederick Jackson Turner, who is best known for his frontier thesis, demonstrated in "The Significance of the Section in American History", sectionalism is as much a characteristic of frontier history as is the advance of settlement westward. Turner not only saw the peopling of the frontier as creating uniquely American traits, but his thesis on sectionalism described newly settled locations as constantly conflicting with older, more established areas. This was frequently in the form of a debtor West confronting a creditor East, a conflict he saw as more important in many ways than the sectional conflict between the North and the South. The West versus East struggle is especially pertinent to the nineteenth-century development of internal improvements and their impact on frontier areas.[1]

Nineteenth-century sectional conflicts over internal improvements gained added importance when considered in relation to varying interpretations of a new and undefined Constitution. Many advocates of a loose interpretation of the Constitution, which would allow federal aid for internal improvements, came from newly settled parts of the country with little access to foreign markets. Not surprisingly, many proponents of strict constitutional construction lived in older, more established coastal areas. Thus, in many ways, sectional conflict over internal improvements involved the ability of the new national government to overcome constitutional strife as well as to compete in a world economy. Much of Turner's work and studies on nineteenth-century internal improvements, such as Carter Goodrich's *Government Promotion of American Canals and Railroads, 1800–1890* and George Rogers Taylor's *The Transportation Revolution, 1815–1860*, recognize the importance of internal improvements in the nineteenth-century United States and the sectional issues involved in their construction.[2]

Turner was among the first to stress the importance of conflict between the West and East over issues such as internal improvements. Yet, as he also pointed out, there were several overlapping layers to sectional strife. Underlying interstate and regional confrontations were local sectional battles fought over projects like the Erie Canal and the Chesapeake and Ohio Canal.[3] Local sectional conflict was also important in earlier internal improvement projects. This was particularly true in Maryland, where the trans-Appalachian West was more accessible than in more northern or southern parts of the

Douglas R. Littlefield is a Ph.D. student in the History Department at the University of California at Los Angeles. An earlier version of this paper won the 1978 prize for best paper on Maryland history awarded by the Pilgrims of St. Mary's County Society.

country.

As Maryland residents recognized, immense benefits followed from being near successful road or river improvement projects. The loss of a proposed project could mean stagnation or a slow death to nascent towns; having a project nearby could dramatically raise real estate values for local landholders. As a result, local boosters lobbied state legislators to enrich their area with a project while denying it to others. Such boosterism not only influenced Baltimore's growth into a prominent seaport but also its votes in the Maryland legislature on the early attempts to improve the Potomac route to the trans-Appalachian West.

The attempt to clear the Potomac River was the first interstate internal improvement project attempted in post-Revolutionary America, but local sectional conflict helped defeat this far-sighted plan. Political rivalries between a young and vigorous Baltimore urban-milling economy, which sought to exploit recently settled frontier areas, and an older, more established Potomac planter/mercantile economy, frequently allied with upriver farming interests, postponed or denied critical state aid to the Potomac effort. This hindered the plan to open the river to frontier regions for over thirty years.

Although late eighteenth- and early nineteenth-century sectional disputes over internal improvements were critical to the growth of frontier Maryland communities, the struggle over improving the Potomac River has not been as thoroughly examined by scholars as battles over later projects. Works like Norman K. Risjord's *Chesapeake Politics, 1781–1800*, Matthew Page Andrews's *History of Maryland: Province and State*, and *Maryland: A History*, edited by Richard Walsh and William Lloyd Fox are surveys of state or regional history which recognize the significance of local sectionalism but only briefly discuss it in relation to early internal improvements. Published monographs examining the Potomac route include Corra Bacon Foster's *Early Chapters in the Development of the Potomac Route to the West*, Clarence P. Gould's *Money and Transportation in Maryland, 1720–1765*, John A. Pickell's *A New Chapter in the Early Life of Washington in Connection with the Narrative History of the Potomac Company*, and George Washington Ward's *The Early Development of the Chesapeake and Ohio Canal Project.* However, these either do not directly address local sectionalism and internal improvements or are dated and lack an interpretive framework. Only Leonard J. Sneddon's "Maryland and Sectional Politics: Canal Building in the Federalist Era" analyzes Maryland's early development as shaped by local sectional politics and internal improvements. Sneddon's treatment, however, is brief, focusing on the general statewide desire for canals; it does not deal substantially with Baltimore's opposition to clearing the Potomac as a route to the West.[4]

Compared to Boston, Charleston, New York, and Philadelphia, Baltimore did not become a major port until relatively late in the colonial period. This late start kept the city from becoming a competitor of the smaller Potomac River ports of Georgetown, Maryland, and Alexandria, Virginia, for many years. Baltimore's slow rise to commercial prominence resulted from the same factors which affected nearly all Maryland tidewater areas. Early town growth in colonial Maryland and Virginia was slow because tobacco, the principal crop of the tidewater area, required little processing before being exported.[5] Moreover, Baltimore's location on the fall line separated it from large tracts of prime tobacco land, much of which had direct access to the Chesapeake Bay. Consequently, for many planters the trip to Baltimore wasted time and increased costs. Tidewater towns along the Potomac such as Alexandria and Georgetown provided better tobacco-related services than Baltimore and prospered accordingly. Residents of these towns saw the potential in opening the Potomac above tidewater, at first for fur trading and easy military access against the French and Indians and later for land speculation and trade with the interior parts of the country.

Despite its inauspicious beginning, Baltimore became a major beneficiary of a change in the tidewater agricultural economy. By the mid–1700s, soil depletion from over-planting tobacco led many planters to abandon tobacco in favor of wheat—a crop that placed fewer demands on the soil.[6] This change and Baltimore's fall-line location, which provided ample water power for milling, gave the city the boost it needed. By the end of the Revolution, Baltimore was becoming the most important milling center and seaport in the Maryland and Virginia area. Georgetown and Alexandria shared in some of the business generated by the new crop, but since both communities had long grown accustomed to an economy based on transshipping tobacco and other goods which required little processing, their attempt to substitute grain without developing a milling industry was not a complete economic success. It was only increasing upriver settlement and land speculation that kept them from being completely overshadowed by Baltimore.[7]

The lack of grist mills in Georgetown and Alexandria brought demands from inland farmers for better roads to Baltimore. But, since land transportation was unreliable and expensive, there was also considerable interest in improving the Potomac to bring crops to market. Goods sent down the Potomac were, of course, more likely to benefit Georgetown and Alexandria than Baltimore, as residents of each community were aware. This created an intense political rivalry in the Maryland state legislature between the economic interests of the Potomac Valley and those of the Baltimore area.[8]

As Baltimore grew, it increasingly dominated the regional economy, but its commercial power was not translated into political clout in the Maryland legislature. The state senate was chosen by an electoral college and, as such, did not necessarily reflect the will of the voting population. The house of delegates, although popularly elected, had four representatives per county (regardless of population), and in a minor concession to more settled urban areas, two additional representatives each from Baltimore City and Annapolis. Thus, lightly populated frontier and planting areas had greater political strength than more heavily settled parts of the state. This was balanced somewhat in that western counties tended to be geographically larger than those in the East, and western representatives frequently were unable to attend legislative sessions held in Annapolis. Nonetheless, assembly representation favored the rural areas, and when western Maryland delegates did get to Annapolis, their votes could be decisive when allied with those of the lower Potomac counties.

As a result of the assembly apportionment, sectional issues were usually determined not on their merits but rather on political trade-offs among

Maryland's geographic factions. The Potomac faction, consisting of the seven counties adjacent to the river (St. Mary's, Charles, Prince George's, Montgomery, Frederick, Washington, and Allegany) with its frequent western shore allies in Anne Arundel and Calvert Counties and the city of Annapolis (who feared domination by nearby Baltimore), could easily prevail over the four upper Chesapeake Bay counties (Baltimore, Harford, Cecil, and Kent) and Baltimore City in any sectional issue, such as internal improvements. The only way northern Chesapeake delegates could prevail over the Potomac faction was to entice the delegates of the Eastern Shore counties (Worcester, Somerset, Dorchester, Caroline, Talbot, and Queen Anne) to join in a mutual effort. (See figure one.) Unfortunately, such coalitions were difficult to achieve, since the Eastern Shore counties frequently had desires independent of or conflicting with both the northern Chesapeake and Potomac factions.[9]

Although sectional conflict over internal improvements was most apparent after the Revolution, it played a significant role in Maryland's colonial politics. Attempts to improve roads or waterways either were defeated in the colonial assembly with two out of three factions opposed to each effort, or if internal improvement bills passed, they inevitably involved political compromises. In 1768, for example, the assembly passed a bill to improve and maintain the Potomac (mostly for fishing purposes) the same day as a bill to conserve fish in the Susquehanna and Patuxent Rivers.[10] Similarly, a 1774 act establishing Maryland's first systematic improvements to roads leading to Baltimore was balanced with other roughly equal appropriations for roads to Georgetown and Annapolis.[11]

While some assembly delegates could reach agreement for improving roads and maintaining rivers for fishing purposes, they could not so readily concur on opening the Potomac as a transportation artery. Virginia, which shared the Potomac with Maryland as a common border, passed a variety of Potomac improvement bills during the colonial period, but these were blocked by Maryland's three-way sectional split.[12] Discussing the earliest of these bills in a letter to Thomas Jefferson, ardent river promoter George Washington noted that sectional interests in both Maryland and Virginia were likely to defeat it.[13] Despite Washington's pessimistic prediction, the Virginia House of Burgesses passed the bill. But it never survived the Maryland legislature. In 1772 Virginia passed a similar Potomac bill. It also was blocked in Maryland by the combined northern Chesapeake and Eastern Shore factions, despite the efforts of Thomas Johnson, later the first governor of the state of Maryland, who appealed to colonial Governor Robert Eden for support.[14]

As a result of the 1772 Virginia act, John Ballendine, a colonial entrepreneur, organized a company to clear the river. He then left for England to study canal technology and seek additional financial support.[15] When he returned in 1774, Maryland still had not approved Virginia's 1772 act, and George Washington and George Mason tried to secure passage of another Virginia bill more attractive to the Maryland legislature. By March 1775, amid growing problems between the colonies and Great Britain, Mason reported that the new bill to improve the Potomac had been drafted, but he was not optimistic about its chances in Maryland. As Mason saw it, "there will be so strong an opposition from Baltemore [sic] & the Head of the Bay, as will go near to prevent its passage thro' the Maryland Assembly in any

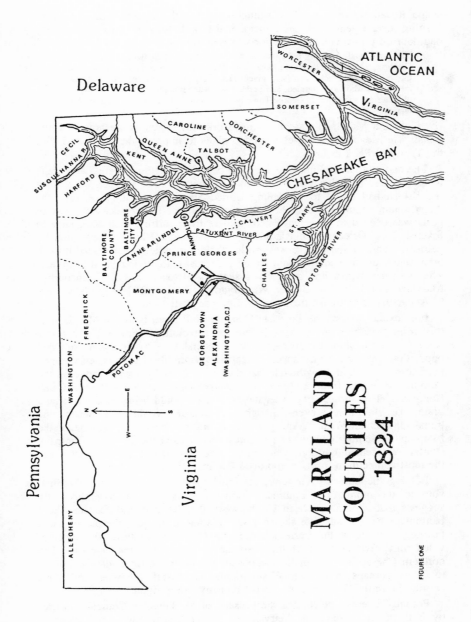

MARYLAND COUNTIES 1824

FIGURE ONE

shape it can be offered."[16] Washington apparently agreed with this view. Writing several years later, he remembered how Baltimore's fear of lost trade had doomed pre-Revolutionary efforts to improve the Potomac:

> The plan to clear the river... was in a tolerably [sic] train when I set out for Cambridge in 1775, and would have been in an excellent way had it not been for the difficulties which was [sic] given (according to report) by the Baltimore merchants; who were alarmed, and perhaps not without cause, at the consequences of water transportation to George Town of the produce which usually came to their market.[17]

Even without Maryland's assent, some work was begun in the area of Little Falls. The Revolution, however, ended plans to improve the river until after the Treaty of Paris in 1783.[18]

The end of the Revolution revived the desire to use the Potomac as a route to the West. The plan was all the more important after independence since the British had ceded to the young United States the territory between the Appalachian Mountains and the Mississippi River. Better access to eastern ports was needed to prevent western settlers from shifting their allegiance to Spanish New Orleans. Legislators in Maryland and Virginia, prompted by patriotism and by speculative western landholdings, quickly introduced bills in both states to incorporate the Potomac Company to undertake the project. The Virginia legislature gave its assent in October 1784; to encourage Maryland to follow suit, George Washington and General Horatio Gates went to Annapolis to lobby for the Potomac Company bill.[19]

For several reasons the Potomac Company bill fared better in Maryland at this point than had similar bills before the Revolution. First, Washington's stature as a Revolutionary hero and his personal visit to Annapolis subdued opposition. Second, some upper Chesapeake assembly delegates, encouraged by Baltimore's rapid growth, felt that they already had gained an edge on the Potomac counties from a 1783 act incorporating the Susquehanna Canal Company. This project, the delegates reasoned, would bring more hinterland grain to Baltimore, even though the canal would not reach the trans-Appalachian West.[20] And perhaps tipping the balance, only one of the Maryland Assembly committee delegates who drafted the Potomac Company charter represented northern Chesapeake counties—areas which would face the most competition from an improved Potomac.[21]

Belying the outward harmony, sectional loyalties still underlay the final vote to incorporate the Potomac Company. The official assembly tally suggests that a deal had been cut between the Potomac and Eastern Shore factions. The roll-call vote shows a strong alliance between the planting and farming interests of the Eastern Shore and Potomac counties, who together voted thirty-five in favor of the Potomac Company and two against. The northern Chesapeake faction was opposed, but not by a large margin—seven to five—perhaps reflecting Washington's successful lobbying and their confidence in the Susquehanna Canal Company. (See figure two.)[22]

Potomac interests celebrated the passage of the Potomac Company charter by both states. Prominent Marylander Daniel Carroll, an initial Potomac Company stockholder who later served the state in a variety of official capacities, typified those who saw great advantages from the improved river. Observing that a "great and important work is to be immediately begun," he exulted that "the vast consequences that must derive to the middle states when [it is] completed cannot be elucidated but by time, the discoverer of all great events."[23]

Northern Chesapeake residents were not so happy, however. Virginia House of Delegates member James Madison recognized this and concluded that "the policy of Baltimore will probably thwart as far as possible, the opening of... [the Potomac]."[24] Baltimore opponents usually based their sentiments on a potential loss of trade to other mid-Atlantic areas. For example, "Planter," writing in the *Maryland Gazette*, objected that the opening of the Potomac would benefit only Virginia. "Answer to Planter" countered by claiming that the project would benefit Maryland more than Virginia since Georgetown was higher on the Potomac than Alexandria; thus, most down-river trade would enhance the Maryland economy. Ignoring the fact that Baltimore boosters were just as concerned about competition with Georgetown as they were with Alexandria, "Answer to Planter" concluded that when his prophecy came true, it would "be probable that no more complaints will come from any Baltimore writers on this score."[25]

With the Potomac Company's incorporation an accomplished fact, such debate rapidly dwindled. Most detractors evidently considered further protest futile, especially as work on the river progressed, albeit sluggishly at times. The company had ten years to build locks and canals around the major obstacles at Little Falls and Great Falls and three years for simple by-pass canals at other rapids. In between these areas, the river was to be dredged, allowing its entire length to be navigable for flat boats drawing one foot of water when fully loaded. Maryland and Virginia each were to buy fifty shares of company stock, and they were to finance roads from the headwaters of the Potomac to those of the Ohio River to open the frontier beyond the Appalachian Mountains.[26]

The project was not an easy one. The company had to constantly battle problems with the weather, labor, and technology. Changes in American foreign policy adversely affected many Potomac Company investors and influenced the marketability of produce brought down the river.[27] But the company's major problem was financial and stemmed in large part from political sectionalism in Maryland and the post-war economy.

After the war, the chaotic new national economy led the earlier Potomac-upper Chesapeake rivalry to take on the tone of a rural-urban animosity. While Baltimore boomed with European credit underwriting the resumption of foreign trade, frontier farmers in western Maryland and planters along the lower Potomac felt pressured as specie drained to the cities to pay taxes and purchase British goods. Besides the lack of specie, these groups were hampered in marketing crops by a lack of reliable transportation to mill sites. The fact that some crops in the 1780s were worth as much as one hundred percent more in coastal ports than in farming areas provided part of the post-war unity of frontier farmers and Potomac planters on internal improvement issues.[28]

By the mid–1780s rural areas of Maryland clamored for paper money to pay taxes and private debts. Baltimore merchants, however, insisted upon payment in specie only since that was what they had to send overseas to pay their creditors. Thus, the pre-war Baltimore-Potomac trade rivalry had now grown to include the additional sectional issue of rural debtor versus urban

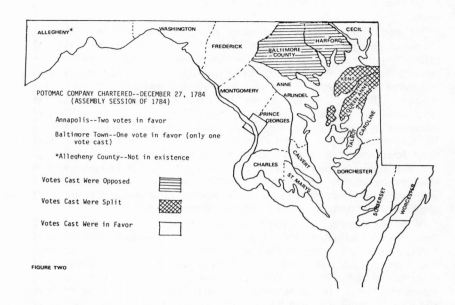

POTOMAC COMPANY CHARTERED--DECEMBER 27, 1784
(ASSEMBLY SESSION OF 1784)

Annapolis--Two votes in favor

Baltimore Town--One vote in favor (only one
vote cast)

*Allegheny County--Not in existence

Votes Cast Were Opposed

Votes Cast Were Split

Votes Cast Were in Favor

FIGURE TWO

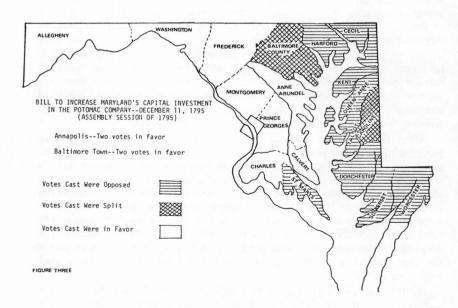

BILL TO INCREASE MARYLAND'S CAPITAL INVESTMENT
IN THE POTOMAC COMPANY--DECEMBER 11, 1795
(ASSEMBLY SESSION OF 1795)

Annapolis--Two votes in favor

Baltimore Town--Two votes in favor

Votes Cast Were Opposed

Votes Cast Were Split

Votes Cast Were in Favor

FIGURE THREE

creditor. And due to the nature of the Maryland economy, this conflict was one where frontier farmers and Potomac planters were pitted against Baltimore merchants and their northern Chesapeake allies.

These economic and sectional problems severely burdened the young Potomac Company. Since company stock was purchased with only a percentage down and the rest due in installments, the crippled finances of western farmers and Potomac planters compounded problems due to weather, labor, the lack of good technical help, and foreign affairs. This was all the more true because many subscribers had speculated heavily in land along the river and had pledged more company shares than they could afford—over ninety percent of the non-state government stock pledged came from subscribers in the Potomac watershed.[29] Such circumstances resulted in missed assessment payments by many investors. Payment delinquency became such a problem that it even brought about an unsuccessful attempt to resell the defaulters' shares.[30]

With these circumstances undermining its efforts, the company eventually had to seek government aid beyond each state's initial stock pledge. Beginning in the 1790s, a series of bills were introduced in the Maryland Assembly to provide funds to the Potomac Company. While Maryland's economy had improved considerably since the 1780s, these bills rekindled the smoldering animosities between the frontier/planting Potomac faction and the urban commercial interests of the northern Chesapeake Bay. Although not all Potomac legislation generated roll-call votes, those that did offer telling evidence of the impact of political sectionalism on the development of the Potomac route to the West. In some cases, even non-roll-call assembly votes, when examined in light of votes on related issues, demonstrate the sectional interests involved.

In late 1795, the Maryland legislature grappled with the first of the Potomac Company financial aid bills when the directors petitioned the state to subscribe to part of a new stock issue. Supporters backed a state pledge to forty shares, and a Potomac-led assembly committee issued a favorable report on the proposal. The state aid was blocked, however, when a coalition of the Eastern Shore and northern Chesapeake delegates defeated a motion to concur with the committee report.[31] Four days later, a motion to reconsider passed but only by a small margin. The Eastern Shore/northern Chesapeake alliance held strong but not enough to offset several defections and a greater show of strength from the Potomac counties.[32] This set the stage for a show-down vote. The final vote was forty to thirty to increase Maryland's stake in the Potomac Company, with thirty of those in favor coming from the Potomac faction. (See figure three.)[33]

The bill's passage not only gave the Potomac Company part of the aid it needed, but the maneuvering and final assembly vote revealed that a major political realignment had occurred which was likely to affect future company aid. Unlike ten years earlier when the Eastern Shore had allied with the Potomac faction to incorporate the Potomac Company, now Eastern Shore delegates lined up behind the upper Chesapeake counties. This new alliance is significant because it suggests that the stagnating Eastern Shore feared the rapidly growing western Maryland farming counties.[34] The upper Chesapeake and Eastern Shore coalition also demonstrated Baltimore's apprehension that with greater inland settlement, the Potomac project might succeed more than had been previously expected. The Eastern Shore and northern Chesapeake counties continued to oppose most subsequent Potomac Company legislation until the incorporation of the Chesapeake and Ohio Canal Company in 1825.

The new stock sale provided some relief to company finances, but it was not enough to complete the charter requirements. In 1797 the Potomac Company directors asked the state for a $60,000 pledge toward more company stock. The request was referred to a Potomac-dominated assembly committee, which began the search for political compromises to speed passage of an aid bill. Northern Chesapeake delegates quickly indicated the extent of their opposition to the Potomac Company request, however, and this shaped the committee's recommendations. After a northern Chesapeake attempt to force the matter out of committee prematurely failed by only four votes, the committee recommended to the full assembly that instead of the $60,000 stock purchase, the state should make less of a commitment and loan the company $72,000 to complete its work at Great Falls. The committee also recommended that if the work was completed within eighteen months, the state was to have the option of converting the loan into 120 additional shares of company stock. Otherwise the state could call in the loan. To counter the committee recommendation, northern Chesapeake delegates tried to tie any new Potomac Company aid to financial help for the foundering Susquehanna Canal Company, but this failed. Unable to reach a compromise, the assembly then tabled the issue until the next legislative session.[35]

The vote to table, however, did not end the matter for the 1797 session. Near the end of the session, after over half of the upper Chesapeake and Eastern Shore delegates had returned to their respective counties, the Potomac faction, in an astute but ethically questionable move, introduced a new resolution to lend the Potomac Company the $72,000. When an attempt to postpone the resolution failed in the face of overwhelming Potomac strength, the few remaining northern Chesapeake and Eastern Shore delegates vehemently protested this political chicanery:

> Resolved that the question relative to the loan to the Patowmack [sic] Company having been disposed of when the house was full, it is politically wrong again to bring it forward at this time after many members have left the house at what they thought a late period of the session, under an impression the business would be left to sleep.[36]

Perhaps fearing later reprisals, the Potomac delegates relented, but only after securing an alternate bill allowing the Potomac Company to collect tolls on the river even though goods had to be portaged around Great Falls.[37]

As the legislative maneuvers of 1795 and 1797–1798 demonstrated, both the northern Chesapeake and the Eastern Shore counties were threatened by rapid western settlement and the advantages it might bring to the Potomac Valley. Yet on at least one occasion, the Potomac faction found itself the beneficiary of Baltimore's economic interests. In 1799 the needs of the struggling Susquehanna Canal Company led to a temporary Potomac/northern Chesapeake alliance. Several factors brought this about. First, with delinquent stock payments still plaguing it, Potomac Company directors realized that the meager income from tolls was not sufficient for work to continue. Reluctantly, they asked the Maryland Assembly to pledge 130 additional shares. This would bring the state's total to 220 of the company's

730 shares. At the same time, the Susquehanna Canal Company had requested a state loan of $30,000. With the proposed Potomac stock investment over twice the loan sought by the Susquehanna Canal Company, the Potomac delegates found it expedient to offer a compromise: the Potomac faction would not block the Susquehanna Canal Company loan if the upper Chesapeake counties would vote for the Potomac stock purchase.[38]

Despite their long antipathy to Potomac needs, northern Chesapeake delegates had several reasons for accepting the deal. First, the Susquehanna Canal Company badly needed funds to continue its project. Second, some upper Chesapeake representatives, like many other Maryland residents, were beginning to suspect that the Potomac project was impossible no matter how much aid might be extended. Finally, Baltimore merchants and millers were greatly concerned about an Eastern Shore proposal for a cross-cut canal connecting the Chesapeake and Delaware Bays. Such a canal, they realized, would direct the Susquehanna Canal trade to Philadelphia, turning Baltimore's pet project into a windfall for its Pennsylvania rival. Although the trade was uneven, compromising with the Potomac faction was the obvious answer to the northern Chesapeake delegates in order to prevent a reunification of the Potomac and Eastern Shore factions. As a result, both the Potomac and Susquehanna bills passed by nearly identical margins one after the other on December 4, 1799. The cross-cut bill passed by an even larger margin. This vote was perhaps an attempt by both the Potomac and northern Chesapeake factions to outbid each other for the future good will of the Eastern Shore delegates. (See figures four and five.)[39]

The unusual support for such a generous Potomac bill caused northern Chesapeake delegates to worry that their constituents might misinterpret the compromise. Attempting to set the record straight, an "observer," who happened to be in Annapolis when the bills passed, wrote to the *Baltimore American* explaining the rationale behind the compromise:

> It will doubtless surprise his constituents that Mr. Johonnot, your active and intelligent representative [from Baltimore City], stands in the affirmative [on both the Potomac and Susquehanna bills]—but such you will perceive was the great majority on the Cross Cut that it alone would have been decided against the Baltimore interests had not... [the Chesapeake and Potomac factions] united to carry their two measures.... [40]

Maryland's new stock pledge proved sufficient to allow the Potomac Company to open the entire river to navigation in 1802. But it was open in name only. Floods first inundated company works, and then drought left them high and dry. During the winter months, ice made the river impassable. Continuing financial problems and the realization that the weather was a more formidable opponent than any political group caused the company to reevaluate its original plan to connect the Potomac with the Ohio River. Instead, the company limited its goal to clearing just the Potomac and its tributaries. This new plan was aimed at exploiting a known and more accessible market than the Ohio Valley.[41]

Even with the modified plan, the company struggled to stay afloat. For the first two decades of the nineteenth century, tolls were barely enough to keep the locks in repair, and the company accomplished little work on the tributaries.[42] A variety of factors thwarted the Potomac Company, including better roads to Baltimore, the company policy of restricting industrial growth

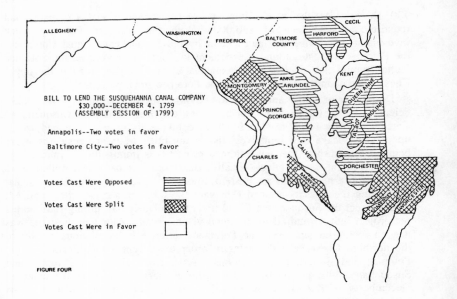

BILL TO LEND THE SUSQUEHANNA CANAL COMPANY
$30,000--DECEMBER 4, 1799
(ASSEMBLY SESSION OF 1799)

Annapolis--Two votes in favor

Baltimore City--Two votes in favor

Votes Cast Were Opposed

Votes Cast Were Split

Votes Cast Were in Favor

FIGURE FOUR

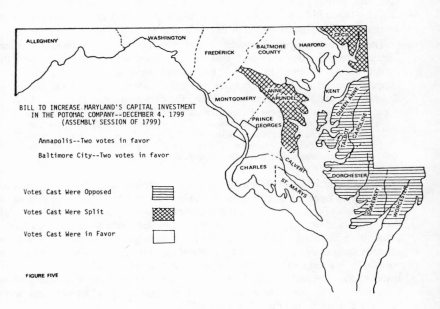

BILL TO INCREASE MARYLAND'S CAPITAL INVESTMENT
IN THE POTOMAC COMPANY--DECEMBER 4, 1799
(ASSEMBLY SESSION OF 1799)

Annapolis--Two votes in favor

Baltimore City--Two votes in favor

Votes Cast Were Opposed

Votes Cast Were Split

Votes Cast Were in Favor

FIGURE FIVE

along the river (directors feared that industrial water use would interfere with the project), the relative decline of Georgetown and Alexandria as major ports, and the reluctance of Maryland and Virginia to extend more state aid. An 1809 attempt to bring in additional funds through a lottery failed miserably, and the company's debts mounted steadily, particularly during the War of 1812.[43]

The War of 1812 further complicated the problems of clearing the river and emphasized their sectional causes. With trade at a near standstill, disgruntled Potomac Valley residents vented their frustrations at the nearest scapegoat— the Potomac Company. Not without some justification, farmers in more recently settled western areas blamed the company for their economic hardships and retaliated in whatever way they could. In 1813, for example, Virginians along the uncleared Shenandoah River convinced their legislature to revoke the Potomac Company's right to improve that tributary and to create a new company for the project. Similarly, in 1815, company subscribers refused to advance any more funds to clear the Antietam, another Potomac tributary, because they thought that the work's estimated cost there was too low.[44]

As in Virginia, increased settlement in western Maryland counties led to dissatisfaction with the Potomac Company's progress. But unlike their neighbors south of the river who lacked easy access to a mill center and port, western Marylanders could take their grain overland to Baltimore. The result was that as westerners' unhappiness with the river increased, so did Baltimore's success. Even after the Potomac was declared open in 1802, overland trade to Baltimore rapidly outpaced that along the river. By 1811— the Potomac Company's most prosperous year—nearly four times the amount of flour that went down the river arrived by road in Baltimore.[45]

With overland trade in Maryland climbing steadily, roads continued to be as much a sectional issue as the Potomac project, although there were attempts to gloss it over. For example, in 1820 an assembly committee composed entirely of northern Chesapeake and western Maryland delegates prefaced its report on a bill to buy a private turnpike from Cumberland, Maryland, to Baltimore with this self-satisfied analysis:

> True it is that for some years jealousies have existed in some parts of the state
> toward Baltimore arising from sectional and partly from political feelings; but it
> must give great satisfaction to every friend of Maryland to find that those jealousies
> are wearing fast away, and that the people of the state are fully convinced and
> ready to acknowledge that whatever public measure benefits Baltimore, it will
> ultimately prove beneficial to the whole state.[46]

The full house of delegates apparently thought differently and tabled the road bill.[47] Recognizing the need for sectional compromise, the delegates sent the road bill to the governor for further study and authorized him to appoint two commissioners to meet with Virginia representatives regarding the Potomac Company's problems. The representatives from the two states were to report on the condition of navigation on the Potomac and make appropriate recommendations.[48]

The joint Maryland/Virginia commission issued its damning report in 1822. The commissioners concluded that the Potomac Company could never achieve its charter goals, that no further aid should be provided by either state, and that a continuous still-water canal next to but separate from the river should be built from Georgetown to Cumberland. At an expense of approximately $1,500,000—over six times the original Potomac Company estimate for its work—such a canal would be less susceptible to floods and drought than the Potomac Company's river-linked works. At the same time, the commissioners recognized the need for upper Chesapeake support for this new project; they recommended that a lateral branch from Georgetown be built to Baltimore, theoretically to funnel Potomac trade to that city.[49] Their recommendation for such an ambitious project was further encouraged by the progress of a potential New York competitor—the Erie Canal, which had been started in 1817. The commissioners' report stimulated renewed interest in improving both the Potomac and the Susquehanna, and it brought out in the open the long dormant northern Chesapeake-Potomac feud over internal improvements. This time the debate focused on two issues—the lateral branch and funding for the new effort. The debate over these two issues demonstrates the impact of the Potomac Company's failure to provide adequate transportation to the rapidly growing interior areas and the sectional interests involved.

The lateral canal proposal was not merely an attempt to appease northern Chesapeake milling and commercial concerns. It was also an idea supported by many inland Maryland settlers. These westerners had concluded that Baltimore offered the best milling and shipping facilities in the region, a belief that was based in large part on dissatisfaction with the Potomac River as a transportation artery. To farmers in the upriver Potomac counties, a new Potomac canal would be acceptable only if the lateral branch to Baltimore was included.[50] Not surprisingly, northern Chesapeake supporters had similar sentiments. Since Baltimore's economic supremacy over Georgetown and Alexandria had been assured years earlier, some Baltimoreans argued that, if anything, the new canal with the lateral branch would further undercut Georgetown's and Alexandria's lagging economies since Baltimore was a better deep-water port with easier access to the sea.[51]

But not all Baltimore residents agreed that a new Potomac canal was the solution, even with a lateral branch. After one of the Baltimore City delegates, John P. Kennedy, voted in favor of the new proposal to improve the Potomac, he felt obliged to write a series of four letters to the *Baltimore American* explaining his actions, which appeared all the more questionable because he owned land through which the proposed lateral branch would pass. Perhaps Baltimore voters either were dissatisfied with his support for the project or his explanation or both. Nevertheless, they did not return him to the assembly in the next session.[52]

The lateral canal may have been controversial, but the question of funding proved to be the downfall of the proposed Potomac Canal Company; it was this question that clearly defined the various sectional attitudes in the state. With a substantial investment in the old Potomac Company, many Maryland delegates were unwilling to fund the new project no matter what its potential for success until reimbursement for money invested in the old Potomac Company could be assured. In seven roll-call votes in the 1822 Maryland Assembly session, the Chesapeake faction continued its long-standing pattern of voting with the Eastern Shore to postpone or block funding. (See figure six.) The Potomac Canal Company bill was finally removed from the House

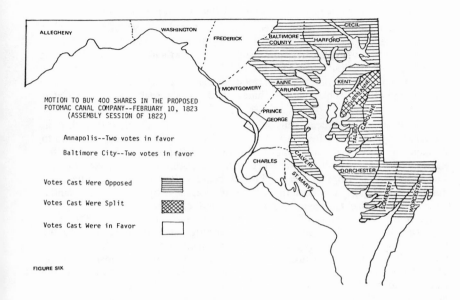

MOTION TO BUY 400 SHARES IN THE PROPOSED
POTOMAC CANAL COMPANY--FEBRUARY 10, 1823
(ASSEMBLY SESSION OF 1822)

Annapolis--Two votes in favor

Baltimore City--Two votes in favor

Votes Cast Were Opposed

Votes Cast Were Split

Votes Cast Were in Favor

FIGURE SIX

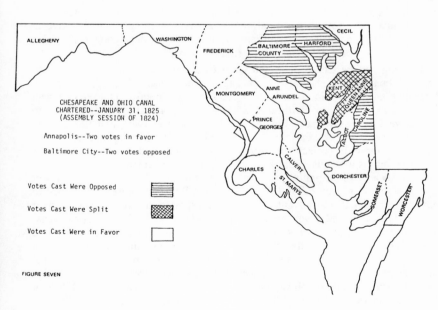

CHESAPEAKE AND OHIO CANAL
CHARTERED--JANUARY 31, 1825
(ASSEMBLY SESSION OF 1824)

Annapolis--Two votes in favor

Baltimore City--Two votes opposed

Votes Cast Were Opposed

Votes Cast Were Split

Votes Cast Were in Favor

FIGURE SEVEN

of Delegates with the weary concurrence of Potomac representatives.[53]

A Potomac-dominated committee, which reported a new bill in the next session to incorporate the Chesapeake and Ohio Canal Company, evidently was impressed by the earlier animosity toward further funding of Potomac efforts without reimbursement for the old Potomac Company investment. To garner support, the committee recommended that Potomac Company stock and bills of credit be exchanged for shares in the Chesapeake and Ohio Canal Company.[54]

This strategy was successful, and it brought about an important shift in sectional alignments. After several attempts by upper Chesapeake delegates to weaken the Chesapeake and Ohio Canal bill, the Potomac faction enticed the Eastern Shore to abandon its alliance with the northern Chesapeake counties and to rejoin its original late eighteenth-century Potomac River allies. In making this change, the Eastern Shore was motivated by more than potential losses to Potomac Company stockholders and creditors. Although Eastern Shore counties were wary of western Maryland competition in the 1790s, they now saw the dwindling strength of all farming interests in relation to the massive power of Baltimore's industrial/merchant economy. Moreover, the Eastern Shore may have sought Potomac support for funds to clear its rivers. This Potomac and Eastern Shore unity resulted in the incorporation of the Chesapeake and Ohio Carral Company by a vote of forty-two to twenty-three.[55] Since Virginia's concurrence with Maryland's version of the act was required, a bill acceptable to both states did not pass in Maryland until January 31, 1825. The final vote was overwhelming, with fifty-five in favor and sixteen against. Significantly, most of the opposition came from northern Chesapeake delegates. (See figure seven.)[56]

Funding for the Chesapeake and Ohio Canal did not come until March 6, 1826, when Maryland voted a package compromise of $500,000 to the Chesapeake and Ohio Canal; $500,000 to a lateral canal to connect Washington, D. C. to Baltimore; $500,000 to a canal from Baltimore to Yorkhaven, Pennsylvania (following the Susquehanna River); and $200,000 to improve rivers on the Eastern Shore. Although the Chesapeake and Ohio Canal was the only project that ultimately was completed, the compromise on this funding is obvious. Unlike the legislative agreement, however, other funding was still strongly sectional in character. Non-state government investments in the new canal demonstrated that Potomac interests continued to have great faith in the advantages better transportation would bring to their valley. The city and town governments of Washington, D. C., Alexandria, and Georgetown together invested three times as much in the Chesapeake and Ohio Canal as did the state of Maryland.[57] These investments indicated that sectional issues would continue to play a prominent role in internal improvements throughout the nineteenth century and strongly suggested that local rivalries would complicate the larger sectional questions raised by federal financial support for projects like the Chesapeake and Ohio Canal.

Sectionalism was a common phenomenon in the nineteenth century, and it is clearly evident in such regional conflicts as the confrontation over slavery between the North and South or the East versus West struggle over federal support for internal improvements. Yet in the late eighteenth and early nineteenth centuries (prior to federal backing for internal improvements) sectionalism on the local level was the dominant force in deciding where roads and canals would be built and which rivers would be improved. This was the case in Maryland where three major sections sought to oppose or profit by Baltimore's rise as a major port. These sectional conflicts were not only geographical in nature, but they also involved shifting antipathies among various urban and rural interests as economic changes occurred in the state. Prior to and shortly after the Revolution, the frontier and planting counties of the Potomac Valley united with the agrarian Eastern Shore against the young and increasingly important northern Chesapeake milling interests. In 1795, however, these sectional alliances changed. With dramatic western Maryland growth, the Eastern Shore wanted protection from agricultural competition and opposed Potomac aid bills in conjunction with the upper Chesapeake interests, which wanted western Maryland's trade to come to Baltimore. Finally, with the incorporation of the Chesapeake and Ohio Canal Company, the Eastern Shore moved back into its former alliance with Potomac agrarian interests. The renewal of this old coalition not only allowed further work on the Potomac route to the West, but because the alliance facilitated the approval of a project with partial federal support, it helped set the stage for the better known national sectional conflicts over internal improvements.

NOTES

The maps accompanying this article were provided by the author.

[1]Frederick Jackson Turner, "The Significance of the Section in American History," *Wisconsin Magazine of History* 8 (1925): 255–280. This article was also published posthumously together with several other of Turner's essays in Turner, *The Significance of Sections in American History* (New York: Henry Holt and Co., 1932). The importance of sectionalism as a factor in shaping western development is also a theme in Turner's *Rise of the New West, 1819–1829* (New York: Harper and Brothers, 1906) and *The United States, 1830–1850: The Nation and its Sections* (New York: Henry Holt and Co., 1935), published after his death. For Turner's frontier thesis, see "The Significance of the Frontier in American History," in the *Annual Report of the American Historical Association for the Year 1893* (Washington: Government Printing Office, 1894). The frontier essay is also reprinted in Turner, *The Early Writings of Frederick Jackson Turner* (Madison: University of Wisconsin Press, 1938) and Turner, *The Frontier in American History* (New York: Henry Holt and Co., 1949). For a recent analysis of the frontier thesis, see Ray A. Billington, *America's Frontier Heritage* (Albuquerque: University of New Mexico Press, 1974).

[2]Carter Goodrich, *Government Promotion of American Canals and Railroads, 1800–1890* (New York: Columbia University Press, 1960); George Rogers Taylor, *The Transportation Revolution, 1815–1860* (New York: Harper and Row Publishers, 1951).

[3]On the Erie Canal, see Nathan Miller, *The Enterprise of a Free People: Aspects of Economic Development in New York State During the Canal Period, 1792–1838* (Ithaca, N. Y.: Cornell University Press, 1962); and Ronald E. Shaw, *Erie Water West: A History of the Erie Canal, 1792–1854* (Lexington: University of Kentucky Press, 1966). For the Chesapeake and Ohio Canal, consult Walter S. Sanderlin, *The Great National Project: A History of the Chesapeake and Ohio Canal* (Baltimore: Johns Hopkins University Press, 1946).

[4]Norman K. Risjord, *Chesapeake Politics, 1781–1800* (New York: Columbia University Press, 1978); Matthew Page Andrews, *History of Maryland: Province and State* (Garden City, N Y.: Doubleday, Doran and Co., 1929); Richard Walsh and William Llyod Fox, eds., *Maryland: A History* (Baltimore: Maryland Historical Society, 1974); Corra Bacon-Foster, *Early Chapters in the Development of the Potomac Route to the West* (Washington: Columbia Historical Society, 1912); Clarence P. Gould, *Money and Transportation in Maryland, 1720–1765* (Baltimore: Johns Hopkins University Press, 1915); John A. Pickell, *A New Chapter in the Early Life of Washington in Connection with the Narrative History of the Potomac Company* (New York: D.

Appleton and Co., 1856); George Washington Ward, *The Early Development of the Chesapeake and Ohio Canal Project* (Baltimore: Johns Hopkins University Press, 1899); Leonard J. Sneddon, "Maryland and Sectional Politics: Canal Building in the Federalist Era," *Maryland Historian* 6 (1975): 79–84. See also Thomas F. Hahn, *George Washington's Canal at Great Falls, Virginia* (Shepardstown, W. V.: American Canal and Transportation Center, 1976); Homer R. Stanford, *The Historic Potomac Beginning in 1740* (Princeton: Princeton University Press, 1940); Rhoda M. Dorsey, "The Pattern of Baltimore Commerce During the Confederation," *Maryland Historical Magazine* 62 (1967): 119–134; Mary Jane Dowd, "The State in the Maryland Economy, 1776–1807," ibid., 57 (1962): 90–132, 229–258.

⁵The Maryland Assembly evidently felt that for future colonial prosperity towns would ultimately be necessary, especially as the economy became more complex. It was with this in mind that the Maryland Assembly passed an act in 1729 creating the town of Baltimore "in and about the place where one John Fleming now lives," at the present site of the city of Baltimore. William Kilty, ed., *The Laws of Maryland to which are Prefixed the Original Charter with an English Translation, the Bill of Rights and Constitution of the State, as Originally adopted by the Convention with the Several Alterations by Acts of the Assembly, the Declaration of Independence, the Articles of Confederation, the Constitution of the General Government and the Amendments made Thereto with an Index to the Laws, the Bill of Rights, and the Constitution*, 2 vols. (Annapolis: Frederick Green, Printer to the State, 1799), vol. 1, 1729 sess., chap. 12, unpaged.

⁶Despite its age, a still useful study on soil exhaustion as it affected Maryland and Virginia tidewater areas is Avery O. Craven, *Soil Exhaustion as a Factor in the Agricultural History of Virginia and Maryland, 1606–1860* (Urbana: University of Illinois Press, 1926).

⁷The lack of mills in Georgetown and Alexandria and the poor quality of most roads to Baltimore contributed to the rise of grain mills in western Maryland counties. By 1810 there were over 150 mills in Frederick and Washington Counties compared to only fifty in Baltimore. These frontier mills helped stimulate economic growth in the West but processed relatively small quantities of grain. Of greater significance is the fact that western Maryland counties annually produced about 350,000 gallons of liquor—an easily transported and non-spoilable product— compared to only 140,000 gallons for Baltimore City. See James S. Van Ness, "Economic Development, Social and Cultural Changes: 1800–1850," in Walsh and Fox, *Maryland: A History*, p. 175; George Terry Sharrer, "Flour Milling and the Growth of Baltimore, 1783–1830" (Ph.D. dissertation, University of Maryland, 1975), pp. 12–34; Sharrer, "Commerce and Industry," in John D. Macon, ed., *Alexandria: A Towne in Transition, 1800–1900* (Alexandria, Va.: Alexandria Bicentennial Commission and Historical Society, 1977), pp. 16–38; George J. Stansfield, "Banks and Banking," in ibid., pp. 39–48; and Dorsey, "The Pattern of Baltimore Commerce During the Confederation," pp. 119–120, 134.

⁸Virginia also had sectional divisions affecting issues such as internal improvements. For a general overview, see Charles H. Ambler, *Sectionalism in Virginia, 1776–1861* (Glendale, Ca.: Arthur H. Clark Co., 1910). For information on how sectionalism and the change to grain farming hurt one Virginia town, see Thomas H. Duffy, "The Decline of the Port of Alexandria, Virginia, 1800–1861" (Master's thesis, Georgetown University, 1965).

⁹Unless indicated otherwise, references to the Potomac faction are intended to include Anne Arundel and Calvert Counties and the city of Annapolis.

¹⁰*Votes and Proceedings of the Maryland House of Delegates*, June 11, 1768, in *Records of the States of the United States*, microfilm (Washington: Library of Congress, 1949), hereafter cited as *Votes and Proceedings*, followed by the appropriate date. See also Kilty, ed., *Laws of Maryland*, vol. 1, 1768 sess., chap. 5.

¹¹Kilty, ed., *Laws of Maryland*, vol. 1, 1774 sess., chap. 21.

¹²John P. Kennedy, ed., *Journals of the House of Burgesses of Virginia, 1766–1769, 1770–1772*, and *1773–1776* (Richmond: n.p., 1906), Dec. 5, 8, 13, 14, 1769, April 11, 1772, and June 14, 17, 21, 1775. See also William Waller Hening, ed., *The Statutes at Large Being a Collection of All the Laws of Virginia from the First Session of the Legislature in the Year 1619*, 13 vols. (Richmond: George Cochran, 1823), 8: 570–579. Details on some of the colonial proposals to clear the Potomac can be found in the George Washington Papers, Minnesota Historical Society, St. Paul, Minnesota. Some of these papers have been published in Grace L. Nute, ed., "Washington and the Potomac: Manuscripts of the Minnesota Historical Society (1754) 1764–1796," *American Historical Review* 28 (1923): 497–519, 702–722.

¹³George Washington to Thomas Jefferson, July 20, 1770, in John C. Fitzpatrick, ed., *The*

Writings of George Washington from the Original Manuscript Sources, 1745–1799, 39 vols. (Washington: Government Printing Office, 1938), 3: 17–21.

[14]Hening, ed., *Statutes at Large*, 8: 570–579; Edward S. Delaplaine, *The Life of Thomas Johnson: Member of the Continental Congress, First Governor of the State of Maryland, and Associate Justice of the United States Supreme Court* (New York: Grafton Press, 1927), pp. 72–75.

[15]Broadside of John Ballendine, Potomac Company Miscellaneous Accounts, Records of the National Park Service, item 179, National Archives, Washington, D. C. Ballendine promoted many entrepreneurial projects before the Revolution. See Randolph W. Church, "John Ballendine: Unsuccessful Entrepreneur of the Eighteenth Century", *Virginia Cavalcade* 8 (1959): 39–46; Arthur G. Burton and Richard W. Stephenson, "John Ballendine's Eighteenth Century Map of Virginia," *Quarterly Journal of the Library of Congress*, 21 (1964): 172–178. Ballendine's supporters included many prominent Maryland and Virginia residents, such as George Washington. Although Washington thought Ballendine's "principles have been loose," he overcame his qualms and subscribed to the proposed project. See George Washington to Thomas Jefferson, May 5, 1772, in Fitzpatrick, *Writings of Washington*, 3: 82–83. Other colonial proponents of the Potomac River as a route to the West included entrepreneur John Semple; British General Edward Braddock; frontiersman Thomas Cresap; Virginia colonial governor John Lord Dunmore; Maryland colonial governor Robert Eden; Virginia Northern Neck proprietor Thomas Lord Fairfax; the state of Maryland's first governor, Thomas Johnson; President of Congress under the Articles of Confederation Richard Henry Lee; statesman and author of the Virginia Declaration of Rights George Mason; and Ohio Company agent George Mercer. Washington frequently noted these plans in both his correspondence and his diaries. In addition to the Washington Papers in the Minnesota Historical Society, see generally Fitzpatrick, *Writings of Washington*, and Fitzpatrick, ed., *The Diaries of George Washington*, 4 vols. (Boston: Houghton Mifflin Co., 1925).

[16]George Mason to George Washington, March 9, 1776, in Robert A. Rutland, ed., *The Papers of George Mason, 1725–1792*, 3 vols., (Chapel Hill: University of North Carolina Press, 1970), 1: 224–225.

[17]Parentheses in the original. George Washington to Thomas Jefferson, March 29, 1784, in Fitzpatrick, *Writings of Washington*, 27: 373–377.

[18]"[Anonymous] to a member of the Present Assembly Now Siting [sic] at Annapolis," and "Recommendations Regarding Ballendine's Paper's," both in the Washington Papers in the Minnesota Historical Society. See also, Hahn, *George Washington's Canal*, p. 6.

[19]Hening, *Statutes at Large*, 11: 510–525.

[20]For Washington's influence in the Maryland Assembly, see *Votes and Proceedings*, Nov. 26, 1784. Although proponents of the Susquehanna Canal contemplated tapping the farming areas in Maryland and nearby Pennsylvania, that project never was the success that Baltimoreans hoped it would be, largely due to Philadelphia merchants, who blocked passage of a Pennsylvania charter that would have allowed the company to extend the canal into their state. See Kilty, ed., *Laws of Maryland*, vol. 1, 1783 sess., chap. 23; Van Ness, "Economic Development," in Walsh and Fox, *Maryland: A History*, p. 173; James W. Livingood, *The Philadelphia-Baltimore Trade Rivalry, 1780–1860* (Harrisburg: Pennsylvania Historical and Museum Commission, 1947), passim.

[21]The one northern Chesapeake delegate was from Kent County. *Votes and Proceedings*, Nov. 26, 1784; J. Thomas Scharf, *History of Baltimore City and County from the Earliest Period to the Present Day including Biographical Sketches of Their Representative Men* (Philadelphia: Louis E. Everts, 1881), p. 52.

[22]*Votes and Proceedings*, Dec. 27, 1784; Dowd, "The State in the Maryland Economy," p. 121.

[23]*Maryland Gazette*, May 26, 1785. See also *Alexandria Gazette*, Feb. 10, 1785, for a similar view by another supporter.

[24]James Madison to Thomas Jefferson, April 25, 1784, in Gaillard Hunt, ed., *The Writings of James Madison Comprising His Public Papers and His Private Correspondence including Numerous Letters and Documents Now for the First Time Printed*, 9 vols. (New York: G. P. Putnam's Sons, 1901), 2: 48.

[25]*Maryland Gazette*, April 21, 1785.

[26]Kilty, ed., *Laws of Maryland*, vol. 1, 1784 sess., chap. 33; Hening, *Statutes at Large*, 11:

510–525. The time limits were extended several times, and both states ultimately bought more than the original fifty shares each. For a collection of all legislation relating to the Potomac Company, see *Acts of the States of Virginia, Maryland, and Pennsylvania, and the Congress of the United States in Relation to the Chesapeake and Ohio Canal Company with the Proceedings of the Convention which Led to the Formation of Said Company. Also, the Acts and Resolutions of the States of Virginia and Maryland Concerning the Potomac Company to which are Appended the By-Laws, Lists of Officers, etc., of the Chesapeake and Ohio Canal Company with a Copious Index* (Washington: Gales and Seaton, 1828), hereafter cited as *Acts of the States*. Virginia also pledged fifty additional shares (as well as one hundred in the James River Company—the political price of the Potomac Company legislation) for George Washington, who was greatly embarrassed by the gifts. See George Washington to Benjamin Harrison, Jan. 22, 1785; Washington to Marquis de Lafayette, Feb. 25, 1785; Washington to Governor Patrick Henry, Feb. 27, 1785; Washington to Nathanael Greene, May 20, 1785; Washington to the Secretary of War, June 18, 1785; Washington to Edmund Randolph, July 30, 1785 and Aug. 13 1785; and Washington to Thomas Jefferson, Sept. 26, 1785; all in Fitzpatrick, *Writings of Washington*, 28: 34–38, 71–76, 89–94, 144–146, 166–169, 214–216, 218–221, and 278–281. See also, Fitzpatrick, *Diaries of Washington*, 4: 158n, and Douglas S. Freeman, *George Washington: A Biography*, 7 vols. (New York: Charles Scribner's Sons, 1948), 7: 231, 275, 586.

[27]Although these problems are not inconsequential, they are beyond the scope of this paper. They are abundantly documented in the Potomac Company Papers, Records of the National Park Service, National Archives. These papers include the Proceedings of the General Meetings of the Potowmack [sic] Company, 1785–1796, (item 159), hereafter cited as Proceedings of the General Meetings, followed by the appropriate date. After 1796 the minutes of the general meetings were recorded in a journal with the Proceedings of the Board of President and Directors of the Potowmack [sic] Company, 1785–1807, (item 160). Minutes of the general meetings after 1796 will be cited as Proceedings of the Board, 1785–1807—General Meeting, and President and Directors Meetings shall be cited as Proceedings of the Board—Meeting of the President and Directors, both followed by the appropriate date. A second and third journal carry Potomac Company business from 1808 to 1822 and from 1822 to 1828, and those dates shall be used in the above citations where appropriate. Other items of regular company business were also included in these same journals and shall be similarly identified. For discussions of the company's problems, consult the works cited in note 4; Sanderlin, *The Great National Project*; Ella May Turner, *James Rumsey: Pioneer in Steam Navigation* (Scottsdale, Pa.: Mennonite Publishing House, 1930). Rumsey was the company's first chief engineer.

[28]On sectionalism and the Maryland economy during the Confederation, see William Arthur O'Brien, "Challenge to Consensus: Social, Political, and Economic Implications of Maryland Sectionalism, 1776–1789" (Ph.D. dissertation, University of Wisconsin, 1979). See also Kathryn L. Behrens, *Paper Money in Maryland, 1727–1789*, (Baltimore: Johns Hopkins University Press, 1923), p. 78; Merrill Jensen, *The New Nation: A History of the United States During the Confederation, 1781–1789* (New York: Alfred Knopf, 1958), pp. 37–39, 314–315; Dorsey, "Pattern of Baltimore Commerce During the Confederation," p. 168; and Richard Walsh, "The Era of the Revolution," in Walsh and Fox, eds., *Maryland: A History*, pp. 131–134.

[29]Subscription books for stock pledges were opened in six towns, three each in Maryland and Virginia. The breakdown of the 403 shares pledged by the first company meeting in 1785 reveals the sectional interest in the project, with nearly all non-state subscriptions from towns along the river. In Maryland, seventy-three shares (including fifty for the state) were pledged in Annapolis, forty-two in Georgetown, and twenty-two in Fredericktown. In Virginia, one hundred (fifty for the state and fifty as a gift for Washington) were pledged in Richmond, one hundred and thirty-five in Alexandria, and thirty-nine in Winchester. See Pickell, *Early Life of Washington*, p. 66, and George Washington to Nathanael Greene, May 20, 1785, in Fitzpatrick, *Writings of Washington*, 28: 144–146.

[30]With little tax revenue, even the state of Maryland temporarily defaulted on its payments. Proceedings of the Board, 1785–1807—Meeting of the President and Directors, March 1 and 2, 1786, April 3, May 25, 1787; Proceedings of the General Meetings, Aug. 7, 1786.

[31]The directors reported the company's economic condition to the stockholders in Proceedings of the General Meetings, Aug. 3, 1795. See also *Votes and Proceedings*, Nov. 23 and 28, 1795. The assembly vote was 35 opposed and 29 in favor.

[32]Ibid., Dec. 2, 1795. The vote was 38 to 30.

[33]Proceedings of the General Meetings, Aug. 3, 1795, and Aug. 1, 1796; *Votes and*

Proceedings, Dec. 11, 1795. Virginia also pledged part of this new stock issue, but sectionalism within that state made it necessary for Potomac supporters to compromise with James River proponents. *Journal of the [Virginia] House of Delegates*, in *Records of the States of the United State*, microfilm (Washington: Library of Congress, 1949), Dec. 21 and 24, 1795; Samuel Sheppard, ed., *The Statutes at Large of Virginia from October Session 1792 to December Session 1806, Inclusive in Three Volumes Being a Continuation of Hening*, 3 vols. (Richmond: n.p., 1835), 1: 375–377.

[34]Three western Maryland counties—Frederick, Washington, and Allegany—swelled in population from 51,422 in 1790 to 72,188 in 1820. In comparision, the entire Eastern Shore—six counties—had a population of 81,178 in 1790 and 94,208 in 1820. The three western Maryland counties had grown from sixty-three percent of the Eastern Shore's population in 1790 to seventy-seven percent in 1820. See, *Fifth Census; or the Enumeration of the Inhabitants of the United States. 1830. To Which is Prefixed a Schedule of the Whole Number of Persons within the Several Districts of the United States, Taken According to the Acts of 1790, 1800, 1810, 1820* (Washington: Duff Green, 1832). The delegates from St. Mary's County may have opposed the Potomac Company's aid because of fears similar to those of the Eastern Shore.

[35]The proposed loan was to be in the form of United States stock. Proceedings of the Board, 1785–1807—General Meeting, Aug. 7, 1797; Potomac Company Broadside, "Entrusted as We Are with the Interests of the Potomack [sic] Company," microprint reproduction (Worcester, Mass.: American Antiquarian Society, 1963); *Votes and Proceedings*, Nov. 30, Dec. 15, 21, 23, 26, 28, 29, 30, 1797, Jan. 5, 12, 13, 1798. Contrary to Norman K. Risjord's findings in *Chesapeake Politics* (p. 479), the delegates from the northern Chesapeake counties did not "back the Potomac subsidy almost to a man." In nine roll call votes (Risjord cites eight)—one on Dec. 15, four on Dec. 28, one on Dec. 30, 1797, two on Jan. 5, and one on Jan. 13, 1798—northern Chesapeake delegates consistently opposed Potomac interests. See the following table for the vote breakdown of the Potomac (P), northern Chesapeake (NC), and Eastern Shore (ES) factions:

| | IN FAVOR | | | | OPPOSED | | | |
	P	NC	ES	TOTAL	P	NC	ES	TOTAL
Dec. 15	5	11	15	31	27	2	6	35
Dec. 28	15	11	4	30	12	4	12	28
Dec. 28	22	2	4	28	6	12	12	30
Dec. 28	23	2	5	30	4	13	11	28
Dec. 28	22	4	2	29	5	10	13	28
Dec. 30	5	14	11	30	22	1	6	29
Jan. 5	5	14	12	31	25	1	4	30
Jan. 5	6	14	12	32	25	1	5	31
Jan. 13	4	2	7	13	22	5	5	32

[36]Ibid., Jan. 12 and 13, 1798.

[37]Ibid., Jan. 17, 1798. The assembly also passed a watered-down Susquehanna bill. There is no indication that the Potomac loan ever passed in the 1797 session of the assembly, although at least one scholar suggests otherwise. See Risjord, *Chesapeake Politics*, p. 479.

[38]Proceedings of the Board, 1785–1807—General Meeting, Feb. 4, 1798, and Aug. 5, 1799.

[39]*Votes and Proceedings*, Dec. 4, 1799. The vote for the Potomac bill was 37 to 29; for the Susquehanna bill 38 to 29; and for the Chesapeake-Delaware Canal, 50 to 15.

[40]*Baltimore American*, Dec. 9, 1799.

[41]Proceedings of the Board, 1785–1808—General Meeting, Aug. 2, 1802, Aug. 1, 1803; Proceedings of the Board, 1808–1822—Report to the Secretary of the Treasury , Jan. 20, 1808. Jay's Treaty in 1794 and Pinckney's Treaty in 1795 had also removed many of the earlier concerns about western settlers' loyalties.

[42]Apparently only two of the tributaries—the Shenandoah and the Monocacy—ever had any extensive work done on them. See Tobias Lear, *Observations on the River Potomack [sic], the Country Adjacent, and the City of Washington* (New York: Samuel Loudon and Son, 1793; reprint ed., Baltimore: Samuel T. Chambers, 1940); and Proceedings of the Board, 1808–1822—Meeting of the President and Directors, Report to the Secretary of the Treasury, Jan. 20. 1808.

[43]In 1808 Potomac Company President John Mason had reported to Secretary of the Treasury

Albert Gallatin that the company was $66,814.90 in debt with only $7,146.47 on hand and that $444,648.80 had been spent on the river—over twice the charter estimate. Mason estimated that the company would need more than $100,000 to complete its work in the Potomac watershed. Ibid.; Proceedings of the Board, 1785–1807—General Meeting, Aug. 3, 1807; P.oceedings of the Board, 1808–1822—General Meeting, April 10, Aug. 5, 1810, Aug. 5, 1811, Aug. 3, 1812, Aug. 2, 1813, Aug. 7, 1816; Proceedings of the Board, 1808–1822—Meeting of the President and Directors, April 10, 1810, Dec. 3, 1816. See also "Report on Roads and Canals" in *American State Papers—Documents, Legislative and Executive of the Congress of the United States*, 10 classes, 38 vols. (Washington: Gales and Seaton, 1832–1861), class 10, vol. 1, pp. 724–921.

[44]Downriver areas were also unhappy with the company. See the *Alexandria Gazette*, Nov. 8, 1816. See also, *Acts of the States*, pp. 108–112, 151–154; Proceedings of the Board, 1808–1822—General Meeting, Nov. 13, 1813, Aug. 7, 1815, Nov. 29, 1816; Proceedings of the Board, 1808–1822—Meeting of the President and Directors, Oct. 3, 1815; United States Congress, *Report of the Committee of the District of Columbia to Whom were Referred Sundry Memorials from the Inhabitants of Pennsylvania, Maryland, and Virginia Praying the Aid of the Federal Government Towards the Improvement of the Navigation of the River Potomac*, House Report 111, 17th Congress, 1 sess., 1822, p. 22; Sanderlin, *Great National Project*, pp. 42–44.

[45]In 1811 the Potomac Company collected tolls on 118,222 barrels of flour, while state inspectors in Baltimore examined 530,000 barrels that same year. See Commissioners of Maryland and Virginia Appointed to Survey the Potomac River, *Letter from the Governor and Council of Maryland Transmitting a Report of the Commissioners Appointed to Survey the River Potomac* (Washington: Gales and Seaton, 1823), appendix B. Hereafter cited as *Commission Report of 1822*. See also S. W. Bruchey, *Robert Oliver: Merchant of Baltimore, 1783–1819* (Baltimore: Johns Hopkins University Press, 1956), p. 104.

[46]*Votes and Proceedings*, Dec. 18, 1820.

[47]Ibid., Dec. 18 and 20, 1820, Jan. 8, 1821.

[48]Ibid., Feb. 16, 1821. For details on why Virginia decided to examine the Potomac project, see Goodrich, *Government Promotion of American Canals and Railroads*, pp. 87–88; Virginius Dabney, *Virginia: The New Dominion* (Garden City, N. Y.: Doubleday and Co., 1971), pp. 212–214; Ambler, *Sectionalism in Virginia*, pp. 93–99, 104–107; Ward, *Early Development of the Chesapeake and Ohio Canal*, pp. 16–17.

[49]*Commission Report of 1822*, pp. 5–24.

[50]*Baltimore American*, July 21, 1823.

[51]Robert Goodloe Harper, *General Harper's Speech to the Citizens of Baltimore on the Expediency of Promoting a Connection between the Ohio at Pittsburgh and the Waters of the Chesapeake at Baltimore by a Canal through the District of Columbia with His Reply to Some of the Objections of Mr. Winchester* (Baltimore: E. J. Coale, 1824), pp. 33–34.

[52]*Votes and Proceedings*, Feb. 6 and 10, 1823; *Baltimore American*, July 18, 23, 26, and Aug. 1, 1823.

[53]*Votes and Proceedings*, Feb. 6, 10, 11, 12, 15, and 17, 1823. Virginia backers of the new Potomac project had to overcome the sectional opposition of th proponents of the James River. *Journal of the [Virginia] House of Delegates*, Feb. 20, 1823, and Jan. 22, 1824.

[54]Bacon-Foster, *Early Chapters in the Development of the Potomac Route to the West*, pp. 149–151; Ward, *Early Development of the Chesapeake and Ohio Canal Project*, pp. 59–65; Hugh Sisson Hanna, *A Financial History of Maryland (1789–1848)* (Baltimore: Johns Hopkins University Press, 1907), p. 79.

[55]*Votes and Proceedings*, Jan. 22 and 24, 1824.

[56]Ibid., Jan. 31, 1825.

[57]The state of Maryland pledged $500,000; Alexandria and Georgetown, $250,000 each; and Washington, $1,000,000. United States Congress, House Committee on Roads and Canals, *Chesapeake and Ohio Canal*, House Report 47, 20th Congress, 1st sess., 1828, pp. 1–39.

The Potomac Company: A Misadventure in Financing an Early American Internal Improvement Project

DOUGLAS R. LITTLEFIELD

¶ *The failure of the Potomac Company—the first interregional internal improvement project attempted in the United States—has been largely neglected by historians. From the mid 1780s to the 1820s, this company struggled unsuccessfully to link the East Coast with the Old Northwest by enhancing the navigability of the Potomac River. In this article, Mr. Littlefield examines this little-known episode, describing how the project was overwhelmed by a combination of factors that included an unstable American economy, unreliable government aid, and interstate rivalries. He concludes that the Potomac Company's failure demonstrated how the absence of federal support could cripple a large-scale internal improvement project, and suggests that its example spurred the U.S. government to become directly involved in the economic development of the young republic.*

In late 1784, approximately a year after the Treaty of Paris ended the American Revolution, George Washington and Horatio Gates arrived in Annapolis, Maryland, to seek that state's assent to a project that had tantalized prominent Virginians and Marylanders for over thirty years—transforming the Potomac River into a major transportation artery to the trans-Appalachian West. Earlier that year, after returning from the West, Washington had written to Virginia governor Benjamin Harrison, urging him to bring the matter before the Virginia Assembly. Washington cited commercial reasons for improving transportation along the river, and he added that the political allegiance of western settlers would soon stray to Spanish New Orleans if communication with the American states were not made easier. Submitting his own estimates of distances from various eastern locations to the Ohio Valley, Washington noted that the Potomac route was by far the shortest, and he suggested that a formal survey be taken. "Upon the

DOUGLAS R. LITTLEFIELD is a doctoral candidate at the University of California, Los Angeles. He wishes to thank Norris Hundley, Larry Lipin, Marilyn Morgan, and two anonymous *Business History Review* referees for helpful comments on earlier drafts of this paper. He also expresses his appreciation for help in selecting and reproducing some of the illustrations to Paul Gardner and the National Park Service staff at Great Falls National Park, Virginia.

Business History Review 58 (winter 1984) © 1984 by The President and Fellows of Harvard College.

whole," he stressed, "the object, in my estimation, is of most commercial and political importance."[1]

Washington's national stature after the Revolution persuaded Governor Harrison to present the letter, together with a petition from citizens of both Maryland and Virginia seeking an improved river, to the Virginia Assembly. The assembly responded by appointing Washington, Gates, and Thomas Blackburn commissioners to seek Maryland's agreement to clear the river of obstructions. Washington's letter to Harrison and his subsequent visit to Annapolis resulted in legislation incorporating the Potomac Company in Maryland in 1784 and in Virginia in 1785.[2]

The newborn Potomac Company was the culmination of several colonial attempts to improve the river. As early as 1749, Marylanders and Virginians had thought of using the Potomac to gain access to the interior for both economic and strategic reasons. Some promoters, such as members of the Ohio Company, had planned to use the river to increase fur trading and to enhance inland real estate values. Others urged its use to transport military supplies for defense against the French and Indians or for settlement of and trade with the region beyond the Appalachian Mountains. These colonial proposals were encouraged by the close proximity of the Potomac's headwaters to those of the Ohio, endless political haggling in colonial legislatures over road locations, and rapid soil depletion from tobacco farming.[3]

Colonial plans to clear the river were frustrated by rivalries among land speculators, a lack of technical knowledge, a severe labor short-

---

[1] George Washington to Thomas Jefferson, 29 March 1784, in *The Writings of George Washington from the Original Manuscript Sources, 1745–1799*, ed. John C. Fitzpatrick, 39 vols. (Washington, D.C., 1931–44), 27:373–77.

[2] Blackburn did not go to Annapolis with Washington and Gates. William Kilty, ed., *The Laws of Maryland to Which are Prefixed the Original Charter with an English Translation, the Bill of Rights and Constitution of the State, as Originally Adopted by the Convention with the Several Alterations of Acts of the Assembly, the Declaration of Independence, the Articles of Confederation, the Constitution of the General Government and the Amendments Made Thereto, with an Index to the Laws, the Bill of Rights, and the Constitution*, 2 vols. (Annapolis, 1799), vol. 1, 1784 sess., chap. 33, unpaged; William Waller Hening, ed., *The Statutes at Large: Being a Collection of All the Laws of Virginia, from the First Session of the Legislature, in the Year 1619*, 13 vols. (Richmond, 1809–23), 11:510–25; Thomas Jefferson to James Madison, 20 Feb. 1784, in *Papers of Thomas Jefferson*, ed. Julian Boyd, 20 vols. (Princeton, 1950–82), 6:544–51; Thomas Jefferson to George Washington, 15 March 1784, in *Papers of Jefferson* 7:25–27; John A. Pickell, *A New Chapter in the Life of Washington, in Connection with the Narrative History of the Potomac Company* (New York, 1856), 44–46.

[3] Among the prominent pre-Revolutionary backers of the Potomac route to the West were entrepreneurs John Ballendine and John Semple; British general Edward Braddock; frontiersman Thomas Cresap; Virginia colonial governor John M. Lord Dunmore; Maryland's last colonial governor, Robert Eden; Virginia Northern Neck proprietor Thomas Lord Fairfax; Maryland's first governor after the Revolution, Thomas Johnson; president of Congress under the Articles of Confederation Richard Henry Lee; statesman and author of the Virginia Declaration of Rights George Mason; Ohio Company agent George Mercer; and, of course, George Washington. Details on some of these early projects can be found in the

age, and conflicts with foreign powers. Yet continuing faith in the usefulness of an improved river prompted many backers of early river plans to participate in later ones as well. This sustained interest in the Potomac route to the West, and it eventually brought about the chartering of the Potomac Company.

Although early enterprises such as the Potomac Company played a significant role in opening back-country areas, few writers have examined pre-nineteenth-century internal improvements in any depth. George Rogers Taylor's *The Transportation Revolution, 1815–1860* (1951) and Carter Goodrich's *Government Promotion of American Canals and Railroads, 1800–1890* (1960) mention such late eighteenth-century mid-Atlantic schemes, either projected or actually begun, as the Chesapeake and Delaware Canal crossing both Delaware and Maryland's Eastern Shore, the Susquehanna Canal Company in Maryland, and the James River and Dismal Swamp canals in Virginia. Both Taylor and Goodrich also briefly discuss the Potomac Company, yet their works are broad studies focusing most heavily on nineteenth-century projects begun after Secretary of the Treasury Albert Gallatin's 1808 report to Congress on internal improvements. Monographs that examine the Potomac as a transportation artery, such as Walter S. Sanderlin's *The Great National Project: A History of the Chesapeake and Ohio Canal* (1946), Corra Bacon-Foster's *Early Chapters in the Development of the Potomac Route to the West* (1912), and John A. Pickell's *A New Chapter in the Early Life of Washington, in Connection with the Narrative History of the Potomac Company* (1856), either study the Potomac Company as a predecessor to the better-known Chesapeake and Ohio Canal Company or are outdated and lack an interpretive framework. All of these general studies and monographs ignore the Potomac Company's path-breaking role as the earliest internal improvement of national importance.[4]

George Washington Papers, Minnesota Historical Society, St. Paul, Minn. Some, but not all, of these papers have been published in Grace L. Nute, ed., "Washington and the Potomac: Manuscripts of the Minnesota Historical Society (1754) 1764–1796," *American Historical Review* 28 (1923): 497–519, 702–22. Washington frequently mentioned Potomac plans in his diaries and correspondence, published respectively in *The Diaries of George Washington, 1748–1799*, ed. John C. Fitzpatrick, 4 vols. (Boston, 1925) and *Writings of Washington*. In secondary sources, see the appropriate chapters in Walter S. Sanderlin, *The Great National Project: A History of the Chesapeake and Ohio Canal* (Baltimore, 1946); George Washington Ward, *The Early Development of the Chesapeake and Ohio Canal Project* (Baltimore, 1899); Corra Bacon-Foster, *Early Chapters in the Development of the Potomac Route to the West* (Washington, D.C., 1912); and Pickell, *New Chapter in the Early Life of Washington*. Of all the colonial schemes, Ballendine's progressed the furthest, only to be interrupted by the Revolution. See the above sources and Randolph W. Church, "John Ballendine: Unsuccessful Entrepreneur of the Eighteenth Century," *Virginia Cavalcade* 8 (1959): 39–46; Richard W. Stephenson, "John Ballendine's Eighteenth Century Map of Virginia," *Quarterly Journal of the Library of Congress* 21 (1964): 172–78.
[4] Taylor and Goodrich also discuss other pre-1800 schemes, such as the Middlesex Canal in Massachusetts, the Western Inland Lock Navigation Company in New York, the Lehigh Canal in Pennsylvania,

Although the Potomac Company was not the only project launched shortly after the Revolution, its incorporation marked the beginning of the first interstate internal improvement project that required the cooperation of more than one state government and contemplated linking two major regions of the country. The undertaking, however, was ultimately a financial disappointment and a technical failure; indeed its significance lies primarily in its demonstration that joint-stock companies were poorly equipped to carry out major internal improvements without massive and reliable government aid, especially during the first few decades after independence. Until well into the early nineteenth century, internal improvement enterprises were extremely vulnerable to a variety of uncontrollable and unpredictable factors that made financial planning and raising capital from private sources difficult at best. Among these were foreign affairs problems, such as competition from European goods and crops, Jefferson's embargo, and the War of 1812. Adding to the difficulties from abroad were domestic natural disasters, like droughts, floods, and insect plagues. All of these contributed to an unstable American economy and rampant land speculation. The economy, in turn, forced private enterprises to rely on pay-as-you-go subscription processes, company-sponsored lotteries, and heavy borrowing to finance their undertakings.

The economic uncertainties were compounded by a significant political problem. Without leadership by the federal government, interstate internal improvement companies had to cajole more than one state government into passing legislation to allow initial chartering and later into providing financial aid when private funding proved inadequate.[5] These economic and political obstacles combined to make corporate planning close to impossible and gave strong support to those who argued that large-scale internal improvements were unlikely to succeed in the new United States without substantial and unified government support. The Potomac Company, then, is an illustration of the inadequacies of eighteenth-century private enterprise to meet the

and the Santee Canal in South Carolina. See George Rogers Taylor, *The Transportation Revolution, 1815–1860* (New York, 1951); Carter Goodrich, *Government Promotion of American Canals and Railroads, 1800–1890* (New York, 1960). On the Potomac, see Sanderlin, *Great National Project*; Bacon-Foster, *Early Chapters in the Development of the Potomac*; Pickell, *New Chapter in the Life of Washington*. Gallatin's report can be found in "Report on Roads and Canals" presented to the Senate by the secretary of the treasury, 4 April 1808, in *American State Papers—Documents, Legislative and Executive, of the Congress of the United States*, 10 classes, 38 vols. (Washington, D.C., 1832–61), class 10, 1:724–921, hereafter cited as Gallatin, "Report on Roads and Canals."

[5] The necessity for Maryland and Virginia to agree on all legislation to clear the Potomac resulted in a series of meetings, which ultimately culminated in the convention to amend the Articles of Confederation and the decision to draft the Constitution. Sanderlin, *Great National Project*, 31n; Bacon-Foster, *Early Chapters in the Development of the Potomac* 142.

needs of interstate internal improvements and a demonstration of the relative importance of reliable government assistance to these projects. The company's experiences, although frustrated by events beyond its control, helped shape the financial plans of its successor, the Chesapeake and Ohio Canal Company, to include federal sponsorship and encouraged a Federalist vision of a country united by a well-integrated, government-supported system of internal commerce and transportation.

THE PROJECT AND THE POSTWAR ECONOMY

Like most contemporary English river-improvement projects, the Potomac effort was to be undertaken by a private company granted extensive monopoly rights by the government—in this case, by the legislatures of both Maryland and Virginia, since the river formed the two states' common border.[6] The Maryland and Virginia acts incorporating the Potomac Company were nearly identical. The company was to raise 50,000 pounds sterling (approximately 220,000 Spanish dollars) in five hundred shares. Stock shares were pledged with only a small percentage down, the remainder to be paid when called for by the company directors—a standard joint-stock company procedure. Because of long-standing strong public support for the project (and perhaps because of legislators' landholdings along the river), each state was to subscribe to fifty shares. In a provision that was to become increasingly troublesome for the Potomac Company as specie became scarce in the postwar economy, subscriptions were to be paid only in Spanish dollars or other foreign silver or gold coin; paper money was unacceptable. Additional capital could be raised through subscriptions to new shares. Subscribers were to make payments and meet any financial deficiencies as work required. The company had three years to clear the upper Potomac and ten years to build bypass canals and locks around the major obstructions at Little and Great falls just above tidewater—a total distance of more than 175 miles. The right to collect "reasonable tolls forever" was granted to subscribers or their heirs on condition that the river be made navigable in dry seasons for flatboats drawing one foot of water when fully loaded. Both Maryland and Virginia passed additional laws to build roads connecting the headwaters

---

[6] For information on river improvements in England, see William T. Jackman, *The Development of Transportation in Modern England* (London, 1962); Edwin A. Pratt, *A History of Inland Transport and Communication in England* (London, 1912); J. R. Ward, *The Finance of Canal Building in Eighteenth Century England* (London, 1974); and T. S. Willan, *River Navigation in England, 1600–1750* (New York, 1964).

GREAT FALLS ON THE POTOMAC RIVER AT LOW WATER, SEPTEMBER 1984

Great Falls was one of the major obstructions to river traffic on the Potomac. The Potomac Company planned to circumvent the falls through a combination of by-pass canals and locks. (Photograph by the author.)

of the Potomac with those of the Ohio, and both states were to ask Pennsylvania for permission to open an additional road from the Potomac to the Youghiogheny, a tributary of the Monongahela.[7]

Given the scope of the project and the state of the postwar economy, there was considerable doubt that all five hundred Potomac Company shares would be pledged in the United States. With inflation soaring and specie rapidly disappearing, even so ardent a supporter as George Washington was forced to admit that "in general the friends of the measure [to open the river] are better stocked with good wishes than

---

[7] The Spanish dollar was the most common form of specie in circulation in America. Its long-standing reliability made it the currency of choice to Potomac Company directors. On currency and exchange rates, see John J. McCusker, *Money and Exchange in Europe and America, 1600–1775: A Handbook* (Chapel Hill, N.C., 1978), 3–26, esp. 7–8. McCusker's conclusions, although focusing on the colonial era, can be applied reasonably to the early national period, particularly before the Constitution gave Congress the power to coin money. On the terms of the Potomac Company's charter, see Hening, *Statutes at Large* 11:510–25; Kilty, *Laws of Maryland*, vol. 1, 1784 sess., chap. 33; George Washington to president of Congress Richard Henry Lee, 8 Feb. 1785, in *Writings of Washington* 28:67–71; James Thomas and T. J. C. Williams, *History of Allegheny County, Maryland* (reprint ed., Baltimore, 1969), 22; T. J. C. Williams and Folger McKinsey, *History of Frederick County, Maryland, with a Biographical Record of Representative Families* (reprint ed., Baltimore, 1967), 146.

with money."[8] Yet generous postwar credit from European manufacturers and American merchants eager to return to prewar business
levels created a temporary illusion of prosperity, although it did not
increase the amount of specie in circulation. Optimism abounded as
residents in newly settled parts of the Cumberland and Shenandoah
valleys—both formed by tributaries of the Potomac—clamored for improved river transportation to downstream markets. Proclaiming the
"great advantages that must inevitably flow to our country [from the
improved river]," the *Alexandria Gazette* voiced the enthusiasm typical of those most likely to benefit from this trade.[9]

The Potomac Company's subscription process and the credit-fueled
postwar boom encouraged investors to sign stock pledges with near
carefree abandon and with little careful analysis of the true state of the
economy or the immense size of the project. The pledge-now, pay-
later subscription process, although a seemingly practical approach to
financing a long-range undertaking, ultimately meant Potomac Company investors had little to lose. If the project were successful, subscribers would hold valuable stock. In addition, those who owned land
along the river (and many did or soon bought it) could expect a dramatic rise in its value. If the project appeared to be failing, subscribers
need only stop making payments, and the company could do little except try to sell the delinquent shares or begin costly litigation to force
payment. Such speculative reasoning resulted in the pledging of more
than 400 Potomac Company shares—each costing over $400—before
the first meeting of the stockholders on 17 May 1785.[10]

Subscription books had been opened in six towns, three in Maryland
and three in Virginia. Most pledges came from residents of communities along the river, particularly the larger downstream towns, which
expected increased trade and real estate values. Table 1 demonstrates
the varying degrees of interest and faith in the project.[11]

Not surprisingly, nationalist merchants and planters near the two
Potomac River ports of Alexandria and Georgetown were willing to

[8] George Washington to Thomas Jefferson, 25 Feb. 1785, in *Writings of Washington* 28:77–81.
[9] *Alexandria Gazette*, 10 Feb. 1785. See also ibid., 25 Nov. 1784; and *Maryland Gazette*, 21 April 1785, for similar views.
[10] George Washington to Nathanael Greene, 20 May 1785, in *Writings of Washington* 28:144–46.
[11] Washington was greatly embarrassed by Virginia's gift to him of fifty Potomac Company shares (as well as one hundred shares in the James River Company—incorporated in that state as the political price for the Potomac Company legislation) because he did not want to be perceived as promoting legislation to benefit himself. For the better part of the next year, he wrote to many people asking for advice about how he might politely turn down the gift without insulting the state legislators. Ultimately, at Washington's request, the Virginia Assembly held the shares in trust for whatever project Washington thought might benefit the public. In the spirit of political compromise in which they were given, Washington eventually decided to donate the James River Company shares to Liberty Hall Academy, which later became Washington and Lee College (near Lexington, Virginia, appropriately on the upper James River). The Potomac Company shares were to have gone to a school in Washington, D.C., but it is unclear whether this transfer ever took place. Both the Potomac Company and the James River Company offered

TABLE 1

Local Support for the Potomac Company

STATE	CITY	SHARES SUBSCRIBED
Maryland	Annapolis	73[a]
	Georgetown	42
	Fredericktown	22
Virginia	Richmond	100[b]
	Winchester	31
	Alexandria	135
TOTAL		403

[a]Fifty for the state.
[b]Fifty for the state and fifty as a gift to Washington.

gamble the most on the river enterprise and subscribed to over a third of the shares. Residents of up-river towns (Winchester and Fredericktown, which according to Tobias Lear were among the largest inland towns in the United States) offered what support they could. Aside from state government pledges, towns not on the river (Richmond and Annapolis) saw little advantage from an improved Potomac. Pledges taken in those towns mostly represented each state's legislatively mandated stock commitment.[12]

With most subscriptions taken, George Washington, who had been chosen the first company president, and the directors toured the river and began the difficult task of hiring workers and a chief engineer. The

Washington their corporate presidencies. Washington accepted the former and, pleading distance from the James River project, declined the latter. For details, see Hening, *Statutes at Large* 11:525; George Washington to Benjamin Harrison, 22 Jan. 1785, in *Writings of Washington* 28:34–38; George Washington to Marquis de Lafayette, 25 Feb. 1785, in ibid., 71–76; George Washington to Governor Patrick Henry, 27 Feb. 1785, in ibid., 89–94; George Washington to Nathanael Greene, 20 May 1785, in ibid., 144–46; George Washington to the Secretary of War, 18 June 1785, in ibid., 166–69; George Washington to Edmund Randolph, 30 July 1785, in ibid., 214–16; George Washington to Edmund Randolph, 13 Aug. 1785, in ibid., 218–21; George Washington to Thomas Jefferson, 26 Sept. 1785, in ibid., 278–81; *Diaries of Washington* 4:158n; Douglas S. Freeman, *George Washington: A Biography,* 7 vols. (New York, 1948), 7:231, 275, 586.

12. Norman K. Risjord examined the occupations, party preferences, and political experience of those ninety-one stockholders who either attended the first company meeting or sent proxies. He found that this group was heavily dominated by planters and merchants. Of those who could be identified by party, all were Federalists, and a substantial number had served in state assemblies, Constitutional ratifying conventions, or city governments. See Risjord, *Chesapeake Politics, 1781–1800* (New York, 1978), 242–43. See also George Washington to Nathanael Greene, 20 May 1785, in *Writings of Washington* 28:144–46; Tobias Lear, *Observations on the River Potomack, the Country Adjacent, and the City of Washington* (New York, 1793; reprint ed., Baltimore, 1940), 15; Pickell, *New Chapter in the Early Life of Washington,* 66.

tour yielded a plan to build moving-water canals and locks around Little and Great falls and simple bypass canals without locks up-river at Seneca, Shenandoah (Payne's), and House's falls. Elsewhere the river would be cleared of obstructions and deepened. Because of the labor shortage, Washington and the directors were forced to employ a mixture of free, indentured, and slave laborers, although they would have preferred a work force composed entirely of free workers, who were believed to be more capable and reliable. To direct the laborers, James Rumsey, well known for his work with steam-propelled river boats, was hired as chief engineer.[13]

As work began, the company issued frequent subscription assessments, but the pay-as-you-go subscription process and the requirement that pledges be paid in specie quickly confronted the realities of the Maryland-Virginia agricultural economy in the 1780s. Drought and insect invasions plagued the area in 1785 and were followed by torrential rains in 1786, which ruined crops and the regional economy. Such natural disasters were made worse by a general American malaise fostered by large war debts and the surplus of commercial credit. As a result, by the end of 1786 less than half of the assessment calls had been met. Even the state of Maryland, with tax revenues dwindling, felt the squeeze and defaulted on payments on its fifty shares.[14]

[13] The Potomac Company faced substantial problems in obtaining both laborers and the technical knowledge necessary to pursue the project. These problems aggravated the company's already severe handicaps. Since this paper focuses on financing, problems in engineering and labor are beyond its scope, but for general background, see Ella May Turner, *James Rumsey: Pioneer in Steam Navigation* (Scottsdale, Pa., 1930); Thomas F. Hahn, *George Washington's Canal at Great Falls, Virginia* (Shepardstown, W. Va., 1976); Bacon-Foster, *Early Chapters in the Development of the Potomac*; Pickell, *New Chapter in the Early Life of Washington*; Sanderlin, *Great National Project*; and Ward, *Early Development of the Chesapeake and Ohio Canal Project*.

[14] George Washington to Thomas Jefferson, 31 Aug. 1788, in *Writings of Washington* 30:80; James Madison to Thomas Jefferson, 20 Aug. 1785, in *Papers of Jefferson* 8:413–17; James Madison to Thomas Jefferson, 12 Aug. 1786, in ibid., 10:229–36; George Washington to Thomas Jefferson 13 Feb. 1789, in ibid., 14:546–49; Pickell, *New Chapter in the Early Life of Washington*, 87. Flooding was a constant problem even after the company was able to clear part of the river. High water either forced work to halt, destroyed what had been accomplished, or compelled the company to use temporary measures, such as wood planks to hold back water, to keep stretches of the river open. See 7 Aug. 1786, 4 Aug. 1788, and 4 Aug. 1794, in Proceedings of the General Meetings of the Potowmack [sic] Company, 1785–96, item 159, Records of the National Park Service, Record Group 79, National Archives, Washington, D.C., hereafter cited as Proceedings of the General Meetings, followed by the appropriate date. The records of the general meetings of the shareholders were kept in a separate journal between 1785 and 1796; thereafter the minutes were recorded in with those of the Proceedings of the Board of President and Directors of the Potowmack [sic] Company, 1785–1807, item 160, Records of the National Park Service, Record Group 79, National Archives. Minutes of the general meetings after 1796 will be cited as Proceedings of the Board, 1785–1807—General Meeting, followed by the date of the meeting. Other items of regular company business were also recorded in this same journal and shall be similarly identified. President and directors meetings shall be cited as Proceedings of the Board—Meeting of the President and Directors, again followed by the date of the meeting. Two additional journals carry company business from 1808 to 1822 and from 1822 to 1828 respectively, and those dates shall be used with the above citations when appropriate.

The company's recourse against defaulters, according to its charter, was to sell their shares. Nonetheless, a 1787 effort to auction fifty-four of the most delinquent shares was a waste of time. No one appeared to bid, despite newspaper advertising. The company then sought, and the Maryland and Virginia legislatures obligingly passed, laws to sue those who missed payments. Lawsuits, however, could not enforce solvency; defaults on subscriptions continued unabated for several more years.[15]

THE IMPACT OF LAND SPECULATION

The Potomac Company's ability to collect assessments was thwarted in the late 1780s by economic problems stemming from the end of the Revolution, the adoption of the Articles of Confederation, and natural disasters. Yet even when the American economy revived in the 1790s after the ratification of the Constitution and the outbreak of European wars slowed foreign competition, the speculative nature of the enterprise itself continued to undermine fund raising. Many Potomac Company investors, who had earlier bought land along the river, now discovered that they no longer could meet pledges because their resources were tied up in real estate. The typical case of Virginia governor Henry "Light-Horse Harry" Lee reveals a serious weakness in the company's pledge-now, pay-later financing method.

Only a few years after the Potomac Company had been chartered and before his election as governor, Lee had noted the real estate and industrial potential of the Great Falls area on the Potomac. Acting before rival land speculators (one of whom was Potomac Company director and former Maryland governor Thomas Johnson), Lee bought five hundred acres at Great Falls, intending to develop the land into a storage depot for goods in transit and a milling and manufacturing center. An improved Potomac, he reasoned, would make such a center extremely valuable. Perhaps also motivated by a desire to have the projected new national capital located on or near his property and by the incorporation of Georgetown in 1789, Lee petitioned the Virginia leg-

---

[15] See Proceedings of the Board, 1785–1807—Meeting of the President and Directors, 1 and 2 March 1786, 3 April, 25 May 1787; Proceedings of the General Meetings, 7 Aug. 1786. See also William P. Palmer and Sherwin McRae, eds., *Calendar of Virginia State Papers and Other Manuscripts*, 11 vols. (Richmond, 1875–93), 5:84; *Acts of the States of Virginia, Maryland and Pennsylvania, and the Congress of the United States in Relation to the Chesapeake and Ohio Canal Company with the Proceedings of the Convention which led to the Formation of Said Company. Also the Acts and Resolutions of the States of Virginia and Maryland Concerning the Potomac Company to which are Appended the By-Laws, Lists of Officers, etc., of the Chesapeake and Ohio Canal Company with a Copious Index* (Washington, D.C., 1828), 103, 130–31, hereafter cited as *Acts of the States*.

islature and was rewarded in 1790 with an act creating at Great Falls the town of Matildaville, named after his wife. Together with Virginia congressman and future president James Madison, Lee organized a company to sell lots in the new town and to build warehouses for produce, which, according to Potomac Company charter goals, soon would be coming down the improved river.[16]

The Potomac Company, however, was not about to concede such a valuable piece of real estate as Great Falls; it was concerned that Lee's town lots might interfere with proposed canals. Moreover, the company wanted the site for its corporate headquarters. When negotiations to purchase the property from Lee proved fruitless, the company used its charter powers to condemn his land. This placed Lee in a difficult financial situation. Because his land was now tied up in condemnation proceedings, he could not sell or develop it. Yet without income from the anticipated land sales or the ability to use the land profitably, Lee was unable (or perhaps unwilling) to make payments on his Potomac Company subscriptions. When the condemnation proceedings yielded a price considerably lower than what Lee expected to earn from his completed town, he fought the decision.

The issue of Lee's land dragged on for some time. In 1792, shortly after he had been elected governor of Virginia, future Supreme Court Chief Justice John Marshall—then a prominent lawyer and member of the Virginia House of Delegates—offered an informal opinion that the company had overstepped its bounds by condemning land not to be used exclusively for its canals. It was not until 1793, however, that Lee and the company agreed on the value of the land and closed the condemnation proceedings.[17] In the meantime the company had begun a legal action of its own against Lee for default on his Potomac Company shares and was unwilling to pay Lee for his property until this case was resolved. Finally, in 1795 a jury ordered that the Potomac Company collect from Lee the amount due on his shares less the value of the land, but even by 1796 Lee was still unable (or still unwilling) to pay.[18]

---

[16] Lee also had obtained rights to cut timber on adjacent land, and he had purchased other valuable property in the area from John Semple, a colonial proponent of the river project. See George Washington to Thomas Jefferson, 13 Feb. 1789, in *Papers of Jefferson* 14:546–49; Henry Lee to Thomas Jefferson 6 March 1789, in ibid., 619–21; George Washington to James Madison, 17 Nov. 1788, in *Writings of Washington* 30:128–31; George Washington to Thomas Jefferson, 13 Feb. 1789, in ibid., 198–202; James Madison to Henry Lee, Jan. 1789, in *The Writings of James Madison Comprising his Private Correspondence, including Numerous Letters, and Documents Now for the First Time Printed*, ed. Gaillard Hunt, 9 vols. (New York, 1900–10), 5:321–24; Hening, *Statutes at Large* 13:170–73.

[17] Proceedings of the Board, 1785–1807, undated but preceding 28 Nov. 1793; John Marshall, "Opinion," 31 Jan. 1792, in *The Papers of John Marshall*, ed. Herbert A. Johnson and Charles T. Cullen, 3 vols. (Chapel Hill, N.C., 1974–79), 2:107–8; Bacon-Foster, *Early Chapters in the Development of the Potomac*, 87.

[18] Proceedings of the General Meetings, 3 Aug. 1795, 1 Aug. 1796.

RICHARD HENRY "LIGHT-HORSE HARRY" LEE

A governor of Virginia, Lee typified many prominent Virginians and Marylanders who overextended themselves in speculative schemes involving the Potomac River. The owner of 500 acres at Great Falls, Lee hoped to develop the land into a town named Matildaville, after his wife. The Potomac Company opposed his plans because they interfered with the company's projected canals and locks and because the company wanted the site for its corporate headquarters. (Photograph courtesy of the Great Falls National Park, Great Falls, Virginia.)

The mere fact that Lee would owe the company money *after* the value of his land was deducted demonstrates the degree to which land speculators overextended themselves in Potomac Company subscriptions.

Lee's case was by no means an isolated example of the Potomac Company's legal problems. Other proceedings involving land or water rights kept lawyers bustling in and out of court until the company formally surrendered its charter to the Chesapeake and Ohio Canal Company in 1828. These battles tied up the company's time and ate into its limited resources. Moreover, the publicity accompanying these cases lessened support from those most likely to provide it—other wealthy investors—and contributed to a general lack of faith in the company's endeavors. The decline in public confidence rapidly grew to crisis proportions, worsening the company's already dismal economic position. By 1795 the company president and the directors unhappily reported to the shareholders that "to procure the necessary funds for prosecuting the business with spirit has ever been the most difficult part of . . . [our] duties."[19]

STATE AID

The economic heritage of the 1780s, legal battles, and the continual need to repair damages from spring floods prompted the company to try selling one hundred new shares to raise funds. Enticing wary investors to subscribe was not easy. Nonetheless, with already heavy stakes in the company, the states of Maryland and Virginia pledged over half the new issue. Forty shares were taken by Maryland, twenty by Virginia, and the remainder by individuals. This influx of capital, however, was not enough to offset escalating expenses caused by a lack of good technical advice, poor planning, labor problems, and frequent repair work.[20]

Even the additional stock sale proved inadequate to keep the river project moving rapidly forward. Work slowed to a crawl by 1797, with only some of the upper river cleared and with temporary wooden locks at Little Falls. The company again was forced to turn its attention to fund raising. At first the president and directors considered mortgaging future tolls. Lacking the legal authority to do so, they decided instead to borrow company stock that had been paid in full and mortgage it. The company soon learned, however, that since the success of the project was in such doubt, the stock was not sufficiently secure as collateral for the loans sought. The president and directors next asked Maryland and Virginia to guarantee loans that would be obtained in Europe, but both states refused. Similarly, neither state was willing to lend the company cash (although Maryland did offer its stock to be mortgaged). Eventually, all that could be borrowed was a mere $6,000, less than half the estimated need of $16,000. Even this amount was

---

[19] Proceedings of the General Meetings, 3 Aug. 1795.
[20] This stock was issued at 130 pounds sterling per share. Ibid.; Proceedings of the General Meetings, 1 Aug. 1796; Tobias Lear to Thomas Jefferson, 13 March 1796, George Washington Papers, Minnesota Historical Society. Such state aid to the Potomac Company frequently had a political price. In both Maryland and Virginia sectionalism prevented financial aid to the Potomac Company unless other river and canal projects were also supported. See Douglas R. Littlefield, "Maryland Sectionalism and the Development of the Potomac Route to the West, 1768–1826," *Maryland Historian* 14 (1983): 31–52; Leonard J. Sneddon, "Maryland and Sectional Politics: Canal Building in the Federalist Era," ibid. 6 (1975): 79–84; Risjord, *Chesapeake Politics*, 478–82; and, more generally, Charles H. Ambler, *Sectionalism in Virginia, 1776–1861* (Glendale, Calif., 1910).

raised only because George Washington and Daniel Carroll, both Potomac Company stockholders, loaned the company their own United States stock to be used as collateral. By 1799 all work ceased while the president and directors made a desperate plea for a "voluntary" payment of $100 per share. When this appeal went unheeded, company supporters, primarily in the Maryland legislature, negotiated a political compromise to secure the necessary funds.[21]

The aid that saved the Potomac Company took two forms. First, both Maryland and Virginia, recognizing the company's dire condition, allowed it to collect tolls on the river provided that goods were hauled around the unopened sections of the river. Second, and more substantially, after a protracted battle in the state legislature, Maryland subscribed to all 130 shares of a third stock issue. Maryland's generous stock pledge was the result of a sectional political trade-off that benefited not only the Potomac Company but also the northern Maryland Susquehanna Canal Company. It was this money that allowed the Potomac Company to complete work at Great Falls and to open the locks to traffic in February 1802. Maryland's investment in the Potomac Company now stood at 220 shares, and Virginia held 120 (50 of these, however, were held in trust for the estate of George Washington, who had died in 1799).[22]

Having nearly exhausted the good will of state legislators and private supporters, the Potomac Company now hoped that tolls would provide financial salvation.[23] These high hopes were not shared by all along the river, however. The previously supportive *Alexandria Gazette*, per-

[21] The extent to which rising costs played a role in the company's distress can be seen by the fact that in 1799 the Potomac Company directors claimed that all the shares from the first two stock issues had been paid in full "except some inconsiderable balances owing by insolvent characters." See Potomac Company Broadside, 2 July 1799, "Entrusted as We Are with the Interests of the Potomack [sic] Company" (microprint reproduction, Worcester, Mass., 1963). See also Proceedings of the General Meetings, 4 Aug. 1794; Proceedings of the Board, 1785–1807—General Meeting, 7 Aug. 1797, 4 Feb. 1798, 6 Aug. 1798, and 5 Aug. 1799; Mary Jane Dowd, "The State in the Maryland Economy, 1776–1807," *Maryland Historical Magazine* 57 (1962): 123; Bacon-Foster, *Early Chapters in the Development of the Potomac*, 95–97. United States stock was the equivalent of present-day government bonds. The stock had been created in 1790 in accordance with Alexander Hamilton's plan to fund the public debt. See Donald F. Swanson, *The Origins of Hamilton's Fiscal Policies* (Gainesville, Fla., 1963), esp. 34–55.

[22] This third Potomac Company stock issue, like the second, was valued at 130 pounds sterling per share. The Susquehanna Canal Company received a $30,000 loan from the state in exchange for the Potomac Company's aid. See *Votes and Proceedings of the Maryland House of Delegates*, in *Records of the States of the United States* (microfilm, Washington, D.C., 1949), 4 Dec. 1799; Proceedings of the Board, 1785–1807—General Meeting, 4 Feb. 1798, 5 Aug. 1799, 2 Aug. 1802; Sanderlin, *Great National Project*, 35–37.

[23] Even before the river was open some stockholders thought that enough had been accomplished to warrant collecting some tolls. In 1796 the stockholders voted to collect tolls since most of the work on the river had been completed except for the locks at Great Falls. The president and directors suspended this decision until they could ascertain if the work met charter requirements. They apparently decided that it did not, since it took a special legislative act in 1799 to allow tolls to be collected despite the fact that Great Falls still had not been opened. See Proceedings of the General Meetings, 1 Aug. 1796; *Acts of the States*, appendix.

haps dismayed by seventeen years of waiting for the project to be completed, cynically marked the opening only with an official notice of toll rates and the admonition that those who might try to cheat the company would be prosecuted to the fullest extent of the law.[24]

The *Gazette*'s cynicism was prophetic. Within seven months of the opening, the president and directors reported to the stockholders that "it was generally expected that [when the locks at Great Falls were completed] the stock of the company would immediately become productive to the holders and we had no doubt of being able to lay before you at . . . [the annual meeting of stockholders] such a state of the tolls as would afford a handsome dividend." Unfortunately, the directors added, despite the extremely successful harvest and large quantities of produce waiting to be sent down the river, the near total lack of snow in the Appalachian Mountains during the winter of 1801–2 and the light spring rains had left the river too low to be navigable except "at short intervals after some of these partial rains." The president and directors thought, perhaps for only psychological reasons, that some dividend was in order, and they recommended a 3 percent payment on each stockholder's capital investment. This was the only dividend ever paid, and most of the money did not come from tolls collected on the river—over half came from Washington's and Carroll's U.S. stock still held by the company.[25]

COMPANY POLICY CHANGES

The weather and international markets clearly were playing a greater role in the company's financial well-being than had been originally expected. Added to these uncertainties were other unanticipated problems arising from land speculation by shareholders. A late realization of these factors may have been partly responsible for two major policy changes in 1802. The first was a decision to abandon the earlier goal of connecting the Potomac with the Ohio Valley and to focus instead on improving the more heavily settled Potomac River area and its tributaries, such as the Shenandoah, the Monocacy, and the Antietam. This decision seemed practical at the time. Jay's Treaty in 1794 and Pinckney's Treaty in 1795 had eliminated many pressing strategic reasons for reaching the West, and the growth of the Potomac wa-

[24] *Alexandria Gazette*, 6 Feb. 1802.
[25] The company received $3,647.96 in tolls and $4,073.77 in income from the U.S. stock in 1802. Proceedings of the Board, 1785–1807—General Meeting, 2 Aug. 1802; Freeman W. Galpin, "Grain Trade of Alexandria, Virginia, 1801–1815," *North Carolina Historical Society Review* 4 (1927): 404–27, esp. 410–12.

tershed offered a known market to exploit. This local market was an attractive alternative to the more distant and largely unknown Ohio Valley trade.

Variability in precipitation led to the second company decision, to discourage water-using industry in the Potomac Valley. The company adopted this policy even though industry would broaden the regional economy, lessening the reliance on agriculture, which was so vulnerable to the weather and foreign events. These policy changes brought a shift in attitude among stockholders, who now preferred to use tolls and additional borrowed money for Potomac watershed expansion rather than receive more dividends and/or raise funds through further capitalization. Accordingly, the dividend voted in 1802 was suspended in 1803 in favor of expansion and improved maintenance, and was never reinstituted.[26]

Despite the new policies, weather continued to complicate problems involving foreign markets. Unfavorable American harvests in 1804–6 combined with extremely good yields in England to cut into the profitability of bringing crops down-river to export. The harvest of 1806 in Virginia was particularly poor because of drought, and Napoleon's Berlin Decree in November 1806 brought the American market to a complete standstill. Yet the following year was more favorable. Napoleon's inability to enforce his decree and a large, successful 1807 harvest teased river project supporters with the hope that a turning point had finally been reached. The company's annual report noted that tolls collected had climbed to the highest levels ever.[27] At the 1807 annual shareholders' meeting, the Potomac Company president and directors optimistically projected that "it is not apprehended that the tolls will at any time hereafter be less than at present; it is confidently believed they will annually increase."[28]

While there was finally some good news for Potomac Company investors, the directors had to recognize that the company was on the brink of disaster. The same year that they seemed so confident to shareholders, the directors answered a questionnaire sent by Secretary

---

[26] Proceedings of the Board, 1785–1807—General Meeting, 2 Aug. 1802, 1 Aug. 1803; Proceedings of the Board, 1808–22—General Meeting, 29 Nov. 1816; Proceedings of the Board, 1808–1822—Report to the Secretary of the Treasury, 20 Jan. 1808.

[27] In 1807 the company collected $15,080 in tolls. Proceedings of the Board, 1785–1807—General Meeting, 3 Aug. 1807; Commissioners of Maryland and Virginia Appointed to Survey the Potomac River, *Letter from the Governor and Council of Maryland Transmitting a Report of the Commissioners Appointed to Survey the River Potomac* (Washington, D.C., 1823), appendix B, hereafter cited as *Commission Report of 1822*. This report is also printed in Senate, *Letter from the Governor and Council of Maryland Transmitting a Report of the Commissioners Appointed to Survey the River Potomac*, 17th Cong., 2d sess., 1823, S. Rept. 23. See also Galpin, "Grain Trade of Alexandria," 412–18.

[28] Proceedings of the Board, 1785–1807—General Meeting, 3 Aug. 1807.

THE GREAT SEAL OF THE POTOMAC COMPANY

Chartered in 1784–85, the Potomac Company planned to improve the Potomac River as a transportation route to the West. The company seal was designed the year after the river was officially declared open, but a multitude of problems caused the company to collapse by the 1820s. (Photograph courtesy of the Great Falls National Park, Great Falls, Virginia.)

of the Treasury Albert Gallatin in preparation for his report to Congress on internal improvements. The directors' replies to Gallatin were not nearly as cheery as their presentation to shareholders had been. Even though the river was technically open, the directors indicated that the Potomac Company was seriously foundering. As of 1 August 1807, the company had spent $444,648.80—over twice the charter estimate of the project's total cost. Most of this expenditure had financed work on the Potomac River itself; work on the tributaries was just beginning. Moreover, the company was $66,814.90 in debt, with only $7,146.47 on hand. The directors estimated that the completed project would require annual maintenance expenditures of over $5,000, which was more money than the company had earned in tolls in most previous years. But most damning of all was their estimate that the company would require an additional $100,000 to complete even its revised plan to open just the Potomac watershed.[29]

The report to Gallatin left no doubt that the company could not withstand many more unpredictable events. But circumstances beyond the company's control once again chipped away at the Potomac watershed's economy and hence the company's financial security. Jefferson's embargo created an extreme financial stringency and a scarcity of hard money in most parts of the United States by early 1808. Surpluses from the large 1807 Maryland-Virginia harvest, which had been such a boost to both the morale and finances of the Potomac Company, forced agricultural prices down and hampered domestic trade. By August 1808 the number of boats on the river had dropped considerably, and tolls were well below the peak of 1807. The company sank deeper in debt than it ever had been. It increasingly needed funds not only for maintenance and a continuation of its work, but also merely to repay creditors.[30]

THE LOTTERY PLAN TO RAISE FUNDS

With investors defaulting and creditors unwilling to lend more, the desperate company decided to sponsor a lottery to raise funds. In the spring of 1809, the company petitioned Congress to grant $100,000 to finish work on the Potomac watershed or alternatively to authorize a lottery to raise the same amount. Congress, which was already embroiled in debate over the constitutionality of federal aid to internal improvements, failed to act on either request. The company then turned to the state of Maryland to approve the lottery, adding that "unless money can be procured in some way or other, the progress of the unfinished work in which the company has been so long engaged and has expended so much money must stop."[31] Since this was not a request for more money, in 1810 the Maryland legislature authorized a series of lotteries to raise up to $300,000.[32]

By 1811 boat traffic on the river had grown heavier because of an increase in the number of settlers and an improved foreign market. The Potomac Valley had been hit by a serious drought and insect in-

[29] Proceedings of the Board, 1808–22—Report to the Secretary of the Treasury, 20 Jan. 1808. See also Gallatin, "Report on Roads and Canals."
[30] Proceedings of the Board, 1785–1807—General Meeting, 3 Aug. 1807; Commission Report of 1822, appendix B; Galpin, "Grain Trade of Alexandria," 414–18.
[31] Proceedings of the Board, 1808–22—General Meeting, 4 May 1809, 7 Aug. 1809.
[32] Proceedings of the Board, 1808–22—General Meeting, 10 April 1810, 5 Aug. 1810; Proceedings of the Board, 1808–22—Meeting of the President and Directors, 10 April 1810.

vasion the previous year, however. With little money to spare, few area residents could afford the considerable price of ten dollars for a lottery ticket. As a result, drawings for the first lottery began "with a large proportion of the tickets remaining on hand unsold." Nonetheless, the company hoped that a few winners of large prizes would encourage sales for the second lottery. But many of the winning tickets had not been sold, and large prizes went unawarded. Ticket sales dropped even more. Credit was authorized to promote wholesale ticket marketing for the second lottery, but as war with England broke out and foreign trade was ruptured, the company decided to accept even personal notes to encourage individual ticket sales. Significantly, payment for all tickets bought on credit was not due until thirty days *after* a particular drawing.[33]

The credit provision was the downfall of the entire lottery scheme. The Potomac Company had accepted the risk that it probably would have some difficulty collecting payment from individuals whose tickets had not won.[34] But the company had not anticipated problems from the wholesale credit provisions for buyers of at least one hundred tickets, especially since this arrangement was aimed at encouraging retail sales by large purchasers. Yet with the War of 1812 raging, wholesalers could not sell the tickets any more easily than the company, and some began to search their unsold ticket supplies for winning numbers. One such wholesaler was Robert Gray, who discovered in 1813 that one of his unsold tickets had won the $20,000 grand prize. He immediately demanded that he be awarded the prize. The Potomac Company refused to pay on the ground that Gray had not yet paid for the 1,200 tickets he had received, and therefore they were still company property. With little to lose and much to gain, Gray sued in U.S. District Court in Alexandria (which, at the time, was part of the District of Columbia). The company was forced to suspend the lottery during the court proceedings, which was probably just as well since it was unlikely to bring in much money in wartime.[35]

The Potomac Company lost in District Court, but in 1816 it was able to arrive at an out-of-court settlement before its appeal reached the Supreme Court. In the settlement, Gray agreed to pay for his 1,200 tickets; until he could raise the necessary $12,000, he would hand over his winning ticket to the Potomac Company as security. Once Gray

[33] Proceedings of the Board, 1806–22—Meeting of the President and Directors, 10 April 1810; Proceedings of the Board, 1806–22—General Meeting, 5 Aug. 1811, 3 Aug. 1812.
[34] Proceedings of the Board, 1806–22—General Meeting, 3 Aug. 1812.
[35] Proceedings of the Board, 1806–22—General Meeting, 2 Aug. 1813; 7 Aug. 1816.

had paid for all his tickets, the Potomac Company would award him the $20,000 prize.[36]

But Gray wanted more than just the $8,000 difference between what he owed the company and what they owed him. He also wanted to be able to sell his remaining lottery tickets—a prospect that was now exceedingly plausible since, by the time the settlement was reached, the War of 1812 had ended and the regional economy had improved. To get the Potomac Company to reinstitute the lottery, Gray offered to buy the tickets in another disputed ticket case, but only on the condition that the company resume drawings. Faced with more costly and embarrassing litigation if it did not accept his offer, the company reluctantly agreed, thus ensuring that Gray would be able to sell most of his remaining tickets and still collect the grand prize. This disastrous episode in the company's history mercifully came to a close in 1817, when the second lottery was completed. The Potomac Company had anticipated earning over $100,000 in profit from the lottery series. But the actual results were nowhere near that figure. In the first lottery, the company earned $15,134.41; in the second, it lost $14,648.38. The company never held the planned third lottery. The net gain after six frustrating years was a paltry $486.03 (before deducting attorneys' fees) and considerable embarrassment.[37]

As the lottery affair ran its course, the company still had financial obligations to meet. In November 1812, the Maryland legislature had voted to lend the Potomac Company $30,000 in U.S. stock until the lottery brought in additional money. In a less than patriotic gesture, the company refused to accept the offer, since the directors feared that the War of 1812 would mean a rapid depreciation in the stock. By 1814, however, desperate to offset lost revenue from the stalled lottery, the company reversed itself and accepted the loan. The fact that the U.S. stock had not depreciated as much as had been expected also played a role in this decision. Thus, by the end of the war, the states of Maryland and Virginia together had provided funding to the Potomac Company totaling approximately $250,000. Maryland legislators, some of whom were also Potomac Company investors and/or land speculators, apparently thought it better to bail out the company at least one more time than to throw away money (both state and personal) already invested. They realized that the war had cut into company tolls, and this

[36] Gray never signed the Potomac Company copy of this agreement, but his acceptance of the settlement is noted in the company records. See Proceedings of the Board, 1808-22—Agreement with Robert Gray, undated.
[37] Proceedings of the Board, 1808-22—Meeting of the President and Directors, 3 Dec. 1816.

helped explain the poor maintenance of the "opened" river; at the same time they became increasingly skeptical of the company's claim that it would completely clear the tributaries.[38]

Potomac watershed residents and legislators began to suspect that even the limited post-1802 goals were more than the company could accomplish. In 1813, prompted by angry constituents along the uncleared Shenandoah River, the Virginia legislature revoked the company's authority to clear that Potomac tributary. A new organization was formed to take over the project, although the Potomac Company was reimbursed for work it had already done.[39] Labor on the Antietam ceased in 1815 when subscribers refused to advance more funds because of the "apprehension and belief (sanctioned by public opinion) that the . . . [estimated cost] of the work was too low."[40] Even Alexandria residents, who had been among the most loyal company supporters, organized a new project to build a still-water canal from Seneca Falls to their town, thus bypassing the problem areas at Little and Great falls. Rightfully concluding that this would only hurt its efforts, the company used its extensive charter rights to block the project.[41]

END OF STATE SUPPORT

In spite of such setbacks, the Potomac Company operated fitfully until the national economy collapsed in 1819. Maryland now demanded that the company begin payments on the long overdue $30,000 U.S. stock loan of 1814 or else pay dividends on the state's 220 shares. The Potomac Company, with nowhere else to go, turned to

---

[38] Proceedings of the Board, 1808–22—General Meeting, 23 Feb. 1813; 1,2 Aug. 1814; Dowd, "The State in the Maryland Economy," 123. There was one unusual attempt to gain federal aid in this period. In 1811 Gouverneur Morris and De Witt Clinton were sent by New York State's Canal Commission to appeal for federal support for the proposed Erie Canal to the Great Lakes. In an attempt to get the widest possible support in Congress, they drafted an omnibus bill to set aside all land in Michigan Territory north of the fortieth parallel and give it, for the purposes of various internal improvements, to twelve states and the Potomac Company. Albert Gallatin, in early 1812, recommended against this proposal because of the nation's financial situation, and the House committee appointed to consider the bill found it "inexpedient for the Congress of the United States to make a donation in land or money" because of the poor state of foreign affairs. This determination was subsequently reinforced by the outbreak of war with England. See Goodrich, *Government Promotion of American Canals and Railroads*, 36–37.

[39] *Acts of the States*, 108–12, 151–54; Proceedings of the Board, 1808–1822—General Meeting, 13 Nov. 1813, 7 Aug. 1815.

[40] Parentheses in the original. Proceedings of the Board, 1808–22—Meeting of the President and Directors, 3 Oct. 1815:

[41] *Alexandria Gazette*, 8 Nov. 1816; Proceedings of the Board, 1808–22—General Meeting, 29 Nov. 1816; U.S. Cong., House, *Report of the Committee of the District of Columbia, to whom were Referred Sundry Memorials from the Inhabitants of Pennsylvania, Maryland, and Virginia, Praying the Aid of the Federal Government towards the Improvement of the Navigation of the River Potomac*, 17th Cong., 1st sess., 1822, H. Rept. 111, 22; Sanderlin, *Great National Project*, 42–44.

Virginia for aid.[42] Unwilling to commit more money blindly to the Potomac Company, the Virginia Assembly directed the chief engineer of its newly created board of public works, Thomas Moore, to provide advice.

Moore's preliminary report, issued in 1821, concluded that a continuous still-water canal from tidewater to the Cumberland coal fields, at a cost of $1,114,300, would be more likely to succeed than the current Potomac effort. Such a canal, he reasoned, would be less susceptible to variations in weather, which had first flooded Potomac Company works and then left them high and dry. In response to Moore's report, Virginia and Maryland appointed commissioners to examine the state of navigation on the river and to determine if the Potomac Company should receive any more aid. The company directors, still hoping for the best, thought that more aid might enable them to liquidate the large debts "in a satisfactory manner."[43]

The Virginia and Maryland commissioners found that the Potomac Company was hopelessly broke. It had spent $729,387.29 over thirty-seven years and had debts totaling $175,886.59. Equally dismaying, the river was navigable only forty-five days of the year. Drought, floods, and ice made it otherwise impassable. The commissioners agreed with Moore's 1821 report that improved water transportation in the Potomac Valley would come only with a still-water canal. The Potomac Company, they concluded, could never fulfill its charter terms, and neither state should provide more aid.[44]

On the basis of the 1822 report, Virginia promptly withdrew its support from the Potomac Company and incorporated a new firm to begin the still-water canal, to be called the Potomac Canal Company to distinguish it from the older enterprise. Maryland, with much larger stakes in the old company, refused to support any new effort until assured that Potomac Company stockholders would be bought out at a fair price.[45] Maryland's concerns led Virginia to pass a revised bill in January 1824 allowing Potomac Company investors and creditors to exchange stock and bills of credit for shares in the new Chesapeake

[42] Proceedings of the Board, 1808–22—General Meeting, 2 Aug. 1819; Proceedings of the Board, 1808–22—Letter to the Maryland Senate and Assembly from President John Mason, 26 Jan. 1820.
[43] House, Report of the Committee of the District of Columbia, 19–27; Acts of the States, 116, 142; Commission Report of 1822, 5; Proceedings of the Board, 1808–22—General Meeting, 5 Aug. 1822; Ward, Early Development of the Chesapeake and Ohio Canal Project, 16–17, 39–41.
[44] Commission Report of 1822; Ward, Early Development of the Chesapeake and Ohio Canal, 45–46.
[45] Maryland's assent to the new project was further slowed by northern Chesapeake Assembly delegates, who were concerned about possible economic competition from Georgetown. See Littlefield, "Maryland Sectionalism," 43–47; Charles Elbert Fisher III, "Internal Improvement Issues in Maryland, 1816–1826" (Master's thesis, University of Maryland, 1972), 20–23; Sanderlin, Great National Project, 50–51; Ward, Early Development of the Chesapeake and Ohio Canal, 45–46.

and Ohio Canal Company. Satisfied it would not have to write off its investment in the Potomac Company, Maryland incorporated the Chesapeake and Ohio Canal Company in early 1825. Congress quickly approved the new company's charter, and Pennsylvania (through which part of the canal would run to the Ohio River) accepted it in 1826. Political struggles over estimated costs of the new canal project delayed government pledges until May 1828, although subscription books had been opened in 1827. With its financial and legislative support gone, the Potomac Company surrendered its charter in August 1828.[46]

CONCLUSION

Although the commissioners appointed in 1822 to examine the state of navigation on the Potomac River concluded that the Potomac Company had failed because of "a want of information" concerning river improvement technology "at the very early period of our existence as a nation, when the company was formed," in reality the reasons were more complex.[47] The national depression immediately after the end of the Revolution automatically gave the newly created Potomac Company a financial handicap. Additionally, the company could not immediately depend on heavy down-river traffic to provide tolls as work progressed because there was little inland settlement. Consequently, investors expected returns from land speculation or from increased produce after long-range settlement could occur. Unfortunately, the very nature of the company's original proposal to connect with the Ohio Valley encouraged land speculation, sometimes at the expense of investments in the company. This problem was compounded by the process of making payments on Potomac Company stock as work required. These factors made financing the project extremely vulnerable to changes in the economy due to weather and foreign events. When the economy soured, speculators scrambled to protect themselves, often at company expense. Government aid was unreliable and sporadic because of strife within states and the relative poverty of state governments. Thus, it is not surprising that in 1802 the Potomac Company abandoned its ambitious charter plan to connect with the Ohio Valley and focused instead on exploiting just the Potomac watershed.

[46] Potomac Company Legal Papers, item 164, Records of the National Park Service, Record Group 79, National Archives, Washington, D.C.; House, Chesapeake and Ohio Canal, 19th Cong., 1st sess., 1826, H. Rept. 228, 25–60; Bacon-Foster, Early Chapters in the Development of the Potomac Route, 149–51; Ward, Early Development of the Chesapeake and Ohio Canal, 59–65; Sanderlin, Great National Project 51–60.
[47] Commission Report of 1822, 7.

That market, however, was too limited (and was kept that way by anti-industrial Potomac Company policies) to provide the money the project ultimately required. Unable to overcome such massive barriers, the Potomac Company eventually was forced to yield to the Chesapeake and Ohio Canal Company—an organization with an allegedly more feasible plan and stronger government backing.

The Potomac Company may have failed to accomplish its charter goals, but its attempt was significant nonetheless. First, the company's efforts demonstrated the importance of participation by the federal government in interstate internal improvements—primarily by the absence of that participation. Had the federal government taken an active role in the Potomac Company, its financial difficulties might have been largely overcome. Moreover, the federal government might have helped coordinate and lead state support. This lesson was not lost on the organizers of the Chesapeake and Ohio Canal Company, who successfully lobbied Congress for major financial support.[48]

The Potomac Company is also important because of the scale of its enterprise. Unlike many other schemes projected or accomplished during this era, the Potomac Company's plan to connect with the Ohio Valley was truly national in scope. Where advocates of other projects were less ambitious, the Potomac Company boldly proposed to unite two major regions of the country. This interregional aspect of the company's plan expressed an early belief in the potential for expanding American commerce and transportation beyond local areas and coastal ports. Despite the Potomac Company's failure, the belief persisted and was endorsed by the company's successor as well as by a general trend toward other major internal improvements. Thus, the Potomac Company's legacy is that its ultimate vision succeeded where its specific plan did not.

---

[48] Congress not only funded the survey of the route for the Chesapeake and Ohio Canal, but it pledged $1 million to the new enterprise and allowed the three District of Columbia cities—Alexandria, Georgetown, and Washington—to pledge $1.5 million more. See Sanderlin, *Great National Project*, 56–57.

THE BALTIMORE RIOTS OF 1812 AND THE
BREAKDOWN OF THE ANGLO-AMERICAN MOB TRADITION

The nature of rioting — what rioters did — was undergoing a transformation in the half century after the American Revolution. A close examination of the extensive rioting in Baltimore during the summer of 1812 suggests what those changes were. Telescoped into a month and a half of rioting was a range of activity revealing the breakdown of the Anglo-American mob tradition.[1] This tradition allowed for a certain amount of limited popular disorder. The tumultuous crowd was viewed as a "quasi-legitimate" or "extra-institutional" part of the political system and was to be tolerated in certain situations as long as its action was circumscribed to an immediate goal with a minimum of violence to persons and property. The idea was predicated on the assumption that the normal process of government was imperfect and that it was occasionally necessary to resort to "politics out-of-doors" to meet the needs of the community. Just enough force was to be provided by the crowd to rectify an obvious injustice which official channels were incapable of handling.[2]

This Anglo-American mob tradition can be seen operating in the English bread riots E.P. Thompson describes; crowds acted to re-establish the "just price," set by custom and ancient law, and violated by profiteering grain merchants.[3] So too, colonial American mobs in the 1760's and 1770's moved to oppose British imperial measures in actions which were generally confined to limited attacks on symbols of that imperial authority, as in the Boston Tea Party. Occasionally a mob might get carried away in the passions of the moment, such as in the destruction of Governor Thomas Hutchinson's house in 1765, but even when it did, it rarely acted in a brutish manner against persons — rages were limited to attacks against property.[4]

Yet there always remained in each riot situation the potential for excessive disorder.[5] This created a tension between the elite, who would reluctantly condone rioting in only the most extreme circumstances, and the lower and middling ranks of society, who were far more willing to countenance collective violence.[6] That tension, which was evident in the attempt of American Whig leaders to bridle the pre-Revolutionary mob activity of the 1760's and 1770's, was resolved through informal means of social control. If the riot did not appear to threaten the prevailing social system unduly, then a kind of temporary license was granted to the mob. When the mob had finished with its attack on its immediate and proscribed object, or when its actions began seriously to challenge the social system, then it was time for the elite to pull in its reins and reassert its authority. No elaborate police powers were thought necessary for this. The Anglo-American mob tradition thrived in small scale pre-industrial communities where contacts between all levels of society were fluid and where social relations were marked by deference and personal recognition.

   Thus, informal mechanisms, combining the personal and public prestige of
local magistrates and members of the elite, were the mainstays of riot control.
Very often the magistrate would simply address the members of the mob, inform
them that they were acting in an overly tumultuous manner, and tell them it was
time to disperse. The riot acts of both England and America were merely a
legalization of this practice; the magistrate would read the act to the disorderly
crowd and then wait for a stipulated time, ordinarily an hour, allowing the mob
ample opportunity to disband.[8] The *posse comitatus* can also be viewed as a
regularization of these informal means of social control. Members of the *posse*
were temporary deputies of the magistrate recruited from the community at large.
Theoretically anyone and everyone could be sworn in as part of the *posse*. More
often than not, however, the *posse* was recruited from men the magistrate knew
would support him and these were usually men of prominence and standing in the
local community whose real value lay in their further bolstering the moral weight
of the magistrate. The militia, too, might be called upon to help supress a riot. But
the militia, which tended to include all able-bodied men in a community, was
likely to be overly sympathetic with the mob and could hardly be expected to turn
out and protect an unpopular cause. More importantly, in both England and
America there was a deeply ingrained fear of the military, inhibiting the use of
both the militia and the regular army, as well as limiting the size and power of the
ordinary police forces of constables and night watch.[9]
   Of course, implicit in every one of the magistrate's possible avenues of action,
be he asserting his authority alone, reading the riot act, with a *posse comitatus*, or
with a detachment of the military at his side, there was always the threat of
coercion. But few magistrates really wanted to be taken up on that threat. They did
not want to be responsible for spilling the blood of men they knew all their lives
and with whom they must continue to deal with long after the riot was over and
whatever force that was mustered had been dismissed.[10] In fact, many magistrates
knew that any force, and especially the army, put an extra burden on local
resources and hurt everyone in the community.[11] Moreover, as E.P. Thompson
has reminded us, "the credibility of the gentry and magistracy" had to be
maintained and this was most effectively done through the "reassertion of
paternalist authority" rather than the use of troops or force.[12] Therefore, the
preferred means of riot control was to "talk the mob down" after the
community's needs had been served by "politics out-of-doors."

   The Baltimore riots of 1812 began in the spirit of this deep-seated tradition.[13]
The vast majority of Baltimore's citizens were Republicans and the publication in
their city of the Federalist partisan news sheet, the *Federal-Republican*, was a
constant irritant to their Jeffersonian sympathies. Threats had long been mouthed
by the Republican papers warning the *Federal-Republican* that its persistent attacks
on Madison's administration and on local Republicans were bound to rouse the
wrath of the citizenry.[14] With the declaration of war against Great Britain in June
1812 the *Federal-Republican* only became more vehement in its assertions. On the
night of June 22 the people of Baltimore acted, as a group of thirty or forty men
dismantled the Gay Street printing office of the *Federal-Republican*. One
Republican paper reported, "Last night between 9 and 10 o'clock, a party of men
and boys began, with great sang froid to demolish the printing office of the Federal
Republican . . . and perservered till they accomplished their purpose. The
business went on as regularly as if they contracted to perform the job for pay."[15]
Demolishing or "pulling down" buildings was a widespread practice of both

English and American mobs in the eighteenth century, while the destruction of the printing press was an activity reminiscent of several American Revolutionary mobs. Obviously this was not a raging, overly destructive mob; rather it was orderly, workmanlike and restricted in its goal.

Little effort was made by the Republican city officials to stop the mob that night. Mayor Edward Johnson, a staunch Republican brewer, made a half-hearted appearance at the scene of the riot.[16] His entreaties to halt the rioting, however, were respectfully declined as one ringleader told the mayor, "Mr. Johnson, I know you very well, no body wants to hurt you; but the laws of the land must sleep, and the laws of nature and reason prevail; that house is the temple of Infamy, it is supported with English gold, and it must and shall come down to the ground!"[17] This one statement sums up the very essence of the Anglo-American mob tradition. First, the rioter knew Johnson personally. Both men were members of the larger Republican community. Political office in Baltimore was still mainly the province of the elite. Edward Johnson was a member of that elite whose base of political power was his close connection with the mechanics and laborers of "Old Town," where he lived and worked, and Fell's Point. On election day the Republican leadership expected Johnson to deliver the workingman's vote.[18] Thus it is not surprising that the rioter knew Johnson and treated him with deference and respect. Secondly, and more importantly, was the declaration that the "laws of the land must sleep, and the laws of nature and reason prevail." This short phrase epitomizes the theoretical justification of the Anglo-American mob tradition. The underlying assumption was that there was a gap between the "laws of the land" and the "laws of nature and reason." It was the people's right, no, it was the people's duty, to assert themselves in unison to bridge that gap even in the most reasoned of governments. Finally, there was the identification of the *Federal-Republican* with the national enemy, for war had been declared, and the implication was that the destruction of the "temple of Infamy" was a patriotic duty.

No doubt Mayor Johnson found it difficult to argue with this statement and was probably not too disturbed by the banishment of this maligning tool of his political opponents. In any case, he did not press the point and, as might be expected in good Anglo-American mob tradition, he retreated for the time being, allowing the people their moment of riot.

The tumult lasted until the early hours of the morning as the mob scoured the streets in pursuit of one of the Federalist editors, Jacob Wagner, who had wisely left town. Wagner's own house and the house of his father-in-law, where his family was staying, were both searched by select members of the mob. In doing this no violence was offered to anyone nor was any private property threatened. Had Wagner been captured he would probably have received some rough treatment, for it had been rumored during the day that he was to be clothed with a terrapin shell and a sheepskin with a pair of horns, but it is unlikely, considering the overall self-control the mob exercised, that they would carry out their threat of putting a bullet through his heart.[19]

So far, then, all the criteria for the traditional Anglo-American mob had been fulfilled: the attack was limited to only the odious object of the *Federal-Republican* printing office; opportunity for doing further violence was declined when the mob had Wagner's house and family at its mercy; and the community apparently gave its tacit approval to the riot — over five hundred persons witnessed the evening's activity, including the mayor who made no arrests. With the "laws of nature and reason" satisfied, and the Federalist newspaper driven from the city, it was time for the "laws of the land," in the guise of the local authorities, to reassert control. There was no anticipated difficulty here and on the next day Mayor Johnson and the city magistrates issued a statement urging "all citizens who were so disposed to preserve the order and peace of the community" to discountenance "all irregular and tumultuous meetings" and aid the civil officers in supressing them. If the riot were to be true to the form of the Anglo-American mob tradition this public statement, combined with the personal surveillance of the mayor, would be sufficient to prevent any further disturbances.[20]

Mayor Johnson soon had a chance to test his informal tools of riot control. On the evening after the destruction of the Federalist newspaper office a mob threatened a Mr. Hutchins for having spoken out against the war effort. Before the 40 or 50 angry Republicans could break any law Mayor Johnson arrived at the scene and persuaded the would-be rioters to leave Hutchins alone. Johnson personally led them away from Hutchins' home to the Market house, several streets away, where he made sure they all dispersed. However, no sooner did the mayor return to his vigil at Hutchins' house, joined by several gentlemen friends, than another and larger mob appeared. Standing in the doorway Johnson was forced to give in and allow an inspection of the premises. But first he made sure that Hutchins escaped out a back door. With Hutchins safely out of the way, Johnson escorted a committee of the mob on its search. Satisfied that Hutchins was not to be found, and leaving his property unmolested, the mob began to disband. Again Mayor Johnson could congratulate himself on his handling of the unruly populace. Yet he was to experience one more scare that night. As the last of the crowd was breaking up Johnson got word "that a few gentlemen, having heard of the riot, had armed themselves, and were probably on the way" to support him. Fearing that such a show of force would antagonize the lingering mob, Johnson "privately withdrew" and went off to intercept his would-be saviors. He met with Samuel Hollingsworth, a Federalist, and two other horsemen, all armed to the hilt, and, after assuring them that he had everything under control, he managed to get them to return home.[21]

In all, Mayor Johnson could view his night's work as success; he had gone face to face with two mobs and prevented both from committing any serious violence. However, Johnson was upset by the efforts of the three armed Federalists and was afraid that bloodshed, and possibly civil war, might be the result of any further popular political disturbances. Definitely committed against the use of force, and rather than simply relying on another public statement, the mayor and city magistrates decided that a more symbolic gesture was needed. Within a few days all of the city's officials and constables were massed together and paraded through the streets in a deliberate attempt to match the theater of the mob with the counter-theater of the elite and to exhibit before the entire Baltimore community their united stand against any further public disorder.[22] In a still largely oral society this physical and dramatic demonstration was calculated to impress the mechanic and laborer as no high sounding proclamation could — for it was with "body language" and the "oral-dramaturgical process" that the elite communicated most effectively with the lower section of society.[23]

Somehow the people of Baltimore were unimpressed with this show of counter-theater and the mob continued to be active. The Anglo-American mob tradition flouished in simple, generally unified communities. Baltimore, however, was no longer this kind of unified community. In the half century before 1812 the city has experienced phenomenal growth and was transformed from a few clusters of houses to a thriving metropolis of fifty thousand. It was a commercial boom town with many different kinds of people — rich and rising merchants on the make, middling tradesmen, native-born and immigrant laborers, and both slave and free blacks.[24] Moreover, the city's work force was undergoing a significant transition as artisans became increasingly reliant on a pool of unskilled laborers; apprentices, slaves, and even women were replacing the journeyman at the work place, creating additional resentment between employer and employee.[25] In such a city there were a great number of diverse interests and some of these were starkly exposed in the following wave of rioting.

Racial antagonism, for instance, was revealed in the tearing down of two houses owned by James Briscoe, a free black. Briscoe had been quoted as saying that "if all the blacks were of his opinion, they would soon put down the whites," and this, combined with a widespread fear of a British-inspired slave conspiracy, was quite enough to provoke the ire of the mob. The action, which was not very violent, seems to have been limited in its goals and might therefore easily be considered as being in the spirit of the Anglo-American riot tradition. However, a more careful examination suggests another conclusion. A magistrate was at the scene of the riot and attempted to prevent the destruction of any property. Not only did he fail to stop the mob from pulling down Briscoe's home, but he was equally powerless when the mob decided that they would "visit the sins of the father upon his generation" and, dragging Briscoe's daughter out of her bed, levelled her house to the ground as well. Harassment of blacks continued thereafter and even the African church was threatened.[26]

Other divisions in society can be seen in the street fighting which erupted between Protestant and Catholic Irish. Mayor Edward Johnson reported "A number of inferior disturbances took place, confined to the Irish alone, who were persecuting each other as orangemen." Alexander Wiley, who was apparently a Protestant Irishman, was twice threatened with tar and feathering and was finally temporarily forced to leave town. The mob claimed he had ridden express for Wagner, but Wiley believed that he was attacked "to gratify private revenge, and that the enmity to him partook of religious animosity." Neither Wiley nor his persecutors knew very much about politics, although they did use "a cant term, 'Tory', which was the signal for insult and violence."[27]

More directly connected to the war effort was the dismantling of several ships bound for the Iberian peninsula and the Spanish possessions in the West Indies. One ship, the schooner *Josepha*, was regularly cleared at the Customs House and set sail on July 7, but was "brought back by armed men, who dismantled her and cut off her rudder." The next morning the Collector put the ship under the protection of the revenue cutter; however, since no carpenter had the "hardihood to make a new rudder" it was thought unlikely she would be able to set sail. The reason given for these depredations was that the Spanish and Portuguese were Britain's allies against Napoleon and that a number of these ships were loaded with grain and were bound to supply Wellington's army in Spain. Just as important, however, was longstanding prejudice against hispanics and resentment against profiteering merchants who seemed willing to trade with the enemy.[28]

Nearly every night, then, after the destruction of the *Federal-Republican* office in late June until late July the mob roamed the streets of Baltimore, striking at a variety of targets. As it did so, the mob's activity ceased to represent the interests of the majority of the Baltimore community and began more and more to represent special and private interests which often reflected the growing animosities in an increasingly heterogeneous community. Screened behind a plea of patriotism the mob could begin to vent its pent up anger and frustration over racial, ethnic, and class issues. To almost all of this the mayor and magistrates continued to use their "gentle" methods of persuasion in dispersing mobs and minimizing violence despite the appearance of some evidence that the elite could not always "talk the mob down."[29]

It was against this background of constant mob activity that the other editor of the *Federal-Republican*, the aristocratic Alexander Contee Hanson, decided to re-establish his paper in Baltimore.[30] The paper, which was being printed in the less volatile Georgetown, was to be distributed from a Baltimore address. Asserting that the "empire of the laws" had been "overthrown" and that society had become "unhinged" and "degraded to a state of nature," Hanson planned to do what he felt Mayor Johnson and the other city officials were failing to do — guarantee the freedom of the press. He had no intention of facing the Baltimore mob alone and at least fifty ardent Federalists were recruited from both the Maryland countryside and Baltimore to help defend Hanson's "natural and constitutional rights."[31]

On Sunday, July 27, the Federalist host quietly collected at No. 45 Charles Street. Although Hanson and company attempted to attract as little attention as was possible, they made no secret of their location — the Charles Street address was defiantly placed on the masthead of the paper. By Monday, the twenty-eighth, everyone in Baltimore knew that Hanson and his *Federal-Republican* were back in town, and the Federalists on Charles Street prepared themselves to meet the onslaught of the mob. Being well armed and committed to stand their ground the Federalists were confident that the cowardly mob would not dare risk a prolonged attack.[32]

That night proved them wrong. A large crowd collected outside the Federalist fortress and a riot broke out as men and boys pelted stones and shouted insults at the Federalist defenders. Warnings to the crowd only intensified the shower of stones and after some debate inside the Federalist fortress a blank volley was fired in the hope of intimidating the mob. The loud blast from the Federalist guns had the desired effect as the street was quickly cleared of the crowd of people. But finding that no harm was done, and angered by the temerity of this new Federalist affront, the mob soon returned and re-commenced its taunting activities. Becoming bolder and bolder, Dr. Gale, a crackpot apothacary, led a rush upon the house. As Gale entered through the battered door the Federalists leveled another, this time lethal, volley. More shots followed and the dying Gale was carried away. Others were hit as they retired to cover. The firing continued intermittently from the house and the mob, which now began to arm itself.[33]

Official reaction to the riot was slow. Mayor Johnson left Baltimore that day for his country residence. Further up Charles Street lived General John Stricker, the commander of the city's militia. He obviously knew something was going on as much of the crowd had to file past his house on their way to the Federalist stronghold. Perhaps he hoped that the events of the night of June 22 would be repeated and once again the Federalist news organ would be expelled from Baltimore. In any case, he and several friends, who were at his house that night, became increasingly alarmed by the constant stream of reports of the intensifying conflict and by the first shots. Finally, after many appeals by Federalists and others, Stricker set the complicated machinery for calling the militia into motion. Before any troops could be mustered he needed the signature of two of the city's magistrates. Unfortunately, magistrates were an extremely rare commodity that night and those who could be found, even Federalists, were reluctant to sign the order for fear of mob retaliation. Four different magistrates were brought to Stricker's house and each managed to disappear before their signatures were secured.[34]

After much delay the proper orders were signed and delivered to Major William Barney around midnight. Two more hours passed before the thirty militia men, out of the two companies called, were ready to move down Charles Street. Both Major Barney and General Stricker were apprehensive of the crowd's reaction to the appearance of the militia. On Stricker's advice Barney removed the proud aristocratic eagle and ribbon of the Order of Cincinnati from his uniform, believing that if Barney wore this insignia he would be attacked by the mob as a "foreigner." By the same token, Barney ignored military eitquette and allowed the more robust and lower class red-feathered Chausseurs to lead ahead of his own white-feathered Hussars because, so he later claimed, the red feathers made less obvious targets.[35] No doubt he also felt that the mob would be less willing to attack the innkeepers, peddlers, butchers, carpenters, and ship joiners of the Chausseurs than the merchants in the Hussars.[36] Barney, who was to lead this expedition, removed his own white feather from his hat. He did not want to wear anything that might antagonize the mob.

Meanwhile the situation was becoming increasingly serious. A cannon had been brought up by the mob and placed opposite the building occupied by the Federalists. It remained unused, but the exchange of musket fire continued. At this critical juncture Barney and his small band of militia arrived. Considering the size of the mob, which some estimates put as large as a thousand persons, and the fortitude of an undetermined number of Federalists defending No. 45 Charles Street, Barney's predicament was extremely delicate. Rather than attempting to use brute force (which he did not have) Barney, stripped of his white feather and emblem of the Cincinnati, resorted to the time-tested method of personal appeal. He pleaded with the mob, declaring himself their *"political* friend," and gave assurances that those inside would not escape. The moment was precarious; hostilities had ceased upon the arrival of the mounted uniformed militia and the mob even temporarily withdrew. But the cannon remained poised to fire upon the Federalists, and the mob, seeing how small Barney's force really was, quickly regathered. Barney stalled for time, believing that reinforcements were bound to come and that the impending dawn would disperse the mob as its members would fear recognition in the growing daylight. He placed his militia between the mob and the defenders with orders to guard every window and door of the building to prevent anyone from entering or leaving. A tense cease-fire was established.[37]

With the mob incensed over the murder of Gale, the wounds of its friends, and the presence of the Federalists, there was nothing for Barney to do but negotiate. Finally, aided by Mayor Johnson, who arrived from the country, General Stricker, and a number of other gentlemen, a compromise was worked out. The Federalist defenders surrendered to the authorities for protection. Since they were to be placed in the jail for safe keeping the mob could be assured that the "murderers" of Gale would not go free.

As daylight arrived one last insult was offered to the people of Baltimore. The Federalists wanted to call for carriages to convey them to the jailhouse. Stricker thought it best to submit this proposal to the sovereignty of the people and asked the mob if they would allow this. The idea of these "murderers" riding to prison in a symbol of wealth and prestige was unacceptable to the crowd. Instead of carriages they shouted that the Federalists should be taken in carts — the common mode of conveyance for criminals and victims of the mob.[38] It was decided that the procession would walk and at about seven o'clock the Federalists filed out of the house they had defended all night. The mob surrounded the twenty-three fearless Federalists and their meager guard.[39] Insults were heaped upon the defenders all the way to the jail house and some stones were thrown at both the guard and their charge. A fife and drum serenaded this odd assemblage with the "Rogue's March."[40]

All in all, the Republican leadership could heave a sigh of relief that Tuesday morning. The situation had been on the brink of disaster, yet somehow that disaster had been averted. The mob appeared satisfied to see the Federalists put into jail. The militia had to be called upon but it had proved unnecessary for them to use force. Ultimately, it was the persuasive powers of the city's leadership which held sway. Furthermore, the Republican politicians, and the populace they represented, were once again assured that the insidious Federalist tabloid was silenced in Baltimore. Two men lay dead — one was only a spectator — but still the Anglo-American mob tradition was left somewhat intact. Had the mob been unrestrained in their attack on the Charles Street fortress and had Major Barney and company failed in quelling the disturbance that night that tradition would have been wholly abandoned.

By no means, however, was the Charles Street disturbance cast completely in the traditional mold of the Anglo-American mob. First of all, the rioters, both the Federalist defenders and the Republicans in the street, were much too violent and preoccupied with inflicting physical damage on one another. Normally, riots in the Anglo-American mob tradition focused on property, not persons. Second, had the informal methods of social control been fully operative, the mob, seeing so many of the city's elite attempting to restrain them, would have feared recognition in the growing daylight and dispersed as Major Barney expected. Instead their numbers doubled after dawn. General Stricker did recognize many of the rioters as being members of his militia brigade but they almost uniformly ignored his entreaties that morning to join the military escort and protect the Federalists. They preferred to remain within the ranks of the mob rather than being recruited for such an obnoxious duty.[41] Finally, the traditional bonds of deference and respect were sorely tested a number of times that night. Before marching down Charles Street, Barney saw a group of men with muskets and a drum heading towards the riot. He ran to intercept them and in the ensuing scrap he was almost bayonetted. In the midst of the fight one lad, 15 or 16 years old, shouted to the man Barney was wrestling with "give me the gun and I'll shoot the son of a bitch in a minute."[42] Neither Barney's social position nor his uniform intimidated this young man. Major Barney was aware of this — hence his removal of the Order of Cincinnati insignia and his aristocratic white feather. These symbols of wealth and prestige, which should have been assets in gaining the deference of the mob, were now considered liabilities which were best discarded. In short, the Baltimore mob appeared ready to transcend the boundaries of accepted riot behavior.

During the day, despite the mob's promises to the contrary, the building at No. 45 Charles Street was destroyed. In marked contrast to the workmanlike demolition of the *Federal-Republican* office in June, this activity was carried on in an unorganized fashion by looters and scavengers who grabbed what they could, down to the bricks and lumber, and then scurried off into the side streets of Baltimore. Talk and rumor were everywhere. Close to one thousand militia men were called for; only about forty reported for duty and since General Stricker felt that the uniforms might anger the Baltimore citizenry they were dismissed without even going near the jailhouse. Crowds milled in and about the jail and gazed at the Federalist prisoners to assure themselves that the "murderers" had not been bailed out.[43]

That evening, after the militia was dismissed, the crowd outside the jail became more hostile and threatened a general assault. Mayor Johnson stood in the front of the door as the mob began to press towards it. Once again he hoped to curb the furor of the mob. As he was being swept aside he declared: "I am the mayor of your city; they are my prisoners, and I must protect them." Johnson recieved several answers, but the one he remembered as the most vicious was "you damn'd scoundrel don't we feed you, and is it not your duty to head and lead us on to take vengeance for the murders committed."[44] For the first time that summer Mayor Johnson completely failed in a face to face confrontation with the mob. His personal authority meant little to the rioters and in a perverse sense of democracy they viewed him as a mere hireling, dependent upon them for his very sustenance and duty bound to lead them in their wild depredations. This separation of personal and political authority left the mayor helpless and with the protection of a few gentlemen friends Johnson beat a hasty retreat.

The mob, with the possible connivance of the turnkey, was instantly inside the jailhouse. Confusion reigned and some of the Federalist prisoners escaped through the crowd unscathed. Others, including Alexander Contee Hanson and the Revolutionary War generals Light Horse Harry Lee and James Maccuban Lingan, did not. All told, eight or nine of these Federalist prisoners fell into the hands of the mob and received a ferocious beating from fists, clubs, and whatever else was handy: penknives were stuck into their faces and hot candle grease dropped into their eyes. General Lingan attempted to address the mob and remind them of his past services to the country, but the mob could not care less about his personal stature and proven patriotism and they turned upon him with renewed vigor. Lingan was beaten until he stopped moving — by then he was dead.[45]

John Hall, one of the Federalist prisoners, vividly described the scene. As Hall tried to run out of the jail he was caught by "two rough looking men" who promised to take "care" of him. "They held me by the wrist for about ten minutes, during which I saw several of my friends knocked down and their blood scattered all over the pavement . . . they either cut off or tore off my coat, leaving none of it on me but the cape and the sleeves. Having thus *secured my pockets*, they tore my shirt leaving my bosom bare." He feared extra torture because he was a resident of Baltimore. "I made another effort but just as I escaped their hands, I received a blow on my head which brought me senseless to the floor. I was revived by some one jumping on my arm . . . ." Hall made yet another attempt to escape with the same results — more and harsher beating. Finally he realized that every time he moved he attracted attention to himself as being alive and decided just to lie there, playing dead. He was then thrown in a heap with the others who had fallen victim to the mob.[46]

Although it may appear that this torture was senseless brutality, all of the mob's actions were symbolically important.[47] Hall may have felt that his coat was torn off him to secure his pockets, but in that moment of riotous excitement, the "rough looking men" who attacked him were probably more concerned with stripping him of that important symbol of Hall's wealth and standing — his clothing. Each of the Federalist victims had their clothes ripped off them and after the "massacre" the jailhouse was strewn with "foreign clothing," "Montgomery coats," and "Virginia Boots."[48] So too, Hall's final realization that the only way for him to survive the ordeal was to play dead is significant. Others among the victims related how they came to the same conclusion;[49] in each case the mob seemed to be demanding that these members of the Federalist elite surrender, at last, to the forceful will of the people. General Lingan alone steadfastly refused to submit and his appeal, based upon his stature as an aged patrician and war hero, was rewarded with the mob's beating the very life out of him.

After piling up their victims in front of the jailhouse the mob searched for Hanson's body, planning special cruelties. But amidst the darkness, blood and gore it was impossible for them to find Hanson in the stack of nearly naked "corpses."[50] In a society where personal recognition was crucial the mob's inability to identify Hanson, who was no stranger to Baltimoreans, is curious. It was almost as if the distinguishing characteristics were purposefully beaten off of the faces of the Federalist victims. For the moment Hanson, Lingan, Lee, Hall, and the others were no longer land owners, Revolutionary War heroes, lawyers, or merchants; they were mere criminals, stripped of clothes and rank, fit only to be surrendered to the city's medical doctors as cadavers for dissection.[51]

Reaction to the "massacre" was terrific. Federalists, with their families, began to leave Baltimore and it was feared that there would be a run on the banks. Newpapers across the country carried accounts of witnesses and some of the victims. Even Republicans were shocked. A few of the party leaders expressed sympathy with the aim of punishing the Federalist "murderers" but almost all were displeased over the way this was done.[52] The mob meanwhile seemed to rule triumphant in Baltimore.

In early August the relentless and intrepid editors of the *Federal-Republican* mailed their paper to subscribers in Baltimore. What Alexander Contee Hanson failed to do was now left to the United States government. Again the mob threatened. This time, however, the authorities moved quickly and exhibited a new willingness to use force. On August 4, without even pausing to get the requisite magistrates' signatures, General Stricker ordered out the militia, which reported in strength. Contrary to the fears of the Republican leaders, there was no mutiny of the militia that night and a charge by two members of a troop of horse was enough to send the mob on its heels. For six nights thereafter the militia was called out to guard the Post Office. Baltimore had had enough of mobs and on one of those nights as many as seven hundred men were in uniform.[53] That the old techniques of riot control, using personal appeal and conciliation, were now abandoned was further indicated when several ringleaders of the "massacre" were arrested a few weeks later. Once again the mob seemed ready to strike, only now with the aim of setting the prisoners free. Several companies of the militia were ordered out and artillery was placed in the hall of the prison.[54] The barrel of a cannon proved to be a far more effective deterrent to mob action than the entreaties of an unarmed mayor. The mob yielded under the show of force and its power waned.

Although the viciousness of the Baltimore riots burnt a deep mark of infamy on the conscience of America, so deep that twenty years later Alexis de Tocqueville would hear of the riots on his visit to America and for generations Baltimore would be known as a "mobtown," the summer of 1812 marks no irreversible break with the past.[55] Mobs would still occasionally be raised in the spirit of the Anglo-American riot tradition as whole communities attempted to purge themselves of undesirables, be they abolitionists, grain hoarders, or criminals.[56] Yet the Baltimore riots of 1812 are an important benchmark in the history of American popular disorder because they suggest the outlines of a new trend of rioting in which the larger community was divided into warring factions of competing sub-communities and because they presage the intense racial, ethnic, and class conflicts of Jacksonian America.[57] Compressed in the shift from the organized and workmanlike destruction of the office of the *Federal-Repulican* in June to the near anarchic and brutal "massacre" at the jailhouse is an example of the disintegration of the traditional Anglo-American mob behavior and the emergence of a new form of rioting representative of the heterogeneous and confused democratic society. As the mob moved from objects which were disapproved by the entire community to objects detested by only one segment of the community new tensions within society were exposed — in Baltimore this was shown by the attacks on blacks, Irishmen, and grain ships. Furthermore, these same tensions could be expressed with an added vehemence and savagery, as in the "massacre" at the jailhouse, which was unlike anything ever experienced under the old norms of the Anglo-American mob tradition. Yet even at its most violent the mob retained a purposefulness in its action, revealed in the demand that the Federalists symbolically surrender their lives, wealth, and prestige or suffer death at the hands of the mob. The Republican elite did not recognize this purposefulness; they only saw a bloodthirsty mob severing its unwritten contract with the elite and offering an unprecedented challenge to the social order. All that the elite city officials could do was to slowly react to this challenge, hesitating because they were loath to give up the deferential perquisites they had enjoyed for so long.

With this failure of the old informal means of social control the mob denied all paternalistic authority and asserted a new, purely democratic order of society.[58] In response the elite had to turn to its one remaining tool to control social disorder — the use of force. But no longer did that force act as a mere bulwark to the personal authority of the magistrate. Nor did that force represent the coercion of some outside power — as did the use of the military in the Shays', Whiskey, and Fries Rebellions. Rather the force used represented divisions within the community. Most adult males in Baltimore in 1812 were in the militia and the failure of that militia to report for duty until after the "massacre," as well as the presence of some militia men in the crowd on Charles Street, indicates that there was a broad level of support for the mob's activities up to the fateful night at the jailhouse. However, after the "massacre" that support was no longer so widespread. By mustering to defend the Post Office in August one segment of Baltimore showed that the consensus behind the mob had ended. Battle lines were drawn, loyalties tested, and luckily for Baltimore, the mob was sufficiently cowed by men in uniform that further bloodshed was avoided.

Under the old Anglo-American mob tradition it was assumed that the entire community shared certain basic values and could agree on when the "laws of the land must sleep." Now, however, the bloodstained halls of the Baltimore jailhouse stood as a gruesome testament to the variety of meaning a diverse and complicated society could have for the "laws of nature and reason." As a result, the mob lost whatever legitimacy it may have once had in the eyes of the elite. The trend towards condemnation of "politics out of doors" became even more evident as the nineteenth century wore on. Rioting, which occurred more often in the early national period than is generally realized, became a major social problem by the Jacksonian era and was an important impetus behind the formation of urban police forces.[59] As the elite's attitude towards the mob hardened there was an increased willingness to use force to supress any disturbance, and the history of the nineteenth century is marred by a continual chronicle of bloody head-to-head combat between the military and the mob.[60]

In the wake of the Baltimore rioting in 1812 a few observers recognized that there had been some great changes in society. George Washington Parke Custis, a Federalist spokesman, gave the funeral oration for the martyred General Lingan. In the "good old Federalist times," declared Custis, no one would have dared touch Lingan, and his venerable presence along would have been enough to hold back the mob. Those halcyon days were now gone, and Custis cautioned, soon every city would have its own Baltimore mob.[61]

Brown University   Paul A. Gilje

FOOTNOTES

1. Some historians reject the term "mob" and prefer the less perjorative "crowd." However, "mob" has been used here because it is what is found in the sources. "Crowd" seldom appears in the primary material and when it does it ordinarily refers to spectators watching riot activity. "Mobs," on the other hand, were the perpetrators of the riot. Furthermore, "mob" was also used as a general slur and tag word for the lower classes. This ambiguity suggests that the elite not only mistrusted the lower classes but feared them as well. For interesting discussions on the definition of "mob" see: William Anders Smith, "Anglo-American Society and the Mob" (Ph.D. diss., Claremont Graduate School, 1965), 10-12; and George Rudé, "The London 'Mob' of the Eighteenth Century," in *Paris and London in the Eighteenth Century: Studies in Popular Protest* (New York, 1971), 293-318.

2. This is but a brief summary of a complex body of literature. The main works include: E.P. Thompson, "The Moral Economy of the English Crowd," *Past and Present*, 51 (1971), 76-136; Thompson, "Patrician Society, Plebian Culture," *Journal of Social History*, 7 (1974), 382-405; Thompson, "Eighteenth-century English Society: Class Struggle Without Class," *Social History*, 3 (1978), 133-165; George Rudé, *The Crowd in History: A Study in France and England, 1730-1848* (New York, 1964); R.B. Rose, "Eighteenth Century Price Riots and Public Policy in England," *International Review of Social History*, 6 (1961), 277-292; John Brewer, *Party Ideology and Popular Politics at the Accession of George III* (Cambridge, 1976), Part III; Pauline Maier, *From Resistance to Revolution: Colonial Radicals and the Development of American Opposition to Britain, 1765-1776* (New York, 1972), 3-48; Gordon S. Wood, "A Note on the Mobs in the American Revolution," *William and Mary Quarterly*, 3d Ser., 23 (1966), 635-642; John Philip Reid, "In a Defensive Rage: The Use of the Mob, the Justification in Law and the Coming of the American Revolution," *New York University Law Review*, 49 (1974), 1043-1091; Smith, "Anglo-American Society and the Mob;" and Charles Tilly, "Collective Violence in European Perspective," in Hugh Davis Graham and Ted Robert Gurr, eds., *The History of Violence in America: Historical and Comparative Perspectives* (New York, 1969), 4-45.

3. Thompson, "Moral Economy," 76-136.

4. Maier, *Resistance*, passim.

5. The elite viewed riot as a "calamity to be avoided if at all possible." Thompson, "Moral Economy," 98, 120-126.

6. E.P. Thompson emphasizes the differences between what he calls patrician society and plebian culture in two recent articles on eighteenth century England. Although he falls short of calling this a class alignment, he does assert "The mob may not have been noted for an impeccable consciousness of class; but the rulers of England were in no doubt at all that it [the mob] was a horizontal sort of beast." Thompson also points out that the gentry tolerated mobs as a part of the price they paid for a limited monarchy and weak state. "Patrician Society, Plebian Culture," 397; and "Eighteenth-century English Society," 145.

7. Some historians have stressed the differences between the aims of the elite and the aims of the people in the riots leading up to the American Revolution. Jesse Lemisch, "The American Revolution Seen From the Bottom Up," in Barton Bernstein, ed., *Towards a New Past: Dissenting Essays in American History* (New York, 1968), 3-45; Lemisch, "Jack Tar in the Streets: Merchant Seamen in the Politics of Revolutionary America," *William and Mary Quarterly*, 3d Ser., 25 (1968), 371-407; Dirk Hoerder, *People and Mobs: Crowd Action in Massachusetts During the American Revolution, 1765-1780* (Berlin, 1971); Hoerder, "Boston Leaders and Boston Crowds, 1765-1776," in Alfred Young, ed., *The American Revolution: Explorations in the History of American Radicalism* (DeKalb, Ill., 1976), 233-271; Hoerder, "'Mobs, A Sort of Them at Least, Are Constitutional;' The American Revolution, Popular Participation, and Social Charge," *Amerikastudien/American Studies*, 21 (1976), 289-306.

8. Of course the original English Riot Act of 1715 was intended to strengthen the magistrate's hand by making riot a felony and allowing the use of coercion without liability. Yet English sensibilities dictated restraining the use of force with the odd result of giving the mob an hour of unmolested freedom after the Riot Act was read. The justice, however, could use that hour to persuade the mob to disperse, that is if he wanted to limit the mob's activity, with the Riot Act and threat of force acting only as an added rationale for his influence over the mob. On the origins of the Riot Act see Max Beloff, *Public Order and Popular Disturbance, 1660-1714* (London, 1938), 136-137.

9. Maier, *Resistance*, 16-20; Thompson, "Patrician Society, Plebian Culture," 403-405; David R. Johnson, *Policing the Urban Underworld: The Impact of Crime on the Development of the American Police, 1800-1887* (Philadelphia, 1979), 13-14.

10. Furthermore, a magistrate, or anyone who would support him, might himself be liable to a suit or criminal charges if excess force were used. Maier, *Resistance*, 19.

11. Thompson, "Moral Economy," 121-126.

12. Thompson, "Patrician Society, Plebian Culture," 404-405.

13. Two articles on the Baltimore riots have recently appeared. Frank A. Cassell, "The Great Baltimore Riot of 1812," *Maryland Historical Magazine*, 70 (1975), 241-258, concentrates on the political conflict and the apparent breakdown of democracy. Donald R. Hickey, "The Darker Side of Democracy: The Baltimore Riots of 1812," *Maryland Historian*, 7 (1976), 1-20, is more concerned with the threat posed to the liberty of the press. Both echo earlier interpretations. Alexis de Tocqueville used the riots as a "striking example of the excesses to which despotism of the majority may lead," J.P. Mayer, ed., *Democracy in America* (Garden City, N.Y., 1969), 252 fn. Henry Adams emphasized the political conflict in his *History of the United States of America: During the First Administration of James Madison*, VI (New York, 1931), 405-408. Gelnn Tucker, *Poltroons and Patriots: A Popular Account of the War of 1812* (New York, 1954), 136-144, focuses on the freedom of the press issue. See also Richard Buel, Jr., *Securing the Revolution: Ideology in American Politics, 1789-1815* (Ithaca, 1972), 286-288; and David Hackett Fischer, *The Revolution of American Conservatism: The Federalist Party in the Era of Jeffersonian Democracy* (New York, 1965), 156-158.

14. *Report of the Committee of Grievances . . . on the Subject of the Recent Riots in the City of Baltimore, Together with the Depositions taken for the Committee* (Annapolis, 1813), 1-2.

15. *Annapolis Maryland Republican*, July 1, 1812. William Gwyn, an eye witness confirms this impression, "The work of the destruction was performed with great regularity and but little noise." *Report . . .* , 21. See also *Annapolis Maryland Gazette*, July 2, 1812; and John Howard Payne to Virgil Maxcy, June 24, 1812, Vol. 31, Galloway-Maxcy-Markoe Mss., Library of Congress.

16. Johnson seldom confronted a mob alone. He was almost always accompanied by a group of "gentlemen" friends who acted as an informal *posse comitatus* and bolstered both his official and unofficial position. The mayor recognized this and told an acquaintance, before attempting to stop a later disturbance, that "if he could be supported by only a few friends at the commencement . . . [of a riot] he might be able to prevent mischief." *Report* . . . , 161.

17. *Report* . . . , 242, 160-161, 199, 336, 344-345. Judge John Scott also made a futile attempt to influence the mob. *Report* . . . , 119-120, 153-154.

18. For Johnson's role in Baltimore politics see William B. Wheeler, "Urban Politics in Nature's Republic: The Development of Political Parties in the Seaport Cities in the Federalist Era" (Ph.D. diss., University of Virginia, 1967), 168-169; and Wilbur H. Hunter, "Baltimore's War: Its Gallant Defence produced America's National Anthem," *American Heritage* 3 (1952), 31. For the general structure of Baltimore's politics see Wheeler, "Urban Politics," 144-120; Dorothy Marie Brown, "Party Battles and Beginnings in Maryland" (Ph.D. diss., Georgetown University, 1961); Lee Loverly Verstandig, "The Emergence of the Two Party System in Maryland" (Ph.D. diss., Brown University, 1970); J.R. Pole, "Constitutional Reform and Election Statistics in Maryland, 1790-1812," *Maryland Historical Magazine*, 55 (1960) 275-292; Frank A. Cassell, "The Structure of Baltimore's Politics in the Age of Jefferson, 1795-1812," in Aubrey C. Land, *et al.*, eds., *Law, Society, and Politics in Early Maryland* (Baltimore, 1977), 277-296; L. Marx Renzulli, Jr., *Maryland, The Federalist Years* (Rutherford, N.J., 1972); Whitman H. Ridgeway, "Community Leadership: Baltimore During the First and Second Party System," *Maryland Historical Magazine* 71 (1976), 334-349; and Victor Sapio, "Maryland's Federalist Revival, 1808-1812," *Maryland Historical Magazine* 64 (1969), 1-17.

19. The terrapin shell was to be used because Maryland had strict laws imposing heavy penalties for tar and feathering. *Report* . . . , 174, 292-296, 321-324; and *New York Evening Post*, July 13, 1812.

20. *Report* . . . , 161, 326-327.

21. *Report* . . . , 3, 63-65, 161-164, 222; and Payne to Maxcy, June 24, 1812, Vol. 31, Galloway-Maxcy-Markoe Mss., Library of Congress.

22. E.P. Thompson examines the role of theater and counter-theater between the elite (patricians) and the mob (plebs). "Patrician Society, Plebian Culture," 382-405; and "Eighteenth-century English Society," 133-165. *Report* . . . , 161-164, 300-320.

23. The term "oral dramaturgical process" is from Rhys Isaac, "Dramatizing the Ideology of Revolution: Popular Mobilization in Virginia, 1774 to 1776," *William and Mary Quarterly*, 3d Ser., 32 (1976), 357-385.

24. Denis Rankin Clark, "Baltimore, 1729-1829: The Genesis of a Community" (Ph.D. diss., The Catholic University of America, 1976); Clarence P. Gould, "Economic Causes of the Rise of Baltimore," in *Essays in Colonial History Presented to Charles Mclean Andrews by his Students* (New Haven, 1931), 225-231; Richard M. Bernard, "A Portrait of Baltimore: Economic and Occupational Pattern in an Early American City," *Maryland Historical Magazine*, 69 (1974), 341-361; Jane N. Garret, "Philadelphia and Baltimore, 1790-1840: A Study of Intra-Regional Unity," *Maryland Historical Magazine*, 55 (1960), 1-13; James S. Van Ness, "Economic Development, Social and Cultural Changes, 1800-1850," in Richard Walsh, *et al.*, eds., *Maryland, A History 1632-1974* (Baltimore, 1974), 156-238.

25. Charles G. Steffen, "Changes in the Organization of Artisan Production in Baltimore, 1790 to 1820," *William and Mary Quarterly*, 3d Ser., 36 (1979), 101-117.

26. *Report* . . . , 3, 149, 160-163, 23; David Hoffman to Maxcy,˙ July 11, 1812, Vol. 31, Galloway-Maxcy-Markoe Mss., Library of Congress.

27. *Report* . . . , 169, 177, 200, 203.

28. *New York Evening Post*, July 13, 1812; *New York Spectator*, July 15, 1812; *Report* . . . , 50-51, 243, 254, 346-347.

29. *Report* . . . , 22-24, 97, 160-162, 337. The militia was called out to protect the African church, but there was no recorded clash or confrontation with the mob. *Report* . . . , 3, 149.

30. For Hanson's background see Joseph Herman Schauinger, "Alexander Contee Hanson, Federalist Partisan," *Maryland Historical Magazine*, 35 (1940), 354-364.

31. *Report* . . . , 3-4; *Niles' Weekly Register* (Baltimore), Aug. 8, 1812; *Georgetown Federal-Republican*, July 27, 1812.

32. *Report* . . . , 5; A.C. Hanson to Robert Goodloe Harper, July 24, 1812, Harper-Pennington Collection, Maryland Historical Society; *An Exact and Authentic Narrative of the Events Which Took Place In Baltimore, on the 27th and 28th of July Last, Carefully Collected From Some of the Sufferers and Eyewitnessess* . . . (n.p., 1812); Grace Overmyer, "The Baltimore Mobs and John Howard Payne," *Maryland Historical Magazine*, 58 (1963), 54-61.

33. *Report* . . . , 56, 282-284, 303-306; Henry Lee, *Correct Account of the Baltimore Mob* (Winchester, 1814), 6-8; *An Exact and Authentic Narrative* . . ., 6-10; *Niles' Weekly Register* (Baltimore) Aug. 8, 1812.

34. *Report* . . . , 25, 230-232, 257-260, 279-280, 308; Jacob Wagner to Alexander C. Magruder, Dec. 3, 1812, from Executive Archives, printed in "Baltimore Riot of 1812," *Maryland Historical Magazine*, 5 (1910), 191.

35. *Report* . . . , 260.

36. A list of the Hussars and Chausseurs of the Baltimore militia for 1814 was examined and the names there checked for occupations in the city directory. Of the 81 Hussars only 32 were not listed. Of the 49 names in the directory, 27 were listed as merchants. A number of others had positions like "cashier of the city," "masonic lottery office," "atty-at-law," "President of the Levy Court and a J.P.," etc. Some had only their address listed, suggesting that they were men of means without an occupation. There were very few tradesmen. In contrast, the 47 Chausseurs were less likely to be listed — only 23 were found in the directory. Other than the officers, a few of whom were merchants, the company had more mundane occupations like those listed in the text. A list of the Baltimore militia by company can be found in *The Citizen Soldiers at North Point and Fort McHenry, September 12 & 13* (Baltimore, 1889); the directory used was John Lakin, *The Baltimore Directory and Register for 1814-1815: Containing the Names, Residence and Occupations of the Citizens* . . . (Baltimore, 1814).

37. *Report* . . . , 27, 150-151, 192-197, 211-213, 235-236, 260-272, 316, 320, 339-343; Lee, *Correct Account* . . ., 8-12; *An Exact and Authentic Narrative* . . ., 10-13; *Niles' Weekly Register* (Baltimore), Aug. 8, 1812.

38. *Report* . . . , 288-289, 312-313. Criminals at this time were executed from a cart. Thomas W. Griffith, *Annals of Baltimore* (Baltimore, 1829?), 227.

39. Twenty-three Federalists were taken into custody. Many others had been in the Charles Street fortress that night but either escaped some time during the night or had been sent out to contact city officials or reconnoiter. Overmyer, "The Baltimore Mobs," 191; *Report* . . . , 16-18, 259, 282-284.

40. *Report* . . . , 118, 191, 211-212, 224-225, 305, 317; *An Exact and Authentic Narrative* . . ., 14-16.

41. *Report* . . . , 79, 165-166.

42. *Report* . . . , 259-260.

43. *Report* . . . , 132, 135, 227-228, 290; *Niles' Weekly Register* (Baltimore), Aug. 8, 1812; *Philadelphia Poulson's American Daily Advertiser*, July 30, 1812.

44. *Report* . . . , 170, 48, 190.

45. *Report* . . . , 7-8, 28, 171; *An Exact and Authentic Narrative* . . . , 27-35, 60-62; *Niles' Weekly Register* (Baltimore), Aug. 8, 1812.

46. *Interesting Papers Illustrative of the Recent Riots at Baltimore* (Philadelphia, 1812), 55-59.

47. Natalie Zemon Davis reminds us that even in the most extreme cases, as in the religious violence she has studied, "crowds do not act in a mindless way." There is symbolic meaning behind the form and occasion of that violence. "The Rites of Violence: Religious Riot in Sixteenth-Century France," *Past and Present* 59 (1973), 51-91, especially 91.

48. Montgomery county was an important Federalist center in Maryland known for its aristocratic gentry. It was also the county Hanson lived in. *Report* . . . , 275, 295.

49. John Thomson, who was taken from the jailhouse, tarred and feathered, as well as tortured, claimed to have feigned death to escape further maltreatment. After the "massacre" Henry Nelson, Peregrine Warfield, Charles Kilgour, Hall, and Hanson all signed a joint statement in which they asserted that they "perfectly retained their senses" throughout the ordeal and that "they sustained without betraying any signs of life, or gratifying their butchers with a groan or murmur, all the tortures that were inflicted on them." *Interesting Papers* . . . , 45; *An Exact and Authentic Narrative* . . . , 29-30.

50. At least one member of the mob said he knew Hanson personally but could not recognize him among the "corpses." *An Exact and Authentic Narrative* . . . , 30.

51. *Report* . . . , 7-8, 294-295; *An Exact and Authentic Narrative* . . . , 28.

52. *Report* . . . , 29, 251; William Lansdale to Maxcy, Aug. 3, 1812, Vol. 31, Galloway-Maxcy-Markoe Mss., Library of Congress; *Philadelphia Poulson's American Daily Advertiser*, July 30, 1812, *New York Evening Post*, July 31, and Aug. 1, 1812. Meetings against the Baltimore mob were held in several Maryland counties, New York City, Boston, and other places. *Interesting Papers* . . . , 66-80. For typical Republic reaction, castigating Hanson *et al.* for provoking the mob while deploring the mob's brutality, see *Annapolis Maryland Republican*, July 29, Aug. 5, 12, 1812.

53. *Report* . . . , 8-9, 155-159, 171, 177, 200-201; Mark Pringle to Robert Smith, Aug. 5, 1812, Letterbook of Mark Pringle, Maryland Historical Society.

54. *Report* . . . , 9, 216-217.

55. De Tocqueville, Mayer, ed., *Democracy in America*, 252 fn. Of course Baltimore would have plenty of other riots in the nineteenth century to reinforce the epithet of "mobtown," but as J. Thomas Scharf points out, the riots in 1812 were "the chief cause of the evil repute into which Baltimore fell." *History of Baltimore City and County From the Earliest Period to the Present Day: Including Biographical Sketches of their Representative Men* (Philadelphia, 1881), 780-781; see also Francis F. Bierne, *The Amiable Baltimoreans* (New York, 1951), 142-155.

56. A number of anti-abolitionist riots were apparently in the spirit of this tradition. The flour riots of New York City in 1837 and the 1863 bread riot in Richmond, Virginia also seem to fit this model, while the long vigilante tradition in America is probably derived from the Anglo-American mob tradition. Leonard Richards, *"Gentlemen of Property and Standing:" Anti-Abolition Mobs in Jacksonian America* (New York, 1970); Richard Hofstadter and Michael Wallace, eds., *American Violence: A Documentary History* (New York, 1970), 126-129; William J. Kimball, "The Bread Riot in Richmond, 1863," *Civil War History* 7 (1961), 149-154; Richard Maxwell Brown, *Strain of Violence: Historical Studies of American Violence and Vigilantism* (New York, 1975).

57. The bulk of rioting in the nineteenth century appears to be of this type. Recent works on Jacksonian rioting which emphasize racial, ethnic, and class divisions include: Michael Feldberg, "Urbanization as a Cause of Violence: Philadelphia as a Test Case," in Allen F. Davis and Mark H. Haller, eds., *The Peoples of Philadelphia: A History of Ethnic Groups and Lower Class Life, 1790-1940* (Philadelphia, 1973), 53-69; Feldberg, "The Crowd in Philadelphia History: A Comparative Perspective," *Labor History* 15 (1974), 323-336; Feldberg, *The Philadelphia Riots of 1844: A Study in Ethnic Conflict* (Westport, Conn., 1975); David Grimsted, "Rioting in its Jacksonian Setting," *American Historical Review* 77 (1972), 361-397; Theodore K. Hammet, "Two Mobs of Jacksonian Boston: Ideology and Interest," *Journal of American History* 62 (1976), 845-868; Vincent P. Lannie and Bernard C. Diethorn, "For the Honor and Glory of God: The Philadelphia Bible Riots of 1840," *History of Education Quarterly* 8 (1968), 44-106; Bruce Laurie, "Fire Companies and Gangs in Southwark: the 1840's" in Davis and Haller, eds., *Peoples of Philadelphia*, 71-87; David Montgomery, "The Shuttle and the Cross: Weavers and Artisans in the Kennsington Riots of 1844," *Journal of Social History*, 5 (1972), 187-218; John Charles Schneider, "Mob Violence and Public Order in the American City, 1830-1865" (Ph.D. diss., University of Minnesota, 1971); Schneider, "Urbanization and the Maintenance of Order: Detroit, 1824-1847," *Michigan History* 60 (1976), 260-281; Paul Weinbaum, "Temperance, Politics, and the New York City Riots of 1857," *New York Historical Society Quarterly* 59 (1975), 246-270.

58. There is some evidence suggesting that even the membership of the mob was changed over the course of the summer. The men arrested in the fall of 1812 for participating in the destruction of the *Federal-Republican* office (N=11) were recruited from a wide spectrum of society, including a keeper of baths worth over $1000, a grocer worth $133, three artisans, an unpropertied druggist and his son, some journeymen, a drummer in the army, a sailor from a privateer, and a number of unidentified others. The men tried with the Charles Street riot (N=16) included a few less men of middling property and a number of journeymen. At the "massacre," however, none of those charged with the murder of General Lingan (N=16) seem to have been artisans or men with property. Those charged with the tar and feathering of John Thomson (N=12), which occurred the night of the "massacre," included a few men who had some property: the same keeper of baths listed above, a grocer worth $255, and a cooper worth $90. There were also a number of unpropertied and unidentified individuals. Thus, despite the overlapping of one or two persons, there seems to be a general shift toward a mob composed of journeymen and the unpropertied.

In each phase of the riot only about half of the men named in the court dockets could be reasonably identified using directories. A tradesman was considered a journeyman if he had less than $100 of taxable property or if he was not listed in the tax records at all. There were others arrested for various intermediate disturbances between the destruction of the *Federal-Republican* office and the "massacre." See Baltimore Court of Oyer and Terminer Dockets,

July and September Tems, 1812, Maryland Hall of Records, Annapolis; William Fry, *The Baltimore Directory for 1810* . . . (Baltimore, 1810), Fry, *Fry's Baltimore Director For the Year 1812* . . . (Baltimore, 1812); James Lakin, *The Baltimore Directory and Register, for 1814-1815* . . . (Baltimore, 1814); Baltimore City Assessment Records, 1813, Baltimore Bureau of Archives.

59. My research on popular disorder in the early national period has revealed nearly 200 instances of riot between 1793 and 1829 in New York City alone. Paul A. Gilje, "Mobocracy: Popular Disturbances in Post-Revolutionary New York City, 1783-1829" (Ph.D. diss., Brown University, forthcoming). For the development of American police see: Roger Lane, *Policing the City: Boston, 1822-1885* (Cambridge, Mass., 1967); James F. Richardson, *The New York Police: Colonial Times to 1901* (New York, 1970); Wilbur R. Miller, *Cops and Bobbies: Police Authority in New York and London, 1830-1870* (Chicago, 1977); Johnson, *Policing the Urban Underworld.*

60. Frederick T. Wilson, *Federal Aid in Domestic Disturbances, 1787-1903* (Washington, D.C., 1903); Robert Rheinders, "Militia and Public Order in Nineteenth Century America," *Journal of American Studies* 11 (1977), 81-101. Ultimately the trend implied in the last stages of the Baltimore riots is seen most starkly in the great draft riots of New York City, 1863, in which the rioters and the military fought pitched battles in the streets. For a nineteenth-century view of that and other disturbances see Joel Tyler Headley, *The Great Riots of New York, 1712-1873.* Introduction by Thomas Rose and James Rodgers (New York, 1970; originally published 1873). The best modern account of the draft riots is Adrian Cook, *The Armies of the Streets: The New York City Draft Riots of 1863* (Lexington, Kentucky, 1974).

61. George Washington Parke Custis, *Oration by Custis* . . . *with an Account of the Funeral Solemnities in honor of* . . . *Lingan* (Washington, D.C., 1812), 13, 18-20.

A BRIDGE, A DAM, A RIVER: LIBERTY AND INNOVATION IN THE EARLY REPUBLIC

John Lauritz Larson

What was the promise of the American revolution? Liberty, equality, and the right to republican governments, we might correctly answer. But how did the inheritors of the revolution understand these terms and live by them? The good patriots of Georgetown, in the new District of Columbia, for example, thought liberty insured them a right to become a rich exporting center, merchandising the produce of the Potomac Valley in the markets of the world. The equally virtuous residents of Alexandria, across the Potomac in Virginia's contribution to the federal district, believed that liberty conveyed to them much the same right. Yet as early as 1802 these sister cities in the only jurisdiction directly governed by Congress were at each other's throats over improvements in the Potomac River, which (each place argued in turn) either secured their liberty or destroyed their freedom to prosper and endure. They couched their arguments in the language of republicanism, which in the last thirty years American historians have recognized as essential to understanding the revolution. Sensitive to the rhetoric of the revolution as well as the complexity of its causes, historians of the early republic now confront, with their subjects, the working out of that legacy, the application of that language, and the resolution of conflicting interests in an experimental nation blessed

Mr. Larson is a member of the Department of History at Purdue University, West Lafayette, Indiana. An earlier version of this article was read at the annual meeting of the Society for Historians of the Early American Republic, Knoxville, Tennessee, July 25, 1986. The author wishes to thank the National Endowment for the Humanities and the American Bar Foundation for financial support; Richard E. Ellis, Joseph H. Harrison, Jr., and A. G. Roeber for critical review; and Earl J. Leland, in whose honor the piece was conceived.

JOURNAL OF THE EARLY REPUBLIC, 7 (Winter 1987). © 1987 Society for Historians of the Early American Republic.

with a republican ideology and the most ambitious, unsettled, and innovative people alive at the dawn of the nineteenth century.

Much important scholarship has already charted the intellectual roots of the new social order and the logical or ideological consequences of a republican revolution. In 1967 Bernard Bailyn started the flow, and since that time Joyce Appleby, Lance Banning, Richard Buel, Edward Countryman, Richard Ellis, Linda Kerber, Drew McCoy, Forrest McDonald, John Murrin, J. G. A. Pocock, Gordon Wood, and many others have contributed vital insights and challenging hypotheses for interpreting the early republican period. Recently Robert Wiebe has published a sweeping book-length essay embracing the experimental period from the constitution to the sectional crisis in a single interpretive framework. An entire number of the *American Quarterly* devoted to republicanism and a recent debate between Lance Banning and Joyce Appleby in the *William and Mary Quarterly* demonstrate the enormous influence and also the possible limits of what some historians call the "republican synthesis" in American historiography. All of these writers have discovered ambiguities in American republicanism, which looked simultaneously forward and backward, incorporated moralistic and rational views, celebrated commonwealth ideals and liberal individualism, nostalgia and hope. Pocock argues that the inherited language of the Atlantic republican tradition defined and restrained the vision of the founders' generation. Appleby counters that it was the emerging spirit of liberal individualism, not classical or utopian republicanism, that truly energized the American people. Whichever held sway, Americans in the first generation after independence faced extraordinary opportunities to reshape their political, social, and material environment, opportunities that reflected both the forces that made the revolution and the consequences that followed.[1]

---

[1] See essays by Joyce Appleby, Linda Kerber, and others in the special issue "Republicanism in the History and Historiography of the United States," *American Quarterly*, 37 (Fall 1985); Robert E. Shalhope, "Toward a Republican Synthesis: The Emergence of an Understanding of Republicanism in American Historiography," *William and Mary Quarterly*, 29 (Jan. 1972), 49-80, and "Republicanism and Early American Historiography," *ibid.*, 39 (Apr. 1982), 334-356; Robert H. Wiebe, *The Opening of American Society: From the Adoption of the Constitution to the Eve of Disunion* (New York 1984); Lance Banning, "Jeffersonian Ideology Revisited: Liberal and Classical Ideas in the New American Republic," *William and Mary Quarterly*, 43 (Jan. 1986), 3-19; and Joyce Appleby, "Republicanism in Old and New Contexts," *William and Mary Quarterly*, 43 (Jan. 1986), 20-34. J. G. A. Pocock, in "Virtue and Commerce," *Journal of Interdisciplinary History*, 3 (Summer 1972), 119-134, and *Politics, Language and Time: Essays on Political Thought and History* (New York 1971), establishes the argument for classical influence; Joyce Appleby rejoins in *Capitalism and a New Social Order: The Republican Vision of the 1790s* (New York 1984).

One way to connect and possibly transcend the contradictory elements in American revolutionary culture is to focus on one of the ideas that united the two in the minds of contemporaries: innovation. Whether they were molded by classical or liberal thought, agricultural or commercial wealth, Americans were preeminently an innovative people. They lived in essentially self-created societies, and they staged a revolution that purposefully repudiated conventional notions of tradition, cyclical history, and cultural equilibrium. Not content to simply throw off a distasteful government and replace it with a better one, they set about creating a wholly new kind of government that could immunize them from the cycles of decay that typified the past while still fostering that spirit of innovation that turned mere change into progress.[2] In the Old World innovation had always seemed dangerous, profoundly disruptive of social harmony and political stability. Since the Renaissance, according to Pocock, Atlantic politicians and political theorists had wrestled with establishing legitimacy in new regimes and changing times. But because Americans had always lived on the edge of the commercial revolution, in a new and changing world, no ancient traditions or static arrangements satisfied their requirements for opportunity *and* stability. Instinctively John Adams tried to couch his revolution in conservative terms, and as late as 1787 James Madison pleaded with the Philadelphia convention to draft a plan of government that could "secure the permanent interests of the country against innovation." Still, extreme nationalists and "little republic" men alike knew that any government they devised would have to give vent to the ambitions of their countrymen or be doomed to speedy extinction.[3]

---

[2] Bernard Bailyn taught historians to "suspend disbelief" in *The Origins of American Politics* (New York 1968), 11; and one of the fruits of that advice is Drew R. McCoy's important treatment of developmental thinking in the eighteenth century in *The Elusive Republic: Political Economy in Jeffersonian America* (Chapel Hill 1980), chapters 1-3. Bailyn's understanding of colonial development is brilliantly summarized in *The Great Republic* (3rd ed., Lexington, Mass. 1985), chapters 1-6. See also Gerald Stourzh, *Alexander Hamilton and the Idea of Republican Government* (Stanford 1970), and Forrest McDonald, *Alexander Hamilton: A Biography* (New York 1979).

[3] Gordon S. Wood, *The Creation of the American Republic* (Chapel Hill 1969), traces the problem of innovation in politics through the American revolutionary generation; J. G. A. Pocock, *The Machiavellian Moment: Florentine Political Thought and the Atlantic Republican Tradition* (Princeton 1975), explores its three hundred-year history; Edward Countryman, *The American Revolution* (New York 1985), neatly summarizes a voluminous literature on changes in the revolutionary era; Richard D. Brown, *Modernization: The Transformation of American Life, 1600-1865* (New York 1976), and Wiebe, *Opening of American Society*, offer two ambitious attempts to carry the theme across the larger picture. Madison's comment is in *Records of the Federal Convention of 1787*, ed. Max Farrand (rev. ed., 4 vols., New Haven 1966), I, 431, and is cited in Wiebe,

The federal Constitution of 1787 was designed to be the final revolutionary settlement for the American people. On the whole it quickly was accepted as such, but confusion lingered over its applied meaning and the degree of elasticity the framers intended. One category of interpretive quarrels fed on the smoldering agenda that gentlemen surrendered but did not abandon in the drafting and ratification of the document itself. But just as important was the shifting ground on which Americans sought to erect their model republic. To most Americans one important goal of their newly won liberty was personal prosperity, and in the New World riches flowed to those who met the challenge in novel ways. Thus, while they talked of securing themselves against further "innovation," they also dedicated their energies to exploiting and "improving" their material world more rapidly than ever. As the crisis of independence and survival passed, a general enthusiasm for public works of "internal improvement" burst forth throughout the country. Roads, bridges, canals, schools, even factories, wharves, and harbor improvements—all were hailed as physical proof of the wisdom of independence and the virtue of republican ways. When they put their shoulders to the wheel, however, in a nationwide campaign to change the face of nature, these enthusiastic improvers saw that public works dramatically (and permanently) altered the conditions on which their personal ambitions and patriotic hopes depended. Exactly where and how improvements were carried forward, therefore, became a serious question among builders of the new nation.[4]

Nothing proved more baffling more quickly for the Americans than the fact that liberty expressed through innovation inexorably collided with liberties already enjoyed by other persons, interests, or communities. The campaign for internal improvements, so universally appealing in the abstract, proved incredibly controversial at all levels of government as soon as workmen struck their spades into the earth. It seems necessary, therefore, for historians to approach the problem with a complete view of details, interests, and local prejudices as well as the grand motives and objectives that accompanied these projects.

Opening of American Society, 9. For Adams' agonies see Wood, *Creation of the American Republic*, 567-592.

[4] The internal improvements movement is sketched briefly in Curtis P. Nettels, *The Emergence of a National Economy, 1775-1815* (New York 1962), chapter 12; and in encyclopedic detail in *History of Transportation in the United States before 1860*, ed. Caroline E. MacGill *et al.* (Washington 1917, rep. New York 1948). See also Carter Goodrich, "American Development Policy: The Case of Internal Improvements," *Journal of Economic History*, 16 (Dec. 1956), 449-460, and *Government Promotion of American Canals and Railroads, 1800-1890* (New York 1960), 1-50.

By the early 1800s literally hundreds of works, large and small, lay before the public at home, in their states, and in the national arena. Mastering the whole issue has proved virtually impossible. Since Joseph H. Harrison's unpublished dissertation in 1954, no scholar has attempted a comprehensive treatment of political, constitutional, financial, and technical questions at the national level. Successful studies of individual projects, local and state campaigns, or topical aspects of internal improvements (usually economics and finance) line the shelves of our libraries; but without the national dimension these cannot adequately incorporate republican nationalism and constitutional issues, which rendered internal improvements so crucial to the success of the Union in its early decades.[5] As an alternative to existing interpretations and the comprehensive view, the present essay explores the possibility of synthesis grounded in an episode small enough to be intimately viewed yet still imbued with the largest national issues.

The battle over a dam and a bridge in the Potomac River was fought in Congress in the years between 1803 and 1808, and it raised incredibly important questions on the backs of the most narrow, selfish, and mundane interests. Georgetown wanted a dam in the river to improve the channel flowing past that city's wharves. Alexandria wanted a bridge to allow its residents access to the capital and a fair share of the prosperity anticipated at the seat of American empire. Congress alone governed the District of Columbia, but the free navigation of the Potomac was perpetually guaranteed by a compact of two states predating the Constitution. Quickly, to the astonishment even of the participants, what began as maneuvering by local interests spun off

---

[5] Joseph H. Harrison, Jr., "The Internal Improvement Issue in the Politics of the Union, 1783-1825" (Ph.D. diss., University of Virginia 1954), chapter 3. The relevant literature includes *Canals and American Economic Development*, ed. Carter Goodrich (New York 1961); Ralph D. Gray, *The National Waterway: A History of the Chesapeake and Delaware Canal* (Urbana, Ill. 1967); Oscar Handlin and Mary Flug Handlin, *Commonwealth: A Study of the Role of Government in the American Economy: Massachusetts, 1774-1861* (Cambridge, Mass. 1947, rev. ed. 1969); Louis Hartz, *Economic Policy and Democratic Thought: Pennsylvania, 1776-1860* (Cambridge, Mass. 1948); Nathan Miller, *The Enterprise of a Free People: Aspects of Economic Development in New York State During the Canal Period, 1792-1838* (Ithaca, N.Y. 1962); Julius Rubin, *Canal or Railroad?* (Philadelphia 1961); Walter S. Sanderlin, *The Great National Project: A History of the Chesapeake and Ohio Canal* (Baltimore 1946); Ronald E. Shaw, *Erie Water West: A History of the Erie Canal, 1792-1854* (Lexington, Ky. 1966), and "Canals in the Early Republic: A Review of Recent Literature," *Journal of the Early Republic*, 4 (Summer 1984), 117-142; and George Rogers Taylor, *The Transportation Revolution* (New York 1951).

constitutional, technical, and political questions that drove petitioners and legislators back to the ideological roots of what they believed was the promise of the American revolution. In short, quarreling constituents forced Congress to define liberty, equality, and republican government in terms of immediate interests and expectations.

Pick up the story on November 28, 1804, when the House of Representatives of the Eighth Congress, second session, dissolved into a committee of the whole to debate a bill authorizing Georgetown to build a dam in the Potomac River. It seems that some years before a sudden spring thaw produced an ice jam that blocked the regular riverbed, and the freshet that followed cut a new direct route down the west side of Mason's Island. The current slowed in Georgetown's channel, and silt accumulated along the city's waterfront. Merchants feared that the mudbanks would destroy their navigation; and when dredging failed they turned to Congress for permission to dam up the new western channel and force the water back to Georgetown's shore.[6]

Immediately John Randolph of Virgnia, a leading Jeffersonian Republican in the House and a passionate ideologue, rose to condemn the bill. Congress had no right, Randolph argued, to act upon the river because, according to a compact made in 1785, the Potomac belonged in common to Maryland and Virginia. Only joint action by these two states could authorize a dam. Confident that was the end of it, Randolph gratuitously snarled that the people of the district should stop wasting Congress's precious time with their petty local problems. Other members reminded Randolph that, unless Congress gave the district back to the states, these people had no other government to pester, and then Virginia Federalist Joseph Lewis, Jr., rose to support the proposition in earnest. Since the "landholders of Georgetown" had "very generally signed the petition," and since "no person out[side] of the walls of this House gave it opposition," Lewis thought the bill should pass. This dam would not injure navigation or the port of Alexandria downstream, but it would definitely benefit Georgetown. In such circumstances, Lewis believed government should act. Roger Nelson, a Republican from Maryland, agreed and implicated the whole exporting population of the Potomac Valley in the benefits of this bill. Hoping to destroy the question of jurisdiction, Nelson sug-

---

[6] *Annals of Congress*, 8th Cong., 2nd sess., 711-721, 792-811. For background on early Washington see Constance McLaughlin Green, *Washington: Village and Capital, 1800-1878* (Princeton 1962); James Sterling Young, *The Washington Community, 1800-1828* (New York 1966); and Linda M. Arnold, "Congressional Government of the District of Columbia, 1800-1846" (Ph.D. diss., Georgetown University 1974).

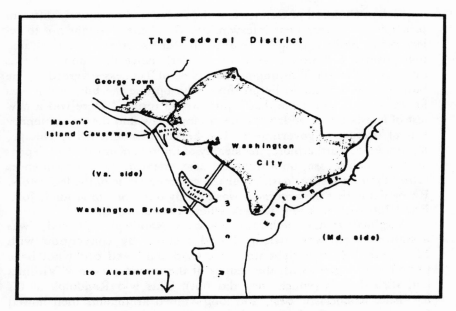

Potomac River Bridge and Dam Sites

gested that the dam could not possibly violate the old Mount Vernon Compact because this dam was an "improvement" not an "obstruction" to navigation.[7]

To this argument House Speaker Nathaniel Macon, a North Carolina conservative Republican and friend of Randolph, responded sharply that the burden of proof for such improvements must lie with the innovators. Frankly, he thought the dam would deprive Alexandria of an excellent route down the western shore, and unless the petitioners could prove their dam was harmless, he thought Congress was bound to assume it was an obstruction for which they had no authority to act. Macon also reminded the committee that the same petitioners who now begged a dam had come before Congress a year ago to block a bridge across the Potomac at Alexander's Island upon similar constitutional grounds! Macon thought he saw a case of shameless special pleading.[8]

---

[7] *Annals of Congress*, 8th Cong., 2nd sess., 711-713.

[8] *Ibid.*, 713-714. The first surviving petition against the bridge at Alexander's Island was signed by Daniel Reintzel and 113 other residents of the District of

Calvin Goddard of Connecticut then advanced an entirely different principle for government intervention. Gentlemen "ought not to reject doing positive good," he argued, "unless it was demonstrated that positive evil would result to counterbalance the good that was intended." George Washington Campbell of Tennessee agreed: "The burden of proof should lie on those who oppose the bill, and it was for them to demonstrate that injury would result." Here was a new test of legislation at odds with the common law and the revolutionary fear of overactive government. The benefit of doubt fell to change, not tradition. Furthermore, the legality of improvements seemed dependent, in such a case, on a technical assessment of their consequences rather than on justice, custom, or the common sense of the legislators. Recognizing that the argument was drifting onto foreign ground, John Randolph rose to bring it back where he wanted it.[9]

Virginia's right of highway in the river, Randolph explained, "was a natural right acknowledged and secured by convention with Maryland." Such a right was "conventional" and could not have passed to Congress with the ceding of the territory even if Virginia had wished it to (which they did not). This was Randolph at his legalistic, iconoclastic best, and long-winded arguments then flowed from attorneys who had cut their teeth on constitution writing and loved nothing more than excavations into the deep soil of organic law. Finally Christopher Clark of Virginia tossed aside Roger Nelson's distinction between improvements and obstructions: "Is not building the wall from Mason's island to the Virginia shore an obstruction, and the improvement at best problematical?" But even this begged the question, Clark said, while greater dangers lurked. This dam might signal the "commencement of a scheme" to monopolize the traffic at Georgetown and usurp the advantages of the Potomac Canal that recently had been completed by Maryland *and* Virginia investors. More seriously, from the moment the Constitution was first presented to people, "some of the best and greatest men who ever had lived" had seen this federal district as "the germ of incalculable mischief, as the ambush from which the masked monarchy of the Constitution was

---

Columbia, Jan. 15, 1802, Records of the United States House of Representatives, Record Group 233, Box HR 7A, Folder 4.2 (National Archives). (These records are quoted here by the gracious permission of Benjamin J. Guthrie, Clerk of the House of Representatives, and are hereafter cited as House Petitions.) A second petition bearing the same arguments was signed by Philip B. Key and 637 other residents of Georgetown, Jan. 30, 1804, in House Petitions, Box HR 10A, Folder 9.3.

[9] *Annals of Congress*, 8th Cong., 2nd sess., 714-715. See Morton J. Horwitz *The Transformation of American Law, 1780-1860* (Cambridge, Mass. 1977).

to spring upon the people." Perhaps this dam was the first step in such a conspiracy? Building upon this fear, Joseph Hopper Nicholson of Maryland declared his eternal and unalterable opposition to dams, bridges, or anything else for which Congress had not expressed authority in the Constitution. "So long as he had the honor of a seat in the House," Nicholson proclaimed, "he would hold up his hands against any measure like the present, which would go to affect the rights of any of the States."[10]

In an afternoon arguments had drifted incredibly from matters of constitutional authority to the benevolent character of improvements, the technical properties of moving water, various theories of property conveyance, utility versus tradition as a measure of legitimacy, the monopolistic ambitions of Georgetown, and monarchist plots against the sovereign states. Tired of such reckless debate the committee rose and adjourned. Ten days of other business intervened before the Georgetown causeway came up again. This time proponents of the dam reiterated their claim that the best justification for government action was the benevolence of the result: if it was good for the people it was legitimate for the people's republican government to do it. Their opponents preferred the high ground of principle, where tyrants lurked behind "innocent" proposals and the government that governed best governed least. Thomas Jefferson had come to power in 1800 on precisely that rhetorical ground, in opposition to the "energetic" governments of George Washington and John Adams. Virginia's John Dawson saw the dam as a dangerous precedent. "If we admit the right to erect a dam, we have the same to build a bridge," and there was no way left to refuse "accommodation" to innovators throughout the district. Seeing a majority forming against him John Randolph declared the question one of loyalty to Old Virginia and her principles, which meant Republican party discipline. Dawson put the question in those spirited terms that had first brought the Jeffersonians into opposition: the measure before the committee was an affront to the cherished doctrine of strict construction, and men must "either adopt the extensive doctrine of *implication* as one of their political tenets, or relinquish that bill." At a stroke he linked Georgetown's improvers to Alexander Hamilton's heresies of loose construction and implied powers, and through that to monarchy, aristocracy, tyranny, and corruption.[11]

Debate was in vain, for the dam passed the House by a comfortable margin. There was nothing especially telling in the alignment

---

[10] *Annals of Congress*, 8th Cong., 2nd sess., 715-721.
[11] *Ibid.*, 791-811.

of forces either for or against the dam. Opposition speakers from Virginia naturally favored Alexandria's view, but three members from Old Dominion voted for Georgetown's improvement. Randolph and Macon were notorious enemies of the federal establishment and loose construction, but their opposition produced no Jeffersonian party response. More than half the Republicans in the House voted for the dam, including most members from Pennsylvania, New York, North and South Carolina (Table I). Federalists nearly all voted for it, but so did two of the four men who still clung to the label Antifederalist. Despite Christopher Clark's and John Dawson's shrill warnings against monocrats and conspirators, the broad consensus lay in favor of innovations for improvement.[12]

At this point ideological fervor among the Jeffersonians appeared to be collapsing in the face of interest group politics and party success. Indeed this was occurring, but an interesting twist in the story was yet to come. Until this juncture both crabby ideologues like Randolph and optimistic improvers like Roger Nelson and George Washington Campbell appeared to square ideology and interests in a sincere fashion. In February 1805, however, ten days after the causeway bill became law, a committee chaired by Pennsylvania Republican Joseph Clay (an enemy of the causeway) reported a bill favoring petitioners for a bridge from Alexander's Island to Washington City.[13]

Alexandria's pleas for the bridge began in 1802 and had been repulsed repeatedly by Georgetown's claim to free navigation on the river, guaranteed by principles of justice and the Mount Vernon Compact. The case for a bridge was simple. The river cut the town off from the life of the capital; a bridge would unite the halves of the District of Columbia and the nation; and a bridge built soon would injure fewer individuals than one built after Georgetown had developed as a port. Although Alexandria bluntly rejected political union under a single Columbian legislature, commercial connection with the capital looked more appealing. The question of congressional jurisdiction and the Mount Vernon Compact had given Alexandria residents pause,

---

[12] Randolph and the arch-conservatives were in the process of breaking with the Jefferson administration. See Norman K. Risjord, *The Old Republicans: Southern Conservatism in the Age of Jefferson* (New York 1965), chapters 2-4; Daniel P. Jordan, *Political Leadership in Jefferson's Virginia* (Charlottesville, Va. 1983), chapters 1-3; also Robert Dawidoff, *The Education of John Randolph* (New York 1979).

[13] *Annals of Congress*, 8th Cong., 2nd sess. 1175-1176.

Table I
Final Dam Votes, 8th Congress, House

Party	Yea	Nay
Republican	28	29
Federalist	27	1
Antifederalist	2	2
Unknown	9	6
Total	66	38

Place	Yea	Nay
New England	23	5
New York	7	5
Pennsylvania	12	5
Delaware-New Jersey	4	2
Maryland	2	1
Virginia	3	12
South	12	4
West	3	4

Source: *Annals of Congress*, 8th Cong., 2nd sess., 810-811.

but now that their rival city on the opposite bank had permission to build a dam, the west shore merchants wanted their due. They were astonished next December when Georgetown once more heaped opposition upon them, arguing as if nothing had changed, that Congress possessed no authority over the river! Leading the charge for Georgetown was none other than Roger Nelson, last year's defender of congressional dam-building now converted to strict construction and the perils of an overactive government.[14]

In the Ninth Congress, first session, a special committee headed by Virginia Republican Philip R. Thompson enthusiastically endorsed the bridge. The causeway bill last year was "declaratory of the right of the Legislature of the United States" to "occlude, in a degree, the navigation of the river within their jurisdiction." Thus relieved of their constitutional obligations, the committee asked two questions of the

---

[14] The first surviving pro-bridge petition was signed by Thomas Swann and 507 other residents of Alexandria County, Dec. 17, 1804, but the earlier counterpetition of Daniel Reintzel *et al.*, Jan. 15, 1802, implies an identical earlier appeal. Additional petitions were submitted in 1804, and all these documents were carried over to the 9th Congress. Georgetown drafted a largely new memorial dated Jan. 11, 1806, which circulated at various times that year. All these petitions are in House Petitions, Box HR 10A, Folder 9.3. See also *Annals of Congress*, 9th Cong., 1st sess., 354-357, 417-428; and Arnold, "Congressional Government," 41-62.

bridge: would it ruin navigation, and would it serve the public interest? If a bridge could be erected "with such a draw as will admit the free passage of vessels of any burden for which there is depth of water in the channel," they believed it would be legal. Furthermore, if last year's dam-builders were correct about accelerated currents deepening the river, then the same effect "might reasonably be expected" between two bridge piles straddling the main channel. In other words, appropriating the "facts" presented by their opponents in the causeway fight, Alexandria's friends concluded that a bridge was not an obstruction but an improvement—just like a dam! Since Maryland's legislature chartered a bridge in 1791 that body surely did not view bridges always as violations of the Mount Vernon Compact. Finally, the "public interests" would be "greatly promoted" by the bridge while little injury resulted to anyone. Outside of Congress, the Alexandria press predicted that an "improvement of such grandeur and general utility" would "go far towards exciting a spirit for similar improvements in every state in the union." The bridge would be a "golden chain of union between the northern and southern states," binding together the parts of the federal district; and it would "sooner or later be taken up by an enlightened congress upon national principles."[15]

The Virginia advocates of Alexandria's bridge carefully blended rhetorical instruments with logical argument as they built their case. They embraced the enlargement of federal power as a *fait accompli* and looked instead toward an evenhanded dispensing of government favor. Phrases like "spirit of improvement" and "golden chain of union" recaptured for these Jeffersonians expansive and patriotic sentiments once exclusively usurped by Federalists. Refusing to be cast as antidevelopers, they laid their own claims to the progressive tradition symbolized by George Washington's original Potomac Canal and (ironically) the Mount Vernon Compact. Georgetown's defenders, however, didn't miss a step in mounting a creative opposition to the challenge of the bridge.

"Conscious of the natural advantages" of their geographical situation, Georgetown's petitioners began, men had invested their treasure at that place and "unremittingly laboured" to remove "those impediments which accidental circumstances had placed in the way of their more immediate growth." Believing themselves "justified from the improving state" of upstream navigations, because of Potomac

[15] *Annals of Congress*, 9th Cong., 1st sess., 354-357; letter signed "Citizen of Columbia," Alexandria *Daily Advertiser*, Jan. 24, 1806.

River improvements, these citizens expected the "most serious and important advantages." The "citizens of George Town, so far from wishing to see any part of the District deprived of its natural advantages," viewed "with pleasure improvements in every part of it." Nevertheless, they hoped that if "liberality" did not produce the "same good wishes" among their neighbors, a "sense of justice would restrain them" from destroying "this Town." Appealing to the impartiality and wisdom of the federal Congress, the petitioners "humbly" submitted the central point: "It is with you to determine whether George Town shall reap the Fruits to which the activity and exertions of her citizens entitles her, or whether she shall be deprived of her natural rights" guaranteed by the Mount Vernon Compact, "and thus be reduced to ruin."[16]

Georgetown's defense neatly offered the "sovereign" Congress a distorted choice between preserving justice and liberality or violating the natural and contractual rights of the people. The constant reuse of the word "natural" to protect Georgetown's claims from any artificial interference called up an ancient and frustrating distinction from the common law. Bridge promoters were condemned for their "prejudices and interests," "passions" that traditionally governed wicked but not virtuous gentlemen. Without attacking the innovative bias they so clearly showed on the causeway issue, Georgetown's leaders appealed to an old moralistic vocabulary to distinguish bad from good alterations in nature. Then, just in case humility and virtue were lost on Congress, these memorialists suggested a hint of conspiracy. The bridge promoters, they wrote, "have not the most remote intention of embarking their funds in so hazardous an enterprise" as a Potomac bridge. They conspired only to profit somehow from the state of insecurity produced at Georgetown by "having the subject frequently before Congress." Congress might possess exclusive right to govern the district, but "that right is never to be exercised to gratify the views of one portion of the citizens at the expense of ruin to another portion."[17]

In Congress, Roger Nelson reiterated Maryland's insistence that Congress had no authority to obstruct—only to improve—the river Potomac. To establish this illegal character in the bridge, Nelson and others rehearsed the fears that silt would collect where the piles blocked

---

[16] Georgetown petition dated Jan. 11, 1806, in House Petitions, Box HR 10A, Folder 9.3.

[17] *Ibid.* See Horwitz, *Transformation of American Law*, 31-40, and Pocock, *Machiavellian Moment*, 3-82, on language of virtue and interests.

the current, that ships could not tack against wind and tide through a narrow draw, and that ice and floods would carry off the structure in the spring, leaving the river choked with debris. Nelson claimed for Congress authority over half the river (the dam) but not the whole width (the bridge); however, this distinction was absurd. The only hope for opponents of the bridge was to establish a principle with which to measure public good and private injury. William Findley of Pennsylvania offered a traditional rule: when in doubt do nothing, lest you unjustly favor one over another. Caught with their own preferential legislation tucked in their pockets, Georgetown's defenders now sought protection from further government action.[18]

Virginia Federalist Joseph Lewis, Jr., himself a conservative advocate of minimal government and rural values, nevertheless took up the cause of the bridge from a consistent and logical commitment to works of internal improvement. He launched a "fair, candid, and impartial investigation" with a promise never to sanction a bridge that injured Georgetown. On the other hand, if that city's objections proved "chimerical" or "emanated from an unfounded jealousy of their neighbors," he would give his "unequivocal approbation" to the bridge. Gentlemen agreed that the burden of proof lay on the "opponents to this measure, and not upon its friends," and the counter-memorialists had offered "bare assertion" in place of proof; still, Lewis would answer the substance of their arguments. This bridge would not destroy Georgetown's commerce any more than bridges at London and Boston had destroyed those great cities. Engineers now generally believed that the pilings on which the bridge rested did no harm and even helped scour the channel between. A properly constructed drawbridge would cause a "very trifling" inconvenience to Georgetown's shipping— much of which, by the way, called not at Georgetown but downriver at wharves in Washington's Eastern Branch. Lewis had done a little figuring, and it appeared to him that fewer than twenty-five vessels per year actually landed at Georgetown, so the magnitude of injury (supposing there *were* any injury) could not be great. Finally, Georgetown had argued that her "natural advantages ought not to be injured by artificial means," but Lewis skillfully turned this upon them as a weapon. Georgetown enjoyed prosperity entirely because of the Potomac Canal, an *artificial* waterway begun by George Washington to remove the *natural* barriers to commerce in the upper

---

[18] *Annals of Congress*, 9th Cong., 1st sess., 417-427. Two days of debates are lost to record, but arguments by Nelson, Findley, and others were reviewed by Joseph Lewis, Jr., speaking Jan. 31, 1806, to which these pages refer.

Potomac. Furthermore, a bridge across the river at Little Falls carried much of Virginia's country produce to the Potomac Canal and thus to Georgetown—produce that naturally belonged to Virginia's ports. In the end, Georgetown's claims arose from "jealousies" in defense of a recent, man-made, competitive advantage, and not from natural right or public interest. Lewis knew not the particular merits of either city's cause and he wished them equally well; but it was the "nation at large" he would promote by this bridge, and "considerations of this kind must yield to public duty."[19]

Both sides clearly wanted improvements and advantages, yet both sides desired protection from the reckless assaults of jealous and ambitious neighbors. For Joseph Lewis the "public duty" favored national improvements the local consequences of which did not concern him. Pennsylvania's Findley preferred a selective application of the common law traditions, falling somewhere between the anti-developmental bias of customary rights and the unrestrained competition of Adam Smith's *laissez-faire*. As the bridge campaign gained momentum the arguments of its opponents ranged widely and grew more desperate. Oddly, the enemies of this particular innovation accepted the burden of proof that traditional law would not have handed them, while men in and out of Congress searched natural law, science, tradition, history, and common sense, for principles that would elicit from a changing world the advantages they sought without either stopping all development or unchaining the beast of avarice among them.[20]

Was a bridge necessarily an obstruction? Arguments from history and tradition suggested that it was. Few commercial cities existed above bridges, and the mercantile community assumed it as a truth, that commerce would not endure the inconvenience of passing the draw if safe harbors could be found below. On the other hand, recent experience with drawbridges at Boston and elsewhere suggested a technological solution to this ancient objection. Hydraulic engineers could not agree whether piers in the current would deepen the channel or silt it up. Benjamin Latrobe, perhaps the most respected engineer in the country, thought that the collision of the river with tidewater, coupled with the heavy burden of silt that followed the clearing of forests upstream, would eventually bar the channel at Georgetown no matter what anybody did to prevent it. Latrobe was correct, but

---

[19] *Ibid.* See also Georgetown's numerous documents "refuting" Lewis' charge that few ships actually ascended the river, in House Petitions, Box HR 10A, Folder 9.3.

[20] See Horwitz, *Transformation of American Law*, 101-139, on the slow transition to competitive values in the private law tradition.

Georgetown had just spent $24,000 to build the Mason's Island Causeway, and their own expert, Thomas Moore, certified in 1807 that the mud bank was already receding. A New York bridge builder, Theodore Burr, sold his expertise first to one side then the other, discrediting all expert opinion and throwing the decision back on the good sense of the people's representatives.[21]

If science was confusing, law proved only slightly less entangling. In January 1807 a group of Washington landholders tried to claim a property right in the perpetual navigation of the Potomac, based on the Mount Vernon Compact and the plan of Washington City. Specific geographical conditions, they argued, had been guaranteed in their titles, and no individual or "Body Politic, no matter how constituted" could alter them. To "extend a bridge across the channel adjoining their scites [sic] for wharves" denied them free intercourse upon the river to which they felt "justly & inalienably entitled." Memorialists from four Maryland counties claimed a similar property right in the "choice of Markets" and the blessings of competition. Inland farmers enjoyed an inalienable "natural and political right" to the "unobstructed navigation of the River Potomac from its source to its mouth." Here rhetorical passion clearly outran good sense. Such traditional guarantees against contingencies threatened the very origins of speculative gain, which is what these memorialists were desperately protecting. Fearing losses at the hands of Alexandria's improvers, the residents of the eastern shore above the bridge wished to elevate conditions from the previous decade to the level of timeless rights, and then lock up the future against change. Perhaps recognizing that these arguments took them backward, not forward, Georgetown's most influential merchants filed a new petition (December 1806) that focused less on law and more on the fairness and wisdom of permitting a bridge.[22]

---

[21] *Annals of Congress*, 9th Cong., 1st sess., 417-427; petition from the Mayor (Daniel Reintzel), Aldermen, and Board of Common Council of Georgetown to the United States Senate, Mar. 24, 1806; petition of John Mason, *et al.*, Dec. 30, 1806; petition of John Mason, *et al.*, Jan. 14, 1807; Benjamin Latrobe to Phillip R. Thompson, Mar. 24, 1806; certificate of Thomas Moore, n.d. [Dec. 1806] regarding soundings at Georgetown; Theodore Burr to Joseph Lewis, Jr., n.d. [Jan. 1806]; Burr to William B. Giles, Jan. 26, 1807; depositions of Joseph Lewis, Jr., and K. K. Van Rensselaer in the Senate, Jan. 21, 1807, regarding Theodore Burr's testimony; all in House Petitions, Box HR 10A, Folder 9.3.

[22] Petition of thirty-eight property holders from northern Washington City, Dec. 4, 1806 (duplicate of one dated Jan. 27, 1806); petition of fifty-one residents of Montgomery, Frederick, Washington, and Allegheny counties in Maryland, Jan. 27,

"God made Rivers and man made roads," was the old saying quoted by the Georgetown petitioners. Nowhere in Europe, where all efforts aimed at commerce and convenience, was a navigable river sacrificed to a road; and if this were a present fancy in New England, "it still remains to be ascertained . . . that the innovation has also been an improvement." It was too soon to build a bridge. Washington didn't require it yet, and perhaps when a genuine need for such convenience had developed there would be capital enough to build a proper bridge. Present traffic across the river could never pay a profit to investors. The plan was so preposterous the "conclusion must be irresistible" that this bridge served motives that did not "meet the Public Eye." Some might argue, petitioners continued, that Alexandria was closer to the sea and offered country produce a more advantageous market; but in reality transporting goods another eight miles downstream constituted a tax upon exporting shippers, while "the same wind that brings a ship from the Sea to Alexandria, will in one or two hours more, bring her to George Town." (How upstream passage could be cheaper than downstream passage they never explained!) Given the magnitude of certain injury, why artificially obstruct the river, to the ruination of Georgetown and the western country, for so little public gain?[23]

Pro-bridge residents of Washington City answered this petition point by point, refuting the assertion that the bridge threatened prosperity upstream. Georgetown's shipping was not as great as its merchants represented, and their wealth had grown dramatically even as their shipping declined. Georgetown's opposition was grounded in "imaginary fears of speculation," not the "just deduction of reason." The claim that "God made Rivers and man made roads" was absurd and irrelevant: who made the vessels that sailed on the rivers? A bridge could not be seen in "any other light than as an improvement upon a ferry," and the "right of the haulers to cross a river" was "as great as the right of the merchants to sail up & down it." The pro-bridge petitioners claimed for Washington City nothing more than legislatures elsewhere "in their wisdom" granted to "promote union." Their opponents, selfish men, urged "continual separation instead."[24]

1806; petition of John Mason, *et al.*, Dec. 30, 1806; in House Petitions, Box HR 10A, Folder 9.3.

[23] Petition of John Mason, *et al.*, Dec. 30, 1806, in House Petitions, Box HR 10A, Folder 9.3.

[24] Petition of Robert Brent, *et al.*, of Washington City, n.d. [Jan. 1807], answering petition of John Mason, *et al.*, Dec. 30, 1806; in House Petitions, Box HR 10A, Folder 9.3.

By January 1807 arguments were approaching a stalemate. Both sets of petitioners and a large majority in the House of Representatives conceded the constitutional issue and became locked in a contest over local advantages and public justice. Fearing the worst, the Corporation of Georgetown hired its own stenographer to track congressional debates. Alexandria's petitioners ventured to argue that it was the purpose of "legislatures to endeavor to reconcile" the "contending rights" of land and water carriers. They would trust the matter to Congress, relatively certain of a victory there. Georgetown's position was more awkward. Any principle that clearly condemned the bridge at least weakened the case for their dam. At the same time any reasonable person could see that the contemplated bridge would drive shipping to the Eastern Branch and the lower Washington shore, abruptly terminating Georgetown's pretensions as a seaport. Unable to prove that this consequence was inevitable or illegal, Georgetown played the only card left in a losing hand: "if the Public faith were pledged" to pay "*all damages* . . . which might arise from the Erection of the Bridge—many objections to it would be removed."[25] Finally there was a basis for a resolution by existing institutions. The political process, embodied in the legislature, would strike a working balance, and the courts could award damages should an interested majority trespass on the liberties of others.

The House of Representatives first passed the bridge bill in January 1806, by a vote of 60 to 48. Despite the desperate efforts of the Georgetown party and the enormous influence of their leader, John Mason, in the Washington community, this margin grew each time the vote was taken. Analysis of the roll calls supports no scheme of party, regional, or ideological interpretation. Parties divided freely, as did delegations from each state. Of the fifty-eight members who voted on both the dam and the bridge, less than half (46%) stood consistently either for or against both forms of improvement (Table II). The remaining members found specific reasons for approving one and opposing the other (Table III). Campbell of Tennessee was all for encouraging improvements, but he thought the bridge too much of an obstruction. William Findley measured his position against the interests of his western Pennsylvania constituents, who might gain by the dam and lose by the bridge. State-rights Virginians who reversed

---

[25] *Ibid.*; petition of John Mason, *et al.*, Jan. 14, 1807, answering Brent, in House Petitions, Box HR 10A, Folder 9.3; Richard P. Jackson, *The Chronicles of Georgetown, D.C.* (Washington 1878), 64-65.

themselves for local interest included Christopher Clark, Peterson Goodwyn, Walter Jones, Thomas Newton, John Randolph, and Philip R. Thompson. Maryland's Nicholas R. Moore condemned the dam but approved the bridge, perhaps because he owned Washington real estate. Joseph Hopper Nicholson, that fiery opponent of federal aggrandizement, supported the bridge either as a favor to his friend Randolph or as an expression of his Eastern Shore's rivalry with Maryland's Potomac region. New members of Congress were sixteen percent more likely to support the bridge than veterans of two sessions or more, which may reflect a difference between the merits of the case and the passions that surrounded the lawmakers in residence. When it was all over Alexandria honored Joseph Lewis with a dinner, but they singled out his "zeal in promoting the interests in the district" and not his Federalist politics for public approbation.[26]

Popularity in the lower chamber did not readily move the Senate; and if William Plumer is to be believed, it was there that the influence of the bridge's enemies was most keenly felt. After a week of debate in April 1806, the senators postponed the bill, claiming lack of time to think. The following winter amid accusations that Theodore Burr had lied and other gentlemen lacked candor, they postponed it once again. Plumer said the "friendship" of John Mason restrained at least one supporter of the bridge, while the whole episode provided "new views" of his fellow lawmakers' "character." John Quincy Adams angrily condemned the bridge (Plumer said he was "utterly unable to speak") and recorded in his diary that it progressed to a third reading "by a sort of agreement of General [Samuel] Smith of Maryland, whose real opposition against it seems a little doubtful." Scraps of evidence indicate a nasty showdown in the Senate, where gentlemen played a less public game. The Maryland legislature sent instructions to their senators, which drew a stinging reminder from the Alexandria press, that federal congressmen were not "embassadors" from the states. If government were a "mere matter of will on any side," lectured "Aristides," the "will of the constituent, without question, ought to be superior"; but "government and legislation" were "matters of

---

[26] *Annals of Congress*, 8th Cong., 2nd sess., 810-811; 9th Cong., 1st sess., 833; 9th Cong., 2nd sess., 166-167; 10th Cong., 1st sess., 1006-1007. See Young, *Washington Community*, 87-153, for an important discussion of lawmakers' behavior. Nicholas R. Moore owned at least two lots in Washington according to the Register of Deeds, Recorder of Deeds, Washington, D.C. See Douglas R. Littlefield, "Maryland Sectionalism and the Development of the Potomac Route to the West, 1768-1826," *Maryland Historian*, 14 (Fall/Winter 1983), 31-52, on intrastate rivalry; and *National Intelligencer*, May 4, 1808, for Lewis' dinner in Alexandria.

reason and judgement, and not of inclination." (Ideas of "virtual representation" were far from dead.) Finally, on January 22, 1808, by a margin of four votes, the senators chartered a corporation to erect the bridge. Unlike a modern corporate charter, this act spelled out in exacting detail the liabilities of the company for debts, damages, and suits at law; set the dimensions of the bridge and draws; called for the relocation of the draws should the river channel shift; fixed precise tolls for each class of traffic; held the company liable for damages arising from disrepair or debris; and dissolved the corporation at the end of sixty years. It was a closely circumscribed grant of authority to intrude upon nature, which later entrepreneurs would have found positively hostile; still, it granted the right to build a bridge.[27]

Subscription books for the Washington Bridge Company opened April 4, 1808, and shares sold out within a week. More significantly, in an era when many improvements were chartered but few constructed, the company let contracts in May and opened the bridge to traffic one year later. Ice did not sweep it away, nor did silt choke up the river. Georgetown and Alexandria experienced neither sudden death nor instant riches. The seaborne trade of Georgetown did shift to places below the bridge, but Georgetown adjusted with less agony than they imagined. The bridge was burned in 1814, one end each by the British and Americans, then was rebuilt and used until 1831, when ice finally ruined the span. Congress then purchased the franchise and built a new bridge under direct public authority.[28] The "spirit of improvement" doubtless was encouraged by the Washington Bridge, and travel through the district was much improved; yet the bridge alone could not bring Alexandria into meaningful intercourse with the government center nor resolve the real and symbolic divisions between the northern and southern states. The significance in the episode, therefore, lies not in the contribution of this or any bridge or dam, but in the complicated process by which innovation met tradition, and liberty prevailed.

This contest over improvements, played out in a ten-mile-square section of the Potomac Valley, reflected in miniature the tangle of

---

[27] *William Plumer's Memorandum of Proceedings in the United States Senate, 1803-1807*, ed. Everett Somerville Brown, (New York 1923), 476, 579, 582, 593-596; John Quincy Adams, *Memoirs*, ed. Charles Francis Adams (12 vols., Philadelphia 1874-1877), I, 492; *Annals of Congress*, 9th Cong., 1st sess., 191, 234; 9th Cong., 2nd sess., 23, 36-49; 10th Cong., 1st sess., 45-52, 98-99, 2826-2829. The act ran to nearly 3,000 words.
[28] *National Intelligencer*, Apr. 4, 1808, Apr. 6, 1808, June 13, 1808, May 22, 1809. See Robert L. Taylor, "History of the Potomac Bridges in the Washington Area," *Arlington Historical Magazine*, 1 (Oct. 1957), 43-48.

Table II
Consistency of Voting on Dam and Bridge

Party	Consistent*	Split
Republican	16	22
Federalist	6	3
Antifederalist	—	3
Unknown	5	3
Total	27	31

Place	Consistent*	Split
New England	7	6
New York	—	2
Pennsylvania	2	6
Delaware-New Jersey	2	1
Maryland	1	1
Virginia	6	6
South	7	4
West	2	5

*Consistent: voted either for or against both bills.

Source: *Annals of Congress*, 8th Cong., 2nd sess., 810-811; 9th Cong., 1st sess., 833; 10th Cong., 1st sess., 1006-1007. N - 58 House members who voted on both bills.

interests, ideals, ambitions, opportunities, hopes, and fears that faced the American people as they set about creating their modern republic. For convenience we try to group these tangled interests into pairs of Federalists and Jeffersonians, nationalists and localists, ideologues and materialists, but the Potomac bridge issue demonstrates how much more shifting and ambivalent were the lines of force. Both Alexandria and Georgetown had worked artfully to secure the federal city on the Potomac, and their mutual interests utterly depended on the rising glory of the nation, the government, and Washington City.[29] Yet their immediate paths to the future diverged, and each city reached for ideological, legal, and constitutional language to defend its special needs. For merchants at Georgetown liberty could only be found in perpetual free navigation of the Potomac (at least as far as Georgetown), and no legitimate government under the Constitution could deprive them of this right. Alexandria residents, on the other hand, found their inclusion in the District of Columbia increasingly absurd because of the

---

[29] For an account of the maneuvering to locate the capital at Alexandria see Donald Sweig, "A Capital on the Potomac," *Virginia Magazine of History and Biography*, 87 (Jan. 1979), 74-104. Georgetown's ambitions are discussed in Littlefield, "Maryland Sectionalism," 36-47.

mile-wide band of water that kept them from participating in the life and profits of the capital. For them no legitimate government would foster Georgetown's glory while Alexandria lay orphaned and neglected. Non-local congressmen used the issue for secondary purposes, while private residents in the district used their last ounce of influence to "corrupt" members of the Senate. What bound everyone together in conflict was the shared recognition that specific fights over bridges and dams were shaping the true meaning of republican government, equality, and liberty.

The incredible challenge facing this first generation after independence was to find among these many contending interests the one "general will" of republican theory. In the early days of the revolution, when society was more completely governed by a small upper class of local notables, this was not impossible to do. The Mount Vernon Compact, for example, to which both cities appealed for their protection, had been drawn up on George Washington's back porch by gentlemen overlooking a river they confidently referred to as theirs. But one of the unanticipated consequences of the revolution these men had made was the decline of deference and the rise of liberated individuals who took self-government into their own hands. At least for some Potomac area residents, the old guarantee of perpetual free navigation now conflicted with the promises of wealth and power it was intended to secure. Each city alternately embraced then rejected the force of this compact between states as its situation changed, thereby claiming the irreconcilable rights to be governed by tradition and still be free to innovate at will.

It would be wrong to conclude in the face of these tortured arguments and passionate ambitions, that ideology and belief simply fell before the juggernaut of private, selfish interests. True, a dam (or a bridge) was not really unconstitutional—this claim was more strategic than sincere—but it surely was wrong for a republic to injure the majority for the greed of a few, and just as wrong for the majority to gratify unjust desires. Language, principles, and precedents were absolutely important in a new revolutionary country. The power of ideology shows through in the way all parties sought to articulate their desires in the rich language of constitutional piety and republican virtue. Alexandria's bridge invariably took on national importance as a "golden chain of union." To obstruct a river or unsettle men's established rights for less was unthinkable. Georgetown's causeway promised, not to enrich local merchants, but to complete George Washington's grand national dream of a Potomac gateway to the interior. Maryland's farmers unwittingly seized both the past and the

Table III
Final Bridge Votes, 10th Congress

Party	House Yea	House Nay	Senate Yea	Senate Nay
Republican	57	27	13	9
Federalist	15	8	3	3
Antifederalist	2	1	—	—
Unknown	11	7	2	2
Total	85	43	18	14

Place	Yea	Nay	Yea	Nay
New England	23	7	6	4
New York	12	3	—	2
Pennsylvania	4	12	—	2
Delaware-New Jersey	6	1	4	—
Maryland	3	5	—	2
Virginia	15	5	1	1
South	16	6	5	1
West	6	4	2	2

Source: *Annals of Congress*, 10th Cong., 1st sess., 98-99, 1006-1007.

future when they claimed a "natural right" to a choice of markets because competition was always a blessing. The first hint of such a doctrine favoring competition had just issued forth from a New York court (*Palmer* v. *Mulligan*, 1805), and it would be another generation before entrepreneurial values stayed the conservative hand of the common law. Innovations in water power, manufacturing, steamboats, turnpikes, canals, and bridges placed enormous strains on legal and constitutional frameworks established in the eighteenth century. Sometimes private law held in check the passions of an overactive legislature; other times courts cleared the way where assemblies feared to go. The cumulative effect was to legitimate competition and change. As in the case of the Potomac bridge and the Georgetown dam, arguments were extremely self-serving and "interested," but the casuistry itself demonstrates the powerful boundaries of revolutionary discourse that defined the American experiment. Rhetoric and reality were one and indistinguishable.[30]

---

[30] The best summary of changing legal views is in Horwitz, *Transformation of American Law*. More detail can be followed for Massachusetts in Handlin and Handlin, *Commonwealth*, and for Pennsylvania in Hartz, *Economic Policy*. See also R. Kent Newmyer, *Supreme Court Justice Joseph Story: Statesman of the Old Republic* (Chapel Hill 1985), especially chapters 4 and 9.

One conclusion emerges clearly from these early contests, and it was not lost upon contemporaries. In an environment of rapid change and innovation, there would be no single way to build a republic and get it right, once and for all. Constitutions might create the structures and set down the principles; but constitutionalism had to become a process of growth, not a framework of absolutes, or constitutions themselves would be destroyed by the innovative liberties they guaranteed. When constitutions tried to fix conditions as well as principles, men quickly chafed at these restraints. There had once been a time when it was reasonable to say that Alexandria would never have a bridge to Washington, because it would obstruct the trade of Georgetown. But by 1806 Joseph Lewis could declare that "a bridge must and will be built, at some time or other, and the sooner it is done the better."[31] Most of his listeners already sensed that this was true; but they wondered, where was liberty for those who wished to have no bridge?

Here was an enduring irony of the revolutionary experiment. Liberty fostered and accelerated changes which effectively destroyed the world that other people loved and thought they had a right to preserve. Deep inside the ambivalent republican creed lay two visions of perfection. One was defensive and moral, the other expansive and vigorous. One saw communities at equilibrium, cast in classical language, centered, perfect, timeless; the other saw a dynamic rising empire, hitched to time itself, demonstrating the progress of the race. One would have its rivers remain in a natural state, while the other would improve them time and time again. Americans recognized both kinds of republics and mixed them up promiscuously as they argued about their futures. Because ambivalence seemed rooted in their highest ideals, they felt no discomfort shaping arguments to suit their transient interests. In fact they came to believe that the genius of republican government was its capacity to endure the clash of interests without disintegrating. While the next generation sifted through ideological variations, scientific discoveries, partisan advantages, economic prospects, and innovative possibilities, they clung to the hope that somehow a procedural commitment to republican government under the federal Constitution would bring liberty and commonwealth together.

Ultimately Americans let the crush of interests in the marketplace resolve these tensions and set the agenda for the future. They chartered bridge companies, turnpikes, canals, banks, and business corporations,

---

[31] *Annals of Congress*, 9th Cong., 1st sess., 421.

and when the exclusive privileges thus granted became restrictive, they chartered new ones to compete. Privileges granted in the name of public service were undercut in the name of competition and further growth. Government gradually withdrew its regulatory hand and the resulting "release of energy" (the phrase is Willard Hurst's) transformed America and the nineteenth century.[32] Constitutionalism became the final line of defense against the hazards of a free competitive society. Not surprisingly, then, throughout the whole period between the election of Jefferson and the sectional crisis of 1850, political discourse mingled freely with constitutional law. Politicians twisted the lexicon of revolutionary America to fit the new age, no matter how absurdly words changed their meanings. There were scarcely any fixed limits to American opportunities, and competitive liberalism rightly appealed to a self-governing and relatively rich population. Yet they clung as well to the republican legacy and to its conservative, defensive vision, as a brake against the whirlwind they created. They locked corporate ideals and individualistic rights in permanent juxtaposition. Traditional rights and vested interests repeatedly battled against innovations even though Americans knew that the future was supposed to defeat the past. In a curious way these people had bound themselves, in the revolutionary generation, to ideals they were bound to change, so they might bridge or dam a river if they wished.

---

[32] James Willard Hurst, *Law and the Conditions of Freedom in the Nineteenth-Century United States* (Madison, Wisc. 1956), chapter 1. This work literally revolutionized American legal history and informs a great deal of literature cited above.

The Formation of the Republican Party in Virginia, 1789-1796

By HARRY AMMON

A LITTLE MORE THAN A QUARTER OF A CENTURY AGO THE late Charles A. Beard arrived at certain conclusions concerning the origin of Jeffersonian democracy, which, after the initial shock of their iconoclastic impact had abated, became the basis of the generally accepted interpretation of the origin of the first political parties in the early Republic.[1] By analyzing the subsequent political affiliations of the members of the Philadelphia convention, by a careful study of the more important political pamphlets of that period, and by a close examination of the proceedings of the first two Congresses, Beard was able to demonstrate that the Federalist and Republican parties arose from the conflict between the mercantile and agrarian interests in the new nation. He also concluded on the basis of his investigations that the party which rallied around Hamilton was "substantially the same party that had supported the Constitution," whereas the Republican party drew its members largely from the anti-federal ranks.[2] Since the latter observation was based principally upon his analysis of the later political careers of the convention members, Beard admitted that this general conclusion might not be true on the state level. In his study Beard did not devote any attention to the specific steps by which the parties came into existence other than to indicate the broad outlines of the issues over which they divided.

It is the purpose of this paper to examine specifically the process by which the Republican party emerged in Virginia, an area of

[1] Charles A. Beard, *Economic Origins of Jeffersonian Democracy* (New York, 1915).
[2] *Ibid.*, 75. Lower case "f" and "a" have been used throughout this article in referring to the federalists and anti-federalists of 1788 in order to avoid confusion with the later Federalist and Republican parties.

particular interest, for not only was it the native state of three of the major figures in the party—Jefferson, Madison, and Monroe—but it was also the scene of one of the greatest political triumphs of the Republicans. From the very beginning the Republicans were in complete control of the Old Dominion, a circumstance which is not surprising in view of the pronouncedly agrarian character of the state. Yet even in this favorable atmosphere Republican dominance was only achieved and perpetuated through the organization of dissatisfaction directed against the Washington administration by a group of skillful practical politicians. Secondly, it is intended to test the main points of the Beard thesis, especially his identification of anti-federalism with Republicanism, on the state level.

Before examining the stages by which the Republican party developed, it seems essential to comment briefly upon the connection between the federalists of 1788 and the Federalists, and between the anti-federalists and the Republicans. As we have noted, Beard concluded, on the basis of an examination of the subsequent political affiliations of the members of the Philadelphia convention, that the Federalists derived their membership from the advocates of the Constitution, while the Republicans drew their members for the most part from the anti-federalists.

The Old Dominion sent six delegates to Philadelphia in 1787—George Washington, James Madison, George Mason, Edmund Randolph, George Wythe, and James McClurg. Washington and Madison signed the Constitution without any hesitation. Although McClurg and Wythe departed before the convention ended its labors and consequently did not sign the final document, both gave it their full approval in the ratifying convention. The remaining two members of the delegation, Mason and Randolph, refused to sign, but only the former can be included in the anti-federalist ranks. Randolph later changed his mind and became one of the leading advocates of the Constitution in the state convention. The later careers of only five members of the Virginia delegation can be traced. Mason died in 1792 before party alignments were sufficiently clear to include him in either party. According to all indications, however, his sympathies were with the "republican interest." Of the five federalists of 1787, Madison,

Randolph, and Wythe became Republicans while McClurg and Washington attached themselves to the Federalist cause.[3]

This ratio of three Republicans to two Federalists suggests that in Virginia the federalists did not all join the Federalist party. This point can be confirmed by an examination of the subsequent political affiliations of the members of the ratifying convention. Of the twenty-two federalist members of that body whose later political careers can be traced, thirteen became Republicans while only nine entered the ranks of the Federalists. The anti-federalists, however, displayed a quite different pattern of distribution. With only two exceptions the fifteen anti-federalists whose later political connections can be identified were all Republicans. The elusive Patrick Henry and Levin Powell, who were pillars of anti-federalism in 1788, were the sole exceptions.[4]

In terms of the prevailing mercantile-agrarian interpretation, the variation from the national trend is easily understandable. The conflict over the Constitution in Virginia was not grounded upon a struggle between agricultural and mercantile interests. The latter were too insignificant to be able to exert a decisive influence on a question of such great import. Actually the conflict was between two wings of the agricultural element which dominated the state. One group, led by Madison, was convinced that a strong Union was essential to the well-being of agriculture, while the other group, directed by Henry and Mason, saw no advantage to the planter or the farmer in a new and stronger government. The Virginia federalists were for the most part agrarian federalists, and when they became convinced that the government which they had helped inaugurate was about to succumb to the eastern commercial interests, they rallied around the banners of the agrarian-minded Republican party, in whose inception, it should not be forgotten, Virginians played a major role. On the other hand, the anti-federalists, who had pointed to the danger that the government would become a tool in the hands of the mercantile interests, inevitably entered the Republican party when they thought they saw their suspicions confirmed by the. events of Washington's first administration.

[3] *Ibid.*, 34 ff.; Harry Ammon, "The Republican Party in Virginia, 1789-1824" (Ph.D. dissertation, University of Virginia, 1948), 49-50, 94-97.
[4] Ammon, "Republican Party," 92-98. There were 168 members in the Virginia ratifying convention.

While it can be generally accepted as valid that the Republicans inherited from the anti-federalists that portion of their political philosophy which related especially to individual rights and to the concept of the sovereignty of the state, they received neither their organization nor their objectives from the anti-federalist group. The latter had achieved no real unity during the contest over the Constitution. The leading anti-federalists had been unable to agree upon either the basis on which they opposed the Constitution or upon the strategy which they should use to defeat it. Mason and Henry, the two chief anti-federalists, were in no closer agreement upon the Constitution than they had been upon any political question during the preceding decade. Mason was a moderate in his views and was willing to accept the Constitution if it were modified. Henry, on the contrary, was opposed to any project leading towards a stronger Union. In the light of this fundamental disagreement the anti-federalists were unable to work out any program before the convention began its sessions, thus giving a substantial advantage to their well-organized opponents.[5]

Once the Constitution was ratified the anti-federalists showed no disposition to prevent the inauguration of the new government, although their majority in the legislature of 1788 would have made such a move possible. The anti-federalists under the direction of Henry joined the federalist minority in unanimously passing the laws providing for the election of representatives to the First Congress and for the election of presidential electors. Both of these laws were necessary for Virginia's participation in the new government. This complaisant attitude was probably engendered as much by disunity in the anti-federalist ranks as by a certain willingness to see how the experiment would work.[6] The

---

[5] *Ibid.*, 59 ff.; Jonathan Elliot (ed.), *The Debates in the Several State Conventions on the Adoption of the Federal Constitution* (5 vols., Washington, 1836-1845), III, *passim;* Hugh Blair Grigsby, *History of the Virginia Federal Convention* (Collections of the Virginia Historical Society, N.S., IX-X [Richmond, 1890-1891]), IX, 71 ff.

[6] Edmund Randolph considered this to be the prevailing attitude in the spring of 1789. Randolph to Madison, March 27, 1789, quoted in Moncure D. Conway, *Omitted Chapters of History Disclosed in the Life and Papers of Edmund Randolph* (New York, 1888), 121. This Assembly, which met in the fall of 1788, had been elected in March, 1788, before the Constitution had been ratified. The ratification of the Constitution may have well caused the anti-federalists to hesitate before launching measures hostile to the new government.

anti-federalists pushed through a resolution requesting Congress to summon a second convention for the purpose of amending the Constitution.[7] They also demonstrated their strength by electing as Virginia's first senators two staunch anti-federalists, Richard Henry Lee and William Grayson. This choice was a major defeat for the federalists who had put forward James Madison.[8]

The triumph of the anti-federalists was short-lived. In the following session of the legislature the position of the two parties was reversed, with the federalists in the ascendant. Henry's influence, which had been unchecked in 1788, was now counterbalanced by that of Edmund Randolph, John Marshall, and Henry Lee.[9] The friendly reception given to the amendments which Madison had introduced in Congress in June, 1789, was a clear indication of the weakening of the anti-federal impulse. Even though they may have been designed as an "anodyne to the discontented," Madison's proposals served to mollify many who had objected to the Constitution on the grounds that it did not contain any guarantees of civil liberties and that it tended to destroy the sovereignty of the states.[10] The Tenth Amendment with its reserved-powers provision was specifically designed to answer the latter criticism. The members of the legislature generally con-

[7] Charles Lee to George Washington, October 29, 1788, in U. S. Bureau of Library and Rolls, *Documentary History of the Constitution, 1787-1870* (5 vols., Washington, 1901-1905), V, 101-103; Grigsby, *Virginia Federal Convention*, X, 190-94. This was a favored project of the anti-federalists, and the only measure upon which the various elements were able to agree.

[8] Henry did everything in his power to defeat Madison, resting his opposition upon Madison's supposed hostility to amending the Constitution. Henry even tried to keep Madison out of the House of Representatives by arranging the counties in Madison's district in such a fashion that the anti-federalists would control a majority. The situation was so serious that Madison, upon the urging of friends, returned to Virginia and campaigned. For the latter task he had a marked dislike, but his appearance in his district won him the election over the anti-federalist candidate, James Monroe. Monroe had reluctantly been persuaded to run against Madison. Charles Lee to Washington, November 9, 1788, in *Documentary History of the Constitution*, V, 110; Burgess Ball to Madison, December 8, 1788; Edward Carrington to Madison, November 26, 1788; Madison to Washington, December 2, 1788; Hardin Burnley to Madison, December 16, 1788, all in Madison Papers (Manuscripts Division, Library of Congress); Gaillard Hunt, *The Life of James Madison* (New York, 1902), 146-47.

[9] The favorable reaction in Virginia to the Constitution during the six months following its ratification was clearly manifested in the congressional elections, when out of a total of ten representatives, seven federalists were chosen. Madison to Jefferson, March 29, 1789, in *Letters and Other Writings of James Madison* (4 vols., Philadelphia, 1865), I, 179; hereinafter cited as Madison, *Letters* (Congress).

[10] The quotation is from Edmund Randolph to Madison, June 30, 1789, in Madison Papers.

demned as "seditious and highly reprehensible" the letter Senators Lee and Grayson had written to the legislature urging that Madison's amendments should be rejected because of their inadequacy. The legislature, which had willingly responded to the direction of Henry in the preceding year by electing Lee and Grayson, now refused to tender them a vote of thanks for their efforts in the Senate to defeat Madison's amendments.[11] Although these amendments fell short of those recommended by the Virginia ratifying convention, they were sufficiently extensive to win over the more moderate anti-federalists.[12]

The legislature of 1789-1790 witnessed a last trifling manifestation of the party animosities that had been engendered in the conflict over the Constitution when Patrick Henry introduced a resolution to postpone the consideration of the amendments until the next session. Without waiting for his resolutions to be acted upon, Henry returned home after attending the session for only a few weeks. Without the support of their sponsor they were summarily rejected.[13] With this last gesture anti-federalism vanished in Virginia, and while men continued to watch closely the conduct of the new government, there was no longer in existence a party pledged to its destruction. When an opposition group did appear, it was not aimed at the government as such, but at the measures proposed during Washington's first administration, and had as its objective the checking of the government's policies rather than the abolition of the federal instrument.

[11] Edward Carrington to Madison, December 20, 1789, ibid.; Dd. Stuart to [Washington], December 3, 1789, in Documentary History of the Constitution, V, 220.

[12] These amendments were not finally ratified until the session of 1791. The delay was caused by a disagreement between the House of Delegates and the Senate over several of the amendments. It is not possible to ascertain the motives of the Senate in this controversy between the two houses. Ammon, "Republican Party," 106.

[13] At this session Patrick Henry seems to have lost all interest in anti-federalism, and his departure was a most agreeable surprise to the federalists who speculated as to its cause. Jefferson advanced the opinion that Henry had retired in disappointment over his inability to prevent the ratification of the proposed amendments. Jefferson to William Stuart, December 14, 1789, in Paul L. Ford (ed.), The Writings of Thomas Jefferson (10 vols., New York, 1892-1899), V, 136 [hereinafter cited as Jefferson, Writings (Ford)]; Carrington to Madison, December 30, 1789, in Madison Papers. Fisher Ames, in reporting a rumor current in New York that Henry was no longer intransigent in his opposition to the new government, seems to have come closer to the truth. Ames to George Richards Minot, January 13, 1790, in Seth Ames (ed.), Works of Fisher Ames (2 vols., Boston, 1854), I, 72.

The immediate cause for the revival of political animosities was Hamilton's Report on Finances of January, 1790. Until the submission of this report the measures of the federal government had met with increasing approval in the Old Dominion. Now, as Hamilton's proposals were translated into law by Congress, there was a growing discontent. The plan as a whole was not condemned, but only those portions relating to the assumption of the state debts and the establishment of a national bank. Hamilton's recommendation that the Continental and foreign debt should be paid was accepted without complaint, for it had been recognized ever since the Constitution was adopted that this would necessarily be one of the first acts of the new government.[14] It was clearly understood that the funding system might lead to the creation of a class of stockholders dedicated to support the government out of self-interest, but this method of financing the debt was accepted as the only possible means.[15] Madison and others, however, were horrified at the proposal that the Continental debt should be funded at par, when, as all knew, the Continental certificates had never sold at face value. To make it worse, speculators, who seemed to have advance information as to the government's plans, had been avidly purchasing these depreciated securities during the winter of 1789-1790. Madison's stubborn fight to prevent the redemption of these certificates at par, while a failure in Congress, won him, according to Henry Lee, the applause of the "landed interest" in Virginia. Naturally, as Lee also pointed out, Madison's course was much "disrelished by the town interest," which had been active in purchasing securities.[16]

The bitterness created by this issue was quickly succeeded by

[14] Jefferson to Madison, November 18, 1788, in Jefferson, *Writings* (Ford), V, 55.

[15] Henry Lee argued in this fashion in a letter to Madison, March 4, 1790, in Madison Papers.

[16] Lee to Madison, March 13, 1790, *ibid.* Randolph confirmed Lee's description of the reaction in Virginia. Randolph to Madison, March 10, 1790, *ibid.* See also Madison to Henry Lee, April 13, 1790, in Gaillard Hunt (ed.), *The Writings of James Madison* (9 vols., New York, 1900-1910), VI, 11 [hereinafter cited as Madison, *Writings* (Hunt)]; and William Cabell Rives, *History of the Life and Times of James Madison* (3 vols., Boston, 1859-1868), III, 79-87. Carrington presented the views of the "town interest" to Madison when he pointed out that the original holder had no claim to the face value for he had originally received them at below par; moreover, the speculator took a risk in purchasing securities which had never been at par. Carrington to Madison, March 2, 1790, in Madison Papers.

the resentment aroused by the plan to assume the state debts, which followed upon the heels of the funding scheme. The assumption proposal caused some of the warmest admirers of the new government to waver in their devotion to the political structure which they had helped to establish and in which they had believed so devoutly. This measure seemed absolutely unnecessary to the average Virginian, for his state had paid off most of its debt, and to him it seemed but an excuse to increase the number of federal stockholders. Assumption, it was believed, would merely add to the financial burdens of the Old Dominion, for according to Madison's calculations the first plan would have required the state to pay one fifth of the total instead of the more equitable one seventh.[17] From the outset the opposition to assumption was total. It was more than just a question of the way in which the measure was to be executed, as it had been in the case of the redemption of the Continental debt. Both Henry Lee and Edward Carrington, who had looked upon the Constitution as the only way to prevent civil discord and who later became Federalists of the steadiest character, questioned the integrity of the proponents of this measure. Lee went so far as to see in it the confirmation of Patrick Henry's prediction of 1788 that the Constitution would create a government dominated by "an insolent northern majority," which would permanently subjugate the agricultural interest—a charge which Lee had certainly not agreed with when it was originally made.[18]

With Madison fully exerting himself, the first assumption plan was defeated in the House of Representatives—a defeat which augmented Madison's reputation in his native state. As Edmund Randolph informed him, many of those who had once distrusted Madison because of his excessive federalism were now inclined to regard him more favorably.[19] The rejection of assumption was only temporary. The story of Hamilton's appeal to Jefferson and the latter's acquiescence in a compromise is too well known to require repetition. As a result of this agreement the capital was located on the Potomac and two members of the Virginia delegation, Richard Henry Lee and Alexander White, changed their

[17] *Annals of Congress*, 1 Cong., 2 Sess., 1590 ff.
[18] Lee to Madison, April 3, 1790; Carrington to Madison, April 30, 1790, in Madison Papers.
[19] E[dmund] R[andolph] to Madison, May 20, 1790, *ibid.*

votes and helped to pass a revised assumption program. Madison was a party to this agreement, although he did not alter his vote. He merely agreed not to agitate unduly against the revised bill.[20] Although Jefferson and Madison believed that the new act, which assumed $3,500,000 for Virginia, would bring neither gain nor loss to their state, their fellow citizens did not view the measure in this light.[21] Both Madison and Jefferson had been warned that the location of the capital on the Potomac would not make assumption palatable in Virginia.[22] The accuracy of these warnings was quite evident when the legislature assembled in November, 1790. Only one topic of conversation was to be heard—the assumption—and the reaction was unfavorable.[23] Resolutions condemning the measure as the exercise of a power not granted to the federal government were quickly passed, and a committee was appointed to draft a memorial of protest to be submitted to Congress. The committee included both former federalists and former anti-federalists. Patrick Henry now found it possible to cooperate with two of his most outspoken opponents in 1788— Francis Corbin and Henry Lee.[24]

The memorial of 1790, which has been attributed to Patrick Henry, ranks in importance with the historic resolutions of 1798 against the Alien and Sedition Laws.[25] For the first time the legislature of Virginia registered a protest against a federal law upon the grounds of its unconstitutionality and proclaimed the right of the state to remonstrate.

The constitutional point of view of the memorialists was stated succinctly:

[20] Jefferson to George Mason, June 13, 1790; Jefferson to T. M. Randolph, June 20, 1790, in Jefferson, *Writings* (Ford), V, 184-85.

[21] Jefferson to T. M. Randolph, July 25, 1790, in Coolidge Papers (Massachusetts Historical Society); Madison to Bishop James Madison, July 31, 1791, in Madison, *Writings* (Hunt), VI, 19-20.

[22] Monroe to Jefferson, July 3, 1790, in Stanislaus Murray Hamilton (ed.), *The Writings of James Monroe* (7 vols., New York, 1898-1903), I, 209; James Dawson to Madison, July 4, 1790, in Madison Papers.

[23] Zachariah Johnston to Archibald Stuart, October 27, 1790, in Stuart-Baldwin Papers (University of Virginia Library).

[24] Virginia General Assembly, *Journal of the House of Delegates for 1790*, pp. 25-44 (November 3-8, 1790). The only prominent person to oppose the resolutions was John Marshall. Albert J. Beveridge, *Life of John Marshall* (4 vols., New York, 1916-1919), II, 65-68.

[25] William Wirt Henry, *Patrick Henry: Life, Correspondence, and Speeches* (3 vols., New York, 1891), II, 453-55, ascribed this memorial to Patrick Henry.

During the whole discussion of the fœderal constitution by the convention of Virginia, your memorialists were taught to believe "That every power not granted, was retained," under this impression and upon this positive condition, declared in the instrument of ratification, the said government was adopted by the people of this Commonwealth; but your memorialists can find no clause in the constitution, authorizing Congress to assume the debts of the states! As the guardians then of the rights and interests of their constituents, as sentinels placed by them over the ministers of the fœderal government, to shield it from their encroachments, or at least to sound the alarm when it is threatened with invasion, they can never reconcile it to their consciences, silently to acquiesce in a measure, which violates that hallowed maxim.[26]

In this brief passage the legislature of Virginia formulated the principle of strict construction which was to become an integral part of the political thinking of every Republican. To some extent the memorial foreshadowed the later doctrine that the state was the proper agent to judge infractions against the Constitution. This doctrine, however, was not to receive its explicit statement until Jefferson drafted the Kentucky Resolutions of 1798.

Apart from the constitutional theory put forward, the memorial is of particular interest because of its frank and clear statement that the assumption measure tended to create a monied interest which was injurious to farmers and planters. In subsequent legislative resolutions and memorials, finespun constitutional and legal arguments predominated to the exclusion of the practical and immediate injuries wrought by the measures under discussion. The memorial declared: "In an agricultural country like this, therefore to erect, and concentrate, and perpetuate a large monied interest, is a measure which . . . must in the course of human events, produce one or other of two evils, the prostration of agriculture at the feet of commerce, or a change in the present form of fœderal government, fatal to the existence of American liberty."

This legislative protest marked the first step in the creation of a party based upon the agricultural element and seeking to wrest

[26] William Waller Hening (ed.), *The Statutes at Large; Being a Collection of all the Laws of Virginia* [1619-1792] (13 vols., Richmond 1809-1823), XIII, 237-39. The full text of the memorial may be conveniently found in Henry S. Commager (ed.), *Documents of American History* (2 vols., 2nd ed., New York, 1940), I, 155-56.

control of the federal government from the hands of the commercial eastern interests which seemed to dominate it.[27] It did not immediately lead to the formation of distinct parties, for many of those who joined in the protest against assumption were later to reaffirm their loyalty to the Washington administration and its measures. Other tests were to be necessary before political affiliations became distinct.

During the third session of the First Congress two other widely unpopular measures were put into effect—the excise on whisky and the establishment of the Bank of the United States. Neither was liked in Virginia, but at the same time neither produced any notable movement of protest. Governor Henry Lee was probably overapprehensive in predicting that there would be armed resistance to the excise in the western parts of the state.[28] Actually, apart from a few petitions and some meetings around Morgantown and Martinsburg, no resistance occurred in Virginia.[29] The bank bill did not then have the central position which it held a few years later. All of the members of the Virginia delegation present in Congress voted against the incorporation of the Bank of the United States. Madison and William Branch Giles, who was just coming into political prominence at this time, distinguished themselves by their opposition to this measure. In their speeches they stressed the constitutional issue, denying that the power to incorporate had been granted to Congress. They insisted that this power could not be inferred from the grant of power to borrow money, for this was not a bill for that purpose; nor did Congress have the power to create a means of borrowing money as a result of the general grant of the power to borrow money. Madison conceded that the bank might be convenient and useful, but he denied that it was absolutely necessary in order to borrow money.[30]

Shortly after the adjournment of the First Congress, in which so many vital measures had been adopted, Madison and Jefferson set out on their famed "botanical" excursion through the eastern

---

[27] In expressing their confidence "in the justice and wisdom of Congress" which would lead that body to repeal the assumption act, the memorialists indicated no desire to destroy the existing frame of government.

[28] Jefferson to Madison, June 21, 1791, in Madison Papers.

[29] Leland D. Baldwin, *Whiskey Rebels: The Story of a Frontier Uprising* (Pittsburgh, 1939), 105-108, 207-208.

[30] *Annals of Congress*, 1 Cong., 3 Sess., 1937 ff.

and northern states.[31] While this was not the first occasion that these close friends had traveled together, the fact that they called upon the leading political figures of the day during their travels lent to their jaunt more than a passing significance. Although the letters of neither traveler reflected any particular concern over political matters, their observations were undoubtedly more searching than those of the casual passer-by. What Madison and Jefferson saw and heard upon this leisurely journey was of great value in plotting the course which they thought must be adopted in the face of the rising eastern interest, which they believed threatened to dominate the Union. Although James Monroe, who was later to be so intimately associated with Jefferson and Madison in creating the Republican party, did not accompany them upon this excursion, he seems to have been well aware of the political interests of his colleagues. Shortly after the conclusion of Jefferson's tour with Madison, Monroe wrote the former:

Upon political subjects we perfectly agree and particularly in the reprobation of all measures that may be calculated to elevate the government above the people, or place it in any respect without its natural boundary. To keep it there is nothing necessary but virtue in a part only (for in the whole it cannot be expected) of the high public servants, and a true developement of the principles of those arts wh. have a contrary tendency. The bulk of the people are for democracy, and if they are well informed the reck [sic] of such enterprizes will inevitably follow.[32]

There is no direct reference in this letter to any precise agreement, but it indicates that a general understanding was in the process of formation among these three leaders. Monroe's emphasis upon the undemocratic tendencies of the government was both a foretaste of subsequent Republican propaganda and an echo of the dire predictions which the anti-federalists had made in 1788.

Although Madison, Jefferson, and Monroe seem to have established a common ground of political opinions in 1791, there was no immediate attempt to transfer these principles to the level of a popular organization. They continued to survey the strength and

[31] See Jefferson's letters of May and June, 1791, in Jefferson, *Writings* (Ford), V, 335 ff.
[32] Monroe to Jefferson, July 17, 1791, in Hamilton (ed.), *Writings of Monroe*, I, 223.

endurance of the recently developed hostility against the new government and attempted to gauge the extent to which the critics of the fiscal program could be relied upon to continue their opposition. During 1791 and 1792 the members of the Virginia triumvirate were indefatigable in visiting and corresponding with their prominent contemporaries. Their correspondents included Henry Lee, Patrick Henry, George Mason, Edmund Randolph, and Edmund Pendleton. The information they obtained reflected an uncertainty on the part of some who were gradually retreating from the extremes of the 1790 protest against assumption. Among those whose afterthoughts led them to regret their previous position were Henry Lee and Patrick Henry. By 1792 both had abandoned their opposition to assumption and adopted the view that it was necessary to support Hamilton's program in order to avoid civil disturbances.[33]

When the Second Congress began its sessions it was obvious that there was an opposition devoted to the principles of strict constructionism, agrarianism, and republicanism. All of the members of the Virginia delegation can be numbered in this group, which was soon labeled the "republican interest." Madison was conspicuous in expounding strict-construction views, while John Page and William Branch Giles presented to Congress the republican and agrarian aspects of the philosophy of the minority. Again and again during the first session of the Second Congress, Page referred to the administration measures as efforts to carry into effect the "projects of Monarchical and Aristocratical juntos."[34]

A thoroughly self-conscious, agrarian economic point of view was advanced by William Branch Giles, with the able assistance of Page, during the debates on a bounty to codfishers. This comparatively unimportant measure drew the fire of both men. Giles saw in the practice of granting bounties the creation of a "separate and distinct interest not wholly between the East and the South, but between the manufacturers and the cultivators of the soil."[35] He warned the sponsors of the bill that the only way in which

[33] Lee to Madison, January 8, 1792; Henry to Madison, January 17, 1792, in Madison, *Writings* (Hunt),VI, 81-83.
[34] Speech on the ratio of representation, November 15, 1791, in *Annals of Congress*, 2 Cong., 1 Sess., 183; see also his speech on the bounty to codfishers, February 7, 1792, *ibid.*, 391-95.
[35] *Ibid.*, 400 (.February 8, 1792).

they could prevent the opposition which was now based only "upon jealousies and suspicions" from becoming a "real" party was by administering the government impartially in the interests of all. Page shared Giles's apprehensions that the commercial elements were being favored by the measure, and in repudiating it he carried his agrarian philosophy to its ultimate conclusion. He informed his fellow congressmen that he believed it would be of far greater service to the nation if the fishermen were to be sent to the West to cultivate unused lands. A nation of farmers, in Page's eyes, was to be preferred to a nation of seamen.[36] Seldom was this point of view given such direct and positive expression.

President Washington was deeply concerned by the activities of the minority in Congress, and in the spring of 1792 he asked Jefferson to outline the principles which motivated the "republicans." Jefferson informed the President that the "republican party" saw in the fiscal system a design to change "the present republican form of government to that of monarchy." This plan, he continued, was contemplated in the Philadelphia convention where its partisans had made no secret of their intent, and now the monarchists together with the "corrupt squadron" of public stockholders possessed a majority in Congress. The great object of the "republicans," therefore, was to "preserve the government in its present form." Jefferson listed a second reason for the formation of the opposition. It arose, he believed, from the continued sacrifice of southern to northern, agrarian to commercial interests in the face of the South's known hostility to the new government when it was first proposed. In this letter Jefferson summarized the basic principles upon which he had agreed with Monroe and Madison the year before. These were the principles upon which the minority in Congress had operated, and they became the guiding theories of the Republican party.[37]

Although there was an active minority in Congress opposing the

[36] *Ibid.*, 391-95 (February 7, 1792). It should be noted that neither Madison nor Jefferson opposed this measure, which Jefferson had recommended in his report on the fisheries. Madison voted for it. *Ibid.*, 395.

[37] Jefferson to Washington, May 23, 1792, in Jefferson, *Writings* (Ford), VI, 1-6. In this letter Jefferson urged Washington to continue in office, for his presence alone would be sufficient to prevent the monarchists from carrying out their plans. Jefferson went over somewhat similar ground in a conversation with Washington reported in Jefferson's "Anas," July 10, 1792, in A. A. Lipscomb and A. E. Bergh (eds.), *The Writings of Thomas Jefferson* (20 vols., New York, 1903-1904), I, 311-12.

Washington administration, and although Jefferson could write to Washington concerning the objectives of the "republican party," there was actually no party as yet on the popular level. No test had been made of the political sentiments of the average Virginian which would unequivocally label him as either a supporter of the "republican interest" or a member of the "governmental" or "ministerial machine." The test had not materialized simply because no suitable issue had presented itself.

It would seem that the Hamiltonian fiscal program should have been the proper measure to select as the rallying point for a popular movement, since this was the question which had produced the first real antagonism against the Washington administration. The "republicans," however, seem to have avoided this particular issue in Virginia, and it was not until after party lines had been drawn upon other measures that the fiscal program became a major point of attack. There were two basic reasons why the "republican interest" shied away from the subject of the Hamiltonian program. The first of these Monroe succinctly stated to Madison in June, 1792:

I found at Richmond a general dissatisfaction to the measures of the government prevailing; in the specification, it harmonized with the sentiments of the minority. Notwithstanding I am well satisfied that in the present state of things the soundest deliberation must be used before any attempt at a change is made. Upon the excise particularly, altho an universal odium exists, yet it seems doubtful whether if the money must be raised, any other mode wod. be preferred. . . . Another mode might bring upon its authors the odium wh. now belongs to the father of this, and if the public censure is to be fix'd on any, who are better objects for it than those who have made the tax necessary[?] [38]

It would be difficult to quarrel with the political strategy formulated in this letter. How, indeed, could the "republicans" attack a measure whose objects they deemed indispensable when they could concoct no other means to the same end likely to be more acceptable? The path of wisdom, therefore, was to await the appearance of some issue which could be attacked from all sides without creating any awkward problems.

A second reason—equally pragmatic—deterred Jefferson and his

[38] Monroe to Madison, June 27, 1792, in Madison Papers.

cohorts. Early in 1792 it was perfectly obvious that many who had joined in the hue and cry against assumption two years before and who had willingly subscribed to the legislative protest were now retreating from their former stand. Both Patrick Henry and Henry Lee after previously inveighing against assumption were now defending the Hamiltonian program. They both argued that it must be accepted, even though objectionable, lest continued opposition beget civil disturbances and turmoil.[39] The "republican interest" could not afford the risk of seeking to discredit the administration by a wholesale attack on the fiscal system, for such action might compel moderate men to support the government in order to avoid civil disturbances and financial chaos.[40] The premature selection of an issue could easily jeopardize the whole movement, and for the moment there was no effort to organize a following on a popular level.

Although no general appeal had been made to the people, the presidential electors of the Old Dominion in 1792 acted with a unanimity that was indicative of the extent of the understanding among the leaders of the state. Every elector cast his second ballot for George Clinton, who had been brought forward by the opponents of the administration as a rival of John Adams, the favorite of all who abhorred the nascent "republicans." On the other hand, in voting solidly for George Washington on their first ballot the electors reflected the policy of Jefferson and his associates of continuing to support Washington. This unanimity of action was the result of the political habits of Virginia, where patterns of aristocratic leadership prevailed. The influence of Jefferson and the other leaders in his party with the members of this dominant class was sufficient to mobilize the electors of the state.[41]

In connection with the political contacts which we have previously noted that the Virginians were most active in making, an incident which occurred on the eve of the election deserves some

[39] Lee to Madison, January 8, 1792; Henry to Madison, January 17, 1792, in Madison, *Writings* (Hunt), VI, 81-83.

[40] Not all joined in this retreat. George Mason, for example, continued to abhor the Hamiltonian program. Mason to Monroe, February 9, 1792, in Monroe Papers (Manuscripts Division, Library of Congress).

[41] Edward Stanwood, *A History of the Presidency* (Boston, 1898), 39. Joseph Dawson, intimate of Monroe and Jefferson, assisted in this process of selection by talking up Clinton among the members of the legislature when it met in 1792. Dawson to Monroe, October 29, 1792, in Monroe Papers (New York Public Library).

comment because of the light it throws upon the political methods of the day, even though it does not relate exclusively to the local scene. In October, 1792, a special messenger arrived in Fredericksburg from an agent of Aaron Burr in New York. The messenger brought a letter to Monroe proposing that Burr be substituted for George Clinton as the "candidate of the republican interest." Monroe sent the letter together with the bearer to Madison. Regarding the suggested change as "truly embarrassing," Madison at once proposed a personal conference with Monroe.[42] Not only does this episode illustrate the extent of the contacts among the Republican leaders, but it reveals their general methods of operation. At this crucial period none of the leaders of the opposition trusted intimate political secrets to the post. Indeed they seem to have avoided writing except when necessary, and confined themselves in their letters to promises to discuss important subjects when they next met. Since Madison, Monroe, and Jefferson lived within easy reach of one another in Virginia, it was possible for them to arrange frequent meetings.

Not only did the leading figures find occasion to meet together, but they also contrived opportunities for visiting and conversing with local political leaders. Jefferson, for example, stopped off at Gunston Hall on his way to Monticello in 1792 to see his old friend George Mason and to sound out his political views.[43] In the same year Madison was able to see William B. Giles, Josiah Parker, and John Page in Fredericksburg, while waiting for Monroe to accompany him to Philadelphia.[44] Such meetings were undoubtedly of common occurrence. Jefferson seems to have taken a lesser part in this activity, for his position as Secretary of State made it necessary for him to avoid open acts of opposition. Monroe, for example, conducted all the arrangements connected with the writing of John Taylor's pamphlet against the Bank of the United States in 1793—transmitting to Taylor Jefferson's compliments and suggestions for revision without, of course, referring to Jefferson by name.[45] Because personal conferences were so im-

[42] Monroe to Madison, October 9, 1792, in Monroe Papers (Library of Congress); Madison to Monroe, October 11, 1792, in Madison Papers. Burr is not mentioned by name in either letter. Unfortunately, the reply which Monroe and Madison agreed upon exists neither in the original nor in drafts.

[43] Jefferson to Madison, October 1, 1792, in Jefferson, *Writings* (Ford), VI, 114.

[44] Madison to ———, October 23, 1792, draft, in Madison Papers.

[45] Monroe to Madison, May 18, 1793, *ibid.*

portant, much of the early history of the Republican party must remain unknown.

It was not until the autumn of 1793 that the leaders of the "republican interest" sought to organize a demonstration of public opinion that would clearly establish the strength and vigor of the opposition to the administration. Even at this juncture one has the impression that they were forced to take steps in this direction somewhat sooner than they had intended. Jefferson and his associates decided to make the occasion of the widespread disapproval of Washington's policy towards France their point of departure. Certainly from a political point of view this issue had none of the embarrassing aspects which Monroe had noted in connection with the fiscal program. The policies of the administration could be attacked without opening upon any vistas of internal disorders as in the case of Hamilton's financial system. By taking up this question the "republicans" were able to vitalize the as yet inarticulate and vague opposition which existed on the popular level.

The course of the French Revolution had been watched with much sympathy in the United States by those attached to the "republican interest," but it was not until the French declaration of war on England in February, 1793, that they took umbrage at the policy of the Washington administration. The particular cause of the "republican" anger was Washington's proclamation of neutrality of April 22, 1793—notable for its careful avoidance of the word "neutral." The proclamation had been drafted after much consultation with members of the cabinet as to the exact obligations of the United States under the treaty of 1778. It had been cautiously worded in an effort to make it more palatable to the Francophiles, who, it was believed, wished the United States to render full aid to France. In this objective it failed completely. The pro-French "republicans" were not so much disappointed because the administration chose to be neutral, but because Washington and his advisers failed to lend the moral weight of the United States in behalf of the French cause. In this moderately worded document the "republicans" saw evidence of what they considered to be the influence of the mercantile element—the pro-British party which desired closer relations with Britain for commercial reasons and who wished to introduce the British system of government in the United States.[46] This issue so sharply divided opinions that Jefferson at last believed it was possible to sort out parties with some accuracy. According to him the French question left no doubt that the fashionable circles of Philadelphia, New York, and Boston, merchants trading on British capital, and the public stockholders were all on the side of the British, whereas the farmers, mechanics, Irish merchants, and merchants trading upon their own capital were warm in behalf of the French.[47] Madison confirmed this judgment as far as Virginia was concerned, noting that the towns were united in approving the President's proclamation, while the farmers universally despised it.[48] The impact of the war in Europe was reflected in the organization of a Republican Society in Norfolk in 1793 which immediately published a set of resolutions identifying the cause of liberty everywhere with the victory of France.[49]

The whole discussion of the proclamation, followed by the enthusiastic reception given Citizen Edmond Genêt during his progress through Virginia, alarmed President Washington. During the summer of 1793 Washington heard rumors that the "Virg[inia] interest, as it is called, designs to attack him." To verify this report and to obtain firsthand information about public opinion there, he sent his fellow Virginian and Secretary of State, Edmund Randolph, to Virginia in July, 1793.[50] This visitation was eagerly seized upon by the leaders of the "republican interest" as an opportunity to impress their point of view more directly upon Washington. To achieve this purpose Jefferson sent specific instructions to Madison as to the necessity of exposing Randolph to

[46] "Firm Republican" presented these arguments in the *Richmond and Manchester Advertiser*, October 28, 1793.
[47] Jefferson to Madison, May 12, 1793, in Jefferson, *Writings* (Ford), VI, 251.
[48] Madison to Jefferson, June 13, 1793, in Madison, *Letters* (Congress), I, 581-82. Monroe made the same observation about Virginia. Monroe to Jefferson, May 8, 1793, in Hamilton (ed.), *Writings of Monroe*, I, 252.
[49] Resolutions of the Republican Society of Norfolk, in Norfolk *Virginia Chronicle*, June 8, 1793. From the available records it does not seem that the Democratic Societies, which played such an important part in the development of the Republican party in some of the other states, were a significant factor in Virginia. The Norfolk Society was the second such organization to be formed and the first in Virginia. The only other societies formed in Virginia were organized in Dumfries and in Wytheville. See Eugene P. Link, *Democratic Republican Societies, 1790-1800* (New York, 1942), *passim*.
[50] John Taylor to Madison, June 20, 1793, in Madison Papers. Taylor received his information concerning Washington's apprehensions from Edmund Randolph.

correct influences: "I have no doubt he is charged to bring back a faithful statement of the dispositions of that state. I wish therefore he may fall into hands which will not deceive him. Have you the time and the means of impressing Wilson [Cary] Nicholas (who will be much with E.R.), with the necessity of giving him a strong and perfect understanding of the public mind?"[51] Madison was unable to see Nicholas before Randolph arrived, and consequently did not carry out Jefferson's recommendations. When Madison finally did see Nicholas after Randolph had departed, he reported to Jefferson that Nicholas seemed to be "right and firm on the French Revolution and free from any taint of heresy," but that in conversing with Randolph he might very well have adapted his views to suit those of his important guest.[52]

Although Nicholas may have been "right" on the French question, he did not prevent Randolph from returning to President Washington with a report that Virginia was basically in accord with the President's policies and that the opposition which existed was limited to a personal antagonism towards Hamilton.[53] Madison and Jefferson were both deeply shocked at Randolph's erroneous observations, which Madison blamed on "tainted sources" whose obvious bias should have induced the President's emissary to be wary of their opinions.[54]

It is impossible to say on the basis of the available evidence whether the Republicans were planning, as Washington suspected, an organized attack on his policies. The Virginia newspapers are not particularly informative on this question. The two principal papers of the state, the *Virginia Gazette and General Advertiser* and the *Richmond and Manchester Advertiser*, both published in Richmond, were weeklies with no decided political preference. Political opinion was indicated only through

[51] Jefferson to Madison, June 2, 1793, in Jefferson, *Writings* (Ford), VI, 278. Randolph was Nicholas' brother-in-law.

[52] Madison to Jefferson, July 22, 1793, in Madison, *Writings* (Hunt), VI, 136.

[53] Jefferson to Madison, July 21, 1793, in Jefferson, *Writings* (Ford), VI, 355.

[54] Madison to Jefferson, July 30, 1793, in Madison, *Writings* (Hunt), VI, 139. Not all "tainted sources" were so biased. Edward Carrington, who was warmly devoted to the administration, gave Hamilton a view of public opinion which corresponded closely to that of the Republicans. Carrington urged Hamilton to see that the French minister should be received in order to prevent the charge that the government was in the hands of an "eastern influence in favor of monarchy in America, consequently, unfriendly to the liberties of France." Carrington to Hamilton, April 26, 1793, in John C. Hamilton (ed.), *The Works of Alexander Hamilton* (7 vols., New York, 1850-1851), V, 555-60.

letters representing both sides. It was in part the political weakness of the Virginia press which led Jefferson to sponsor Philip Freneau's *National Gazette*. Only a few letters appeared in these papers prior to the public demonstrations against the foreign policy of the Washington administration which began in the autumn of 1793.

Whatever the plans of the Republicans may have been in the spring, developments late in the summer compelled them to act. The need for an organized anti-administration campaign which would clearly indicate the pro-French sentiments of the people seems to have been brought home to the "republican" leaders by the effect of a public meeting held in Richmond on August 17, 1793. This assembly was presided over by Chancellor George Wythe, while two strong administration men, John Marshall and James McClurg, were on the committee which drafted resolutions that were highly laudatory of Washington's policy.[55] By the end of the month similar sets of resolutions were adopted at Norfolk and in King William County.[56] Madison immediately ascribed their activities to the influence of the "Philadelphia cabal," by which he meant the pro-English mercantile group dominated by Hamilton and against which he had been contending since 1791. Prompted by these resolutions Monroe and Madison immediately conferred and concluded that a misconception of Virginia's sentiments would prevail if there were not "an early and well digested effort for calling out the real sense of the people." They agreed that the best counteroffensive would be to set "on foot expressions of the public mind in important counties . . . under the auspices of respectable names." With this object in mind Madison wrote John Taylor of Caroline late in August enclosing a set of resolutions with the request that they be adopted at a meeting in Caroline County under the sponsorship of Edmund Pendleton.[57] Taylor acted with such promptitude that within two weeks a meeting was arranged and he was able to make a favorable report to Madison: "Instantly upon the re-

---

[55] Richmond *Virginia Gazette and General Advertiser*, August 21, 1793.

[56] *Ibid.*, September 4, 1793; Norfolk *Virginia Chronicle*, September 21, 1793.

[57] Madison to Jefferson, August 27, 1793, in Madison, *Letters* (Congress), I. 595-96. Monroe also wrote to Taylor to much the same effect, and urged him to prevent the other counties from being led astray. Monroe to Taylor, August 30, 1793, in *Proceedings of the Massachusetts Historical Society* (Boston, 1791-   ), 3rd Ser., XLII (1908), 321.

ceipt of yours from Albemarle, notifications were dispersed, and in five days resolutions were formed by a very numerous meeting. They are in some papers, and will appear in many others. I hope you will approve of them. I wish they may differ enough from those of the [state] to avoid suspicion of their being coined in the same mint."[58] Edmund Pendleton, as Madison had wished, presided at this meeting, thus lending the dignity of the name of the chancellor of the Court of Appeals of Virginia to the resolutions.[59]

The resolutions adopted in Caroline, and with changes in the other counties, demanded the preservation of the alliance with France, on the ground that repudiation would be deliberately to draw the United States closer to Great Britain. The resolutions did not suggest military aid to France, but only proclaimed that the spectacle of a nation—and in particular one to which the United States owed such a debt of gratitude—struggling for its liberty should arouse the sympathy of the people. They attributed the anti-French propaganda to those men who "desire a closer union with Britain and [who] desire to alter the government of the United States to a monarchy." The framers of the protest were careful to include a declaration of loyalty to Washington and to condemn the activities of Citizen Genêt, though without mentioning the latter by name. This policy was entirely in accord with Republican views at this time, for Genêt's intemperate conduct had made him a liability rather than an asset. The resolutions provided an ideal opportunity for the Republicans to detach themselves from any direct connection with the French minister.[60]

While one set of resolutions was being considered in Caroline, similar sets appeared in other counties. Madison sent one copy to Albemarle, and Monroe rode off to the Staunton court with another. In Staunton Monroe was able to obtain the adoption of his resolutions under the patronage of Archibald Stuart, a prominent leader of the Valley. Monroe's arrival in Staunton was especially timely, for he was able to prevent the adoption of a set of pro-administration resolutions which were about to be proposed as a

---

[58] J[ohn] T[aylor] to Madison, September 25, 1793, in Madison Papers.
[59] The meeting was held September 10, 1793. Resolutions were printed in the Richmond *Virginia Gazette and General Advertiser*, September 25, 1793.
[60] Jefferson and Madison had agreed early in August that they must abandon Genêt before he did irreparable damage to their cause. Jefferson to Madison, August 3, 1793, in Jefferson, *Writings* (Ford), VI, 361; Madison to Jefferson, August 5, 1793, in Madison, *Writings* (Hunt), VI, 139.

result of John Marshall's influence. By the end of September resolutions corresponding in the main to the original pattern had been adopted in Culpeper, New Kent, Williamsburg, King William, Fredericksburg, and Albemarle, in addition to those approved in Caroline and at Staunton.[61]

With the organization of the protest against Washington's policy toward France the opposition entered upon a new phase. Prior to 1793 it had been confined to a relatively small group of political figures who had relied upon the tradition of aristocratic leadership and the common point of view of an agrarian state to sustain their program, without any attempt to define their objectives in a precise fashion. The resolutions, however, marked a realization of the need to mold and guide the public dissatisfaction against the policies of Washington's administration in a more direct and obvious fashion. From this point on the Republicans, assured of the support of a self-consciously Republican segment of the electorate, began to operate more openly. In their activities in Virginia it is undeniable that they were not only concerned with consolidating public opinion behind them, but also with using the Virginia demonstration to strengthen their following in other states. The confidence resulting from the attack on Washington's foreign policy led the Republicans to subject Hamilton's fiscal program to an extensive critical scrutiny. Among the most important of the pamphlets written on this topic were those of John Taylor of Caroline, the ranking agrarian political theorist of the state, who contributed two works on the fiscal system. The first, published late in 1793, exposed the personal speculations of members of Congress in the public securities; the second, which appeared in 1794, presented an unfavorable appraisal of the Bank of the United States.[62]

The second major issue which solidified party lines in Virginia arose from the treaty which John Jay negotiated with Great Britain in 1794 and which was submitted to the Senate in March, 1795. The decision of the Washington administration to attempt to obtain a treaty from the British was in large measure prompted

[61] Monroe to Madison, September 25, 1793, in Madison Papers; Madison to Jefferson, September 2, 1793, in Madison, *Letters* (Congress), I, 597; Monroe to Jefferson, October 14, 1793, in Hamilton (ed.), *Writings of Monroe*, I, 278; Richmond *Virginia Gazette and General Advertiser*, September 4, 25, October 2, 23, 1793; *Richmond and Manchester Advertiser*, October 24, 1793.
[62] These pamphlets are ably analyzed in Beard, *Economic Origins*, 196 ff.

by Madison's determined efforts during the Third Congress to impose commercial restrictions upon the British in order to compel them to execute the treaty of 1783 and to grant favorable trade concessions to Americans. Madison's resolutions were applauded by the planters and farmers of Virginia, and the repercussions of this approbation undoubtedly made the need for a new treaty seem imperative.[63]

From the very moment when Jay was appointed the Republicans had little hope that an acceptable treaty would be negotiated, for, as John Nicholas observed, he was "a man perfectly British in his affections."[64] The results were indeed in accordance with expectations. Shortly after the treaty was submitted to the Senate and before its contents were made public, criticisms of it appeared in the press.[65]

Following the publication of the text of the treaty, the Republicans organized a series of meetings at which resolutions unfavorable to the document were adopted. These resolutions requested the Senate to reject the treaty because it made no compensation for the slaves removed by the British during the Revolution, contained no protection of neutral rights, and granted no commercial advantages to the United States.[66] Chancellor George

[63] *Annals of Congress*, 3 Cong., 1 Sess., *passim*. Spencer Roane and others commented upon the favorable reaction in Virginia to Madison's proposals. Roane to Monroe, January 25, 1794, in Monroe Papers (Library of Congress); Joseph Jones to Madison, January 25, 1794; John Dawson to Madison, February 12, 1794, in Madison Papers. The mercantile interests in Virginia, while disapproving the failure of the British to execute the treaty, were not in favor of commercial restrictions. Robert Gamble to Wilson Cary Nicholas, February 24, 1794, in Nicholas Papers (University of Virginia Library). Resolutions approving Madison's proposals were adopted in Charlotte and Halifax counties. *Richmond and Manchester Advertiser*, May 26, 1794.

[64] John Nicholas to W. C. Nicholas, April 30, 1794, in Nicholas Papers (University of Virginia Library).

[65] Most of these criticisms revealed a reasonably thorough knowledge of the contents of the treaty. Madison, for instance, was able to give Monroe a fairly accurate summary in a letter from Philadelphia, March 26, 1795, in Madison Papers. The treaty was finally released to the public on June 29, 1795, by Stevens Thomson Mason, senator from Virginia. The Senate had voted to release the treaty while he was present, but later, in his absence, reversed itself. Mason chose to ignore the second ballot and undoubtedly released it in the interests of the Republicans who were convinced that the secrecy was based upon the Federalist fear that publicity would make ratification impossible. Madison to Monroe, December 20, 1795, copy, in Madison Papers; S. T. Mason to B. F. Bache, editor of the Philadelphia *Aurora*, June 29, 1795, enclosing a copy of the treaty, printed in Fredericksburg *Virginia Herald and Advertiser*, July 7, 1795.

[66] Meetings were held in Petersburg, Caroline, and Amelia. *Richmond and Manchester Advertiser*, August 8, 15, September 15, 1795.

Wythe presided over the meeting held in Richmond—a circumstance which was highly gratifying to the Republicans since he had been in the chair of the assemblage which had approved of Washington's proclamation in 1793.[67] The campaign might have reached considerable proportions had not the treaty been ratified late in August.[68]

When the legislature convened in October, 1795, the Republicans prepared to continue their war on the treaty. Resolutions were promptly introduced approving the conduct of Senators Henry Tazewell and Stevens Thomson Mason in voting against the treaty. This rather negative approach was probably chosen to avoid the implication of a personal attack on Washington, who had given his approval to Jay's handiwork.[69] In spite of the powerful opposition of John Marshall and Henry Lee, the resolution was approved by a vote of 100 to 50—a division which clearly indicated the relative strength of the two parties at this time. The Senate later altered the resolution with the concurrence of the House to include a phrase praising the "integrity and patriotism" of Washington and specifically exempting him from any censure in connection with the treaty.[70]

Bolstered by the disapproval of their state, the Virginians in the House of Representatives during the Fourth Congress joined in the efforts to nullify the treaty by blocking the passage of the necessary laws to carry it into effect.[71] Although the Virginia Republicans carried on the battle ably in Congress, the campaign at home was neglected. While the treaty was being debated in the House, the Federalists mustered their forces during the spring of

---

[67] Madison to Jefferson, August 6, 1795, in Madison, *Letters* (Congress), II, 43.

[68] This was the reason given for the cancellation of a proposed meeting in Goochland County. John Guerrant to Wilson C. Nicholas, September 10, 1795, in Nicholas Papers (Division of Manuscripts, Library of Congress). It is significant that Guerrant, who was an active Republican, felt that some explanation was necessary. Nicholas in the next few years became one of the most important figures in the Republican party in Virginia.

[69] Joseph Jones, a member of the legislature, pointed out this difficulty to Madison in a letter, October 29, 1795, in Madison Papers. Jones also expressed a wish to see Madison in order to consult with him on the steps to be taken in the legislature. If this meeting took place, Madison undoubtedly helped shape the final resolution.

[70] Virginia General Assembly, *Journal of the House of Delegates for 1795*, pp. 20, 27-29 (November 20-21, 1795), 71 (December 4, 1795).

[71] *Annals of Congress*, 4 Cong., 1 Sess., 976-1291, *passim*. An unusually large number of the delegation participated in the debates—Madison, John Nicholas, William B. Giles, Andrew Moore, John Heath, and Thomas Rutherford.

1796 and organized a series of meetings to express sentiments favorable to the treaty and to condemn the policy of the Republicans in the House.[72] The meeting held in Richmond was a master stroke arranged by John Marshall and took the Republicans completely by surprise.[73] Of this gathering, which was attended by about four hundred persons, Edmund Randolph, who was now definitely committed to the Republican side, sent an agitated account to Madison:

... a large proportion ... [of those present] were British merchants, some of whom pay for the British purchases of horses,—their clerks,—officers, who hold posts under the President at his will,—stockholders—expectants of offices—and many without the shadow of a freehold. Notwithstanding this, the numbers on the republican side though inferior, were in a small degree only; and it is believed on good grounds, that the majority of freeholders were on the side of the house of representatives. Campbell and Marshall were the principal combatants. . . . Marshall's argument was inconsistent, and shifting; concluding every third sentence with the horrors of war. Campbell spoke elegantly and forcibly; and threw ridicule and absurdity upon his antagonist with success. Mr. Clopton [member of Congress] will receive two papers; one signed by the treaty men, many of whom he will know to have neither interest nor feeling in common with the citizens of Virginia, and to have been transplanted hither from England or Caledonia since the war; interspersed pretty considerable with fugitive ones, who have returned under the amnesty of peace.
The notice, which I sent you the other day, spoke of instructions and a petition; but Marshall, suspecting, that he would be outnumbered by freeholders, and conscious that none should instruct, except those, who elect, quitted the idea of instructions, and betook himself to a petition, in which, he said, all the inhabitants of Richmond, tho' not freeholders, might join.[74]

As disturbing as these measures were, the Republicans made no countermove, for the petitions pouring in from Virginia and

[72] Meetings were held in Staunton, Portsmouth, Richmond, and in Augusta and Prince William counties. Alexandria *Columbian Mirror*, May 10, 1796; *Richmond and Manchester Advertiser*, May 18, 1796. Meetings were organized by the Federalists throughout the nation, and Congress was deluged with resolutions favorable to the treaty.
[73] John Marshall to Rufus King, April, 1796, in Charles R. King (ed.), *The Life and Correspondence of Rufus King* (6 vols., New York, 1894-1900), II, 45-46.
[74] E[dmund] R[andolph] to Madison, April 25, 1796, in Madison Papers.

the other states were more than adequate to create an impression that could not be easily overcome.[75] The Republicans also realized that there was no alternative to the treaty other than war—a course which they certainly did not favor. The Virginia Republicans contented themselves with voting against the treaty in the House (with the exception of one member of the state's delegation) and did not pursue their opposition any further through the medium of popular meetings.[76]

The methods used by the Republicans in conducting their campaigns against Washington's foreign policy and against Jay's Treaty became an established political formula which remained unchanged until 1800. During the next four years the party did not undergo any major changes in the organization and procedures which had been developed since 1791. On every important issue meetings were organized at which resolutions were adopted. These in turn were echoed by the legislature.[77] Although these public assemblies seemed spontaneous, actually they were summoned at the behest of the leaders of the party, who were able to direct the affairs of the Republicans without any of the complex machinery of semi-public committees and caucuses which we consider essential today. The conferences held by the party leaders at this time were casual and informal and were not publicized. The strength of the leaders rested on the *entente cordiale* which prevailed between them and the locally important political figures in Virginia. The task of controlling the party without any generally recognized policy- or strategy-making bodies was tremendously simplified by the small electorate, and the prevalence of what might be termed a "natural aristocracy" of leadership on the local level, whereby political power rested in the hands of a small group of well-to-do citizens.

From the evidence presented in this paper it seems that some rather definite conclusions may be drawn concerning the organization and background of the Republican party in Virginia. First, there is no significant connection between the anti-federalists of 1788 and the Republicans, nor between the federalists and the

[75] Madison to Jefferson, May 22, 1796, draft, *ibid.*
[76] The exception was George Hancock of Botetourt County, who had taken no part in the debate. *Annals of Congress,* 4 Cong., 1 Sess., 1291 (April 30, 1796).
[77] The famous Republican attack on the Alien and Sedition Laws was conducted in this manner. Ammon, "Republican Party," 176.

subsequent Federalist party. It is true that the anti-federalists joined the Republicans almost to a man, but the majority of the Virginia federalists made the same choice. The fundamental issues of 1788 were quite different from those of the 1790's, and therefore a new alignment of parties upon the basis of the new issues is not surprising. Second, it seems clear that, although the Hamiltonian fiscal program figured largely in arousing the hostility, or at least the distrust of Virginians toward Washington's administration, the opposition did not seek to exploit this question as a general political rallying point. Rather, the Republicans chose to concentrate upon the perplexing problem of Franco-American relations as a much safer issue. Thus in drawing party lines in Virginia the most important test was not based upon Hamilton's financial schemes, but upon the more general question of the French Revolution. In making this decision, as has been noted, Jefferson and his associates seem to have been governed largely by reasons of expediency. This is not to minimize the importance of the hostility of an agrarian region to the financial policy designed to benefit the eastern merchants, for this sentiment was fully expressed in the correspondence of the leading Republicans, but rather to emphasize that in organizing public sentiment they did not place primary emphasis upon this element. The crystallization of the Republican party from a vague opposition was achieved by concentrating upon a safer and in some ways seemingly less significant issue which required no constructive counterproposal.

The Evolution of Political Parties in Virginia, 1782-1800

NORMAN K. RISJORD

AND

GORDON DENBOER

How and when did the first American party system develop? One way to answer this question is by a roll call analysis of legislative behavior. That, of course, will not tell the whole story, but it will provide an index of party loyalty and organization, at least among the leadership élite. Although scholars have subjected Congress to numerous quantitative analyses, comparatively little work has been done on state legislatures.[1] This is unfortunate, not only because American politics in the post-Revolutionary era was state oriented but also because the state assemblies involved a sort of second-echelon élite. Thus a careful study of assemblies would enable historians to move closer to an understanding of the political attitudes of the "common man."

Another difficulty with many recent analyses of early national politics is that they either begin or end with the Constitution. Historians have made the Constitution appear as an epochal break in history, but to contemporaries it was part of a chain of important political events. Those who built the first

Norman K. Risjord is professor of history in the University of Wisconsin, Madison. Gordon DenBoer is employed with the Atlas of Early American History, Newberry Library. The authors acknowledge the financial assistance of the American Council of Learned Societies.

[1] Noble E. Cunningham, Jr., *The Jeffersonian Republicans: Formation of Party Organization, 1789-1801* (Chapel Hill, 1957); Manning J. Dauer, *The Adams Federalists* (Baltimore, 1953); Kenneth R. Bowling, "Politics in the First Congress, 1789-1791" (doctoral dissertation, University of Wisconsin, 1968). Richard R. Beeman analyzes the Virginia assembly in the 1790s but includes in the program only those legislators who served three consecutive terms. Richard R. Beeman, *The Old Dominion and the New Nation: 1788-1801* (Lexington, Ky., 1972). Mary P. Ryan confirms at the congressional level many of the conclusions reached concerning Virginia politics in the 1790s. Her thesis, that significant blocs of partisan voting can be found as early as 1789, is a graphic demonstration of the need for a closer look at the state and congressional politics of the previous decade. Mary P. Ryan, "Party Formation in the United States Congress, 1789 to 1796: A Quantitative Analysis," *William and Mary Quarterly*, XXVIII (Oct. 1971), 523-42.

political parties in the 1790s recalled and were influenced by personal and regional rivalries that had emerged in the previous decade. A roll call analysis of the Virginia House of Delegates from 1782 to 1800 was undertaken to determine just how and when voting behavior fell into patterns of agreement that might be called parties.[2] This essay also traces contemporary observers' perceptions of this process.

The task of roll call analysis was complicated by the size of the House of Delegates and by the turnover resulting in part from annual elections (see Table I).[3] Until the Adams administration when the Quasi War caused un-

TABLE I

Session	Number of Delegates	"New" Members	Percent "New"
1782	150	95	63
1783	152	83	55
1784	152	80	53
1785	156	78	50
1786	160	79	49
1787	168	80	48
1788	170	82	48
1789	173	80	46
1790	179	74	41
1791	183	86	47
1792	171	73	43
1793	171	62	36
1794	177	76	43
1795	177	71	40
1796	177	68	38
1797	177	91	51
1798	179	83	46
1799	179	82	46
1800	183	73	40

usual turnover in house membership, there was a decline in "new" members, from about three fifths of the house at the end of the Revolution to about two fifths by the mid-1790s. In all, 1,287 individuals served in either the

[2] The analysis was confined to the lower house because the senate was elected on a district system; analysis of the senate suffers from some of the same disadvantages as an analysis of congressional voting. Furthermore, the senate recorded few roll call votes.

[3] Each county elected two delegates, and the boroughs of Richmond, Williamsburg, and Norfolk sent one each. The increase in the number of delegates resulted from the creation of new counties; the decrease in 1792 marks the statehood of Kentucky. "New" members are those who did not serve in the previous session, even though they might have served some years before.

legislature or the ratifying convention or both between 1782 and 1800. There was, however, a group of men, perhaps as many as twenty in any given session, whose service spanned a number of years and who provided continuity, experience, and often leadership for the legislative system.

This analysis was also complicated by the paucity of roll call votes, seldom more than ten or fifteen per session. In order to obtain enough roll calls for statistical comparisons, the sessions were grouped 1782-1784, 1785-1787, 1788-1792, 1793-1796, and 1797-1799. Delegates who did not register at least three votes on party issues, or six votes overall (about one third of the members in most sessions) were excluded from the analysis. The voting records of the remaining two thirds were compared with those of a dozen or more "leaders," who were selected either on the basis of number of votes cast or attributed prominence in the assembly. To compare each delegate's voting record with that of every other would involve an unmanageable amount of data. In selecting "leaders" care was taken to insure that each region was represented, in order to determine whether personal and regional subgroups existed.[4]

During the years 1782-1784 the assembly was relatively disorganized. A few prominent men, such as Patrick Henry and Richard Henry Lee, commanded personal followings, but it is unlikely that these factional groups included more than half of the house membership. Contemporaries used vague terms in assessing the relative size of each faction, and the large number of new men who won seats in the annual spring elections increased the problem of identification. In each of the three year periods for which statistics were compared more than half of the delegates had not served in the previous assembly. Governor Benjamin Harrison saw in this rapid turnover a general "opposition to the old members," and others noted the appearance of an unusual number of younger men and former army officers.[5]

[4] The number of individuals involved and the high rate of absenteeism precluded the use of such methods as Guttman scaling. Some scaling was attempted where the number of roll calls on related issues seemed to justify it. Though scaling failed to reveal any persistent subgroups or personal alliances, it did reveal some regional blocs within the parties—for example, a bloc of western, debtor-oriented Federalists in the 1790s. Susan Lee Foard attempted to determine the degree of prominence among legislators through service on key committees. Susan Lee Foard, "Virginia Enters the Union, 1789-1792" (master's thesis, College of William and Mary, 1966). For an alternative method, see Norman K. Risjord, "The Virginia Federalists," *Journal of Southern History*, XXXIII (Nov. 1967), 486-517.

[5] Benjamin Harrison to Thomas Jefferson, April 16, 1784, Edmund Randolph to Jefferson, April 24, 1784, William Short to Jefferson, May 14, 1784, Julian P. Boyd, ed., *The Papers of Thomas Jefferson* (18 vols., Princeton, 1951-), VII, 102-03, 116-17, 257; Beverley Randolph to James Monroe, May 14, 1784, James Monroe Papers (Manuscript Division, Library of Congress). Analyzing the 1783 session, for example, Edmund Randolph identified three "corps" in the assembly; Patrick Henry, Richard Henry Lee, and

Most of the problems facing the assembly in these years stemmed from the Revolutionary War and the postwar depression. Of primary importance were economic issues involving debtor relief and taxation: postponement of tax collections, payment of taxes in kind, relief of sheriffs delinquent in tax collections, and regulation of relationships between private debtors and creditors. Henry was the acknowledged leader of a debtor-oriented faction in the assembly, although his absenteeism and the extensive turnover of delegates make it difficult to determine the precise size of his following. There were nine roll calls involving economic issues. Henry voted only four times. Twenty-eight delegates, most from the West and the region south of the James River, agreed with Henry on at least three of the four votes.[6] On the six roll calls that involved only domestic debts and taxation a substantial group of debtor-oriented delegates is apparent, but there is no regional pattern among them. The lack of such a pattern and the absence of a creditor-oriented group indicates the broad support for debtor-relief measures in these years. One explanation for Henry's apparent influence was that he articulated popular measures and reflected the views of a large majority of the assembly.[7] Even his erstwhile rival Richard Henry Lee generally voted for debtor-relief measures until 1784. Not until James Madison entered the assembly in that year did the opponents of debtor relief have a leader to rival Henry.[8]

The sharpest divisions in the 1782-1784 sessions involved the prewar debts owed to British merchants.[9] Virginia courts were closed to British creditors during the war, but the peace settlement required the removal of impediments to debt collection. The issue involved not only the sanctity

Speaker John Tyler each led a faction. Henry's was the most numerous, Randolph thought, while Tyler's was "but a temporary bubble." Edmund Randolph to Jefferson, May 15, 1784, Boyd, ed., *Papers of Thomas Jefferson*, VII, 257.

[6] The Southside includes all the counties south of the James River, from the seacoast to the Blue Ridge. The Piedmont is here defined as the counties west of the fall line, from Spotsylvania to Henrico, and between the Rappahannock and the James. The Middle Tidewater includes the counties along the bay between those two rivers, as well as the Eastern Shore. The Northern Neck includes the area north of the Rappahannock and east of the Blue Ridge. The West embraces the area beyond the Blue Ridge.

[7] Observers agreed that Henry was still "all powerful." George Mason to Henry, May 6, 1783, Robert A. Rutland, ed., *The Papers of George Mason, 1725-1792* (3 vols., Chapel Hill, 1970), II, 769-73; Edmund Pendleton to James Madison, May 17, 1783, David John Mays, ed., *The Letters and Papers of Edmund Pendleton: 1734-1803* (2 vols., Charlottesville, 1967), II, 446.

[8] Edmund Randolph to Jefferson, May 15, 1784, Short to Jefferson, May 14, 1784, Boyd, ed., *Papers of Thomas Jefferson*, VII, 257, 259-61.

[9] For state and congressional action on the debts, see Benjamin R. Baldwin, "The Debts Owed by Americans to British Creditors, 1763-1802" (doctoral dissertation, Indiana University, 1932).

of private contracts but also national treaty obligations.[10] John Marshall objected to the law impeding British debt collection "because it affords a pretext to the British to retain possession of the forts on the lakes but much more because I ever considered it a measure tending to weaken the federal bonds which in my conception are too weak already."[11] Others recognized that it would be difficult to attract European investment capital in the future if past debts were not paid.[12] Thus, while a pro-creditor attitude on the payment of debts owed to the British went hand in hand with nationalism, there is almost no correlation between voting behavior on the debts issue and domestic debts and taxes.

The issue involved three roll call votes, one in 1783 and two in 1784, and efforts to remove the impediments to British suits were rejected by large majorities. Support for compliance with the debt repayment provisions of the peace treaty came principally from the Northern Neck and lower James River counties. Of the eighteen delegates in this group, thirteen subsequently voted for the Constitution (ten remained Federalist, three later became Republicans), one became an Antifederalist/Republican, and the other four cannot be subsequently identified. Thirty-four delegates voted with Henry against compliance (on three of three or two of two roll calls). Of the twelve whose subsequent affiliation is known, two voted for the Constitution and later became Republicans; ten were Antifederalists in 1788.

Congress' request for authority to place an impost on imported goods for twenty-five years created a furor in 1783, but it was approved without a roll call vote. The political leadership divided along essentially the same lines as on the British debts issue, with the exception of Richard Henry Lee. Lee opposed the amendment because he was suspicious of congressional power and feared that Virginians would pay a disproportionate share of the tax.[13]

[10] Richard Henry Lee thought the "impeding laws" ought to be repealed "for the honour of our country." Richard Henry Lee to Madison, Nov. 26, 1784, James Madison Papers (Manuscript Division, Library of Congress). Edmund Randolph rejoiced for the national honor when Congress asked the states to comply with the debt provisions of the treaty. Edmund Randolph to Madison, April 4, 1787, *ibid.* See also George Washington to George William Fairfax, June 30, 1786, George Washington Papers (Manuscript Division, Library of Congress); Beverley Randolph to St. George Tucker, Nov. 29, 1784, Tucker-Coleman Papers (College of William and Mary); William Grayson to Madison, May 28, 1786, Madison Papers.

[11] John Marshall to Monroe, Dec. 2, 1784, Monroe Papers. For a similar concern see Washington to Richard Henry Lee, Dec. 14, 1784, Washington Papers; Richard Henry Lee to Madison, Nov. 20, 1784, Madison to Monroe, Dec. 24, 30, 1784, Madison Papers; Richmond *Virginia Gazette, or the American Advertiser,* July 12, 1786.

[12] William Lee to Thomas Lee, March 26, 1786, Lee-Ludwell Papers (Virginia Historical Society); George Mason to Arthur Lee, March 25, 1783, Rutland, ed., *Papers of George Mason,* II, 765-67.

[13] Richard Henry Lee to Landon Carter, June 3, 1783, Lee-Ludwell Papers. For an analysis

Lee and his following also associated the impost with their old enemy Robert Morris. They had led an unsuccessful fight against the amendment when Morris first proposed it in 1781 and persuaded the assembly to withdraw its approval in 1782.

On other roll calls in the 1782-1784 sessions alignments varied with the issue, and there is no correlation among them. Religious issues, such as the move to incorporate the Episcopal church and the effort to assess taxpayers for religious purposes, produced divisions that followed regional lines. Anti-establishment feeling was strongest among delegates from the transmontane West and the northern Piedmont, where religious dissenters were particularly strong. A series of four votes defining citizenship—aimed at preventing certain Loyalists from returning to the state—revealed a rather lenient attitude toward the returnees. Tolerance for Loyalists was greatest in the counties near urban centers such as Alexandria, Richmond, Williamsburg, and Norfolk. Although the issue revealed some lingering bitterness, the voting alignments have no particular relationship to those on other issues.

Henry's move from the assembly to the governorship in November 1784 and Madison's rapid ascendancy in the assembly encouraged fiscal conservatives and nationalists. In autumn 1785 George Washington outlined a program in a letter to David Stuart: an additional grant of power to Congress to regulate commerce, legislation that would encourage the development of Virginia seaports, improvement in the court system to accelerate civil suits, continuation of current taxation policies with no further delays in collection, and state support for projects to improve inland navigation.[14] The appearance of such a comprehensive, issue-oriented program marked a significant change from the piecemeal approach to issues and the emphasis on personalities that had characterized the 1782-1784 sessions. At the opening of the 1785 session Madison watched with bemused indifference while the partisans of John Tyler and Harrison engaged in complicated "intrigues" for the speaker's chair. By 1786 Madison's following was clearly in control. Joseph Prentis of Williamsburg, who subsequently became a Federalist, won the speakership over Theodorick Bland, an ally of Henry

of political attitudes on the issue, see Edmund Randolph to Madison, May 9, June 28, 1783, Joseph Jones to Madison, May 25, June 8, 1783, Madison Papers; Thomson Mason to John F. Mercer, June 27, 1783, John F. Mercer Papers (Virginia Historical Society); Jefferson to Madison, May 7, June 17, 1783, Madison to Jefferson, Dec. 10, 1783, Boyd, ed., *Papers of Thomas Jefferson*, VI, 266, 277, 377.

[14] George Washington to David Stuart, Nov. 30, 1785, John C. Fitzpatrick, ed., *The Writings of George Washington* (39 vols., Washington, 1931-1944), XXVIII, 328-29. Archibald Stuart thought Madison's power in the assembly was "almost absolute." Archibald Stuart to Jefferson, Oct. 17, 1785, Boyd, ed., *Papers of Thomas Jefferson*, VIII, 645-46.

and an Antifederalist, by a vote of 49 to 37. Edmund Randolph was chosen governor by a "considerable majority" over Bland and Richard Henry Lee.[15] Furthermore, the congressional delegation was solidly pro-Madison.[16]

Clearly, an issue-oriented coalition was beginning to form. Madison welcomed the election of George Mason in 1786 as "an inestimable acquisition on most of the great points," but concluded that when the interests of Mason's locality were involved "he is to be equally dreaded." Madison also suspected that Mason was not "fully cured of his antifederal prejudices."[17] Henry was still to be feared, especially if he should endorse some popular measure such as paper money, but by 1787 Madison was able to count votes shortly after the spring elections and determine that Henry would be "powerfully opposed" on such issues in the House of Delegates.[18]

The development of Madison's coalition between 1785 and 1787 can be seen by comparing votes on two key issues—the commerce amendment and British debts. In 1785 a proposal to grant Congress authority to regulate commerce for thirteen years was rejected in two successive votes.[19] Tactical maneuvers caused some realignment, but if those who participated in both roll calls are regarded as either "pro" or "anti" Congress, the geographical distribution was clear (see Table II). As in earlier sessions, personalities

TABLE II

Region	Pro-nationalist	Anti-nationalist
Northern Neck	3	10
Middle Tidewater	9	11
Piedmont	4	4
Southside	2	22
West	4	16

were still important: the votes of delegates from the Northern Neck reflect the continuing influence of the Lees on this particular issue; the West was voting with Patrick Henry.

By 1787 both regions were solidly aligned with the nationalists. This can be seen in the controversy over British debts, which was revived in that year

[15] Madison to Jefferson, April 27, 1785, Boyd, ed., *Papers of Thomas Jefferson*, VIII, 110-16; Jan. 22, 1786, *ibid.*, IX, 194-95; Dec. 4, 1786, *ibid.*, X, 577; Oct. 23, 1786, *Journal of the House of Delegates of Virginia, 1776-1790* (Richmond, 1827-1828).
[16] The delegates were William Grayson, Edward Carrington, Henry Lee, Joseph Jones, and Madison.
[17] Madison to Monroe, May 13, 1786, Monroe Papers. Ill health prevented Mason from serving. Note the early use of the term "antifederal."
[18] Madison to Jefferson, April 24, 1787, Boyd, ed., *Papers of Thomas Jefferson*, XI, 310.
[19] Nov. 30, Dec. 1, 1785, *Journal of . . . Delegates . . . 1785-1786*, pp. 65-67.

by a congressional resolution calling on the states to repeal all laws in conflict with the peace treaty. The request seemed like congressional dictation to some Virginians, and the issue was discussed in the assembly when measures dealing with the proposed Constitution—calls for a state ratifying convention and a second federal convention—were generating heated feelings. The close correlation between voting behavior on the British debts issue and later stands on the Constitution suggests that the issue was, as it had been in 1783-1784, as much a federal-state question as an economic one.[20]

The repeal measure requested by Congress finally passed, but only after strenuous efforts by opponents to weaken it. The bill, in its final form, suspended repeal until Britain evacuated the Northwest posts and compensated Virginians for slaves carried off during the war. The four roll calls on the issue (counting only those delegates who voted consistently on four of four or three of three) disclose three distinct groups. The creditor/nationalist element favored repeal of all state laws interfering with payment of the debts and opposed all efforts to dilute the resolution of compliance. Westerners unanimously favored this stand, evidently in the belief that strict adherence to the peace treaty would induce the British to evacuate the Northwest posts and thus reduce the Indian menace on the frontier.[21] A group of twenty-eight delegates wanted to suspend the repeal measure or attach conditions that would impede payment. They were willing, however, to pay the debts in installments (conceivably recognizing that ultimate payment was inevitable and this was one means to delay it). The third group, led by Henry, opposed all measures to repay the debts, even by installments. There was also a regional and political distribution (see Tables III and IV).

Issues involving domestic debts—primarily efforts to delay payment of taxes—show less clear divisions. Five roll calls were spread over the three sessions, 1785-1787; and because of high turnover relatively few delegates registered the four or five votes necessary to establish a pattern. Eleven men favored strict tax collections on at least four of the five votes: five from the West, six from the Tidewater. Seven became Federalists; two became Anti-

---

[20] For a discussion of this relationship, see Emory G. Evans, "Private Indebtedness and the Revolution in Virginia, 1776 to 1796," *William and Mary Quarterly*, XXVIII (July 1971), 349-74. It could be argued, of course, that American debts owed to British creditors were still fundamentally an economic matter and that one's subsequent stand on the Constitution was determined by indebtedness or lack of it. This may have influenced some delegates, but the Constitution posed so many issues—political as well as economic—that it seems unlikely that stands for or against ratification were dictated by the single issue of indebtedness to the British.

[21] Jackson Turner Main, *The Antifederalists: Critics of the Constitution 1781-1788* (Chapel Hill, 1961), 229.

TABLE III

Region	Creditor/ nationalists	Moderate debtor/ anti-nationalists	Henryite debtor/ anti-nationalists
West	21	0	0
Northern Neck	9	1	0
Middle Tidewater	5	6	0
Piedmont	1	6	1
Southside	6	15	8
Total	42	28	9

TABLE IV

Subsequent Party Affiliation			
Federalists	20	4	0
Antifederalists	1 (Mason)	17	7
Middle-of-road	2	0	0
Unknown	19	7	2
Total	42	28	9

federalists; and the affiliations of two are unknown. Although this is a very small sample, it indicates that some westerners were creditor-minded on domestic taxation as well as on foreign debts.

Conversely, of the fourteen who voted against strict tax collections, five were from the Southside, four from the Piedmont, three from the Tidewater, and two from the West. Eight became Antifederalists; two became Federalists; and the affiliations of four are unknown. Again the sample is very small, but the regional division complements the votes on the British debts issue. The spectrum of economic issues—involving both domestic and foreign debts—presents a vaguely defined dichotomy between debtor-oriented antinationalism, concentrated in the Southside and Piedmont, and a creditor-oriented nationalism, concentrated in the Tidewater—or more specifically the Northern Neck—and the West.

Closely related to these economic issues were four roll calls dealing with judicial reform. In general, they involved efforts led by Madison to establish additional courts and to speed up the judicial process. Again, only a few delegates registered a significant pattern because the votes occurred in all three sessions, but there are some interesting correlations, even if the analysis is limited by counting only those who voted consistently on four of four or three of three roll calls (see Table V). The similarity of this

TABLE V

Region	Favored Judicial Reform	Opposed Judicial Reform
West	4	2
Northern Neck	4	0
Middle Tidewater	3	2
Piedmont	0	4
Southside	3	7
Lower James River	4	0
Total	18	15
Subsequent Party Affiliation		
Federalists	12	3
Antifederalists	1	7
Unknown	5	5
Total	18	15

breakdown to that involving debt issues is apparent—only one of the delegates opposed to judicial reform was creditor-oriented on debt and taxation issues, while all those who favored judicial reform also favored paying debts and taxes. Both sides clearly felt that the establishment of additional courts would facilitate the collection of debts.

Thus by the time the Constitutional Convention assembled in Philadelphia to draft a blueprint for a stronger central government, two coalitions based on regional interests could be clearly discerned in the Virginia assembly. The conflict involved mostly economic issues[22]—domestic and foreign debts, taxation, and the judiciary—and the Constitution affected every one of these in one way or another. Therefore, it was assumed that popular reaction to the Constitution would follow the regional and partisan lines evident in the assembly. One of Madison's Federalist friends thought it certain "that the honest part of the community whether merchants or planters are for it. People in debt, and of dishonesty and cunning in their transactions are against it. This will apply universally to those of this class who have been members of the legislature."[23] By December 1787—three months before the election of delegates and six months before the ratifying convention met—Madison was able to predict the regional distribution of the vote on the Constitution with considerable accuracy.[24]

[22] Roll calls on social issues such as religion and slavery (private manumission bills) followed regional patterns that bore little relation to votes on other issues; apparently they had no effect on party development.

[23] Washington to Henry Knox, Oct. 15, 1787, Washington Papers; Benjamin Hawkins to Madison, Feb. 14, 1788, Madison Papers.

[24] Madison to Jefferson, Dec. 9, 1787, Boyd, ed., *Papers of Thomas Jefferson*, XII, 408-12.

At that point Madison could distinguish three basic "parties" (the term was beginning to lose its pejorative connotation, for Madison applied it to his friends as well as his opponents). One party favored ratification of the Constitution as it stood. A second party, led by Mason and Randolph, approved the substance of the Constitution but desired "a few additional guards in favor of the Rights of the States and of the People." Then there was a "third Class, at the head of which is Mr. Henry. This class concurs at present with the patrons of amendments, but will probably contend for such as strike at the essence of the System. . . ."[25] The middle group embraced a wide assortment of attitudes, ranging from those who desired some minor additions delineating the rights of citizens to those who would delete some of the substantive powers of Congress. But this middle group had to sort itself out before long because only two responses were ultimately possible— yea or nay.[26]

James Monroe subsequently claimed that he was elected to the ratifying convention without formally committing himself on the Constitution. If this is true, he was almost the only one who was.[27] Washington, noting that delegates were chosen on the basis of their stand, anticipated that the fate of the Constitution would be known as soon as the election results were tallied.[28] Indeed, even before the March elections were completed "an accurate list" of delegates, together with the stand of each on the Constitution, was circulating in Richmond.[29] When the balloting ended, the Winchester *Virginia Centinel* listed thirty-eight counties for the Constitution, twenty-five against, three divided, and seventeen (including six of the seven Kentucky counties) as doubtful. With somewhat more precision Charles Lee estimated that the Federalists had a majority of ten or twelve.[30]

The debate over ratification focused attention on issues—rather than personalities—polarized opinion, and enhanced the importance of the electorate. Both sides carefully tested the political temper, and the voters, in turn, were unusually quick to express their views. Shortly after the Constitution

---

[25] *Ibid.*
[26] For examples of this sorting process, see Jefferson to Edward Carrington, Dec. 21, 1787, Jefferson to Alexander Donald, Feb. 7, 1788, Boyd, ed., *Papers of Thomas Jefferson*, XII, 445-47, 570-72; John Page to Jefferson, March 7, 1788, *ibid.*, XII, 650-54; Joseph Jones to Madison, Oct. 29, 1787, Monroe to Madison, Oct. 13, 1787, Feb. 7, 1788, Madison Papers.
[27] Monroe to Jefferson, July 12, 1788, Boyd, ed., *Papers of Thomas Jefferson*, XIII, 351-53. Carrington complained that some of the Southside candidates were evasive on the question. Edward Carrington to Madison, Feb. 10, April 8, 1788, Madison Papers.
[28] Washington to John Jay, March 3, 1788, Washington to Benjamin Lincoln, March 10, 1788, Washington Papers.
[29] Winchester *Virginia Centinel, or the Winchester Mercury*, April 2, 1788.
[30] *Ibid.*, April 9, 1788; Charles Lee to Richard Henry Lee, April 6, 1788, Washington Papers.

was published, Madison was informed that "The freeholders of Fairfax have, in the most pointed terms directed Col. Mason to vote for a convention [in the assembly], and have as pointedly assured him he shall not be in it."[31] Mason wisely moved over to neighboring Stafford County, where he possessed additional property, to run for a seat in the ratifying convention. But George Nicholas of Albemarle County, who had been one of Henry's chief lieutenants in the early 1780s, evidently sampled local opinion and decided to support the Constitution "however contrary it may be to his own opinions."[32] Political rivalry was clearly expanding beyond the narrow confines of the assembly chamber.

The controversy over ratification also revealed a growing sophistication in political techniques—the ability to identify interests, predict votes, and secure commitments on voting behavior. Yet the "parties"—to use Madison's term—that divided over the Constitution were political coalitions, not parties in any modern sense. The requirement that the delegates vote "on the single question of Union or No Union," as Governor Randolph put it, concealed a wide variety of opinions. On June 25 the convention ratified by a vote of 89 to 79, after the Federalists agreed to attach amendments to the act of ratification. Some were concerned only with guarding the procedural rights of citizens and some were substantive alterations in the powers of the new government, but all obtained considerable support. Approving an amendment that would curtail the federal power to tax, for instance, were sixteen delegates who had voted for the Constitution, including Randolph himself and such erstwhile Madison allies as Edmund Pendleton, William Fleming, and Paul Carrington.[33] Madison pushed the Bill of Rights through Congress in the summer of 1789 in the hope of undercutting the Antifederalists' demand for amendments, but his limited procedural safeguards did not satisfy their desire for changes in the structure and powers of the government. As a result, the twin demands for a second federal convention and substantive amendments to the Constitution agitated the Virginia assembly for the next five years.

The debate on the Constitution also provided a national forum for political divisions. Federalists developed an interstate network for exchanging views and information during the ratification process, and the Antifederalists belatedly imitated their methods. In this respect the first federal election

[31] John Dawson to Madison, Oct. 19, 1787 Madison Papers. See also Instructions from a Committee of Voters in Fairfax County [Oct. 2, 1787], Rutland, ed., *Papers of George Mason*, III, 1000-01.
[32] James McClurg to Madison, Sept. 10, 1787, Madison Papers.
[33] David Robertson, *Debates and Other Proceedings of the Convention of Virginia . . . June 1788 . . .* (Richmond, 1805), 470-75.

was a continuation of the contest, as both sides recognized the importance of controlling the new government. "To be shipwrecked in sight of the port," warned Washington, "would be the severest of all possible aggravations to our Misery. . . ."[34] Thus began the transformation from Federalists-as-framers to Federalists-as-party controlling the executive and legislature of the new government.

"The parties feds and anti have in most transactions been pretty distinguishable," reported Joseph Jones when the Virginia assembly met in the fall of 1788.[35] But Henry and his allies were in solid control of the house, and this presented two problems for the Federalists. The assembly was certain to elect two Antifederalists to the United States Senate, and it might design the congressional districts to the advantage of the Antifederalists. Since two senators were to be chosen, each legislator would cast two ballots; and Federalists hoped Madison would get enough second votes to slip in. Antifederalist ranks held firm, however, and the result was ninety-eight for Richard Henry Lee, eighty-six for William Grayson, seventy-seven for Madison, twenty-six for Henry (who was not a candidate), and the rest scattered. Edward Carrington concluded that "two thirds of the assembly are anti's who meditate mischief against the Govt."[36]

Madison accordingly ran for a seat in the House of Representatives, and the assembly, as expected, manipulated his northern Piedmont district to include as many Antifederalist counties as possible. "The party" even persuaded Madison's old friend Monroe to run against him.[37] By an ingenious combination of new and old tactics, Madison's friends kept him informed of the sentiment in each county of the district, identified the wavering regions, and enlisted prominent members of the gentry to endorse him at strategic moments. Such "electioneering"—distasteful as it was—succeeded, and Madison won by a substantial majority.[38] He even managed to remain on good terms with Monroe.[39]

[34] Washington to Madison, Sept. 23, 1788, Washington Papers.
[35] Jones to Madison, Nov. 21, 1788, Madison Papers.
[36] Theodorick Bland to Richard Henry Lee, Nov. 9, 1788, Richard Henry Lee Papers (University of Virginia); Edward Carrington to Madison, Nov. 9, 1788, Madison Papers.
[37] Madison to Jefferson, Dec. 8, 1788, Boyd, ed., *Papers of Thomas Jefferson*, XIV, 340; Edward Carrington to Madison, Nov. 15, 1788, Joseph Jones to Madison, April 5, 1789, Madison Papers; Bland to Richard Henry Lee, Nov. 9, 1788, Richard Henry Lee Papers; James Duncanson to James Maury, Feb. 17, 1789, James Maury Papers (University of Virginia).
[38] Edward Carrington to Madison, Dec. 30, 1788, Henry Lee to Madison, Jan. 14, 1789, Edward Stevens to Madison, Jan. 31, 1789, Madison Papers. The vote was 1308 to 972. Fredericksburg *Virginia Herald*, Feb. 12, 1789.
[39] Monroe to Jefferson, Feb. 15, 1789, Boyd, ed., *Papers of Thomas Jefferson*, XIV, 557-59; Monroe to Madison, April [26], 1789, Madison Papers.

It was anticipated that the congressional contest would be close every-where, except in the Southside where no Federalist was even willing to step forward.[40] As a result, both sides developed some rudimentary nominating procedures in order to avoid internal divisions. In the northern congressional districts, Henry Lee reported, "It is probable that each party will fix on one man, & that the election will decide the will of the people, provided the districts have not been artfully designated."[41] The Antifederalists in the assembly even drew up a slate of ten candidates for Congress and twelve presidential electors, which they then circulated around the state.[42] In the end, eight Federalists and two Antifederalists were sent to Congress. The balloting clearly reflected a feeling that the new government ought to be given a chance, sentiment that also marked the transition from Antifederal-ist-critic-of-the-Constitution to Republican-critic-of-the-administration.

The political issues presented by the Constitution—a possible second con-vention, amendments, arrangement of congressional districts, and an act disqualifying federal officials from serving the state—agitated the assembly for the next two years. For a time Henry ruled, and the assembly passed resolutions endorsing a second convention and substantive amendments. But the smooth establishment of the federal government and congressional passage of the Bill of Rights undermined his support. In 1789 an effort to add to the Bill of Rights the substantive amendments suggested by the Virginia ratifying convention was defeated on three successive votes. Henry went home in the middle of the session—disappointed at his lack of sup-port, so Federalists said.[43]

Alexander Hamilton's fiscal system, especially the proposal that the federal government assume the war debts of the states, created new contro-versies in 1790. Virginians disliked Hamilton's proposals because it seemed to them that speculators in the public debt, most of them northern merchants, would get an undeserved windfall at the expense of taxpayers. The pro-posal was particularly obnoxious because Virginia had paid off much of its war debt; it now appeared that the state would be taxed again to pay the debts of others. Even so staunch a Federalist as Henry Lee, who was not

---

[40] Edward Carrington to Madison, Dec. 19, 30, 1789, Madison Papers; Bland to St. George Tucker, Feb. 8, 1789, Tucker-Coleman Papers.

[41] Henry Lee to Madison, Dec. 8, 1788, Madison Papers. For examples of conscious efforts to settle on candidates, see Henry Lee to Madison, Dec. 8, 1788, Jan. 14, 1789, Madison Papers; Washington to David Stuart, Dec. 2, 1788, Washington to Henry Knox, Jan. 1, 1789, Washington to Henry Lee, Dec. 12, 1788, Washington Papers; Isaac Avery to John Cropper, Dec. 29, 1788, Jan. 30, 1789, John Cropper Papers (Virginia Historical Society).

[42] Duncanson to Maury, Feb. 17, 1789, James Maury Papers.

[43] Edward Carrington to Madison, Dec. 20, 1789, Madison Papers; David Stuart to Wash-ington, Dec. 3, 1789, Washington Papers.

above speculating in lands at the falls of the Potomac in the hope that the President would locate the nation's capital there, denounced the funding system for perverting the Constitution and placing the country in the hands of merchants.[44] Henry was considered a prophet for having predicted that northern mercantile interests would dominate the new government, and even the "strongest antifederalists" praised Madison for his opposition to Hamilton's proposals.[45] In the assembly, Henry's resolution denouncing assumption of state debts as "repugnant to the Constitution" passed by a vote of 75 to 52.[46]

Madison's creation of an anti-administration following in Congress and Henry's transformation from critic to interpreter of the Constitution laid the foundation for a new political alignment. Toward the end of 1791 Madison's brother William transmitted the news that Henry desired to open a correspondence. Madison replied cautiously that he was gratified by any "friendly sentiments" Henry might have, but since he had never written to Henry in his life he feared that the "abrupt commencement" of a correspondence might seem odd.[47] Henry, in short, would have to write the first letter, and he never did. Madison had no reason to regret it. Henry was an unpredictable ally and a potential rival for leadership. Madison had won Henry's following—where else could they go? What the new Republican party needed was more disaffected Federalists.

How many did they get? To what extent was there continuity from the factional contest of the late 1780s to the parties that divided over national issues in the 1790s? Treating the 1788-1792 assembly sessions as a unit, there were eight roll calls during these years on issues that determined party. These ranged from Federalist/Antifederalist splits over amendments and a second convention to Federalist/Republican divisions over assumption of state debts and the establishment of new congressional districts after the census of 1790.[48] A total of 426 men served in the House of Delegates during these five sessions. Of these, 150 cast enough votes to be identified: Federalist, 41; leaning Federalist, 10; middle of the road, 5; leaning Antifederalist/Republican, 6; and Antifederalist/Republican, 88.[49]

[44] Henry Lee to Madison, March 4, 1790, Madison Papers; Henry Lee to [a member of Congress], Jan. 8, 1792, Charles Carter Lee Papers (Virginia State Library, Richmond).

[45] Henry Lee to Madison, April 3, 1790, Edward Carrington to Madison, April 30, 1790, Edmund Randolph to Madison, May 20, 1790, Madison Papers.

[46] Nov. 3, 1790, *Journal of . . . Delegates . . . . 1790*, pp. 35-36.

[47] William to James, Dec. 3, 1791, James to William, Dec. 13, 1791, Madison Papers.

[48] On the districting bill, Francis Corbin thought that "Party wish runs higher than I ever knew it before upon any Legislative arrang[ement] whatever." Corbin to Madison, Jan. 7, 1792, *ibid*.

[49] The record of each legislator was compared with that of several known Federalists and

The rigidity of party lines is quite remarkable, especially in view of the fact that the Federalists lost substantial support as a result of Hamilton's fiscal policies. The five middle-of-the-roaders, for example, were all professed Federalists—such as Henry Lee and Francis Corbin—who opposed assumption of state debts. But the relatively small number of "trimmers" suggests that there was no major shift among the delegates from one party to another during these years. When voters became unhappy with Federalist policies, they merely elected new men. The extent of continuity can be discerned (see Table VI).[50]

TABLE VI

	Creditor faction of 1785–1787	Debtor faction of 1785–1787
Pro-Constitution in 1788–1789	26	4[a]
Anti-Constitution in 1788–1789	6[b]	28
Unknown	16	9
	——	——
	48	41

[a] Two remained Federalists; two became Republicans.
[b] Two of the six voted Federalist in 1793–1794.

There are 316 men whose stand on the Constitution is known, either through participation in the ratifying convention or through their voting in the assembly on the issues of a second convention and radical amendments. Their subsequent party affiliation can be identified (see Table VII).

TABLE VII

Federalists in 1788		Antifederalists in 1788	
Remained Federalists	68	Became Federalists	5
Became Republicans	31	Became Republicans	49
Unknown	62	Unknown	101

Lines of historical continuity are never perfect, but there does seem to be, in Virginia at least, a rather continuous pattern of party evolution. There

Republicans who agreed among themselves 100 percent of the time. Those classified by party agreed with the party models at least 80 percent of the time. Those listed as "leaning" voted with a party on 60 to 80 percent of their votes; those in the middle of the road agreed with either party less than 60 percent. Two hundred and seventy-six men voted fewer than three times or split their votes 2-1. Percentages were calculated only for those who voted more than five times; if a delegate cast fewer votes he had to side consistently with either one party or the other in order to be classified with a party.
[50] The totals in each case are higher than in Tables III and IV because they also include a few delegates who were identified only by their votes on domestic debts and taxes.

were shifts, of course, especially among supporters of the Constitution who became Republicans. But it is also clear that a substantial majority of the Republican party were former Antifederalists. In general, it can be said that the party system that appeared in the 1790s as a result of differences over national policies, domestic and foreign, was superimposed upon the existing factional alignment in Virginia.

The outbreak of war in Europe, Washington's neutrality proclamation, and the mission of Edmond Genet in the spring of 1793 created new sources of controversy among Virginians, but did not seriously disrupt existing political alignments. Their main effect was to stimulate party organization at the local level.[51] Mass meetings and petition campaigns were not new, but never before had they been so well managed or so successful in mobilizing opinion. On August 17, 1793, Federalists organized a "numerous meeting" of Richmond citizens, chaired by aging George Wythe. It passed resolutions submitted by Marshall which endorsed the neutrality proclamation and denounced foreign influence that might "lead to the introduction of foreign gold and foreign armies."[52] Popular meetings in neighboring counties soon passed similar resolutions. The language and tone differed somewhat in each case, but the extent of Federalist collusion was evident. By early September their apparatus had spread to the Shenandoah Valley. A meeting in Staunton passed resolutions drafted by Archibald Stuart—Madison's ally in the 1780s—that were virtually identical to the Richmond set.[53]

Republicans were surprised and dismayed at this Federalist initiative. Madison suspected "the cabal at Philadelpia" was behind it, but he suggested that Republicans sponsor similar meetings to determine "the real sense of the people."[54] The first was held in Caroline, where Pendleton presided over a meeting that passed resolutions vaguely endorsing the President and neutrality while denouncing all efforts to drive a wedge between the United States and France. Similar resolutions were adopted in other counties, and though the tone was vague and defensive the Republicans could count on general public support.[55] When the Federalists tried to organize another meeting in Staunton, Monroe rode across the Blue Ridge with one of Madison's addresses in hand and managed to "effectually change the current and give it a direction against the anti-Republican faction."[56]

[51] Harry Ammon, "The Genet Mission and the Development of American Political Parties," *Journal of American History*, LII (March 1966), 725-41.
[52] Richmond *Virginia Gazette and General Advertiser*, Aug. 21, 1793.
[53] *Ibid.*, Sept. 4, 11, 25, Oct. 2, 1793.
[54] Madison to Jefferson, Aug. 27, 1793, Madison Papers.
[55] Richmond *Virginia Gazette*, Sept. 25, Oct. 17, 23, 1793.
[56] Monroe to Madison, Sept. 25, 1793, Madison Papers.

During the next two years national issues continued to dominate Virginia politics. When Governor Henry Lee led a detachment of Virginia troops to suppress the Pennsylvania whiskey rebels in the fall of 1794, Republicans in the House of Delegates introduced a resolution claiming the governor had violated the statute which prohibited officials from holding positions under both state and federal governments. The house thereupon declared the office of governor vacant and elected Republican Robert Brooke over Federalist James Wood by a vote of 90 to 60.[57] This was the first time national issues dictated the selection of a governor.

The Whiskey Rebellion coincided with a crisis in Anglo-American relations brought on by British depredations on American commerce and lingering disputes over planter debts, retention of the Northwest posts, and intrigues among the Indians. Henry's son-in-law, Spencer Roane, told Monroe that if war became necessary, "a pretty strong Expedition into Canada, paid with the money due to british creditors, could scarcely fail. . . ."[58] In Congress, Madison introduced resolutions to curtail trade with Britain as a measure of retaliation; and, when Washington dispatched Chief Justice John Jay to negotiate a settlement, Republicans expected the worst. They disliked the use of a judge for executive embassies, and they distrusted Jay for his suggestion a decade earlier that navigation of the Mississippi be abandoned to Spain in return for commercial concessions that would have benefited the North.[59] Rumors that came out of England during Jay's negotiations were not reassuring, and Virginia Republicans were fully prepared to be dismayed at the result.[60]

After Jay returned, Washington delayed several months before submitting the treaty to the Senate; and then the Senate voted to keep its provisions secret until it was fully ratified. On June 24, 1795, Senator Henry Tazewell summarized Virginia's objections to the treaty. It set up mechanisms for the restoration of confiscated Loyalist property and the recovery of British debts without providing compensation for Negroes allegedly carried off by the British during the Revolution. It regulated the nation's trade by executive agreement, thereby depriving Congress of some of its power over commerce (notably the power to retaliate against Britain through nonintercourse). And it was likely to damage American relations with France, while restoring a colonial dependence upon Britain.[61] In objecting

[57] Nov. 21, 1794, *Journal of . . . Delegates . . . 1794*, p. 28.
[58] Spencer Roane to Monroe, Jan. 25, 1794, Monroe Papers.
[59] Madison to Jefferson, April 28, 1794, Madison Papers; Resolutions of the Democratic Society of Wythe County, Richmond *Virginia Gazette*, July 23, 1794.
[60] Jones to Madison, Nov. 16, 1794, Madison to Jefferson, Feb. 15, 1795, Madison Papers.
[61] Thomas J. Farnham, "The Virginia Amendments of 1795: An Episode in the Opposition to Jay's Treaty," *Virginia Magazine of History and Biography*, 75 (Jan. 1967), 75-88.

to the treaty Jefferson and Madison were preoccupied with neutral rights and national pride, but other Virginia Republicans focused on the provisions involving British creditors and Loyalist estates.[62] Virginia Federalists, however, generally approved the treaty because it kept the peace, honored old debts, and removed the British from the Northwest.[63]

Each of these issues of national policy was debated in the Virginia assembly. In the period of 1793-1796 there were eleven roll calls involving party divisions, including resolutions on Washington's French policy in 1793, commentary on Congressman William Branch Giles' efforts to investigate the treasury department, attempts to add new amendments to the Constitution, the removal of Governor Henry Lee for accepting a federal command against the whiskey rebels, and a succession of votes expressing the opinion of the house on the Jay Treaty. A total of 360 men served during these four sessions, of whom 197 (54 percent) can be identified by party, a substantial increase over previous sessions.[64] The growth of party cohesion is also evident in the decline of the middle. Only twenty delegates failed to agree with one party or the other as much as 75 percent of the time, while 114 voted with a party 100 percent of the time. There were 102 Republicans and seventy-five Federalists, which is roughly the same proportion that the two parties possessed in the 1788-1792 sessions. This suggests that the Genet mission, the Whiskey Rebellion, and the Jay Treaty were not quite as disastrous to Federalist strength in Virginia as historians commonly assume.[65] The regional breakdown was also similar to that which had existed since the Constitution (see Table VIII). The solidification of party strength in the Piedmont, Southside, and West evidenced the polarizing effect of domestic and foreign issues that arose in 1793 and after. The Middle Tidewater remained as mixed as ever, and the only important shift is in the stance of the Northern Neck. Federalist gains there were the result mostly of the party organization built in the mid-1790s by Alexandria merchant Levin Powell. He was particularly successful in the Loudoun/Fairfax/Fauquier part of the northern Piedmont, coun-

---

[62] Paul Varg, *Foreign Policy of the Founding Fathers* (East Lansing, 1963), 111-12. For examples, see Daniel Hylton to Jones, Jan. 17, 1795, Robert Atkinson to Jones, Sept. 7, 1795, Joseph Jones Papers (Duke University); Stevens T. Mason to Henry Tazewell, Oct. 6, 1795, Henry Tazewell Papers (Virginia State Library); Joseph Neville to Madison, Dec. 8, 1795, Madison Papers.

[63] Risjord, "The Virginia Federalists," 499-501.

[64] One Republican and two Federalists voted on all eleven roll calls; their records were used as models. The minimum standard was three out of four agreements (75 percent), but there were only thirteen of these.

[65] It is possible, of course, that the Federalists were more conscientious in attendance and voting and, therefore, more likely to be identified. This could not be tested without undertaking to count members who cast only two ballots on the key issues. This was not statistically defensible.

TABLE VIII

	1788–1792 Sessions			1793–1796 Sessions		
Region	Fed	Anti- fed/Rep	Middle	Fed	Anti- fed/Rep	Middle
Northern Neck	10	12	1	13	4	2
Middle Tidewater	7	16	2	15	12	3
Piedmont	4	11	0	6	19	3
Southside	7	37	0	2	52	3
West	22	18	1	37	15	9
Urban	1	0	1	2	0	0
Totals	51	94	5	75	102	20

ties that were solidly Federalist through these years. The Federalist complexion of the Northern Neck is also reminiscent of its creditor stance in the 1780s. Indeed, the aberration is the mixed record of the area in the 1788-1792 period; and this was probably the result of personal influence more than anything else—the strong antipathy to the Constitution voiced by Mason, Grayson, and Richard Henry Lee.

In addition to the various votes which determined party loyalty in the 1793-1796 sessions, there were eight roll calls involving economic issues: four on taxation and four on various forms of debtor relief. Republican cohesion was remarkable. Using as a model William Boyce, the one Republican who voted on all eight issues, a total of fifty-one Republicans, five Federalists, nine middle-of-the-roaders, and two of unknown party agreed with him at least 75 percent of the time. It is not always clear from the *Journal* what issues were involved in the debtor-relief votes, but on the other four votes the Republicans consistently favored tax reduction or postponement.

Federalists were more divided on economic issues. One group that voted the reverse of the above Republican position on all issues contained twenty-one Federalists, five Republicans, and five in the middle. The Federalists were mostly from the Shenandoah Valley and the Tidewater, especially the Northern Neck and lower James River regions. Another group of eleven Federalists, mostly from western Virginia, voted with Republicans on tax issues but with eastern Federalists on debtor-relief issues. Despite the return of prosperity in the 1790s partisan voting still extended to economic issues. Thus the state divided regionally along roughly the same lines that it did in the 1780s, and since the political parties followed similar lines there is substantial correlation between partisan and economic voting behavior.

By the end of Washington's administration the first party system had taken shape in Virginia, and there remained only the perfection of techniques—disciplining party ranks in the legislature and improving the local machinery for mobilizing the electorate. The political tensions of the Adams administration—including the XYZ Affair, the undeclared war with France, and the alien and sedition laws—afforded both parties plenty of opportunity to perfect their organizations. At the same time they eroded Federalist strength, for the administration's belligerence toward France, its moves to enlarge the army, and its efforts to silence the Jeffersonian press were generally unpopular in Virginia. In the 1797-1799 sessions there were twenty-one roll calls involving party issues (twice as many as in any previous period), itself an indication of the increase in partisanship. The issues included statements on John Adams' conduct of foreign policy, changes in the state's presidential electoral system, and numerous resolutions protesting the alien and sedition laws and increases in the military establishment. The increased number of roll calls enables the identification of a higher percentage of the house than before (270 out of 330, or 81 percent), and it permits some assessment of the degree of party fervor (see Table IX).[66]

TABLE IX

Republicans	149
Moderate Republicans	8
Middle-of-road	7
Moderate Federalists	12
Federalists	94

The amount of internal cohesion among both parties evidences the final development of the system. The legislature was virtually polarized; there was no longer much room for moderates or inconsistent behavior. The fate of John Pierce of James City County is a case in point. In the 1788-1792 period Pierce voted Antifederalist five of six times, but then in the 1793-1796 sessions he voted with the Federalists on ten of twelve roll calls. Republican Littleton Waller Tazewell, who defeated him in the spring election of 1798, observed triumphantly that Pierce had "met the reward for his inconsistency."[67] Tazewell, at least, kept track of Pierce's voting record and evidently thought the electorate did too.

Considering the dramatic changes in national public attitudes during these years—from the patriotic burst that greeted the XYZ Affair to the shrill criticism of federal taxation and the military establishment—one might

[66] A minimum of 80 percent agreement was required for party categorization; "moderates" were those who voted with a party 60 to 80 percent of the time. Those who cast only three or four votes were not included unless they were perfectly consistent.

[67] Littleton W. Tazewell to Henry Tazewell, Feb. 16, 1798, Tazewell Papers.

expect more shifts in party allegiance. Yet, of the Federalists, only four had voted Republican in previous sessions, and among the Republicans only seven had previously voted Federalist. To the extent that public opinion changed in Virginia it was reflected in the turnover among the delegates, which was higher in these years than at any time since the Constitution went into effect. Evidently, when a delegate was out of tune with his county he was quickly replaced.

The development of the party system thus enhanced the importance of the electorate. In earlier years candid appeals to the voters for support were considered bad form, but by the late 1790s democratic sentiments were creeping into the political rhetoric.[68] When John Page lost his congressional seat in 1797 to a Federalist from the Eastern Shore, he ascribed his defeat to the influence of "the Aristocrats" in the district. (Page was master of "Rose-well," a plantation of 1,750 acres and thirty slaves on the York River, while his opponent, Thomas Evans, possessed 516 acres and six slaves in Accomac.)[69] Nevertheless, Page reassured a Williamsburg friend, "I have so perfectly trained my mind to republican Principles that it instantly sub-mits to the will of the Majority. I am therefore perfectly reconciled to the Decision of the Electors. I thank you and your Friends who went to York to vote for me."[70]

When the spring elections of 1799 were over, Marshall observed, "There are from fifty to sixty new members. Unfortunately the strength of parties is not materially varied. The opposition maintains its majority in the house of Delegates. The consequence must be an antifederal Senator & Gover-nor."[71] The assembly had been sending former Antifederalists to the Senate since the first federal election, but the gubernatorial election, except for Henry Lee's dismissal in 1794, was not a partisan affair. Indeed, the incum-bent James Wood, a veteran of the Indian wars, was a Federalist. The gov-ernor had few powers under the constitution of 1776, but installing a Re-publican in the post, thought John Taylor of Caroline, would be "of immense importance by the influence it will have on public opinion." Another Republican thought the state needed a change because a "truely

[68] For examples of how electioneering was equated with demagoguery, see Pendleton to Richard Henry Lee, March 14, 1785, Lee Family Papers (University of Virginia); Archi-bald Stuart to John Breckinridge, Oct. 21, 1785, Breckinridge Papers (Manuscript Division, Library of Congress); Madison to Randolph, Nov. 23, 1788, Madison Papers; "Aristides to the Freemen of the State of Virginia," Richmond *Virginia Independent Chronicle*, March 21, 1787; "Observer to the Freeholders of the Commonwealth of Virginia," *ibid.*, March 28, 1787.

[69] Tax lists, Gloucester (1797), Accomac (1793, 1800) (Virginia State Library).

[70] John Page to St. George Tucker, March 30, 1797, Tucker-Coleman Papers.

[71] Marshall to Washington, May 16, 1799, Washington Papers.

Republican Executive" would provide "a sure foundation for the Election of the next President."[72]

When the assembly met in the autumn, Monroe was elected governor over Federalist James Breckinridge by a vote of 111 to 44, and Federalists were purged from all offices—speaker, clerk, and public printer.[73] The Republican majority then proceeded to change the rules of the electoral system. It abolished the district system of choosing presidential electors in favor of a winner-take-all approach, thereby preventing a repetition of the two electoral votes which Virginia Federalists had cast for Adams in 1796. It also eliminated oral voting in the choice of presidential electors, so that each voter had to write in the name of each of the twenty-one electors allotted to the state. The effect was to give an advantage to the party with the best local organization. A week after these changes were adopted the Republicans held a party caucus. This meeting selected prominent figures in each county to serve as a local committee, and then it created a standing committee to supervise the activities of the county committees. The purpose behind the changes in the electoral laws became evident when the central committee distributed printed ballots containing the names of the Republican electors. It even suggested that local committees could hand them out to freeholders to be used as genuine ballots on election day.[74]

The Federalists were slightly less organized and considerably more defensive, aware that the Adams administration was quite unpopular in the state. In May 1800, they printed a list of candidates for the electoral college. An accompanying "Address to the Voters" avoided any reference to the national party, even to the point of styling itself "The American Republican Ticket." It appealed to the name of the recently deceased Washington and called for support of his "virtuous successor" without mentioning Adams by name. Avoiding any mention of such unpopular policies as the alien and sedition laws, increases in the military, and heavy taxation, it concentrated instead on Republican changes in the electoral rules which placed the choice of President in the hands of a few "imposing names."[75]

The election of 1800 thus represents the ultimate maturity of the first party system. Party loyalty was a major criterion for appointment to both

---

[72] John Taylor to Jefferson, Feb. 15, 1799, *John P. Branch Historical Papers of Randolph-Macon College*, II (1908), 278-81; John Guerrant to Monroe, Oct. 14, 1799, Monroe Papers.

[73] Beeman, *Old Dominion and the New Nation*, 212-13.

[74] Cunningham, *Jeffersonian Republicans*, 194-96; Beeman, *Old Dominion and the New Nation*, 221-22.

[75] "An Address to the Voters for Electors of President and Vice President of the United States, in the State of Virginia," May 26, 1800, John Cropper Papers.

executive and legislative offices. Nearly all members of the legislature and all candidates for the electoral college were identified by party. Each side was actively appealing to the people for support or at least giving lip service to the principle of democracy, and each was developing sophisticated organizations to mobilize that support on election day.

Thus, from essentially personal factions in the early 1780s there evolved by 1800 political organizations with a disciplined membership, able to formulate a comprehensive program and appeal to the electorate for support. The process was gradual, with each new coalition and each new political technique built upon earlier alliances and methods. The economic issues and congressional politics of the Confederation, the Constitution, Hamilton's fiscal system, and the diplomatic problems of the 1790s—each contributed to the evolutionary process by focusing attention on issues, stimulating public debate, and engendering popular organizations.

Even in its maturity, however, the first party system was comparatively primitive by modern standards. Much would still be done by later organizers to develop more effective means of party discipline and a rhetoric that would enable the "common man" to identify with the political system. Nor should the first party system be judged by the example of a practitioner as profound and analytical as Madison. Probably a more typical product and observer of the system was the assembly "back bencher" from the Shenandoah Valley who wrote to a neighbor: "I hop that I shall be at home against Crismus not that I am tired of the buesness it is the Best Scool that I ever was at I am verry happy if I could engoy my little famuley, I have a grate oppertunity of knowing the ways of the Town. I hope that Mr. Jefferson will be Elected praesedent. . . ."[76]

[76] William Lemon to Henry Bedinger, Nov. 23, 1796 [copy], Danske-Dandridge Papers (Duke University).

ON THE LIBERTY OF THE PRESS
IN VIRGINIA

From Essay to Bludgeon, 1798-1803

by STEVEN H. HOCHMAN*

THE extent of liberty of the press in America remained uncertain even after the Sedition Act expired on March 3, 1801, and the presidency passed to Thomas Jefferson.[1] Merely because Jefferson and the Republican party had opposed the act of 1798, it did not follow that they therefore favored an unlimited press. To be sure, no Republican ever said he opposed liberty of the press, but then neither had any Federalist. The definition of the concept was still murky.

While the Republicans had denied any power in the federal government to impose restrictions on the press, they had recognized that such a power might be exercised by the states. Since the Federalist party maintained political control in a number of states, they could continue at that level to use criminal prosecutions to stifle Republican opposition. The Republicans, of course, possessed the same option where they were in control. To determine how much freedom actually existed, it is necessary to study the records of the individual states.[2]

Early in Jefferson's administration a clear perversion of freedom of the press by an embittered journalist forced Virginians to re-examine their principles. James Thomson Callender, whom Republicans had defended

* Mr. Hochman is assistant to Dumas Malone, biographer-in-residence at the University of Virginia.

[1] Leonard W. Levy, *Legacy of Suppression: Freedom of Speech and Press in Early American History* (Cambridge, Mass., 1960), pp. 297-307; Dumas Malone, *Jefferson the President: First Term, 1801-1805* (Boston, 1970), pp. 227-235; *Jefferson the President: Second Term, 1805-1809* (Boston, 1974), pp. 371-391; Merrill D. Peterson, *Thomas Jefferson and the New Nation: A Biography* (New York, 1970), pp. 714-718.

[2] Even the exception to this rule, the 1806 libel cases instituted in the United States District Court in Connecticut, is best understood in the context of state rather than national politics. Local Republicans prosecuted the cases in the only court they controlled, in order to retaliate for Federalist-inspired prosecutions in the state courts there. Republican principles ultimately triumphed. The cases were dismissed, except for *United States* v. *Hudson and Goodwin*, which went to the Supreme Court as a test case. The decision finally reached in 1813 denied to the federal courts jurisdiction at common law. Therefore, a common-law crime such as criminal libel could not be prosecuted (Malone, *Jefferson: Second Term*, pp. 371-391; Peterson, *Jefferson*, pp. 716-717).

from the Sedition Act,[3] turned against his former party and embarked upon a campaign of character assassination. One man who tried to stop Callender had earlier defended him as counsel. George Hay, known as one of the foremost advocates of a free press, now sought to curb its abuses. His rage against Callender determined his actions, but it was his attempt to reconcile these with his theories that makes worthwhile an examination of the conflict between them, its background and consequences.

It was by a contribution to free-press theory that George Hay had first merited notice.[4] In January 1799, six months after the Federalist-dominated Congress passed the Sedition Act, Hay, in Virginia, composed a series of 'addresses to the president and to the people of the United States challenging its constitutionality. Under the pseudonym Hortensius, the series was published in the leading Republican paper in the nation, the Philadelphia *Aurora*, then almost immediately was reprinted in pamphlet form as *An Essay on the Liberty of the Press*.[5] Hay, a Richmond lawyer, was a participant in a larger Virginia campaign of protest against the Sedition Act. In his essay he attempted to expound the principles just voiced in the resolutions of the Virginia General Assembly and its counterpart in Kentucky.[6]

First, Hay argued that Congress was *"not warranted"* by the Constitution in prescribing a punishment for libels, since Congress was not expressly granted such a power. This was the fundamental contention of the Republicans, based on a strict literal interpretation of the Constitution. The second part of Hay's argument, that Congress was *"expressly forbidden"* by the First Amendment to punish printed libels, was therefore immaterial, as he subsequently noted. "But," he wrote, "as the 'freedom of the press,' has never yet been accurately defined, and as there is no subject in which the

---

[3] The authoritative account of this trial and others under the act is in James Morton Smith, *Freedom's Fetters: The Alien and Sedition Laws and American Civil Liberties* (Ithaca, N. Y., 1956, emended edition 1966).

[4] Hay, born December 15, 1765, became an important Virginia political and legal figure, but there is no adequate account of his life.

[5] Published in five installments in the *Aurora*, February 2-11, 1799. An advertisement on February 13 announced that the pamphlet, *An Essay on the Liberty of the Press; Respectfully Inscribed to the Republican Printers Throughout the United States*, would be published the following day, and be sold for fifteen cents.

[6] The Virginia Resolutions were adopted December 21-24, 1798, and may be seen in Gaillard Hunt, editor, *Writings of James Madison*, VI (New York, 1906), 326-331. The Alien and Sedition Acts, and the campaign of protest against them, have inspired a considerable body of impressive scholarship. An important article is Adrienne Koch and Harry Ammon, "The Virginia and Kentucky Resolutions: An Episode in Jefferson's and Madison's Defense of Civil Liberties," *William and Mary Quarterly*, 3rd ser., V (1948), 145-176. See also the works previously cited by Levy, Peterson, and Smith, as well as Malone, *Jefferson and the Ordeal of Liberty* (Boston, 1962).

welfare of society is more essentially concerned, my original undertaking shall be fully performed." [7] It is in this second part of the essay that Hay presented what Leonard Levy describes as the first publication of "new and original libertarian doctrines." [8]

The Federalist party considered freedom of the press to mean "laying no *previous* restraints upon publications." This was the definition given by William Blackstone in his *Commentaries on the Laws of England.* "Every freeman has an undoubted right to lay what sentiments he pleases before the public," Blackstone wrote, "to forbid this, is to destroy the freedom of the press: but if he publishes what is improper, mischievous, or illegal, he must take the consequences of his own temerity." [9] In fact, the Federalist Congress maintained that it had advanced beyond Blackstone in the sedition statute by allowing truth as a defense, for according to the English common law it was immaterial whether a seditious libel was true or false. [10]

Hay also thought, but for a different reason, that whether or not a libel was true did not matter. He argued "that if the words freedom of the press, have any meaning at all, they mean a total exemption from any law making any publication whatever criminal." Hay claimed that freedom of the press must be absolute. [11] However, his definition of "absolute freedom" had a significant qualification. The press, he wrote, "may do whatever it pleases to do, uncontrolled by any law, *taking care however to do no injury to any individual.* This injury," he said, "can only be by slander or defamation, and reparation should be made for it in a state of nature as well as in society." Since he made this qualification, derived almost certainly from his study of John Locke, he should have explained its application. It would have saved him from future charges of inconsistency. But he was not bothering with careful distinctions here. At this point, as a champion of the "sacred cause of liberty and truth," he was attempting to preserve the spirit of inquiry and

---

[7] *Essay on the Liberty of the Press,* pp. 5, 21. Citations are to the most easily accessible edition, the Richmond reprint of 1803, which has been reproduced by Da Capo Press, New York, 1970.

[8] Levy, editor, *Freedom of the Press from Zenger to Jefferson: Early American Libertarian Theories* (Indianapolis, 1966), p. 186.

[9] London, 1791 edition, pp. 150-153.

[10] Smith, *Freedom's Fetters,* pp. 128-129, 421-422.

[11] *Essay on the Liberty of the Press,* pp. 23, 26. Leonard Levy argues that until the Republican protest against the Sedition Act in 1798, the Blackstone concept of freedom of the press was unchallenged in America, and that the new libertarianism of Hay and others represented a sudden breakthrough. However, James Morton Smith disputes this view, in part, in a new preface to *Freedom's Fetters* (1966). He contends that the new legal theory was a gradual development out of the Revolution.

discussion, which he believed must be given "absolute protection, even in its excesses." [12]

Hay later claimed that it was this dedication to the principle of a free press that led him to volunteer to defend James T. Callender when he was indicted in Virginia under the Sedition Act in 1800.[13] In 1793, at the age of thirty-five, Callender had fled his native Scotland under indictment for seditious libel. Settling in Philadelphia he took up his pen against the Federalist administration, wielding it with such virulence that the day before the signing of an American sedition act, he fled once again in fear of prosecution.[14] Ironically, the Federalists, by attempting to suppress the Republican press in the North, assured Callender a welcome in the South. Virginia, where the Republicans were the majority, had possessed a mild press. But to insure the maintenance of the Republican cause they established an effective partisan print in December 1798, the *Examiner*, edited by Meriwether Jones.[15] Callender began writing for it early the next year. By August local Federalists had formed an "association" to run him out of Richmond, but threats of counterviolence from Republicans cooled this movement. However, when it came to his indictment in the Federal District Court for seditious libel, Virginia Republicans attempted to defend him by legal means. The presiding judge, Samuel Chase, did not make this easy. He refused to allow counsel to argue the constitutional issues or even to try to prove that the alleged libels were true. The best that Hay and his fellow lawyers could do was to resign from the case in protest. On June 3, 1800, Callender was

---

[12] *Essay on the Liberty of the Press*, pp. 23, 28, 30. Since Leonard Levy points out that John Locke's "claim of writing in behalf of 'ABSOLUTE LIBERTY' was overstated and even unjustifiable," it is strange that he is not more critical of Hay's definition of absolute liberty. He calls Hay an "absolutist." To Hay and to Locke, "absolute liberty" did not imply license. Even in a state of nature none possessed the right to harm another, and therefore according to Locke, an offender of the law of nature deserved punishment, and the injured party deserved reparation. Hay only mentioned reparation for injury in his essay, so Levy does have reason to claim that at this time Hay only believed that injuries could be redressed civilly by a suit for damages. Yet Locke on this topic was so familiar to the readers of his essay that Hay might have assumed that they would simply think he was following Locke on punishment as well (John Locke, *Of Civil Government*, Book Two [London, 1924 edition], ch. II, sections 6-11; Levy, *Legacy*, pp. 101, 270-273).

Very likely Hay had not thought the problem through. His *Essay* is an important historical document, but it does not actually present either a sound legal argument or a first-rate exposition of libertarian theory. For these see James Madison, *The Virginia Report of 1799-1800*; and Tunis Wortman, *A Treatise Concerning Political Enquiry, and the Liberty of the Press* (New York, 1800), both in Levy, *Freedom of the Press*, pp. 197-284.

[13] *Recorder* (Richmond), December 15, 1802; *Virginia Gazette* (Richmond), January 8, 1803.

[14] Charles A. Jellison, "That Scoundrel Callender," *Virginia Magazine of History and Biography*, LXVI (1959), 295-298; Smith, *Freedom's Fetters*, pp. 335-337.

[15] *The Examiner's* predecessor, Dixon's *Observatory*, was moderately partisan.

fined and sentenced to nine months' imprisonment. The "Scots Correspondent in the Richmond Jail" was not silenced. He continued to lambaste his oppressors, perhaps with even more effect during his martyrdom.[16]

Callender, however, did not plan to be a martyr all his life. He expected a reward for his political services, a public office, but it was not forthcoming. The Republicans neglected him, he wrote Jefferson after the election, "because I had gone farther to serve them than some dastards durst go to serve themselves. . . . I have been equally calumniated, pillaged, and betrayed by all parties." [17]

"I am not the man who is either to be oppressed or plundered with impunity," Callender warned James Madison on April 27, 1801. His letter revealed a man in a terrible emotional state, deep in self-pity and breathing hostility towards those who he believed had abandoned him. Jefferson and the Republicans of Virginia had not actually done so. They still offered him support, but he perversely refused what he felt were crumbs.[18]

Callender set out to prove he was not a man who was to be taken lightly. He did this through the *Recorder*, a Richmond periodical which was founded in October 1801, by Henry Pace, as a weekly "Lady's and Gentleman's Miscellany." The paper was insipid until Pace acquired his new assistant, whom he made a partner early in 1802. Soon after, the masthead reference to gentility was dropped.

The *Recorder* carried little advertising, and left foreign and domestic news to other papers. It was devoted almost exclusively to the humiliation of Callender's victims—primarily the Republicans with whom he had been most intimate. Callender did not hesitate to attack men at their most vulnerable points; and there was no limit to his scurrility. Although his defamations of Jefferson are best known, he dealt as brutally with others. Not only did the *Recorder* quickly develop one of the largest circulations in America but its stories were reprinted by the Federalist press. This was taking place, it must be remembered, in an era and in a state in which personal honor and privacy were almost an obsession.[19]

---

[16] Jellison, "Scoundrel Callender," *VMHB*, LXVI, 298-300; Smith, *Freedom's Fetters*, pp. 338-358.

[17] To Madison, January 23, 1801, to Jefferson, February 23, April 12, 1801, *New England Historical and Genealogical Register*, LI (1897), 22-25; Malone, *Jefferson: First Term*, pp. 207-209.

[18] To Madison, April 27, 1801, *New England Historical and Genealogical Register*, LI, 153-155; *Examiner*, July 27, 1803. For detailed accounts of Jefferson's relations with Callender see Malone, *Ordeal of Liberty; Jefferson: First Term*; and Peterson, *Jefferson*.

[19] *Examiner*, November 6, 1802; *Recorder*, February 2, 1803. It does not seem necessary to repeat Callender's libels here.

The *Recorder* continued throughout 1802 to attack whomever Callender wished, and he gloried in his power. On December 15, "Mr. George Hay" was the heading for a column. Callender claimed he had never given offense to Hay, and had even ignored insults from him the previous winter, attributing his behavior to partisanship. But now, he said, Hay had gone too far by insulting his partner Pace. Callender therefore had sent a gentleman to inform Hay that he was to receive "a dressing" in the *Recorder*. This had brought Hay to the office.

Callender noted the details of their interview—how Hay had not removed his gloves to shake hands with him; how he had accused Hay of writing a series of letters against him in the *Examiner* (which Hay denied) and of publicly proclaiming that Hay defended him from the Sedition Act not out of feeling for a "scoundrel" but for the sake of principle. "I said more," Hay had burst out. "I said that if your treatment of some other persons had been applied to me, YOU SHOULD NOT BE LIVING." When they parted, Hay had said, "Pursue your course, and I will pursue mine." It should be noted that this was taking place just as Hay was being put forward for election to his first public office, membership on the state privy council.[20] In the next week's *Recorder*, Callender described Hay's response.

On December 20, according to Callender, he stepped down to Darmstadt's store to have some Dutch translated. He was attempting to read to the bookkeeper when "I felt a violent stroke to my forehead." This was repeated three or four times, before he saw his attacker. "The cowardly villain [it was George Hay], came behind my back!" Hay intended to commit murder, Callender charged in the *Recorder* of the 22nd. Only a high crowned hat protected him from Hay's bludgeon and saved his life. "He fears me," Callender said of Hay, because of what would be told.

Whatever Callender planned to reveal about Hay had to be postponed, as their conflict moved immediately into a new arena—the courts. Under the common law, a man who could establish that he had just cause to fear physical injury from another, could demand that that person be legally bound to keep the peace. Callender used this routine procedure against Hay by appealing to the Richmond mayor, John Foster, who in town possessed the magisterial powers of a justice of the peace. Hay, when confronted by Foster on December 23, offered to pledge his honor that he would not molest Callender "unless he gave the first attack," but he learned with indignation that he was to be required to provide security for his recognizance

---

[20] Hay qualified for the Council of State on December 24, 1802 (*Calendar of Virginia State Papers*, edited by H. W. Flournoy, IX [Richmond, 1890], 340).

like any common brawler. Hay determined therefore that he would require the same of Callender. He could not maintain that a recognizance to keep the peace was applicable, since Callender did not threaten violence, but he could maintain that the editor fell under a second species of recognizance requiring good behavior. This law was something of a catchall, but Hay's interpretation was uncustomary in Virginia.[21]

Hay applied to Foster for a warrant to commit the editors of the *Recorder* to jail unless they gave security that they would publish nothing that reflected adversely on Hay or any citizen of Virginia. Foster said Hay "*demanded it*. I informed Mr. Hay," Foster continued, "that it was a new case, and that I had my doubts whether such a warrant could legally be granted; that I must have time to consider the subject, and obtain the best legal opinion I could." Hay read the mayor the act of Assembly he relied on and, supported by Alexander MacRae as his lawyer, insisted Foster had the power. But the mayor decided he needed further advice. Such a proceeding appeared to be an infringement on the liberty of the press. The three lawyers he applied to all counseled him against issuing the warrant. Before he could refuse Hay, however, he was informed that a warrant had been obtained elsewhere.[22]

Hay had turned from the Federalist mayor to a Republican magistrate of Henrico County, Gervas Storrs, who required Callender and Pace to answer Hay's complaint in the county court the next morning. Serving the editors as counsel were William Marshall, state's attorney, and James Rind. John Wickham and Alexander MacRae appeared with Hay. Storrs, William Price, Pleasant Younghusband, and Joseph Selden sat as magistrates.[23]

Alexander MacRae opened the hearing by contending that Callender and Pace "should be bound over from publishing libellous matter, as being per-

---

[21] The legal system of this era can be understood rather well by referring to three books: William Waller Hening, *The New Virginia Justice, Comprising the Office and Authority of a Justice of the Peace, in the Commonwea'th of Virginia* (Richmond, 1795); Blackstone's *Commentaries;* and the current collection of acts of the General Assembly. In 1803 an annotated edition of Blackstone by St. George Tucker, and a new collection of acts printed by Samuel Pleasants and Henry Pace were published (4 *Blackstone* 18, 252-256; *Recorder*, December 22, 29, 1802; *Virginia Gazette*, December 29, 1802; January 12, 1803).

[22] *Ibid.;* John Foster to Mr. A. Davis, December 30, 1802, *ibid.*, January 1, 1803.

[23] The account of this proceeding is drawn from two Richmond papers: *Virginia Gazette*, December 29, 1802; *Virginia Argus*, December 29, 1802, reprinted in the *Aurora*, January 5, 1803. Marshall was also clerk of the federal Circuit Court and a Federalist. Rind, the son and brother of newspaper editors, seems to have been a Republican who broke with the party. Wickham, a Federalist, was probably the most successful lawyer in the state. MacRae, a Republican, later appeared in the Burr trial of 1807. Storrs and Selden were both on the Richmond Republican Committee.

sons of bad fame." He said he could prove by the bundle of *Recorders* in his hand that Callender and Pace were men of that description, and that Callender in particular had libeled "almost every respectable person in the state of Virginia."

When the defense presented their case, they first objected that the magistrates of Henrico County were not empowered to take cognizance of this question between two citizens of Richmond. The argument was answered by Hay's counsel, and the magistrates ruled "that their authority as justices of Henrico extended all over the county, although the city court in some instances has concurrent jurisdiction." Rind next contended that the character of bad fame could not apply since both men were industriously employed, and "could not be charged with publishing libels, as no jury had found them guilty of that crime." Properly, he said, Hay should prosecute for defamation and a jury should determine the extent of the offense. If the magistrates bound the editors, they would be acting as judges of the nature of publications. Rind charged "that the exploded common law of England, which all good democrats had abused as a system of tyranny . . . was attempted to be used as an engine of oppression by the very man who had written an excellent treatise to prove the unconstitutionality of the sedition law, and in vindication of the liberty of the press."

Hay replied by claiming he was not acting inconsistently with the doctrines of Hortensius. He said he had never argued the right of publishing private scandal and destroying the peace of private families. John Wickham pointed out that Hay himself had been compelled by Callender to give security without a trial by jury. The object was "preventive justice." Since Hay's hands were tied, it was only proper that Callender and Pace be prevented from printing lies. As for the comments on the common law—this was not a United States court and the common law certainly was in effect in Virginia. He contended also that the remedy would be no restraint on a free press since the editors would still be at liberty to publish what they wished. Their recognizance could not be forfeited unless they published libelous matter which would remain to be determined by a jury.

The magistrates found against Callender and Pace and required each to enter into a personal recognizance for $500 and to obtain securities to post an equal amount. Pace complied, with William Marshall and William Richardson as securities. Callender refused. The legality of the magistrates' decision was to be reviewed at the regularly monthly session of the county court on January 3. Until that date Callender was committed to jail.[24]

---

[24] The act regarding conservators of the peace passed October 17, 1792 (*Acts*, p. 94).

Before that session took place, the story of the previous transactions exploded in the newspapers. On December 29, a half-sheet, black-bordered *Recorder* addressed "the Citizens of the United States . . . From My Old Quarters in Richmond Jail." In the *Virginia Gazette* the headline of the same day proclaimed "The Liberty of the Press Invaded." Callender dwelt mostly on his personal sufferings, but the *Gazette* account presented the larger issues and a thorough report of the hearing. The author reminded his readers of the article of the Virginia Declaration of Rights—"That the freedom of the press is one of the great bulwarks of liberty, and can never be restrained but by despotic governments." Identifying the magistrates of the court as "anti-federal" or "democratic," he wrote that "this decision furnishes, the most decided proof of the real principles of the present ruling party, and of those men who are perpetually bawling about liberty and republicanism."

In the *Virginia Argus* of the same day, George Hay anticipated and denied this charge in a signed address to "the People of Virginia." He recognized "the arrest . . . will probably be denounced as a party measure, for which the republicans generally, are responsible. . . . This will not be just." Hay asserted the action was exclusively his. He also confronted the issue of his personal inconsistency, and stated, as he had in court, that he had never believed that freedom of the press should be used to protect vicious libelers of personal character. Because this case was still before the courts, he postponed a fuller explanation.

The *Examiner*, on January 1, 1803, supported Hay's denial of a Republican persecution. It said the various statements which had appeared regarding the trial were generally accurate, but that the *Virginia Gazette* had left out the argument of John Wickham, the Federalist counsel of Hay, and was mistaken in claiming that all the magistrates were Republicans. According to the *Examiner*, Younghusband, who favored the restrictions, was "an ardent Federalist." The others were Republicans, but one of them, Joseph Selden, opposed the surety.

The case naturally received national attention, and disapproval of Hay's actions was not limited to Federalists. William Duane of the Philadelphia *Aurora*, which had published Hortensius, regretted that Hay had taken notice of Callender. "The press had indeed been prostituted to the basest purposes by Callender, but we doubt much whether the method taken to

According to the common law as defined in both Hening and Blackstone, the justices of the county courts also act as enforcement officers (*Virginia Argus*, January 5, 1803; Henrico County Order Book, No. 10 [1801-1803], microfilm from the Virginia State Library, 483).

correct the evil will have any other effect than the contrary of what was intended, and whether the freedom of the press is not much endangered by it." Hay had dragged before the public, thought Duane, a man whose libels were beginning to be ignored.[25]

However, it was more than a coincidence that when Hay returned to court on January 3, he reached into Pennsylvania for support of his actions, quoting Governor Thomas McKean's recent speech in which he had alluded to the "unparalleled licentiousness" which threatened to annihilate the benefits of "the noblest invention of man"—the printing press. "It is time, then," McKean had said, "that the good sense of our fellow citizens, aiding the authority of the magistrate, should interpose to rescue us from a tyranny, by which the wicked, and the obscure, are enabled to prey upon the fame, the feelings, and the fortunes of every conspicuous member of the community." [26]

Hay told the court that some people were "such philosophers, or could conceal their thoughts so well, as to bear with every symptom of indifference, all the attacks which malice or calumny could attempt against them." He owned this was not his situation, that he both felt and was wounded by the slanders of the *Recorder*. Hay included in his three-hour argument extensive remarks on the particular events that had occurred. Although he had been called assassin, he said he had met Callender by accident, that the supposed "bludgeon" was only his walking stick, and that he would not have killed Callender, though he did believe him "the most unprincipled man in existence." If he had simply charged Callender with libel, for eighteen months to two years he would have had calumny and slander heaped upon him. What satisfaction would the fine and imprisonment have been then, he asked. Hay said that in his character as an official he would be vulnerable to attack, but not as a private man.[27]

The next day in the packed courtroom, William Marshall answered the final point. The private characters of candidates for public office were legitimate subjects of inquiry, he said, otherwise unprincipled men would

[25] *Aurora*, January 5, 1803. John W. Eppes in a private letter to his father-in-law Thomas Jefferson reporting events in Richmond also said Callender was sinking into obscurity (December 23, 1802, University of Virginia).

[26] *Virginia Gazette*, January 5, 1803; *Aurora*, December 14, 1802. Pennsylvania Republicans were seriously divided on the issue of freedom of the press as on many others. McKean attempted to use very similar tactics against Duane who was a bitter critic. The legislature did not support him, however (Sanford W. Higginbotham, *The Keystone in the Democratic Arch: Pennsylvania Politics, 1800-1816* [Harrisburg, 1952], pp. 114, 123-125).

[27] *Virginia Gazette*, January 5, 1803.

be elected. James Rind agreed. He did not defend Callender's accuracy, but argued his right to criticize public figures.

A new set of Henrico justices of the peace sat on this court. To them all cases stated as precedents appeared inapplicable to Virginia and in opposition to the state Bill of Rights. The propriety of restraining the press, they believed, was a subject to be considered by the legislature and not by them. Callender was discharged late Tuesday the 4th of January.[28]

On the next Monday, Hay attempted to obtain a discharge from his recognizance. Before the Court of Hustings of Richmond he declared, "I did what I then thought was proper; what I now think was right; and what I shall always consider to have been justified." But he was willing to pledge he would not molest Callender unless attacked. Callender, however, testified that he still dreaded danger from Hay. When Hay asked Callender if he dreaded danger if he did not make the first attack, Callender declined to answer unless forced. The result was that the court refused to discharge Hay's recognizance, and he was still bound to keep the peace for twelve months.[29]

This was not the end of the incident. Hay suffered a torrent of personal abuse from Callender, assaults on his principles from the Federalist press as a whole, and even a chiding from his fellow Republicans. Callender began a campaign on January 12 that appeared in every issue of the *Recorder* into April. He asked his readers to excuse his incoherence, for he was "half nerveless and half blind" as a result of Hay's attack. A variety of charges and innuendoes were offered.

His first attack revealed much about the nature of his resentment towards Hay, for he asked who was Hay, and then answered his question by a comparison with himself. One, he said, was the son of a Scots tobacconist; the other, Hay, was "the son of a bankrupt Scots carpenter." Hay and his whole family had been objects of charity, Callender emphasized. Besides this subject, Callender took up two others, first, that Hay suppressed testimony in an official investigation he conducted, and second, that he was an unethical gambler, if not a cheat. Attacks on Hay from other newspapers were also reprinted.[30]

---

28 *Ibid.*, January 8, 12, 1803; Henrico County Order Book, 486. The magistrates were Bowler Cocke, William Mayo, Richard Adams, and William Randolph—Federalists; and Daniel Hylton, Hezekiah Henley, and Thomas Williamson—Republicans. There is no statement that this involved a party vote (*Examiner*, January 8, 1803).

29 *Virginia Gazette*, January 12, 1803; Richmond City Hustings Court Order Book, microfilm from the Virginia State Library. Hay posted bond for $500 and Peter Carr and Alexander MacRae posted $250 apiece as securities.

30 *Recorder*, January 12–March. At the request of Governor James Monroe, Hay had in-

More significant historically than Callender's abuse of Hay was a series of articles on the liberty of the press submitted to the *Virginia Gazette.* To a large extent these essays reiterated the arguments presented in court by counsel for Callender and Pace, but on at least two points they seemed to take new stands.[31] In fact, these essays may have advocated the broadest construction of freedom of the press that appeared in the early national period. Their author, commenting that he had forgotten the substance of the 1799 Hortensius essay, stated that if Hay was accurately restating its principles, "I will venture to say they will never more be remembered by any man of common sense, who really values the principles of free government, but to be most cordially execrated." He had always believed that it was the right of every free man to call into question the conduct and character of candidates for office. Furthermore, "I contend, that it is the right and duty of every man in society, to expose to *public* view all the vices and improper practices, even of private men, that threat or tend in the smallest degree to injure that society." The essayist had moved beyond Republican theory with that sentence, for the concern of the founding fathers had been with threats to liberty from the power of government. This man would extend the guarantee of freedom of the press to exposure of dangers from the private sector.[32] Again he suggested a position beyond that of the Republican party on the significance of the guarantee of freedom of the press in the United States Constitution. He pointed out that if the states possessed the power to abridge the liberty of the press, then the first amendment was actually of little value. He believed that the Constitution was the "supreme law of the land" and questioned whether the federal Bill of Rights could be rendered null by state governments. If it was true that it could be, then in consistency they should amend the Constitution again to prohibit the states from abridging that liberty.[33]

vestigated a magistrate in Norfolk, Dr. Read, who was accused of surrendering a British mutineer without first giving him the protection of the laws (Monroe to Hay, April 29, 1800, Monroe to the speakers of the General Assembly, December 1, 1800, Stanislaus Murray Hamilton, editor, *The Writings of James Monroe,* III [New York, 1900], 177-179, 228-230). Callender called Hay a "semi-mendicant protegée of Edmund Randolph," who had taught Hay the law. Hay seems to have been an active loo player.

[31] James Rind may have been the author. The arguments are similar to those reported from him in court. Also he had opposed the Sedition Act (Charles T. Cullen, "St. George Tucker and Law in Virginia, 1772-1804," Ph.D. dissertation, University of Virginia, 1971, p. 219).

[32] *Virginia Gazette,* January 15, 22, 29, 1803.

[33] *Ibid.* It should be noted that Madison had originally wanted freedom of speech guaranteed from the states as well, but his amendment wording was not accepted. The Republicans as a whole were too dedicated to states' rights and strict interpretation of the Constitution to agree.

George Hay had certainly lost his position as champion of a free press. John Taylor of Caroline, a leading Republican ideologist, was quoted in the press as denying that any law existed to warrant Hay's measures, and that if it did, "the present legislature ought never to go home until it should be repealed." [34] Hay withdrew from the arena for a time. Not until August 27 did he again address the people of Virginia. The series of articles which appeared through October 5 in the *Virginia Argus* defended his actions and his consistency. In October, the series and Hay's letter of December 26, 1802, were published in pamphlet form as *An Essay on the Liberty of the Press, Shewing, That the Requisition of Security for Good Behavior from Libellers, Is Perfectly Compatible with the Constitution and Laws of Virginia*. The printer, Samuel Pleasants, bound it with a reprint of Hay's 1799 piece.[35]

In his new essay, Hay stated flatly that freedom of the press was not unlimited, and that this was "a truth which must command, and has commanded, universal assent. There is not a man in the commonwealth of Virginia, who has ever ventured even to suggest, that according to the constitution and laws of our country, damages cannot be recovered from a printer, for the publication of a libel, or that such a publication is not an indictable offense." If a modern student of civil liberties is correct, Hay himself had denied that libel was a criminal offense in his 1799 pamphlet. Nevertheless, Hay was right in saying that Virginians still believed libel to be criminal. St. George Tucker in an appendix to his 1803 edition of Blackstone's *Commentaries* presented an authoritative opinion that this was so, and Thomas Jefferson in private letters and his second inaugural address indicated that prosecutions would be in order to curb a licentious press.[36]

Because libel was a common-law crime, Hay said he could not understand why it would be considered an invasion of rights to require a calumniator to give security as a pledge that he would not violate the law. Certainly in the case of other suspected crimes, security was in order. He said that his opponents at the bar admitted that after a conviction for libel, security for good behavior could be required. "How arbitrary, how monstrous then is it to say, that security for good behaviour cannot be required before con-

34 *Virginia Gazette*, January 8, 1803.

35 Hortensius was reprinted first in the *Examiner*, January 15, 19, 22, 29, February 2, 1803, and *Virginia Argus*, August 27-October 5, 1803. The first advertisement for the pamphlet appeared October 1, 1803. It should be noted that the reprint of Hortensius and the new essay were bound together with separate pagination but continuous signatures.

36 Hay, *Security*, p. 25; Levy, *Legacy of Suppression*, p. 273; Tucker, *Blackstone*, in Levy, *Freedom of the Press*, pp. 324-325; and Jefferson, Second Inaugural, *ibid.*, 367-368.

viction, because *it is a restraint*, but, that after conviction, it may be required, because *it is not* a restraint, on the freedom of the press." Hay did not deny that public officers or candidates were subject to examination and that "whatever is true, however degrading, may be stated with impunity." But he said he would never admit that they were to be "left entirely to the mercy of every miscreant, who writes for a newspaper." [37]

Hay's essay met little but silence. Commenting on it in December, "Marcellus" attributed the lack of reaction to a general conviction that Hay had "entirely failed of his object." [38] Doubtless, Virginians were aware that the journalism of Richmond was undergoing major reform without the coercion of the law. On July 7, James Callender was found dead in the James River. According to the coroner's inquest, he was bathing in a state of intoxication and drowned accidentally. But the editor of the *Examiner* said Callender had been threatening for three weeks to put an end to his life, and conjectured that he had got himself excessively drunk for that express purpose. Whether or not it was conscious suicide, the man had died in a "paroxism of frenzy and despair." Without Callender, the *Recorder* soon expired, and it was not long until the *Examiner*, which had lately fallen to Callender's level, followed.

Not only did the most scurrilous newspapers die, but the quality of journalism in Richmond rose perceptibly. On May 9, 1804, Thomas Ritchie founded *The Enquirer*, a newspaper destined to become in Jefferson's opinion, "the best that is published or ever has been published in America." [39] Ritchie, in August 1806, was reminded of the Callender-Hay episode. Selleck Osborne, a Republican journalist in Connecticut, was undergoing imprisonment rather than post a bond similar to that debated in the complaint against Callender. Ritchie recalled the earlier incident:

The innumerable circumstances which combined to favour that motion, made the advocates of the press tremble for its liberty. No man was more personally obnoxious, at that moment, than the wretched defendant. Few men were so well calculated to give due weight to the motion which he advocated as the complainant himself, whose legal acquirements were entitled to universal respect; whose celebrated letters of Hortensius had already raised him above the suspicion

---

[37] Hay, *Security*, pp. 26, 37, 41.

[38] *Virginia Argus*, December 7, 1803. Six Marcellus letters appeared December 7-24, which were located with the generous assistance of Dr. Helen Cripe at the American Antiquarian Society. "A Citizen of Halifax" also replied to Hay (*Virginia Gazette*, November 12, 1803).

[39] *Examiner*, July 27, 1803; Thomas Jefferson to William Short, September 8, 1823 (A. A. Lipscomb and A. E. Bergh, editors, *The Writings of Thomas Jefferson*, XV [Washington, 1903], 468-469).

of entertaining any hostile sentiments towards the liberty of the press. Among the most splendid talents of the Richmond Bar were raised on the side of the prosecution. But the constitution of Virginia and the liberty of the press triumphed over all these considerations. . . .

In spite of the notorious treachery of Callender, at that time beginning to burst forth upon the public view, the republicans of Virginia triumphed in the decision. They regarded it as a sincere tribute of respect paid to our Bill of Rights, and to the liberty of the press.[40]

Even more than Ritchie recognized, the dismissal of the complaint against Callender marked a watershed for freedom of the press in Virginia. For the rest of the early national period, prosecutions there against journalists disappeared. While the courts might not have upheld the more extreme libertarian theories that had been advanced by Hay and his critics, they did not have to because complaints were not brought. All newspapers did not practice self-restraint, nor did all men attacked by the press satisfy themselves by public refutation. As George Hay had said, not everyone was a philosopher. Economic and social pressures were exerted against offending papers, and the final resort for redress of grievances was violence, by bludgeon or pistol. Libertarian Virginia was a place where one would not be fined or jailed for what one wrote, but one might be killed for it.[41]

---

40 *The Enquirer* (Richmond), August 8, 1806.

41 In the case of the *Commonwealth of Pennsylvania* v. *William Duane*, Chief Justice William Tilghman ruled that though he would not place an absolute prohibition upon the practice, it was "most agreeable to the spirit of our constitution, and most conducive to the suppression of libels, to adopt it as a general rule, not to demand surety for good behaviour before conviction" (*Aurora*, August 12, 1806; Higginbotham, *Keystone*, p. 114). The case of the *Commonwealth of Virginia* v. *John Morris, Jr.* was decided in the General Court of Virginia on June 12, 1811. The decision upheld the right to offer truth as a justification for libel in the case of public officers or candidates for public office. However, libelous matter which did not tend to show that a person was unfit for office could not be justified, nor could truth justify libels of private persons (Judges [William] Brockenbrough and [Hugh] Holmes, *A Collection of Cases Decided by the General Court of Virginia* . . . [Philadelphia, 1815], pp. 176-181; see also Norman L. Rosenberg, "The Law of Political Libel and Freedom of the Press in Nineteenth Century America: An Interpretation," *American Journal of Legal History*, XVII [October 1973], 336-352).

Legislative Privilege in Post-Revolutionary South Carolina

Michael E. Stevens

IN the decade after the Revolutionary War, American legislators found themselves in a position to define their own privileges and prerogatives. Schooled in the adversarial politics of the late colonial era that pitted the lower houses against the executive, state legislative leaders had become accustomed to equate the growth of their privileges with popular rights. With the collapse of royal power in America these old assumptions suddenly became obsolete, yet lawmakers were not always attuned to the new political realities. Those who failed to move with the times suddenly found themselves targets of harsh public criticism directed against their claims of special privilege. This is seen vividly in South Carolina, where the lower house was the arena for three important political battles between 1784 and 1794 that led to a major redefinition of legislative privilege in that state. The following account of the ways in which these cases were resolved not only fills a gap in our knowledge of legislative and legal history but also sheds light on the changing relationship of legislators to their constituents in post-Revolutionary America.

Legislative privilege, an amorphous concept, refers to rights claimed and exercised by a legislative body. In Anglo-American tradition, these rights most commonly included freedom of speech on the legislature's floor, freedom of members from molestation by outsiders, the right of the legislature to determine its membership and select its officers, and its right to punish anyone, even nonmembers, who infringed its privileges. It was this last claim—the legislature's authority over nonmembers—that created a political uproar in South Carolina.

In England, the rights of the House of Commons evolved to protect that body from undue influence by the crown as well as from other external pressures. Freedom of debate was formally claimed as early as 1541, and freedom from arrest and molestation was won in 1604, although during the Tudor and Stuart eras these privileges were not so well developed that they could not be challenged. As the Commons struggled to establish its position against the crown and the royal courts, it did whatever was

Mr. Stevens is Assistant State Archivist at the State Historical Society of Wisconsin. Acknowledgments: I would like to thank Herbert J. Hartsook, David Moltke-Hansen, Donald W. Rogers, George C. Rogers, Jr., Wylma Wates, and Robert M. Weir for reading drafts of this article and for making helpful suggestions.

necessary to protect its members on the ground that they should not be distracted from their duties by outside pressures. For instance, the seizure of a member's property in payment for a debt could be regarded as an attempt to keep him from attending the House, thus infringing its liberties. To enforce its privileges, the House either reprimanded or jailed offenders.

Although James I maintained that the House's privileges existed by royal sufferance, the House of Commons claimed them as a matter of right and insisted on being the judge of what constituted breach of privilege. The latter argument was vital to the Commons's independence because the House of Lords was the final tribunal for appeals from the law courts. Thus the Commons could not permit cases involving parliamentary rights to be adjudicated in a fashion that, by permitting appeals to the Lords, would imply the subordinate status of the Commons. As a result, if citizens believed they were unjustly imprisoned by the Commons, they could not obtain their freedom with a writ of habeas corpus.

The Commons condemned as breaches of privilege a great variety of offenses, ranging from cutting timber on a member's estate to unauthorized publication of its debates. Not surprisingly, abuses developed, especially in the years following the Glorious Revolution. With its own freedom well protected, the House at times acted arbitrarily. In the late eighteenth century, questions of privilege were often at the center of English politics; they were, for example, the hinges for controversies over John Wilkes's publication of his *North Briton* No. 45, his repeated exclusion from a seat in Parliament, and his protection of London printers in their battles with the Commons. Thus the history of legislative privilege in England on the eve of the American Revolution was a mixed one in which privilege was "used to champion the cause of the people" but at the same time "became the greatest oppressor of the subject's liberty."[1]

Colonial legislatures in British America exercised their privileges as fully as Parliament ever did. The most ample study of the subject is Mary Patterson Clarke's *Parliamentary Privilege in Colonial America,* published in 1943. Clarke demonstrated that colonial legislatures repeatedly invoked their privileges, including the right to punish nonmembers who violated them. Assemblies were quick to take offense, and "anything that injured the feelings or offended the sensibilities of representatives was likely to be considered an affront to their dignity, and hence a breach of their collective privilege." Clarke argued that in both England and America

---

[1] Carl Wittke, *The History of English Parliamentary Privilege* (Columbus, Ohio, 1921), *passim,* quotations on p. 15. See also Mary Patterson Clarke, *Parliamentary Privilege in the American Colonies* (New Haven, Conn., 1943), 1-13; Jack P. Greene, *The Quest for Power: The Lower Houses of Assembly in the Southern Royal Colonies, 1689-1776* (Chapel Hill, N.C., 1963), 212; and P.D.G. Thomas, *The House of Commons in the Eighteenth Century* (Oxford, 1971), 336-338. For background on the cases involving Wilkes, see Raymond Postgate, *"That Devil Wilkes"* (London, 1956), 50-58, 75-76, 137-147, 173-177, and Wittke, *History of Parliamentary Privilege,* 115-125.

legislative privilege was "defended as one of the chief means of upholding and preserving the liberty of the subject," although she also pointed out the oppressive propensities of assemblies. Attempts to restrict the powers of assemblies were viewed by them as assaults on the body politic—that is, on the people themselves.[2] Clarke's work has been employed by other scholars to illuminate early American politics. Jack P. Greene has shown that the assemblies used claims of privilege in their struggle to establish authority comparable to that of the House of Commons.[3] Leonard W. Levy in *Legacy of Suppression* and *Emergence of a Free Press* has demonstrated that the assemblies, using privilege to suppress dissent, were far more oppressive than executives or judges in their treatment of the press.[4]

In South Carolina, the Commons House of Assembly asserted its privileges as strongly as any other colonial legislature. In contests with the crown it developed a tradition of defining and defending its prerogatives. The Commons House maintained that it had the same authority vis-à-vis members and nonmembers as did the British House of Commons, including freedom from external restraints on debate and the right to commit to jail any person who infringed the House's privileges. In 1722, for example, it jailed twenty-eight merchants for libeling the House; yet most of its battles were fought against the royally appointed governor and his Council. In these conflicts the Commons House perceived itself as the champion of popular rights. For instance, between 1726 and 1733, the House arrested five royal officials—the provost marshal, the chief justice,

---

[2] Clarke, *Parliamentary Privilege*, 2, 223, 269.

[3] Greene, *Quest for Power*, 212-216, 219.

[4] Levy, *Emergence of a Free Press* (New York, 1985), *passim*, esp. 16-61, and *Legacy of Suppression: Freedom of Speech and Press in Early American History* (Cambridge, Mass., 1960), *passim*, esp. 18-87. For other discussions of legislative privilege in colonial America see Levy, "Did the Zenger Case Really Matter? Freedom of the Press in Colonial New York," *William and Mary Quarterly*, 3d Ser., XVII (1960), 35-50; Jeffrey A. Smith, "A Reappraisal of Legislative Privilege and American Colonial Journalism," *Journalism Quarterly*, LXI (1984), 97-103, 141; and Harold L. Nelson, "Seditious Libel in Colonial America," *American Journal of Legal History*, III (1959), 160-172. Little has been written on the use of privilege by state legislatures after the Revolution. See C. S. Potts, "Power of Legislative Bodies to Punish for Contempt," *University of Pennsylvania Law Review*, LXXIV (1925-1926), 716-719, for an enumeration of fewer than a dozen cases between 1781 and 1837 in Virginia, Pennsylvania, and New York. Richard Buel, Jr., *Securing the Revolution: Ideology in American Politics, 1789-1815* (Ithaca, N.Y., 1972), 247, asserts, but does not prove, that after the Revolution legislative punishment of libel through the claim of privilege was no longer defensible. He also states, in "Freedom of the Press in Revolutionary America: The Evolution of Libertarianism, 1760-1820," in Bernard Bailyn and John B. Hench, eds., *The Press and the American Revolution* (Worcester, Mass., 1980), 60, 75, that after 1760 the lower houses largely abandoned the practice of punishing printers for breach of privilege.

the clerk of the Council, the surveyor general, and the deputy surveyor general—for offenses ranging from defiance of its orders to insolence.[5]

With the coming of the Revolution, South Carolinians reestablished their political institutions without rethinking the theory of legislative privilege. Members of South Carolina's Provincial Congress asserted that they had "no love of innovation" and declared in the constitution they wrote in 1776 that the lower house had "all other privileges which have at any time been claimed or exercised by the Commons house of Assembly."[6] When the legislature adopted a new constitution in 1778, it used this same wording to define the House's privileges.[7] This sweeping definition of legislative privilege gave the House power to imprison citizens while it was in session without right of appeal to any court. Nonetheless, it was one thing to claim power in the constitution and quite another to use it.

Following the British evacuation of Charleston in 1782, the House tried to exercise its privileges in the same fashion as had the colonial assembly, but in the new political climate engendered by the Revolution it could not do so without sparking public debate.[8] As a result of that debate, the privileges of the House came to be defined in a narrower and more explicit fashion than they had been in 1776. This redefinition was prompted by cases involving breach of privilege in 1784 and 1789, established in the state's new constitution of 1790, and confirmed in a case of 1794 and two later minor ones.

A private dispute in 1784 between John Rutledge, member of the House and prominent Charleston attorney, and William Thompson, a Charleston tavernkeeper, set the stage for the first post-Revolutionary controversy over legislative privilege. Rutledge had played a leading role in South Carolina politics since the early 1760s and had served as the state's wartime governor in exile during the British occupation. Thompson, a captain in the Continental Line during the Revolution and a supporter of the city's radical democratic element, operated the City Tavern, an important gathering place for Charlestonians. During 1783 and 1784 Charleston was agitated by conflicts over the treatment of tories. At the 1782 meeting of the General Assembly, held in the town of Jacksonboro because Charleston was still occupied, numerous tory sympathizers had been banished and their estates confiscated, but in the next two years many of these men petitioned the legislature for clemency and

---

[5] Greene, *Quest for Power*, 215-216.

[6] William Edwin Hemphill and Wylma Anne Wates, eds., *Extracts from the Journals of the Provincial Congresses of South Carolina, 1775-1776* (Columbia, S.C., 1960), 60; Thomas Cooper and David J. McCord, eds., *The Statutes at Large of South Carolina*, 10 vols. (Columbia, S.C., 1836-1841), I, 131.

[7] Cooper and McCord, eds., *Statutes*, I, 141.

[8] Because few private manuscripts from this period have survived, the principal documentation for this debate appears in the journals of the House, in pamphlets, and in Charleston's newspapers.

were permitted upon paying a fine to return to the state with their property restored. Furthermore, British merchants who had come to the city during the occupation were given permission to stay after the war ended, and a number of them were granted citizenship. Many citizens of Charleston, especially merchants and mechanics who had aligned themselves with the patriot cause and now faced competition from their former enemies, believed that the old order was being restored. Demonstrations, riots, and vitriolic political rhetoric led some conservative Charlestonians to fear general disorder. Opponents of the tories, under the leadership of Alexander Gillon, formed the Marine Anti-Britannic Society, which led the protests. It was within this explosive context that Rutledge and Thompson confronted each other in March 1784.[9]

Exactly how the dispute started is unclear, for the combatants offered differing accounts. Rutledge said that he had sent a slave with an oral message for Thompson to convey to the Sons of St. Patrick, one of several fraternal organizations in Charleston, explaining that Rutledge could not join them at their St. Patrick's Day dinner. Thompson did not deliver the message to the Sons nor did he permit the slave to deliver it. Rutledge thereupon sent his slave to ask Thompson to visit him and explain his misconduct.[10]

Thompson told a remarkably different story. He said that a black woman named Beck came to his house on St. Patrick's Day and asked permission to go upstairs so that she could see the artillery firing in honor of the ratification of the definitive treaty of peace. Thompson was so "provoked at the insolence of such a request, from one of her colour," that he ordered her to be gone, "execrating her for her impertinence." According to Thompson, Beck gave no indication that she had a message from Rutledge. Shortly afterwards, Thompson was summoned to Rutledge's home, where he was accused of sending an insolent message back to Rutledge with the slave. Thompson claimed that the slave had lied, but Rutledge, in the presence of Beck, told Thompson that "I must BELIEVE THE WENCH BEFORE YOU." Thompson left in anger, declaring that Rutledge had used him ill because "HE HAD PREFERRED A NEGRO'S EVIDENCE TO HIS."[11]

The next day Thompson sent Rutledge a letter demanding a public

[9] For Charleston politics in the years after the war see Jerome J. Nadelhaft, *The Disorders of War: The Revolution in South Carolina* (Orono, Me., 1981), 87-124, and "'The Snarls of Invidious Animals': The Democratization of Revolutionary South Carolina," in Ronald Hoffman and Peter J. Albert, eds., *Sovereign States in an Age of Uncertainty* (Charlottesville, Va., 1981), 62-94; Richard Walsh, *Charleston's Sons of Liberty: A Study of the Artisans, 1763-1789* (Columbia, S.C., 1959), 111-124; and George C. Rogers, Jr., *Evolution of a Federalist: William Loughton Smith of Charleston (1758-1812)* (Columbia, S.C., 1962), 97-111.

[10] Theodora J. Thompson and Rosa S. Lumpkin, eds., *Journals of the House of Representatives, 1783-1784* (Columbia, S.C., 1977), 581-582, hereafter cited as *Journals of the House, 1783-1784.*

[11] *Gazette of the State of South-Carolina* (Charleston), Apr. 29, 1784.

apology while making clear that he was not proposing a duel. Rutledge replied in writing that it was he who was entitled to an apology because of Thompson's "rash and inconsiderate Measure." If one was not forthcoming, he threatened to lay both letters before the House of Representatives to decide "whether his or Mr. Thompson's [conduct] deserves Reprehension."[12] A third party tried to arrange a compromise, but Thompson rejected it, asserting that if Rutledge "meant to *skreen* himself behind *privilege*, as his *rampart*, he was welcome to do it."[13]

On March 19 Rutledge turned Thompson's letter over to the House, where it was referred to the committee on privileges and elections.[14] When Thompson appeared at the committee hearing that same day, he raised questions about what constituted a breach of privilege. He denied knowing that Rutledge was a member of the House (which, given Rutledge's prominence, was highly unlikely), said that he considered the dispute a private matter between two citizens, and asked to be represented by his attorneys before both the committee and the whole House.[15] The committee denied the right to counsel and declared that the "House alone were the Sole Judges of their Own Privileges." Holding that Thompson's letter was "a gross Insult on, and undeservedly injurious to an Honorable Member of this House, and a flagrant Violation and breach of the privileges thereof," the committee recommended that Thompson be required to apologize both to the House and to Rutledge or else be confined in the city jail.[16]

The following day the House unanimously agreed to the committee report and summoned Thompson to attend. He again asked for and was denied the right to counsel. Thompson said that he was willing to apologize to the House but not to Rutledge. Thomas Bee, one of Thompson's strongest critics on the committee, cited British precedents and argued that the House had shown leniency by not requiring Thompson to ask pardon on his knees. When Thompson refused to apologize to Rutledge, he was jailed for the remaining week of the session.[17]

Thompson's punishment ended when the House adjourned, but the event sparked economic warfare in the city. Shortly after the close of the session, the Marine Anti-Britannic Society adopted a resolution of thanks to Thompson "for his *spirited, manly*, and *patriotic* conduct, by the defence of his fellow citizens rights and privileges, violated in his own person; when *Aristocratical principles* endeavoured to subvert and destroy every *genuine idea* of *real republicanism*."[18] The society asked the city's newspa-

[12] *Journals of the House, 1783-1784*, 580-582.
[13] *Gazette of the State*, Apr. 29, 1784.
[14] *Journals of the House, 1783-1784*, 578.
[15] *Ibid.*, 580; *Gazette of the State*, Apr. 15, 29, 1784.
[16] *Journals of the House, 1783-1784*, 580.
[17] *Gazette of the State*, Apr. 29, 1784.
[18] *Ibid.*, Apr. 1, 1784.

pers to publish its resolve. When the state printer, John Miller, refused, the society's members agreed not to take advertisements in his paper.[19]

Rutledge, for his part, used his influence to attempt to ruin Thompson's business. He was accused of getting his friends to move banquets, meetings, and dances out of the City Tavern.[20] The Charleston Library Society, which had scheduled its quarterly meeting for April 7 at the City Tavern, decided in late March to meet instead at McCrady's Tavern.[21] Likewise, dances that once had been held at the City Tavern now took place at the State House.[22] What Rutledge could not do with his influence, others sought to accomplish by rumormongering. A writer sympathetic to Thompson charged that Miller, "the Puppet Printer of this Commonwealth," had spread a report among the city's women that the City Tavern was infected with smallpox, which was "calculated to prejudice Mr. *Thompson's* Business, and but the feeble effort of a most malicious, but disappointed Faction of *Upstart Lordlings.*"[23]

More significant for the present purpose was the concurrent newspaper debate over legislative privilege that at times descended to scurrilous personal attacks on the integrity of the state's leadership. One satirist used sexual innuendo to explain Rutledge's readiness to believe his slave over Thompson, writing that "J——n sent a maiden, even an *Ethiopian* damsel, whom he loved, unto the house of *William;* and the *Ethiopian* was beautiful to look upon."[24] Thompson himself went public with his own account of the incident at the end of April. In vitriolic language he assailed "the NABOBS of this State, their servile *Toad-eaters,* the BOBS,—and the servilely-servile tools and lick-spittles of Power to *both,* the BOBBETS." Thompson contrasted the House's harsh treatment of him with the leniency granted to tories, especially on the issue of representation by counsel. He was outraged that the privilege granted "to a *Williamson* and *other Traitors,* was refused to me, tho' a *Citizen* and *Soldier.*"[25]

In Thompson's mind, the issue no longer was a dispute between Rutledge and himself but rather centered on who would control the

---

[19] *Ibid.,* Apr. 8, 1784.

[20] *Ibid.,* Apr. 15, 1784.

[21] *South-Carolina Gazette, and Public Advertiser* (Charleston), Mar. 20-24, 24-27, 1784.

[22] Henry Peronneau to Benjamin Guerard, Apr. 14, 1784, and Guerard to Peronneau, Apr. 14, 1784, in *Gazette of the State,* May 6, 1784.

[23] *Ibid.,* May 27, 1784.

[24] *Ibid.,* Apr. 15, 1784.

[25] *Ibid.,* Apr. 29, 1784. Andrew Williamson, a general in the South Carolina militia during the Revolution, took British protection after the fall of Charleston in 1780. Called the "Arnold of the Carolinas," he lost his estate by confiscation in 1782 but regained it in 1784. On Mar. 14, 1784, he was granted the right to be heard by counsel before the House. See Walter B. Edgar *et al.,* eds. and comps., *Biographical Directory of the South Carolina House of Representatives,* 4 vols. (Columbia, S.C., 1974-1984), III, 769-771; Cooper and McCord, eds., *Statutes,* VI, 632, 635; and *Journals of the House, 1783-1784,* 553.

state—the people or the pro-British aristocrats. To Thompson, it was not "the *privilege of the House* which *one active Framer*, at least, of the report had so much in view, as the humiliation of a *Publican*, a *stranger*, a *wretch* of no higher rank in the Common-wealth than that of a *Common-Citizen;* for having dared to dispute with *a John Rutledge*, or any of the *NABOB Tribe.*" He had offended "the *great John Rutledge*," and the aristocrats were determined to use claims of privilege to make an example of him. He stressed that privilege resided in the people and maintained that his refusal to apologize to Rutledge stemmed not from personal pride but from his fear that "it would be an insult on the people's majesty, and on the privileges of every citizen within the land, had I administered to them *so odious a precedent.*"[26]

Thompson also raised the fear of an even more odious precedent—namely, that the "nabobs" might banish at will anyone who dared to criticize them. He charged that a banishment bill aimed at himself had been drafted by Thomas Bee, who, while working to lift the banishment of tories, sought to deprive a free white man of his citizenship. By offering such a clearly oppressive proposal Bee played into the hands of critics who argued that the aristocrats through their exercise of legislative privilege were plotting to establish a tyrannical government.[27]

Christopher Gadsden, writing as "A Steady and Open Republican," replied to Thompson's arguments but did not deny that a banishment bill had been proposed. Instead, he merely asked whether the assembly as a whole could be blamed "for what any single member *may have talked of.*" Responding to Thompson's charge that legislative privilege was merely a subterfuge to impose an aristocracy, Gadsden stated that the dispute was not with Rutledge the private citizen but with Rutledge the member. He insisted that if the reverse had been the case, Thompson should have waited to confront Rutledge until after the House had adjourned. Gadsden argued that if members of the House did not have individual privileges as well as collective ones, freedom of debate would be endangered, but he ignored the central question of how far those rights extended and whether Thompson's actions really were a threat to the House.[28]

Replying to Gadsden, William Hornby, a Charleston brewer writing as "Democratic Gentle-Touch," charged that the legislature had sacrificed Thompson "at the shrine of John Rutledge." In one of the few analyses of the nature of legislative privilege that went beyond mere assertion, he

[26] *Gazette of the State*, Apr. 29, 1784.

[27] *Ibid.* The House journal does not record the formal introduction of a banishment bill. In July 1784 a writer using the pseudonym "Civis" again accused Bee of seeking to banish Thompson, charging that "you were the *person* who proposed it, and sounded the sentiments of several in the Legislature on that subject." "Civis" threatened to produce witnesses if Bee denied the charge. See Civis to Thomas Bee, *ibid.*, July 15, 1784.

[28] Richard Walsh, ed., *The Writings of Christopher Gadsden, 1746-1805* (Columbia, S.C., 1966), 202-203.

denied that the House had authority to send for and imprison nonmembers. Like Bee, who had cited British precedents on the House floor to justify the jailing of Thompson, Hornby also turned to British practice. He maintained that John Wilkes's refusal to honor a summons from Parliament proved his point, "yet our omnipotent House of Assembly pretend to that power, contrary to our Constitution."[29]

Thomas Tudor Tucker, a lowcountry physician and later a member of Congress under both the Articles of Confederation and the Constitution, offered the most sophisticated analysis of the meaning of the Thompson case in light of the theory of legislative privilege. In December 1784 Tucker argued for the calling of a state constitutional convention. The Thompson-Rutledge case was only one incident cited by Tucker, but he used it as a springboard to examine the role of the legislature in state politics and sketched out the principal arguments that would later be used in opposing legislative privilege. Referring to the affair as the recent incident "that made much noise," Tucker said that many saw in it an attempt on the part of the House "to fix their own privileges too high, to stretch their authority too far, and to establish in the State an aristocratical plan of government." He did not believe that the members of the House had intended to make an unconstitutional seizure of power, yet he thought that they had committed an error. Unlike Hornby, he conceded that the state constitution granted the House the power to define its privileges; rather, his argument was with the constitution itself and the relationship that it implied between the people and their representatives.[30]

Before Tucker's pamphlet, critics and defenders of the House's interpretation of legislative privilege had cited British precedents, but Tucker held these irrelevant. He feared that South Carolinians were "too apt to derive our notions of government from the British constitution, which certainly is not in any one of its parts built on principles of true freedom." And while he conceded that the House could constitutionally defend its claim to privilege, he asked, "But who gave them this power? Not the people, but the Legislature themselves." This granting of power, "whether intentional or not," was "a great error, and leaves them by far too much latitude in judging of their own privileges. The mysterious doctrine of undefinable privileges, transcendent power, and political omnipotence, so pompously ascribed to the British parliament, may do very well in a government where all authority is founded in usurpation, but ought

[29] *Gazette of the State*, May 13, 1784. For the identity of the author see Walsh, ed., *Writings of Gadsden*, 206.
[30] "Philodemus" [Thomas Tudor Tucker], *Conciliatory Hints* . . . (Charleston, S.C., 1784), 9-12, 20, quotations on p. 9. For the authorship and dating of the pamphlet see Christopher Gould and Richard Parker Morgan, *South Carolina Imprints, 1731-1800: A Descriptive Bibliography* (Santa Barbara, Calif., 1985), 158. For a sketch of Tucker see Edgar *et al.*, eds. and comps., *Biographical Directory*, III, 725-726.

certainly to be for ever banished from a country that would preserve the freedom of a commonwealth."[31]

Tucker was not opposed to the concept of privilege in a properly drafted constitution, for he conceded that protection had to be offered to members of the legislature. This security, however, was designed primarily for the sake of the public. If a member was not shielded from arrest or molestation, he might miss part of a legislative session and the people of a district would thus be deprived of representation. For Tucker, who believed in the right of constituents to instruct their representatives, the lack of such protection would violate the people's right to participate in their government. Nonetheless, legislators were entitled to claim only such privileges as were "demonstrably essential to the freedom and welfare of their constituents." He also maintained that the House should not be the judge of its own privileges, because this would blend executive, legislative, and judicial power in the same men. Tucker thus turned the debate back to the basic rights of freedom of speech and freedom from molestation that were at the heart of disputes over privilege in the sixteenth and seventeenth centuries, while adding a new dimension by using the theory of popular sovereignty to limit the claims of legislative bodies.[32]

The publication of Tucker's pamphlet concluded the formal debate over the affair, although the arguments that he and others raised would influence the development of the doctrine of legislative privilege during the following decade. As in later privilege cases, the House's leadership preferred to let the controversy die a slow, quiet death rather than rouse the populace by formally replying to its critics. Public debate profited only Thompson and his allies, whereas the nabobs' interests were better served by maintaining the pretense that the House alone could define its privileges. Furthermore, the House had ceased to be a party in the dispute, for its power to imprison for breach of privilege expired when it adjourned. Besides, Rutledge and his allies, with their considerable economic and political power, were able to have the final word in the dispute with Thompson. In the month following the House's adjournment, the *Gazette of the State of South Carolina* carried this telling ad, which informed those who would challenge the nabobs that they could do so only at a high price: "TO BE LET. THE CITY TAVERN. Enquire of Cudworth & Waller."[33]

The House did not attempt to enforce its privileges for another five years. Then, in 1789, it tried to claim immunity from satirical criticism in the press. In this case the House did not concern itself with the honor of an individual member but took higher ground by dealing with an insult to

[31] [Tucker], *Conciliatory Hints*, 10.
[32] *Ibid.*, 11.
[33] *Gazette of the State*, Apr. 8, 15, 1784.

the whole body. The case led to one of the earliest American defenses of unlimited freedom of the press.

Throughout the postwar period debtor relief was a divisive issue in South Carolina. Upcountry citizens regularly petitioned for stay laws, valuation laws, and paper money emissions, at times obtaining some relief.[34] In 1786 the state issued £100,000 in paper money; in the succeeding years several stay laws were passed, the most recent in 1788.[35] In 1789 the House studied additional debtor relief, and a committee of seven upcountry representatives chaired by James Lincoln urged emission of £300,000 in paper money. The proposed emission differed from the earlier one in that the paper would have been made legal tender and would have been issued in each of the state's seven judicial districts rather than exclusively in Charleston, so "that the poorer Class of our Citizens should have equal benefit from such paper emission as the rich lately had." Despite strong upcountry support, the House decisively rejected the plan.[36]

Even before the House debate on the report, Lincoln delivered a copy to the *City Gazette, or the Daily Advertiser,* a Charleston paper published by John Markland and John McIver, who printed it on February 13. That same day, Samuel Beach, a young graduate of the College of New Jersey who had moved to Charleston in 1785, wrote a biting satire on the report under the pseudonym "A,B,C" and carried it to McIver. At Beach's insistence, the editor printed it in the next day's paper. The essay mimicked the style and wording of the report to make it seem that the committee had recommended emission of £5,000,000 and charged that the advocates of paper money sought to defraud creditors of their property.[37]

Lincoln was outraged and introduced a motion in the House declaring the satire a misrepresentation of the report and a breach of privilege. The House voted 86 to 32 that it constituted a breach of privilege, with the upcountry supporting the motion 57 to 3 and the lowcountry dividing 29 to 29. The House adjourned over the weekend, and the members had time to cool their tempers.[38] When the House convened again on

[34] I define the lowcountry as the three coastal judicial districts of Beaufort, Charleston, and Georgetown, and the upcountry as the four inland districts of Camden, Cheraw, Ninety Six, and Orangeburg.

[35] For background on debtor relief in South Carolina see Robert A. Becker, "Salus Populi Suprema Lex: Public Peace and South Carolina Debtor Relief Laws, 1783-1788," *South Carolina Historical Magazine,* LXXX (1979), 65-75.

[36] Michael E. Stevens and Christine M. Allen, eds., *Journals of the House of Representatives, 1789-1790* (Columbia, S.C., 1984), 127, 169-171, hereafter cited as *Journals of the House, 1789-1790.*

[37] *Ibid.,* 146-147; *City Gazette, or the Daily Advertiser* (Charleston), Feb. 13, 14, 1789. For a fuller account of the affair see *Journals of the House, 1789-1790,* xi-xiv. For a biographical sketch of Beach see Richard A. Harrison, *Princetonians, 1776-1783: A Biographical Directory* (Princeton, N.J., 1981), 397-400.

[38] *Journals of the House, 1789-1790,* 138-142.

Monday, Lincoln wanted the matter dropped since the author of the essay "was so contemptible as not to be worthy of the notice" of the House. Other members disagreed, fearing that "an improper licentiousness of the press might follow."[39]

The House summoned McIver for questioning. He denied writing the piece and named Beach as the author. Although some members were then ready to let McIver go, John Rutledge and his younger brother Edward questioned his release. The Rutledge-Thompson affair was only five years past, and the elder Rutledge may have felt that he had to show that the House's privileges did not concern his personal honor alone. He insisted that the printer not be so easily excused, because the printing of the essay was itself a breach of privilege. If the House did nothing, in the future "he might publish what he pleased" and simply escape punishment by naming an author. Edward Rutledge went to the heart of the brothers' concern— namely, that breach of privilege cases concerned more than the offended honor of the lowcountry nabobs as critics had charged. He "wished to convince the gentlemen of the upper country that any indignity offered to them would be as warmly resented by the lower country members, as if offered to themselves." Ironically, it was James Lincoln who spoke up to defend the publishers, stating that they "had acted as printers of a free paper" and that he bore no malice against them.[40]

After dismissing McIver from its custody, the House summoned Beach, who was permitted to read a paper in his defense. He said that he was sorry the House had misunderstood his intentions but insisted that he was exercising his right to comment on public issues. He also said that he had "meant not to reflect upon the Honor, the Integrity or the Dignity of the House or of the Gentlemen who composed the Committee." After Beach withdrew, the House voted that he had not made a sufficient apology but declined to adopt a resolution charging that he had "maliciously misrepresented the Report." Beach was again called before the House and made a further apology, which the House again rejected as inadequate. Rawlins Lowndes, a member from Charleston, urged that Beach be given a third chance. Beach reappeared, saying, "I give up my own Opinion to that of

[39] *City Gaz.*, Feb. 18, 1789.
[40] *Ibid.* Edward Rutledge's position contrasted sharply with his efforts on behalf of the patriot cause nearly two decades earlier. In a curious twist of fate, Rutledge had risen to prominence by defending a colonial printer against breach of privilege charges in 1773. Thomas Powell, a printer jailed for printing part of the Council's proceedings, employed Rutledge, who successfully argued for his release. Rutledge's defense, which endeared him to the patriot cause, ignored the issue of freedom of the press and centered on his contention that the Council was not a legislative body. See Jack P. Greene, ed., *The Nature of Colony Constitutions: Two Pamphlets on the Wilkes Fund Controversy in South Carolina by Sir Egerton Leigh and Arthur Lee* (Columbia, S.C., 1970), 31-32; David Duncan Wallace, *The History of South Carolina*, 4 vols. (New York, 1934), II, 97-98; and *South-Carolina Gazette* (Charleston), Sept. 13, 1773.

the House," and asked its pardon. This was deemed sufficient, and he was released.[41]

Unlike the Thompson case, this time the House seems to have wanted to extricate itself from the matter without losing face. It was not ready to back off once it had decided that a breach of privilege occurred, but neither was it willing to jail a critic. Furthermore, the House was divided on the seriousness of Beach's actions. As with the Thompson case, the Beach affair sparked a newspaper debate, though a less heated one. Beach published a notice promising to comment on the matter after the House adjourned, when he would be safe from further charges of breach of privilege. Another writer, calling himself "A Friend to the Liberty of the Press," charged that the House was more "attentive to its privileges" even than Parliament and chided the representatives for wasting four days at a cost of £400 in prosecuting Beach.[42]

After the House adjourned, three unsigned essays on the affair appeared in the *City Gazette*. From their style and evidence of intimate knowledge of the case, we may conjecture that they were written by Beach himself. He examined the theory of legislative privilege and made a bold defense of unlimited freedom of the press. Citing British precedents, he argued that there were clear boundaries beyond which claims of privilege could not operate and concluded "that privilege of parliament is not in truth so *high and mighty* in its nature, as some have represented it to be." Accordingly, a mere vote of the House "cannot take away or impair any right of the citizen which he holds under any express law." In every case the law of the land was higher than any vote of a legislative body. More important, the essays denied the right of the House to determine "arbitrarily and at pleasure . . . what is a breach of privilege," a right that the House had insisted upon in the Thompson case. Here Beach repeated the argument, made earlier by Thomas Tudor Tucker, that the House should not be the judge of its own privileges.[43]

After disposing of the House's claim to privilege, Beach insisted upon the unlimited right of a citizen to comment on his country's laws and to criticize its rulers. As Leonard W. Levy has noted, American attacks on the concept of seditious libel were rare until the very close of the eighteenth century. Seditious libel, whose definition was as vague as that of legislative privilege, referred to criticism that lowered the public's esteem for the government; in colonial America it was usually prosecuted by legislatures as a breach of privilege. After the Revolution, state legislatures did not abandon the doctrine of seditious libel in theory, but in practice they often tolerated scurrilities against the government. Although Beach's argument was not fully developed, it is important in that it represents an embryonic stage of the argument that Levy found in the following decade. Indeed, Beach's defense preceded by seven years the case of William Keteltas, a

41 *Journals of the House,* 1789-1790, 156-162.
42 *City Gaz.,* Feb. 21, Apr. 29, 1789.
43 *Ibid.,* Mar. 16-18, 1789.

New York lawyer who was imprisoned for a publication deemed a breach of privilege and whose writings are cited by Levy as "the first major criticism of the use of the 'privilege' to muzzle offensive publications or remarks."[44] Beach, however, went even beyond Keteltas, who restricted his arguments to denying that his actions were comprehended by the theory of legislative privilege but did not deny the doctrine of seditious libel.

Beach found the meaning of the Revolution in unlimited freedom of expression. If the right to criticize the government were destroyed, he wrote, "the substantial part of liberty is gone, and independence is only a name which may serve to amuse the vulgar on every returning 4th of July." He anticipated arguments that the House did not restrain liberty of the press, but only its *"licentiousness."* The question, as he aptly put it, was "how shall we fix the bounds between liberty and licentiousness? How can we determine the exact line where the one ends and the other commences? Here lies the difficulty." For Beach, the answer could be found only in unrestricted liberty. He argued that it would be far "better for the public to suffer all the inconveniences & evils even of a licentious press, than for the freedom of it to be restrained by any legislative interference." If individuals were slandered, they could recover damages through civil suits. If a public body was criticized as "ignorant, interested, dishonest, unprincipled, or oppressive," the writer could stand trial in the court of public opinion. If the charges were false, no innocent persons would suffer, since the world, knowing the truth, would not think worse of them. If the charges were true, it would be more honorable for the assembly to be silent in face of the abuse than to use its powers to suppress the publication.[45]

[44] Levy, *Emergence of a Free Press*, 296. For additional background on libel law in the colonial and early national period see Clifton O. Lawhorne, *Defamation and Public Officials: The Evolving Law of Libel* (Carbondale, Ill., 1971), 1-56, and Norman L. Rosenberg, *Protecting the Best Men: An Interpretive History of the Law of Libel* (Chapel Hill, N.C., 1986), 12-78.

[45] The House was faced with what seemed another assault on its privileges during the 1789 session, yet failed to act. On the morning of Jan. 17, Albert Aerney Muller, a representative from St. Matthew's Parish, was making his way through the streets of Charleston to attend a meeting of the House when he was waylaid by John Christian Smith, who accosted him "in very scurrilous language," shot him, and fled. Muller survived but did not return to the House until 1790. Late on the day of the shooting the House, "after some time spent in debate," rejected a motion directing the governor to offer a £100 reward for the apprehension of Smith. It is not clear why the House failed to pursue Muller's assailant, who later returned to Charleston and operated a shop there. A possible explanation can be found in the 1791 House journal, where John Christian Smith reappears as a petitioner asking for a divorce from his wife. Smith claimed that his wife had yielded "to the Artful persuasions of a Seducer and lived for a considerable length of time in the habitual violation of her Marriage vows." Mrs. Smith's infidelity had become a matter of public record by her voluntary confession in a criminal case, the records of which are lost. We do not know

One effect of the Thompson and Beach cases was a clearer definition of legislative privilege. When a convention met in the new state capital of Columbia in 1790 to rewrite the state constitution, it replaced the broad claims of privilege in the constitutions of 1776 and 1778 with a very explicit definition of the House's privileges. Sections 12, 13, and 14 of Article 1 reflect responsiveness on the part of the state's leadership to public criticism of the House's actions. Section 12 defined the House's power over its own members, permitting it to punish them for disorderly behavior and to expel them with the concurrence of two-thirds of the House. Section 14 protected members and their estates during, ten days before, and ten days after the session. This privilege, however, did not extend to members charged with treason, felony, or breach of the peace. The key provisions defining the House's powers over nonmembers are found in Section 13. The House could imprison, during its sitting, nonmembers "who shall be guilty of disrespect to the house, by any disorderly or contemptuous behaviour in its presence—or who, during the time of its sitting, shall threaten harm to body or estate of any member, for any thing said or done in either house; or who shall assault any of them therefor; or who shall assault or arrest any witness or other person ordered to attend the house, in his going to or returning therefrom; or who shall rescue any person arrested by order of the house."[46] Under this carefully circumscribed definition neither Thompson nor Beach could have been imprisoned. Thompson, by explicitly disavowing a desire for "what the Law Calls a *Challenge*,"[47] did not threaten harm against Rutledge, and while Beach's essay was disrespectful, it did not constitute an action done in the presence of the House. The right of the House to summon persons and papers before its committees, however, remained undefined and became the subject of yet another challenge to its rights.

On December 2, 1793, the House appointed a committee "to examine into, and ascertain the Truth of a Report, that an Armed Force is now levying within this State, by persons under a Foreign Authority without the permission and contrary to the express prohibition of the Government of the United States and of this State."[48] The committee reported that several citizens of the state had accepted military commissions from

---

whether her testimony was given in an adultery trial or as a defense in an attempted murder or manslaughter case. The House's failure to treat this incident as a breach of privilege may indicate that Muller had wronged Smith in a way that called for a personal, rather than a formal legislative, response. See *City Gaz.*, Jan. 19, 1789, Apr. 5, 1792; *Journals of the House, 1789-1790*, 46; and Michael E. Stevens and Christine M. Allen, eds., *Journals of the House of Representatives, 1791* (Columbia, S.C., 1985), 52-54.

[46] Cooper and McCord, eds., *Statutes*, I, 187.
[47] *Journals of the House, 1783-1784*, 581.
[48] Journals of the House of Representatives, Dec. 2, 1793, engrossed copy, South Carolina Archives, Columbia, S.C.

Citizen Genet, French minister to the United States, to raise troops to invade Spanish territories. Among those named was Stephen Drayton, a leading member of one of the state's Republican societies and personal secretary to Gov. William Moultrie. According to the committee, this "daring and dangerous attempt by a Foreign Minister to intermeddle in the Affairs of the United States" threatened to "disturb the internal Tranquillity of the United States, and to involve them in Hostilities with Nations with whom they are now at peace." The House resolved that Drayton and others were "Guilty of High Crimes and Misdemeanours" and should be prosecuted in court.[49]

In searching for evidence the House issued a warrant to Sheriff Wade Hampton of Camden District to examine the papers of Drayton and Maj. John Hamilton, a Revolutionary War veteran who had been named as one of the conspirators. Hampton carried out the order with dignity and propriety. On being presented with the warrant, Drayton protested that a search would be "an infringement of his Privilidges as a free man, and a violation of his most sacred rights." Hampton then asked him if he had a trusted friend who would look for incriminating papers and keep the contents of the rest confidential. Clerk of Court Thomas Hall made the search, during which Hampton was forced to break a lock, which he did "with all the delicacy and tenderness possible due to the Citizen of a free Country." No incriminating evidence was found in Drayton's papers, but in Hamilton's the sheriff discovered the military regulations for Genet's American Revolutionary Legion.[50]

The House met in special session in May 1794 to consider unfinished business. Among the items on its agenda was its response to a suit for $60,000 brought by Drayton against the members of the committee for violating the privacy of his records. In selecting an attorney Drayton made a controversial choice by retaining Alexander Moultrie, former attorney general of the state, who had been impeached in 1792 and convicted in 1793 for embezzling state funds. Holding unanimously that its privileges had been violated because Drayton's suit infringed on "freedom of debate and the liberty of acting without the external restraint of fear or influence," the House resolved that "it is essential and inherent in the Legislature that the Members thereof acting in either House are not liable and cannot legally be questioned elsewhere for their conduct or the motives thereof," and "that while each House necessarily possesses the right of censuring or punishing improper conduct in any of its Members it is equally the province of the House to protect the Members thereof from Molestation from any other person, or in any other place." Because these privileges had "always been the received and known usage of the Legislature of this Country," the House determined that anyone infringing

---

[49] *Ibid.*, Dec. 6, 1793.

[50] *Ibid.*, Dec. 18, 1793; *City Gaz.*, Dec. 14, 1793; Report of Wade Hampton to Robert Anderson, Dec. 13, 1793, Records of the General Assembly, Miscellaneous Communications, 1793, No. 10, S.C. Archs.

them was "in open Contempt and Defiance of the Rights, powers and privileges of the Legislature." Finally, the House resolved that Drayton and Moultrie had "knowingly, wilfully and flagrantly violated the Rights, Powers, and privileges of the House of Representatives," and that any attorney bringing suit against any member for anything said or done in the House ought to be disbarred.[51]

The Drayton case differed from earlier ones in several ways. First, the House was responding to an attack on its members for actions done on the House floor. In such instances there were ample precedents for taking steps to protect its members. Second, instead of simply asserting its rights as it had done in earlier cases, the House now went to great lengths to justify its actions. It not only explicitly reclaimed the right to punish nonmembers in cases of molestation but, more important, sought to justify its position as part of an effort to protect popular rights. According to the resolutions, the House's privileges "form the strongest palladium of the rights of the People." Having been cast in the role of oppressor of the public in earlier cases, the House now adopted the justification set forth by Tucker a decade earlier. In doing so, it executed a remarkable turnabout in the manner in which it claimed its rights.[52]

Summoned by the House, Moultrie and Drayton set out for Columbia, but Moultrie suffered an attack of the gout on the road (a "painful situation, which none but gouty men can judge of"), and the pair did not arrive at the capital until two days after the legislature adjourned.[53] Because of their failure to appear, the House again found them "guilty of a flagrant Contempt of the Authority of this House." The House also passed another resolution defending its right to arrest any citizen of the state charged with breach of privilege and declaring that the refusal of any citizen to assist when instructed was itself an act of contempt of the House.[54]

Although the House may have hoped to forestall criticism by portraying itself as a defender of the public, condemnation of its actions filled the newspapers. Essayists not only defended Drayton's efforts to raise an army but questioned the House's use of privilege. Through a series of rhetorical questions "An Inquirer" probed the nature of legislative privilege and arrived at conclusions that were quite similar to those offered by the House's critics in 1784 and 1789. Citing the three crimes for which legislators were not protected under Article 1, Section 14, the writer asked whether "the privileges *allowed* the members of the legislature (*by the people*) exempt them from punishment or censure, for committing treason, felony, or a breach of peace?" Members should be no more secure

[51] Journals of the House, May 3, 1794.
[52] *Ibid.*
[53] Alexander Moultrie, *An Appeal to the People, on the Conduct of a Certain Public Body in South-Carolina, Respecting Col. Drayton and Col. Moultrie* (Charleston, S.C., 1794), 16.
[54] Journals of the House, May 12, 1794.

from prosecution than any other citizen except during the sitting of the legislature. "Inquirer" defended the right of any citizen who believed himself wronged by the state to seek redress in the courts. Furthermore, he questioned whether legislators had "an exclusive right to define their own privileges," which had been one of the central issues in 1784 and 1789.[55]

Republican societies throughout the state were also critical of the House. The Republican Society of Charleston, of which Drayton and Moultrie were members, asserted that the House's proceedings against the pair were "founded on principles and doctrines subversive of the political freedom of this country" and resolved that "any attempt made by the representatives of the people, in their legislative capacity, to accuse, try, convict and condemn any citizen for any imaginary crime, is unjust, arbitrary, and in direct violation of the constitution of this state." The society further resolved that freedom from external restraint applied only when the House was acting as a legislature, not while it was performing judicial functions. In language reminiscent of that used by the legislature when defending its privileges, the society found that the "liberties, privileges and immunities of the citizens have . . . been grossly and flagrantly violated" in the actions taken against Drayton and Moultrie.[56]

Alexander Moultrie wrote the most complete attack on the House's claims of legislative privilege in a pamphlet called *An Appeal to the People*, published by Markland and McIver, the same printers who had published Samuel Beach's controversial essay in 1789. To Moultrie, the case was a personal vendetta in which "the managers were behind the curtain, and the actors and their parts were chosen." In these machinations he saw "features of party, and motives of *personal* pursuit." While the House had every right to summon public officers and send for public papers, Moultrie insisted that it could not lawfully demand the appearance of private persons or seize personal papers. Such actions struck at "the very root of our free constitution" because they violated the principle of separation of powers. The former attorney general then went on to cite the limitations in sections 12-14 of Article 1. This "novel creed of privilege" adopted by the House was erroneous because, "as all power is derived from the people," legislators "can have no further *extent of power or privilege* than is thereby expressly *created with them,* by the people, as essential to their *nature and functions.*" Thus the House's privileges were restricted to those specified in the constitution, and it did not have the right of defining them. Moultrie denied that the House could arrest persons for actions not committed in its presence or during its sitting. He argued that the House's 1793 actions were invalid and that its 1794 resolves violated Drayton's right to obtain redress in the state's courts. He contended that because he and Drayton had been declared guilty of breach of privilege without a

[55] *City Gaz.,* May 13, 1794.
[56] *Ibid.,* June 28, 1794. For another critic of legislative arrest of citizens see "A Republican's Creed," *ibid.,* May 21, 1794.

hearing, their right to trial before a jury of their peers had been denied.[57]

In earlier breach of privilege cases, House members had turned to British precedents to buttress their claims, but Moultrie, like Thomas Tudor Tucker, denied that these had any bearing on the case, for if they did, then "I say, to our shame, we, that moment are *under British government*, and have not any of our own. What then, my fellow citizens, have we been these ten long years contending for at the price of so much blood!" Moultrie charged that his opponents believed that laws were made by leaders for the people, not by the people for themselves. These men needed "to be told that all mankind are, by nature free and equal."[58]

Before adjourning, the House had urged the new legislature, which met in November 1794, to summon Drayton and Moultrie, but when Genet's adventure ended with his recall, the issue was allowed to die.[59] The new House that met in the fall did not even acknowledge the incident and failed to assert its privileges by punishing Drayton and Moultrie for not appearing. Drayton's legal problems also quietly disappeared. Although the grand jury of the federal circuit court of the district of South Carolina indicted him in May 1794 "for entering into the service of the French Republic, and attempting to engage the citizens of the United States, to enter into the said service," the government dropped its case the following May when its witnesses failed to appear.[60]

The three cases described here are important for what they tell about the changing politics of the post-Revolutionary era. A brief look at the House's response in two later cases reveals a political leadership that, becoming sensitive to its use of privilege, adopted the narrow and very explicit definition of privilege advocated by earlier critics. The changes wrought in the 1780s and 1790s meant that privilege was no longer a tool for settling private grievances. William Boone Mitchell, a lowcountry planter who represented St. Paul's Parish in the House, unsuccessfully sought to invoke privilege twice after the Drayton incident. In doing so, he encountered a new House majority that could not easily be provoked into claiming its privileges. In 1795 Mitchell complained that a creditor had seized some of his slaves. The House agreed that a forced sale of his property during the sitting of the House would be illegal but concluded that there was nothing to prevent a creditor from detaining slaves who had been seized before the beginning of the session and then selling them after the House had adjourned.[61]

[57] Moultrie, *Appeal to the People,* 4, 7-8, 9-12, 14-16.
[58] *Ibid.,* 18-19.
[59] Journals of the House, May 12, 1794.
[60] *Columbia Gazette,* May 12, 1794; Journal of the U.S. Circuit Court for the District of South Carolina, 1790-1809, pp. 56, 73, Records of the District Courts in the United States, Record Group 21, Federal Area Records Center, East Point, Ga.
[61] Journals of the House, Nov. 23, 26, 1795. For a biographical sketch of Mitchell see Edgar *et al.,* eds. and comps., *Biographical Directory,* IV, 405-406.

Six years later Mitchell again tried vainly to invoke the privileges of the House in a private matter. The details of the affair are very sketchy; what little we know about the case has to be pieced together from the questions that were put to the witnesses during the House hearing. On December 5, 1801, Mitchell complained to the House that a certain William Conyers had violated his privileges. Apparently, Conyers and Mitchell had got into an argument on the steps of the statehouse, which ended when Mitchell retreated to the House chamber for safety. Mitchell had called Conyers a "damned Rascal," and Conyers in turn threatened to whip one of Mitchell's slaves. What is striking about this episode is the difference between the treatment of Conyers and that of William Thompson in 1784. Conyers was not only permitted to retain an attorney but was granted an extension of time to prepare his case. When the House considered the matter, he was allowed to cross-examine witnesses, including Mitchell himself. After taking testimony from several witnesses, the House voted 53 to 45 that Conyers had not committed a breach of privilege and dismissed him from custody. Thompson had not been permitted to have an attorney with him, but in this case every effort was made to ensure that the accused's right to due process was not violated. The questions asked in the House indicate that the issue of privilege hinged on whether the incident occurred in the hearing or sight of the House. The House did not now concern itself with assaults on a member's honor but was interested only in whether the business of the House was disturbed by the so-called "fracas."[62] In its unwillingness to act and in its new concern for the rights of the accused, the House accepted the definition of privilege set forth earlier by its critics.

Changing interpretations of legislative privilege were the result of the post-Revolutionary political and social situation in South Carolina. During the decade after the war, the state's political leadership was forced to redefine its role. Before the Revolution, when the struggle between the royal governor and the assembly supplied "the dynamics of politics,"[63] the Commons House had actively defended its rights against the crown and its placemen. In doing so it had set itself up as the defender of popular rights, for the two were so closely intertwined as to be seen as one and the same. After the war, the House claimed the same privileged position. British precedents were cited, and the Speaker even ordered from London a black satin gown made in the "exact pattern of that worn by the speaker of the British house of commons."[64] Yet the removal of the royal adversary created a political vacuum, which the lower house rushed to fill. As Tucker pointed out, "after lopping off the monarchical part, we vainly imagined

[62] Journals of the House, Dec. 5, 9, 1801; Records of the General Assembly, Petitions, 1801, Nos. 30, 31, S.C. Archs.
[63] Robert M. Weir, " 'The Harmony We Were Famous For': An Interpretation of Pre-Revolutionary South Carolina Politics," WMQ, 3d Ser., XXVI (1969), 479.
[64] City Gaz., Jan. 18, 1791.

that we had arrived at perfection";[65] yet merely continuing business as usual would not work. The aggressiveness of the lower house, whose expanding claims of privilege cut into the prerogatives of the royal governor, made sense before 1776. Now, with a weak governor who was the creature of the legislature, lacking both veto and appointive powers, the principal rationale for privilege was gone. Critics saw claims of privilege as mere excuses to impose a rule as arbitrary and oppressive as England's had been.

The challenge came from men who were developing new attitudes about government. Jerome Nadelhaft has found a new spirit in South Carolina, flowing from the Revolutionary experience, that was exemplified by the citizens of Pendleton County who declared the idea of petitioning the legislature "a gross absurdity." The logic of popular sovereignty militated against a humble approach by free citizens when addressing their representatives; after all, they asked, "Shall the people petition the people!"[66] It also forced the theory of legislative privilege to imply that the people needed protection against themselves, which to a free citizen of a republic was an absurdity. Republican conceptions of politics, rejecting the relevance of British constitutional theory, demanding careful definitions of power in a written constitution, insisting on the importance of due process, and stressing the separation of powers, generated bold attacks on the theory of legislative privilege as it had been practiced in colonial America.[67]

Within a decade, South Carolinians developed a new theory of legislative privilege. The House had jailed Thompson and forced Beach to apologize, but did so only at the cost of public criticism. There was, as a result, an escalation of issues, a higher exploding point, each time the House demanded its privileges. At stake in the Thompson case was the honor of a single member; in the Beach affair, the honor of a House committee; in the Drayton-Moultrie case, the freedom of members from suits for actions taken in the House. The decisive change, however, occurred with the implementation of the constitution of 1790, which adopted the theory set forth by the House's critics. The House's unwillingness to assert its rights after Drayton and Moultrie failed to appear and its refusal to let Mitchell hide behind claims of privilege attest that legislative practice now conformed with the new constitutional theory. Indeed, when the House contended for its privileges in 1794, it felt compelled to set forth its justification for taking action, something that had been unnecessary in earlier cases when the "House alone were the Sole Judges of their Own Privileges."[68]

[65] [Tucker], *Conciliatory Hints,* 20.
[66] Representation of the People of Pendleton County, July 10, 1794, quoted in Nadelhaft, *Disorders of War,* 216.
[67] For the changing intellectual climate of American politics see Gordon S. Wood, *The Creation of the American Republic, 1776-1787* (Chapel Hill, N.C., 1969).
[68] *Journals of the House, 1783-1784,* 580.

At the same time that political ideas were changing, new views of society were coming into conflict with older views. These are seen most graphically in the dispute between John Rutledge and William Thompson, who held very different conceptions of the meaning of the American Revolution. Thompson stressed his equality with Rutledge, even though he was well aware of the differences in their economic and social status. He argued that the "day is Arrived when *goodness,* and not *Wealth,* are the only Criterions of *greatness.*" Rutledge's offense—crediting the testimony of a slave over that of a free white war veteran—was "an insult on human-nature" itself.[69] In Thompson's view, the Revolution had transformed American public life; in the act of fighting for Independence, all citizens had achieved a new equality. Deference was now at a discount.[70] John Rutledge had a very different notion of the changes wrought by the Revolution. Although he was described by a contemporary as "the proudest and most imperious man in the United States," his patriotism could not be questioned.[71] In the darkest days of the war, when the state was occupied by British troops, he personified the rebel government as its chief executive. Nonetheless, in his reply to Thompson, he denied that the Revolution mandated new standards of public behavior. He agreed that goodness was the measure of greatness, "but he Cannot think that the day is only Just now arrived when it has become so, for he Considered it ever was."[72] According to Rutledge, the Revolution had changed little in the political or social relations of men. It was precisely that view which Thompson and his supporters feared and which was at the heart of disputes over legislative privilege.

[69] *Ibid.,* 581.

[70] For another example of new attitudes about deference see Alfred F. Young, "George Robert Twelves Hewes (1742-1840): A Boston Shoemaker and the Memory of the American Revolution," *WMQ,* 3d Ser., XXXVIII (1981), 561-623.

[71] Clinton Rossiter, *1787: The Grand Convention* (New York, 1966), 130.

[72] *Journals of the House, 1783-1784,* 582.

DONALD J. RATCLIFFE

The Experience of Revolution and the Beginnings of Party Politics in Ohio, 1776-1816

The American Revolution would scarcely be worth the name if it signified nothing more than separation from Great Britain. In fact, it was the beginning of an experiment to create a republic in which a free people could be governed justly without resort to the traditional sources of state power: hereditary right and ancient prescription. The new republic, however, did not take shape overnight; as several recent historians have argued, domestic politics even after 1800 were still preoccupied with working out the problems posed by the Revolution.[1] The new nation was torn by internal rivalries and differing conceptions of what the character of the republic should be; at the same time, the United States was drawn into the revolutionary ferment that enveloped Europe after 1789. Its integrity was jeopardized as much in 1812 as the colonies' had been before 1775. Throughout this long period of crisis, Americans were less united than they had been at the time of independence, and needed to create a stable order that would hold the nation together without compromising the principles of the Revolution. As it happened, Americans evolved a system of ordering their conflicts that would become the most distinctive feature of political life in the United States: the American system of mass political parties, in most of its essentials, was the creation not of the Age of Jackson, but of the Age of Revolution.[2]

1. For the search for a "republic" during the Revolution, see Gordon S. Wood, *The Creation of the American Republic, 1776-1787* (Chapel Hill, 1969). The theme is continued into the early nineteenth century by, among others, Roger H. Brown, *The Republic in Peril: 1812* (New York, 1964); David H. Fischer, *The Revolution of American Conservatism: The Federalist Party in the Era of Jeffersonian Democracy* (New York, 1965); Linda K. Kerber, *Federalists in Dissent: Imagery and Ideology in Jeffersonian America* (Ithaca, 1970); and, especially, Richard E. Ellis, *The Jeffersonian Crisis: Courts and Politics in the Young Republic* (New York, 1971).
2. For recent writings on the early party system, see, in addition to works cited below, Joseph E. Charles, *The Origins of the American Party System* (Williamsburg, 1956); William N. Chambers, *Political Parties In A New Nation: The American Experience, 1776-1809* (New York, 1963); Paul Goodman, "The First American Party System," William N. Chambers and Walter D. Burnham, eds., *The American Party Systems: Stages of Political Development* (New York, 1967); and Norman K. Risjord, ed., *The Early American Party System* (New York, 1969).

Ohio's Revolution

Surprisingly perhaps, it is appropriate to speak of the Age of Revolution in Ohio. The state, of course, played no part in the political events of the 1760s and 1770s, but, even so, the memory of the Revolution and its ideals was strongly established in the territory by the pioneers from New England, Pennsylvania, and the South who settled there in the late 1780s and 1790s. Moreover, these memories were reinforced by the early political experience of the region, which in many ways repeated the original American Revolution.[3]

The first stage of Territorial government provided by the Northwest Ordinance of 1787 established a system of colonial rule much like that of the British Empire. It is true that the Ordinance gave a promise of ultimate political equality and participation in the imperial (or federal) government such as Great Britain had never given before 1776; yet, initially at least, the Territory was ruled with a tighter grip than Britain had ever managed. The governor and the Territorial judges were appointed by the federal government, and together they provided a legislature which represented the nation as a whole rather than the settlers it governed and taxed. Still, the pioneers in the Territory, like their colonial counterparts, had reason to be thankful for the interest of an external power for so long as they were threatened by hostile Indians encouraged by the support of a rival European power. These restraints were removed (as in 1759 and 1763) by the military and diplomatic victories of 1794-1795, secured by the federal government through General Anthony Wayne and John Jay. In both the colonial and Territorial cases, though, American success was ensured by the rapid increase in white settlement, fostered by the liberal policies of the colonizing power.

When the second stage of Territorial government was finally reached in 1798, the introduction of a locally elected representative assembly merely heightened the parallel with the British colonial system. The appointed governor was still the chief executive, enjoying full power to convene, prorogue, and dissolve the assembly and to veto its legislation as he thought fit. Moreover, since the federal government paid his salary, the Territorial governor was more independent than most of his colonial predecessors; but, like them, his influence with the metropolitan government was countered by the appointment of a "colonial agent"—in the Territorial case, a delegate who possessed the right to sit

---

3. The following discussion of Territorial politics is based primarily upon Randolph C. Downes, *Frontier Ohio, 1788-1803* (Columbus, 1935); it is supplemented by Alfred B. Sears, *Thomas Worthington, Father of Ohio Statehood* (Columbus, 1958), 3-108; and Beverley W. Bond, Jr., *The Foundations of Ohio*, vol. I of Carl Wittke, ed., *The History of the State of Ohio* (Columbus, 1941), 396-476.

and speak, though not vote, in the supreme legislature.[4] The governor often found himself torn between the conflicting demands of local interests and those of the empire (or nation) as a whole, while he occasionally chose to defend the interests of the underprivileged and of minority groups against the demands of the powerful local landed and mercantile interests which quickly learned how to make themselves heard politically.[5] In "colonial" Ohio as in the British empire, the demand for local autonomy was voiced most effectively by self-confident and successful men like Nathaniel Massie and Thomas Worthington, who had already established their social and economic predominance.[6]

Protests in the Territory against this system of government echoed colonial complaints against British rule. As early as 1793 newspapers in Ohio complained that the Territorial government denied basic civil liberties and imposed taxation without "the free consent of the people or their legal representatives." Victims of executive tyranny quickly resorted to "the Language of 1774-'75 of Liberty Privilege & ca & ca & ca." In 1797 some Cincinnatians claimed that migration to the Northwestern Territory had deprived them of rights they had enjoyed in the East as citizens and ratifiers of the United States Constitution.[7] As the demand for statehood broadened after 1800, its main impulse came from the desire to throw off the arbitrary rule of an executive unaccountable to the people of Ohio, for Governor Arthur St. Clair had vetoed many of the laws passed by the first Territorial legislature and had arbitrarily prorogued the second. Early statehood was recognized as bringing some disadvantages with it, notably extra financial burdens, but at least it would make possible a government sensitive to its subjects and would prevent the continuation of an aristocracy of office-holders appointed by external authority. Understandably, the charges presented to President Thomas Jefferson in 1802 against the governor were reminiscent of those against George III in the Declaration of Independence.[8] As Thomas Worthington said, the main issue in the statehood contest was whether the Territory would become an "independent state" or remain

4. Bond, *Foundations*, 437-38.
5. William H. Smith, *The St. Clair Papers: The Life and Public Services of Arthur St. Clair* (Cincinnati, 1882), I, 191-92; 221-22, II, 425-26, 472-73, 480; Jacob Burnet, *Notes on the Early Settlement of the North-Western Territory* (Cincinnati, 1847), 496-97; Beverley W. Bond, Jr., *The Correspondence of John Cleves Symmes* (New York, 1926), 15, 22; and *Idem, Foundations*, 422-23.
6. Sears, *Worthington*, 3-93; David M. Massie, *Nathaniel Massie, A Pioneer of Ohio* (Cincinnati, 1896).
7. John D. Barnhart, *Valley of Democracy: The Frontier versus the Plantation in the Ohio Valley, 1775-1818* (Bloomington, 1953), 145-47; Downes, *Frontier Ohio*, 142, 184-85.
8. Smith, *St. Clair Papers*, II, 563-70.

"under the present arbitrary government, better fitted for an English or Spanish colony than for citizens of the United States."[9]

In the end, however, Ohioans escaped from their "colonial system" without a war for independence. They benefitted from exactly the kind of revolution in the "metropolis" that colonial radical leaders had hoped for, in vain, in the early 1770s.[10] The triumph of Jefferson and his followers brought to power in Washington a government sympathetic to the statehood cause, and this new ruling party in Congress positively thrust greatness on Ohio by means of the Ohio Enabling Act of 1802. Yet even though, in the end, there was no imperial resistance to overcome, the achievement of "independence" was still associated with something akin to an internal revolution. The statehood party after 1800 appealed, with its popular Revolutionary rhetoric, to the public at large, including those who did not qualify to vote in assembly elections under the restricted franchise laid down by the Ordinance.[11] The statehood men resorted to extra-legal actions which were sanctioned by public opinion though resisted by the Territorial government, while the sentiments of people unrepresented in the legislature were used to put pressure on key decision-makers. This support from the people, as distinct from the constituted authorities of the Territory, was ultimately the secret of the statehood party's success in 1802.[12]

The opponents of statehood recognized the advantage that its proponents gained from their rhetorical appeal to the memory of the Revolution. St. Clair's allies, to their embarrassment, saw many of their friends turn against him. Even those who remained firm disapproved of his arbitrary acts, but insisted that his offences were exaggerated by his enemies. Similarly, they claimed that the evils of Territorial status were bearable, and more than compensated for by the financial help given by

9. Thomas Worthington to Abraham Baldwin, November 30, 1801, reprinted in Sears, *Worthington*, 64. For Worthington's reluctant turning to statehood as a result of St. Clair's vetoes, see the letters quoted in Massie, *Massie*, 154, 193; and Israel W. Andrews, *Washington County, and the Early Settlement of Ohio: Centennial Historical Address* (Cincinnati, 1877), 28.

10. Pauline Maier, *From Resistance To Revolution: Colonial Radicals and the Development of American Opposition to Britain, 1765-1776* (London, 1973), 228-70.

11. The franchise was restricted to adult males owning fifty acres freehold, or town lots of equivalent value. Freeholders whose titles were in doubt were not allowed to vote, most notably in the Symmes Purchase. Chilton Williamson, *American Suffrage From Property To Democracy* (Princeton, 1960), 117, 212; Smith, *St. Clair*, I, 215, II, 436-38.

12. Downes, *Frontier Ohio*, 182-85, 205-16; Smith, *St. Clair*, 549-50, 560, 572. Some writers, notably Smith, *St. Clair Papers*, I, 229, and William E. Gilmore, *Life of Edward Tiffin, First Governor of Ohio* (Chillicothe, 1897), 35, 51, 62, 77-78, argue that statehood was unpopular and that its advocates deliberately avoided reference to the people. This view overlooks the success of the statehood petition campaigns, the plebiscitary nature of the 1802 elections for the convention, and the final conviction of even Federalist politicians that public opinion made any other course fruitless.

the central government in paying the salaries of the officers of the Territory. With the passage of the Enabling Act in 1802, however, the terms of the argument changed. Now the opponents of statehood could denounce Congress's action "as an act of legislative usurpation of power properly the province of the Territorial Legislature, bearing a striking similarity to the course of Great Britain imposing laws on the provinces." Congress could be branded as ignoring the compact (i.e., the Ordinance) on the basis of which settlers had entered the Territory, and as interfering in internal affairs over which it had had no legal control since the beginning of the representative stage. Far better, said leading opponents, for the people of the Territory to ignore Congress, form their own government in their own time, and then apply for statehood on their own terms. Not only would the new state benefit financially, it would also avoid the onerous conditions that Congress was seeking to impose. Such doctrines of prudence, though couched in the language of independence, could, however, be too easily ridiculed as scantily disguised subservience, and the people showed every bit as much impatience as the statehood leaders "to throw off the shackles of colonial dependence."[13]

The process of securing statehood, like independence two or three decades before, resulted in increased public participation in political decisions. Already the Territorial legislature had brought local government and the administration of justice closer to the people, and had extended the practical opportunity to vote by increasing the number of polling places. This measure alone was expected to change the political complexion of the Territorial legislature, should by chance statehood be deferred and a new assembly become necessary.[14] The legislature's request that the Ordinance be amended so as to allow adult male taxpayers to vote in Territorial as well as local elections was not, however, satisfied until Congress incorporated it in the Enabling Act of 1802. This provision was then included in the new state constitution, which restricted the suffrage to whites but extended it to all required to work on the roads, and so ensured that this taxpaying franchise amounted to resident white manhood suffrage.[15]

13. Burnet, North-Western Territory, 321-22, 338-51, 361-69, 374-81, 494-501; Smith, St. Clair, I, 227-28, 239, II, 515-16, 571-72, 576, 581, 594-97; Julia P. Cutler, ed., Life and Times of Ephraim Cutler (Cincinati, 1890), 59-61; Massie, Massie, 202; Sears, Worthington, 62-63. The quotations are from the protest of a Dayton public meeting, reprinted in Burnet, North-Western Territory, 501; and from Zanesville Express, March 31, 1813.
14. Smith, St. Clair, II, 531, 560; Downes, Frontier Ohio, 207, 212, 244.
15. Williamson, American Suffrage, 216, 219, acknowledges that the increase in voting places and the shift from freehold to tax-paying qualifications effectively democratized the suffrage, but fails to recognize the significance of the clause (IV, 5) allowing the vote to all who worked on the roads, as all adult males were to be obliged to do.

Embodying these democratic gains, the state constitution expressed the best Revolutionary principles, occasionally in their most innocent form. As with men of 1776, the Fathers of Ohio reacted against their experience of executive tyranny by making the governor "a mere dummy," enjoying little patronage and less power.[16] Authority was concentrated in the bicameral legislature, which controlled almost all appointments and was unrestricted by executive veto. Both houses were popularly elected, the House annually and the Senators and Governor every two years. This constitutional set-up was, according to some, so thoroughly "bepeopled" that it denied the Founding Fathers' preference of 1787 for a mixed or balanced government rather than a simple democracy.[17] In fact, the first great issue of state politics was to concern the powers of this unrestrained popularly-elected legislature, for what happened if it violated the constitutional safeguards of liberty, property, and justice? By 1812 Ohio was to experience a reaction toward balanced government such as the older states had undergone in the decades following their Revolution.

One thing Ohioans had not done was to choose their national loyalty and then fight for it. Living in a Territory of the United States, they had no choice but to accept its sovereignty, and the achievement of statehood involved the acceptance of the United States Constitution. But then in 1806 the Aaron Burr conspiracy offered the opportunity, as Harmon Blennerhassett put it, of completing the American Revolution and establishing a new western republic.[18] The decisive action of the state government convinced observers that the people of Ohio "will cling to the assurer [?] of Safety, the Union of American States," though Governor Edward Tiffin himself believed there were important pockets of dissidence in the state.[19] Loyalty to the nation was again tested as relations with Britain came to a crisis. Ohio once more rallied, and was claimed the firmest supporter of the War of 1812, after Kentucky. Yet this war threatened Ohio's territorial integrity, even after the invasion of Ohio by British troops and hostile Indians had been repelled in 1813; in the peace negotiations of 1814, Britain attempted to transform her overall military and naval superiority into specific advantages, including

16. As Governor Tom Corwin described the post in 1840. James H. Hitchman, ed., "John J. Janney's 'Recollections of Thomas Corwin,' " *Ohio History*, LXXIII (Spring 1964), 109.

17. Levin Belt to Paul Fearing, December 3, 1802, quoted in William T. Utter, *The Frontier State, 1803-1825*, vol. II of Carl Wittke, ed., *The History of the State of Ohio* (Columbus, 1942), 14.

18. Marietta *Ohio Gazette*, September 18, 1806; Marshall Smelser, *The Democratic Republic, 1801-1815* (New York, 1968), 116; Norris F. Schneider, *Blennerhasset Island and the Burr Conspiracy* (Columbus, 1966).

19. Wyllys Silliman to Worthington, January 20, 1807, Edward Tiffin to Worthington, January 25, 1807, The Papers of Thomas Worthington, Ohio Historical Society.

the creation of an independent Indian state in northwest Ohio and the territories to the west and north. With her future growth and security threatened by such demands, Ohio could well see the war developing, after its outbreak, into her own war for survival and independence.[20]

Thus in the decade after statehood Ohio shared fully in the experience of the nation, debating the relationship between judiciary and legislature, and fighting the nation's enemies. Moreover, throughout this period the state had its first experience of party politics, an experience which was more protracted than is usually recognized. Indeed, by the time of the War of 1812 the supposedly defunct Federalist party was undergoing a distinct revival in Ohio, sharpening the partisan conflict at a moment of national crisis and raising questions about the fundamental character of the republic. This development was perhaps the most significant in the politics of the period, and signified that, forty years after the Declaration of Independence, Ohioans were still debating the mighty issues of the Age of Revolution.

The Crisis of Party Formation

The beginnings in Ohio of the great national division between Federalist and Republican actually predated the contest over statehood. As opposition began to express itself across the nation, first to Alexander Hamilton's financial measures and then after 1793 to George Washington's pro-British foreign policy, the orthodox New England settlers in Ohio expressed their loyalty to the administration. At the same time the extremism of the French revolutionaries in the crisis of 1793-1795, while horrifying conservatives, was defended by radicals in Cincinnati, who toasted "The Sans Culottes of France and the cause of Liberty triumphant."[21] As divisive as events in Europe was the Whiskey Rebellion in western Pennsylvania in 1794 which attracted sympathy among many Pennsylvanian emigrants to eastern Ohio, but sparked off the Federalist commitment of nationalists like the young Charles Hammond.[22] For most Ohioans, however, national party attachments were first formed in the East and then conveyed to the West. For example, young lawyers like Calvin Pease and Benjamin Tappan had already taken their stand "on the democratic side" in the party

20. *Muskingum Messenger*, October 20, 1813, January 11, 18, 1815; Harry L. Coles, *The War of 1812* (Chicago, 1965); Bradford Perkins, *Castlereagh and Adams: England and the United States, 1812-1823* (Berkeley, 1964).

21. Downes, *Frontier Ohio*, 178-80. See also William H. Smith, "A Familiar Talk about Monarchists and Jacobins," *Ohio Archaeological and Historical Quarterly*, II (1888), 187, 193-94, and *St. Clair*, I, 186-87, 203-05.

22. Roswell Marsh, *The Life of Charles Hammond, of Cincinnati, Ohio* (Steubenville, 1863), 12; Edward T. Heald, *Bezaleel Wells, Founder of Canton and Steubenville, Ohio* (Canton, 1942), chap. 1; Steubenville *Western Herald*, October 11, 1806.

The personal, political, and ideological conflicts between Thomas Jefferson (left) and Alexander Hamilton (right) at the national level promoted the development of political parties and carried over into Ohio politics. SOCIETY COLLECTION

conflicts of their native New England and had every intention of supporting the party cause in their new homes in Ohio.[23]

This cleavage of opinion, however, had little influence on Territorial politics in the 1790s. The elections of 1798 and 1800 to the Territorial legislature were fought largely without regard to party considerations, even while "the States were rent, and almost torn asunder, by party strife." According to Jacob Burnet, "this calmness and unanimity, was ascribable, principally, to the fact, that the people of the Territory had no voice in electing the officers of the General Government, and the Government had but little patronage to distribute among them."[24] A further reason was that, as in the seaboard colonies earlier, the effective center of power and patronage within the Territory was beyond the reach of electoral politics. The governor did not depend on votes in the Northwest for his continuance in office, while he had absolute discretion in his bestowal of office and place and other advantages, such as his much-disputed right to select county seats. The result was that ambitious politicians, of whatever political persuasion, were tempted to ac-

23. Donald J. Ratcliffe, ed., "The Autobiography of Benjamin Tappan," *Ohio History*, LXXXV (Spring 1976); Letters of 1798-1800, The Papers of Benjamin Tappan, Library of Congress.
24. Burnet, *North-Western Territory*, 289, 314, 342n; Beverley W. Bond, Jr., ed., "Memoirs of Benjamin Van Cleve," *Quarterly Publications of the Historical and Philosophical Society of Ohio*, XVII (1922), 64; Samuel P. Hildreth, *Pioneer History: Being An Account of . . . the Early Settlement of the Northwest Territory* (Cincinnati, 1848), 347-48; Massie, *Massie*, 66-67; Gilmore, *Tiffin*, 31-32.

commodate to St. Clair's Federalist views in order to win his favor: thus men whose first instincts were Jeffersonian secured personal political advantages by tempering their views and associating themselves with Federalism in a way which confused both contemporaries and historians.[25]

Moreover, the leading issue of Territorial politics after 1799 was sectionally divisive and so also cut across party lines. Opposition to early statehood came primarily from those who wished to see the boundaries of the future state altered for the sake of local advantage. Thus Chillicothe's liking for a state defined like the modern one with a convenient capital on the Scioto, was countered by those interested in a division along the line of that river, which would increase the chances of Marietta's and Cincinnati's both becoming state capitals. For this reason early Republican demands in Cincinnati for statehood became muted as the city's leaders plotted with St. Clair and Marietta; in the area east of the Scioto, sympathisers with Republicanism found themselves, sometimes to their embarrassment, forced to associate with extreme Federalists who proclaimed the partisan advantages of dividing the territory at the Scioto. Against this sectional log-roll the Chillicothe interest could mobilize back-country areas, notably in Hamilton County, which disliked the subjection of their local interests to those of established county seats like Cincinnati.[26] However, in the long run the dominant Cincinnati-Marietta alliance was doomed to fail, partly as a result of the extension of voting facilities to the backcountry, but mainly because its scheme of division ran counter to the prescription of the Northwest Ordinance. Congressmen, regardless of party persuasion, were inclined to regard that fundamental document as a compact, which had guaranteed from the start that the first Northwestern state would have a western boundary running north from the mouth of the Miami River; even Federalists in Congress felt obliged, therefore, to accept arrangements favorable to the Chillicothe party.[27]

25. Supporters of Jefferson who at times were identified as Federalists include Samuel Huntington, Jr., and George Tod from the Western Reserve, and William Henry Harrison and William Macmillan from Cincinnati. Smith, *St. Clair*, II, 483, 488, 548; Burnet, *North-Western Territory*, 342n; Elbert J. Benton, ed., "Letters from the Samuel Huntington Correspondence, 1800-1812," *Tracts of the Western Reserve Historical Society*, XCV (1915), 63-75; Cutler, *Ephraim Cutler* 67, 69; Gilmore, *Tiffin*, 31-32; Downes, *Frontier Ohio*, 190, 194, 208n, 221; Sears, *Worthington*, 52, 61, 110-11; Dorothy B. Goebel, *William Henry Harrison, A Political Biography* (Indianapolis, 1926), 42-43, 49-52; Mary Lou Conlin, *Simon Perkins of the Western Reserve* (Cleveland, 1968), 14, 31, 59, 164.

26. Downes, *Frontier Ohio*, 177-239. See also Smith, *St. Clair*, II, 450, 482-83, 527-28, 547-48; Massie, *Massie*, 163-64, 166-68; Benton, ed., "Huntington Correspondence," 69-72.

27. A Federalist-dominated Congress passed the Act of 1800 dividing the Northwest Territory along this line, and Federalists joined Republicans in the Congress of 1801-1802 in voting down the territorial legislature's request that this dividing-line be moved east to the Scioto. Sears, *Worthington*, 55-56, 77.

Even so, the statehood contest would finally be cast in partisan terms. The most deeply committed Jeffersonians, convinced that Federalism threatened the destruction of the republican system of government, believed that the Territorial system was an embodiment of Federalist ideals and had to be overthrown. Even in Cincinnati, then, the Republican Societies were willing to prefer early statehood to an advantageous division of the Territory.[28] Furthermore, the closely-contested Presidential contest of 1800-1801 made partisans consider carefully the effect that the admission of a new state would have on the fine balance between the parties; all agreed that Ohio would probably be Republican.[29] Since the Republicans by 1801 had secured control of both the Presidency and Congress, the most effective tactic of the statehood forces was to identify their cause with Democratic Republicanism, while their most intelligent opponents tried to deny that it was a party question. When, in the 1802 session, the "agents from Chillicothe" influenced the "Democratic members very strongly in their cause," they were "able to carry any thing" through Congress, and so gained Congress' authorisation to call a constitutional convention.[30] The campaign which followed was fought primarily along party rather than sectional lines, with the Federalists opposing not so much statehood as the terms offered by Congress. Though on most issues the constitutional convention was marked by harmony and consensus rather than bitter partisan disagreements, the members were, for the most part, clearly identified as members of particular political parties. As one member of the convention remarked, "though it might not be expected that general politics would have found their way across the Allegany [*sic*], yet the line that divides parties in the States is as distinctly drawn here as there."[31]

This partisan conflict took place within a political system which was rapidly becoming remarkably democratic. One sign of this was the dramatic increase in the number of men voting in the decisive election campaigns of 1802 and 1803, which were expected to determine the future political character of the state. In Hamilton County, for example, six times as many people voted in 1802 as two years earlier, the turnout being of the order of eighty-three percent of adult white males. Over the state as a whole, only thirty percent voted for a governor in January 1803, but in the more important race for congressman in the summer,

---

28. Downes, *Frontier Ohio*, 239-42. See also "Oration, 4th July 1801, Deld. at Hudson," Tappan Papers.
29. Smith, *St. Clair*, I, 238; Sears, *Worthington*. 64.
30. Paul Fearing to Cutler, January 18, 1802, reprinted in Cutler, *Ephraim Cutler*, 61-65. See also Smith, *St. Clair*, II, 548, 557-59; Burnet, *North-Western Territory*, 331, 335-37.
31. Samuel Huntington, Jr., to Turhand Kirtland, December 3, 1802, reprinted in Conlin, *Perkins*, 53-54. See also Gilmore, *Tiffin*, 34, 68; Cutler, *Ephraim Cutler*, 68-80.

more than seventy percent went to the polls.[32] This surprisingly high level of turnout reflected, of course, the broadening of the suffrage and the extension of voting facilities, but it also indicated that the character of politics was changing with the introduction of democratic, partisan techniques similar to those developed on the seaboard during the previous four years.[33]

Traditionally, political leaders had depended for electoral success upon their connections with men of local influence. They had attracted their support by satisfying their interests and by appointing them to public office. By these means, and by appealing to the socially dominant elite in the urban centers, St. Clair had secured reasonably pliable legislatures, which had given a Federalist cast to the politics of the Territory. In the "town and neighbourhood" of Cincinnati, that "den of Aristocracy," the "officers of the colonial government were the monied men" and bore down the interests of Republicans.[34] In eastern Ohio immediately south of the Western Reserve, Federalist land speculators and town proprietors were particularly influential, and Federalist victory there in 1802 was prophesied on the grounds that the governor's "pets are chiefly in office," which "will give them a greater weight."[35] For this reason the opposition campaigned strongly in 1800 and 1801 for St. Clair's removal by the President; and his ultimate dismissal in December 1802 was greeted by relief that St. Clair would at last be "forsaken as he has not the loaves & fishes any longer at his disposal." But if control of the patronage now passed firmly into Republican hands, it served to reinforce their political position rather than to establish it, for in the last resort the Republicans depended upon a broad appeal to the voters for their electoral success.[36]

32. Figures for 1802 taken from Downes, *Frontier Ohio*, 207, 246, and Massie, *Massie*, 171; and those for 1803 from Utter, *Frontier State*, 26, 30. In the latter case it was necessary to work out what proportion of the total population would be adult white males. Colonial historians traditionally assume the proportion to be about one-fifth, but in frontier areas the proportion was undoubtedly much higher. Yet the official count of eligibles in 1815 suggested that the true ratio was not far off one in five. To be on the safe side, I have assumed that two people out of every nine were qualified to vote in Ohio, which was what Hezekiah Niles worked out the proportion to be in 1823. *Niles' Weekly Register*, X (June 29, 1816), 299; *Ibid.*, XXV (September 13, 1823), 18.

33. Noble E. Cunningham, *The Jeffersonian Republicans: Formation of Party Organization, 1789-1801* (Chapel Hill, 1957), 144-261.

34. William Goforth to Worthington, August 29, 1803, The Papers of Charles E. Rice, Ohio Historical Society. Smith, *St. Clair*, I, 242, II, 538, 575, 442-43, 431-32, 484-85.

35. James Pritchard to Worthington, March 23, 1802, quoted in Downes, *Frontier Ohio*, 217. The influence of Federalists in towns like Steubenville and Canton is suggested by Heald, *Wells*, 1-100 *passim*.

36. John Smith to Massie, January 22, 1803, reprinted in Massie, *Massie*, 222. Downes argues (*Frontier Ohio*, 216-25) that federal patronage played an essential role in building up the Republican party, yet he does not reveal whether the applications for office which he refers to were ever successful and he ignores the fact that most removals were made by the President *after* the decisive elections of 1802.

St. Clair, it is true, initially believed that the power of the Chillicothe-centred opposition arose from the influence which great landowners like Massie could exert over their tenants and debtors. This was the reason why he preferred a freehold franchise and advocated the ballot in place of *viva voce* voting. But by 1802 he had come to see the enemy, not as overmighty subjects, but as partisan organization directed at securing partial interests and endeavoring to mislead the people.[37] Politics were, in truth, becoming marked more by agitation than deference, while envy of the wealthy and prominent was sometimes exploited against them. As a large landowner on the Western Reserve complained in 1805, "we have a singular kind of Republicanism in this County, i.e., that no man whose property is above mediocrity (and if so much it is very dangerous) is safe to be trusted."[38]

The political system was, in fact, becoming dominated by the need to win popular support, and the wishes of constituents increasingly governed the behavior of elected representatives. Even under the Territorial government public opinion had made itself felt. Jacob Burnet, for example, argued that the Territorial Assembly would never have allowed the introduction of slavery in any shape or form, even had it had the power, because of the "universal" hostility of the people.[39] Constituents were able to exercise such power because legislative proceedings were published and, at the request of any member, votes recorded; Americans had already made what a writer of the Jacksonian era was to describe as "the'glorious invention' of taking the yeas and nays . . . this strong link between representatives and constituents, and the happy means of insuring that precious quality among republicans, RESPONSIBILITY."[40] In fact, liberal politicians considered that the representative was bound to follow the people's wishes. In December 1800 a Republican committee suggested that, because the issue of statehood had arisen since the elections to the second Territorial legislature, the inhabitants of the area east of the Miami line should hold meetings to decide their attitude toward statehood and then "instruct their representatives . . . to govern themselves accordingly."[41] Before the elections to the constitutional convention in Ross and Hamilton Counties, candidates were compelled to answer questions publicly defining their at-

37. Smith, *St. Clair*, I, 218, II, 482, 505-06, 587-90, 593.
38. Simon Perkins to Benjamin Gorham, September 3, 1805, quoted in Conlin, *Perkins*, 57.
39. Burnet, *North-Western Territory*, 306, 332-33.
40. *Niles' Weekly Register*, XXXIII (January 12, 1828), 316. The Territorial legislature instructed its delegate in Congress, regularly took the "yeas" and "nays," and issued addresses to the people; Smith, *St. Clair*, I, 214, II, 451, 543-47.
41. Smith, *St. Clair*, II, 524-25, 565.

titudes to statehood, slavery, and the Republican party; and those
whose votes in the Convention gave dissatisfaction "lost much credit"
and were even defeated in the subsequent election to the state legislature.[42] Consequently, legislative bodies became ever more conscious of
outside opinion, and their members accordingly spent much time "manufacturing speeches . . . to fill the papers for their constituents."[43]

The critical election of 1802, in which most voters first took their
stand, was marked by demagogic, populistic appeals. The various
candidates began early "to break ground in the electioneering field."
One began "to preach, which is generally a symton [sic] of an election
not being far off." Others took to the "stump," though the phrase was
not used at the time. Chillicothe was reported as "glutted with hand bills
and long tavern harangues." Newspapers published appeals to the
voters, appeals directed to prejudice and passion as much as to reason.[44]
At the same time the parties organized to stimulate voting and coordinate action. In Cincinnati, as early as 1797, Republicans had organized a
committee of correspondence, which by 1802 had spawned seventeen
Republican Societies throughout the county. Each society was called on
to elect delegates to a county nominating convention which met in
August 1802 and named a ticket for the constitutional convention. Such
delegate conventions were, however, called by Republicans only in
counties like Hamilton and Belmont where the result was expected to be
a close run thing.[45]

The Federalists, optimistic about their chances of success in 1802, did
not rely simply on their traditional advantages but also adopted more
populistic measures. Indeed, "the extraordinary exertions" made by
the Federalists in preparation for the 1802 elections were used by the
Republicans as justification for their own organized efforts. Federalists
in Washington County called the first delegate conventions in June 1801
and August 1802; even the second one met in advance of any Republican
convention in the Territory. In addition, they campaigned actively for
popular support, and certainly in Cincinnati and its vicinity they canvas-
sed from door to door. At times they descended to the level of scurrility,
as when they accused leading Republicans of wanting to introduce
slavery into Ohio. Such claims created "hot times about slavery" in
Athens County, where the Federalists, though weak, were said to be

42. Downes, *Frontier Ohio*, 199, 243, 247; Sears, *Worthington*, 104. See also Ratcliffe,
"Autobiography of Tappan."
43. Tiffin to Worthington, December 9, 1808, Worthington Papers.
44. Sears, *Worthington*, 86-87; Ratcliffe, "Autobiography of Tappan"; Smith, *St.
Clair*, I, 242, II, 591.
45. Downes, *Frontier Ohio*, 182, 241-45.

"damned saucy."[46] Furthermore, the Federalists were willing to modify their political stance in the light of public opinion: in the convention all but one voted in favor of immediate statehood, almost certainly because they were "influenced by popular motives."[47]

Moreover, in the constitutional convention the Federalists worked to establish a reasonably democratic form of government. Already Federalists in the Territorial Assembly had supported the extension of the suffrage, while even St. Clair had no objection to popular participation through the ballot box; his main fear had been that the Republicans would establish a government which was "democratic in form and oligarchic in its execution."[48] According to Ephraim Cutler, the Federalist minority in the convention worked to give the constitution "a strong democratic tendency" and establish a "perfect . . . republican system, giving . . . complete individual freedom." They not only approved of the tax-paying suffrage requirements, but even fought to deprive the governor of his veto and to provide cheap and convenient justice for the people. Though some Federalist lawyers were subsequently critical of the judicial arrangements, their leaders in the convention were, in general, well pleased with the constitution. They undoubtedly differed with the Republicans on a number of issues, but could not be called enemies of popular rights. Indeed, the Federalists insisted the constitution should be submitted to the people for their approval, but this "strictly republican" proposal was turned down by a Republican majority eager for speedy admission to the Union.[49]

Yet, despite this willingness to organize and campaign and accommodate, the Federalists, to their chagrin, found themselves thoroughly defeated. The Republicans not only secured a four-to-one majority in the convention but also achieved easy victories in the statewide elec-

46. Massie, *Massie*, 205-10; Smith, *St. Clair*, I, 241, 242, II, 524, 529, 575, 588; Benton, ed., "Huntington Letters," 80-81. Andrews, *Washington County: Centennial Address*, 27; Cutler, *Ephraim Cutler*, 54, 65-66. It should be stressed that the evidence used by Fischer (*Revolution of American Conservatism*, 409) to show the organizational vitality of the Ohio "Young Federalists," especially Ephraim Cutler, from 1802 through 1814 (so he implies), is almost all drawn from 1802 rather than from a later period. *Cf.* Lisle A. Rose, *Prologue to Democracy: The Federalists in the South, 1787-1800* (Lexington, 1968); and Cunningham, *Jeffersonian Republicans, 1789-1801*.

47. Jacob Burnet to Cutler, September 26, 1847, quoted in Cutler, *Ephraim Cutler*, 68-69; Burnet professed there was probably some higher motive, but could not think what it was. Cutler, who cast the one negative vote, did so not only from personal conviction, but also to express the views of his constituents.

48. Smith, *St. Clair*, II, 480; Bond, *Foundations*, 458-60, 465-66.

49. Cutler, *Ephraim Cutler*, 68-82, 59; Burnet, *North-Western Territory*, 356-59; Downes, *Frontier Ohio*, 248-49. For an account of the convention stressing Federalist conservativism, see Barnhart, *Valley of Democracy*, 152-59. The Federalists opposed the extension of the suffrage to those who worked on the roads, while they provided firm support for Negro rights; *Ibid.*, 156-57.

tions for governor and congressman in 1803. Even in Washington County where the local interests of Marietta had ensured Federalist success as long as the question of statehood was in doubt, the Republicans succeeded thereafter by a two-to-one margin, at worst.[50] This result partly reflects the fact that the process of migration tended, for some reason, to bring more Republicans to Ohio than Federalists. Pioneers from Pennsylvania and Kentucky were overwhelmingly Republican, and so, surprisingly, were most New Englanders who came after about 1799. Certainly the settlers of the Western Reserve were far more prone to Republicanism than their fellows who stayed in New England, while farther south a Marietta correspondent told Jefferson in 1801 that "these days there is not an Emigrant from Connecticut within this county, but what is really a friend to your honor and a true Republican."[51] This selective process of migration reinforced a general swing against the Federalists on the part of previously uninvolved voters everywhere, including Ohio. "High Federalist" extremism in national affairs between 1798 and 1800 had identified the party with illiberal and militaristic measures and, more disastrously, with high direct taxation. Such policies turned most farming communities outside New England toward the Republicans, who in 1801 and 1802 had reversed these policies and established a government devoted to economy.[52] In addition, they had rescued the people of Ohio from colonial status and given them all the advantages of statehood. Those who had brought the state the blessings of "independence" and full self-government were rewarded with the continuing trust of the people.

The "Dual" Party System

This overwhelming Republican predominance was the main feature of party politics in the first decade of Ohio statehood. Recognizing that in any confrontation they would inevitably lose, the Federalists withdrew from statewide contests—in other words, from elections for governor, congressman, and also for presidential electors, since the general ticket system was adopted from the start. As the Chillicothe *Supporter* commented in 1809, "the federalists of Ohio not being ignorant that their opponents outnumber them, I think I may say five to one, never have made any general effort against their enemy."[53] Even at the county level

50. Utter. *Frontier State*, 26.
51. J. Cook to Jefferson, October 21, 1801, quoted in Fischer, *Revolution of American Conservatism*, 218n; Smith, *St. Clair*, II, 556.
52. Fischer, *Revolution of American Conservatism*, 201-26; Manning J. Dauer, *The Adams Federalists* (Baltimore, 1953).
53. Chillicothe *Supporter*, December 16, 1809. In the presidential election of 1804 the Federalists polled only 364 votes. Basic references for this period are Sears, *Worthington*, 108-202, and Utter, *Frontier State*, 3-120.

they faced defeat and exclusion from local as well as state and federal office. The inevitable consequence was the withdrawal of Federalists from politics in 1804 and their growing disillusionment at the political prospects of the country.[54] No wonder men suspected Federalists in Ohio of disloyalty and involvement in Aaron Burr's mysterious enterprise.[55]

In these circumstances "party spirit" could not long endure "at its meridian height" of 1802 and 1803.[56] According to a Republican commentator in 1806, "there has for the last two years been no party who dared to make head against the republicans." As a result, the General Assembly of that year had "one of the most agreeable sessions ever experienced in this or any other State as there was not the least appearance of any thing like party during the whole time."[57] In these circumstances voter turnout declined considerably in statewide elections, while strict party voting probably became rarer than it had once been. Yet this did not mean that party action had ceased or that the party system was dead, on the contrary, party considerations continued to dominate Ohio's politics. All that happened was that state political questions soon began to create a line of partisan cleavage which did not coincide with the more easily recognizable division arising from national politics.

For the most part, the dominant Republican party maintained the organization it had developed in the crisis of statehood. In areas where the Republicans were easily predominant, as in Ross County, nominations were made informally by various party gatherings and by interested individuals through newspaper announcements. On the other hand, county conventions were more widely used than is usually assumed, being the normal method of nomination not only in the Cincinnati region but also in many parts of eastern Ohio. Moreover, the conventions ceased to represent members of the Republican Societies, and instead were attended by delegates elected by the people in their various townships at the time announced well in advance by the party committee at the county seat.[58]

54. Cutler, *Ephraim Cutler*, 84, 114; Rowena Buell, ed., *The Memoirs of Rufus Putnam* (Boston and New York, 1903), 125; Heald, *Wells*, 45; Mrs. Charles P. Noyes, *A Family History in Letters and Documents* (St. Paul, 1919), I, 272.

55. Sloane to Tappan, May 10, 1806, Tappan Papers; Peter Hoffman and Son to Clay, December 18, 1806, in James F. Hopkins and Mary W.M. Hargreaves, eds., *The Papers of Henry Clay* (Lexington, 1959), I, 263-64.

56. Steubenville *Western Herald*, August 23, 1806.

57. John Sloane to Tappan, January 1, January 30, 1806, Tappan Papers.

58. Cunningham, *The Jeffersonian Republicans in Power, 1801-1809* (Chapel Hill, 1963), 196-200, which concentrates on the Cincinnati region. For examples from eastern Ohio, see *Marietta Ohio Gazette*, September 18, 1806; Sloane to Worthington, August 20, October 3, 1808, Worthington Papers; *Western Herald*, September 20, 1806, September 12, 1807.

The strength of political organization in this period was concentrated primarily at the county level. Poor communications and regional rivalries guaranteed that problems of coordination would arise in statewide elections. From the start the Republicans used legislative caucuses to nominate candidates for these elections, as the one occasion when representatives from all over the state had a chance to confer together and then convey news of the decision back to their counties. The first caucus was held toward the close of the constitutional convention and, in effect, chose Edward Tiffin as first governor. At the close of the first session of the General Assembly, Jeremiah Morrow was named as congressional candidate "at the earnest solicitation of a large majority of the republican members." Once it had been agreed "to support him in the different counties," it was impossible to change the plan without producing confusion among Republicans and risking the election of a Federalist.[59] Morrow succeeded convincingly in 1803 and thereafter he was regularly re-elected as Ohio's sole congressman down to 1812.

The decisions of the caucus, however, were not always well-publicized, their authority was frequently questioned, and there was no central committee authorized to make new nominations should the need arise. In February 1804 the caucus named three candidates for presidential elector; in May the Cincinnati corresponding committee treated the question as still being open to discussion by the various corresponding societies; and in September the removal of one of the nominees to Indiana caused great confusion as to who should be supported in his place.[60] Frequently the official nomination had to be buttressed by the publication of reports secured by the corresponding committee as to whom other counties were intending to support. Thus in September 1806 the Marietta paper eagerly published news from Chillicothe that the delegates from all the townships in Muskingum County, meeting in Zanesville, had determined unanimously to support the caucus's nominee for Congress![61] This need to confirm that the caucus decision would be obeyed revealed organizational difficulties, and also the fact that the lack of Federalist opposition reduced the pressure for common action and allowed the assertion of local rivalries among the Republicans.

59. Worthington to William Goforth, May 25, 1803, reprinted in *American Pioneer*, II (1843), 89.

60. Tiffin to Worthington, February 17, 20, 1804, The Papers of Edward Tiffin, Ohio Historical Society; David Symmes *et al.* to Worthington, May 31, 1804, Rice Papers; Massie, *Massie*, 230.

61. Marietta *Ohio Gazette*, September 18, 1806. See also Wyllys Silliman to Worthington, July 29, 1808, Worthington Papers.

A prime source of confusion arose from Cincinnati's continuing resentment of Chillicothe's claims to political pre-eminence. In 1802 the strongly organised Hamilton County party sought to secure the first term as governor for one of their own men; Massie was thought to be "the only Person (out of the County of Hamilton) who will be able to command their votes."[62] Though Tiffin finally secured their support, they were unwilling to back Morrow for Congress and instead pressed the claims of their own candidate. Similarly, in both 1804 and 1808 they asserted a right to name one of the three electoral candidates, regardless of the caucus's decision, though they were perfectly willing to accept men they were not entirely happy with as the other two candidates, "that we may be united on the day of Election throughout the State."[63] Marietta also could act independently, and in 1807 Chillicothe Republicans felt that their candidate for governor could succeed only if he first came to terms with Marietta's leading Republican, Return J. Meigs, Jr., especially as "by securing Meigs, we can have the Marietta press." However, Meigs ran in competition with the Chillicothe candidate, and in September received the support of the Cincinnati Republican Corresponding Society.[64] The final contest appears the epitome of personal and local rivalry, with each side accusing the other of partisan disloyalty and the legislature ultimately deciding to disallow the election.

Regional resentments prevented unity even in national elections. In 1806, for instance, James Pritchard tried to exploit eastern Ohio's resentment at its exclusion from the great offices in his unsuccessful bid to contest Morrow's re-election. Similarly, in 1808 "a nomination of [presidential] electors did not take place while the representatives of the people were together," because of a disagreement between the Chillicothe politicians and those from elsewhere over one of the three nominees.[65] At all levels local and personal rivalries tended to disrupt party unity, and make log-rolling a prime form of political activity. On the Western Reserve, for example, the dominant question became the contest over county boundaries and the struggle between Warren and Youngstown to become the county seat.[66]

Yet out of these petty divisions among Republicans arose what amounted to a new system of party conflict at the state level. As in New

62. Charles W. Byrd to Massie, May 20, 1802, reprinted in Massie, *Massie,* 205-06.

63. Daniel Symmes *et al.* to Worthington, May 31, 1804, Rice Papers; Sloane to Tappan, October 1, 1808, Tappan Papers.

64. Tiffin to Worthington, February 5, 1807, Worthington Papers; *Western Herald,* September 12, 1807. Meigs was regarded at this time as a sound regular Republican.

65. *Western Herald,* August 23, 1806; Worthington to Huntington, July 29, 1808, in Benton, ed., "Huntington Correspondence," 121-22, 124.

66. Chillicothe *Supporter,* January 26, 1809; Conlin, *Perkins,* 55-59; Tappan to Nancy Tappan, October 6, 1806, Tappan Papers.

York and Pennsylvania, and at Washington, those Republicans who were dissatisfied with the party's leadership began to be identified as a coherent group dubbed "Quids." These men were considered to be willing, for the sake of office, to divide the Republican interest and co-operate with Federalists, thus risking everything gained by the victory of 1800.[67] The existence of such a group was demonstrated at Chillicothe in January 1807 when a "rank Federalist," Philemon Beecher, received one-third of the votes cast by the assembly in an election to the United States Senate, while a prominent moderate Republican was nominated for the governorship by a caucus of Federalists and "Mongrel Republicans."[68] Though only a handful of politicians were considered true Quids—only five or six in the Assembly of 1807-1808—their amalgamation with Federalists and their willingness to exploit dissatisfactions made them a potentially dangerous force.[69] At last in 1808 the statewide elections were seen as a contest between a true Republican and an amalgamationist ticket for governor and congressman. Both the Quid candidates tried to pass as friendly to Republicanism, but the known Federalist failed for Congress while the Quid candidate to whom all paid lip-service as a Republican, Samuel Huntington, was elected governor. There was no doubt that his leading opponents were correct in considering Huntington the preferred candidate of the Federalists, who were much gratified by his success.[70] The appearance of this hard-fought gubernational campaign, which saw the number of votes cast double over the election of 1807, rather contradicts Nathaniel Macon's earlier belief that party contests as regards state affairs occur usually only where the governor is allowed much power.[71]

If this breach within the Ohio Republican party arose as much from personality as from principle, it aroused so much passion and interest because it quickly became involved in a dispute over fundamental issues. As Richard Ellis has argued, neither the Revolution nor the Jeffersonian victory of 1800 had settled the difficult question of the role

67. Sloane to Tappan, October 1, November 13, 1808, Tappan Papers; Massie, *Massie*, 233-34.
68. Tiffin to Worthington, January 3, 6, 25, February 5, 1807; Silliman to Worthington, January 6, 1807, Worthington Papers. The moderate was Massie, who certainly received Federalist support in the election. Massie, *Massie*, 248.
69. Sloane to Tappan, January 25, October 1, 1808, Tappan Papers.
70. Sloane to Worthington, July 7, August 6, October 3, November 13, 1808, Silliman to Worthington, July 29, 1808, Tiffin to Worthington, December 2, 9, 1808, Tappan to Worthington, September 15, 1808, Worthington Papers; Sloane to Tappan, July 11, 1808, Tappan Papers; James Hedges to J. H. Larwill, October 26, 1808, The Larwill Family Papers, Ohio Historical Society; Huntington to Burnet, October 30, 1808, Rice Papers.
71. See Macon's letter of 1802 to Worthington, in Utter, *Frontier State*, 17-18, 48. Of course, a stronger executive would have been more worth winning and so would have encouraged fuller party organization.

and power of the judiciary in a republican society. In Ohio as in many other states, much popular hostility endured against lawyers and a legal system which seemed designed to boost professional fees rather than secure justice and individual rights. The popular demand for cheap justice in civil cases had been voiced in territorial days and had been met by repeated extensions of the power of justices of the peace to hear cases for the recovery of debts in their local courts, where decisions would be quick and expenses low. Initially their power had been restricted to debts below ten dollars; the level had been gradually raised during the 1790s; and the state legislature met popular demands by further raising the level to fifty dollars in 1804, and even seventy dollars in 1809. But the justices' decisions were often amateurish and certainly arbitrary, being made without a jury, while the United States Constitution, ever conscious of the need to safeguard property, had forbidden trials without jury in cases involving debts greater than twenty dollars. Accordingly, in 1806 an Ohio state judge, Calvin Pease, declared the fifty-dollar law unconstitutional, and, in so doing, made a claim to the right of judicial review identical to John Marshall's innovative claim in the famous *Marbury* vs. *Madison* decision in the United States Supreme Court in 1803.[72]

Such a claim offended many of the more extreme Republicans who believed in the right of the people to political supremacy. Indeed, so convinced were many politicians that this principle was what the party stood for that they preferred to refer to themselves as "Democrats" and to their constituency as "the Democracy." Before statehood a meeting on the Western Reserve had lectured St. Clair on the duty of even a Territorial governor to accept nominations made by popular meetings; immediately after statehood the officers of the Hamilton County artillery company, who had been appointed under the Territorial government, resigned their posts and requested elections, because these good republicans felt "impressed, that in all civil governments, particularly in a republic like ours, the people ought to enjoy the privilege of appointing their own officers." On exactly these grounds the Democrats justified the use of delegate conventions for deciding party nominations: they were the most appropriate means by which to "procure the sense of the people" and "the will of the Populous [*sic*]."[73] From this arose the

72. For this issue nationally, see Ellis, *Jeffersonian Crisis;* and, locally, William T. Utter, "Judicial Review in Early Ohio," *Mississippi Valley Historical Review*, XIV (1927), 3-24; and *Idem*, "Ohio and the English Common Law," *Ibid.*, XVI (1929), 321-33. For origins of the issue in Ohio, see Burnet, *North-Western Territory*, 311; Smith, *St. Clair*, I, 191, II, 506; Downes, *Frontier Ohio*, 155-62.

73. Ratcliffe, "Autobiography of Tappan"; William McFarland *et al.* to Tiffin, June 20, 1803, Tiffin Papers; Daniel Symmes *et al.* to Worthington, May 31, 1804, Rice Papers.

belief that the people's representatives were the supreme power in the state and the only possible interpreters of a constitution established through popular sovereignty. Hence Democrats were unwilling to accept that laws passed by the people's legislature could be declared unconstitutional by "the Judiciary, [that] dictatorial court of infallibility, whose decision is paramount to [the] voice of the great mass of the people and their constituent sages." They feared lest "the majesty of the people . . . be dethroned and prostrated at the feet of our judges."[74]

Not all Republicans agreed, however. A number of them believed that Pease's nullifying of "a favorite law of many" was erroneous as a decision, but legitimate as an exercise of judicial power. The House of Representatives in 1807 divided evenly on the question of whether the judiciary had absolute discretion in declaring laws unconstitutional.[75] Then, later in the year, the state Supreme Court itself nullified the fifty-dollar law and so brought forth a newspaper controversy and a stream of popular protests from the "upper and middle" parts of the state. In the assembly of 1808 "the question relative to the unwarrantable conduct of the Judges was one that was more warmly contested than any that has ever come before the legislature." Now the two houses disagreed.[76] By the following session the Democratic faction gained a majority which they used to impeach the erring judges, but the impeachment failed narrowly to gain the necessary two-thirds vote in the Senate. The frustrated Democratic leaders, therefore, decided to use an ambiguity in the state constitution to declare—by a simple majority—that the terms of office of all appointive state officers had expired, and then elected new Judges who possessed a proper sense of their own subservience to the will of the people.[77] So arbitrary appeared this *Sweeping Resolution* of 1810 that its opponents promised that "every exertion will be used to produce a change in the sentiment of representations next session."[78] In many counties the old judges refused to withdraw, the authority of new judges was resisted, and "the whole state was thrown into utter confusion for a time."[79]

74. Ephraim Quinby to Worthington, December 24, 1808, Worthington Papers; Sloane to Tappan, September 4, 1807, Tappan Papers.
75. Tiffin to Worthington, January 3, 9, 1807, Worthington Papers. For this whole paragraph, see Utter, "Judicial Review," 8-9, 12-15, 18, 22-24.
76. Sloane to Tappan, January 25, 1808, Tappan Papers.
77. Stephen Wood to Brown, January 6, 1809, The Papers of Ethan Allen Brown, Ohio Historical Society; Ratcliffe, "Autobiography of Tappan."
78. John Thompson to J. H. Larwill, June 5, 1810, The Larwill Family Papers, Western Historical Manuscript Collections, University of Missouri.
79. Caleb Atwater, *History of Ohio, Natural and Civil* (Cincinnati, 1838), 185. See also John W. Campbell, *Biographical Sketches, With Other Literary Remains* (Columbus, 1838), 70-71; David Griffin to Samuel Williams, June 22, 1811, The Records of the Tammany Society of Ohio, Ohio Historical Society.

This dispute quickly became identified with the growing cleavage between the "regulars" and the "amalgamationists," though some individuals found themselves forced to change sides by the raising of the issue. Even the 1807 gubernational election had a bearing on the dispute, since the supposed Quid candidate had been one of the first to protest against unconstitutional legislation, while in 1808 the successful Quid candidate, Huntington, was himself one of the offending judges. In some areas to oppose Huntington meant incurring "the displeasure of the high Court party . . . and their sycophantic gentry."[80] And in the county elections there was "a very great political struggle this fall: 'Law or no Law,' 'Lawyer or no lawyer.' "[81] The "Democratic" Republicans found their popular support mainly among the debtor interest, long a politically significant force, especially in Ohio where, before 1820, most land was bought on credit. The "Judge Killers" also won support in the middle counties settled by Virginians and Kentuckians, and in eastern Ohio where there was "much of the Democracy of Pennsylvania," a state which was experiencing similar contests. The conservative cause probably suffered from the support it received from lawyers, since they were considered interested parties, but it apparently appealed strongly to settlers from New England, almost regardless of their politics. Most Federalists, in fact, felt that the radicals were placing "the controversy upon such grounds as left them no alternative but to oppose them," and it was their intervention which probably gave the conservative side the advantage in the elections of 1810 and 1811.[82]

Worried by the threats to their position, the Democratic leadership reinvigorated, indeed rebuilt, their political machine. The *Sweeping Resolution* threw open all the civil offices subject to legislative appointment, including the county courts, and enabled the regulars to put sound men in positions of influence. In addition, Tammany Societies were established in 1810, on the New York and Philadelphia pattern, to provide a close bond of fraternity and co-operation for "citizens of known attachment to the political rights of human nature." Their object was "to make nominations and control elections. The elements of their doings were secrecy and concert; and to insure the fidelity of members,

80. Sloane to Tappan, September 4, 1807, Tappan Papers; Ephraim Quinby to Worthington, December 24, 1808, Tappan to Worthington, September 15, 1808, Worthington Papers.

81. John Thompson to J. H. Larwill, September 27, 1808, Larwill Family Papers, University of Missouri.

82. Chillicothe *Supporter*, August 11, 1810; Campbell, *Biographical Sketches*, 70-71; Conlin, *Perkins*, 58-59. See also Utter, "Judicial Review," 12, 13, 20-21, 24; and Ellis, *Jeffersonian Crisis*, 250-66.

the obligations of an oath were imposed."[83] Besides working to ensure the nomination and election of genuine Democratic Republicans, the Tammany Society at the state capital also endeavored to keep the legislature on the straight and narrow. Too often new representatives had been misled in the early days of a session by designing "pretended Republicans." Tammany, therefore, operated as a means of influencing legislators elected in 1810 in those counties where the *Sweeping Resolution* had not been the critical issue, with the result that the attempts, in the assembly of 1810-1811, to rescind the *Sweeping Resolution* were all defeated.[84] Then in 1811, in order to strengthen the supporters of the government "of this state as now administered," leading Democrats at Zanesville, the temporary state capital, proposed the establishment of a state newspaper to harmonize and unite the Democratic Republicans and "GIVE A TONE TO OTHER REPUBLICAN PAPERS."[85]

The Democrats were, in fact, attempting to preserve their position by exercising control over the established party machinery and asserting the duty of all Republicans to support regular nominations. They were trying to use national party loyalties to gain factional advantage on a local issue. As a consequence, the breach in the party induced many Republicans to refuse to submit to party dictation, and they set themselves up as "Independent Republicans." Sometimes the authority of delegate nominations was challenged; sometimes the factions struggled to control the county convention, with the disappointed faction rejecting the nomination and making an alternative one, sometimes by means of a second convention. Even the "Independent Republicans" at times put forward a full ticket containing anti-Tammany candidates for the most minor county offices. If anything, voter interest now revived, with about one eligible voter in three usually attending the polls.[86]

83. "Constitution of the Tammany Society or Columbian Order," March 1810. Records of the Tammany Society of Ohio; Campbell, *Biographical Sketches,* 71. For Tammany's fortunes in Ohio, see Samuel W. Williams, "The Tammany Society in Ohio," *Ohio State Archaeological And Historical Publications,* XXII (1913), 349-70, and William T. Utter, "St. Tammany in Ohio: A Study In Frontier Politics," *Mississippi Valley Historical Review,* XV (1928), 321-40. The society's "Jacobinism" is perhaps demonstrated by its dropping of the Christian calendar: its constitution is dated "Month of Worms, the year of discovery 318," i.e. March 1810.

84. Sloane to Tappan, January 25, 1808, Tappan Papers; Utter, *Frontier State,* 59.

85. Political broadside signed by Isaac Van Horne *et al.,* Zanesville, July 8, 1811, Ohio Historical Society. For the Zanesville Tammany men's attempt to prevent the election of "disaffected men" in 1810, see *Zanesville Express,* August 3, 1815.

86. *Lebanon Western Star,* September 29, October 13, 1810; John F. Edgar, *Pioneer Life in Dayton and Vicinity, 1796-1840* (Dayton, 1896), 92, 141, 148-49; Cunningham, *Jeffersonian Republicans in Power,* 198. It is difficult to assess voter turnout before 1810 because of the lack of reliable estimates of the size of population. In addition, the only reasonably systematic returns are for the gubernatorial election, which never in itself

The rightfulness of party organization now tended to replace the judicial question as the leading issue of the day. Party managers were denounced as "aristocrats" endeavoring to control the votes of the people, while "Independent Republicans" proclaimed the virtue of allowing the people a free choice without "the *few dictating to the many*"—a doctrine which naturally encouraged Federalist support.[87] In particular, this campaign was directed against the Tammany Societies, which were widely denounced as "secret, midnight, aristocratic— political institutions." The "persecuting storms" which raged against this secret organization, with its secrecy, rationalism and pseudo-Indian ritual, are, in fact, reminiscent of the crusade against Freemasonry twenty years later. By 1811 this controversy dominated the state political scene. As a Chillicothe conservative reported in June:

the middle and western part of the State is in an uproar in opposition to the Tammany Society. The establishment of this institution has produced more warmth and division than anything that has occurred since the organization of the State Government. The fears of the people have been justly excited against this Infernal institution. . . .The Tammany scenes that were acted last winter have been laid open to the people and justly exposed. Many good men that have drawn into the institution are abandoning it. . . .The only names of distinction now used are "Tammany & Anti Tammany."[88]

Faced by this popular revolt, the Democrats tried to defend "the new order of things." They warned that "the opposition to the Tammany Society originates from a concealed plan to pull down the leading Democratic Republicans, and with their seventy dollar law to rescind the resolution, and give judges the unlimited right to set aside law."[89] The current of popular feeling could not, however, be stayed. After a close legislative contest, the *Sweeping Resolution* was repealed in January 1812, with men who were eager for popular support in the Congressional elections shifting conspicuously to the opposition. The Democratic or Tammany regulars had lost complete control of the state to their amalgamationist foes, and their radical constitutional doctrines never again

---

attracted much interest. In 1808, however, the governor began to be elected in the same poll as the congressman and county officers, with the result that his election began to reflect the interest provoked by contests for the other offices. My generalization is based on county returns for the gubernational elections of 1808 and 1810, with the number of eligibles being assessed as 2/9ths of the county populations reported in the census of 1810. See n. 32.

87. *Muskingum Messenger*, September 4, 1811.

88. William Creighton, Jr., to George Tod, June 2, 1811, Benton, ed., "Huntington Correspondence," 157-58. Opposition was particularly embittered in the Chillicothe and Cincinnati regions; see John Hamm to Brown, June 7, 1811, Brown Papers; items for 1811 in Records of the Tammany Society of Ohio; and n. 99.

89. Chillicothe *Scioto Gazette*, July 10, 1811.

held sway in Ohio.[90] The regulars quickly dropped the issue, apparently because of their concern to maintain party unity during the war against Britain. In 1814, for example, Tammany men in Cincinnati publicized their desire "to harmonize the Republicans of the state generally" over the coming gubernational election by supporting the most widely acceptable man. Yet the cleavage in the party still survived, and some Tammany Societies persisted, until at least 1819 in Cincinnati and 1821 in Butler County.[91] In Coshocton County the local elections of 1814 were fought between Tammany and the opponents of "the Great Council Fire." In neighboring Muskingum County, the war years were marked by a continuing internal conflict between the champions of "regularity" and the amalgamationist protagonists of "independence."[92] If statewide politics were no longer a contest between two "state parties," the Republicans were clearly still far from united upon local questions.

Indeed, for some time leading radical Republicans had feared that the conflict at the state level would undermine Ohio's Republicanism on national questions. After all, in 1808 Huntington's supporters were associated with a Federalist candidate for Congress and with opposition to Madison's presidential candidacy; for a time some Republicans feared that the confusion surrounding their party's electoral nomination might enable Federalists and dissidents to secure one of Ohio's electoral votes for Madison's rivals. However, public sentiment made such a result unlikely. Huntington himself supported Madison and all the measures of the administration, including the Embargo, while at least some supporters of Monroe and Clinton, when they found "what public sentiment is," were "very noisy for Madison."[93] Again in 1812 a Democratic leader feared that opposition to the *Sweeping Resolution* "will eventually give the Federalists an ascendancy in the Election of Members to Congress. My principle [sic] ground of hope, however, is that in

90. See letters from Zanesville to Worthington, December 1811, January 1812, Worthington Papers; Ratcliffe, "Autobiography of Tappan."
91. Daniel Symmes *et al.*, "Circular," Cincinnati, August 11, 1814, political broadside, Ohio Historical Society. Items relating to the Cincinnati society, 1810-1819, are in the Records of the Tammany Society of Ohio. For Butler County, see "Friends To Liberty," September 24, 1821, political broadside, Ohio Historical Society.
92. C. Johnston to Jeremiah McLene, October 13, 1814, The Papers of Othniel Looker. Ohio Historical Society; *Zanesville Express*, 1812-1815, and *Messenger*, 1813-1815. The returns for the election of 1814 in Muskingum reveal a relatively high degree of ticket voting; *Messenger*, October 19, 1814. In the state legislature the factions still struggled to elect U.S. Senators. Van Horne *et al.* to Brown, December 7, 1814, Brown Papers.
93. Benton, ed., "Huntington Correspondence," 121-24, 134-35; Silliman to Worthington, July 29, 1808; Sloane to Worthington, August 6, October 3, 1808, Worthington Papers; Sloane to Tappan, July 11, October 1, 1808, Tappan Papers.

the selection of Candidates, they and the Quids may split." In order to promote this end the Democrats introduced a loyal address to the President, which, however, failed to divide their opponents since even supposed Federalists decided to vote for it.[94] The Federalists and Quids clearly recognized that the overwhelming majority of Ohioans remained loyal to the national Republican administration, and that nothing could destroy that allegiance on national issues. Significantly, in the presidential election of 1812 each "state party" named its own electoral ticket pledged to Madison; the voters, while for the most part rejecting Tammany candidates for other offices, overwhelmingly preferred the ticket offered by the "regulars," for their loyalty to the administration could not be impugned. Clearly, however much Ohio Republicans had divided over matters of political organization and governmental powers, most of them still agreed on national questions and regarded themselves as members of the same party. In other words, Ohio possessed that surprisingly common American phenomenon, a "dual" party system.[95]

The Federalist Revival
But what stood in the way of a fuller and more complete reconciliation between "Quids" and "Feds"? What prevented the absorption of the Federalist minority into the two Republican "state parties"? It was not merely the prejudice of the Republicans, as Homer C. Hockett suggested; for the Republicans on both sides were willing to welcome apostates from Federalism and even place them at the head of their tickets.[96] The truth was that most Federalists, especially at the grassroots, refused to be absorbed, feeling ever more certain that the disastrous policies of the Republicans must be opposed. Indeed, Federalism, as David H. Fischer has demonstrated, was undergoing a considerable revival in Eastern states after 1807 and seemed capable even of threatening Republican predominance nationally.[97] This revival served not merely to buoy Federalist hopes in Ohio, but also to teach Republicans the danger of risking Federalist success in national elections.

94. Van Horne to Worthington, January 4, March 11, 1812, John Hamm to Worthington, December 2, 1811, Worthington Papers.
95. The term is borrowed from Richard P. McCormick, *The Second American Party System: Party Formation in Jacksonian Era* (Chapel Hill, 1966), 11, though he considers "no-party" to be a better description of politics in Ohio before 1824. *Ibid.*, 257-61.
96. Homer C. Hockett, *Western Influences on Political Parties* (Columbus, 1917), 62. For typical comments on the Republican reception of apostates, who included John Stark Edwards, Ebenezer Buckingham, Jr., and William Woodbridge, see *Zanesville Express*, February 16, August 3, 1814, October 5, 1815.
97. Fischer, *Revolution of American Conservatism;* Sloane to Worthington, July 7, 1808, Jeremiah Morrow to Worthington, January 16, 1810, Worthington Papers.

Even in Ohio Federalism was becoming conspicuously more active. In 1807 and 1808 newspapers were established in Marietta and Chillicothe which were frankly Federalist in sentiment, and although the former soon collapsed, it was quickly replaced by Caleb Emerson's embittered *Western Spectator,* which for over two years (1810-1813) was the only paper published in Marietta. After 1812 at least three more Federalist prints appeared, at Franklinton, Zanesville, and St. Clairsville. The last was the most formidable of all, the *Ohio Federalist,* edited by the talented Charles Hammond, whose command of the language of argument and abuse made him a cruel enemy and formidable critic of the administration and its policies. Such papers were, in fact, innovative in that they contained more editorial comment than was customary.[98] As Federalists became more vociferous, so they became passionately intolerant, even in religious and social matters. Republican devotees of St. Tammany were ejected from the Methodist Church in Chillicothe, while in Steubenville Federalist ladies refused for a whole year to call on a newly-arrived lady of means and accomplishment who happened to be married to a Republican.[99]

Contemporaries had no doubt that this Federalist revival derived from discontent with the policies of the national administration. Intelligent Republicans bemoaned the fact that patriotism had declined since the Revolution, for men were unwilling to undergo the material deprivations necessary in order to preserve the country's independence of foreign tyrants; in other words, the administration's attempt to exert diplomatic pressure by means of the Embargo had produced a politically dangerous degree of economic suffering.[100] Marietta, for example, had developed since 1801 an important ship-building industry, which produced ships even for the Mediterranean trade. According to a distinguished local Republican and historian, the restrictions on overseas commerce after 1807 ended ship-building, rope walks, and hemp growing. "Town property, as well as farms, sunk in value; a stop was put to improvements in

98. Information, not altogether accurate, may be found on these newspapers in Utter, *Frontier State,* 37, 98-100; Osman C. Hooper, *History of Ohio Journalism, 1793-1933* (Columbus, 1933), 24-46; Arthur S. Mink, *Union List of Ohio Newspapers Available in Ohio* (Columbus, 1946). See also extant original copies, and *Marietta Register,* May 15, June 12, October 30, 1863. For Hammond, see Francis P. Weisenburger, "Charles Hammond, the First Great Journalist of the Old Northwest," *Ohio State Archaeological and Historical Quarterly,* XLIII (1934), 344-48. Fischer, *Revolution of American Conservatism,* 409, errs in describing David Everett, who founded the Marietta *American Friend* in 1813, as a Federalist. He had previously edited the *Boston Yankee and Pilot* and was firmly Republican. *Zanesville Express,* April 21, 28, 1813; *American Friend,* April 24, 1813.

99. *Muskingum Messenger,* September 4, 1811; Samuel W. Williams, *Sketches of Early Methodism in Ohio* (Cincinnati, 1909), 187-214; Ratcliffe, "Autobiography of Tappan."

100. Silliman to Worthington, July 29, 1808, Worthington Papers.

building and Marietta . . . retrograded as fast as it had ever advanced."[101] The local Republican press supported government policies, and Republican candidates suffered. The Federalists came within a whisker of carrying the county in 1811, and, in a special election for state senator in December 1814, they actually did so.[102]

Dissatisfaction with the conduct of foreign relations became even more pronounced in southeastern Ohio with the outbreak of war in 1812. In some counties in this area local Republican politicians feared that the departure of volunteers—almost certainly Republican—would jeopardize continued party success; hence some Federalists claimed that the authorities resorted to the draft in order to remove Federalist voters as well.[103] Antagonism to the war was most pronounced in areas settled by Quakers; traditionally Federalist when not apathetic, the Quakers had been willing to support Republican attempts to preserve peace.[104] Once war broke out and the General Assembly refused to allow Quakers exemption from military duty, they opposed the war, refused to serve, and became Federalists "as a matter of course."[105] In Belmont and Jefferson Counties Quaker votes elected Federalist representatives to the Assembly, where they protested vigorously against the war.[106] As late as 1816, the Federalists in Jefferson were considered unusually heated, while in Belmont they were still *"as a party"* running their own candidates for the legislature—and winning.[107]

The Federalist revival was most obvious not only in the Quaker areas, but also in those communities settled by orthodox New Englanders. Places like Granville, Putnam, and parts of Franklin County were all marked by acute opposition to the Republicans, whereas the more heterodox and less developed settlements of New Englanders on the

101. Samuel P. Hildreth, *Genealogical and Biographical Sketches of the Hildreth Family, 1652-1840* [Marietta, c. 1911], 191-97; Andrews, *Washington County: Centennial Address*, 64.

102. Marietta *Ohio Gazette*, March 14, May 11, June 16, 23, 1808. In 1811 the Federalist candidate for the House lost the county by 20 votes; the candidate for the Senate carried it 413-346, but ran 107 votes behind in the associated Athens County. In the regular elections of 1813 and 1814 Federalists ran less well, taking about 42% of the vote. *Marietta Register*, June 12, 1863, and *American Friend*, October 30, 1813, October 22, 1814. For the special election, see *Zanesville Express*, January 5, 1815.

103. *History of Washington County, Ohio* (Cleveland, 1881), 133-34. See also Marietta *Western Spectator*, May 12, 1813; Nahum Ward to Caleb Emerson, April 11, 1814, The Caleb Emerson Family Papers, Western Reserve Historical Society.

104. Sloane to Worthington, August 6, 1808, Worthington Papers.

105. William Cooper Howells, *Recollections of Life In Ohio, 1813-1840* (Cincinnati, 1895), 17, 33-34; Conlin, *Perkins*, 77; *Zanesville Express*, January 6, 1813; Ohio General Assembly, *Senate Journal, 1812-1813*, 187-90.

106. *Senate Journal, 1813-1814*, 340-44; Utter, *Frontier State*, 113.

107. Hammond to John C. Wright, September 19, 1816, The Papers of Charles Hammond, Ohio Historical Society; Steubenville *Western Herald*, September 20, 1816.

Western Reserve remained loyal to the administration.[108] Throughout eastern Ohio south of the Reserve the Federalists began to become more active and so revitalized the party system. As early as the presidential election of 1808, Federalists there turned out better than Republicans and seemed well-drilled in how to vote in order to deprive Madison of an electoral vote.[109] Their support was angled for by dissident Republicans, as in Coshocton in 1812,[110] and they no doubt helped to produce the statewide "amalgamationist" successes of 1808-1812. But more significant was their willingness to run their own candidates in local elections, for this aroused the Republicans to coordinated efforts and revived party conflict like that of 1802-1803. In Washington County, for instance, there was a series of strict party contests which lasted from at least 1811 until 1815. Each party named a full party ticket, which was voted for with the strictest regularity on both sides.[111] In those eastern counties where Federalists threatened success, voter turnout now passed the fifty percent level and even rose past seventy percent, a level maintained as late as 1816. Indeed, bitter partisan feeling continued briefly after the war, with both parties striving to establish strictly partisan newspapers, especially at Columbus, the new state capital. Further, after the July Fourth celebration in Zanesville in 1815, some drunken Republicans fired a cannon loaded with rocks at the Federalist celebration across the river in Putnam.[113]

The Federalists of eastern Ohio even tried to capture a congressional seat during the war. The reapportionment of 1812 had increased Ohio's congressional representation from one to six, and the Assembly decided

108. Henry Bushnell, *The History of Granville, Licking County, Ohio* (Columbus, 1889), 12; Norris F. Schneider, *Y-Bridge City* (Cleveland, 1950), 48-49, 59, 65, 70, 178; Utter, *Frontier State*, 113; Conlin, *Perkins*, 90-94, 99. Elections on the Reserve at this time were marked by local preferences rather than partisan or ticket voting. Poll books for Ashtabula County, October 1813, Vertical File Material, Ohio Historical Society.

109. Sloane to Worthington, November 13, 1808, Tappan to Worthington, September 15, 1808, Worthington Papers.

110. William Craig to James Pritchard, September 8, 1812, Tappan Papers.

111. Marietta *American Friend*, October 30, 1813, October 22, 1814.

112. Voting figures have been taken from newspapers and also, in the case of gubernatorial elections, from the General Assembly journals. Turnouts for 1815 and 1816 were assessed on the basis of the census of adult white males carried out in 1815 to 1816. The number of eligibles for 1810 was assessed on the basis of 2/9ths of the population in each county, as revealed in the census of 1810. A constant rate of increase in the population was assumed in order to estimate the number of eligibles in any intervening year. See n. 32.

113. *Zanesville Express*, July 13, 27, August 10, 1815; *Messenger*, March 29, 1815. The *Western Herald* at Steubenville was revitalized under James Wilson in 1815, and the *Ohio Monitor* was established at Columbus by David Smith in 1816. These Republican successes were countered by the establishment of a moderate Federalist press at Canton, the *Ohio Repository*, and by an abortive attempt to set up a paper called the *Columbian Gazette* at the new state capital. *Express*, April 20, 1815.

to elect these congressmen by districts rather than by general ticket. This decision immediately encouraged Federalist ambitions in the district stretching from Steubenville through the Quaker regions to Coshocton and Zanesville. Yet both parties were embarrassed by a sectional conflict within the district over the routing of the National Road: the northern area wished the Road to strike the Ohio River opposite Steubenville, while the southern portion, from St. Clairsville to Zanesville, preferred Wheeling. In 1812 and 1814 the Federalists nominated the distinguished Bezaleel Wells of Steubenville, who received much support in both northern and southern parts of the district. The Republicans, even in the Steubenville region, supported the official nominee, James Caldwell, who was identified with southern interests, although Republican candidates from Steubenville had offered to run. Standing united, the Republicans carried the day on both occasions, and it is significant that in 1812 this was the only congressional election in which the party as a whole accepted Tammany leadership; as in the presidential contest, Federalist opposition strengthened the hand of the regulars. This willingness to ignore local interest and accept official party nominations offers the best proof of the force of the national party division in eastern Ohio during the War of 1812. Partly as a result of it, the National Road was built to Wheeling, and Steubenville Republicans found they had made "a great sacrifice at the altar of party."[114]

In this struggle of the old parties, Republican nominating machinery regained, or preserved, much of its prestige and authority. Throughout eastern Ohio south of the Reserve delegate conventions were regularly summoned, and their nominations were well supported wherever the Federalist threat seemed serious. Even after 1816 delegate conventions continued to be called in several of these counties, and, if their nominations were less consistently supported as time went on, politicians clearly felt that the traditional machinery had an authority which influenced the voting behavior of many loyalists. Indeed, during this decade local conventions began to be almost as fully developed as ever in the Jacksonian period. In 1812 the first Congressional district convention was called. In 1812 the district convention's authority was accepted, though in 1816 it failed to hold the party together in the face of sectional strains. Moreover, in both district and county conventions, seats and votes began to be allotted according to the size of population in each constituent unit. Such means ensured that the people's will could be

114. *Western Herald,* September 20, 1816. See also letters of August and September, 1812, Tappan Papers; Zanesville *Express,* September 28, 1814, April 11, 1816; *Messenger,* October 5, 26, 1814.

accurately determined, and that the people's votes could be concentrated behind the candidate most acceptable to the "democracy."[115]

By 1816 some Democrats even began to consider the desirability of using delegate conventions to nominate presidential candidates. Followers of the doctrinaire Pennsylvanian William Duane argued that caucuses ought never to make a nomination, since all nominations should directly represent the popular will. Congressional caucuses were particularly objectionable, since the nomination was tantamount to election and congressmen were not only often directly interested but also far removed from their constituents. When the Steubenville newspaper argued on these lines, it was shrewdly answered by the "regular" argument that not only was party integrity the prime consideration, but a national convention might be no freer from objections:

The mode of nominating a candidate by the Republicans in Congress I have thought (if not the least exceptionable) the least inconvenient to them as a party; and I may add, the most likely to meet the public sentiment—for if we should adopt the mode of sending delegates from each state for the express purpose, the inattention of some, and the intrigues of others, would be more likely to excite irritation & scism [sic], and consequently less liable to meet the public opinion.[116]

For the time being, national conventions were no doubt difficult to organize because of transportation difficulties, yet there could be no doubt that the dictation of the congressional caucus was now widely regarded "with a kind of sullen and silent contempt." In 1816 it was tolerated, so some said, because it had merely confirmed the favorite choice of the people. As one commentator said after the 1816 election, "the caucus business is now in its last stage. I do not believe our next President will be nominated by a caucus."[117]

If the Ohio Republicans were on the point of fully realizing the party institutions of the Jacksonian period, the Federalists of the war years found themselves in an ambivalent situation. Cooperation with Republican amalgamators usually required the denunciation of party procedures. Hence they preferred to nominate their candidates in private meetings rather than use delegate conventions. Yet, whenever success

115. Hammond to J. C. Wright, September 19, 1816, Hammond Papers; *Western Herald*, September 20, 1816. The organization of conventions and their theoretical justification is fully revealed in the *Muskingum Messenger* and *Western Herald* during the campaigns of 1816, 1817, and, to a lesser degree, 1818.

116. Van Horne to Tappan, February 16, 1816, Tappan Papers. See also *Western Herald*, May 10, 31, July 5, 1816, for Republican criticism of the caucus; and *Zanesville Express*, January 25, 1815.

117. St. Clairsville *Ohio Federalist*, December 12, 1816; *Muskingum Messenger*, April 17, June 13, 1816.

seemed within their grasp, they were willing to adopt Republican techniques. In Marietta, for example, the Federalists were urged to act with greater discipline and outdo their opponents in loyalty to the official ticket.[118] Most notably, the Federalists introduced the Washington Benevolent Society, a Federalist counterpart to St. Tammany. Devoted ostensibly to promoting humanitarian welfare, this organization was openly described by its members as an attempt to promote the Federalist cause, at least by encouraging cooperation if not by actually electioneering. The Society "for the County of Washington and State of Ohio" was founded in August 1813 in Marietta, and immediately began to encourage the foundation of other branches. By May 1814 there were six branch societies in Washington County, one of them boasting 387 members in 1816, and a further branch in the New England settlement of Putnam in Muskingum County. These societies lasted until at least 1816, when the members could consider their principles to require the ending of partisan distinction.[119]

All considered, the Federalist revival must be seen as a failure. Restricted to a handful of counties, it was important more for alarming Republicans and enforcing their unity than for any lasting electoral victories. On the whole, Federalists found themselves in such a minority that they were better advised to exploit the divisions of Republicans than to take an independent stand. In Muskingum County, for example, the regular Democrats down to 1812 enjoyed "an increasing majority annually, against a host of Fedl. Tavern keepers store keepers &c. &c. whose intrigues and exertions . . . are not exceeded in any other County in the state."[120] When a Federalist paper, the *Express,* was finally established in December 1812, it carefully adopted a moderate tone and pursued a nominally non-partisan course. The reward came when Republican dissidents opposed the regular nomination in 1813, for the *Express* could act as spokesman for an amalgamationist movement which broke the regulars' control of the county. Faced by disaster, the regular newspaper, the *Muskingum Messenger,* launched a partisan crusade designed to expose the rank Federalism of the *Express,* so

118. "Pelopidas," "To Citizens of Washington County, Friends to Good Order and a Washingtonian System of Government," Caleb Emerson Family Papers, Western Reserve Historical Society.

119. The records of the Washington Benevolent Society can be found in the Caleb Emerson Family Papers. For the society elsewhere, see William A. Robinson, "The Washington Benevolent Society in New England: A Phase of Politics During the War of 1812," *Proceedings of the Massachusetts Historical Society,* XLIV (1915-1916), 274-86, and Fischer, *Revolution of American Conservatism,* 110-28, which, however, errs with regard to Ohio (p. 119).

120. Van Horne to Worthington, December 9, 1812, Worthington Papers.

hypocritically cloaked by pseudo-Republican language. At the same time the *Express* came under pressure from hard-line Federalists, who wished it to take a more openly partisan line and reveal more frankly the iniquities and incompetence of the party in power. In 1814 the Federalists ran their own ticket, but the Democratic regulars won the election. Thereafter, as in most other parts of Ohio, the Federalists returned to a policy of exploiting Republican differences rather than competing in their own right.[121]

An interesting feature of all Federalist appeals at this time was their deliberate exploitation of social as well as political dissatisfactions. The Federalists attacked the men in power and so naturally sympathised with others whose interests were too often overlooked; they shared an interest with "the clod-hoppers of the country, who consider more making their bread than of *managing* their fellow-citizens." In 1813 Hammond successfully directed his electoral appeal in Belmont County to farmers and "producers" against "lawyers, doctors, merchants and idle-young men."[122] In Muskingum County in 1815 the "Republican Farmers and Mechanics" not only refused to attend the July Fourth celebration organized by their party leaders, but even called their own rival nominating convention. The reason was, they said, the "general complaint among the laboring part of the community, who are the source of government, that the nomination heretofore has been made by a designing few, in Zanesville and its vicinity"; instead, "the honest farmer and mechanic . . . ought to rule the destinies of this country in future." The regular Republicans denounced this movement as playing the Federalist game, even if that party had no ticket in the field, but in the end this uprising of "the common people," backed by the Federalist press, succeeded in defeating the officeholding "aristocracy" which men believed dominated the county.[123]

The Federalists may have found it necessary to stay in the background in order not to damn an independent movement by their support, yet their spokesmen still acted as defenders of the people's interests against politicians who had held power too long. They supported critics of the congressional caucus of 1816. They criticized officeholders who secured new offices while holding others which disqualified them, and legislators who appointed themselves to offices they had just created. Hammond was especially severe on legislators who raised their own rates of pay, launching his thunderbolts against the notorious Compensation Law of 1816 which raised congressmen's wages to six dollars a day. Such

121. *Zanesville Express*, 1812-1816; *Muskingum Messenger*, 1810, 1811, 1813-1816.
122. *Ohio Federalist*, March 2, 1814, September 29, 1813.
123. *Zanesville Express*, September 7, July 6, and June-October, 1815.
124. *Zanesville Express*, April 11, May 30, November 21, 1816; *Ohio Federalist*,

Federalist agitation forced Democrats to take a stand against the measure, refuse re-election to those who had voted for it, and insist on pledges of repeal from all candidates.[124] Not surprisingly, therefore, radical Republicans soon discovered that a man like Hammond who called himself a Federalist might, in reality, be "a better Democrat than many of those who bawled democracy the loudest."[125] Exclusion from power had, in fact, put the Federalists in a position which made them the natural champions and supporters of all movements of discontent and resentment—a posture in some ways like that of the later Jacksonian Democrats.

Democracy, Party and Tyranny

In the course of the revitalized conflict between 1812 and 1816, the parties talked as if fundamental differences of political ideology divided them. They even refused to celebrate July Fourth together, for fear that they might become associated with unpalatable views on the meaning of the Revolution. During this debate the Federalists offered a most interesting assessment of the political state of the nation. They evidently regarded themselves as the guardians of original principles, the principles fought for in the Revolution and embodied in the United States Constitution. The dire straits to which the United States had sunk during the war with Britain demonstrated that something had gone wrong, and that the nation must once more return to the happier days of "Washingtonian" men and measures. In the course of their search for the source of degeneration, they produced a striking critique of the political system as it had operated for the last fifteen years, and they concluded that the root of the problem lay in the dogmas of Jeffersonian democracy and the prevalence of partisan behavior.[126]

The most striking fault of Republican rule, for them, was its weakness and incompetence. The Jefferson and Madison administrations had

January 5, 1814, March 28, June 13, October 31, 1816, February 5, April 9, 1818; *Western Herald,* August 23, September 13, 20, 1816.

125. James Wilson to W. D. Gallagher, October 1, 1840, Hammond Papers. Both Wilson and Hammond later opposed the Jacksonian Democrats.

126. This section is based primarily on the St. Clairsville *Ohio Federalist,* 1813-1816, the *Zanesville Express,* 1812-1816, supplemented by samples of other Federalist papers and by the *Zanesville Muskingum Messenger,* 1811, 1813-1816, and the *Steubenville Western Herald,* 1815-1816. Further insight may be derived from Charles R. King, ed., *The Life and Letters of Rufus King* (New York, 1898), especially vol. V, and William P. Cutler and Julia P. Cutler, eds., *Life, Journals and Correspondence of Manesseh Cutler* (Cincinnati, 1888), II, 43-194, 279-80, 314-21, 325-34, 345-47. For July Fourth celebrations, see Thomas E. Powell, *The Democratic Party of the State of Ohio, 1803-1912* (Columbus, 1913), I, 20.

destroyed valuable national institutions, including some that were absolutely essential for the defence of the country. Then they had completely mishandled America's relations with the warring European powers, wrongly identifying the main source of danger and approaching diplomatic problems with an inept mixture of belligerence and pusillanimity. In the end they had irresponsibly forced a defenceless country into a completely unnecessary war with Britain. The farcical extreme of irresponsibility, however, was reached closer to home, in Zanesville, where Democratic leaders cashed in on popular enthusiasm in 1812 by forming themselves into the Silk Stocking Company of volunteers, named for a famous troop of that name in the Revolutionary war. Then when Governor Return J. Meigs called the Silk Stockings to the front after Hull's surrender, these good patriots refused to go on the grounds that their services were needed at home to win the election for the administration! In this instance as in general, the country had to be saved from dire peril by loyal Federalists who served their turn in a war for which they bore no responsibility.[127]

The root cause of these failures was the willingness of Republicans to curry popular favor at the cost of national welfare. They had won power by blaming every imagined grievance on the Federalists, by exaggerating the evils of John Adams' "Reign of Terror," and by promising lower taxes. They had then tried to govern in accordance with the popular but impractical principle that economy in government was the highest good in a democratic society. Throughout they pandered to popular prejudices and disregarded their duty to tell unpalatable home truths. Instead of providing responsible and determined leadership of integrity, elected officials tended to "run yelping at the heels of the majority,"[128] sacrificing every principle before the constantly shifting mood of the people. This operated to prevent the election of truly capable leaders, for nominations generally went to the most popular rather than the most capable man. So the successful politician was the man who "always *crept* behind the public sentiment, and . . . thus contrived to be drawn into stations he was never born to occupy."[129] Men who did their duty simply were never elected.

The Federalists believed the true republican relationship between politician and constituent was, in fact, being reversed. The people should acquiesce in the decisions of their leaders, and intervene in

127. *Zanesville Express*, February 17, 1813, October 5, 12, 1814, August 15, 1816, September 3, 1822; Schneider, *Y-Bridge City*, 69.
128. Said of Alfred Kelley. Hammond to Tappan, December 14, 1814, Tappan Papers.
129. *Ohio Federalist*, September 22, 1813, quoted in *Marietta Register*, May 15, 1863. See also *Express*, February 29, 1816; *Ohio Federalist*, July 2, 1818.

politics only during elections. Their concern then should be to choose a talented, loyal, honest, and experienced man, not to dictate policies to their representative. He should be allowed to vote in the legislature "according to the dictates of his conscience, and in pursuance of a judgment maturely formed." If he voted counter to his constituents' wishes, thus rejecting "the *path* of ambition and the way [of] popularity," they should applaud "the independence of his *mind*" and "the rectitude of his heart."[130] Thus the Federalists rejected the "right of instruction" to which most Democrats paid lipservice. In 1816, while General William H. Harrison and "his Tammany squad at Cincinnati" insisted that a representative was obliged "to conform to the directions, and even as far as they can be ascertained, to the wishes and feelings of his constituents," editor Hammond argued that the representative was in a position to gain more information and form a maturer judgment than were the people at home, and so should be allowed to form his opinion on the merits of each issue debated before the legislature.[131] There was, however, some ambiguity as to whether this meant a candidate should not make his views known during an election campaign, since the people needed to have the information upon which to judge the merits of their would-be representatives.

If the Federalists really believed the people should simply re-elect a man of proven integrity, regardless of his views, then they seemed— certainly to the Democrats—to be denying the purpose of elections and representation. Yet the Federalists never proposed that popular rights be limited in any way; their panacea was to improve the moral condition of society, so that the people would judge rightly and statesmen lead nobly. Hence their emphasis on supporting societies for the encouragement of religion and the eradication of sin; hence the emphasis on the educative function of their press and the work of social uplift intended, if not performed, through the Washington Benevolent Societies.[132] If they disliked the way the political system was being operated, then they must learn from their own dictum that "History demonstrates that the form of government must accommodate to the moral and political state of the people for whom it is made."[133]

When they criticized contemporary "democracy," the Federalists made it clear they did not object to "a *legitimate* democracy," which they thought "the most desirable feature in our constitution." Their objection was to the "kind of bastard Jacobinic democracy" imported,

130. *Express,* January 20, 1813.
131. *Ohio Federalist,* September 26, 1816.
132. *Express,* December 1, April 28, 1813, February 2, April 20, 1815. See also the Constitution of the Washington Benevolent Society, Caleb Emerson Family Papers.
133. *Express,* July 29, 1814.

along with atheism, from revolutionary France. This was "a leveling, prostrating principle," subversive of the republican fabric established by the Founding Fathers.[134] The Democrats failed to make the vital distinction between a "republic" and a "democracy," insisting the United States was a republic based on representative democracy, since "the supreme power resides in the people."[135] The Democrats did not believe all men are equally capable of governing, but they did think the people should be trusted to make important decisions. "The people may err mistakenly, but never intentionally."[136] With this sort of faith, the Democrats could see no contradiction between democracy and liberty, since both were the rights of the people. They assumed such rights could be menaced only by monarchy and aristocracy; they denied the possibility of a *"Tyranny of Democracy."* [137] Yet, as the Federalists pointed out, this was exactly what the Founding Fathers had sought to safeguard against when they imposed restrictions and restraints on the power of the more popular elements in the Constitution.

Afraid, therefore, that supporters of a "Frenchified" democracy might jeopardize liberty, the Federalists turned after 1800 to the defence of balanced government and constitutional restraints. As defenders of the Constitution, they relied upon the judiciary as the safeguard of popular rights against the excesses of "Democratic" legislators. Hence they were alarmed in 1802 to hear "Jacobins . . . declare that our judges have no right to adjudge a law unconstitutional, but if the legislature pass an act, it becomes really a law, and that the people and judges must abide by it. If that be the case, our constitution is at an end, and a French convention can do no more than an American Congress."[138] So, when the issue of whether the judiciary should be "under the check of the sovereign opinion of the people" arose in Ohio, the Federalists had no hesitation in supporting the conservative Republicans. They had no doubt the judges should be kept independent of political pressures and should not be prevented from doing their duty by fear of losing popularity. As a writer in a Chillicothe paper said in 1810, the Federalists, "lawyers and all," believed that if the judiciary has not the power of declaring legislative acts unconstitutional, "a written constitution is of no real or essential value."[139] In a sense, the Federalists believed the

134. *Express*, August 10, 1814, March 16, 1815.
135. *Western Herald*, May 10, May 24, June 28, 1816; *Ohio Federalist*, May 16, June 13, 1816.
136. *Muskingum Messenger*, May 31, 1815, September 21, 1814.
137. *Messenger*, September 4, 1811, September 21, 1814.
138. Fearing to Cutler, February 19, February 3, 1802, reprinted in Cutler, *Ephraim Cutler*, 64.
139. Chillicothe *Supporter*, August 11, 1810. See also Burnet, *North-Western Territory*, 357-58.

Founding Fathers had encapsulated political truth in the Constitution and that its meaning was perfectly clear to learned men: hence they were justified in seeing "*a government of laws* and an independent judiciary" as superior to the constantly changing whims of a Democratic majority.[140]

The main threat to constitutional republicanism came not from the perversity of the "Democracy" as much as from their proclivity to see everything in party terms. The Republicans retained the people's allegiance by constantly reviving memories of the "Reign of Terror" and by branding the Federalists as "monarchists" and "aristocrats." This appeal to popular prejudices prevented the electorate from seeing political affairs in their true light. As a result, the people gave power to a group of politicians they considered their exclusive friends, and not even the greatest disasters had shaken popular faith in them. Moreover, party machinery worked to perpetuate these inferior men in power. Devices like conventions created the illusion of popular control, and made it difficult for Republican voters to oppose the nomination if they disliked it, since they were afraid of appearing "singular." This deprived the community of the services not only of the excellent men who happened to be labelled "Federalists" but also those who had alienated the party managers by their independence of mind. If conventions had to be held, the Federalists suggested, nominations should at least be considered recommendations rather than binding decisions, and the people should be encouraged to feel free to reject the advice of those who usually controlled the party.[141]

As it was, conventions too often served merely to keep power within a few restricted hands. The whole object of such nominations, it was argued, was to restrict the voters' freedom of choice in performing "the only sovereign act" permitted them. "Every attempt to abridge the freeness of suffrage . . .," said one Federalist, "is treason against the community, and subversive of genuine republicanism—all Tammany principles and delegated tickets are a direct attack on this privilege."[142] Moreover, even popularly chosen conventions were often devices merely to ratify a ticket already secretly chosen by the party managers. This was particularly apparent in Muskingum County, the chief stronghold of Republican party regularity throughout the war; for here "certain gentlemen about Zanesville, men of wealth and holders of offices[,] used to appoint meetings of the people to make arrangements previous to the elections." Controlling the party machinery, these gentlemen saw

---

140. *Express,* July 11, 1816. See also *Ohio Federalist,* September 5, 1816.
141. *Express,* September 15, 1813, October 5, 1814, August 3, 1815.
142. *Express,* August 25, 1813, August 31, 1814.

that their friends gained ''good snug fat offices,'' and behaved as though they had a prescriptive right, as *legitimate* as the claims of European monarchs, to continue controlling the process of nomination.[143] Thus, in effect, party machinery operated to create a new aristocracy, which was governed by ''certain partialities and family sympathies'' and excluded from nomination ''all that were not within the pale of their peculiar and favorite influence.'' So the equal rights of the people were ignored, and the principle of rotation in office honored only in the breach.[144]

This loyalty to men established as party leaders both locally and nationally tended to produce not only ''aristocracy,'' but also potential tyranny. For party men tended to support their leaders; they would ''give their silent vote to carry into effect every hint of their master.'' A democrat ''reprobates *'the divine right of kings,'* but would cloath [*sic*] the head of his party with all the attributes of infallibility.'' This submissiveness prepared the way for ''some favorite Democrat,'' contemptuous of the interests of his country, to ''rise up (Bonaparte like)'' and establish an absolute rule.[145] This remark of 1802 had even more point a decade later when many Ohio Democrats seemed to favor the French Emperor. As a Federalist editor wrote, anyone who admires Bonaparte ''cannot be a republican, or a friend to equal rights, but is ready to join some such adventurer as him in the prostration of his country's liberties.''[146] Already in 1815 Federalists were watching Andrew Jackson's meteoric rise to fame with some apprehension.[147]

Partisan attitudes could also lead to tyranny by encouraging discrimination and oppression. Party men damned as traitors all who would not accept party dictation, even Revolutionary heroes, and so good men were excluded from office. Moreover, the power of government was abused, as when the draft was used to discriminate against Federalists or when tax assessors chose ''to oppress the refractory minority people.'' The Democrats may not have passed laws like the Alien and Sedition Acts, but they had tried to suppress dissidence by the force of government influence and the pressure of majority opinion.[148] Such intolerance

143. *Express*, September 7, 1815. See also August 3, September 1, 1813.
144. *Express*, September 29, 1813, August 15, 29, 1816.
145. Fearing to Cutler, February 3, 1802, reprinted in Cutler, *Ephraim Cutler*, 64; *Ohio Federalist*, June 29, 1814.
146. *Express*, June 1, 1815; *Ohio Federalist*, June 8, 29, 1814. For an example of unrestrained admiration for Napoleon, see Henry Brush to Brown, June 17, 1815, Brown Papers.
147. *Express*, April 20, May 18, 1815; Heald, *Wells*, 127.
148. *Express*, November 16, January 19, 1814; *Messenger*, May 31, 1815. For objections to the arbitrary execution of the draft, see *Express*, July 28, October 27, 1813; N. T.

arose because Democrats were so convinced of their own righteousness and rightfulness that they doubted the legitimacy of opposition, especially at times of national crisis. One of their editors was shrewdly described as belonging to

that class of politicians who identify their party with the country, and who consider every measure directed against the party as a species of high treason. He looks upon the agents employed or appointed to administer the government, as the government itself, and hence he interprets every attempt to expose the imbecility and wretchedness of the administration, as an attack upon the government.[149]

The Federalists, in fact, insisted on a careful distinction between the system of government and the men who administered it, and, in so doing, made an important contribution to the development of the concept of a loyal opposition. Hammond later said that he began the *Ohio Federalist* because he objected to the Democratic doctrine that criticism must not be allowed in time of war; so "by the exercise of my rights I practically demonstrated their existence."[150] This Federalist insistence on the right to express opposition in the face of intolerance was, indeed, almost as important a contribution to political liberty as that of the Jeffersonians in 1798-1800. Ironically, it also helped to ensure the ultimate acceptance of the legitimacy of political parties.[151]

Republican intolerance of the Federalists and mistrust of their purposes clearly arose from their identification with England at a time of war with that power. Initially, many Republicans had hoped that Federalists would drop their opposition to the administration for the duration, and the fact that they continued to voice criticisms was seen as irrefutable evidence of Federalist subservience to Britain. They were assumed to admire the institutions of that country, where "office and emolument is exclusively confined to a pampered nobility, clergy, and pensioners of the crown, who have . . . no reluctance at furnishing the crown liberally with the national resources."[152] This was typical of the way in which the identification of Republicanism with France and Federalism with Britain tended to heighten the sense of difference between the two parties: the party conflict seemed to represent but a

Clough to Emerson, March 18, 1813, Caleb Emerson Family Papers.

149. *Ohio Federalist*, June 29, 1814. See also *Muskingum Messenger*, June 15, July 6, 1814.

150. *Ohio Federalist*, July 2, 1818. See also *Express*, March 31, 1813, July 20, 1814.

151. This aspect of the subject is overlooked by Richard Hofstadter in his excellent *The Idea of a Party System: The Rise of Legitimate Opposition in the United States, 1780-1840* (Berkeley, 1969).

152. *Muskingum Messenger*, December 22, 1813, May 25, 1814; Van Horne to Worthington, December 12, 1811, December 9, 1812, Worthington Papers; Van Horne to Tappan, February 16, 1816, Tappan Papers.

continuation of the struggle taking place in Europe. This identification arose more from suspicion of the other side's motives than from an accurate diagnosis of its outlook. The Republicans, or most of them, had no great liking for Napoleon, even if he was the great self-made man of the age, but they saw him as fighting America's battles against British usurpation, and his downfall in 1814 was therefore to be deplored. The Federalists themselves believed that "a war with England is not so much to be deprecated as an Alliance (its necessary consequence) with France," for France had shown an insatiable appetite for gobbling up friendly republics.[153] With the fate of the world in balance and the outcome of an age of revolutions to be decided, both parties felt they could not allow the fate of the Republic to be left in the hands of those whose purposes were, at least potentially, un-American.

Thus, ultimately, both partisan standpoints had the same end in view. As moderates on both sides saw, in the last resort both parties in Ohio were loyal to the independence and integrity of the United States. Most Federalists in Ohio, outside the Quaker areas, supported the war, especially when the nation's integrity seemed most threatened in the latter part of 1814. Indeed, many Ohio Federalists were undoubtedly embarrassed by the apparent disloyalty and disunionism of fellow Federalists in New England.[154] At bottom the differences between Democrats and Federalists were not fundamental, since both sides accepted the sanctity of the Constitution, the value of the Union, and the practice of democratic elections. As the *Zanesville Express* insisted, Jefferson had been right when he said "we are all federalists, we are all republicans": in the simplest sense of those terms, almost all Americans were.[155] In that realization, and in the growing belief on the part of many moderates that partisan attachments should be sacrificed for the sake of union, lay the bases for the subsequent all-too-brief Era of Good Feelings.

Yet, if there was general agreement on the basic outlines of the federal republic, the disagreement over aspects of its working was still very real, and in a sense has never been settled. In the decades which followed, politicians increasingly emphasized the populistic character of the polity and paid lip-service to the will of the sovereign people; yet all were quick to emphasize and use constitutional restraints on the will of the majority when it suited their purposes. The United States has, in fact, remained ambivalent in its politcal character. American democracy has always been distinctly more populistic in its style and procedure

153. Benjamin Ives Gilman to Winthrop Sergeant, December 25, 1812, Rice Papers; *Express*, December 30, 1812.

154. *Express*, April 21, 1813, November 16, 1814.

155. *Express*, May 11, 1814, December 8, 1813; *Ohio Federalist*, September 12, 1816.

than other democracies of the West. Yet the United States has never been a "democracy" in the sense that the will of the majority rules, since that will has always been restrained by constitutional protections afforded to minorities and to individuals. Of course, in the long run the popular majority has usually been able to see its own view of the meaning of the Constitution adopted, but that view has itself been tempered by an awareness of the value of the liberties fought for and won by the Revolutionary generation. In a sense the Federalists were right: the United States remains a "republic" rather than a "democracy."

The Child of Revolution?

A prime purpose of this essay has been to emphasize the extent to which party politics substantially like those of the Jacksonian period existed in Ohio even before the battle of New Orleans. Already in the Jeffersonian era politicians had to keep their eye on public opinion, instead of feeling confident that a deferential people would follow wherever they led. Populistic appeals were made to voters, and popular discontents exploited. Rotation in office was advocated, but the enjoyment of office reserved for members of the victorious party. Party managers were already regarded as the new political elite. Many newspapers had become proponents of a strict party line, designed to ensure the continuing loyalty of party supporters. Devices of party organization usually associated with Jacksonian Democracy were already being widely used; when county conventions were called in the later period, they were seen as a return to the good old Jeffersonian techniques of ensuring political righteousness, while the attempt to introduce more extensive, centralized control of the Democratic party in 1833-1834 was identified as an attempt to reintroduce St. Tammany.[156] Even the name "Democrat" was not new, but an attempt to identify the Jacksonians with Jefferson's party. Moreover, the level of popular involvement, as indicated by voter turnout, on several occasions in the earlier period matched that of Jacksonian days, with the important difference that presidential elections in the later period drew out as many voters as did

156. *St. Clairsville Gazette*, February-October, 1826; Zanesville *Democratic Union*, August 2, 1834; *Columbus Sentinel*, May 9, 1833; Campbell, *Biographical Sketches*, 151-52. See also Harry R. Stevens, *The Early Jackson Party in Ohio* (Durham, 1955), 155. The significance of the early development of the convention is overlooked by James Stanton Chase, "Jacksonian Democracy and the Rise of the Nominating Convention," *Mid-America*, XLV (1963), 229-49.

local contests.[157] The Second Party System in Ohio developed more thorough organizational techniques basically because the electorate was more evenly divided between the national parties than in the Jeffersonian era, and because by the late 1830s the main divisions over state issues corresponded closely with the party cleavage over national politics.

But if there was less difference between the politics of Jeffersonian Democracy and those of Jacksonaian Democracy than historians often assume, it remains true that parties in the earlier era were less firmly based. After all, the Jacksonian parties in Ohio tended to maintain an existence even when the issues which had given them meaning had passed away, while the First Party System apparently disintegrated in an Era of Good Feelings. This decline of party behavior after 1816 obviously owed much to the fact that many Americans were unwilling to accept the permanence of party divisions. On both the Republican and Federalist sides, men had clearly demonstrated their unease at submitting to party dictation and their disquiet at some of its consequences; and they assumed that party differences had ended with the coming of peace in Europe and the growth of a new spirit of nationalism at home. Yet the disappearance of party feeling is partly an illusion, since the old passions and loyalties persisted for many Ohioans, while, in any case, within a decade new party divisions had appeared. For many politicians and voters, this new party system was but a revival of the old contests, with the difference that now the scantily-disguised Federalist menace was far more formidable since it drew on the experience and support of so many former Jeffersonian Republicans.[158]

While some Ohio historians have insisted on seeing the development of a new kind of politics in the Jacksonian era, others have been perfectly willing to accept that a democratic form of politics was created at an earlier stage in Ohio history. They have seen this as arising from the democratizing force of the frontier experience, which first created democracy in the West and then passed it on, in the 1820s, to the rest of the nation.[159] These conditions bred also a liking for Jeffersonian democracy, especially since the widespread availability of cheap land

157. Richard P. McCormick. "New Perspectives on Jacksonian Politics," *American Historical Review*, LXV (1960). 288-301. which, however, concentrates upon statewide totals and overlooks the Congressional race of 1803, which on any reckoning saw a turnout of well over 50 percent.

158. See Donald J. Ratcliffe. "The Role of Voters and Issues in Party Formation: Ohio, 1824," *The Journal of American History*, LIX (1973), 847-70.

159. Downes, *Frontier Ohio;* Barnhart, *Valley of Democracy*. The development of a new style of politics, "Jacksonian Democracy," is argued by. among others, Francis P. Weisenburger, *The Passing of the Frontier in Ohio, 1825-1850*, vol. III of Carl Wittke, ed., *The History of the State of Ohio* (Columbus, 1941).

made it relatively easy for most men to become property owners, thus reducing the influence of the large proprietors. From the democratic constitution set up on attaining statehood inevitably arose a populistic style of politics, if not necessarily of party politics.[160]

Yet the "frontier" thesis finally fails to satisfy, if only because it is lacking in perspective. After all, the *French* frontiersmen of Vincennes, Illinois, and Detroit somehow were untouched by the liberal, democratic influences of this environment, for they preferred arbitrary rule to the greater demands of representative self-government.[161] In most practical ways, the needs of frontier society were best suited by a continuance of direct rule, as even the Republican advocates of statehood in Ohio acknowledged.[162] As for the prevalence of Jeffersonianism, that was a characteristic Ohio shared with most agricultural areas of the country, especially those which were uncommercialized or expanding rapidly, including many areas which had long passed the frontier stage.[163] Indeed, what happened in Ohio generally reflected developments elsewhere. Its constitution was copied from those of other states, while its generous suffrage provisions were no more liberal than those already being introduced in the East. The party division was basically derived from national affairs, while the political machinery the parties adopted had been created in the seaboard states. Even the great *state* issue debated in the first decade of statehood was a matter of controversy in other states too, and the conclusion that the "frontiersmen" in Ohio came to was just as conservative and anti-majoritarian as the general verdict of the nation as a whole.[164]

The formative influences upon the development of a party system in Ohio were, in fact, common to the American people everywhere. The belief in the value of representative self-government was central to the Anglo-American political tradition, and it was in defence of that principle that Americans had finally chosen to break their ties with Britain. In the process, the Revolution created a belief in popular responsibility, which found expression at first primarily in the doctrine that the people were the proper constituent power in all free governments. But this

160. Smith, *St. Clair*, I, 197-205, II, 394-96, 417-20, 433; Conlin, *Perkins*, 54; Downes, *Frontier Ohio*, 55-88, 147-252.

161. Bond, "Correspondence of Symmes," 290; Smith, *St. Clair*, II, 489; Downes, *Frontier Ohio*, 172-75; Barnhart, *Valley of Democracy*, 161-63.

162. Andrews, *Washington County: Centennial Address*, 28; Massie, *Massie*, 167; Bond, *Foundations*, 461.

163. Fischer, *Revolution of American Conservatism*, 211-18; Dauer, *Adams Federalists*, 7, 18-25, 275-87.

164. Barnhart, *Valley of Democracy*, 157-58; Williamson, *American Suffrage*, 117-222; Cunningham, *Jeffersonian Republicans; Ellis, *Jeffersonian Crisis*.

belief also encouraged a significant widening of the regular suffrage and the spread of the idea that in American conditions a broad manhood suffrage was appropriate. With these developments, and the accompanying increase in popular participation in politics, came the development of party formations in the various state legislatures during the first decade of independence.[165] Whatever the Federalists may have said later about Jacobin influences, the development of some sort of party action seems to have been inevitable in a political system based on "frequent elections by the mass of our citizens, in whom the sovereignty of this happy government resides."[166]

The growth of *national* parties was prompted when the Constitution of 1789 established a center of national power which could be captured by whatever forces managed to win enough popular elections. At the same time the controversies over liquidating the financial problems created by the Revolutionary War, and over adopting a suitable national posture during Europe's revolutionary conflicts, ensured that opinion throughout the country would be divided and control of the new center of power seem of transcendent importance. Inevitably, Americans resorted once more to the techniques of coordinating action, attracting public support and winning power that they had used in the struggle for independence. Committees of correspondence, popular tribunals, and public demonstrations were pressed into service once more, together with other techniques more appropriate to the new constitutional situation. The result was the development of a party system which few people really approved of, but which was to prove the most effective means of reconciling the internal antagonisms of the nation. Ironically, the Age of Revolution was to end, not with an agreement about the character of the new republic, but with the development of a system for ensuring, as far as possible, that differences and divisions did not destroy the republic the Revolution had created.

165. Jackson T. Main, *Political Parties Before The Constitution* (Chapel Hill, 1973).
166. *Muskingum Messenger,* May 25, 1814.

ANDREW R. L. CAYTON

"A Quiet Independence": The Western Vision of the Ohio Company

Speculative schemes and idealistic visions merged in post-Revolutionary America to produce many new towns in the rapidly expanding Northwest Territory. A group of New England veterans of the American Revolution, organized as the Ohio Company of Associates, established the first such community on April 7, 1788, at the confluence of the Ohio and Muskingum rivers, some 200 miles downstream from Pittsburgh. They called their town Marietta. Within the next several years, many of the 594 associates of the Ohio Company cleared land, built homes, settled their families, and sought fortune and security in or near this city. Above all, they attempted to protect and stablize their financial and ideological investment in what they called "the western world" by providing Marietta with a pervasive and enduring form and character.[1]

Indeed, the construction of Marietta was the culmination of a long contemplated effort by a highly organized elite to establish a community designed to secure individual fortune within the context of communal order. In a 1790 letter seeking to obtain increased protection from Indians, to gain the opening of the Mississippi River, and to assuage eastern fears about depopulation, Ohio Company Superintendent Rufus Putnam told Congressman Fisher Ames that the "Genus" and "education" of no other people was "as favorable to a

Andrew R. L. Cayton is a Ph.D. candidate in history at Brown University and an Instructor in the history department at Harvard University.

1. "A Contemporary Account of Some Events," in James M. Varnum, *An Oration Delivered at Marietta, July 4, 1788* (Newport, 1788), in Samuel Prescott Hildreth, *Pioneer History: Being an Account of the First Examination of the Ohio Valley and the Early Settlement of the Northwest Territory* (Cincinnati, 1848), 515. Hildreth is a detailed account of the founding of Marietta by an early resident. For a concise, modern narrative, see Beverley W. Bond, Jr., *The Foundations of Ohio*, Carl Wittke, ed., *The History of the State of Ohio* (5 vols., Columbus, 1941), I, 275-90.

republican Government" as that of Massachusetts. But in the 1780s Putnam and his colleagues had been less sanguine about the "morrals, relegion and policy" of the East. Then, without the reassuring presence of Putnam's friend and mentor George Washington as president under a strong federal Constitution, some Americans appeared to the founders of the Ohio Company to be repudiating or distorting the tenets of republican government as they defined them. Bitter frustration and disgust with their perception of the United States in the 1780s made the development of Marietta crucial to the associates. Far more than a source of profit, the city was to serve as "a wide model" for the "regular" and "judicious" settlement of the West.[2]

In the East, the veterans had sensed the imminent disintegration of their inseparable personal and public worlds. Believing themselves poorly paid for military service in the Revolution, outraged at a perceived loss of status when they had expected increased respect and prestige, self-pitying but genuinely frightened by post-Revolutionary America, the associates of the Ohio Company sought to escape what they saw as the contentious anarchy of the East and to bring order and stability to their lives in a prosperous but controlled West. Mixing materialism and idealism inextricably, the Marietta founders' negative view of their economic and social positions in the 1780s nurtured positive hopes for a certain, harmonious existence based on a regular city and landed wealth.

Assuming that stability could be produced by a relatively egalitarian dispersal of land among the virtuous and by the example of an orderly city, this self-appointed elite hoped to control the evolution of western society. In this task, they clearly failed. For the boats carrying the people who would settle and develop the West generally passed by Marietta, their passengers perhaps put off by its very regularity and pretensions and interested in individual fortune without the elitist notions of stability and harmony that guided the Marietta founders. Yet, if the story of early Marietta is ultimately one of failure, it nonetheless provides a crucial example of the motives of some early immigrants to the Northwest Territory.

Historians have generally seen the Ohio Company, which was

2. Rufus Putnam to Fisher Ames, 1790, Rowena Buell, ed., *The Memoirs of Rufus Putnam and Certain Official Papers and Correspondence* (Boston, 1903), 246; Manasseh Cutler, *An Explanation of the Map which delineated that part of the Federal Lands, Comprehended between Pennsylvania, the Rivers Ohio and Scioto, and Lake Erie; confirmed to the United States by sundry Tribes of Indians, in the Treaties of 1784 and 1786, and now ready for Settlement* (Salem, 1787), 14.

organized as a joint stock corporation by eleven veterans of the
American Revolution on March 1, 1786, in Boston, as the climax of a
persistent but basically economic effort by New England officers to
obtain payment for their wartime service. Certainly, director Manasseh Cutler and secretary Winthrop Sargent's handling of the
purchase of 1,500,000 acres from Congress in 1787 and their close
association with speculators like William Duer and speculations
like the Scioto Company tend to confirm that judgment. No one can
doubt that the associates were interested in getting land and money.
Many, like Alexander Hamilton, had no immediate intention of settling in the West. Because the company seems so much like a speculative venture, its rhetoric, while not without defenders, especially
among local historians, has often been dismissed as propaganda
designed to gain favors from Congress or to attract settlers to the
purchase. One of the five directors of the company, Manasseh Cutler, even found something redeeming about Shays' Rebellion:
"These commotions," he told Winthrop Sargent, "will tend to promote our plan and incline well-disposed persons to become adventurers." But it was not merely the force of their rhetoric that the
associates believed would convince other people to join. "For," as
Cutler himself noted about Massachusetts in 1786, "who would wish
to live under a Government subject to such tumults and confusions."
Generally believing the assumptions and fears that lay behind
much of their exaggerated public prose and anxious private letters,
the associates expected many others to be receptive to their charac-
terizations of eastern society and their hopes for the West. They did
not reject American society so much as they wanted to stabilize it.
Largely soldiers or their sons who were gambling on building, or
rebuilding, a more predictable life, the active participants in the
westward migration were indeed speculators — in the future as well
as land. Like Captain Joseph Rogers, who had "served honorably
through the Revolution" and then resided some time with his
friends," these veterans believed that they had "cast" their "Bread
upon the Waters of the Revolution" in vain, and now, like "many an
Old Soldier," marched "toward the setting sun in hopes to find it in
the West."[3]

3. Manasseh Cutler to Winthrop Sargent, October 8, 1786, quoted in Sidney Kaplan, "Veteran Officers and Politics in Massachusetts, 1783-1787," *William and Mary
Quarterly,* IX (1952), 43; Joseph Rogers is quoted in George J. Blazier, ed., *Joseph
Barker: Recollections of the First Settlement of Ohio* (Marietta, 1958), 11. The associates are portrayed as speculative entrepreneurs in Sidney Kaplan, "Pay, Pension,
and Power: Economic Grievances of the Massachusetts Officers of the Revolution,"
Boston Public Library Quarterly, III (1951), 15-34, 127-42, and Kaplan, "Veteran

The earliest origins of Marietta lay in the increasing material and social distress felt by its founders. Insistent upon describing themselves as "reputable, industrious, well-informed" men with status in society, the members of the Ohio Company assured congressmen that "many of the subscribers are men of very considerable property and respectable characters." If the associates were certain that they were "distinguished for wealth, education, and virtue," events and other people appeared to them to be threatening that crucial self-image. Long-standing discontents with the evolution of New England society came to a head in the 1780s as the future Mariettans saw ubiquitous challenges to their security and social status.[4]

Generally sons of substantial farmers and artisans, most of the future emigrants came from towns in an arc around Boston, in eastern Connecticut, and in Rhode Island undergoing the pangs of commercial growth and the disruption of what seemed in retrospect, at least, to have been a more personal, communal world. Such predominantly agricultural towns as Pomfret, Connecticut, and Stoughton, Massachusetts, experienced increasing population accompanied by a growing number of neighborhood disputes and stronger connections with the more commercial and cosmopolitan worlds of Boston and Providence.

Officers," 29-57. For discussions of the congressional negotiations and land grant, with emphasis on the speculative nature of the Ohio Company, see Joseph S. Davis, "William Duer, Entrepreneur, 1747-1799," *Essays in the Early History of American Corporations* (2 vols., Cambridge, 1917), II, 131-45; Merrill Jensen, *The New Nation: A History of the United States during the Confederation, 1781-1789* (New York, 1950), 355-59; Richard H. Kohn, *Eagle and Sword: The Federalists and the Creation of the Military Establishment in America, 1783-1802* (New York, 1975), 99-100; Shaw Livermore, *Early American Land Companies* (New York, 1939), 136-46; and Frederick Merk, *History of the Westward Movement* (New York, 1978), 104-05. Not all historians have seen the associates as economic men, however. The most complete and admiring study of the motives of the associates is Archer Butler Hulbert's introduction to *The Records of the Original Proceedings of the Ohio Company* (2 vols., Marietta, 1917). Hulbert viewed the Company as the democratic, "uniquely unselfish and thoroughly American" (I, ciii) carrier of New England idealism, piety, and patriotism to the West. Other writers who emphasize the communal nature and New England origins of the company include: Ray Allen Billington, *Westward Expansion: A History of the American Frontier*, 3rd ed. (New York, 1967), 212-20, esp., 218; Beverley W. Bond Jr., *The Civilization of the Old Northwest* (New York, 1934), 9-12; Daniel Boorstin, *The Americans: The National Experience* (New York, 1965), 53-54; Ralph Brown, *Historical Geography of the United States* (New York, 1948), 215-19; Thomas D. Clark, *Frontier America: The Story of the Westward Movement* (New York, 1959), 149-51; and Malcolm J. Rohrbough, *The Trans-Appalachian Frontier: People, Societies, and Institutions, 1775-1850* (New York, 1978), 66-70.

    4. Varnum, *An Oration*, 507; Manasseh Cutler to Nathan Dane, March 16, 1787, William Parker Cutler and Julia Perkins Cutler, eds., *Life, Journals, and Correspondence of Rev. Manasseh Cutler* (2 vols., Cincinnati, 1888), I, 507.

The Inauguration of Territorial Government at Marietta, Ohio. ﹙SOCIETY COLLECTION﹚

Certainly, economic difficulties haunted several future associates who came of age in the troubled 1760s. Manasseh Cutler's experience as a young Yale graduate was not uncommon. A native of Killingly, Connecticut, a town beset with "wrangles and church feuds," Cutler unsuccessfully tried life as a merchant on Martha's Vineyard before hesitantly turning to the ministry in the late 1760s. Rufus Putnam and Benjamin Tupper, both the youngest of several sons, found their efforts at farming interrupted by service in the French and Indian War and by the necessity of supplementing their income through milling and tanning. Such insecurity combined with land scarcity to cause many future Ohioans to consider migration from New England in the early 1770s. Hoping to receive land as compensation for their military service, the cousins Israel and Rufus Putnam participated in a surveying expedition to the Mississippi River in 1773. They were intensely disappointed by the Crown's decision to refuse their petition.[5]

5. Ellen D. Larned. *Historic Gleanings in Windham County, Connecticut* ﹙Providence, 1899﹚, 76; Cutlers, *Manasseh Cutler,* I, 73, 89. See also, Buell, *Rufus Putnam.* 7, 53; Samuel Prescott Hildreth, *Biographical and Historical Memoirs of the Early Pioneer Settlers of Ohio* ﹙Cincinnati, 1852﹚; and Julia Perkins Cutler, *The Founders of Ohio* ﹙Cincinnati, 1888﹚. The future Mariettans' problems and frustrations were part

The American Revolution dramatically raised the expectations of such frustrated men. Among the first to respond to Lexington and Concord, the future emigrants with near unanimity enthusiastically participated in the 1775 siege of Boston. Not only did the war provide the identifiable enemy and social solidarity in the battle to "restore peace, tranquility . . . Union and liberty" to America, it confirmed at a critical moment the future pioneers' previously insecure status as leaders in personal communities. For the Ohio Company directors Rufus Putnam and Benjamin Tupper of Massachusetts, James Varnum of Rhode Island, and Samuel Holden Parsons of Connecticut, arrived at Boston as chief officers of local and state militia, indisputable evidence of their social standing and the respect and confidence of their neighbors. Further military service, in the officers' minds at least, only accorded them formal deference within the strictly hierarchical society of the army.[6]

In the end, however, fighting for American independence and republican ideals seemed to make economic and social disaster a distinct possibility for many of the future emigrants. Sometimes enfeebled and rarely paid, many of those who served their new country spent family fortunes in mere survival. The failure of Congress to pay them, claimed Major-General Samuel Holden Parsons, was intensely frustrating to men who "have expended their estates, have

of a larger pattern in New England society resulting from an expanding population and declining resources, especially land. See, Richard Bushman, *From Puritan to Yankee: Character and the Social Order in Connecticut, 1690-1765* (New York, 1967); Philip J. Greven, Jr., *Four Generations: Population, Land and Family in Colonial Andover, Massachusetts* (Cambridge, 1970); Robert A. Gross, *The Minutemen and Their World* (New York, 1976), 10-29, 66-108; James A. Henretta, *The Evolution of American Society, 1700-1815: An Interdisciplinary Analysis* (Lexington, 1973), 5-39, 114-15; and Kenneth Lockridge, "Land, Population and the Evolution of New England Society, 1630-1790," *Past and Present*, No. 39 (April, 1968), 62-80.

6. [James Mitchell Varnum], "Ministerial Oppression, with The Battle of Bunker Hill: A Tragedy," [1775], The Harris Collection, The John Hay Library, Brown University, Providence, Rhode Island. The future of Mariettans' revolutionary motives seem to correspond with the patterns outlined in Rowland Berthoff and John M. Murrin, "Feudalism, Communalism, and the Yeoman Freeholder: The American Revolution Considered as a Social Accident," Stephen G. Kurtz and James H. Hutson, eds., *Essays on the American Revolution* (Chapel Hill, 1973), 256-88; Richard L. Bushman, "Massachusetts Farmers and the Revolution," Richard M. Jellison, ed., *Society, Freedom, and Conscience: The American Revolution in Virginia, Massachusetts, and New York* (New York, 1976), 77-124; Gross, *The Minutemen*, 30-66; Kenneth Lockridge, "Social Change and the Meaning of the American Revolution," *Journal of Social History*, 6 (Summer, 1973), 403-09; Stephen E. Patterson, *Political Parties in Revolutionary Massachusetts* (Madison, 1973); Gordon S. Wood, *The Creation of the American Republic, 1776-1787* (New York, 1969), 46-124; and Michaĕl Zuckerman, *Peaceable Kingdoms: New England Towns in the Eighteenth Century* (New York, 1970), 220-58.

hazarded their lives and health, and sacrificed the just expectations of their families for the salvation of their country."[7]

Although their fears were often exaggerated, the difficulties of the future associates did seem to escalate in the 1780s. More crucial than what was actually happening to these soldiers was their perception of what was happening to them. By their standards, postwar America seemed unfamiliar and unfair. A successful lawyer and a member of the Connecticut legislature before the war, Parsons, for example, believed himself "nearly impoverished" and in bad health at its end. Despite his election to the Connecticut legislature in the 1780s, his fortune consisted solely of the government securities he received in lieu of pay and his hopes of profiting from "the future disposal of the land" he surveyed in 1786 in a "subordinate" position. "Insolvent" despite his investment in the Ohio Company, Parsons died in 1789 bewailing "the multiplied troubles which have fallen to my lot."[8]

Unsuccessful "mercantile" ventures were not infrequent, as the former soldiers found it difficult to adjust to a more complex economy. Colonel Ebenezer Spoat, a prewar farmer of substantial means, for example, tried his hand at "mercantile affairs" in the 1780s. "Being entirely unacquainted" with trade and having "no taste for his new business . . . in a short time he failed; swallowing up his wife's patrimony, as well as his resources."[9]

While not all of the future associates suffered financially in the 1780s, many complained bitterly of poor opportunities and inequities. Solomon Drowne, a Rhode Island veteran and future associate, spent several years preparing for a medical career only to find no demand for his services. Reduced to running a pharmacy with his sisters, the ambitious Drowne protested being "superseded or supplanted in so many instances, or to experience almost every species of slight and neglect." "Rust and obscurity" seemed his fate, he lamented, "after devoting the best years of my life to study, and spending a pretty good estate to qualify myself in the best possible manner for the exercise of an important position."[10]

7. Samuel Holden Parsons to Colonel Root, August 29, 1779, Charles S. Hall, *Life and Letters of Samuel Holden Parsons: Major-General in the Continental Army and Chief Judge of the Northwestern Territory, 1737-1789* (Binghamton, 1905), 266.

8. Hall, *Samuel Holden Parsons*, 581; Parsons to his wife, October 18, 1788, Hall, *Parsons*, 533.

9. Hildreth, *Biographical and Historical Memoirs*, 235.

10. [William Drowne], "A Brief Sketch of the Life of Solomon Drowne, M.D.," The Drowne Papers, The Rhode Island Historical Society, Providence, R.I.; Solomon Drowne to Theodore Foster, July 25, 1790, William Drowne, "A Brief Sketch," 71. See

Not the lack of profit but the lack of prestige that followed from his relative poverty was what really rankled Drowne. A graduate of Brown University, a man who had studied in Philadelphia and Europe and dined with Thomas Jefferson, Drowne fretted that his economic failure was undoing his quest for social prominence. Some historians have criticized the associates of the Ohio Company for their seemingly crass pursuit of land, their angry demands for pay from Congress and the states, and their careful attention to the fluctuations in the price of the securities they received in lieu of pay. The associates were indeed frantic for money, but their "grasping" was essentially the pursuit of "a quiet independence" that would accord them a position consonant with the standing they believed they held, or should hold, in society. To Commodore Abraham Whipple, a future Mariettan, his approaching "misery and ruin" were incompatible with his election to the Rhode Island legislature in the 1780s. A respected man hardly mortgaged his farm "for a temporary support," had it sued out of his possession, and then faced the prospect of being "turned out into the world . . . destitute of a house or a home," even if he had lost much of his money fighting for his country's independence. To Whipple, his land was the foundation of his personal independence, of his position as a recognizable community leader.[11]

In 1783, feeling neglected and slighted, the officers of the Continental army organized the Society of the Cincinnati, partly to serve as a lobbying agency to get some sort of payment from Congress, but primarily to perpetuate the formal status they had held as army officers into a socially and economically uncertain postwar society. The medal given to each of its members revealed their intense longing for order, tranquility, and respect. The decoration

also, Julia Perkins Cutler, *Life and Times of Ephraim Cutler* (Cincinnati, 1890), 15; and Rufus Putnam to George Washington, April 5, 1784, Buell, *Rufus Putnam,* 224-25.

11. "Petition of settlers of Belpre, Ohio to George Washington," March 14, 1793, The Samuel Prescott Hildreth Papers, I, The Dawes Memorial Library, Marietta College, Marietta, Ohio; "Copy of an Address from Abraham Whipple to Congress," The Whipple Papers, The Rhodes Island Historical Society. Status anxiety was suggested as a motive for the associates' migration in Jacob Burnet, *Notes on the Early Settlement of the Northwestern Territory* (Cincinnati, 1847), 45. For other examples of the postwar difficulties of veterans, see, Frederick S. Alvis, Jr., ed., *Guide to the Microfilm Edition of the Winthrop Sargent Papers* (Boston, 1965), 10; Roger J. Champagne, *Alexander McDougall and the American Revolution in New York* (Schnectady, 1975), 199-200, 216; Cutlers, *Manasseh Cutler,* I, 155; and especially, George Washington to the Secretary of War, October 2, 1782, Louise B. Dunbar, *A Study of "Monarchical" Tendencies in the United States from 1776 to 1801* (New York, 1970), 47. Kohn, *Eagle and Sword,* contains an unsympathetic analysis of the officers' response to their problems; see Kohn, 9-39.

featured Cincinnatus, the Roman hero, in a field and "his wife standing at the door of their cottage; near it with a plough and instruments of husbandry." Three senators were offering Cincinnatus a sword, calling him back to the defense of the Roman republic. Around the edge of the whole ran the inscription, "OMNIA RELIQUIT SERVARE REM PUBLICAM." On the reverse was pictured the sun rising over an "open city" with "Fame crowning Cincinnatus" and the legends "VIRTUTIS PRAEMIUM" and "ESTO PERPETUA."[12]

The importance of Cincinnatus as an ideal figure to the participants in the Ohio Company was immense. Of the eleven men who met in Boston in March 1786 to organize the company, six were members of the society, as were four of the company's five directors and its secretary. To the associates, Cincinnatus was a model of ideal behavior in an ideal world — for Cincinnatus, living on the land far away from the tumult and corruption of cities and sacrificing his happiness so that the republic might survive the chaos of war and enjoy the pleasure and prosperity of peace, made a powerful comparison with their own positions. Cincinnatus was the embodiment of the independent virtuous republican. Firm fighters for the American republic in war, the Cincinnati envisioned themselves as its staunchest farmer-citizens in peace. They had had, claimed Mariettan Joseph Barker, "a second education in the Army of the Revolution, where they heard the precept of wisdom and saw the example of Bravery and Fortitude. They had been disciplined to obey, and learned the Advantages of subordination to Law and good order in promoting the prosperity and happiness of themselves and the rest of Mankind." A self-proclaimed elite in the defense of harmonious republicanism, the Cincinnati sternly warned that they would expel any member "who, by conduct inconsistent with a gentleman and a man of honor, or by opposition to the interests of the community in general, or the society in particular, may render himself unworthy to continue a member."[13]

To their disgust, however, the officers believed that the Revolution had not only threatened the economic base on which their sta-

12. [C. M. Storey, ed.], *Massachusetts Society of the Cincinnati: Minutes of all Meetings of the Society up to and including the meeting of October 1, 1825* (Boston, 1964), xxviii.

13. Blazier, *Joseph Barker,* 50; [Storey], *Massachusetts Society,* xxvi. On the relationship of the associates of the Ohio Company and the Society of the Cincinnati see, Mrs. L. A. Alderman, *The Identification of the Society of the Cincinnati with the First Authorized Settlement of the Northwest Territory at Marietta, Ohio, April 7, 1788* (Marietta, 1888), 24; and Hulbert, *The Records of the Original Proceedings,* I, xl-xlii.

tus rested, it had released anarchic and insubordinate elements. Only symptomatic was the virulent scorn directed at the Cincinnati, as the pretensions and hereditary characteristics of the society raised a storm of protest throughout New England. Mass meetings and memorials condemned the organization as anti-republican and elitist. Shocked at such treatment, Samuel Holden Parsons found the veterans of Connecticut exposed to "daily Insults" and "contemptuous malignant Neglect." "Without honor," he said, they could no longer live in New England and were seeking homes in New York or farther west. To these veterans, it seemed clear that something had gone wrong in the course of revolution.[14]

Everywhere they looked in the mid-1780s, the associates of the Ohio Company found ingratitude and growing anarchy in the East making a prospective settlement in the West alluring and idyllic. To Samuel Holden Parsons, the West represented "the Rewards of our Toils" in the Revolution and "a Safe Retreat from the Confusions and Distress into which the Folly of our Country may precipitate us." The essential problem with the East, according to Major General James Varnum, was that too rapid change and local prejudices were leading to disorder and potential despotism. Indeed, the prevalence of the former made the latter almost necessary. Manasseh Cutler summarized the general feeling when he wondered to Winthrop Sargent, the company secretary, in 1786 if "mankind are in a State for enjoying all the natural rights of humanity and are possessed of virtue sufficient for the support of a purely republican government." "Dishonesty, Villainy, and extreme ignorance" were rampant. America, he complained, "is the first nation" that could make "a fair experiment of equal liberty in a civil Community," but it seemed to be failing in its calling.[15]

Benjamin Tupper, who believed in 1787 that monarchy was "absolutely necessary" to save the United States from total chaos, saw, as did many of the associates, a climax to his personal and public discontents in Shays' Rebellion in late 1786. Coming after the actual formation of the Ohio Company, the rebellion only confirmed

14. Samuel Holden Parsons to Alexander McDougall, August 20, 1783, quoted in E. James Ferguson, *The Power of the Purse: A History of American Public Finance, 1776-1790* (Chapel Hill, 1961), 156fn. On the public reaction to the Society, see Wallace E. Davies, "The Society of the Cincinnati in New England, 1783-1800," *William and Mary Quarterly,* V (1948), 3-25.

15. Samuel Holden Parsons to Winthrop Sargent, June 16, 1786, The Winthrop Sargent Papers, The Massachusetts Historical Society (microfilm); Manasseh Cutler to Winthrop Sargent, November 6, 1786, The Sargent Papers. See also, Wood, *The Creation of the American Republic,* 391-467.

the disillusionment and fears of the associates. In such a crisis, Tupper cried, "The old Society of the Cincinnati must once more consult and effect the salvation of a distracted country." The Cincinnati did pledge their support of the Massachusetts government, partly because the uprising threatened the value, even the existence, of the securities on which rested the hopes of many to recoup or build fortunes. But their personal economic problems symbolized a more general imperiling of the republican experiment in freedom. Not all of the Ohio Company associates merely decried the rebellion. Many, such as Rufus Putnam and Benjamin Tupper, actively joined General Benjamin Lincoln "against the Insurgents." Others sold their farms in utter disgust. Cutler was right when he argued that "these commotions will tend to promote our plan and incline well disposed persons to become adventurers for who would wish to live under a Government subject to such tumults and confusions."[16]

In short, the veterans sought the security of a well-ordered life. Escaping the conflicts of an increasingly unfamiliar and contentious society, they would find "the assaults of passion . . . subdued by the gentler sway of virtuous affection" in the West. Solomon Drowne hoped that "much-eyed Peace" would "wave her Olive-branch over the earth and at last compose the dispositions of perverse mankind!" Above all, "infatuated mortals" would "learn that happiness is not the offspring of contention, but of mutual concession and accomodation." Marietta, Varnum argued, would be "a safe, an honorable asylum" where equal protection under the law and "the labor of the industrious will find the reward of peace, plenty, and virtuous contentment."[17]

Thus, unrewarded service, personal economic insecurity, and a frightening perspective on the events of the 1780s led the associates of the Ohio Company to forsake what they perceived as an increasingly perverse world. In the West they would build anew along the guidelines of eastern models, but with control and stability inherent in the structure of society. In the 1790s, when the United States seemed more secure under Federalist rule and the associates confronted new problems in the West, they would find much more to praise in the East. But on the eve of their actual migration, disgust and disillusionment prevailed. When Winthrop Sargent met some old war friends on a surveying trip in the West, they determined, in

16. Benjamin Tupper to Henry Knox, April, 1787, quoted in Kaplan, "Veteran Officers," 55; Beull, *Rufus Putnam*, 103; Manasseh Cutler to Winthrop Sargent, October 6, 1786, quoted in Kaplan, "Veteran Officers," 43.

17. Varnum, *An Oration*, 505, 508; Solomon Drowne to Dr. Levi Wharton, January 21, 1792, William Drowne, "A Brief Sketch," 80; Varnum *An Oration*, 506.

summarizing the feelings of the associates, that the lands of the Ohio would be a place "where the veteran soldier and honest Man should find a Retreat from ingratitude" and vowed, once settled, never again to visit the East "but in their children and like Goths and Vandals to deluge a people more vicious and villainous than even the Praetorian Band of Ancient Rome."[18]

The pioneers, however, were well aware that migration and rhetoric would not solve their problems, for social and economic chaos could travel west just as easily as virtue. Reform must begin at the foundations of society. As Samuel Holden Parsons declared, "the habits of an old world are in some degree to be corrected in forming a new one of the old materials. The different local prejudices," he added, "are to be done away and a medium fallen upon which may reconcile all." Thus, the particular value of the Ohio Country for erecting a more stable society was that it was largely virgin land. There, proclaimed Manasseh Cutler, "in order to begin *right* . . . will be no *wrong* habits to combat, and no inveterate systems to overturn — there is no rubbish to remove, before you can lay the foundation." In Ohio, the associates planned to create an orderly society based on equality and security of property, and on the institutions of the school, church, and government, all firmly entrenched in the purity of a natural, regular setting. Rhetorically, the founders of Marietta articulated their version of hopes and ideals that had echoed in New England for a century and a half.[19]

There were to be no economic jealousies, inequities, or insecurities in the West. Near equality would mark company holdings and the virtue of all men would be firmly grounded in the "quiet independence" of landed property. The price of an individual share was set as $125 in gold or $1000 in continentals, each share entitling the owner to a city lot and farm acreage of proportional size. The company further decreed that no person was to own more than five

18. Winthrop Sargent, "Diary," July 19, 1786, The Sargent Papers. New England society looked more appealing to the associates in the 1790s, perhaps because it seemed more stable. See, for example, Gross, *The Minutemen,* 153-88; and Van Beck Hall, *Politics Without Parties; Massachusetts, 1780-1791* (Pittsburgh, 1972), esp. 347-50.

19. Samuel Holden Parsons to William S. Johnson, November 24, 1788, Hall, *Parsons,* 534; Cutler, *An Explanation . . .,* 20. See also, Henry Nash Smith, *Virgin Land: The American West as Symbol and Myth* (Cambridge, 1975). A harmonious, orderly, corporate society had, of course, long been a goal in New England society. See, for example, Bushman, *From Puritan to Yankee,* Kenneth Lockridge, *A New England Town: The First Hundred Years* (New York, 1970), and Zuckerman, *Peaceable Kingdoms.*

shares — within the ranks of the elite, all were to be as economically equal as possible. After the area had been surveyed, plots and numbers were drawn and matched by lot; again the design was to insure a rough equality. Natural leaders would be recognized on the basis of merit rather than wealth and every member of society would have an independent stake in the perpetuation of order. To a large extent, the goal of equality of holdings was achieved, at least on paper. In 1796, when the Ohio Company had virtually ceased to exist, it included 594 stockholders owning a total of 496 shares. The average share per person was .835 with a majority of stockholders owning one share; only forty men owned more than three shares.[20]

Also of supreme importance was a traditional New England emphasis on education and religion. Marietta, Solomon Drowne said in 1789, presented a "noble opportunity for advancing knowledge of every kind," and for training "rising sons of science." Just as important, associate Thomas Wallcut declared, religion was "the most solid foundation" and "the surest support of government and good morals." Thus, one of the first orders the company gave was for the directors to pay close attention immediately "to the Education of Youth and the Promotion of Public Worship." Even a university was planned.[21]

As for government, Rufus Putnam extolled it in his charge to the first grand jury in Marietta, "Government is absolutely necessary for the well being of any people, and the General Happiness of Society", he said, "and I believe it will be found true that all national prosperity in every age of the world has generally, if not always, been enjoyed in proportion to the rectitude of their government and the due administration of its Laws." Hoping to dominate the West ideologically and materially, the people of Marietta futilely begged Major General Arthur St. Clair, first governor of the Northwest Territory, to live in Marietta rather than Cincinnati.[22]

Manasseh Cutler summarized the feelings of the associates in a sermon delivered during his short visit to Marietta in August, 1788. He spoke of the coming "bright day" when "science, virtue, pure

20. Hulbert, *The Records,* I, 6-10, 23-39, II, 234-42.
21. Solomon Drown[e], *An Oration, Delivered at Marietta, April 7, 1789 in Commemoration of the Commencement of the Settlement Formed by the OHIO COMPANY* (Worcestor, 1789), in Hildreth, *Pioneer History,* 522; George Dexter, ed., "Journal of Thomas Wallcut," Massachusetts Historical Society, *Proceedings,* XVII (1879-1880), 191; Hulbert, *The Records,* I, 40.
22. Rufus Putnam, "Charge to the Grand Jury at the September Term, 1788," quoted in Arthur L. Buell, "A History of Public Address in the First Permanent Settlement of the Northwest Territory from 1788 to 1793," (doctoral dissertation, Ohio University, 1965), 152.

religion, and free government shall pervade the western hemisphere" and argued that the settlers could not overlook the "cultivation of the principles of religion and virtue" if they intended to insure their "civil and social happiness." Religion and education provided "the greatest aid to civil government" and "lay the foundation for a well-regulated society." Only with such cultivation would people "conform to . . . the community's laws and regulations" out of "principles of reason and custom."[23]

But the greatest advantage of the West in building a more profitable, equitable, and thus stable, society was its natural setting. Like Cincinnatus, the associates hoped to draw virtue and prosperity primarily from the soil. In fact, these New Englanders were ecstatic about the advantages of an agricultural regime both in attracting settlers and in ordering society. In a hyperbolic promotional pamphlet, Manasseh Cutler praised "the deep, rich soil" that would yield riches for an industrious, agricultural people and the natural waterways that would convey their productions to markets. "The toils of agriculture," he wrote, will in Ohio "be rewarded with a greater variety of productions than in any part of America." The possibilities of the land were often the most significant thing settlers noted upon arriving in the West. Associate and merchant John May, for example, journeying home to New England for a visit, whiled away the tedious trip by remembering that "delightful country whose swelling soil will doubly reward the industrious planter."[24]

The land received its fullest tribute in a speech by Solomon Drowne on April 7, 1789 — the first anniversary of the founding of Marietta. Drowne's address was an extended paean in praise of agriculture. Indeed, he credited the "virgin soil" with luring the settlers "from your native homes" with "charms substantial and inestimable." The Ohio Country, said Drowne breaking into verse, was far from the chaos of the East:

> The rage of nations and the crush of states
> Move not the man who from the world escaped,
> In still retreats and flowering solitudes
> To nature's voice attends from month to month.

23. Manasseh Cutler, "Sermon at Marietta," August 24, 1788, Cutlers, *Manasseh Cutler*, I, 344.

24. Cutler, *An Explanation . . .* , 14; John May, August 10, 1788, Dwight L. Smith, ed., *The Western Journals of John May: Ohio Company Agent and Business Adventurer* (Cincinnati, 1961), 73.

Husbandry, Drowne continued, is "the best occupation of mankind" and "the country['s] . . . most estimable" virtue was that it could be practiced "under the auspices of firmly established liberty, civil and religious, and the mild government of natural laws." Like Cutler, Drowne noted that agriculture was a "profitable" enterprise. But more important, it was an "honorable . . . art" that had been "the delight of the greatest men."[25]

Agricultural isolation, however, was not the goal of the early Mariettans. As detailed in Cutler's pamphlet, they envisioned a wide-ranging commerce for their settlement with the East, Florida, and the West Indies. The bulk of their exports down the Mississippi or back across the mountains would be agricultural products like "corn, flour, beef, lumber, etc." Yet Cutler noted the advantages of small-scale manufacturing, as long as it was guided by a landed elite. "Instead of furnishing other nations with raw materials," he argued, "companies of manufacturers from Europe could be introduced and established in this inviting situation, under the superintendence of men of property." Far from turning their backs on profit, commerce, and industry, the associates embraced its orderly and regular development. As in all other things, the early Mariettans did not reject commercial development so much as they wanted to prevent its potentially disruptive and perverting side effects. Their effort was not to create an insulated asylum, but to restructure the world they had grown up in to make it more stable, predictable, and fair. And to achieve that goal, the associates believed that society's leading members had to ground their lives, ideals, and fortunes securely, if not exclusively, in the land. For farming was the most independent of pursuits and a clear antidote to social contention and economic upheaval. "To have a good farm," Manasseh Cutler told his Ohioan son in 1797, "to establish a good landed interest in preference to trade, or any other object," was of supreme importance, "for there is nothing in this country that will render a man so completely independent and secure against the difficulties which arise from the changes which the times, the state of the country, and other contingencies may occasion, and which are and always will be taking place in the world." "Freedom and tranquility," concluded Solomon Drowne, "may be enjoyed to perfection, if a person be qualified with virtue and a competence." The years of uncertainty and contention would end in the solid, predictable rhythms of farming.[26]

25. Drowne, *An Oration*, 519, 523.
26. Cutler, *An Explanation* . . . , 13. 20; Mannaseh Cutler to Ephraim Cutler, 1797, Julia Cutler, *Ephraim Cutler*, 35fn; Solomon Drowne, December 26, 1799, William

With the philosophy of republicans and the institutions of education, religion, and government firmly founded on economic quality and the practice of husbandry, Mariettans seemed to have little to do but build their model society along the guidelines enunciated in their rhetoric. While "rejoicing nature all around us glows," they would watch

> . . . the spires of Marietta rise,
> And domes and temples swell to the skies;
> Here, justice reigns, and foul dissensions cease,
> Her walks be pleasure and her paths be peace . . .
> In harmony and social virtue blend
> Joy without measure, rapture without end.

In sum, said the inhabitants of Marietta to Governor St. Clair in the summer of 1788, "May we here find a peaceful and happy retreat after the toils of a calamitous war! May we enjoy the richest fruit of a glorious revolution!"[27]

Nowhere was the nature of the society the Ohio Company envisioned better reflected than in the physical plan of Marietta. Because the city was to dominate and epitomize the new world, on nothing more than its structure did the nature and future of the associates' hopes depend. The plan of Marietta was drawn in Boston in the fall of 1787. If not radically innovative, the design nonetheless reflected the associates' strong emphasis on regularity and order. The agents of the company reserved 5,760 acres of the 1,500,000 they had purchased from Congress at the confluence of the Ohio and Muskingum rivers for a city of sixty rectangular blocks in the general form of ten blocks wide and six deep. All the streets were to be 100 feet wide except for a main one of 150 feet. Of the sixty blocks, the agents appropriated four for public use, while

Drowne, "A Brief Sketch," 120. See Ephraim Cutler's comments on the relationship of land and character in Julia Cutler, *Ephraim Cutler,* 89-90. On the nature of the early American farms and the relationship of commerce and virtue see, respectively, James Henretta, "Families and Farms: Mentalite in Pre-Industrial America," *William and Mary Quarterly,* 35 (1978), 3-32; and Drew R. McCoy, "Republicanism and American Foreign Policy: James Madison and the Political Economy of Commercial Discrimination, 1789-1794," *William and Mary Quarterly,* 31 (1974), 633-46.

27. Return Jonathan Meigs, "Fragment of a Speech on July 4, 1789," Buell, "A History of Public Address," 149; "Inhabitants on the Muskingum to Governor St. Clair," July 16, 1788, Clarence E. Carter, ed., *The Territorial Papers of the United States* (26 vols., Washington, 1934), II, 133. On the early government of Marietta, see Rohrbough, *The Trans-Appalachian Frontier,* 368-70; and on the early government of the Northwest Territory, see Jack Ericson Eblen, *The First and Second United States Empires: Governors and Territorial Government, 1784-1912* (Pittsburgh, 1968).

the other fifty-six were to be divided into "house Lots" of 90 by 180 feet.[28]

In the Ohio Country, Rufus Putnam laid out the basic gridiron pattern specified by the agents, but in so doing he took advantage of "the situation of the Ground" and put it to use as a virtuous foundation for the orderly city. The most striking feature of the land the Ohio Company bought was a group of ancient Indian mounds. The huge piles of dirt, relics of the civilization of the Adena group of mound-builders and more than a thousand years old, intrigued the New Englanders. Winthrop Sargent, for example, spent days measuring and preparing descriptions of the mounds. The first thing Cutler went to see when he arrived for his brief visit in the fall of 1788 was the most curious of the ancient monuments, a large cone-shaped mound surrounded by a ten-foot moat. The early Mariettans were obsessed with speculation about the origins of the mounds. Solomon Drowne, interested in attaching some classical virtue to them, suggested that they were not unlike the burial mounds of the ancient Trojans, the ancestors of the Roman republicans. Certainly there had been an elaborate civilization on the spot of the Ohio Company settlement, and the Mariettans felt a primitive nobility exuding from its remnants. What the agents resolved about the future of the cone-shaped mound applied for all of "the ancient works." "Every prudent measure," they decided, "ought to be adopted to perpetuate the figure and appearance of so majestic a Monument of Antiquity." Eventually, they made it the center of their cemetery.[29]

More than merely preserving the mounds, however, Putnam built the town around them, superimposing the regular plan of the company on the Indian ruins. The larger mounds became the centers of public squares. Naming these blocks proved simple, for there was no better way to secure the prominence of virtue than to mark the relics of primitive grandeur and nobility with names from the Roman republic. The agents named the land around the burial mound Conus, and reserved blocks called Capitolium and Quadranou focus-

28. Hulbert, *The Records*, I, 15, 20. See also, John Reps, *Town Planning in Frontier America* (Princeton, 1969) 282-91. The comments of Manasseh Cutler and Winthrop Sargent on contemporary cities reveal an intense appreciation of "regularity" and a dislike of the "haphazard" in urban planning. See, for example, Cutler's 1787 observations in his diary in Cutlers, *Manasseh Cutler*, I, 215, 248, 285, 306-07, 393, 429; Sargent, "Diary," July 4, 1786, The Sargent Papers; and G. Turner to Sargent, November 6, 1787, The Sargent Papers.

29. Drowne, *An Oration*, 522; Hulbert, *The Records*, II, 209. For travellers' observations on Indian mounds, see John A. Jakle, *Images of the Ohio Valley: An Historical Geography of Travel, 1740 to 1860* (New York, 1977), 68-71.

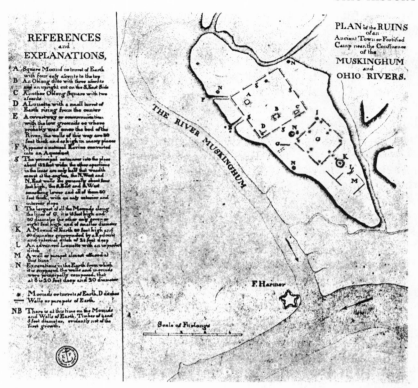

1788 plan of the Marietta earthworks drawn by Rufus Putnam. (SOCIETY COLLECTION)

ing on two rectangular mounds. Putnam and the agents established the final of the requisite four public squares at the confluence of the rivers and named it Cecilia. Completing the reminders of ancient Rome, the New Englanders christened their temporary stockade Campus Martius.[30]

The company did not rely altogether on what the land provided, however, to mark their city. They planned a large role, for example, for trees that they would plant. The agents in Boston had ordered rows of mulberry trees placed along both sides of the city streets. Placed ten or fifteen feet from the houses, the trees' duties, according to Cutler, were "to make an agreeable shade, increase the salubrity of the air, and add to the beauty of the streets." The rows of trees would also create natural sidewalks, leaving streets of the

30. Hulbert, *The Records*, I, 51. See also, Reps. *Town Planning*, 285.

Taken from a painting done in 1795, this early view of the Marietta site depicts the confluence of the Muskingum and the Ohio Rivers and the pre-historic earthworks which fascinated the founding company. (SOCIETY COLLECTION)

spacious width of seventy feet. The importance of trees in adding to the beauty and regularity of the city was most clearly reflected in the strict rules for the temporary leasing of the public squares for clearing and other improvements until the danger of Indian attacks had passed. A "Mr. Woodbridge," for instance, was given a lease on the Capitolium in 1791 for eight years on the condition that he "surround the whole with Locust Trees, except at each corner there shall be an Ash — that the lines a, a, a, be Mulberrys and the lines b, b, Weeping willows, that the trees be set out within two years." The elevated mound on the Capitolium, moreover, "with the Ascents leading to the same," was to be "immediately put into Grass and hereafter occupied in no other way."[31]

The names of the city streets were chosen to reinforce the virtue of the residents of the regular city by perpetuating the fame of its founders and their contemporaries. While the associates gave the streets parallel to the Muskingum River numerical names, the names of modern Cincinnati marked the perpendicular avenues.

31. Manasseh Cutler to Ebenezer Hazard, September 18, 1787, Cutlers, *Manasseh Cutler,* I, 331; Hulbert, *The Records,* II, 80.

Appropriately, the Mariettans called their main street Washington. Those streets to the south of it they named Knox, Worcester, Scammel, Tupper, Cutler, Putnam, Butler, and Greene; to the north were St. Clair, Warren, Montgomery, and Marion. The only break in the ranks was Sacra Via, which ran in two parallel strips from Quadranou west to the Muskingum River just above Washington Street, and preserved part of the noble Indian works.

Idealistically, the associates envisioned a diffusion of themselves and the institutions of republican virtue throughout the city. The random drawings of house lots would place the associates throughout the city to watch over new arrivals and to lead by example. A church and a courthouse were planned and built away from the main street and the central mounds and public square, unlike a typical New England town where everything focused on the central green. The virtuous elite and institutions were to be omnipresent so that no sore could fester into degeneracy and chaos.[32]

The final component of the Marietta plan was the agricultural one, for most of the pioneers intended to become, or to reassume a role as, Jefferson's virtuous laborers "in the earth." While they would live, or at least maintain a home, in Marietta, the shareholders would farm their land for the inseparable goals of profit and independence. No matter how noble farming was, however, it required markets to make it economically secure. Many had moved to Marietta explicitly "to live in a Country where they can maintain their families from the produce of their lands better than where they" had lived. For the first few years Putnam and Cutler looked to "the Constant coming in of new settlers" to provide "a good market." By 1800, Mariettans were building ships and trying to develop an ocean-going commerce. With a cargo of flour and pork, Commodore Abraham Whipple temporarily quit his farm in 1800 to pilot "the first rigged vessel ever built on the Ohio River" to New Orleans, Havana, and Philadelphia. By 1808, approximately twenty ships of 150 to 450 tons had cleared from the "port" of Marietta. By providing an outlet for agricultural products and a means of securing other items, this trade was designed to reinforce both the viability and pervasiveness of an essentially agrarian life and the commercial hegemony of Marietta.[33]

32. The church was built at Front and Putnam Streets; the courthouse at Second and Putnam. Quadranou was located at the head of Sacra Via, and Capitolium at Fifth and Washington Streets.
33. E. Haskell to Winthrop Sargent, February 28, 1786, The Sargent Papers; Hildreth, *Biographical and Historical Memoirs,* 160-61. On the early commercial de-

The Ohio Company greatly emphasized the equality of the quantity of the land each associate received. The agents divided the land grants into several plots rather than one large farm in order to make their settlement in "the most compact manner," and to equalize land grants in terms of both actual size and distance to Marietta. The associates were very sensitive about reassuring that their goal of equality was realized. When Rufus Putnam and some of the first group of settlers argued that "the first actual Settlers should take their choice" of sixty-four acres "of the best land on the Ohio and other navigable streams," they were abruptly overruled. Later, after the agents had been in Ohio for a while and seen the contours of the land with which they were dealing, they resolved that they should have the power to divide the land "as equal[ly] as may be, by dividing greater Quantities of Land to some Lots, and less to other Lots, to do more equal Justice." But they later rescinded this resolution on the ground that equalizing quality would require arbitrary decisions and might lead to favoritism and corruption. Eventually, most felt, the company would build "10 or 12 Towns" up the Muskingum "which will give handsome farms to every right in the Propriety." Return Jonathan Meigs told fellow associate Thomas Wallcut that "the plan" was "to proceed regularly down the Ohio and up the Muskingum" in expanding the hegemony of the company. The point, as always with the Ohio Company, was that a rough egalitarianism was to be preserved at all times among the associates. The "perfect harmony" of the Jeffersonian idea was to be maintained by a democracy of independent farmers guided by the example of an elite and the order and beauty of the town.[34]

Indeed, Marietta fulfilled all the requirements necessary for the "perfect harmony" enunciated in the rhetoric of its builders. The gridiron pattern of the city gave it regularity, order, and predictability. These same values, as well as the ideal of controlled egalitarianism, were reinforced by the uniformity of the house lots and the land grants. Only the preservation of the mounds broke up Marietta's regularity, but even they were made to serve the same functions.

velopment of the Ohio Valley, see, Randolph C. Downes, "Trade in Frontier Ohio," *The Mississippi Valley Historical Review*, XVI (1930), 467-94; Archer Hulbert, "Western Ship-building," *American Historical Review*, XXI (1915-1916), 720-33; Rohrbough, *The Trans-Appalachian Frontier*, 93-114; and William T. Utter, *The Frontier State, 1803-1825*, Carl Wittke, ed., *The History of the State of Ohio* (5 vols., Columbus, 1942), II, 146-82, 229-62.

34. Buell, *Rufus Putnam*, 106; Hulbert, *The Records*, I, 83; Samuel Holden Parsons to Manasseh Cutler, August 24, 1787, The Sargent Papers; Return Jonathan Meigs to Thomas Wallcut, February 26, 1790, Dexter, "Journal of Thomas Wallcut," 190.

Unlike other western and New England cities, Marietta focused on the natural setting for ideological reasons as well as convenience. Not only did this put tangible virtue on display, it also gave no particular part of the city exclusive status. Certainly Washington Street was the "main" one, but why live there when one could live facing the public squares or along the rivers? The institutions of republican virtue were spread throughout the city. Marietta had no "center," in a New England sense.

Above all, the Ohio Company's city had space and an intended simple elegance. The broad avenues, lined with trees, many of them named after modern Cincinnati, and the several open, naturally ornamented squares emphasized the natural setting and the beauty of the area, uniting classical virtue and primitive nature. A conscious effort was made to hide vice and unlovely things like stables in alleys. Finally, the inhabitants of the city were to perform agricultural functions and own their own land to maintain a secure independence. Not a radical innovation in urban planning, Marietta represented a readjustment of the virtues and flaws of contemporary cities fitted to a powerful natural setting in an attempt to preclude anarchy and institutionalize order in the physical structure of society.

More was necessary to make the Mariettans' world complete, however, for they saw themselves as the progenitors of a stable society. Their efforts would be successful only if they converted everyone coming west to the philosophy of order and agrarian independence. Regular Marietta, with its mounds, avenues, and commercial hegemony was to serve that role. In this spirit, James Varnum reminded Mariettans in the summer of 1788 that their "bright example" must "add to the felicity of others" who "having formed their manners upon the elegance of the simplicity, and the refinements of virtue, will be happy in living with you in the bosom of friendship."[35]

The confederation government heartily approved of the notion that Marietta should "serve as a wide model for the future settlement of all the federal lands." Congress had long been concerned about people crossing illegally into the Ohio Country from Pennsylvania and Virginia without paying for the government-owned lands of the Northwest Territory. Wanting the money from land sales to help pay off the war debt, the government as early as 1785

35. Varnum, *An Oration*, 507.

dispatched Ensign John Armstrong and a troop of soldiers to drive such "squatters," "a banditti whose actions are a disgrace to human nature," back across the Ohio River. Later, forts were erected along the Ohio, including Fort Harmar at the mouth of the Muskingum River, to prevent further intrusions.[36]

On a 1786 surveying trip to the Ohio Country, Winthrop Sargent feared that this *"powerful* and *dangerous"* "lawless Banditti" would steal "the most eligible situations and valuable Tracts of land on the Ohio." Without the army, the land would have no "Security" whatsoever. Fearful of anarchy and disorder pursuing them to the West, the associates discovered that these supposed evils were beating them there. Cutler hoped that settling so near Pennsylvania would leave "no vacant lands exposed to be seized by such lawless banditti." In general, the Mariettans could only have faith, as Thomas Wallcut put it, that "our people will be the means of introducing more ambition and better taste," and that their prosperous and regular settlement would still make the Ohio Country, in Cutler's words, "the garden of the world, the seat of wealth, and the centre of a great Empire." As such, Marietta would epitomize "the ideas of order, citizenship, and the useful sciences." To preserve their status and exercise the leadership reserved for society's elite, precluding the growth of anarchy in the West was both a duty and a necessity.[37]

But the prolongation of the Indian wars to 1795 kept the associates from executing their plans as quickly as they would have liked. The company gave land to settlers willing to protect its purchase from both Indians and squatters. Sometimes, the Mariettans acted more forcefully. When, in 1797, an unauthorized group of people settled near present-day Athens, Ohio, some fifty miles to the northwest of Marietta, Rufus Putnam immediately dispatched a contingent of "men possessing firmness of character, courage, and sound discretion" to prevent the land from being "overrun" and "to establish a peaceable and respectable settlement." Not the least of the Mariettans' worries was that they had long ago set aside the Athens' township for a university that "promised most important results." The "substantial men" Putnam sent pushed out a "large portion of

36. Cutler, *An Explanation* . . . , 14; Ensign John Armstrong to Colonel Josiah Harmar, in Harmar to President of Congress, May 1, 1785, William H. Smith, *The Life and Public Services of Arthur St. Clair* (Cincinnati, 1882), II, 4fn.

37. Winthrop Sargent, "Diary," September 7, 1786, The Sargent Papers; Cutler, *An Explanation* . . . , 14; Thomas Wallcut to George Minot, [draft], October 31, November 3, 1789, Dexter, "Journal of Thomas Wallcut," 175. On the general relationship of squatters, government, and land companies, as well as the early settlement of the Ohio Country, see John D. Barnhart, *Valley of Democracy: The Frontier versus the Plantation in the Ohio Valley, 1775-1818* (Lincoln, 1970), 121-47.

the disorderly population," and established Athens' "character as an orderly and respectable community." They introduced, in sum, "a mild and refined state of manners and feelings," and gave order to an area that was being developed with no other principle than that "might makes right."[38]

Marietta, however, was not itself always a paragon of virtue. Squabbles over land and personal grievances had split the company directors until the deaths of Varnum and Parsons in 1788 and 1789. More crucial was unanticipated trouble within the new city. The members of the Ohio Company had settled on their arrival in 1788 in a stockade about a mile up the Muskingum River from the Ohio to avoid floods, but a group of buildings soon grew up at the confluence of the rivers, built by a mixture of discontented associates and itinerants who were allowed temporary housing. These people erected walls and named the cluster the Picketed Point. Attuned to river traffic, the Point became blatantly commercially oriented, sporting a store and a tavern.

To the associates lodged up the Muskingum in Campus Martius, the Point seemed reminiscent of the East they had fled in disgust. In February, 1790, a Marietta grand jury debated four grievances arising from events at the Point. The jury resisted a demand for the abolition of duelling on the ground that the practice "would discourage cowards, and we want brave men." But a second demand, for the incorporation of the city to provide for "the poor and sick strangers," passed, as did a request for a law "licensing and regulating taverns." The jury also condemned the practice of slavery. In the same year, Thomas Wallcut felt outraged enough by behavior at the point to write to Governor St. Clair complaining about a particular tavern keeper. Wallcut wanted "the inordinate passions of oppressive, cruel, and avaricious men" restrained. The "disorderly, riotous, and ill-governed house" of Isaac Mixer, Wallcut concluded, was "destructive of peace, good order, and exemplary morals upon which not only the well-being but the very existence of society so much depends." It was not the pursuit of profit that annoyed the associates, but the lack of control and regularity that characterized the point in their eyes. Thus, what Wallcut requested from St. Clair was simply a law "licensing and regulating taverns."[39]

38. Ephraim Cutler, "The First Settlement of Athens County," Hildreth, *Biographical and Historical Memoirs,* 410, 408, and 413.
39. Thomas Wallcut, February 2, 1790, Dexter, "Journal of Thomas Wallcut," 181; Wallcut to Arthur St. Clair, [draft], 1790, Dexter, 182fn. Picketed Point is described in Hildreth, *Pioneer History,* 325.

Rufus Putnam. (SOCIETY COLLECTION)

Despite several efforts, the company did not gain control over the point until the conclusion of the Indian wars in 1795 and the beginning of serious building. The hegemony of the virtuous elite within orderly Marietta was then relatively secure. They brought their plan to fruition and suppressed "the lawless Banditti" in or near their settlement. According to Samuel Prescott Hildreth, an early Marietta physician and historian, with the end of the Indian wars "few events of interesting character transpired. . . . Each man took possession of his lands, and commenced clearing and cultivating his farm."[40]

To an extent, then, the Ohio Company succeeded in obtaining financial independence for many of its associates and in building a harmonious city. But physical structure could not insure that the example of Marietta would lead the entire West to a consistently ordered existence. The second goal was as crucial to the associates as the first. If Marietta failed to set the "tone" of the West, it would remain a utopian oasis, and a fragile one at best. Yet, the "banditti" were not easily controlled outside the confines of the

40. Hildreth, *Pioneer History,* 345.

Ohio Company purchase. Organic growth, controlled by a self-proclaimed elite, was simply out of place in the West, as the development of the ironically named Cincinnati — the second permanent, American settlement in the Ohio Country — testifies.

Founded in 1788, Cincinnati grew rapidly because of its position as the center of government and military operations against the Indians. The development of the city quickly became uncontrolled and haphazard. Commercially-oriented Cincinnati grew along the river with waterfront land at a premium. Like Marietta and other western cities being built in this era, Cincinnati had a gridiron pattern. But neither it nor any other community could match the Mariettans' obsession with virtue and regularity. The preservation of the Indian mounds and their incorporation in the Marietta plan, for example, were almost unique in American town planning.

The speculators and profit-oriented merchants who began to dominate Cincinnati seemed to the Mariettans to lack the requisite intense commitment to the secure independence of landed property and controlled, organic growth. Consequently, Winthrop Sargent, moving to Cincinnati in 1791 to assume the position of secretary of the Northwest Territory, found the situation not unlike the East in the 1780s. He despaired that the people of Cincinnati and Marietta "seem never to have been intended to live under the same government — the latter are very like our Forefathers and the former (generally) very licentious and too great a portion indolent and extremely debauched." To protect himself, Sargent found it necessary to surround his Cincinnati home with, of course, a garden. John Reps, the historian of American town planning, concludes that an 1815 "plan of Cincinnati . . . reveals nothing very remarkable. Indeed, it shows every indication of being laid out . . . as a speculative enterprise and little more." "What is more," says Reps, "in its design," Cincinnati "resembled hundreds of similar towns that were soon to spring up throughout southern and central Ohio as the region began to attract land hungry settlers from the east." Commercial and haphazard Cincinnati, not agrarian and regular Marietta, became the model for western development.[41]

People going to cash in on the prosperity of booming towns like Cincinnati and Louisville passed Marietta in growing numbers in the 1790s. The soldiers at Fort Harmar, across the Muskingum from Marietta, counted the passing flatboats into the thousands. Cincin-

41. Winthrop Sargent to Timothy Pickering, September 30, 1796, quoted in Benjamin Pershing, "Winthrop Sargent: A Builder of the Old Northwest," (doctoral dis-

nati, and not Marietta, became the center of the Ohio Valley, largely for geographic and economic reasons. Moreover, the controlled and systematic development of Marietta to secure an elite's notion of virtue and stability was anachronistic, and no doubt contributed to its failure to dominate the West. Even by the early nineteenth century, many people believed that making money and pursuing their own best interest would lead to virtue and communal improvement. The "invisible hand" of laissez-faire economics, not the self-appointed members of the Cincinnati, nor Indian mounds, nor regular streets, would bring out the best in society.

By 1824, the year of Rufus Putnam's death, George Ogden, a Quaker merchant from New Bedford, Massachusetts, had found evidence to support that contention on a trip down the Ohio River. Ogden praised Marietta for its "delightful" location, but little else. The city, claimed Ogden, "was until within a few years one of the most flourishing towns in the state," rivalling Cincinnati in "elegance" and "enterprising spirit." But now Marietta wore "quite a different aspect, and" was "rapidly declining." It lacked "commercial energies," and thus, "grandeur," Ogden complained. Cincinnati, in contrast, was the "largest and the handsomest town in the state," the product of its "flourishing energies." For Ogden, Cincinnati had prospered, whatever its origins; Marietta had declined, despite its noble beginnings — the better place was obviously the city that was wealthy and successful. The worst fears of the Ohio Company had come to pass.[42]

The first Mariettans belonged to a world of community and of a harmonious, regular society that was dying — if it ever had really existed — as Marietta was being designed to institutionalize it. Only aged comrades understood any more, including the Marquis de Lafayette who during his 1825 tour of America stopped in Marietta and walked over the graves of his fallen friends in Mound Cemetery. "I knew them well," Lafayette told their descendents, "I saw them fight for their country. They were the bravest of the brave. Better men," he concluded wistfully, "never lived." If so, they held an archaic vision in which regularity, order, and communal virtue counted for as much as individual gain, where even merchants built

sertation, University of Chicago, 1927), 46-147; Reps, *Town Planning*, 292. On early urban experience in the Northwest, see Jakle, *Images of the Ohio Valley*, 122-57, esp. 143-56; Rohrbough, *The Trans-Appalachian West*, 352-60, esp. 353-54; and Richard C. Wade, *The Urban Frontier* (Chicago, 1959), esp. 11, 15-16, 19-20, 22-30.

42. George W. Ogden. *Letters from the West* (New Bedford, 1823); Reuben G. Thwaites, ed., *Early Western Travels, 1748-1846* (32 vols., Cleveland, 1904) XIX, 34-135.

homes first for "the benefit of the community" and then for themselves and "profit." A contemporary account of the July 4, 1788, festivities in Marietta emphasized that the inhabitants were in "high spirits, and extremely happy" and only needed "their tender companions, whom they have left beyond the mountains, to participate with them in the rising glories of the western world." Happy and hopeful the original Mariettans may have been, but those glories were to be of a kind that they could never imagine and thus would go to others.[43]

43. Lafayette is quoted on a tablet in Mound Cemetery, Marietta, Ohio; John May, July 11, 1788, Smith, *Journal,* 62; "A Contemporary Account of Some Events," Hildreth, *Pioneer History,* 515.